SO-BPP-663

THE EARTH AND ITS PEOPLES
A GLOBAL HISTORY

SECOND EDITION

VOLUME B

From 1200 to 1870

Richard W. Bulliet
Columbia University

Pamela Kyle Crossley
Dartmouth College

Daniel R. Headrick
Roosevelt University

Steven W. Hirsch
Tufts University

Lyman L. Johnson
University of North Carolina–Charlotte

David Northrup
Boston College

Houghton Mifflin Company   Boston   New York

Editor-in-chief for history and political science: Jean L. Woy
Sponsoring editor: Nancy Blaine
Senior development editor: Jennifer E. Sutherland
Associate editor: Julie Dunn
Editorial associate: Gillie Jones
Senior project editor: Carol Newman
Senior designer: Henry Rachlin
Senior production/design coordinator: Jill Haber
Senior manufacturing coordinator: Marie Barnes
Senior marketing manager: Sandra McGuire

Cover design: Anthony L. Saizon
Cover image: *The Zocalo, Mexico City,* 17th c. by Casimiro Castro. Schalkwijk/Art Resource, NY.

Part opener credits

Pt. 4, p. 321: Bibliothèque nationale de France; Pt. 5, p. 441: Library of Congress; Pt. 6, p. 569: © Hulton-Deutsch/Corbis.

Chapter opener credits

Ch. 12, p. 297: Justin Kerr; Ch. 13, p. 324: Bodleian Library, Oxford, Ms. Marsh 144, f. (to come); Ch. 14, p. 347: Imperial Household Collection, Kyoto; Ch. 15, p. 369: Victor Englebert; Ch. 16, p. 393: Giraudon/Art Resource, NY; Ch. 17, p. 417: G. Dagli Orti; Ch. 18, p. 444: The Metropolitan Museum of Art, Rogers Fund, 1919. (19.164). Photograph © 1998 The Metropolitan Museum of Art; Ch. 19, p. 471: Archivo General de la Nacion, Buenos Aires; Ch. 20, p. 496: From William Clark, *Ten Views in the Islands of Antigua,* 1823. British Library; Ch. 21, p. 521 : University Library, Istanbul/The Art Archive Limited; Ch. 22, p. 545: Novosti; Ch. 23, p. 572: Bibliothèque nationale de France/The Bridgeman Art Library, London and New York; Ch. 24, p. 598: Elton Collection, Ironbridge Gorge Museum Trust; Ch. 25, p. 620 : *Estracion de Orizaba, 1877.* From Casimiro Castro, *Album del Ferro-Carril Mexicano: Coleccion de Vista Pintadas* (Victor Debray and Company, 1877); Ch. 26, p. 647: Eyre and Hobbs House Art Gallery; Ch. 27, p. 673: Courtesy, Rizzoli.

Copyright © 2001 by Houghton Mifflin Company. All rights reserved.

All rights reserved. No part of this work may be reproduced or transmitted in any form or by any means, electronic or mechanical, including photocopying and recording, or by any information storage or retrieval system without the prior written permission of Houghton Mifflin Company unless such copying is expressly permitted by federal copyright law. Address inquiries to College Permissions, Houghton Mifflin Company, 222 Berkeley Street, Boston, MA 02116-3764.

Printed in the U.S.A.

Library of Congress Catalog Card Number: 00-132429

ISBN: 0-618-00075-5

 2 3 4 5 6 7 8 9-VH-04 03 02 01 00

BRIEF CONTENTS

CONTENTS

MAPS

ENVIRONMENT AND TECHNOLOGY

SOCIETY AND CULTURE

PREFACE

History is not easy. We met ten years ago in a conference room at Houghton Mifflin: six professional historians seated around a table hammering out our ideas on what a global history textbook at the start of a new millennium should be. Together we brought to the project a high level of knowledge about Africa, the Americas, Asia, Europe, the Middle East. We argued; we made up over dinner; we debated some more.

But there was no short cut. We were determined to write the best history we could. That meant testing ideas aloud; considering alternatives put forward by smart, articulate colleagues; and bargaining over what to include and what, with regret, to pass over. We believe the result was worth the sweat.

So began the Preface to the first edition of this book. Then came the wait for responses and a fresh wave of satisfaction as teachers and students from a wide variety of institutions reported positive results from the classroom. Unalloyed praise, however, was too much to hope for from a first edition. Users of the book spotted many possibilities for improvement, and these became our mandate for preparing the second edition.

Our overall goal remains the same: to produce a textbook that not only speaks for the past but speaks to today's student and today's teacher. Students and instructors alike should take away from this text a broad vision of human societies beginning as sparse and disconnected communities reacting creatively to local circumstances; experiencing ever more intensive stages of contact, interpenetration, and cultural expansion and amalgamation; and arriving at a twenty-first century world in which people increasingly visualize a single global community.

Along this trajectory, different parts of the world have moved or paused at different points in time, and each has followed its own path. Domestication of plants and animals in the Western Hemisphere developed independently of the analogous process in the Eastern Hemisphere, as did the growth of empires. Similarly, industrialization of western Europe and North America preceded by a century or two industrialization elsewhere. Yet the world all came together in the late twentieth century, a paradoxical period of global political and economic forces confronting intensified reassertions of particular national and cultural identities. People who speak today of an emerging global community are answered by others who insist on their own distinctive identities.

Process, not progress, is the keynote of this book: a steady process of change over time, at first differently experienced in various regions but eventually entangling peoples from all parts of the globe. Students should come away from this book with a sense that the problems and promises of their world are rooted in a past in which peoples of every sort, in every part of the world, confronted problems of a similar character and coped with them as best they could. We believe our efforts will help students see where their world has come from and learn thereby something useful for their own lives

CENTRAL THEME

We subtitled *The Earth and Its Peoples* "A Global History" because the book explores the common challenges and experiences that unite the human past. Although the dispersal of early humans to every livable environment resulted in myriad different economic, social, political, and cultural systems, all societies displayed analogous patterns in meeting their needs and exploiting their environments. Our challenge was to select the particular data and episodes that would best illuminate these global patterns of human experience.

To meet this challenge, we adopted a central theme to serve as the spinal cord of our history. That theme is "technology and environment," the commonplace bases of all human societies at all times and a theme that grants no special favor to any cultural group even as it embraces subjects of the broadest topical, chronological, and geographical range.

It is vital for students to understand that technology, in the broad sense of experience-based knowledge of the physical world, underlies all human activity. Writing is a technology, but so is oral transmission from generation to generation of lore about medicinal or poisonous plants. The magnetic compass is a navigational technology, but so is Polynesian mariners' hard-won knowledge of winds, currents, and tides that made possible the settlement of the Pacific islands.

All technological development has come about in

interaction with environments, both physical and human, and has, in turn, affected those environments. The story of how humanity has changed the face of the globe is an integral part of our central theme.

Yet technology and the environment do not by themselves explain or underlie all important episodes of human change and experience. Discussions of politics, culture, and society constantly interweave with our central theme to reveal additional historical patterns. Most notable among these is the interplay of dominance—whether political, economic, social, religious, or gender—with human variety. When narrating the histories of empires, for example, we describe a range of human experiences within and beyond the imperial frontiers without assuming that the imperial institutions are a more fit topic for discussion than the economic and social organization of pastoral nomads or the life patterns of peasant women.

CHANGES IN THE SECOND EDITION

Our overriding concerns in conceiving the second edition were updating the scholarship, better unifying the presentation, and addressing issues raised by instructors and students who had used the first edition. The most obvious change is the adoption of a full-color format, which not only brightens the page but makes maps clearer and more effective. The opening pages of each part of the text were similarly reconceived to give students a geographic and chronological overview of what is to come. The timelines and world maps that now accompany the part-opening essays are designed to focus student's attention on broad themes and historical benchmarks. Consolidated timelines within each chapter enable students to see at a glance the sorts of comparisons being made in the text.

Guides to the pronunciation of uncommon words and foreign terms, previously at the back of the book, now appear at the bottom of each page. Key terms are boldfaced in the text, listed at the end of each chapter, and defined in the Glossary at the end of the book. In addition, focus questions at the end of the vignette opening each chapter call attention to the main themes of the chapter. We believe that these unobtrusive changes will improve students' understanding of the main narrative and make it easier for them to grasp the main points of each chapter, as well as to review for examinations.

We sifted through a mass of helpful suggestions on how to revise and reorganize the content itself. Along with hundreds of minor revisions and clarifications, we effected a number of major changes:

- To facilitate comparison among different regions of the globe, we moved discussion of the earliest periods of Western Hemisphere history from Chapter 12 to Chapter 4.
- We greatly increased the coverage of Russian history, including entirely new sections in Chapter 10 (Chapter 9 of the first edition) and Chapter 22.
- Intellectual history gained increased attention with expanded coverage of Confucianism and Legalism in China; scholasticism, the Renaissance, and the Enlightenment in Europe; and twentieth-century modernism.
- Chapters 9 and 10 in the first edition were reversed, so the discussion of the rise of Islam now precedes that of Christian Europe.
- Coverage of the Industrial Revolution was revised to take in a broader geographical purview.
- The organization of twentieth-century history (Chapters 30–35) was completely reconceived to strengthen the chronological narrative.
- Suggested Reading lists were updated with recent scholarship.

The full-color format favored substantial changes in the illustration program, and many of the feature essays also were changed. Topics for the eleven new "Environment and Technology" essays include water engineering in Rome and China, Inca roads, Vasco da Gama's fleet, biomedical technologies, and global warming. The primary-source document feature of the first edition has been renamed "Society and Culture" to emphasize its complementarity with "Environment and Technology." Topics for the thirteen essays new to this edition include the Babylonian New Year's festival, the status of women in Indian literature, everyday law in Ming China, Charles Babbage, Ada Lovelace, and the "Analytical Engine," self-government in Africa, and "Silent Spring."

ORGANIZATION

The *Earth and Its Peoples* uses eight broad chronological divisions to define its conceptual scheme of global historical development. In **Part One: The Emergence of Human Communities, to 500 B.C.E.,** we examine important patterns of human communal organization. Early human communities were small, and most parts of the world were populated sparsely, if at all. As the human species spread worldwide, it encountered and responded to enormously diverse environmental conditions. Humans' responses gave rise to many technologies, ranging from implements for meeting daily needs—such as acquiring and handling foods, fabricating clothing and shelter, and utilizing the natural forces of fire, wind, and animal power—to the compilation of exhaustive lore about plants, animals, the climate, and the heavens.

Part Two: The Formation of New Cultural Communities, 1000 B.C.E.–400 C.E., introduces the concept of a "cultural community," in the sense of a coherent pattern of activities and symbols pertaining to a specific human community. Although all human communities develop distinctive cultures, including those discussed in Part One, historical development in this stage of global history prolonged and magnified the impact of some cultures more than others. In the geographically contiguous African-Eurasian landmass, as well as in Mesoamerica and the Andean region of the Western Hemisphere, the cultures that proved to have the most enduring influence traced their roots to the second and first millennia B.C.E.

Part Three: Growth and Interaction of Cultural Communities, 300 B.C.E.–1200 C.E., deals with early episodes of technological, social, and cultural exchange and interaction on a continental scale both within and beyond the framework of imperial expansion. These are so different from earlier interactions arising from more limited conquests or extensions of political boundaries that they constitute a distinct era in world history—an era that set the world on the path of increasing global interaction and interdependence that it has been following ever since.

In **Part Four: Interregional Patterns of Culture and Contact, 1200–1550,** we take a look at the world during the three and a half centuries that saw both intensified cultural and commercial contact and increasingly confident self-definition of cultural communities in Europe, Asia, and Africa. The Mongol conquest of a vast empire extending from the Pacific Ocean to eastern Europe greatly stimulated trade and interaction. In the West, strengthened European kingdoms began maritime expansion in the Atlantic, forging direct ties with sub-Saharan Africa and beginning the conquest of the civilizations of the Western Hemisphere.

Part Five: The Globe Encompassed, 1500–1750, treats a period dominated by the global effects of European expansion and continued economic growth. European ships took over, expanded, and extended the maritime trade of the Indian Ocean, coastal Africa, and the Asian rim of the Pacific Ocean. This maritime commercial enterprise had its counterpart in European colonial empires in the Americas and a new Atlantic trading system. The contrasting capacities and fortunes of traditional land empires and new maritime empires, along

with the exchange of domestic plants and animals between the hemispheres, underline the technological and environmental dimensions of this first era of complete global interaction.

In **Part Six: Revolutions Reshape the World, 1750–1870,** the word *revolution* is used in several senses: in the political sense of governmental overthrow, as in France and the Americas; in the metaphorical sense of radical transformative change, as in the Industrial Revolution; and in the broadest sense of a perception of a profound change in circumstances and world-view. Technology and environment lie at the core of these developments. With the rapid ascendancy of the Western belief that science and technology could overcome all challenges—environmental or otherwise—technology became not only an instrument of transformation but also an instrument of domination, to the point of threatening the integrity and autonomy of cultural traditions in nonindustrial lands.

Part Seven: Global Dominance and Diversity, 1850–1945, examines the development of a world arena in which people conceived of events on a global scale. Imperialism, world war, international economic connections, and world-encompassing ideological tendencies, such as nationalism and socialism, present the picture of a globe becoming increasingly interconnected. European dominance took on a worldwide dimension, seeming at times to threaten the diversity of human cultural experience with permanent subordination to European values and philosophies, while at other times triggering strong political or cultural resistance.

For **Part Eight: The Perils and Promises of a Global Community, 1945–2000,** we divide the last half of the twentieth century into three time periods: 1945–1975, 1975–1991, and 1991–2000. The challenges of the Cold War and post-colonial nation building dominated the period as a whole and involved global economic, technological, and political forces that became increasingly important factors in all aspects of human life. Technology plays a central role in this part, because of its integral role in the growth of a global community and because its many benefits in improving the quality of life seem clouded by real and potential negative impacts on the environment.

FORMATS

To accommodate different academic calendars and approaches to the course, *The Earth and Its Peoples* is issued in three formats. There is a one-volume hardcover version containing all 35 chapters, along with a two-volume paperback edition: Volume I: *To 1550* (Chapters 1–17), and Volume II: *Since 1500* (Chapters 17–35). For readers at institutions with the quarter system, we offer a three-volume paperback version: Volume A: *To 1200* (Chapters 1–12); Volume B: *From 1200 to 1870* (Chapters 12–27); and Volume C: *Since 1750* (Chapters 23–35).

A new introduction to Volume II has been written for this edition to recapitulate themes contained in Volume I and lay a groundwork for students studying only the period since 1500.

SUPPLEMENTS

We have assembled with care an array of text supplements to aid students in learning and instructors in teaching. These supplements, including *@history* web site, *GeoQuest: World CD-ROM*, a *Study Guide*, an *Instructor's Resource Manual, Test Items, Computerized Test Items,* and *Map Transparencies,* provide a tightly integrated program of teaching and learning.

Houghton Mifflin's *@history* web site provides a wealth of text-based materials for students and instructors. For students, this site offers primary sources, text-specific self-tests, and gateways to relevant history sites. In addition, *History WIRED: Web Intensive Research Exercises and Documents,* prepared by Jonathan Lee of San Antonio College, offers text-specific links to visual and written sources on the World Wide Web, along with exercises to enhance learning. Additional resources are provided for instructors, including historical maps suitable for classroom presentation or assignments.

A New CD-ROM, *GeoQuest: World,* features thirty interactive maps that illuminate world history events from the days of the Persian Empire to the present. Each map is accompanied by exercises with answers and essay questions. The four different types of interactivity allow students to move at their own pace through each section. Four demo maps can be viewed on the Houghton Mifflin *@history* web site.

The *Study Guide,* authored by Michele G. Scott James of MiraCosta College, contains learning objectives, chapter outlines (with space for students' notes on particular sections), key-term identifications, multiple-choice questions, short-answer and essay questions, and map exercises. Included too are distinctive "comparison charts" to help students organize the range of information about different cultures and events discussed in each chapter. The *Study Guide* is published in two volumes, to correspond to Volumes I and II of the textbook: Volume I contains Chapters 1–17; Volume II, Chapters 17–35.

The *Instructor's Resource Manual,* prepared by Harold M. Tanner of the University of North Texas, provides useful teaching strategies for the global history course and tips for getting the most out of the textbook. Each chapter contains instructional objectives, a detailed chapter outline, lecture topics with pertinent suggested readings, discussion questions, paper topic suggestions, and audio-visual resources. The revised preface contains new information on journal writing, as well as contact information for organizations, multimedia distributors, and journals.

Each chapter of the *Test Items,* revised by Jane Scimeca of Brookdale Community College, offers 20 to 25 key-term identifications, 5 to 10 essay questions with answer guidelines, 35 to 40 multiple-choice questions, and 3 to 5 history and geography exercises. We also provide a computerized version of the *Test Items,* to enable instructors to alter, replace, or add questions. Each entry in the *Computerized Test Items* is numbered according to the printed test items to ease the creation of customized tests.

In addition, a set of *Transparencies* of all the maps in the textbook is available on adoption.

ACKNOWLEDGMENTS

In preparing the second edition, we benefited from the critical readings of many colleagues. Our sincere thanks go in particular to the following instructors: Henry Abramson, Florida Atlantic University; Paul V. Adams, Shippensburg University/University of San Carlos; Maria S. Arbelaez, University of Nebraska at Omaha; William J. Astore, United States Air Force Academy; Fritz Blackwell, Washington State University; Thomas Borstelmann, Cornell University; Byron Cannon, University of Utah; David A. Chappell, University of Hawaii; Nancy Clark, California Polytechnic State University at San Luis Obispo; Lee Congdon, James Madison University; James Coolsen, Shippensburg University; Bruce Cruikshank, Hastings College; Linda T. Darling, University of Arizona; Susan Deans-Smith, University of Texas at Austin; Gregory C. Ference, Salisbury State University; Alan Fisher, Michigan State University; Donald M. Fisher, Niagara County Community College; Cathy A. Frierson, University of New Hampshire; Rosanna Gatens, Belmont University; Lorne E. Glaim, Pacific Union College; Matthew S. Gordon, Miami University; Steve Gosch, University of Wisconsin at Eau Claire; Kolleen M. Guy, University of Texas at San Antonio; James R. Hansen, Auburn University; Randolph C. Head, University of California at Riverside; David Hertzel, Southwestern Oklahoma State University; Richard J. Hoffman, San Francisco State University; Catherine M. Jones, North Georgia College and State University; Joy Kammerling, Eastern Illinois University; Carol A. Keller, San Antonio College; Jonathan Lee, San Antonio College; Miriam R. Levin, Case Western Reserve University; Richard Lewis, St. Cloud State University; James E. Lindsay, Colorado State University; Charles W. McClellan, Radford University; Andrea McElderry, University of Louisville; Stephen L. McFarland, Auburn University; Gregory McMahon, University of New Hampshire; Mark McLeod, University of Delaware; Stephen S. Michot, Mississippi County Community College; Shawn W. Miller, Brigham Young University; Kalala Joseph Ngalamulume, Central Washington University; Patricia O'Neill, Central Oregon Community College; Chandrika Paul, Shippensburg University; John R. Pavia, Ithaca College; Thomas Earl Porter, North Carolina A&T State University; Jean H. Quataert, SUNY at Binghamton; William Reddy, Duke University; Thomas Reeves, Roxbury Community College; Dennis Reinhartz, University of Texas at Arlington; Richard Rice, University of Tennessee at Chattanooga; Jane Scimeca, Brookdale Community College; Alyssa Goldstein Sepinwall, California State University at San Marcos; Deborah Shackleton, United States Air Force Academy; Anita Shelton, Eastern Illinois University; David R. Smith, California State Polytechnic University at Pomona; Mary Frances Smith, Ohio University; George E. Snow, Shippensburg University; Charlotte D. Staelin, Washington College; Paul D. Steeves, Stetson University; Yi Sun, University of San Diego; Willard Sunderland, University of Cincinnati; Thaddeus Sunseri, Colorado State University; Sara W. Tucker, Washburn University; John M. VanderLippe, SUNY at New Paltz; Mary A. Watrous-Schlesinger, Washington State University; Eric Van Young, University of California at San Diego; and Alex Zukas, National University, San Diego.

We also want to extend our collective thanks to Lynda Schaffer for her early conceptual contributions as well as to the history departments of Shippensburg University, the United States Air Force Academy, and the State University of New York at New Paltz for arranging reviewer conferences that provided crucial feedback for our revision of the book. Individually, Richard W. Bulliet thanks Jack Garraty and Isser Woloch for first involving him in world history; Pamela Kyle Crossley wishes to thank Gene Garthwaite, Charles Wood, and David Morgan; Steven W. Hirsch extends his gratitude to Dennis Trout and Peter L. D. Reid; Lyman L. Johnson extends his to Kenneth J. Andrien, Richard Boyer, Grant D. Hones, William M. Ringle, Hendrik Kraay, Daniel Dupre, and Steven W. Usselman; and David Northrup thanks Allen Howard and Prasanan Parthasarathi. Lyman Johnson also thanks the members of the Department of History of North Carolina A&T University for their many helpful and pertinent suggestions.

The three people who kept us on course in preparing the second edition deserve our special thanks: Jean L. Woy, Editor-in-Chief for History and Political Science; Nancy Blaine, Sponsoring Editor; and Jennifer E. Sutherland, Senior Development Editor. In carrying out our task, we got to know and value the work of several new staff at Houghton Mifflin: Carol Newman, Senior Project Editor; Julie Dunn, Associate Editor; Gillie Jones, Editorial Associate; Jennifer O'Neill, Editorial Assistant; and Henry Rachlin, Senior Designer. We also had the pleasure of working again with several people who helped so much with the first edition, including Charlotte Miller, Map Editor; Carole Frolich, Photo Researcher; Anthony L. Saizon, Design Director; Jill Haber, Senior Production/Design Coordinator; and Marie Barnes, Senior Manufacturing Coordinator.

We thank also the many students whose questions and concerns, expressed directly or through their instructors, shaped much of this revision. We continue to welcome all our readers' suggestions, queries, and criticisms. Please contact us at our respective institutions or at this e-mail address: college. hmco. com/history.

ABOUT THE AUTHORS

Richard W. Bulliet   Professor of Middle Eastern History at Columbia University and Director of its Middle East Institute, Richard W. Bulliet received his Ph.D. from Harvard University. He has written scholarly works on a number of topics: the social history of medieval Iran (*The Patricians of Nishapur*), the historical competition between pack camels and wheeled transport (*The Camel and the Wheel*), the process of conversion to Islam (*Conversion to Islam in the Medieval Period*), and the overall course of Islamic social history (*Islam: The View from the Edge*). He is the editor of the *Columbia History of the Twentieth Century*. He has published four novels, co-edited *The Encyclopedia of the Modern Middle East,* and hosted an educational television series on the Middle East. He was awarded a fellowship by the John Simon Guggenheim Memorial Foundation.

Pamela Kyle Crossley   Pamela Kyle Crossley received her Ph.D. in Modern Chinese History from Yale University. She is Professor of History, Rosenwald Research Professor in the Arts and Sciences, and Chair of Asian and Middle Eastern Studies at Dartmouth College. Her books include *A Translucent Mirror: History and Identity in Qing Imperial Ideology, The Manchus,* and *Orphan Warriors: Three Manchu Generations and the End of the Qing World.* Her research, which concentrates on the cultural history of China, Inner Asia, and Central Asia, has most recently been supported by the John Simon Guggenheim Memorial Foundation and the National Endowment for the Humanities.

Daniel R. Headrick   Daniel R. Headrick received his Ph.D. in History from Princeton University. Professor of History and Social Science at Roosevelt University in Chicago, he is the author of several books on the history of technology, imperialism, and international relations, including *The Tools of Empire: Technology and European Imperialism in the Nineteenth Century, The Tentacles of Progress: Technology Transfer in the Age of Imperialism, The Invisible Weapon: Telecommunications and International Politics,* and *When Information Came of Age: Technologies of Knowledge in the Age of Reason and Revolution, 1700–1850.* His articles have appeared in the *Journal of World History* and the *Journal of Modern History,* and he has been awarded fellowships by the National Endowment for the Humanities, the John Simon Guggenheim Memorial Foundation, and the Alfred P. Sloan Foundation.

Steven W. Hirsch   Steven W. Hirsch holds a Ph.D. in Classics from Stanford University and is currently Associate Professor of Classics and History at Tufts University. He has received grants from the National Endowment for the Humanities and the Massachusetts Foundation for Humanities and Public Policy. His research and publications include *The Friendship of the Barbarians: Xenophon and the Persian Empire,* as well as articles and reviews in the *Classical Journal,* the *American Journal of Philology,* and the *Journal of Interdisciplinary History.*

Lyman L. Johnson   Professor of History at the University of North Carolina at Charlotte, Lyman L. Johnson earned his Ph.D. in Latin American History from the University of Connecticut. A two-time Senior Fulbright Hays Lecturer, he also has received fellowships from the Tinker Foundation, the Social Science Research Council, the National Endowment for the Humanities, and the American Philosophical Society. His recent books include *The Faces of Honor* (with Sonya Lipsett-Rivera), *The Problem of Order in Changing Societies, Essays on the Price History of Eighteenth-Century Latin America* (with Enrique Tandeter), and *Colonial Latin America* (with Mark A. Burkholder). He also has published in journals, including the *Hispanic American Historical Review,* the *Journal of Latin American Studies,* the *International Review of Social History, Social History,* and *Desarrollo Económico.* He recently served as president of the Conference on Latin American History.

David Northrup   Professor of History at Boston College, David Northrup earned his Ph.D. in African and European History from the University of California at Los Angeles. He has published scholarly volumes on precolonial Nigeria, on precolonial and colonial Congo, on the Atlantic slave trade, and on Asian, African, and Pacific Islander indentured labor in the nineteenth century. His recent work appeared in the *Oxford History of the British Empire, Revue française d'histoire d'outre-mer, Slavery and Abolition,* and the *Journal of World History.* He currently serves on the Executive Council of the World History Association and has received research support from the Fulbright-Hays Commission, the National Endowment for the Humanities, and the Social Science Research Council.

Note on Spelling and Usage

Where necessary for clarity, dates are followed by the letters C.E. or B.C.E. The abbreviation C.E. stands for "Common Era" and is equivalent to A.D. (*anno Domini,* Latin for "in the year of the Lord"). The abbreviation B.C.E stands for "before the Common Era" and means the same as B.C. ("before Christ"). In keeping with our goal of approaching world history without special concentration on one culture or another, we chose these neutral abbreviations as appropriate to our enterprise. Because many readers will be more familiar with English than with metric measurements, however, units of measure are generally given in the English system, with metric equivalents following in parentheses.

In general, Chinese has been romanized according to the *pinyin* method. Exceptions include proper names well established in English (e.g., Canton, Chiang Kaishek) and a few English words borrowed from Chinese (e.g., kowtow). Spellings of Arabic, Ottoman Turkish, Persian, Mongolian, Manchu, Japanese, and Korean names and terms avoid special diacritical marks for letters that are pronounced only slightly differently in English. An apostrophe is used to indicate when two Chinese syllables are pronounced separately (e.g., Chang'an).

For words transliterated from languages that use the Arabic script—Arabic, Ottoman Turkish, Perisan, Urdu—the apostrophe indicating separately pronounced syllables may represent either of two special consonants, the *hamza* or the *ain.* Because most English-speakers do not hear the distinction between these two, they have not been distinguished in transliteration and are not indicated when they occur at the beginning or end of a word. As with Chinese, some words and commonly used place-names from these languages are given familiar English spellings (e.g., Quran instead of Qur'an, Cairo instead of al-Qahira). Arabic romanization has normally been used for terms relating to Islam, even where the context justifies slightly different Turkish or Persian forms, again for ease of comprehension.

There is an ongoing debate about how best to render Amerindian words in English. It has been common for authors writing in English to follow Mexican usage for Nahuatl and Yucatec Maya words and place-names. In this style, for example, the capital of the Aztec state is spelled Tenochtitlán, and the important late Maya city-state is spelled Chichén Itzá. Although these forms are still common even in the specialist literature, we have chosen to follow the scholarship that sees these accents as unnecessary. The exceptions are modern place-names, such as Mérida and Yucatán, which are accented. A similar problem exists for the spelling of Quechua and Aymara words from the Andean region of South America. Although there is significant disagreement among scholars, we follow the emerging consensus and use the spellings khipu (not quipu), Tiwanaku (not Tiahuanaco), and Wari (not Huari). However, we keep Inca (not Inka) and Cuzco (not Cusco), since these spellings are expected by most of our potential readers and we hope to avoid confusion.

THE EARTH AND ITS PEOPLES

A GLOBAL HISTORY

PEOPLES AND CIVILIZATIONS OF THE AMERICAS, 200–1500 C.E.

Classic-Era Culture and Society in Mesoamerica, 200–900 •
The Postclassic Period in Mesoamerica, 900–1500 • Northern Peoples •
Andean Civilizations, 200–1500

ENVIRONMENT AND TECHNOLOGY: Inca Roads

SOCIETY AND CULTURE: Acllas

Maya Scribe   Maya scribes used a complex writing system to record religious concepts
and the actions of their kings. This picture of a scribe was painted on a ceramic plate.

I n late August 682 C.E., the Maya° princess Lady Wac-Chanil-Ahau° walked down the steep steps from her family's residence and mounted a sedan chair decorated with rich textiles and animal skins. As the procession exited from the urban center of Dos Pilas°, her military escort spread out through the fields and woods along her path to prevent ambush by enemies. Lady Wac-Chanil-Ahau's destination was the Maya city of Naranjo°, where she was to marry a powerful nobleman. Her marriage had been arranged to reestablish the royal dynasty that had been eliminated when Caracol, the region's major military power, had defeated Naranjo. Lady Wac-Chanil-Ahau's passage to Naranjo symbolized her father's desire to forge a military alliance that could resist Caracol. For us, the story of Lady Wac-Chanil-Ahau illustrates the importance of marriage and lineage in the politics of the classic-period Maya.

Smoking Squirrel, the son of Lady Wac-Chanil-Ahau, ascended the throne of Naranjo as a five-year-old in 693 C.E. During his long reign he proved to be a careful diplomat and formidable warrior. He was also a prodigious builder, leaving behind an expanded and beautified capital as part of his legacy. Mindful of the importance of his mother and her lineage from Dos Pilas, he erected numerous stelae (carved stone monuments) that celebrated her life.[1]

When population increased and competition for resources grew more violent, warfare and dynastic crisis convulsed the world of Wac-Chanil-Ahau. The defeat of the city-states of Tikal and Naranjo by Caracol undermined long-standing commercial and political relations in much of southern Mesoamerica and led to more than a century of conflict. Caracol, in turn, was challenged by the dynasty created at Dos Pilas by the heirs of Lady Wac-Chanil-Ahau. Despite a shared culture and religion, the great Maya cities remained divided by the dynastic ambitions of their rulers and by the competition for resources.

As the story of Lady Wac-Chanil-Ahau's marriage and her role in the development of a Maya dynasty suggests, the peoples of the Americas were in constant competition for resources. Members of hereditary elites organized their societies to meet these challenges, even as their ambition for greater power predictably ignited new conflicts. No single set of political institutions or technologies worked in every environment, and enormous cultural diversity existed in the ancient Americas. In Mesoamerica (Mexico and northern Central America) and in the Andean region of South America, Amerindian peoples developed an extraordinarily productive and diversified agriculture.[2] They also built great cities that rivaled the capitals of the Chinese and Roman Empires in size and beauty. The Olmecs of Mesoamerica and Chavín° of the Andes were the first great civilizations of the Americas (see Chapter 4). In the rest of the hemisphere, indigenous peoples adapted combinations of hunting and agriculture to maintain a wide variety of settlement patterns, political forms, and cultural traditions. All the cultures and civilizations of the Americas experienced cycles of expansion and contraction as they struggled with the challenges of environmental changes, population growth, social conflict, and war.

As you read this chapter, ask yourself the following questions:

- How did differing environments influence the development of Mesoamerican, Andean, and northern peoples?
- What technologies were developed to meet the challenges of these environments?
- How were the civilizations of Mesoamerica and the Andean region similar? How did they differ?
- How did religious belief and practice influence political life in the ancient Americas?

Maya (MY-ah)
Wac-Chanil-Ahau (wac-cha-NEEL-ah-HOW)
Dos Pilas (dohs PEE-las)   **Naranjo** (na-ROHN-hoe)

Chavín (cha-VEEN)

CHRONOLOGY

	Mesoamerica	Northern peoples	Andes
100	**100** Teotihuacan founded	**100–400** Hopewell culture in Ohio River Valley	
			200–700 Moche culture of Peruvian coast
	250 Maya early classic period begins		
400			
			500–1000 Tiwanaku and Wari control Peruvian highlands
700		**700–1200** Anasazi culture	
	ca. 750 Teotihuacan destroyed **800–900** Maya centers abandoned, end of classic period **968** Toltec capital of Tula founded	**919** Pueblo Bonito founded	
1000			
		1050–1250 Cahokia reaches peak power	
	1156 Tula destroyed	**1150** Collapse of Anasazi centers begins	**1200** Chimú begins military expansion
1300			
	1325 Aztec capital Tenochtitlan founded		
			1438 Inca expansion begins **1465** Inca conquer Chimú
1500	**1502** Moctezuma II crowned Aztec ruler	**1500** Mississippian culture declines	**1500–1525** Inca conquer Ecuador

CLASSIC-ERA CULTURE AND SOCIETY IN MESOAMERICA, 200–900

Between 200 and 900 C.E. the peoples of Mesoamerica created a remarkable civilization. Despite enduring differences in language and the absence of regional political integration, Mesoamericans were unified by similarities in material culture, religious beliefs and practices, and social structures. Building on the earlier achievements of the Olmecs and others, the peoples of what is now Central America and south and central Mexico developed new forms of political organization, made great strides in astronomy and mathematics, and improved the productivity of their agriculture. During the classic period, population grew, a greater variety of products were traded over longer distances, and social hierarchies became more complex. Great cities were constructed, serving as centers of political life and as arenas of religious ritual and spiritual experience.

Classic-period civilizations built on the religious and political foundations established earlier in Olmec centers. The cities of the classic period continued to be dominated by platforms and pyramids devoted to religious functions, but they were more impressive and diversified architecturally. They had large full-time pop-

Map 12.1   Major Mesoamerican Civilizations, 1000 B.C.E.–1519 C.E.   From their island capital of Tenochtitlan, the Aztecs militarily and commercially dominated a large region. Aztec achievements were built on the legacy of earlier civilizations such as the Olmecs and Maya.

ulations divided into classes and dominated by hereditary political and religious elites who controlled nearby towns and villages and imposed their will on the rural peasantry.

The political and cultural innovations of this period did not depend on the introduction of new technologies. The agricultural foundation of Mesoamerican civilization had been developed centuries earlier. The major innovations in agriculture such as irrigation, the draining of wetlands, and the terracing of hillsides had all been in place for more than a thousand years when great cities were developed after 200 C.E. Instead, the achievements of the classic era depended on the ability of increasingly powerful elites to organize and command growing numbers of laborers and soldiers. What had changed was the reach and power of religious and political leaders. The scale and impressive architecture found at Teotihuacan°

Teotihuacan (teh-o-tee-WAH-kahn)

or at the great Maya cities illustrate both Mesoamerican aesthetic achievements and the development of powerful political institutions.

Teotihuacan

Located about 30 miles (48 kilometers) northeast of modern Mexico City, **Teotihuacan** (100 B.C.E.–750 C.E.) was one of Mesoamerica's most important classic-period civilizations (see Map 12.1). At the height of its power, from 450 to 600 C.E., Teotihuacan was the largest city in the Americas. With between 125,000 and 200,000 inhabitants, it was larger than all but a small number of contemporary European and Asian cities.

Religious architecture rose above the city center. Enormous pyramids dedicated to the Sun and Moon and more than twenty smaller temples devoted to other gods were arranged along a central avenue. The people recognized and worshiped many gods and lesser spirits. Among the gods were the Sun, the Moon, a storm-god, and Quetzalcoatl°, the feathered serpent. Quetzalcoatl was a culture-god believed to be the originator of agriculture and the arts. Like the earlier Olmecs, people living at Teotihuacan practiced human sacrifice. More than sixty sacrificial victims were found during the excavation of the temple of Quetzalcoatl at Teotihuacan. Sacrifice was viewed as a sacred duty toward the gods and as essential to the well-being of human society.

The rapid growth in urban population was the result of the forced relocation of farm families from small villages in the region. More than two-thirds of the city's residents continued to work in agriculture, walking out from urban residences to their fields. The elite of Teotihuacan used the city's growing labor resources to bring marginal lands into production. Swamps were drained, irrigation works were constructed, terraces were built into hillsides, and the use of chinampas was expanded. **Chinampas°,** sometimes called "floating gardens," were narrow artificial islands anchored by trees and created by heaping lake muck and waste material on beds of reeds. Chinampas permitted year-round agriculture—because of subsurface irrigation and resistance to frost—and thus played a crucial role in sustaining the region's growing population. The productivity of the city's agriculture made possible its accomplishments in art, architecture, and trade.

As population grew, the housing of commoners underwent dramatic change. Apartment-like stone buildings were constructed for the first time. Among the residents of these early apartment blocks were the craftsmen who produced the pottery and obsidian tools that were the most important articles of long-distance trade. Teotihuacan pottery has been found throughout central Mexico and even in the Maya region of Guatemala. More than 2 percent of the urban population was engaged in making obsidian tools and weapons.

The city's role as a religious center and commercial power provided both divine approval of and a material basis for the elite's increased wealth and status. Members of this elite controlled the state bureaucracy, tax collection, and commerce. Their prestige and wealth were reflected in their style of dress and diet and in the separate residence compounds built for aristocratic families. The central position and great prestige of the priestly class were evident in temple and palace murals. Teotihuacan's religious influence drew pilgrims from as far away as Oaxaca and Veracruz. Some of them became permanent residents.

Unlike the other classic-period civilizations, the people of Teotihuacan did not concentrate power in the

Teotihuacan Polychrome Mask   Masks made from many different materials, including semiprecious stones and clay, were an important part of ritual life at Teotihuacan. Some were attached to burial shrouds. This mask shows the large earspools and nose ornament worn by members of the elite.   (Enrique Franco-Torrijos)

hands of a single ruler. Although the ruins of their impressive housing compounds demonstrate the wealth and influence of the city's aristocracy, there is no clear evidence that individual rulers or a ruling dynasty gained overarching political power. In Teotihuacan the deeds of the rulers were not featured in public art, nor were their images represented by statues as in other Mesoamerican civilizations. In fact, some scholars suggest that Teotihuacan was ruled by alliances forged among elite families or by weak kings who were the puppets of these powerful families. Regardless of what form political decision making took, we do know that this powerful classic-period civilization achieved regional preeminence without subordinating its political life to the personality of a powerful individual ruler or lineage.

Historians debate the role of the military in the development of Teotihuacan. The absence of walls or other defensive structures before 500 C.E. suggests that Teotihuacan enjoyed relative peace during its early development. Archaeological evidence, however, reveals that the city created a powerful military to protect long-distance trade and to compel peasant agriculturalists to transfer their surplus production to the city. The discovery of representations of soldiers in typical Teotihuacan dress in the Maya region of Guatemala suggests to some that Teotihuacan used its military to expand trade relations. Unlike later postclassic civilizations, however, Teotihuacan was not an imperial state controlled by a military elite.

It is unclear what forces brought about the collapse of Teotihuacan about 650 C.E. Weakness was evident as

Quetzalcoatl (kate-zahl-CO-ah-tal)
chinampas (chee-NAM-pahs)

early as 500 C.E., when the urban population declined to about 40,000 and the city began to build defensive walls. These fortifications and pictorial evidence from murals suggest that the city's final decades were violent. Early scholars suggested that the city was overwhelmed militarily by a rival city located nearby or by nomadic warrior peoples from the northern frontier. More recently, investigators have uncovered evidence of conflict within the ruling elite and the mismanagement of resources. This, they argue, led to class conflict and the breakdown of public order. As a result, most important temples in the city center were pulled down and religious images defaced. Elite palaces were also systematically burned and many of the residents killed. Regardless of the causes, the eclipse of Teotihuacan was felt throughout Mexico and into Central America.

The Maya

During Teotihuacan's ascendancy in the north, the **Maya** developed an impressive civilization in the region that today includes Guatemala, Honduras, Belize, and southern Mexico (see Map 12.1). Given the difficulties imposed by a tropical climate and fragile soils, the cultural and architectural achievements of the Maya were remarkable. Although they shared a single culture, they were never unified politically. Instead, rival kingdoms led by hereditary rulers struggled with each other for regional dominance, much like the Mycenaean-era Greeks (see Chapter 3).

Today Maya farmers prepare their fields by cutting down small trees and brush and then burning the dead vegetation to fertilize the land. This swidden agriculture can produce high yields for a few years, but it uses up the soil's nutrients, eventually forcing people to move to more fertile land. The high population levels of the Maya classic period (250–900 C.E.) required more intensive forms of agriculture. Maya living near the major urban centers achieved high agricultural yields by draining swamps and building elevated fields. They used irrigation in areas with long dry seasons, and they terraced hillsides in the cooler highlands. Nearly every household planted a garden to provide condiments and fruits to supplement dietary staples. Maya agriculturists also managed nearby forests, favoring the growth of the trees and shrubs that were most useful to them, as well as promoting the conservation of deer and other animals hunted for food.

During the classic period, Maya city-states proliferated. The most powerful cities controlled groups of smaller dependent cities and a broad agricultural zone by building impressive religious temples and creating rituals that linked the power of kings to the gods. Classic-era cities, unlike earlier sites, had dense central precincts visually dominated by monumental architecture. These political and ceremonial centers were commonly aligned with the movements of the Sun and Venus. Open plazas were surrounded by high pyramids and by elaborately decorated palaces often built on high ground or on constructed mounds. The effect was to awe the masses drawn to these centers for religious and political rituals.

The Maya loved decoration. Nearly all of their public buildings were covered with bas-relief and painted in bright colors. Religious allegories, the genealogies of rulers, and important historical events were the most common motifs. Beautifully carved altars and stone monoliths were erected near major temples. This rich legacy of monumental architecture was constructed without the aid of wheels—no pulleys, wheelbarrows, or carts—or metal tools. Masses of men and women aided only by levers and stone tools cut and carried construction materials and lifted them into place.

The Maya cosmos was divided into three layers connected along a vertical axis that traced the course of the Sun. The earthly arena of human existence held an intermediate position between the heavens, conceptualized by the Maya as a sky-monster, and a dark underworld. A sacred tree rose through the three layers; its roots were in the underworld, and its branches reached into the heavens. The temple precincts of Maya cities physically represented essential elements of this religious cosmology. The pyramids were sacred mountains reaching to the heavens. The doorways of the pyramids were portals to the underworld.

Rulers and other members of the elite served both priestly and political functions. They decorated their bodies with paint and tattoos and wore elaborate costumes of textiles, animal skins, and feathers to project both secular power and divine sanction. Kings communicated directly with the supernatural residents of the other worlds and with deified royal ancestors through bloodletting rituals and hallucinogenic trances. Scenes of rulers drawing blood from lips, ears, and penises are common in surviving frescoes and on painted pottery.

Warfare in particular was infused with religious meaning and elaborate ritual. Battle scenes and the depiction of the torture and sacrifice of captives were frequent decorative themes. Typically, Maya military forces fought to secure captives rather than territory. Days of fasting, sacred ritual, and rites of purification preceded battle. The king, his kinsmen, and other ranking nobles actively participated in war. Elite captives were nearly always sacrificed; captured commoners were more likely to be enslaved.

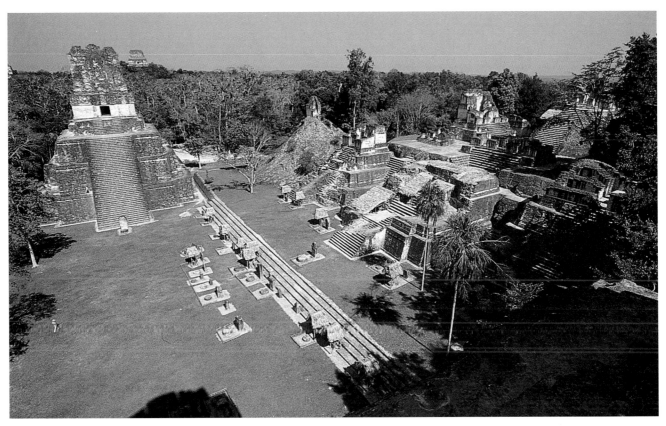

The Great Plaza at Tikal   Still visible in the ruins of Tikal, in modern Guatemala, are the impressive architectural and artistic achievements of the classic-era Maya. Maya centers provided a dramatic setting for the rituals that dominated public life. Construction of Tikal began before 150 B.C.E.; the city was abandoned about 900 C.E. A ball court and residences for the elite were part of the Great Plaza.   (Martha Cooper/Peter Arnold, Inc.)

Only two women are known to have ruled Maya kingdoms. Maya women of the ruling lineages did play important political and religious roles, however. The consorts of male rulers participated in bloodletting rituals and in other important public ceremonies, and their noble blood helped legitimate the rule of their husbands. Although Maya society was patrilineal (tracing descent in the male line), there is evidence that some male rulers traced their lineages bilaterally (in both the male and the female lines). Like Lady Wac-Chanil-Ahau's son Smoking Squirrel, some rulers emphasized the female line if it held higher status. Much less is known about the lives of the women of the lower classes, but scholars believe that they played a central role in the household economy, maintaining essential garden plots and weaving, and in the management of family life.

Building on what the Olmecs had done, the Maya made important contributions to the development of the Mesoamerican calendar and to mathematics and writing. Their interest in time and in the cosmos was reflected in the complexity of their calendric system. Each day was identified by three separate dating systems. Like other peoples throughout Mesoamerica, the Maya had a calendar that tracked the ritual cycle (260 days divided into 13 months of 20 days) as well as a solar calendar (365 days divided into 18 months of 20 days, plus 5 unfavorable days at the end of the year). The concurrence of these two calendars every 52 years was believed to be especially ominous. The Maya, alone among Mesoamerican peoples, also maintained a continuous "long count" calendar, which began at a fixed date in the past that scholars have identified as 3114 B.C.E., a date that the Maya probably associated with creation.

These accurate calendric systems and the astronomical observations on which they were based depended on Maya contributions to mathematics and writing. Their system of mathematics incorporated the concept of the zero and place value but had limited notational signs.

Maya writing was a form of hieroglyphic inscription that signified whole words or concepts as well as phonetic cues or syllables. Aspects of public life, religious belief, and the biographies of rulers and their ancestors were recorded in deerskin and bark-paper books, on pottery, and on the stone columns and monumental buildings of the urban centers. In this sense every Maya city was a sacred text.

Between 800 and 900 C.E. many of the major urban centers of the Maya were abandoned or destroyed, although a small number of classic-period centers survived for centuries. This collapse was preceded in some areas by decades of urban population decline and increased warfare. Some experts have argued that the earlier destruction of Teotihuacan after 650 C.E. disrupted trade, thus undermining the legitimacy of Maya rulers who had used these goods in rituals. Other scholars suggest that growing population pressure led to environmental degradation and declining agricultural productivity. This environmental crisis, in turn, might have led to social conflict and increased levels of warfare as desperate elites sought to acquire additional agricultural land through conquest. Although little evidence has been found, some scholars have proposed that epidemic disease and pestilence were the prime causes of the catastrophe. Most probably, a combination of factors caused the end of the classic period.

THE POSTCLASSIC PERIOD IN MESOAMERICA, 900–1500

The division between classic and postclassic periods is somewhat arbitrary. Not only is there no single explanation for the collapse of Teotihuacan and many of the major Maya centers, but these events occurred over more than a century and a half. In fact, some important classic-period civilizations survived unscathed. Moreover, the essential cultural characteristics of the classic period were carried over to the postclassic. The two periods are linked by similarities in religious belief and practice, in architecture, in urban planning, and in social organization.

There were, however, some important differences between these periods. There is evidence that the population of Mesoamerica expanded during the postclassic period. Resulting pressures led to an intensification of agricultural practices and to increased warfare. The governing elites of the major postclassic states—the Toltecs and the Aztecs—responded to these harsh realities by increasing the size of their armies and by developing political institutions that facilitated their control of large and culturally diverse territories acquired through conquest.

The Mesoamerican Ball Game   From Guatemala to Arizona, archaeologists have found evidence of an ancient ball game played with a solid rubber ball on slope-sided courts shaped like a capital T. Among the Maya the game was associated with a creation myth and thus had deep religious meaning. There is evidence that some players were sacrificed. In this scene from a ceramic jar, players wearing elaborate ritual clothing—which includes heavy, protective pads around the chest and waist—play with a ball much larger than the ball actually used in such games. Some representations show balls drawn to suggest a human head.   (Dallas Art Museum/Justin Kerr)

The Toltecs

Little is known about the **Toltecs°** prior to their arrival in central Mexico. Some scholars speculate that they were originally a satellite population that Teotihuacan had placed on the northern frontier to protect against the incursions of nomads. After their migration south, the Toltecs borrowed from the cultural legacy of Teotihuacan and created an important postclassic civilization. Memories of their military achievements and the violent imagery of their political and religious rituals dominated the Mesoamerican imagination in the late postclassic period. In the fourteenth century, the Aztecs and their contemporaries erroneously believed that the Toltecs were the source of nearly all the great cultural achievements of the Mesoamerican world. As one Aztec source later recalled:

> In truth [the Toltecs] invented all the precious and marvelous things. . . . All that now exists was their discovery. . . . And these Toltecs were very wise; they were thinkers, for they originated the year count, the day count. All their discoveries formed the book for interpreting dreams. . . . And so wise were they [that] they understood the stars which were in the heavens.[3]

In fact, all these contributions to Mesoamerican culture were actually in place long before the Toltecs gained control of central Mexico. The most important Toltec innovations were instead political and military.

The Toltecs created the first conquest state based largely on military power, and they extended their political influence from the area north of modern Mexico City to Central America. Established about 968 C.E., Tula°, the Toltec capital, was constructed in a grand style (see Map 12.1). Its public architecture featured colonnaded patios and numerous temples. Although the population of Tula never reached the levels of classic-period Teotihuacan, the Toltec capital dominated central Mexico. Toltec decoration had a more warlike and violent character than the decoration of earlier Mesoamerican cultures. Nearly all Toltec public buildings and temples were decorated with representations of warriors or with scenes suggesting human sacrifice.

Two chieftains or kings apparently ruled the Toltec state together. Evidence suggests that this division of responsibility eventually weakened Toltec power and led to the destruction of Tula. Sometime after 1000 C.E., a struggle between elite groups identified with rival religious cults undermined the Toltec state. According to legends that survived among the Aztecs, Topiltzin°—one of the two rulers and a priest of the cult of Quetzalcoatl—and his followers bitterly accepted exile in the east, "the land of the rising sun." These legendary events coincided with growing Toltec influence among the Maya of the Yucatán Peninsula. One of the ancient texts relates these events in the following manner:

> Thereupon he [Topiltzin] looked toward Tula, and then wept. . . . And when he had done these things . . . he went to reach the seacoast. Then he fashioned a raft of serpents. When he had arranged the raft, he placed himself as if it were his boat. Then he set off across the sea.[4]

After the exile of Topiltzin the Toltec state began to decline, and around 1156 C.E. northern invaders overcame Tula itself. After its destruction, a centuries-long process of cultural and political assimilation produced a new Mesoamerican political order based on the urbanized culture and statecraft of the Toltecs. Like Semitic peoples of the third millennium B.C.E. interacting with Sumerian culture (see Chapter 2), the new Mesoamerican elites were drawn in part from the invading cultures. The Aztecs of the Valley of Mexico became the most important of these late postclassic peoples.

The Aztecs

The **Mexica°**, more commonly known as the **Aztecs,** were among the northern peoples who pushed into central Mexico in the wake of the collapse of Tula. At the time of their arrival they had a clan-based social organization. In this new environment they began to adopt the political and social practices that they found among the urbanized agriculturalists of the valley. At first, the Aztecs served their more powerful neighbors as serfs and mercenaries. As their strength grew, they relocated to small islands near the shore of Lake Texcoco and began the construction of their twin capitals, **Tenochtitlan°** and Tlatelolco (modern Mexico City), around 1325 C.E.

Military successes allowed the Aztecs to seize control of additional agricultural land along the lakeshore. With the increased economic independence and greater political security that resulted from this expansion, the Aztecs transformed their political organization by introducing a monarchical system similar to that found in more powerful neighboring states. Clans survived to the era of Spanish conquest but increasingly lost influence to monarchs and hereditary aristocrats. Aztec rulers did not have absolute power, and royal succession was not based on primogeniture. A council of

---

Toltec (TOLL-tek)   Tula (TOO-la)   Topilitzin (tow-PEELT-zeen)

Mexica (meh-SHE-ca)   Tenochititlan (teh-noch-TIT-lan)

Costumes of Aztec Warriors
In Mesoamerican warfare individual warriors sought to gain prestige and improve their status by taking captives. This illustration from the sixteenth-century Codex Mendoza was drawn by an Amerindian artist. It shows the Aztecs' use of distinctive costumes to acknowledge the prowess of warriors. These costumes indicate the taking of two (top left) to six captives (bottom center). The individual on the bottom right shown without a weapon was a military leader. As was common in Mesoamerican illustrations of military conflict, the captives, held by their hair, are shown kneeling before the victors. (The Bodleian Library, Oxford, Ms. Arch. Selder. A.I. fol. 64r)

powerful aristocrats selected new rulers from among male members of the ruling lineage. Once selected, the ruler was forced to renegotiate the submission of tribute dependencies and then demonstrate his divine mandate by undertaking a new round of military conquests. War was infused with religious meaning, providing the ruler with legitimacy and increasing the prestige of successful warriors.

As the power of the ruler and aristocracy grew, the authority of kinship-based clans declined. As a result, social divisions were accentuated. These alterations in social organization and political life were made possible by Aztec military expansion. Territorial conquest allowed the warrior elite of Aztec society to seize land and peasant labor as spoils of war (see Map 12.1). In time, the royal family and highest-ranking members of the aristocracy possessed extensive estates that were cultivated by slaves and landless commoners. The Aztec lower classes received some material rewards from imperial expansion but lost most of their ability to influence or control decisions. Some commoners were able to achieve some social mobility through success on the battlefield or by entering the priesthood, but the highest social ranks were always reserved for hereditary nobles.

The urban plan of Tenochtitlan and Tlatelolco continued to be organized around the clans, whose members maintained a common ritual life and accepted civic responsibilities such as caring for the sick and elderly. Clan members also fought together as military units. Nevertheless, the clans' historical control over common agricultural land and other scarce resources, such as fishing and hunting rights, declined. By 1500 C.E. great inequalities in wealth and privilege characterized Aztec society.

Aztec kings and aristocrats legitimated their ascendancy by creating elaborate rituals and ceremonies to distinguish themselves from commoners. One of the Spaniards who participated in the conquest of the Aztec Empire remembered his first meeting with the Aztec ruler Moctezuma° II (r. 1502–1520): "many great lords

Moctezuma (mock-teh-ZU-ma)

walked before the great Montezuma [Moctezuma II], sweeping the ground on which he was to tread and laying down cloaks so that his feet should not touch the earth. Not one of these chieftains dared look him in the face."[5] Commoners lived in small dwellings and ate a limited diet of staples, but members of the nobility lived in large, well-constructed two-story houses and consumed a diet rich in animal protein and flavored by condiments and expensive imports like chocolate. Rich dress and jewelry also set apart the elite. Even in marriage customs the two groups were different. Commoners were monogamous, great nobles polygamous.

The Aztec state met the challenge of feeding an urban population of approximately 150,000 by efficiently organizing the labor of the clans and additional laborers sent by defeated peoples to expand agricultural land. The construction of a dike more than 5½ miles (9 kilometers) long by 23 feet (7 meters) wide to separate the fresh and saltwater parts of Lake Texcoco was the Aztecs' most impressive land reclamation project. The dike allowed a significant extension of irrigated fields and the construction of additional chinampas. One expert has estimated that the project consumed 4 million person-days to complete. Aztec chinampas contributed maize, fruits, and vegetables to the markets of Tenochtitlan. The imposition of a **tribute system** on conquered peoples also helped relieve some of the pressure of Tenochtitlan's growing population. Unlike the tribute system of Tang China, where tribute had a more symbolic character (see Chapter 11), one quarter of the Aztec capital's food requirements was satisfied by tribute payments of maize, beans, and other foods sent by nearby political dependencies. The Aztecs also demanded cotton cloth, military equipment, luxury goods like jade and feathers, and sacrificial victims as tribute. Trade supplemented these supplies.

A specialized class of merchants controlled long-distance trade. Given the absence of draft animals and wheeled vehicles, this commerce was dominated by lightweight and valuable products like gold, jewels, feathered garments, cacao, and animal skins. Merchants also provided essential political and military intelligence for the Aztec elite. Operating outside the protection of Aztec military power, merchant expeditions were armed and often had to defend themselves. Although merchants became wealthy and powerful as the Aztecs expanded their empire, they were denied the privileges of the high nobility, which was jealous of its power. As a result, the merchants feared to publicly display their affluence.

Like commerce throughout the Mesoamerican world, Aztec commerce was carried on without money and credit. Barter was facilitated by the use of cacao,

quills filled with gold, and cotton cloth as standard units of value to compensate for differences in the value of bartered goods. Aztec expansion facilitated the integration of producers and consumers in the central Mexican economy. As a result, the markets of Tenochtitlan and Tlatelolco offered a rich array of goods from as far away as Central America and what is now the southwestern border of the United States. Hernán Cortés (1485–1547), the Spanish adventurer who eventually conquered the Aztecs, expressed his admiration for the abundance of the Aztec marketplace:

> One square in particular is twice as big as that of Salamanca and completely surrounded by arcades where there are daily more than sixty thousand folk buying and selling. Every kind of merchandise such as may be met with in every land is for sale. . . . There is nothing to be found in all the land which is not sold in these markets, for over and above what I have mentioned there are so many and such various things that on account of their very number . . . I cannot detail them.[6]

The Aztecs succeeded in developing a remarkable urban landscape. The combined population of Tenochtitlan and Tlatelolco and the cities and hamlets of the surrounding lakeshore was approximately 500,000 by 1500 C.E. The island capital was designed so that canals and streets intersected at right angles. Three causeways connected the city to the lakeshore.

Religious rituals dominated public life in Tenochtitlan. Like the other cultures of the Mesoamerican world, the Aztecs worshiped a large number of gods. Most of these gods had a dual nature—both male and female. The major contribution of the Aztecs to the religious life of Mesoamerica was the cult of Huitzilopochtli°, the southern hummingbird. As the Aztec state grew in power and wealth, the importance of this cult grew as well. Huitzilopochtli was originally associated with war, but eventually the Aztecs identified this god with the Sun, worshiped as a divinity throughout Mesoamerica. Huitzilopochtli, they believed, required a diet of human hearts to sustain him in his daily struggle to bring the Sun's warmth to the world. Tenochtitlan was architecturally dominated by a great twin temple devoted to Huitzilopochtli and Tlaloc, the rain god, symbolizing the two bases of the Aztec economy: war and agriculture.

War captives were the preferred sacrificial victims, but large numbers of criminals, slaves, and people provided as tribute by dependent regions were also sacrificed. Although human sacrifice had been practiced

---

Huitzilopochtli (wheat-zeel-oh-POSHT-lee)

since early times in Mesoamerica, the Aztecs and other societies of the late postclassic period transformed this religious ritual by dramatically increasing its scale. There are no reliable estimates for the total number of sacrifices, but the numbers clearly reached into the thousands each year. This form of violent public ritual had political consequences and was not simply the celebration of religious belief. Some scholars have emphasized the political nature of this rising tide of sacrifice, noting that sacrifices were carried out in front of large crowds that included leaders from enemy and subject states as well as the masses of Aztec society. The political subtext must have been clear: rebellion, deviancy, and opposition were extremely dangerous.

NORTHERN PEOPLES

By the end of the classic period in Mesoamerica, around 900 C.E., important cultural centers had appeared in the southwestern desert region and along the Ohio and Mississippi river valleys of what is now the United States. In both regions improved agricultural productivity and population growth led to increased urbanization and complex social and political structures. In the Ohio Valley Amerindian peoples who depended on locally domesticated seed crops as well as traditional hunting and gathering developed large villages with monumental earthworks. The introduction of maize, beans, and squash into this region from Mesoamerica after 1000 B.C.E. played an important role in the development of complex societies. Once established, these useful food crops were adopted throughout North America.

As growing populations came to depend on maize as a dietary staple, large-scale irrigation projects were undertaken in both the southwestern desert and the eastern river valleys. This development is a sign of increasingly centralized political power and growing social stratification. The two regions, however, evolved different political traditions. The Anasazi° and their neighbors in the southwest maintained a relatively egalitarian social structure and retained collective forms of political organization based on kinship and age. The mound builders of the eastern river valleys evolved more hierarchical political institutions: groups of small towns were subordinate to a political center ruled by a hereditary chief who wielded both secular and religious authority.

Anasazi (ah-nah-SAH-zee)

Southwestern Desert Cultures

Immigrants from Mexico introduced agriculture based on irrigation to present-day Arizona around 300 B.C.E. Because irrigation there allowed the planting of two crops per year, the population grew and settled village life soon appeared. Of all the southwestern cultures, the Hohokam of the Salt and Gila river valleys show the strongest Mexican influence. Hohokam sites have platform mounds and ball courts similar to those of Mesoamerica. Hohokam pottery, clay figurines, cast copper bells, and turquoise mosaics also reflect Mexican influence. By 1000 C.E. the Hohokam had constructed an elaborate irrigation system that included one canal more than 18 miles (30 kilometers) in length. Hohokam agricultural and ceramic technology spread over the centuries to neighboring peoples, but it was the Anasazi to the north who left the most vivid legacy of these desert cultures.

Archaeologists use **Anasazi,** a Navajo word meaning "ancient ones," to identify a number of dispersed though similar desert cultures located in what is now the Four Corners region of Arizona, New Mexico, Colorado, and Utah (see Map 12.2). Between 450 and 750 C.E. the Anasazi developed an economy based on maize, beans, and squash. Their successful adaptation of these crops permitted the formation of larger villages and led to an enriched cultural life centered in underground buildings called kivas. Evidence suggests that the Anasazi may have used kivas for weaving and pottery making. They produced pottery decorated with geometric patterns, learned to weave cotton cloth, and, after 900 C.E., began to construct large multistory residential and ritual centers.

One of the largest Anasazi communities was located in Chaco Canyon in what is now northwestern New Mexico. Eight large towns were built in the canyon and four more on surrounding mesas, suggesting a regional population of approximately 15,000. Many smaller villages were located nearby. Each town contained hundreds of rooms arranged in tiers around a central plaza. At Pueblo Bonito, the largest town, more than 650 rooms were arranged in a four-story block of residences and storage rooms. Pueblo Bonito had 38 kivas, including a great kiva more than 65 feet (19 meters) in diameter. Social life and craft activities were concentrated in small open plazas or

Map 12.2 Culture Areas of North America In each of the large ecological regions of North America, native peoples evolved distinctive cultures and technologies. Here the Anasazi of the arid southwest and the mound-building cultures of the Ohio and Mississippi river valleys are highlighted.

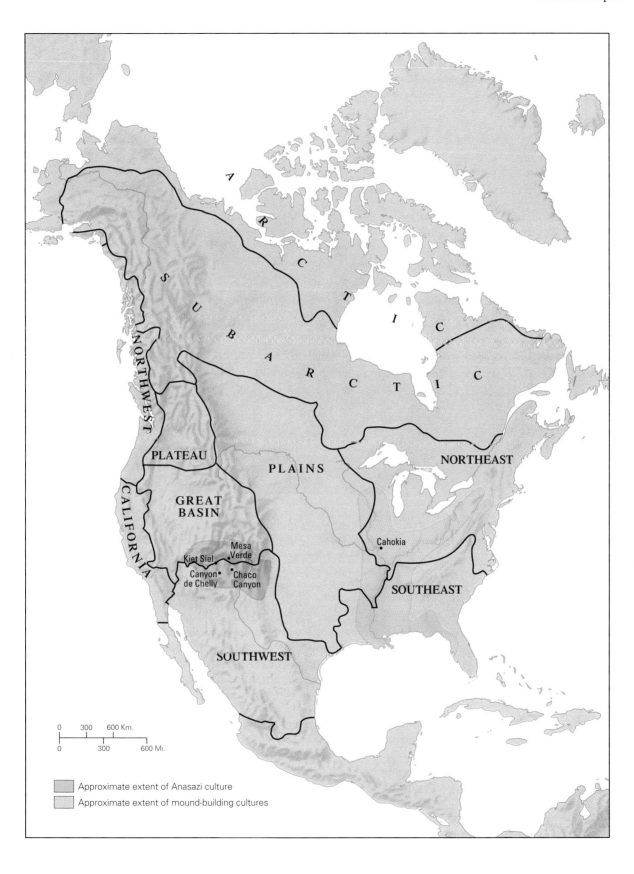

ARCTIC

SUBARCTIC

NORTHWEST

PLATEAU

PLAINS

NORTHEAST

CALIFORNIA

GREAT
BASIN

Kiet Siel •   Mesa
             Verde •

Canyon •   • Chaco
de Chelly   Canyon

• Cahokia

SOUTHEAST

SOUTHWEST

0   300   600 Km.

0   300   600 Mi.

Approximate extent of Anasazi culture

Approximate extent of mound-building cultures

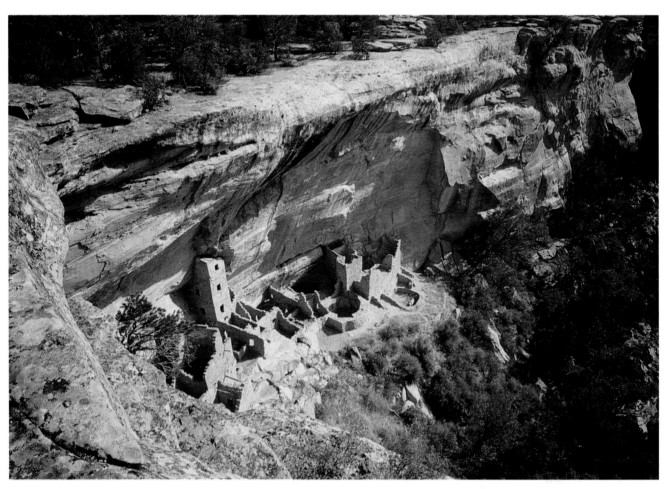

Mesa Verde Cliff Dwelling   Located in southern Colorado, the Anasazi cliff dwellings of Mesa Verde hosted a population of about 7,000 in 1250 C.E. The construction of housing complexes and religious buildings in the area's large caves was probably prompted by increased warfare in the region.   (David Muench Photography)

common rooms. Hunting, trade, and the need to maintain irrigation works often drew men away from the village. Women shared in agricultural tasks and were specialists in many crafts. They also were responsible for food preparation and childcare. If the practice of modern Pueblos, cultural descendants of the Anasazi, is a guide, houses and furnishings may have belonged to the women who formed extended families with their mothers and sisters.

The high-quality construction at Chaco Canyon, the size and number of kivas, and a system of roads linking the canyon to outlying towns suggest that Pueblo Bonito and its nearest neighbors exerted some kind of political or religious dominance over a large region. Some archaeologists have suggested that the Chaco Canyon culture originated as a colonial appendage of Mesoamerica, but the archaeological record provides little evidence for this

theory. Merchants from Chaco provided Toltec-period peoples of northern Mexico with turquoise in exchange for shell jewelry, copper bells, macaws, and trumpets. But these exchanges occurred late in Chaco's development, and more important signs of Mesoamerican influence such as pyramid-shaped mounds and ball courts are not found at Chaco. Nor is there evidence from the excavation of burials and residences of clear class distinctions, a common feature of Mesoamerican culture. Instead, it appears that the Chaco Canyon culture developed from earlier societies in the region.

The abandonment of the major sites in Chaco Canyon in the twelfth century most likely resulted from a long drought that undermined the culture's fragile agricultural economy. Nevertheless, the Anasazi continued in the Four Corners region for more than a century after the abandonment of Chaco Canyon. There were major centers at Mesa Verde in present-day Colorado and at Canyon de Chelly and Kiet Siel in Arizona. Anasazi settlements on the Colorado Plateau and in Arizona were constructed in large natural caves high above valley floors. This hard-to-reach location suggests increased levels of warfare, probably provoked by population pressure on limited arable land. Elements of this cultural tradition survive today among the Pueblo peoples of the Rio Grande Valley and Arizona who still live in multistory villages and worship in kivas.

Mound Builders: The Adena, Hopewell, and Mississippian Cultures

The Adena people of the Ohio River Valley constructed large villages with monumental earthworks from about 500 B.C.E. This early mound-building culture was based on traditional hunting and gathering supplemented by limited cultivation of locally domesticated seed crops. Most, but not all, of the Adena mounds contained burials. Items found in these graves indicate a hierarchical society with an elite distinguished by its access to rare and valuable goods such as mica from North Carolina and copper from the Great Lakes region.

Around 100 C.E. the Adena culture blended into a successor culture now called Hopewell, also centered in the Ohio River Valley. The largest Hopewell centers appeared in present-day Ohio; but Hopewell influence, in the form of either colonies or trade dependencies, spread west to Illinois, Michigan, and Wisconsin, east to New York and Ontario, and south to Alabama, Louisiana, Mississippi, and even Florida (see Map 12.2). For the necessities of daily life Hopewell people were dependent on hunting and gathering and a limited agriculture inherited from the Adena.

Hopewell is an early example of a North American **chiefdom**—territory that had a population of as much as 10,000 and was ruled by a chief, a hereditary leader with both religious and secular responsibilities. Chiefs organized periodic rituals of feasting and gift giving that established bonds among diverse kinship groups and guaranteed access to specialized crops and craft goods. They also managed long-distance trade, which provided luxury goods and additional food supplies.

The largest Hopewell towns in the Ohio River Valley served as ceremonial and political centers and had several thousand inhabitants. Villages had populations of a few hundred. Large mounds built to house elite burials and as platforms for temples and the residences of chiefs dominated major Hopewell centers. Chiefs and other members of the elite were buried in vaults surrounded by valuable goods such as river pearls, copper jewelry,

and, in some cases, women and retainers who seem to have been sacrificed to accompany a dead chief into the afterlife. As was true of the earlier Olmec culture of Mexico, the abandonment of major Hopewell sites around 400 C.E. has no clear environmental or political explanation.

Hopewell technology and mound building continued in smaller centers that have been linked to the development of Mississippian culture (700–1500 C.E.). As in the case of the Anasazi, some experts have suggested that contacts with Mesoamerica influenced Mississippian culture, but there is no convincing evidence to support this theory. It is true that maize, beans, and squash, all first domesticated in Mesoamerica, were closely associated with the development of the urbanized Mississippian culture. But these plants and related technologies were probably passed along through numerous intervening cultures.

The development of urbanized Mississippian chiefdoms resulted instead from the accumulated effects of small increases in agricultural productivity, the adoption of the bow and arrow, and the expansion of trade networks. An improved economy led to population growth, the building of cities, and social stratification. The largest towns shared a common urban plan based on a central plaza surrounded by large platform mounds. Major towns were trade centers where people bartered essential commodities, such as flint used for weapons and tools.

The Mississippian culture reached its highest stage of evolution at the great urban center of Cahokia, located near the modern city of East St. Louis, Illinois (see Map 12.2). At the center of this site was the largest mound constructed in North America, a terraced structure 100 feet (30 meters) high and 1,037 by 790 feet (316 by 241 meters) at the base. Areas where commoners lived ringed the center area of elite housing and temples. At its height in about 1200 C.E., Cahokia had a population of about 30,000—about the same population as the great Maya city Tikal.

Cahokia controlled surrounding agricultural lands and a number of secondary towns ruled by subchiefs. Burial evidence suggests that the rulers of Cahokia enjoyed an exalted position. In one burial more than fifty young women and retainers were apparently sacrificed to accompany a ruler on his travels after death. As at Hopewell sites, no evidence links the decline and eventual abandonment of Cahokia (which occurred after 1250 C.E.) with military defeat or civil war. Experts argue that climate changes and population pressures undermined its vitality. After the decline of Cahokia, smaller Mississippian centers continued to flourish in the southeast of the present-day United States until the arrival of Europeans.

ANDEAN CIVILIZATIONS, 200–1500

The Andean region of South America was an unlikely environment for the development of rich and powerful civilizations (see Map 12.3). Much of the region's mountainous zone is at altitudes that seem too high for agriculture and human habitation. Along the Pacific coast an arid plain posed a difficult challenge to the development of agriculture. And, to the east of the Andes Mountains, the hot and humid tropical environment of the Amazon headwaters also offered a formidable obstacle to the organization of complex societies. Yet the Amerindian peoples of the Andean area produced some of the most socially complex and politically advanced societies of the Western Hemisphere. Perhaps the harshness of the environment compelled the development of the administrative structures and social and economic relationships that became the central features of Andean civilization.

Map 12.3 Andean Civilizations, 200 B.C.E.–1532 C.E. In response to environmental challenges posed by an arid coastal plain and high interior mountain ranges, Andean peoples made complex social and technological adaptations. Irrigation systems, the domestication of the llama, metallurgy, and shared labor obligations helped provide a firm economic foundation for powerful, centralized states. In 1532 the Inca Empire's vast territory stretched from modern Chile in the south to Colombia in the north.

Cultural Response to Environmental Challenge

People living in the high mountain valleys and on the dry coastal plain were able to overcome the challenges posed by their environment through the effective organization of human labor. The remarkable collective achievements of Andean peoples were accomplished with a recordkeeping system more limited than the one found in Mesoamerica. A system of knotted colored cords, **khipus°,** was used to aid administration and record population counts and tribute obligations. Large-scale drainage and irrigation works and the terracing of hillsides to control erosion and provide additional farmland led to an increase in agricultural production. Andean people also undertook road building, urban construction, and even textile production collectively.

The sharing of responsibilities began at the household level. But it was the clan, or **ayllu°,** that provided the foundation for Andean achievement. Members of an ayllu held land communally. Although members claimed descent from a common ancestor, they were not necessarily related. Ayllu members thought of each other as brothers and sisters and were obligated to aid each other in tasks that required more labor than a single household could provide. These reciprocal obligations provided the

model for the organization of labor and the distribution of goods at every level of Andean society. Just as individuals and families were expected to provide labor to kinsmen, members of an ayllu were expected to provide labor and goods to their hereditary chief.

With the development of territorial states ruled by hereditary aristocracies and kings after 1000 B.C.E., these obligations were organized on a larger scale. The **mit'a°** required members of ayllus to work the fields and care for the herds of llamas and alpacas owned by religious establishments, the royal court, and the aristocracy. Each allyu contributed a set number of workers for specific tasks each year. Mit'a laborers built and main-

khipus (KEY-pooz) ayllu (aye-YOU)

mit'a (MEET-ah)

tained roads, bridges, temples, palaces, and large irrigation and drainage projects. They produced textiles and goods essential to ritual life such as beer made from maize and coca (dried leaves chewed as a stimulant and now also a source of cocaine). The mit'a system was an essential part of the Andean world for more than a thousand years.

Work was divided along gender lines, but the work of men and women was interdependent. Hunting, military service, and government were reserved largely for men. Women had numerous responsibilities in textile production, agriculture, and the home. One early Spanish commentator described the responsibilities of Andean women in terms that sound very modern:

> [T]hey did not just perform domestic tasks, but also [labored] in the fields, in the cultivation of their lands, in building houses, and carrying burdens. . . . [A]nd more than once I heard that while women were carrying these burdens, they would feel labor pains, and giving birth, they would go to a place where there was water and wash the baby and themselves. Putting the baby on top of the load they were carrying, they would then continue walking as before they gave birth. In sum, there was nothing their husbands did where their wives did not help.[7]

The ayllu was intimately tied to a uniquely Andean system of production and exchange. Because the region's mountain ranges created a multitude of small ecological areas with specialized resources, each community sought to control a variety of environments so as to guarantee access to essential goods. Coastal regions produced maize, fish, and cotton. Mountain valleys contributed quinoa (the local grain), as well as potatoes and other tubers. Higher elevations contributed the wool and meat of llamas and alpacas, and the Amazonian region provided coca and fruits. Ayllus sent out colonists to exploit the resources of these ecological niches. Colonists remained linked to their original region and kin group by marriage and ritual. Historians commonly refer to this system of controlled exchange across ecological boundaries as vertical integration, or verticality.

The historical periodization of Andean history is similar to that of Mesoamerica. Both regions developed highly integrated political and economic systems long before 1500. The pace of agricultural development, urbanization, and state formation in the Andes also approximated that in Mesoamerica. However, in the Andean region unique environmental challenges led to distinctive highland and coastal cultures with separate periodizations. Here, more than in Mesoamerica, geography influenced regional cultural integration and state formation.

Moche and Chimú

Around 200 C.E., some four centuries after the collapse of Chavín (see Chapter 4), the **Moche°** developed cultural and political tools that allowed them to dominate the north coastal region of Peru. Moche identity was cultural in character. They did not establish a formal empire or create unified political structures. The most powerful of the Moche urban centers, such as Cerro Blanco located near the modern Peruvian city of Trujillo (see Map 12.3), did establish hegemony over smaller towns and villages. There is also evidence that the Moche extended their political and economic control over their neighbors militarily.

Archaeological evidence indicates that the Moche cultivated maize, quinoa, beans, manioc, and sweet potatoes with the aid of massive irrigation works. At higher elevations they also produced coca, used ritually. Archaeological excavations reveal the existence of complex networks of canals and aqueducts that connected fields with water sources as far away as 75 miles (121 kilometers). These hydraulic works were maintained by mit'a labor imposed on Moche commoners and on subject peoples. The Moche maintained large herds of alpacas and llamas to transport goods across the region's difficult terrain. Their wool, along with cotton provided by farmers, provided the raw material for a thriving Moche textile production. Their meat provided an important part of the diet.

Evidence from surviving murals and decorated ceramics suggests that Moche society was highly stratified and theocratic. The need to organize large numbers of laborers to construct and maintain the irrigation system helped to promote class divisions. Wealth and power among the Moche was concentrated, along with political control, in the hands of priests and military leaders. Hierarchy was further reinforced by the military conquest of neighboring regions. The residences of the elite were constructed atop large platforms at Moche ceremonial centers. The elite literally lived above the commoners. Their power was also apparent in their rich clothing and jewelry, which confirmed their divine status and set them further apart from commoners. Moche rulers and other members of the elite wore tall headdresses. They used gold and gold alloy jewelry to mark their social position: gold plates suspended from their noses concealed the lower portion of their faces, and large gold plugs decorated their ears.

These deep social distinctions also were reflected in Moche burial practices. A recent excavation in the Lambeyeque Valley discovered the tomb of a warrior-priest who was buried with a rich treasure that included gold,

Moche (MO-che)

Moche Portrait Vase   The Moche of ancient Peru were among the most accomplished ceramic artists of the Americas. Moche potters produced representations of gods and spirits, scenes of daily life, and portrait vases of important people. This man wears a headdress adorned by two birds and seashells. The stains next to the eyes of the birds represent tears. (Museo de Arqueologica y Antropologia, Lima/Lee Bolton Picture Library)

silver, and copper jewelry, textiles, feather ornaments, and shells. Also buried with this powerful man were two women° and three men. Each retainer had one foot amputated to ensure her or his continued subservience and dependence in the afterlife.

Most commoners devoted their time to subsistence farming and to the payment of labor dues owed to their ayllu and to the elite. Both men and women were involved in agriculture, care of llama herds, and the household economy. They lived with their families in one-room buildings clustered in the outlying areas of cities and in surrounding agricultural zones.

The high quality of Moche textiles, ceramics, and metallurgy indicates the presence of numerous skilled artisans. As had been true centuries earlier in Chavín, women had a special role in the production of textiles; even elite women devoted time to weaving. Moche culture developed a brilliant representational art. Moche craftsmen produced highly individualized portrait vases that today adorn museum collections in nearly every city of the world. Ceramics were also decorated with line drawings representing myths and rituals. The most orig-

inal of Moche ceramic vessels were decorated with explicit sexual acts. The Moche also were accomplished metalsmiths, producing beautiful gold and silver objects devoted to religious and decorative functions or to elite adornment. Metallurgy served more practical ends as well: artisans produced a range of heavy copper and copper alloy tools for agricultural and military purposes.

Since we have no written sources, a detailed history of the Moche can never be written. The archaeological record makes clear that the rapid decline of the major centers coincided with a succession of natural disasters in the sixth century and with the rise of a new military power in the Andean highlands. When an earthquake altered the course of the Moche River, major flooding seriously damaged urban centers. The Moche region also was threatened by long-term climate changes. During the sixth century a thirty-year period of drought expanded the area of coastal sand dunes, and powerful winds pushed sand onto fragile agricultural lands, overwhelming the irrigation system. As the land dried, periodic heavy rains caused erosion that damaged fields and weakened the economy that had sustained ceremonial and residential centers. This succession of disasters undermined the authority of the religious and political leaders, whose privileges were based on their ability to control natural forces through rituals. Despite massive efforts to keep the irrigation canals open and the construction of new urban centers in less vulnerable valleys to the north, Moche civilization never recovered from these environmental disasters. In the eighth century, the rise of a new military power, the **Wari°,** also contributed to the disappearance of the Moche by putting pressure on trade routes that linked the coastal region with the highlands.

At the end of the Moche period the **Chimú°** developed a new and more powerful coastal civilization. Chan Chan, capital of the Chimú Empire, was constructed around 800 C.E. near the earlier Moche cultural center. After 1200 C.E. Chimú began a period of aggressive military expansion. At the apex of its power, Chimú controlled 625 miles (1,000 kilometers) of the Peruvian coast.

Within Chan Chan was a series of walled compounds, each one containing a burial pyramid. Scholars believe that each ruler built his own compound and was buried within it upon his death. Sacrifices and rich grave goods accompanied each royal burial. As with the Moche, Chimú's rulers separated themselves from the masses of society by their consumption of rare and beautiful textiles, ceramics, and precious metals as a way of suggesting the approval of the gods. Some scholars suggest that the Chimú dynasty practiced split inheritance: goods and lands of the deceased ruler went to sec-

Wari (WAH-ree)   **Chimú** (chee-MOO)

ondary heirs or for religious sacrifices. The royal heir who inherited the throne was forced to construct his own residence compound and then undertake new conquests to fund his household. After the Inca conquered the northern coast in 1465, they borrowed from the rich rituals and court customs of Chimú.

Tiwanaku and Wari

After 500 C.E. two powerful civilizations developed in the Andean highlands. At nearly 13,000 feet (3,962 meters) on the high treeless plain near Lake Titicaca in modern Bolivia stand the ruins of **Tiwanaku°** (see Map 12.3). Initial occupation may have occurred as early as 400 B.C.E., but significant urbanization began only after 200 C.E. Tiwanaku's expansion depended on the adoption of technologies that increased agricultural productivity. Modern excavations provide the outline of vast drainage projects that reclaimed nearly 200,000 acres (8,000 hectares) of rich lakeside marshes for agriculture. This system of raised fields and ditches permitted intensive cultivation similar to that achieved by use of chinampas in Mesoamerica. Fish from the nearby lake and llamas added protein to a diet largely dependent on potatoes and grains. Llamas were also crucial for the maintenance of long-distance trade relationships that brought in corn, coca, tropical fruits, and medicinal plants.

The urban center of Tiwanaku was distinguished by the scale of its construction and by the high quality of its stone masonry. Large stones and quarried blocks were moved many miles to construct a large terraced pyramid, walled enclosures, and a reservoir—projects that probably required the mobilization of thousands of laborers over a period of years. Despite a limited metallurgy that produced only tools of copper alloy, Tiwanaku's artisans built large structures of finely cut stone that required little mortar to fit the blocks. They also produced gigantic human statuary. The largest example, a stern figure with a military bearing, is cut from a single block of stone 24 feet (7 meters) high.

Little is known of the social structure or daily life of this civilization. Neither surviving murals nor other decorative arts offer the suggestive guidance found in the burial goods of the Moche. Nevertheless, it is clear that Tiwanaku was a highly stratified society ruled by a hereditary elite. Most women and men devoted their time to agriculture and the care of llama herds. However, the presence of specialized artisans is evident in the high-quality construction in public buildings and in locally produced ceramics. The distribution of these ceramics to distant places suggests the presence of a specialized merchant class as well.

Many scholars portray Tiwanaku as the capital of a vast empire, a precursor to the later Inca state. It is clear that the elite controlled a large, disciplined labor force in the surrounding region. Military conquests and the establishment of colonial populations provided the highland capital with dependable supplies of products from ecologically distinct zones. And Tiwanaku cultural influence extended eastward to the jungles and southward to the coastal regions and oases of the Atacama Desert in Chile. But archaeological evidence suggests that Tiwanaku, in comparison with contemporary Teotihuacan in central Mexico, had a relatively small full-time population of around 30,000. It was not a metropolis like the largest Mesoamerican cities; it was a ceremonial and political center for a large regional population.

The contemporary site of Wari was located about 450 miles (751 kilometers) to the northwest of Tiwanaku, near the modern Peruvian city Ayacucho. The culture and technology of Wari were clearly tied to Tiwanaku, but the exact nature of this relationship remains unclear. Some scholars argue that Wari began as a dependency of Tiwanaku. Others suggest that they were joint capitals of a single empire. However, there is little evidence for either position. Clearly there were sustained cultural contacts between the two societies, but each had a unique cultural signature.

The site of Wari was larger than Tiwanaku, measuring nearly 4 square miles (10 square kilometers). The city center was surrounded by a massive wall and included a large temple. The center had numerous multifamily housing blocks. Less-concentrated housing for commoners was located in a sprawling suburban zone. Wari's development, unlike that of most other major urban centers in the Andes, appears to have occurred without central planning.

The small scale of its monumental architecture and the near absence of cut stone masonry in public and private buildings distinguish Wari from Tiwanaku. It is not clear that these characteristics resulted from the relative weakness of the elite or the absence of specialized construction crafts. Wari ceramic style also was different from that of Tiwanaku. This difference has allowed experts to trace Wari's expanding power to the coastal area earlier controlled by the Moche and to the northern highlands. Wari's military expansion occurred at a time of increasing warfare throughout the Andes. As a result, roads were built to maintain communication with remote fortified dependencies. Perhaps as a consequence of military conflict, both Tiwanaku and Wari declined to insignificance by about 1000 C.E. The Inca inherited their political legacy.

Tiwanaku (tee-wah-NA-coo)

The Inca

In little more than one hundred years, the **Inca** developed a vast imperial state, which they called "Land of Four Corners." By 1525 the empire had a population of more than 6 million inhabitants and stretched from the Maule River in Chile to northern Ecuador and from the Pacific coast across the Andes to the upper Amazon and, in the south, into Argentina (see Map 12.3). In the early fifteenth century the Inca were one of many competing military powers in the southern highlands, an area of limited political significance after the collapse of Wari. Centered in the valley of Cuzco, the Inca were initially organized as a chiefdom based on reciprocal gift giving and the redistribution of food and textiles. Strong and resourceful leaders consolidated political authority in the 1430s and undertook an ambitious campaign of military expansion.

The Inca state, like earlier highland powers, was built on traditional Andean social customs and economic practices. Tiwanaku had relied in part on the use of colonists to provide supplies of resources from distant ecologically distinct zones. The Inca built on this legacy by conquering additional distant territories and increasing the scale of forced exchanges. Crucial to this process was the development of a large, professional military. Unlike the peoples of Mesoamerica, who distributed specialized goods by developing markets and tribute relationships, Andean peoples used state power to broaden and expand the vertical exchange system that had permitted ayllus to exploit a range of ecological niches.

Like earlier highland civilizations, the Inca were pastoralists. Inca prosperity and military strength depended on vast herds of llamas and alpacas, which provided food and clothing as well as transport for goods. Both men and women were involved in the care of these herds. Women were primarily responsible for weaving; men were drivers in long-distance trade. This pastoral tradition provided the Inca with powerful metaphors that helped to shape their political and religious beliefs. They believed that the gods and their ruler shared the obligations of the shepherd to his flock—an idea akin to Old Testament references to "The Lord is my Shepherd."

Collective efforts by mit'a laborers made the Inca Empire possible. Cuzco, the imperial capital, and the provincial cities, the royal court, the imperial armies, and the state's religious cults all rested on this foundation. The mit'a system also created the material surplus that provided the bare necessities for the old, weak, and ill of Inca society. Each ayllu contributed approximately one-seventh of its adult male population to meet these collective obligations. These draft laborers served as soldiers, construction workers, craftsmen, and runners to carry messages along post roads. They also drained swamps, terraced mountainsides, filled in valley floors, built and maintained irrigation works, and built storage facilities and roads. Inca laborers constructed 13,000 miles (20,930 kilometers) of road, facilitating military troop movements, administration, and trade (see Environment and Technology: Inca Roads).

Imperial administration was similarly superimposed on existing political structures and established elite groups. The hereditary chiefs of ayllus carried out administrative and judicial functions. As the Inca expanded, they generally left local rulers in place. By leaving in place the rulers of defeated societies, the Inca risked rebellion, but they controlled these risks by means of a thinly veiled system of hostage taking and the use of military garrisons. The rulers of defeated regions were required to send their heirs to live at the Inca royal court in Cuzco. Inca leaders even required that representations of important local gods be brought to Cuzco and made part of the imperial pantheon. These measures promoted imperial integration while at the same time providing hostages to ensure the good behavior of subject peoples.

Conquests magnified the authority of the Inca ruler and led to the creation of an imperial bureaucracy drawn from among his kinsmen. The royal family claimed descent from the Sun, the primary Inca god. Members of the royal family lived in palaces maintained by armies of servants. The lives of the ruler and members of the royal family were dominated by political and religious rituals that helped to legitimize their authority (see Society and Culture: Acllas). Among the many obligations associated with kingship was the requirement to extend imperial boundaries by warfare. Thus each new ruler began his reign with conquest.

Tenochtitlan, the Aztec capital, had a population of about 150,000 in 1520. At the height of Inca power in 1530, Cuzco had a population of less than 30,000. Nevertheless, Cuzco was a remarkable place. The Inca were highly skilled stone craftsmen: their most impressive buildings were constructed of carefully cut stones fitted together without mortar. The city was laid out in the shape of a giant puma (a mountain lion). At the center were the palaces that each ruler built when he ascended to the throne, as well as the major temples. The richest was the Temple of the Sun. Its interior was lined with sheets of gold, and its patio was decorated with golden representations of llamas and corn. The ruler made every effort to awe and intimidate visitors and residents alike with a nearly continuous series of rituals, feasts, and sacrifices. Sacrifices of textiles, animals, and other goods sent as tribute dominated the city's calendar. The destruction of these valuable commodities, and a small number of human sacrifices, helped give the impression

Inca Roads

From the time of Chavín (900–250 B.C.E.), Andean peoples built roads to facilitate trade across ecological boundaries and to project political power over conquered peoples. In the fifteen and sixteenth centuries, the Inca extended and improved the networks of roads constructed in earlier eras. Roads were crucially important to Inca efforts to collect and redistribute tribute paid in food, textiles, and chicha (corn liquor).

Two roads connected Cuzco, the Inca capital in southern Peru, to Quito, Ecudaor, in the north and Chile farther south. One ran along the flat and arid coastal plain, the other through the mountainous interior. Shorter east/west roads connected important coastal and interior cities. Evidence suggests that administrative centers were sited along these routes to expedite rapid communication with the capital. Rest stops at convenient distances provided shelter and food to traveling officials and runners who carried messages between Cuzco and the empire's cities and towns. Warehouses were constructed along the roads to provide food and military supplies for passing Inca armies or to supply local laborers working in construction projects or cultivating the ruler's fields.

Because communication with regional administrative centers and the movement of troops were the central objectives of the Inca leadership, routes were selected to avoid natural obstacles and to reduce travel time. Mit'a laborers recruited from nearby towns and villages built and maintained the roads. Roads were commonly paved with stone or packed earth and often were bordered by stone or adobe walls to keep soldiers or pack trains of llamas from straying into the fields of farmers. Whenever possible, roadbeds were made level. In mountainous terrain some roads were little more than improved paths, but in flat country three or four people could walk abreast. Care was always taken to repair damage caused by rain runoff or other drainage problems.

The achievement of Inca road builders is clearest in the mountainous terrain of the interior. They built suspension bridges across high gorges and cut roadbeds into the face of cliffs. A Spanish priest living in Peru in the seventeenth century commented that the Inca roads "were magnificent constructions, which could be compared favorably with the most superb roads of the Romans."

Source: Quotation from Father Bernabe Cobo, *History of the Inca Empire. An account of the Indians' customs and origin together with a treatise on Inca legends, history, and social institutions* (Austin: University of Texas Press, 1983), 223.

Inca Road The Inca built roads to connect distant parts of the empire to Cuzco, the Inca capital. These roads are still used in Peru. (Loren McIntyre/Woodfin Camp & Associates)

Acllas

Acllas (AK-yahz) were young virgins selected by representatives of the Inca ruler to serve the cult of the Sun or be given as marriage partners and concubines to the ruler himself or to Inca nobles and favored nobles from dependencies. These young women were commonly chosen for their beauty from among the daughters of local rulers.

Our understanding of the acllas' lives comes primarily from Spanish-era sources. We know these women lived within the closely guarded walls of convent-like buildings located in the large towns of the empire and that their lives were dedicated to religious observances and the production of fine textiles.

Felipe Guaman Poma de Ayala wrote the following account in the early seventeenth century. After long neglect, his illustrated history of Inca and early Spanish colonial society has become a fundamental source for Andean history. In this text, the word Inca *refers both to the people and to their ruler. Although Guaman Poma is obviously proud of his descent from a high-ranking indigenous noble family, his description of ancient images of gods as "idols" suggests the depth of cultural change among Amerindian people after the Spanish conquest.*

During the time of the Incas certain women, who were called acllas or "the Chosen," were destined for lifelong virginity. Mostly they were confined in houses and they belonged to one of two main categories, namely sacred virgins and common virgins.

The so-called "virgins with red cheeks" entered upon their duties at the age of twenty and were dedicated to the service of the Sun, the Moon, and the Day-Star. In their whole life they were never allowed to speak to a man.

The virgins of the Inca's own shrine of Huanacauri were known for their beauty as well as their chastity. The other principal shrines had similar girls in attendance. At the less important shrines there were older virgins who occupied themselves with spinning and weaving the silk-like clothes worn by their idols. There was a still lower class of virgins, over 40 years of age and no longer very beautiful, who performed unimportant religious duties and worked in the fields or as ordinary seamstresses.

There was yet another class of aclla or "chosen," only some of whom kept their virginity and others not. These were the Inca's (the ruler of the Inca people) beautiful attendants and concubines, who were drawn from noble families and lived in his palaces. They made clothing for him out of material finer than taffeta or silk. They also prepared a maize spirit of extraordinary richness, which was matured for an entire month, and they cooked delicious dishes for the Inca. They also lay with him, but never with any other man.

Thus chastity was greatly prized in our country. It was the Inca who received our girls from the Sun and who allotted them, always as virgins, to his subjects. Until that time the man did not know the woman nor the woman the man. The man might be in Quito or Chile and might be assigned a woman from quite a different region but a contract of marriage was made with the help of the woman's brother.

What special qualities were most valued in the young women selected to be acllas? What categories of aclla does Guaman Poma describe? What were the lives of acllas like? What does this description of the Inca ruler's relationship with the acllas tell us about how he was viewed?

Source: Felipe Guaman Poma de Ayala, *Letter to a King: A Peruvian Chief's Account of Life Under the Incas and Under Spanish Rule,* ed. and trans. Christopher Dilke (New York: Dutton, 1978), 84–86.

of splendor and sumptuous abundance that appeared to demonstrate the ruler's claimed descent from the Sun.

Inca cultural achievement rested on the strong foundation of earlier Andean civilizations. We know that astronomical observation was a central concern of the priestly class, as in Mesoamerica; the Inca calendar, however, is lost to us. All communication other than oral was transmitted by the khipus borrowed from earlier Andean civilizations. In weaving and metallurgy, Inca technology, building on earlier regional developments, was more advanced than in Mesoamerica. Inca craftsmen produced utilitarian tools and weapons of copper and bronze as well as decorative objects of gold and silver. Inca women produced textiles of extraordinary beauty from cotton and the wool of llamas and alpacas.

Although the Inca did not introduce new technologies, they increased economic output and added to the region's prosperity. The conquest of large populations in environmentally distinct regions allowed the Inca to multiply the yields produced by the traditional ex-

Inca Tunic   Andean weavers produced beautiful textiles from cotton and from the wool of llamas and alpacas. The Inca inherited this rich craft tradition and produced some of the world's most remarkable textiles. The quality and design of each garment indicated the weaver's rank and power in this society. This tunic was an outer garment for a powerful male.   (From *Textile Art of Peru*. Collection created and directed by Jose Antonio de Lavalle and Jose Alejandro Gonzalez Garcia [L. L. Editores, 1989])

changes between distinct ecological niches. But the expansion of imperial economic and political power was purchased at the cost of reduced equality and diminished local autonomy. The imperial elite, living in richly decorated palaces in Cuzco and other urban centers, was increasingly cut off from the masses of Inca society. The royal court held members of the provincial nobility at arm's length, and commoners were subject to execution if they dared to look directly at the ruler's face.

After only a century of regional dominance, the Inca Empire faced a crisis in 1525. The death of the Inca ruler Huayna Capac at the conclusion of the conquest of Ecuador initiated a bloody struggle for the throne. Powerful factions coalesced around two sons whose rivalry compelled both the professional military and the hereditary Inca elite to choose sides. Civil war was the result. The Inca state controlled a vast territory spread over more than 3,000 miles (4,830 kilometers) of mountainous terrain. Regionalism and ethnic diversity had always posed a threat to the empire. Civil war weakened imperial institutions and ignited the resentments of conquered peoples. On the eve of the arrival of Europeans, the destructive consequences of this violent conflict undermined the institutions and economy of Andean civilizations.

CONCLUSION

The indigenous societies of the Western Hemisphere developed unique technologies and cultural forms in mountainous regions, tropical rain forests, deserts, woodlands, and arctic regions. In Mesoamerica, North America, and the Andean region the natural environment powerfully influenced cultural development. The Maya of southern Mexico, for example, developed agricultural technologies that compensated for the tropical cycle of heavy rains followed by long dry periods. On the coast of Peru the Moche used systems of trade and mutual labor obligation to meet the challenge of an arid climate and mountainous terrain while the mound builders of North America expanded agricultural production by utilizing the rich flood plains of the Ohio and Mississippi rivers. Across the Americas, hunting and gathering peoples and urbanized agricultural societies both produced rich religious and aesthetic traditions as well as useful technologies and effective social institutions in response to local conditions. Once established, these cultural traditions proved very durable.

The Aztec and Inca Empires represented the culmination of a long developmental process that had begun before 1000 B.C.E. Each imperial state controlled extensive and diverse territories with populations that numbered in the millions. The capital cities of Tenochtitlan and Cuzco were great cultural and political centers that displayed some of the finest achievements of Amerindian technology, art, and architecture. Both states were based on conquests and were ruled by powerful hereditary elites who depended on the tribute of subject peoples. In both traditions religion met spiritual needs while also organizing collective life and legitimizing political authority.

The Aztec and Inca empires were created militarily, their survival depending as much on the power of their armies as on the productivity of their economies or the wisdom of their rulers. Both empires were ethnically and environmentally diverse, but there were important differences. Elementary markets had been developed in Mesoamerica to distribute specialized regional production, although the forced payment of goods as tribute remained important. In the Andes reciprocal labor obligations and managed exchange relationships were used to allocate goods. The Aztecs used their military to force defeated peoples to provide food, textiles and even sacrificial captives as tribute, but they left local hereditary elites in place. The Incas, in contrast, created a more centralized administrative structure managed by a trained bureaucracy.

As the Western Hemisphere's long isolation drew to a close in the late fifteenth century, both empires were challenged by powerful neighbors or by internal revolts. In earlier periods similar challenges had contributed to the decline of great civilizations in both Mesoamerica and the Andean region. In those cases, a long period of adjustment and the creation of new indigenous institutions followed the collapse of dominant powers such as the Toltecs in Mesoamerica or Tiwanaku in the Andes. With the arrival of Europeans, this cycle of crisis and adjustment would be transformed, and the future of Amerindian peoples would become linked to the cultures of the Old World.

■ Key Terms

Teotihuacan	khipu
chinampas	ayllu
Maya	mit'a
Toltecs	Moche
Aztecs	Chimú
Tenochtitlan	Tiwanaku
tribute system	Wari
Anasazi	Inca
chiefdom	acllas

■ Suggested Reading

In *Prehistory of the Americas* (1987) Stuart Fiedel provides an excellent summary of the early history of the Western Hemisphere. Alvin M. Josephy, Jr., in *The Indian Heritage of America* (1968), also provides a thorough introduction to the topic. *Canada's First Nations* (1992) by Olive Patricia Dickason is a well-written survey that traces the history of Canada's Amerindian peoples to the modern era. *Early Man in the New World*, ed. Richard Shutler, Jr. (1983), provides a helpful addition to these works. *Atlas of Ancient America* (1986) by Michael Coe, Elizabeth P. Benson, and Dean R. Snow is a useful compendium of maps and information. George Kubler, *The Art and Architecture of Ancient America* (1962), is a valuable resource, though now dated.

Eric Wolf provides an enduring synthesis of Mesoamerican history in *Sons of the Shaking Earth* (1959). A good summary of recent research on Teotihuacan is found in Esther Pasztori, *Teotihuacan* (1997). Linda Schele and David Freidel summarize the most recent research on the classic-period Maya in their excellent *A Forest of Kings* (1990). The best summary of Aztec history is Nigel Davies, *The Aztec Empire: The Toltec Resurgence*

(1987). Jacques Soustelle, *Daily Life of the Aztecs,* trans. Patrick O'Brian (1961), is a good introduction. Though controversial in some of its analysis, Inga Clendinnen's *Aztecs* (1991) is also an important contribution.

Chaco and Hohokam (1991), ed. Patricia L. Crown and W. James Judge, is a good summary of research issues. Robert Silverberg, *Mound Builders of Ancient America* (1968), supplies a good introduction to this topic.

A helpful introduction to the scholarship on early Andean societies is provided by Karen Olsen Bruhns, *Ancient South America* (1994). For the Moche see Garth Bawden, *The Moche* (1996). *The History of the Incas* (1970) by Alfred Metraux is dated but offers a useful summary. The best recent modern synthesis is María Rostworowski de Diez Canseco, *History of the Inca Realm,* trans. by Harry B. Iceland (1999). John Murra, *The Economic Organization of the Inca State* (1980), and Irene Silverblatt, *Moon, Sun, and Witches: Gender Ideologies and Class in Inca and Colonial Peru* (1987), are challenging, important works on Peru before the arrival of Columbus in the Western Hemisphere. Frederich Katz, *The Ancient Civilizations of the Americas* (1972), offers a useful comparative perspective on ancient American developments.

■ Notes

1. This summary follows closely the narrative offered by Linda Schele and David Freidel in *A Forest of Kings: The Untold Story of the Ancient Maya* (New York: Morrow, 1990), 182–186.
2. Before 1492 the inhabitants of the Western Hemisphere had no single name for themselves. They had neither a racial consciousness nor a racial identity. Identity was derived from kin groups, language, cultural practices, and political structures. There was no sense that physical similarities created a shared identity. America's original inhabitants had racial consciousness and racial identity imposed on them by conquest and the occupation of their lands by Europeans after 1492. All of the collective terms for these first American peoples are tainted by this history. *Indians, Native Americans, Amerindians, First Peoples, and Indigenous Peoples* are among the terms in common usage. In this book the names of individual cultures and states are used wherever possible. *Amerindian* and other terms that suggest transcultural identity and experience are used most commonly for the period after 1492.
3. From the Florentine Codex, quoted in Inga Clendinnen, *Aztecs* (New York: Cambridge University Press, 1991), 213.
4. Quoted in Nigel Davies, *The Toltec Heritage: From the Fall of Tula to the Rise of Tenochtitlán* (Norman: University of Oklahoma Press, 1980), 3.
5. Bernal Díaz del Castillo, *The Conquest of New Spain,* trans. J. M. Cohen (London: Penguin Books, 1963), 217.
6. Hernando Cortés, *Five Letters, 1519–1526,* trans. J. Bayard Morris (New York: Norton, 1991), 87.
7. Quoted in Irene Silverblatt, *Moon, Sun, and Witches: Gender Ideologies and Class in Inca and Colonial Peru* (Princeton, NJ: Princeton University Press, 1987), 10.

PART FOUR

INTERREGIONAL PATTERNS OF CULTURE AND CONTACT,

1200–1550

n Eurasia, overland trade along the Silk Road, which had begun before the Roman and Han Empires, reached its peak during the era of the Mongol empires. Beginning in 1206 with the rise of Genghis Khan, the Mongols linked Europe, the Middle East, Russia, Central Asia, and East Asia with threads of conquest and trade. In the century and a half of Mongol domination, some communities in Eurasia thrived on the continental connections that the Mongols' hold on the overland routes made possible, while others groaned under the tax burdens and physical devastation of Mongol rule. But whether for good or ill, Mongol power was based on the skills,

strategies, and technologies of the overland trade and life on the steppes.

The impact of the Mongols was also felt by societies that remained outside Mongol rule. In Europe, Egypt, Southeast Asia, and Japan, the Mongol challenge stimulated societies that had already begun to urbanize, develop new industries, and undertake political centralization, and it accelerated many of these changes.

By 1500, Mongol dominance was past, and new powers were emerging. A new Chinese empire, the Ming, was expanding its influence in Southeast Asia. The Ottomans had captured Constantinople and

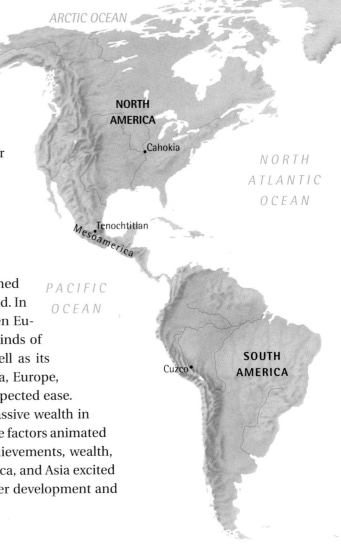

overthrown the Byzantine Empire. And Christians had defeated Muslims in Spain and were laying the foundations of a new overseas empire. With the fall of the Mongol Empire, Central Asia was no longer a major crossroads of trade.

As the great overland trade of Eurasia faded, merchants, soldiers, and explorers took to the seas. The most spectacular of the early state-sponsored long-distance ocean voyages were undertaken by the Chinese admiral Zheng He. The 1300s and 1400s also saw African exploration of the Atlantic and Polynesian colonization of the central and eastern Pacific. By 1500 the navigator Christopher Columbus, sailing for Spain, had reached the Americas, and the Portuguese had sailed around the world. In earlier centuries travelers had considered a journey between Europe and East Asia as crossing the whole world. But new kinds of ships and better knowledge of the size of the globe as well as its shorelines made sub-Saharan Africa, the Indian Ocean, Asia, Europe, and finally the Americas accessible to each other with unexpected ease.

The great overland routes of Eurasia had generated massive wealth in East Asia and growing hunger for commerce in Europe. These factors animated the development of the sea trade, too. Exposure to the achievements, wealth, and resources of societies in the Americas, sub-Saharan Africa, and Asia excited the interest of the emerging European monarchies in further development and control of the seas.

	1200	1250	1300	1350
Americas	• **1200** Population of Cahokia reaches 30,000 **1200–1300** Collapse of Anasazi centers			• **1325** Aztecs found Tenochtitlan
Europe	• **1215** Magna Carta • **1240** Mongol conquest of Russia • **1241** Mongol invasion of Europe	• **1286** Champagne fairs begin to promote regional trade • **1300** First clocks	• **1347** Black Death **1337–1453** Hundred Years War	
Africa	Kingdom of Benin founded ca. 1250 • **1240–1500** Mali Empire	• **1270** Solomonic dynasty founded in Ethiopia	• **1324–1325** Mansa Musa's pilgrimage to Mecca brings Islamic learning to Mali	
Middle East	• **1221** Mongols attack Iran	• **1260** Mamluks defeat Mongols at Ain Jalut • **1258** Mongols take Baghdad, end Abbasid Caliphate	• **1300** Emergence of Ottomans in Anatolia **1295–1304** Rule of Muslim Il-khan Ghazan	**1370–1405** Reign of Timur
Asia and Oceania	• **1200** Polynesians settle New Zealand **1206–1227** Reign of Genghis Khan • **1206** Delhi Sultanate founded in India	• **1274, 1281** Mongol attacks on Japan Polynesians settle Hawaii **1300** • **1265–1294** Reign of Khubilai Khan	• **1336** Ashikaga Shogunate founded Yuan Empire in China **1279–1368** Ming Empire founded in China **1368** •	

ARCTIC OCEAN

EUROPE
• Moscow

ASIA
• Karakorum

Rome
• Constantinople
Anatolia

Portugal Spain
Morocco

• Samarkand

Korea
Japan

Baghdad
Iran

China

MIDDLE EAST
Egypt

• Delhi

India

AFRICA

Goa •

PACIFIC OCEAN

Mali

Ethiopia

Benin

Kongo

INDIAN OCEAN

• Malacca

Great
Zimbabwe •

SOUTH
ATLANTIC
OCEAN

AUSTRALIA

New Zealand

0	1000	2000	3000 Km.
0	1000	2000	3000 Mi.

1400   **1450**   **1500**   **1550**

1438–1533 Inca Empire   • **1533** Pizarro conquers Inca Empire

• **1520** Cortés conquers Aztec Empire

• **1492** Columbus reaches Caribbean

Voyages of Henry the Navigator **1418–1460** **1462–1505** Ivan III unites Russia   Portugal establishes trading empire
                                                                                    In Indian Ocean **1499–1572**
• **1454** Gutenberg Bible printed

1400 1550 Italian Renaissance   • **1492** Christian reconquest of Spain

1400–1450 Great Zimbabwe at its peak   • **1471** Portuguese establish Elmina   • **1526** Christian king of Kongo urges end of slave trade
                                         • **1486** Benin and Portugal initiate trade
                         Vasco da Gama rounds Africa **1499** •
                                                                            • **1539** Portuguese aid Ethiopia

• **1415** Portuguese seize Morocco

• **1453** Ottomans take Constantinople

• **1517** Ottomans conquer Egypt

1405–1433 Voyages of Zheng He   Annam conquers Champa **1500** •   • **1510, 1511** Portuguese seize Goa, Malacca

• **1482** Japanese invasion of Korea

• **1392** Yi kingdom founded in Korea   • **ca. 1449** Ulugh Beg builds observatory in Samarkand

13

WESTERN EURASIA,
1200–1500

The Rise of the Mongols, 1200–1260 • The Fall and Rise of Islam, 1260–1500 •
Local Solidarity in Response to the Mongols
ENVIRONMENT AND TECHNOLOGY: Horses
SOCIETY AND CULTURE: Dueling Pieties

Gemini   This Persian schematic from a collection of constellations was based
on the notebooks of the Il-khan academy at Maraga.

When the Mongol leader Temüjin° was a boy, his father was murdered by a rival group. Though Temüjin's mother tried hard to shelter him (and protect him from dogs, which he feared), she could not find a safe haven for him. At the age of fifteen Temüjin sought a place for himself in the care of Toghoril°, leader of the Keraits°. Among the many warring confederations of Mongolia, the Keraits were Turkic speakers who had a strong interest in both Christianity and Buddhism. During his years with them, Temüjin learned much that would be fundamental to the power and the scope of the empire he would someday build: the charisma of personal strength, courage, and intelligence; the importance of religious tolerance; the necessity to show no mercy to determined enemies; and the versatility of the cultural and economic institutions of Central Asia.

In 1206, Temüjin was acknowledged as **Genghis Khan°**, or supreme leader, of the **Mongols** and their allies. He counted among his advisers adherents of all the major religions of the Middle East and East Asia, as well as speakers of many of the region's languages. All were able to guide him in making his rule more effective among and more appealing to the diverse civilizations of Eurasia. A contemporary historian recorded the following as Genghis's deathbed speech. It can hardly be literally true, but it captures the strategy behind Mongol success: "If you want to retain your possessions and conquer your enemies, you must make your subjects submit willingly and unite your diverse energies to a single end."[1]

Although scholars today recognize the importance of Temüjin and his successors (see Figure 13.1 on page 330) for the development of the later medieval world, the common view of the Mongols is still the one expressed in European and Asian sources of the time. The association of the Mongols with death, gore, suffering, and conflagration is nearly overwhelming. It is true that the Mongol conquests were bloody encounters, involving levels of slaughter previously unknown in many areas. It is also true that the rapid movement of Mongol soldiers, their equipment, and their captives accelerated the spread of virulent diseases, including the plague.

But Mongol rule also provided many advantages. By 1250 the Mongol Empire stretched from Poland to Siberia (see Map 13.1). By unifying much of the Eurasian landmass, the Mongol Empire promoted the movement of people and ideas from one end of Eurasia to the other. Specialized skills that had developed in various parts of the world in the preceding centuries spread rapidly throughout the Mongol domains. Trade routes improved, markets expanded, and the demand for products grew in both the Middle East and East Asia. The Silk Road was reinvigorated.

Though the period from 1200 to about 1350 is often considered the age of Mongol domination, the Mongols themselves are only one part of the story. The Mongols had limited economic and strategic interest in the areas they controlled. In most cases they permitted local cultures to survive and to continue to develop. Regions tended to become better defined in the Mongol period, partly as a result of Mongol unification of large territories, and partly because of local reactions against Mongol domination. Thus, while it is true that the Mongols stimulated economic and cultural exchange among widely separated regions, they also provoked the local reactions that allowed China, Russia, Iran, and other areas to refine their sense of difference and their search for self-rule. This was not nationalism in our modern sense of the word, but it was a stage of loyalty formation that was crucial to modern nationalism.

As you read this chapter, ask yourself the following questions:

- What accounts for the size and speed of the Mongol conquests?
- What benefits resulted from the integration of Eurasia achieved by the Mongol empire?
- What was the impact of the Il-khan Mongols' conversion to Islam?
- What was the impact of Mongol rule on Russia, Central Asia, and the Middle East?

Temüjin (TEM-uh-jin) Toghoril (TOE-hoe-rill)
Keraits (keh-rates) Genghis Khan (GENG-iz KAHN)

Map 13.1 The Mongol Domains in Eurasia in 1300 After the death of Genghis Khan in 1227, his empire was divided among his sons and grandsons. Son Ögödei succeeded Genghis as Great Khan. Grandson Khubilai expanded the Domain of the Great Kahn into eastern China by 1279. Grandson Hülegü was the first Il-khan in the Middle East. Grandson Batu founded the Khanate of the Golden Horde in southern Russia. Son Jagadai ruled the Jagadai Khanate in Central Asia. (From John King Fairbank, et al., *East Asia: Tradition and Transformation*, rev. ed., pp. 172, 196. Copyright © 1989 by Houghton Mifflin Company. Used by permission.)

THE RISE OF THE MONGOLS, 1200–1260

Large federations of nomads had dominated the **steppes** (dry, high plains) and deserts of Central Asia many times since the beginnings of recorded history. The environment, economic life, cultural institutions, and political traditions of the steppes and deserts all contributed to the expansion and contraction of empires. Similarly, the rise of the Mongols can be attributed at least as much to the long-term trends and particular pressures of Central Asia as to any special abilities of Genghis Khan and his followers.

Nomadism in Central Asia

Nomadism is a way of life forced by a scarcity of resources. Nomadic groups have by far the lowest rates of population density. To find pastures and water for their livestock, they are continually on the move. In the course of their migrations they frequently come into contact with other nomadic groups seeking the same resources, and the outcome of these encounters is commonly warfare, alliance, or both. In times of drought, conflicts increase. The result is the extermination of small groups, the growth of alliances, and frequent outmigration from groups that have grown too large. Historians believe that such a period of environmental stress afflicted northern Eurasia around 1000 C.E. and contributed to the dislocations and conflicts out of which the Mongols eventually

CHRONOLOGY

	Central Asia	Middle East	Russia
1200	**1206** Temüjin chosen Genghis Khan of the Mongols **1227** Death of Genghis Khan **1227–1241** Region of Great Khan Ögödei	**1221–1223** First Mongol attacks in Iran	**1221–1223** First Mongol attacks on Russia **1240** Mongols sack Kiev **1242** Alexander Nevskii defeats Teutonic Knights
		1250 Mamluk regime controls Egypt and Syria **1258** Mongols sack Baghdad and kill the caliph **1260** Mamluks defeat Il-khans at Ain Jalut	**1260** War between Il-khans and Golden Horde
1300		**1295** Il-khan Ghazan converts to Islam	
		1349 End of Il-khan rule **ca. 1350** Egypt infected by plague	**1346** Plague outbreak at Kaffa
	1370–1405 Reign of Timur		
1400		**1453** Ottomans capture Constantinople	**1462–1505** Ivan III unites Russia under rule of Moscow, throws off Mongol rule (1480)

emerged. Some agricultural lands became disastrously wet in this period, but lands in northern Eurasia became unusually dry, and nomadic peoples began to move south in search of new pastures.

Nomadic groups in Central Asia frequently engaged in violence, so every man was a full-time herdsman, hunter, and warrior. Like all their predecessors on the steppes, the Mongols were superb riders. They continued the ancient tradition of putting their infants on goats to accustom them to riding. And like all Central Asian warriors the Mongols were adept at shooting arrows from a galloping horse (see Environment and Technology: Horses).

Because nomads are constantly moving but also always under pressure to make their movements efficient and accurate, centralized decision making is a necessary part of their life. The relative independence of Mongol individuals and their families forced decision making to be public, and many people voiced their views. Even at the height of a military campaign nomad warriors moved with their families and their possessions and, if they disagreed with a decision, sometimes struck off on their own. The political structures of the Central Asian empires were designed to accommodate the conflicting centralizing and decentralizing forces of traditional nomadic life. Mongol groups had strong hierarchies, but the leader—the *khan*—was always required to have his decisions ratified by a council of the leaders of powerful families.

Competition for resources reinforced slavery and tribute in Central Asia. Many of the men and women captured during warfare or raids became slaves and were forced to do menial work in nomadic camps. Some individuals evidently entered into slavery willingly, to avoid starvation. Slaves were valuable for their labor and also as currency. Weak groups secured land rights and protection from strong groups by providing them with

ENVIRONMENT + TECHNOLOGY

Horses

Before the rise of the Mongols, many breeds of horses in Eurasia had been improved and specialized by crossbreeding with the large, quick, graceful horses of the Caucasus and the Middle East. The Mongols, however, preserved a form of domesticated horse that looked not very different from the prehistoric horses that Paleolithic peoples had painted on cave walls.

Mongol ponies were an excellent example of the adaptation of traditional technology (in this case horse breeding) to environment. Because they remained semiwild, they were uniquely able to survive the very cold, dry climate of Mongolia. The Mongols never fed or sheltered them, so by natural selection the breed was able to forage in snow, and to survive the plunging night temperatures.

During the Tang Empire (618–907), Central Asian ponies were crossbred with specialized strains from the Middle East to produce larger, stronger, more beautiful horses. Occasionally such horses were brought to Mongolia by the Turks and bred with the local horses. But only after the time of Genghis did the numbers of the Mongolian pony decline dramatically. The breed, or a near relative of it, now survives only in game preserves.

Charioteers, who for a time dominated warfare in ancient Middle East and East Asia, were no match for well-coordinated and well-armed light horsemen, and chariot driving disappeared as a war art wherever extensive campaigns against Central Eurasian riders occurred. The Parthians of eastern Iran, whose riding skills astonished the empires of the Middle East, were legendary for their ability to shoot arrows at the enemy while retreating from them. In China, the Xiongnu drove out the chariot and forced Chinese soldiers to fight on horseback. For similar reasons, the Huns were a revelation to Europe, which adopted the iron stirrup from them.

Central Eurasian riding skills fundamentally altered the social significance of the horse. In the ancient Middle East, the use of horse teams and chariots in warfare was extremely expensive and demanded a select group of warriors wealthy enough to maintain their equipment and powerful enough to control grazing land for their animals. Horses had to be carefully bred to be large enough to pull the chariots and carefully trained to manage their loads with rather inefficient harnessing. In Central Asia, riding was an ability that all men and women in good health possessed. It required only a rudimentary saddle and experience. The deployment of riders in warfare blurred the distinction between a riding herdsman (or hunter) and a riding soldier, and there was no specialization of function along class lines. Because Central Asians did not enclose their herds but left them to forage, no question of individual landownership arose.

In Russia, the Middle East, and East Asia, the skills necessary for the use of the horse, including breeding, tacking, and military riding, were all adapted from the nomads. The use of riders for such varied activities as postal service and military scouting changed the speed of communications and some patterns of military strategy. During the Mongol period and for centuries after, the breeding, raising, training, and maintenance of horses for warfare, in particular, dominated the government economies of all countries north of the tropics.

Mongolian Pony   This resting pony wears a head collar, as specified by Ghenghis's law.   (National Palace Museum, Taipei, Republic of China)

slaves, livestock, weapons, silk, or cash. Many powerful groups (such as the one to which Genghis Khan's father belonged) found that they could live almost entirely off tribute, so they spent less time and fewer resources on herding and more on the warlike activities that would secure greater tribute.

As each group grew in numbers and wealth, its political institutions became more complex. Federations arose, based on an increasing number of alliances among groups, almost always expressed in arranged marriages between the leading families. Children frequently became pawns of diplomacy: their marriages were arranged in childhood—in Temüjin's case, at the age of eight. Because of the relationship between marriage and politics, women from prestigious families were often very powerful in negotiation and management. And, when things became violent, they were just as likely as men to suffer assassination or execution.

The long-distance, seasonal movements of the Central Asia nomads created powerful channels for trade and communication. The result was great cultural diversity. Nomads aided in the spread of Manichaeism, Judaism, Christianity, Buddhism, and Islam across Central Asia. On the steppe, it was not unique to find within a single family believers in two or more of those religions, in combination with traditional shamanism (ancient practices by which special individuals visited and influenced the supernatural world). This plurality of religious practice reflected the fact that Central Eurasian nomads did not always associate ideas about rulership with ideas about religion.

Since very early times, Central Asian societies had been permeated by the idea of world rulership by a khan, who, with the aid of his shamans, would speak to and for an ultimate god, represented in Central Asia as Sky or Heaven. It was believed that this universal ruler, by virtue of his role as the speaker for Heaven, would transcend particular cultures and dominate them all. For the Mongols, the idea of universal rule was centrally important—as the words attributed to Genghis on his deathbed reflect. It permitted them to appeal to any and all religions to legitimate their conquests. And it authorized them to claim superiority over all religious leaders.

Nomads strove for economic self-sufficiency by attempting to restrict their diet to foods they could provide for themselves—primarily meat and milk—and by wearing clothes produced from pastoral animals—felt (from wool), leather, and furs. Women generally oversaw the breeding and birthing of livestock and the preparation of furs, both of which were fundamental to the nomadic economy. Nomads, however, never lived completely independent of the settled regions.

Animal Husbandry   In nomadic societies, it was common for men and boys to tend to the herds in the pastures. The more technical tasks associated with animal husbandry—breeding, birthing, shearing, milking, and the processing of pelts—were usually peformed by women who worked together in teams and passed their knowledge from older to younger members of the community. Various activities are depicted in this contemporary painting.   (Ulan Bator Fine Arts Museum)

Iron was crucially important to Central Asian nomads. They used it in bridles and stirrups, wagons, and weapons. Nomads did not develop large mining enterprises, but they eagerly acquired iron implements in trade and reworked them to suit their own purposes. As early as the 600s, the Turks' large ironworking stations south of Mount Altai were famous. Agricultural empires in East Asia and the Middle East attempted to restrict the export of iron in any form to Central Asia, but these attempts were never successful. On the contrary, Central Asians improved many of the sedentary technologies, such as iron forging, and then exported them back to the agricultural regions. The Mongols retained the traditional Central Asian reverence for iron and the secrets of ironworking. Temüjin, Genghis Khan's personal name, means "blacksmith," and several of his prominent followers were sons of blacksmiths. The name of a later conqueror, Timur, means "iron" in Turkish.

In addition to iron, the Central Asian nomads also traded with agricultural societies to acquire wood, cotton and cotton seed, silk, vegetables, and grains. In

Figure 13.1   Mongol Rulers, 1206–1260   This is the family chart of the founders of the Mongol empires. All the names of those who succeeded to the position of Great Khan are shown in bold type. Those who founded the regional khanates are listed with their dates of rule.

exchange they offered wool, leather, and horses. Many nomads learned the value of permanent settlements for the farming of grains and cotton, as well as for the working of iron, and they established villages—often with the help of migrants from the agricultural regions—at strategic points. The result was extensive frontier regions, particularly east of the Caspian Sea and in northern China, where nomadic peoples and agricultural peoples interacted and created economically as well as culturally pluralistic societies.

Despite the mutual dependence of nomadic pastoralists and the settled agriculturalists, conflict between them was common. When farming societies needed land, their soldiers tried to claim additional territory. When nomads needed agricultural goods or slaves, they resorted to raiding or even large-scale invasion. Warfare tended to break out when normal trade relations between the nomads and the agriculturalists were interrupted.

The Mongol Conquests

Shortly after he was acclaimed "Great Khan" in 1206, Genghis began to carry out his plan to convince the kingdoms of Eurasia to surrender tribute to him. The next two decades saw the bursting forth of Mongol aggression. The earliest sustained action was westward, against Central Asia, the Middle East, and Russia.

Genghis Khan died in 1227, possibly of the effects of alcoholism. His son and successor, the Great Khan

Ögödei°, continued the campaigns seeking domination of China (see Figure 13.1). The Tanggut and then the Jin Empires were destroyed, and their territories were put under Mongol governors (see Chapter 14). In 1236 Genghis's grandson Batu° (d. 1255) launched a major offensive into the Russian territories and took control of all the towns along the Volga° River (see Map 13.1). Within five years he conquered Moscow and Kievan Russia, Poland, and Hungary and was ready to strike at Central Europe. Under siege by the Mongols by the 1230s, Europe would have suffered grave damage in 1241 had the Mongol forces not lifted their attack because of the death of the Great Khan Ögödei, and the necessity to head east to the Mongol capital at Karakorum for the election of a new Great Khan. After the installation of the new Great Khan, Genghis's grandson Güyük°, in 1246, Mongol pressure on the Middle East intensified. It climaxed in 1258 with the sacking of Baghdad and the murder of the last Abbasid caliph (see Chapter 9).

Historians often ask why the Mongols, who were not great in number, were able to defeat some of the most formidable armies of the time. Part of the answer lies in the combination of their extraordinary abilities on horseback and the special properties of their bows. The Mongol bow could shoot arrows one-third farther (and was significantly more difficult to pull) than Middle Eastern and European bows of the same period. The

Ögödei (ERG-uh-day)   Batu (BAH-too)   Volga (VOHL-gah)
Güyük (gi-yik)

composite structure of the Mongol bow and a jade thumb-ring that allowed the archer's hand to withstand the tremendous tension of the drawn bowstring also gave the archer an advantage.

Mounted Mongol archers rarely used all of the five dozen or more arrows they carried in their quivers. At the opening of battle, they shot a volley of arrows from a distance to destroy the ranks of enemy marksmen. Then they rode their swift horses nearly without challenge into sword, lance, javelin, and mace combat against the enemy's infantry. The Mongol cavalry met its match only at the Battle of Ain Jalut°, where it confronted Mamluk forces, whose war techniques also reflected the riding traditions of Central Asia. Thus it was Central Asian knowledge that stopped the Mongol advance toward the Mediterranean.

Another reason for the Mongols' success was their use of Genghis's principles of adaptability and inclusiveness. They changed their techniques for penetrating sophisticated fortifications. A typical Mongol attack began with a volley of flaming arrows, after which the Mongols hurled enormous projectiles—frequently on fire—from catapults. The first Mongol catapults were taken from the Chinese. Though easy to transport, they had short ranges and poor accuracy. From the defeated Khwarazmshahs° in Central Asia the Mongols adapted a catapult design that was half again as powerful as the Chinese catapult. They used this improved weapon against the cities of Iran and Iraq.

Residents of cities under Mongol attack faced immediate slaughter if they opened their gates to fight or slow starvation followed by slaughter if they did not. As a third alternative, the Mongols offered their prospective victims food, shelter, and protection if they surrendered without a fight. The terrible bloodletting that the Mongols inflicted on cities such as Balkh° (in present-day northern Afghanistan) in their early conquests gave staggering force to these appeals, and throughout the Middle East the Mongols found populations willing to acknowledge their overlordship in return for life. With the capture of each city the "Mongol" armies swelled in number. The conquest in the Middle East was accomplished by a small Mongol elite overseeing armies of recently recruited Turks, Iranians, and Arabs.

Through their experiences with so many different cultures the Mongols quickly learned about the rivalries among neighboring groups and found ways to take advantage of them to further the conquest. In their campaigns against the cities of Central Asia the Mongols exploited Muslims' resentment against nonbelievers. In the Middle East, where Muslims were a solid majority, the Mongols exploited Christian resentment of Muslim rule in their seizure of cities in Syria (where Christians were a large group), forcing the conversion of mosques to churches. When Hülegü° captured Baghdad in 1258, he agreed to the requests of his Christian wife that Christians be sought out and put in prominent posts.

Overland Trade and the Plague

The cosmopolitan nature of the Mongol conquests underscores the influence of the Mongols in the transmission of military technology and related scientific knowledge across Eurasia. The overland connections of the time were similarly important to the spread of civil technologies and artistic styles. A spectacular example of their importance is the leap forward in textile manufacture and trade—particularly in silk. Like their aristocratic predecessors in Central Asia, Mongol nobles had the exclusive right to wear silk, almost all bought from China. The unprecedented commercial integration of Eurasia under the Mongols brought new styles and huge quantities of silk westward. Since the material was used not only for clothing but also for wall hangings and furnishings, the presence of silk throughout the Middle East and Europe transformed the daily life of the elite and urban groups. At the same time, the trading of designs brought a mixing and merging of artistic motifs from Japan and Tibet to England and Morocco.

This trade was protected by Mongol control of the overland routes and promoted by Mongol tax policies, but it was carried out by a collection of very different peoples from all over Eurasia. Merchants hoping for wealth and prestige joined political ambassadors, learned men, and religious missionaries over long distances to the Mongol courts. These journeys produced travel literature that gives us vivid insights into the Eurasian world of the thirteenth century. Some narratives, such as that of the Venetian traveler Marco Polo° (1254–1324), freely mixed the fantastic with the factual, to the delight of the audience (Map 13.1 shows Marco Polo's route). Most important, these books left an image of the inexhaustible wealth of the Mongols, and of Asia generally, that created in Europe a persisting ambition to find easier routes to Asia for trade and conquest.

Though the accounts of these travelers mesmerized readers for centuries, their unembellished experiences were not rare for their time. In the towns they visited in Central Asia or China, they regularly encountered other

---

Ain Jalut (ine jah-LOOT)　**Khwarazmshah** (hwa-RAZZ-um-shah)
Balkh (bahlk)

Hülegü (HE-luh-gee)
Marco Polo (mar-koe POE-loe)

Passport   The Mongol Empire that united Eurasia in the mid-1200s provided good roads and protection for the movement of products, merchants, and diplomats. Individuals traveling from one culture area to another encountered new languages, laws, and customs frequently. The *paisa* (from a Chinese word for "card" or "sign"), with its inscription in Mongolian, proclaimed to all that the traveler had received the ruler's permission to travel through the region. Europeans later applied the practice to travel through their small and diverse countries. The paisa was thus the ancestor of modern passports. (The Metropolitan Museum of Art, purchase bequest of Dorothy Graham Bennett, 1993 [1993.256]. Photograph 1997 The Metropolitan Museum of Art)

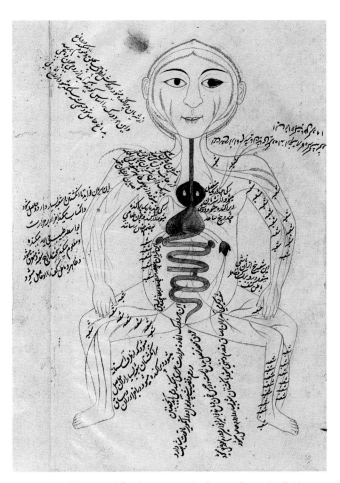

Anatomy   Illustrated Persian anatomical texts from the Il-khan and Timurid periods were based on ancient Greek ideas about the functions of the body. Here, the digestive and arterial systems are depicted together because it was assumed that heat generated by digestion forced circulation of the blood. The nervous system, which was not well understood, is not included. Diagrams such as these became very important in Europe a few centuries later, as European scientists continued to build on the anatomical and physiological knowledge of the Islamic world.   (Bodleian Library, Oxford, Ms. Fraser 201 fol. 104r)

Europeans, sometimes from their own home regions. Some were travelers and some were captives, but all were part of a steady flow of people across Eurasia. The economic, political, and cultural benefits of this traffic were great. Technical knowledge, whether of pharmacology, engineering, mathematics, or financial management, flowed between China and Iran.

Mongol policy and occasionally Mongol competition also widened the steady stream of knowledge between Europe and the Middle East. For instance, the wish of the Mongols in the Middle East (in the Il-khan Empire) to drive the Mongols of Russia out of the Caucasus in the 1260s helped create a half-century of complex diplomacy in which Muslims often allied themselves with the European sponsors of the Crusader states—sometimes against Christians, sometimes against the Mongols. Or to use a different case, when the Mongols in Russia granted a special trade charter to merchants from

Genoa, the Mongols in the Middle East granted a similar privilege to traders from Venice. And it was probably also by this route that the cosmological ideas and technical knowledge of scholars working under Mongol patrons were communicated to Europe and helped to profoundly change its intellectual life.

There were also great dangers to the exchange. Europe had been free of **bubonic plague** since about 700. The Middle East had seen no plague since about the year 1200. In southwestern China, however, the plague had festered in Yunnan province since the early Tang period.

In the mid-thirteenth century, Mongol troops arrived in Yunnan and established a garrison. From that point, military and supply traffic in and out of Yunnan provided the means for flea-infested rats carrying plague to be carried from Yunnan to central China, to northwestern China, and across Central Asia. Along the routes, marmots and other desert rodents were infected and passed the disease to dogs and people. The caravan traffic across Central Asia infected the oasis towns when rats and fleas disembarked from the overloaded camels, covered wagons, and the wagon-mounted felt tents of the nomads. The Mongols themselves were incapacitated by the plague during their assault on the city of Kaffa° in Crimea° in 1346. They withdrew, but the plague infiltrated Crimea. From Kaffa, both Europe and Egypt were repeatedly infected by fleas from rats on ships bound across the Mediterranean.

Bubonic plague was only one of the diseases at work weakening the resistance of urban populations in particular and unleashing new waves of latent illness. Typhus, influenza, and smallpox traveled with the plague. The combination of these and other diseases created what is often called the "great pandemic" of 1347–1352. The human and cultural damage that resulted was far greater than any of the direct consequences of the Mongol military conquests. It is tempting to associate the social disorder of conquest and the plague as twin illnesses, but it was not the Mongol invaders who brought the disease westward. Rather, disease was transmitted by the trade encouraged by Mongol protection of the Eurasian land routes. Peace and profit were the channels by which pandemic illness terrorized Eurasia in the mid-fourteenth century.

THE FALL AND RISE OF ISLAM, 1260–1500

By 1260 two distinct Mongol realms had been established in western Eurasia: the **Il-khan**° Empire and the Khanate of the **Golden Horde** (also called the Kipchak° Khanate; see Map 13.1). The Mongols under Genghis's grandson Hülegü controlled parts of Armenia and all of Azerbaijan, Mesopotamia, and Iran. The Mongols who had conquered southern Russia settled north of the Caspian Sea, establishing their capital at Sarai° on the Volga River. They became known as the Golden

Kaffa (KAH-fah)   Crimea (cry-MEE-ah)   Il-khan (IL-con)
Kipchak (KIP-chahk)   Sarai (sah-RYE)

Celebrating Battle   The Mongols were in a long line of Central Asian warriors who mastered the art of shooting arrows from a galloping horse. They were renowned not only for their mobility but also for the unusual distance and accuracy their archers could attain with their distinctive compound bows. This detail from a painted bowl of the early Il-khan period illustrates a contemporary portrayal of the military skills of shooting from horseback, as well as depicting the violence of the battlefield. But it carefully avoids a fact of war in the thirteenth-century Middle East: the slaughter, starvation, and enslavement of civilians are not shown.   (Courtesy of the Freer Gallery of Art, Smithsonian Institution, Washington, DC.)

Horde, and quickly established a close relationship with the Muslim Turkic nomads who had frequented the area for centuries. By the 1260s Batu's successor as leader of the Golden Horde had declared himself a Muslim, announced his intention of avenging the murder of the caliph, and claimed the Caucasus—the region between the Black and Caspian Seas—also claimed by the Il-khans.

Mongol Rivalry

There is evidence that some members of the Mongol imperial family were believers in Islam before the Mongol assault on the Middle East, and Mongols frequently relied on Muslims as advance men and intermediaries. Muslims in the region known as Transoxiana played this critical role. In addition, certain of the Il-khans showed favoritism toward some Muslim groups. The Il-khan Hülegü, for instance, was a Buddhist but often gave privileges to the Muslim Shi'ite sect to which his most trusted adviser belonged. As a whole, however, the Mongols under the command of Hülegü were slow to become exposed to the Muslim religion.

Tensions between individual Mongols and Muslims paralleled tensions between Muslim principles and Mongol culture. Many Muslims could not forgive the murder of the last Abbasid caliph. In accordance with Mongol customs for the execution of high-born persons, the caliph had been rolled in a rug and trampled to death by horses to prevent his blood from spilling on the ground. The Mongols considered the elimination of the supreme religious leader of the Muslims a necessity for their control of the region. Muslims were shocked and outraged.

The passage of time did little to reconcile Islamic doctrines with Mongol ways. Muslims were repelled by the Mongols' worship of idols, which is fundamental to shamanism but at odds with Islamic teachings on the proper use of art. Another point of contention was rituals governing animal slaughter. The shamanic method of the Mongols forbade the spilling of blood; and the Islamic code of cleanliness, *halal°*, required the draining of blood from the carcass. Litigation on this and closely related matters flooded the law courts of the Il-khans.

Islam posed other dangers to the Mongol mission in the Middle East. At the time that Hülegü was leading the Mongol armies into Iran and Iraq, Mongols were also conquering southern Russia, north of the Caspian Sea. By the 1260s the Mongol leader—Genghis's grandson Batu—in Russia had declared himself a Muslim, announced his intention to avenge the last caliph, and claimed the Caucasus, between the Black and Caspian Seas. By this route, the Mongols of the Golden Horde could gain direct access to the Il-khan territories, and particularly to the Il-khan capital at Tabriz° (see Map 13.2).

The conflict was the first between Mongol domains, and the fact that one of the parties—the Mongols of the Golden Horde—was avowedly Muslim led the leaders of Europe to believe that they could enlist the other party—the Il-khans, who were Buddhists—to drive Muslims out of contested religious sites in Syria, Lebanon, and Palestine. The result was a brief diplomatic correspondence between the Il-khan court and Pope Nicholas IV (r. 1288–1292) and an exchange of ambassadors that sent two Christian Turks—Markuz° and Rabban Sauma°—on a remarkable tour of western Europe as Il-khan ambassadors in the late 1200s.

The Buddhist Il-khans attempted to enlist the aid of European countries to eject the Golden Horde from the Caucasus. Many Christian crusaders enlisted in the Il-khan effort, and the pope later excommunicated some for doing so. For their part, the Mongols in Russia attempted to forge an alliance with the Muslim Mamluks in Egypt against the crusaders and the Il-khans. The net result was to extend the life of the Crusader kingdoms in Palestine and Syria and European influence there; the Mamluks did not succeed in completely ejecting the crusaders until the fifteenth century.

Before the Europeans could realize their plan of allying with the Mongols, the new Il-khan ruler, Ghazan° (1271–1304) declared himself a Muslim in 1295. His prime minister and confidant, **Rashid al-Din°,** a convert from Judaism to Shi'a Islam, had convinced the Il-khan to convert. In the following decades the Il-khans and the Golden Horde promoted Islam throughout their domains.

The public stance of the Il-khans as Muslims radically changed the relationship of state and religion in the Middle East. The Il-khans declared themselves the protectors and advocates of Islam, and all Mongols in the Il-khan Empire were ordered to convert to Islam. The Il-khan legal code was brought into agreement with the principles of Islam. Years passed before the Il-khans made the crucial decision to support Sunna and not Shi'a Islam.

Islam and the State

The goal of the Il-khans was to extract wealth from their domain by peaceful means whenever possible but in any case to extract the maximum. This goal was most efficiently achieved through taxation, and the Mongols became masters of extraction. The method they used is generally called **tax farming,** a practice well developed in the Middle East before the coming of the Mongols. The government sold tax-collecting contracts to small corporations, most of which were owned by merchants who might work together to finance the caravan trade, small industries, or military expeditions. The winners of the contracts were the groups that agreed to generate the most revenue for the government. They could use whatever methods they chose to collect the tax and could keep anything over the contracted amount.

The short-term results for the government were good, for with a minimum of bureaucratic overhead the state received large amounts of grain, cash, and silk. The long-term results were different. The exorbitant rates charged by the tax farmers drove many landowners into

---

halal ((haa-LAAL) **Tabriz** (taw-BREEZE) **Markuz** (MARK-uhz) **Rabban Sauma** (rahb-bahn SAU-ma)

Ghazan (haz-zan) **Rashid al-Din** (ra-SHEED ad-DEEN)

Map 13.2   Western Eurasia in the 1300s   This map of the Mongol domains in the Middle East demonstrates the delicate balance of power that was upset by Ghazan's conversion to Islam in 1295. During the conflict between the Il-khans and the Golden Horde in the 1260s, European leaders hoped to ally themselves with the Il-khans against Muslim defenders in Palestine. These hopes were abandoned after Ghazan's conversion to Islam in 1295, and the powerful alliance between the Mamluks and the Golden Horde kept the Il-khans from advancing west. Europeans hoped to exploit the conflict by enlisting the Il-khans against the Mamluks, but realized the cause was lost after Ghazan became Muslim. The Mamluks and the Golden Horde remained allies against the Il-khans, which aided Europeans in retaining their lands in Palestine and Syria.

debt and servitude and prevented the reinvestment necessary to maintain productivity. Because many taxes were collected in kind, the price of grain rose so much that the government had difficulty procuring supplies for the soldiers' granaries. As a consequence the state was forced to appropriate land to grow its own grain. This land, like religious land grants, was tax-exempt, so the tax base shrank even though the demands of the army and the Mongol nobility for revenue continued to grow.

Economic troubles were acute when Ghazan became Il-khan in 1295 and converted to Islam. To address the economic crisis, Ghazan cited the humane values of

Islam and announced his intention to lessen the government's tax demands. He also took advantage of the Mongols' international contacts to seek new methods of economic management. He believed he found one in the Chinese practice of using paper money, and he ordered the use of paper money in his domain. But the peoples of the Middle East had no previous exposure to paper money and no confidence in its value, and the economy quickly sank into a depression that lasted until after the end of the Il-khan period in 1349.

After Ghazan, the Il-khan regime experienced a slow decline that was like the decline of Mongol regimes elsewhere. The extraction of revenues for the support of the

Mongol military elite caused widespread popular unrest and resentment among local elites. Mongol nobles in the Middle East competed fiercely among themselves for the decreasing revenues, and fighting among Mongol factions destabilized the government. The fragmentation of Il-khan power aroused the expansive ambitions of the Mongols north of the Caspian. In the mid-fourteenth century, Mongols from the khanate of the Golden Horde moved through the Caucasus into the western regions of the Il-khan Empire and soon into the Il-khan's central territory, Azerbaijan. The Mongols from Russia participated in the dismemberment of the Il-khan Empire and briefly occupied its major cities.

As the power of the Il-khans in the Middle East and of the Golden Horde in Russia weakened in the fourteenth century, a new power emerged in Central Asia. The Mongol rulers there were descendants of Genghis's son Jagadai (d. 1242). Under the leader **Timur°**, the Jagadai° Khanate (see Map 13.1) drew on the political traditions of the Mongols and on Islam. The campaigns of Timur in western Eurasia were even more brutal than earlier Mongol campaigns had been. By the late fourteenth century much of the Middle East was united under his rule, and he hoped to add China. The Timurids (descendants of Timur) held the Middle East together long enough to deepen and consolidate Sunni Islamic influence, and they laid the groundwork for the later establishment in India of a Muslim Mongol regime, the Mughals, in the sixteenth century.

Timur (r. 1370–1405) was the last great Central Asian conqueror. After his time Central Asia was no longer the crossroads of Eurasia, as it had been since the earliest times.

Art and Science in Islamic Eurasia

Thanks partly to the wide-ranging cultural exchange fostered by the Mongols, the Ilkhans and Timurids presided over a brilliant period in Islamic civilization. Many of the intellectual developments of the era had a strong direct effect on Europe. Others had an indirect but equally important influence. The sharing of artistic trends and political ideas between Iran and China created the illusion in European eyes that east of the Mediterranean there existed an "Orient" that was uniform in its tastes and political cultures. In fact, the intimacy of Iran and China was a product of the centuries of Silk Road trade and only more recently of the Mongol Empire. It was not evidence of any fundamental "Oriental" character. Although Timur was not successful in his wish to reunite Iran and China, at Samarkand he made possible the advancement of some specific arts because of his practice, followed by his descendants, of forcibly concentrating scholars, artists, and craftsmen in his capital.

The historian Juvaini°, who noted Genghis Khan's deathbed speech, was a central figure in literary development. His family came from the city of Balkh, which the Mongols devastated in 1221. At that time the family switched allegiance to the Mongols, and both Juvaini and his older brother assumed high government posts. Il-khan Hülegü, seeing an opportunity to both immortalize and justify the Mongol conquest of the Middle East, enthusiastically supported Juvaini's historical projects. The result was the first comprehensive narrative describing the rise of the Mongols under Genghis Khan.

Juvaini's work and his methods—he often was critical of his subjects—inspired Rashid al-Din, the prime minister of Il-khan Ghazan, to attempt the first history of the world. It contains the earliest known general history of Europe, based on information from European monks. Editions of Rashid al-Din's world history were often richly illustrated. Pictures adapted from European paintings depicted European persons and events, and pictures adapted from Chinese paintings depicted Chinese persons and events. In this way, Chinese principles of watercolor composition and portraiture were introduced into Iran. The reproduction and distribution of Rashid al-Din's work spread throughout Eurasia knowledge of the arts and histories of the lands under Mongol rule.

The cosmopolitan influence of Rashid al-Din's world history was personified by Rashid himself. As a Jew converted to Islam, serving the Mongols and traveling very widely in their service, he was aware of many cultures and many points of view. He was in constant touch with Mongol officials in Central Asia and China. When he could not see them in person, he often wrote letters to them explaining his ideas on economic management. It was partly as a result of these lines of communication that similar financial and monetary reforms occurred at roughly the same time in Iran, Russia, and China. Rashid was above all practical. It was he who advocated conducting government in accord with the moral principles of a majority of the population, and it was he who convinced Ghazan to convert to Islam.

Under the Timurids, the magnificent achievement of the Il-khan historians was augmented. Timur himself was acquainted with the greatest historian and geographer of the age, **Ibn Khaldun°** (1332–1406), a Moroccan. Like his Mongol predecessors, Timur was an enthusiastic supporter of historical narratives in which he himself

---

Timur (tem-EER) **Jagadai** (jahg-ah-die)

Juvaini (joo-VINE-nee) **Ibn Khaldun** (ee-bin hal-DOON)

acted as the primary informant. In a scene reminiscent of the times when Ghazan had sat patiently answering Rashid al-Din's questions on the history of the Mongols, Timur and Ibn Khaldun sat in Damascus, exchanging historical, philosophical, and geographical viewpoints. Like Genghis, Timur saw himself as a world conqueror, so the story of his conquests was necessarily the story of the world. At their capitals of Samarkand and Herat (in modern-day Afghanistan), later Timurid rulers sponsored historical writing in both Persian and Turkish. Under them, the art of illustrating historical and fictional works, employed so strikingly in Rashid al-Din's history, reached a very high point of development.

Juvaini had accompanied Hülegü in 1256 in the campaigns against the Assassins, a radical religious sect, and he worked to preserve the historical archives that the Assassins maintained at Mount Alamut°. It was possibly the archives and libraries of the Assassins that had drawn a multitalented Shi'ite believer, **Nasir al-Din Tusi°**, to Mount Alamut, where Mongol forces took him into custody. Nasir al-Din quickly charmed Hülegü and became one of his most trusted advisers.

Nasir al-Din was interested in history, poetry, ethics, and religion, but his outstanding contributions were in mathematics and cosmology. He drew on the work of the great poet and mathematician of the Seljuk° period, Omar Khayyam° (1038?–1131), to lay the foundations for complex algebra and trigonometry. The impact of Nasir al-Din's work was considerable. A group of his followers, working at their observatory at Maraga°, an academy near the Il-khan capital of Tabriz, were able to solve a fundamental problem in classical cosmology.

Islamic scholars had preserved and elaborated on the insights of the Greeks in astronomy and mathematics. They adopted the cosmological model of Ptolemy°, which assumed a universe with the earth at its center and the sun and planets rotating around the earth in circular orbits. Astronomers knew Ptolemy's model was flawed, because the motions of the five visible planets were not in agreement with its predictions. Since Ptolemy's time, astronomers and mathematicians of the Middle East had been searching for mathematically consistent explanations that would account for the movement of the planets and reconcile them with Ptolemy's model.

Nasir al-Din proposed such a model. His approach was based on a concept of small circles rotating within a large circle, changing vectors in such a way as to account for their movement when viewed from the earth. A student of Nasir al-Din reconciled the model with the ancient Greek idea of epicycles (small circles rotating around a larger circle) to explain the movement of the moon around the earth, and here occurred the breakthrough that changed cosmological thought. The mathematical tables and geometric models of this student were later transferred in their entirety to Europe and became known to Nicholas Copernicus (1473–1543), a Polish monk and astronomer. The means of transmission is still one of the tantalizing unknowns in world history.

Astronomy and Engineering   Throughout Eurasia, observational astronomy went hand in hand not only with mathematics and calendrical science but also with engineering, as the construction of platforms, architecture for solar measurement, and armillary spheres became more sophisticated. Publication of instruction manuals helped refine the science and the technology. This manual in Persian (completed in the 1500s but illustrating activities that occurred in the Il-khan period) provides instruction on the establishment of a plumb line for an enormous outdoor armillary sphere.   (Istanbul University Library)

Alamut (ah-lah-moot)   **Nasir al-Din Tusi** (nah-zer ad-DEEN toos)
Seljuk (SEL-jook)   **Omar Khayyam** (oh-mar KIE-yam)
Maraga (mah-rah-gah)   **Ptolemy** (TOHL-uh-mee)

Copernicus adopted the lunar model as his own, virtually without revision. He then proposed that the model of lunar movement developed under the Il-khans was the proper model for planetary movement also—with the planets moving around the sun.

Europe was indebted to the Il-khans not just for cosmological insights. Perhaps because of the Central Asian nomads' traditional dependence on the stars to guide their movement, or because of the suitability of high, dry Central Asia for astronomical observation, Central Asian empires—particularly the Uigurs° and the Seljuks—had excelled in their sponsorship of observational astronomy and the making of calendars. Under the Il-khans, Maraga became a sort of world center for the prediction of lunar and solar eclipses. Astrolabes, armillary spheres, three-dimensional quadrants, and other instruments in use there were much more precise than those used earlier.

The Il-khans made a deliberate attempt to amass at their observatory astronomical data from all parts of the Islamic world, as well as from China. In this way they achieved unprecedented accuracy in the prediction of eclipses. The predictions of the Il-khan astronomers were translated into Arabic for use in the hostile Mamluk territories. Byzantine monks took them to Constantinople and translated them into Greek. They were taken to Muslim Spain and translated into Latin. They were taken to India, where the sultan of Delhi ordered them translated into Sanskrit. The Great Khan Khubilai° (see Chapter 14) was so impressed that he demanded a team of Iranians to come to Beijing to build an observatory for him. The Timurids continued to sponsor large observatories. Indeed, the Timurid ruler Ulugh Beg° (1394–1449) was an astronomer and actively participated in the construction of a great observatory at Samarkand.

Such work required a system for writing numbers that would give mathematical calculations a precision that was not possible with the numerical systems inherited—in both the Middle East and Europe—from the Greeks. By the 700s, Middle Eastern scholars had adapted the Indian numerical system, including the symbol for zero, to their own script. This advance made possible work on the level of the Nasir al-Din group. Until Leonardo of Pisa (also called Fibonacci°, the discoverer of Fibonacci's Numbers) studied Iranian texts and used them to introduce Europeans to the abacus in the 1200s, Europeans were still using the clumsy Roman numerals to do their calculations. In his text, Leonardo adapted the "Arabic" numerals of the Middle East and in this way introduced columnar calculation. With this technology, Europeans were finally able to participate again in the study of complex mathematics, astronomy and astrology, music theory, and logic—scholarship that had begun in the ancient Greek world and had been advanced in Islamic and Indian civilizations.

The Timurids continued the Seljuk and Il-khan policies of sponsoring advanced work in astronomy and mathematics that integrated the traditions of Eurasia, and they underwrote another major advance in mathematics. Ghiyas al-Din Jamshid al-Kashi°, in his studies of Chinese calendars, noted that Chinese astronomers had long used a unit for the measurement of new moons that was calculated as 1/10,000th of a day. It appears that this was the inspiration for al-Kashi's use of the decimal fraction, by which quantities less than 1 may be represented by the manipulation of a marker to show place value (a technology to which the zero was also crucial). With this means for representing decimal fractions, al-Kashi went on to propose a far more precise calculation for *pi* (π) than had been achieved since the value was established in classical times. This innovation was transmitted to Europe by way of Constantinople, where al-Kashi's famous work on mathematics was translated into Greek in the fifteenth century.

REGIONAL DEFINITION IN RESPONSE TO THE MONGOLS

Major features of Iran and Iraq under the Il-khans were present in many other regions that the Mongols occupied. One was a marked disparity between the fortunes of the cities and the countryside. After the conquest, the volume of safe, reliable overland trade throughout Eurasia stimulated many of the commercial cities of Iran and Iraq. But the countryside, subjected to extensive damage in the conquest, sporadically continuing violence, and crushing taxes, suffered terribly. Although from the time of Ghazan the Il-khan policy changed from maximum extraction from the rural sector to a policy that was more constructive and protective, the change came too late to stop the decline in population and further deterioration of agriculture.

There also were distinctive cultural changes under the Il-khans and Timurids. Both empires were inclined

---

Uigur (WEE-ger)   Khubilai (KOO-bih-lie)
Ulugh Beg (oo-look bek)   Fibonacci (fee-bo-NACH-chee)

Ghiyas al-Din Jamshid al-Kashi
(gee-YASS ad-DIN jam-sheed ak-KAHSH)

to promote the use of the written Persian language, often in connection with popular forms of writing such as poetry, epic writing, and songs. Similarly, both showed a strong interest in popular religious practices, especially the mystical form of Islam known as Sufism°. This interest was somewhat at odds with the official stance of the later Il-khan and the Timurid courts as adherents of Sunna orthodoxy. The elements of Persian language and steadfast devotion to Islam became indispensable to the rulers of the region.

Russia and Rule from Afar

The first conflict between Kievan Russia and the Mongols occurred in 1223, when the Mongols defeated a combined Russian and Kipchak (a Turkic people) army in southeastern Russia. The great Mongol onslaught led by Batu came in the late 1230s, when a series of defeats for the Russians culminated in the Mongol capture and pillage of the town of Riazan°. Unlike others who invaded Russia before and after, the Mongols were capable of successful winter campaigning and found that only the springtime mud of Russia hindered their cavalry. The Russian princes failed to unite to oppose the invaders, and in 1240 the central town of Kiev° fell. The princes of Hungary acknowledged the superiority of Batu shortly afterward, and the entire region came under Mongol domination.

Batu and his descendants established their own regime on the southern Russia steppe and, as discussd earlier, were known as the "Golden Horde" (see Map 13.1). This was really a collection of small khanates, many of which survived when others died out at the end of the 1300s. The White Horde, for instance, ruled much of southeastern Russia until the 1480s, and the khan of Crimea was not overthrown until 1783.

The Mongols placed their capitals at the ends of the overland caravan routes, which were the infrastructure of their empires. But in Russia only the region at the mouth of the Volga River could be connected to the steppe networks. Thus the Mongols of the Golden Horde settled well to the south and west of their Russian domains, first at (Old) Sarai just north of the Caspian Sea (see Map 13.1). As part of their rule-from-afar, the Mongols granted great privileges to the Orthodox Church, which then helped to reconcile the Russian people to their distant Mongol masters. Old Church Slavonic was revived, but chronicle-writing in Russian remained vigorous, and the Greek language was shunned by Russian scholars even though the khans of the Golden Horde permitted renewed contacts with Constantinople. The Russian language for the first time became the dominant written language of Russia. The Golden Horde also enlisted Russian princes to act as their agents (primarily as their tax collectors and census takers) and frequently as their ambassadors to the court of the Great Khans at Karakorum in Mongolia.

The Mongols' primary concern in Russia, as in their other domains, was the extraction of wealth. The flow of silver and gold into Mongol hands starved the local economy for currency. Like the Il-khans, the khans of the Golden Horde attempted to introduce paper money as a response to the currency shortage. So vivid was the impression left by this Mongol innovation that the word in Russian for money (*denga*°) comes from the Mongolian word for the stamp (*tamga*°) used to create paper currency.

Mongol domination strongly affected urban development and population movement in Russia, in part because of the role played by **Alexander Nevskii**° (ca. 1220–1263), the prince of Novgorod. Alexander aided in the Mongol conquest by persuading many of the Russian princes that it would be better to submit to the Mongols than to resist them. In recognition of his service, the Mongols favored both Novgorod (under Alexander's rule) and the emerging town of Moscow (under the rule of Alexander's brother Daniel). These towns eclipsed devastated Kiev as political, cultural, and economic centers during the period of Mongol domination. This, in turn, encouraged people to move northward, away from the Mongol pasture lands in the southwest, and it led to the opening of new agricultural land far north of the Caspian Sea. During the 1300s, Moscow emerged as the new center of Russia, and control of Moscow became equivalent to control of the entire country (see Map 13.2).

Russia preserved reminders of the Mongol presence for many years. Some regions of southern Russia, particularly Crimea, remained breeding grounds for the bubonic plague long after the caravans that the Mongols encouraged and protected had introduced the disease. In the late Kievan period, (1000–1230) Ukraine° had been a fertile and well-populated region. But under the Mongols, Ukraine underwent a severe loss of population. The Mongols crossed the region repeatedly in their campaigns against eastern Europe and raided it continually to punish villages that were slow to hand over their tax payments.

Sufism (SOO-fiz-uhm)   **Riazan** (ree-AH-zahn)
Kiev (kee-yef)

denga (DENG-ah))   *tamga* (TAHM-gah)   **Nevskii** (nih-EFF-skee)
Ukraine (you-CRANE)

Transformation of the Kremlin   Like many peoples of northern medieval Europe, the Russians of the Kievan period preferred to build in wood, which was easy to handle and comfortable to live in. But the fortifications of important political centers, which were vulnerable to assault, had to be made of stone. In the 1300s, the city of Moscow emerged as a leading political center, and its old palace, the Kremlin, was gradually transformed from a wooden to a stone structure. The process is depicted in this contemporary drawing.   (Novosti)

Historians debate the effect of the Mongol period of domination on the shaping of Russia. The destructiveness of the Mongol capture of Riazan, like the capture of Balkh seems to many to be typical of the Mongol conquests. In the opinion of many historians the Mongol conquest of Russia and parts of eastern Europe isolated Russia from the great currents of development in early modern Europe. These historians refer to the "Mongol yoke" and hypothesize a sluggish economy and a dormant culture under the Mongols.

Other historians offer a different interpretation. In response to the hypothesized economic damage, they point out that the Kievan economy was in decline before the coming of the Mongols and that the Kievan princes had already ceased to mint money. In addition, even though the Mongols' demands were high and their internationally oriented monetary measures sometimes inappropriate, the Russian territories regularly managed to pay their taxes in silver. These tax payments in silver suggest regular surpluses in income and an economy sufficiently well developed to make the conversion of goods to cash convenient. It also is clear that the tax burden was significantly increased not by the Mongols directly but by their tax collectors—Russian princes who often exempted their own lands from the tax and shifted the additional burden to the peasants. When the princes requested and received a lowering of the tax rate from the Mongols, the outcome was not necessarily more money in the hands of the common people.

In response to the hypothesized cultural isolation of Russia, skeptical historians point out that before the Mongol invasion, Russia was under the domination of the Byzantine Empire, which was not greatly affected by the Renaissance in western Europe. The Orthodox Church, which was strongly oriented toward Constantinople and did not encourage relations of any sort with western Europe, would have protected Russia from outside influences, with or without the influence of the Mongols.

To enhance their ability to control the country, the Mongols in Russia tended to undermine the local elites or alter the status of individuals within the elite. It does not appear that the Mongols destroyed the traditional forms of elite participation in government. There is good evidence that the structure of local government in Russia did not change significantly in this period. On the regional level, the princely families continued to battle among themselves for dominance as they had in the past. The Mongols were merely an additional factor in those struggles.

Ivan° III, the prince of Moscow (r. 1462–1505), established himself as an autocratic ruler in the late 1400s. Before Ivan, the title **tsar** (from "caesar"), by which the rulers of Russia after the Mongols were known, was used only for foreign rulers (whether the emperors of Byzantium or the Turkic khans of the steppe) dominating the disunited Russian principalities. After throwing off Mongol dominion in 1480, Russian leaders adopted the title *tsar* to show that Russia should be ruled by Russians and not from afar.

There were strong similarities between the effects of Mongol domination in Russia and in the Middle East. In Russia the Mongols ended the dominance of Kiev and

Ivan (ee-VAHN)

encouraged the rise of Moscow. In the Middle East the Mongols ended the political and cultural dominance of Baghdad and encouraged the emergence of new centers of power and commerce. Like the Mongols who first occupied Iran, the Mongols in Russia had little interest in the dominant religious system. The distance between the Mongols and the local people in Russia, prevented the Mongols from attempting to become patrons of the local religion. The result was the survival of the Russian Orthodox religious hierarchy and the strong association of the Russian Orthodox Church with Russian identity and aspirations to independence. Also, in Russia as elsewhere, the Mongols were an impetus to centralization. In the aftermath of the Mongol period, Russia's strongest leaders and its most centralized political system emerged.

Social Change and Centralization in Europe and Anatolia

Parallel to the division of the western part of the Mongol Empire between the Golden Horde and the Il-khans was the division of Europe at the same time between the political forces of the papacy and those of Frederick II of the Hohenstaufen family, who was the Holy Roman Emperor and hereditary ruler of the German territories. Raised in Sicily, Frederick (r. 1212–1250) was sympathetic to Muslim culture. When the pope threatened him with excommunication unless he participated in the Crusades in Palestine and Syria, Frederick conspired with the Mamluk rulers of Egypt and Syria to present the illusion of capturing Jerusalem.

With Europe divided between the pope and the Holy Roman Emperor, the kingdoms of eastern Europe—particularly Hungary and Poland—dealt with the onslaught of the Golden Horde on their own. Many of the eastern European princes chose to capitulate and went to (Old) Sarai to declare themselves slaves of Batu. One of the minority of the eastern groups unwilling to capitulate was the Teutonic° Knights.

Like the Knights Templar in the Middle East, the Teutonic Knights had been sent on crusade. Their goal was to Christianize the Slavic and Kipchak populations of northern Europe. Also like the Knights Templar, the Teutonic Knights were licensed to colonize their conquered territories. They imported thousands of German-speaking farmers, artisans, and clerics to populate their kingdoms. Alexander Nevskii, the prince of Novgorod, led the Mongol campaigns against the Teutonic Knights and their Finnish allies, who in 1242 lost so many of their

Teutonic (two-TOHN-ik)

Pope and Emperor   In the world history overseen by Rashid al-Din, the narratives are based on information that is often drawn from original European sources. But many of the illustrations capture the tendency of Persians to see Europeans as projections of themselves. Here, Holy Roman Emperor Frederick II—a well-known figure in the Islamic world, though not a friend to the Il-khans—and Pope Gregory IX are depicted in Persian dress and postures, their features drawn according to the artistic principles of Persian portraitists and painters of miniatures.   (Topkapi Saray Museum)

number through the ice at Lake Chud (see Map 13.2) that their power was broken and the northern Crusades virtually ceased.

Alexander Nevskii's role in the defeat of the Teutonic Knights is a reminder that the "Mongol" armies that the Europeans encountered were barely Mongol at all. Most commanders were Mongols, and historians rank one of them—Sübüdei, who was Batu's chief general in western Eurasia—as a military genius. But Mongol policies of recruitment and conscription created an international force of Mongols, Turks, Chinese, Iranians, Europeans, and at least one Englishman, who went to the Middle

East as a crusading knight and, through capture or capitulation joined the Mongol forces and turned up in the Hungarian campaigns.

Eastern Europe came under direct assault from these forces in the winter of 1241, when the Danube River froze. Sübüdei's troops rode across it and inflicted a series of dazzling defeats on the eastern European kingdoms. Mongol forces appeared at the foot of the Alps, apparently menacing northern Italy and possibly Venice. They also were on the outskirts of Vienna. Poles, Hungarians, Austrians, and Bohemians struggled frantically to safeguard themselves and mount some resistance. The rest of Europe was panicked by the sudden, terrifying onslaught.

Rumors and some written accounts described the Mongols as having bodies that were part dog. They were theorized to have come from Hell or from the caves where, it was said, Alexander the Great had banished the monsters of ancient times. They were said to be cannibals. People in Germany claimed that the Mongols were the lost tribes of Israel returned, and in the eastern German territories Jews who were thought to be in secret alliance with the invaders were lynched. In Hungary, the recently Christianized Kipchaks were accused of aiding the Mongols; some were imprisoned, and some were killed. The king of France resigned himself to the destruction of his country, accepting it as the will of God. The pope, despite his wish to keep pressure on Frederick II, authorized a crusade against the Mongols, and the liturgies for daily worship were altered to include a line begging God for deliverance from them.

It seemed that the prayers were answered. Before the Europeans could mount a united force to repel the Mongols, Sübüdei's forces withdrew in December 1241. The Great Khan Ögödei had died, and the Mongol princes wished to return to Mongolia to participate in election of Ögödei's successor as Great Khan.

After the sudden retreat of Batu's troops from Europe, several European leaders attempted to open peaceful channels of communication with the Il-khan, hoping through him to reach the Great Khan in Mongolia. Some kings of Europe, trade federations, and the pope sent embassies to Iran, and many diplomats and merchants traveled eastward toward the Mongol capital. The Mongol rulers often received merchants and craftsmen favorably, but they welcomed ambassadors from kings or from the Vatican only if they brought messages of submission from their lords (see Society and Culture: Dueling Pieties).

European embassies to the Golden Horde and to the Great Khan in Mongolia increased in number through the thirteenth century. As Europeans learned to utilize the Mongol trade routes, and to exploit Mongol divisions in the Middle East, their terror of the Mongols was replaced by their awe of, and eventual idealization of, the wealth and power of the Mongol khanates. From their contacts with the Mongols the Europeans gained their first systematic knowledge of Eurasian geography, cultural patterns, natural resources, and commerce. They learned about the use of diplomatic passports, the mining and uses of coal, movable type, high-temperature metallurgy, efficient enumeration and higher mathematics, gunpowder, and, in the fourteenth century, the casting and use of bronze cannon.

Nevertheless, Europe suffered greatly from the effects of Mongol domination of eastern Europe and Russia. The terror created by the Mongol invasions combined with other factors, such as the outbreak of bubonic plague in the late 1340s (see Chapter 16), to ignite a storm of religious questioning and anxiety, especially in regions of eastern and Central Europe that had been virtually under the hooves of the Mongol horses.

In the fourteenth century, the Mongol grip on eastern Europe was weakened, and several regions emerged from the century of Mongol pressure considerably centralized. Lithuania° was one region of Europe energized by the Mongol threat (see Map 13.2). In the mid-thirteenth century, just as Russia fell to the Mongols and eastern Europe was first invaded, Lithuania was undergoing an unprecedented degree of centralization and military strengthening. Like Alexander Nevskii, the Lithuanian leaders struck a deal with the Mongols and were able to maintain their independence. In the late 1300s, when Mongol power in Russia was waning, Lithuania capitalized on its privileged position to dominate its neighbors—particularly Poland—and ended all hopes of a revival of the power of the Teutonic Knights in eastern Europe.

In the Balkans, independent and well-organized kingdoms separated themselves from the chaos of the Byzantine Empire and thrived until the Turkic Ottomans conquered them in the 1500s and 1600s. In the history of the Mongol period we can see basic connections among eastern Europe, the Balkans, and Anatolia (then under the control of the Byzantine Empire).

Communications between the Il-khans and Constantinople gave Europe a second doorway (Spain provided the first) to the scientific and philosophical achievements of Islamic culture. Because direct Il-Khan conquests did not extend into Anatolia, the Byzantine Empire survived, and Anatolia became a haven for Turkic groups pushed eastward by the Mongols.

Lithuania (lith-oo-WAY-nee-ah)

Dueling Pieties

Much of the written communication between Europe and the Mongols survives, but only as a result of an extraordinarily complex process. Europeans wrote to the Mongols in Latin, which was normally translated into Persian when the parties reached the Il-khan territories. On the route to the Mongol capital at Karakorum, a means had to be found to translate the Persian into Mongolian. Translation could be done orally if the ambassadors received an audience with the Great Khan or his representatives. For messages going from east to west, the process was reversed.

The messages were not complicated, but each side found the other's ideas so bizarre that mistakes in translation were very often suspected. This passage in a letter from Pope Innocent IV to the Great Khan in 1245 is typical. (Innocent did not know that there was no one to receive the letter, for Ögödei had died in 1241 and Güyük had not yet been installed as the next Great Khan.)

It is not without cause that we are driven to express in strong terms our amazement that you, according to what we have heard, have invaded many countries belonging both to Christians and to others and are laying them waste in a horrible desolation, and with a fury still unabated you do not cease from breaking the bond of natural ties, sparing neither sex nor age, you rage against all indiscriminately with the sword of chastisement.

Like popes before and after him, Innocent explained that he was sending monks to convert the Great Khan to Christianity, to baptize him, and to make him not a waster of the Christian lands but their protector. Group after group of Christian missionaries tried to convert the Mongols, but all were disappointed.

When Güyük was proclaimed Great Khan in 1246, he answered Innocent's letter. He expressed befuddlement at the idea that he should be chastised for invading Christian lands and at the suggestion that he himself should be baptized. Güyük questioned Innocent's arrogance in presuming to know God's intentions:

Though you also say that I should become a trembling Christian, worship God, and be an ascetic, how do you know whom God absolves, or in truth to whom He shows mercy? How do you know that such words as you speak are with God's approval? From the rising of the sun to its setting, all the lands have been made subject to me. Who could do this contrary to the command of God?

The Great Khans shared the traditional Central Asian belief that Heaven shows its will in the unfolding of history, that victors are necessarily the messengers of Heaven's will, and that the supreme victor is the supreme messenger. As often as the popes warned the Great Khans to be baptized and submit to the guidance of the Vatican, the Great Khans responded with the simple message that they were not about to submit to the church and that all Europe had best submit to the Great Khans—or suffer the consequences.

Güyük sternly closed his letter to Innocent:

If you do not observe God's command, and if you ignore my command, I shall know you as my enemy. Likewise I shall make you understand. If you do otherwise, God knows what I know.

In 1254, the Great Khan Möngke (MERNG-keh)—the last to rule the united Mongol Empire in Eurasia—used similarly ringing rhetoric on Louis IX of France:

If, when you hear and understand the decree of the eternal God, you are still unwilling to pay attention and believe it, saying "Our country is far away, our mountains are mighty, our sea is vast," and in this confidence you bring an army against us—we know what we can do: He who made what was difficult easy and what was far away near, the eternal God, He knows.

What did the popes regard as the primary evidence that the Mongols were evil? What did the Mongols see as the basic test of their supreme righteousness?

Source: Adapted from Christopher Dawson, ed., *Mission to Asia*, Medieval Academy Reprints for Teaching Series (Toronto: University of Toronto Press, 1981), 75, 85–86, 204. Archaic language has been amended to make the quotations more readable.

Among such groups were the ancestors of the **Ottomans,** Turks who had come to Anatolia in the same wave of migrations as the Seljuks. The Ottomans maintained their independence because the Il-khans were preoccupied with preventing Golden Horde invasions from the north and then, in later times, Timurid incursions from the east. By 1400 the Ottomans were expanding their territory and were in conflict with the Byzantines. In 1453, the Ottomans conquered Constantinople and killed the last of the Byzantine emperors based there. The Christians of eastern Europe and Russia were stunned, and for centuries the rulers of those regions yearned to regain Constantinople from the Islamic Ottomans. But the city, renamed "Istanbul," remained the capital of the Ottoman Empire for nearly five centuries.

Stabilization of Mamluk Rule in Egypt

In the Middle East, the **Mamluks°** are the outstanding example of a government that became stronger and more centralized by, and even gained some international support for, its resistance to the Mongol advance. (In Abbasid times, *mamluk* was a term used for military slaves; the Mamluks who established an empire in Egypt and Syria in 1250 used the name "Mamluk" for their regime and its ruling class.) The Mamluks retained control of their base in Egypt and their lands in Syria (see Map 13.2). During the campaigns against the Il-khans in the 1250s and 1260s, the crusaders allowed the Mamluks to cross Palestine to maintain lines of supply and command. The Mamluks were brilliantly successful in their campaigns against the Il-khans. This same strength was evident in the later defeat and destruction of the Crusader kingdoms. It also was demonstrated in the Mamluks' ruthless suppression of the well-organized and violent Assassins in their last remaining centers in northern Syria, which made the Mamluks one of the pillars (far more reliable than the Il-khans) of Sunni orthodoxy in the Middle East.

Mamluk society, particularly in Egypt, became very diverse. In the Abbasid and Seljuk eras, Mamluks had been Turkic immigrants from Central Asia. By the thirteenth century the military servants who gave their name to the regime were drawn from sub-Saharan Africa, from parts of Europe, and from far-flung regions of the Middle East. Under Mamluk rule, Egypt remained a military dictatorship until the forces of the Ottoman Empire conquered it in the 1500s.

The Mamluks were cosmopolitan and practical in outlook (they remained the dominant elite in Egypt until the end of the eighteenth century). They continued their friendship with the Hohenstaufen family and sent the Syrian diarist and judge Jamal al-Din Muhammad ibn Salim° as ambassador to Frederick's son Manfred in Italy. Mamluk links with the Golden Horde, established during the conflict with the Il-khans, kept a steady stream of people and goods moving by ship between Cairo and the port of Kaffa in Crimea, the primary point of embarkation for carriers of bubonic plague to the Mediterranean.

From the late 1300s to the very end of the 1700s, the Mamluks and their successors continued to import soldiers from Crimea. At the height of the fourteenth-century pandemic, around 1350, Egypt may have lost as much as a third of its population. Lebanon, Palestine, and Syria all had many towns receiving caravan traffic from the east and ship traffic from the Mediterranean. The plague spread swiftly through the populations of those towns, but the epidemic was brief there. Egypt, however, was continually reinfected by the traffic from Crimea, where plague lingered into the modern period.

CONCLUSION

Basic features of nomadic society afforded the Mongols the military capabilities and the organizational habits to begin their conquests in Central Asia. They were ready to adopt any useful technologies and to incorporate men from anywhere into their forces. The decentralized structure of the Mongol Empire facilitated even more innovation, because the regional khans were free to forge their own relationships with local elites, cultures, and economies.

This freedom to innovate on the part of the regional Mongol leaders was complemented by communications with very distant regions. The combination of distant influences and local interactions explains much of the change in western Eurasia during this time. The Il-khans' involvement in Iranian society eventually led them to listen to Rashid ad-Din's advice and convert to Islam. In Russia, however, the Mongols were removed from Russian society, both physically and politically, and never developed an interest in or identification with the local culture. On the surface it may appear that these are two opposite results—in one case the Mongols converted to the local religion and in another they had little contact with it—but actually they are not so very different. In

---

Mamluk (MAM-look)

ibn Salim (ee-bin sah-leem)

both the Islamic Middle East and Christian Russia, the local population was free to practice its religion as in earlier times.

Yet this should not be understood as meaning that the Mongols had no important impact. During the Il-khan period, the local language, Persian, became more influential as a literary language in Iran. Similarly, Russian emerged as a literary language in Russia. In both cases, local spoken languages that had had inferior status in comparison to foreign, classical languages became more established, and the amount written in them increased. The Mongol governments contributed to these changes by weakening traditional elites.

The effects of the bubonic plague in Europe parallel effects of Mongol domination in Iran and Russia. Traditional elites were weakened, and Latin lost some ground to local vernacular languages. In all these areas, the effects on literature and literacy would survive for centuries.

In Iran, the Timurids, by their patronage of Sunni doctrine, inspired their opponents to identify with Shi'ism and often with ecstatic sects such as Sufism. Thus, both positively and negatively, the period of Il-khan and Timurid domination established the terms of regional definition. Similarly, it was both by positive and negative influences that the Mongols helped to establish the terms of regional definition in Russia. To efficiently control the Russian territories, the Mongols stabilized the rule of the Russian princes and solidified the control of powerful families over certain towns and cities. In this way, native control was unbroken during Mongol domination of Russia and parts of eastern Europe.

To understand the full impact of the Mongol conquests, it is important to compare the experiences of the Mongol domains to the Mongol peripheries. The directly controlled domains frequently gained local definition and cultural coherence under the Mongols, and many sectors of the economy benefited from their participation in the Eurasian trade system. But in general their century or so of subjugation left them drained of wealth, sometimes demographically depressed, and deprived of the technological stimulation they might have gained had the Mongols not imposed on them nearly a century of peace.

The peripheries, in contrast, frequently integrated themselves with the Mongol trade networks and enjoyed a flow of information, experience, and often wealth (as in the cases of Genoa and Venice) that aided in their growth. Under military pressure from the Mongols they often tightened and strengthened their leadership (as in the cases of Lithuania, the Ottomans, and the Mamluks), or they explored new working alliances (as between the Mamluks and the Holy Roman Emperor).

■ Key Terms

Genghis Khan	tax farming
Mongols	Timur
steppe	Ibn Khaldun
nomadism	Nasir al-Din Tusi
bubonic plague	Alexander Nevskii
Il-khan	tsar
Golden Horde	Ottomans
Rashid al-Din	Mamluks

■ Suggested Reading

An enormous amount has been written on the history of the Mongol Empire. An accessible recent introduction, now available in paperback, is David Morgan's *The Mongols* (1986). A more specialized study is Thomas T. Allsen, *Mongol Imperialism: The Policies of the Grand Qan Möngke in China, Russia, and the Islamic Lands, 1251–1259* (1987). Also in paperback is René Grousset's classic *The Empire of the Steppes: A History of Central Asia* (1970; reprint, 1988). Two accessible but scholarly texts link early and modern Mongol history and culture: Sechin Jagchid and Paul Hyer, *Mongolia's Culture and Society* (1979), and Larry Moses and Stephen A. Halkovic, Jr., *Introduction to Mongolian History and Culture* (1985). Tim Severin's *In Search of Chinggis Khan* (1992) is a fascinating revisit by a modern writer to the paths of Genghis's conquest. The demographic effects of the Mongol conquests are outlined by William H. McNeill in *Plagues and Peoples* (1976), and Joel Mokyr discusses the technological effects in *The Lever of Riches: Technological Creativity and Economic Progress* (1990). For a thesis of global development that connects commercial development in Europe to the Eurasian trade routes of the Mongol era, see Janet L. Abu-Lughod, *Before European Hegemony: The World System A.D. 1250–1350* (1989).

The history of Central Asia during the Mongol period, when it first came under the rule of the Jagadai Khanate, is important but difficult. An interesting overview is S. A. M. Adshead, *Central Asia in World History* (1993). The most recent scholarly study of Timur is Beatrice Manz, *The Rise and Rule of Tamerlane* (1989).

The only "primary" document relating to Genghis Khan, *Secret History of the Mongols,* has been reconstructed in Mongolian from Chinese script and has been variously produced in scholarly editions by Igor de Rachewilz and Francis Woodman Cleaves, among others. Paul Kahn produced a readable prose English paraphrase of the work in 1984. Also of interest is the only version of the *Secret History* by a modern Mongol author: *The History and the Life of Chinggis Khan: The Secret History of the Mongols, Translated and Annotated by Urgunge Onon* (1990). Outstanding among recent biographies of Genghis Khan are Leo de Hartog, *Genghis Khan, Conqueror of the World* (1989); Michel Hoang, *Genghis Khan,* trans. Ingrid Canfield

(1991); and Paul Ratchnevsky, *Genghis Khan: His Life and Legacy*, trans. and ed. Thomas Nivison Haining (1992), which is most detailed on Genghis's childhood and youth.

The best single volume in English on the Mongols in Russia is Charles Halperin, *Russia and the Golden Horde: The Mongol Impact on Medieval Russian History* (1987). A more detailed study is John Lister Illingworth Fennell, *The Crisis of Medieval Russia, 1200–1304* (1983), and those with a special interest might consult Devin DeWeese, *Islamization and Native Religion in the Golden Horde* (1994).

No single volume in English has yet been devoted to a history of the Il-khans. David Morgan, cited above, is a Persianist, and his chapters on the Il-khans in *The Mongols* (1986) are presently the best general introduction to the history of the Il-khans in Azerbaijan and Iran. Interestingly, the great historians of the Il-khan period have been translated into several European languages. Available in English are Juvaini's history of the Mongols, Joveyni, 'Ala al-Din 'Ata Malek, *The History of the World-Conqueror*, translated from the text of Mirza Muhammad Qazvini by John Andrew Boyle (1958); a small portion of Rashid al-Din's work translated by David Talbot Rice, *The Illustrations to the World History of Rashid al-Din*, ed. Basil Gray (1976); and *The Successors of Genghis Khan*, trans. John Andrew Boyle (1971). Equally important as illustrative reading are works re-lated to Ibn Battuta. See C. Defremery and B. R. Sanguinetti, eds., *The Travels of Ibn Battuta, A.D. 1325–1354*, translated with revisions and notes from the Arabic text by H. A. R. Gibb (1994), and Ross E. Dunn, *The Adventures of Ibn Battuta, a Muslim Traveler of the 14th Century* (1986).

For Europe, a lively and well-known narrative is James Chambers, *The Devil's Horsemen: The Mongol Invasion of Europe* (1979). Many of the individuals who traveled from Europe to the Mongol courts—not only Marco Polo but also the Franciscan friars John of Plano Carpini and William of Rubruck—have had their accounts translated and annotated in modern editions. Christopher Dawson, ed., *Mission to Asia* (1955; reprint, 1981), is a compilation of some of the best known. But see also Frances Wood, *Did Marco Polo Really Go to China?* (1995). There is also some published material on the travels of Rabban Sauma, a Christian Turk, to Europe; the most recent and most comprehensive is Morris Rossabi, *Visitor from Xanadu* (1992).

■ Note

1. Quotation adapted from Desmond Martin, *Chingis Khan and His Conquest of North China* (Baltimore: The John Hopkins Press, 1950), 303.

14

EASTERN EURASIA,
1200–1500

Mongol Domination in Eastern Eurasia, 1200–1368 • The Early Ming Empire,
1368–1500 • Centralization and Militarism in East Asia, 1200–1500
ENVIRONMENT AND TECHNOLOGY: From Gunpowder to Guns
SOCIETY AND CULTURE: Everyday Law in Ming China

Defending Japan   Japanese warriors board Mongol warships with swords to prevent
the landing of the invasion force, its cavalry, and siege machines.

fter the Mongols conquered northern China in the 1230s, Great Khan Ögödei° told his newly recruited Confucian adviser, Yelu Chucai°, that he planned to turn the heavily populated North China Plain into a pasture for livestock. According to the records, Yelu reacted calmly to this startling plan but argued that taxing the existing cities and villages would bring greater wealth. The Great Khan chose the gentler approach, though the tax system that he instituted was not the fixed-rate method traditional to China but the oppressive tax farming already in use in the Il-khan Empires in the Middle East.

In the early years of the Mongol occupation the Chinese suffered under this system. But there were also benefits, particularly in trade, science, and technology. The Mongols secured routes of transport and communication. They also forced the exchange of experts and advisers between eastern and western Eurasia. These practices led to the rapid spread of information, ideas, and skills.

The effects of the Mongol domination of eastern Eurasia varied from one region to another. China and in some ways Korea gained new unity and definition from the Mongol interlude but suffered great losses of agricultural wealth and population. Japan and northern Vietnam (then called Annam) shared—in very different ways—the complex effects of being at the margins of the Mongol Empire. Song° China and Korea were able to resist the Mongols for decades; Japan and northern Vietnam were attacked by the Mongols but not conquered. This resistance prolonged the warfare in eastern Asia through nearly the entire thirteenth century, a far longer period than in western Eurasia.

The Mongols rapidly appropriated technological developments, particularly in warfare, and carried them westward. As a consequence, the Mongol period of the technologies of gunpowder, metal casting, and the building of wagons and bridges were refined and spread, and large-scale trade in iron ore, sulfur, coal, and copper created new economies in eastern Eurasia. China and Korea were beneficiaries of the techno-

logical developments of the century of warfare in the 1200s, though their societies struggled for decades to recover from the social impact of the Mongol century.

As you read this chapter, ask yourself the following questions:

- What were the major effects of Mongol rule on Chinese government, economy, and culture?
- What stimulated the economic growth of the early Ming period?
- What impact did developments of the Mongol period have on state formation in Korea, Japan, and Vietnam?

MONGOL DOMINATION IN EASTERN EURASIA, 1200–1368

The Mongol conquest of southern China in 1279 marked the end of the prolonged struggle of the Southern Song Empire (1127–1279) against northern invaders—a struggle that had produced a new centralization of government and many technological advances. After destroying the Tanggut and Jin Empires in northern China, Genghis's grandson Khubilai° established a new empire based in China, the Yuan°. Integrating Korea into his empire and maintaining close relations with the Il-khans, Khubilai created a system that allowed technologies improved in the Song period to be disseminated throughout Eurasia, while technologies and sciences of the Islamic world became more accessible in China than at any time since the Tang° Empire (618–906).

The Mongol Conquests, 1206–1279

In 1206 Temüjin° became Genghis Khan, supreme leader of the Mongols. In less than ten years the Mongols subdued other powerful federations of the steppes, and in 1215 Genghis Khan led the attack on the Jin capital at Beijing°. The first Mongol invasions of Russia and the Middle East (see Chapter 13) were occurring about the same time as the extensive campaigns

---

Ögödei (ERG-uh-day) Yelu Chucai (yay-loo CHOO-tsye)
Song (soong)

Khubilai (KOO-bih-lie) Yuan (yu-wenn) Tang (tahng)
Temüjin (TEM-uh-jin) Beijing (bay-JING)

CHRONOLOGY

	Central Asia and Mongolia	China and Southeast Asia	Korea and Japan
1200	**1206** Temüjin chosen Genghis Khan of the Mongols **1227** Death of Genghis Khan **1265** Khubilai becomes last Great Khan; destruction of Karakorum	**1234** Mongols conquer northern China **1271** Founding of Yuan Empire **1279** Mongol conquest of Southern Song **1283** Yuan invades Annam **1293** Yuan attacks Java	**1258** Mongols conquer Koryo rulers in Korea **1274, 1281** Mongols attack Japan
1300		**1368** Ming Empire founded	**1333–1338** End of Kamakura Shogunate in Japan, beginning of Ashikaga **1392** Founding of Yi kingdom in Korea
1400	**1405** Death of Timur	**1403–1424** Reign of Yongle **1405–1433** Voyages of Zheng He **1449** Mongol attack on Beijing **1471–1500** Annam conquers Champa	

against the Tanggut and Jin Empires in the early 1220s. Genghis died in 1227, but the conquest of China continued under his son Ögödei. By 1234, the Mongols controlled most of northern China and were threatening the Southern Song.

Although the earliest purpose of the Mongol campaigns was not to conquer these regions but to convince the rulers to render tribute, Ögödei was far more interested in ruling the territories. He established the Mongol imperial capital at Karakorum°, and between 1240 and 1260 it attracted merchants, ambassadors, missionaries, and adventurers from all over Eurasia. When the European missionary Giovanni di Piano Carpini (John of Plano Carpini) visited Karakorum in 1246, he found it isolated (see Map 14.1) but well populated and cosmopolitan.

The Mongol Empire was united from 1206 to about 1265, and during that period the khans of the Golden Horde, the khans of the Jagadai domains in Central Asia, and the Il-khans in the Middle East were subordinate to the Great Khan in Mongolia. The Great Khan was chosen in gatherings of Mongol aristocrats that took years to come to a conclusion. While they were deliberating and

Karakorum (kah-rah-KOR-um)

debating, the widow of the deceased Great Khan sometimes acted as head of the government. After Ögödei's death in 1241, the Mongol Empire began to disintegrate. When Khubilai declared himself Great Khan in 1265, the descendants of Jagadai and other lineages refused to accept him. Karakorum was destroyed in the fighting, and Khubilai created a new capital for himself at what is now Beijing. In 1271 he declared himself founder of the **Yuan Empire.**

The Jagadai descendants continued to dominate Central Asia, where they nursed a hatred of Khubilai and the Yuan Empire. The political prestige of the Jagadai Khanate and the ability of the Jagadai Mongols to defend themselves prevented the absorption of Central Asia by the Yuan. Moreover, the independence of the Jagadai khans contributed to the tendency of Central Asian Mongols to continue to strengthen their ties to Islam and to Turkic language and culture. Both the Islamic and the Turkic links were important to the rise of Timur (r. 1370–1405) in the later fourteenth century (Timur's empire is described in Chapter 13). The long-standing enmity between the Jagadai ruling family and the Yuan Empire may also have inspired Timur's unfulfilled wish to conquer China.

Map 14.1   The Ming Empire and Its Allies, 1368–1500   The Ming Empire controlled China but had a hostile relationship with peoples in Mongolia and Central Asia who had been under the rule of the Mongol Yuan emperors. Mongol attempts at conquest by sea, which are marked on this map, were continued by the Ming mariner Zheng He. Between 1405 and 1433 he sailed to Southeast Asia and then beyond, to India, the Persian Gulf, and East Africa.

After the Yuan Empire destroyed Southern Song in 1279, the state of Annam—in what is now northern Vietnam—was the next logical target. Mongol troops crossed south of the Red River and attacked Hanoi three times. On each occasion they occupied the city, attained an agreement for the paying of tribute, and then withdrew. In 1283 Kubilai's forces moved farther south, invading Champa in what is now southern Vietnam and making it a tribute na-tion as well. Then Khubilai attempted to subjugate Java. In 1293 a combined Mongol, Uigur, and Chinese force, num-bering perhaps forty thousand, set out from the southeast China coast. They arrived in Java but became embroiled in an internal dispute and wasted their resources with-out conquering the island. In Southeast Asia, as in east-ern Europe, the ultimate extension of Mongol effort and the limits of Mongol war techniques were reached.

Partly because of their experiences with the formal Islamic and Christian heirarchies in the Middle East and Russia, the Mongols were quick to communicate with religious leaders in eastern Eurasia. In China, Buddhist and Daoist leaders visited the Great Khan and, like the Muslims and Christians from western Eurasia, believed that they had all but convinced him to accept their beliefs. But only the religious leaders of Tibet seem to have exercised real influence over the Mongol rulers. The Tibetan idea of a militant universal ruler, bringing the whole world under control of the Buddha and thus pushing it nearer to salvation, was in agreement with the ancient idea of universal rulership in Central Asia.

The Mongol Great Khan personally oversaw the governance of Tibet and reinforced the dominance of Lamaism, a Tibetan variant of Buddhism. A **lama**° was a teacher of special techniques for contacting the deities. Tibetan Buddhism became increasingly familiar to Mongol nobles during the 1200s and 1300s.

The Yuan Empire, 1279–1368

Khubilai Khan was the Mongol ruler who best understood the advantages of the Chinese traditions of imperial rule. He gave his oldest son a Chinese name and had Confucianists participate in the boy's education. In his public announcements and often in the ways he allowed the law to be crafted, Khubilai was careful to see that Confucian conventions were acknowledged. He made **Beijing,** in northern China, his capital in 1265.

Like the capitals of the Il-khans and of the Golden Horde, Beijing was located at a critical spot on the overland trade routes that were the infrastructure of the Mongol world. The city was the eastern terminus of the caravan routes that began near Tabriz and Sarai. The routes were reinforced by the imperial horseback courier system, which established hundreds of stations and protected trails over Central Asia.

Khubilai created the spirit, if not all the features that remain today, of Beijing, naming it his Great Capital (Dadu) or, as it was also called, City of the Khan (*khan-balikh*°, Marco Polo's "Cambaluc"). Khubilai ordered massive mud walls of rammed earth built around Beijing, and a tiny portion of them can still be seen. The main streets were made wider and broader. Khubilai's engineers developed linked lakes and artificial islands at the city's northwest edge as a closed imperial complex. As a summer retreat, Khubilai maintained the palace and parks at Shangdu°, now in Inner Mongolia. This was "Xanadu°" celebrated by the English poet Samuel Taylor Coleridge; its "stately pleasure dome" was the hunting preserve where Khubilai and his courtiers practiced the traditional skills of riding and shooting.

When the Mongols came to Chinese territory in the 1220s, there was no "China" as we think of it today. Northern China was under the control of the Tanggut Empire and of the Jin. China south of the Yellow River was ruled by the Southern Song. Part of southwestern China was controlled by the state of Nanzhao. These states had different languages, different writing systems, and different forms of government. Each had a distinctive elite culture. The Great Khans destroyed all these regional regimes and encouraged the restoration or preservation of many features of Chinese government and society, creating a reunited China that was to survive long after the end of Mongol rule.

The Mongols did not merely copy and perpetuate the style of government that had developed under the Song. They introduced many distinctive practices and large numbers of immigrant professionals. As they had in the Middle East, they put primary emphasis on counting the population and collecting taxes. In the early period, direct taxation was replaced by tax farming in the Middle Eastern style. For this purpose the Yuan government brought Persian, Arab, Uigur, and Turkic administrators to China to staff the offices of taxation and finance. The Yuan relied on Muslim scholars to lead the offices of calendar making and astronomy.

By law, the status of individuals was dictated by where they or their ancestors had come from. Mongols had the highest social ranking; below them were Central Asians and Middle Easterners, northern Chinese, and finally southern Chinese. This apparent racial ranking, it should be noted, was also a hierarchy of functions. The Mongols were the conquering caste, the warriors of the empire. Central Asians and Middle Easterners contributed the highly valued political functions of census taking, tax collection, and managing the calendar. The northern Chinese had come under Mongol control almost two generations before the southern Chinese and thus outranked them. The southern Chinese, the last to be conquered, were strongest in their attachment to the principles of Confucian thought.

Despite Khubilai's attempts to include "Confucians" (a formal and hereditary status under the Yuan Empire) in the Yuan government, most saw that their role was much weaker than it had been before the Mongols came. Many were alienated from the Yuan government because of their comparatively low status and their philosophical objections to the conquest. The Confucians, for instance, criticized the elevation in status of merchants. In the Yuan Empire, merchants were a privileged group,

---

lama (LAH-mah)   *khan-balikh* (kahn-BAL-ik)
Shangdu (shahng-DOO)   **Xanadu** (ZAH-nah-doo)

and most were of Central Asian or Middle Eastern origin or were northern Chinese. Similarly, the Confucians regarded doctors as at best technicians and at worst heretical practitioners of Daoist mysticism. The Yuan, however, encouraged the practice of medicine, and the very long process of integrating the medical and herbal knowledge of China and the rest of Eurasia began under the Yuan.

In China as in the Middle East, the Mongols redistricted the country for purposes of census taking and administration. The Mongols organized China into provinces that were much larger than earlier units had been and were under the jurisdiction of provincial governors, tax collectors, and garrison commanders. The creation of the provinces—a strong assertion of Mongol ownership—marked a radical change and increased central control over selected matters.

The impact of Mongol rule on the economy is difficult to assess because of the scarcity of contemporary records and the hostility of later Chinese accounts of the period. Many cities seem to have prospered—the cities of north China that were on the caravan routes, the cities of the interior that were on the Grand Canal, and the well-developed cities along the coast. The reunification of the country revitalized trade between north and south China, fulfilling the original purpose of the Grand Canal. Early in the Yuan period, Khubilai discovered that it was more economical to move grain from south China to Beijing by sea than by land, so the ports of eastern China also were invigorated. The reintegration of East Asia (though not Japan) with the overland Eurasian trade further stimulated the urban economies.

The privileges and prestige that merchants enjoyed under the Mongols changed urban life and the economy of China. The old Chinese elites were eligible for only a limited number of posts in the government, so the great families who in the past had spent their fortunes on educating their sons for government service needed to find other uses for their money. Many gentry families chose to enter the world of commerce, despite their sense of a loss of prestige.

Most commercial activities, from the financing of caravans to tax farming to lending money to the Mongol aristocracy, were managed through corporations—groups of individual investors who behaved as single commercial and legal units and shared the risk of doing business. The forerunners of these corporations were caravan-financing groups in Central Asia and the Middle East, and early Yuan-period corporations were operated mostly by Central Asians and Middle Easterners. Chinese quickly began to purchase an interest in them, however; and soon most corporations were mixed in membership and many were entirely Chinese-owned.

Credit was a great issue in the Yuan period, partly because Mongol conquests damaged the agricultural base from which taxes were drawn, and partly because

Mongol Couple Mongols who settled in China adopted many of the country's practices, including the use of tombs and of portraits on tomb walls, of the sort depicted here. In accordance with Mongol custom, which for a time became influential among northern Chinese, the man and woman are portrayed side by side. (From *Wenwu*, 1986, #4, pp. 40–46)

the Mongol aristocracy absorbed much more wealth than it ever generated. The imperial government issued paper money in an attempt to solve its economic shortages. Small amounts of paper money had been used in China for centuries, but the massive amounts of unsecured notes issued by the Yuan failed to earn the trust of the population.

The improved stability of copper coins partially offset the failure of the paper currency. During the Song, exports of copper coins to Japan had caused a severe coin shortage in China. The shortage elevated the coins' value and distorted the price ratio of copper to silver. The Mongols cut off trade with Japan, which coincidentally stabilized the value of copper coins, somewhat encouraging trade and credit throughout the Yuan Empire.

The financial and commercial life of Yuan China inspired the gentry to live in cities rather than in the countryside, a change from earlier times. Cities began to cater to the tastes of merchants instead of the traditional scholars. Specialized shops selling clothing, grape wine, furniture, and properly butchered meats (reflecting customers' religious convictions) were common. Teahouses thrived—particularly those featuring sing-song girls, drum singers, operas, and other arts previously considered coarse. One result was a lasting linguistic change: the rise of literature written in the style of everyday speech and the increasing influence of the northern, Mongolian-influenced Chinese language that in the West is often called Mandarin.

In the countryside, where 90 percent of the people lived, **cottage industries** linked to the urban economies continued to advance. The cultivation of mulberry trees and cotton fields and the construction of new irrigation systems (encouraged by the Mongols, who favored the irrigation systems of the Middle East), dams, and water wheels were all common features of village technology. Some of the most famous treatises on planting, harvesting, threshing, and butchering were published in this period. Villagers continued to worship as local gods technological innovators such as Huang Dao Po°, who in the Yuan period brought her special knowledge of cotton growing, spinning, and weaving from her native Hainan Island to the fertile Yangzi Delta.

Overall, however, the Yuan period was a dark one for farmers and other residents of the rural villages. The vast majority of farmers depended on staple crops. After the initial conquests, the Mongol princes evicted many farmers. Those who remained were subjected to the exactions and the brutality of the tax farmers, their agents, and their enforcers. There is evidence that by the end of

the 1200s the Mongol government in China, as in Iran, had begun to change its policy from exploitation of farmers to protection and encouragement. But the change came too late. Many farmers had been forced into servitude or homelessness, and dams and dikes had been so neglected that flooding, particularly of the Yellow River, was recurring and disastrous.

The hardships in the countryside took a toll on the size of the population. If Song records of population levels before the Mongol conquest and the Ming census taken after the overthrow of the Mongols are reliable (each may be exaggerated in one direction or another), China may have lost as much as 40 percent of its population in the eighty years of Mongol rule. Many localities in northern China may have lost as much as five-sixths of their populations during the 1200s and early 1300s.

The reasons were complex. One was the continuous warfare of the 1220s due to effective resistance by the Southern Song. Another was the massive, continuous, southward movement of people attempting to flee not only the Mongols but the flooding of the Yellow River. This migration might explain why population losses in northern China were greater than in southern China and why the population along the Yangzi River markedly increased.

Perhaps more important was the effect of bubonic plague and its attendant diseases, which were spread by the constant population movements of the period. The Mongol opening of Yunnan° to first-time rule by a government based in China exposed the lowlands to plague (see Map 14.1). Cities may have been better equipped to lessen or avoid outbreaks than the countryside. Rural portions of northern China were extensively affected by plague in the 1300s, and it is probable that the south was exposed before then. Privations in the countryside may have been extreme enough to depress the rate of population growth, particularly if the traditional practice of female infanticide was employed.

Scientific Exchange

During the Mongol period, technological, medical, mathematical, and astronomical knowledge was vigorously shared from one end of Eurasia to the other. Khubilai in China and Hülegü° in Iran were brothers, and their primary advisers were constantly in touch. The economic and financial policies of the Yuan Empire and the Il-khans were similar, and so was their devotion to the sponsorship of engineering, astronomy, and mathematics.

Huang Dao Po (hwahng DOW poh)

Yunnan (YOON-nahn) **Hülegü** (HE-luh-gee)

Il-khan science and technology were exported to China and Korea. Muslims from the Middle East oversaw most of the weapons manufacture and engineering projects for Khubilai's armies.

From China, the Il-khans imported scholars and texts that helped them understand technological advances new to them. These included the use of sighting tubes for isolating astronomical objects, stabilized on sling-shot-shaped equatorial mounts; mechanically driven armillary spheres; and new techniques for measuring the movement of the moon. Khubilai commissioned a team of Iranians to come to Beijing to construct an observatory and an institute for astronomical studies similar to the Il-khans facility at Maraga. For the remainder of the imperial period in China, maintaining and staffing the observatory was considered an imperial responsibility.

In mathematics as well, the Yuan Empire promoted an integration of Chinese skills with new ideas from the Middle East. The Chinese had contributed the concept of fractions to Middle Eastern mathematics, and Middle Easterners coming to China brought with them the latest developments in algebra and trigonometry. Chinese mathematicians were encouraged to develop and publish their treatises.

The influence of Islamic doctors and Persian medical texts—particularly in anatomy, pharmacology, and opthalmology—was also strong in China during the Yuan. The Yuan emperors—particularly Khubilai, who suffered from alcoholism and gout—gave doctors an influential position. Chinese scholarship on herbs, drugs, and potions was well developed before the Mongol period, but the introduction of new seeds and formulas from the Middle East stimulated an explosion of experimentation and publication.

Dispersal of the Mongols

In the 1340s, power contests among the Mongol princes shredded the political fabric of the Yuan Empire. By the 1360s China was engulfed in local rebellions by farmers and local civil wars by Mongols. In the chaos a charismatic Chinese leader, Zhu Yuanzhang°, was able to mount a massive campaign that ultimately destroyed the Yuan Empire and in 1368 brought China under control of his new empire, the Ming. Though the Ming government was unfriendly to the memory of the Yuan Empire, many Mongols—as well as the Muslims, Jews, and Christians who had come with them—remained in China, some as farmers, some as shepherds, and some as high-ranking scholars and officials. In most cases their descendants took Chinese names and became part of the diverse cultural world of China.

Mongol power in Eurasia did not come to an end in 1368. New Mongol leaders prevented Ming armies from controlling Mongolia and Turkestan, and Timur held much of Central Asia and Iran. The reconcentration of Mongols on the steppes fostered Mongol unity. Islam united some Mongol groups; Tibetan Buddhism, others.

When the Yuan Empire disintegrated, some retreating Mongols joined Tungusic-speaking peoples of northeastern Asia who depended on hunting, gathering, and fishing. The Tungus—some of them were reindeer-riding nomads—were often seen in trading villages. Their languages and their dress were slightly affected by the Mongols, but in general the Tungus were too scattered and mobile to be effectively subjugated. In extreme northeastern Asia, they continued their traditional way of life and, by means of the Aleutian Islands, maintained contact with the peoples of Alaska, who were their cultural and linguistic distant relatives.

Manchuria (see Map. 14.1), with strong linguistic and cultural ties to the Tungus, was more thickly populated than extreme northeastern Asia and had a good number of farmers. Since the 600s a steady influx of Chinese and Korean settlers had worked to develop the agriculture and towns of the region. Manchuria came under Mongol control and became the Mongols' steppingstone to Korea. Using Mongolian terms and Mongol organizational institutions, the dominant indigenous people—the Jurchens, who had once ruled the area as part of the Jin Empire—made gains in economic and military power. By the late 1400s the Jurchens were a challenge to control of Manchuria by the Ming Empire in China.

Warfare among these groups became increasingly frequent after the disintegration of the Yuan Empire. The growing disorder hindered overland Eurasian trade, which remained an important economic resource for the Mongols of Central Asia.

The Mongols controlling Central Asia were less technologically innovative than their ancestors of the Genghis era, but they were superb traditional warriors and posed a persistent threat to agricultural areas. This meant trouble for Ming China, which hoped to bring all the Mongols under its domination and to convince them to participate in the tributary system. The Mongols did participate, but only to the extent that doing so made it easy for them to trade with the Chinese. Otherwise, they were hostile. Ming attempts to suppress a resurgence of Mongol power led, in the mid-1400s, to a disastrous war in which the Mongols captured the Ming emperor and in 1449 attacked Beijing.

Zhu Yuanzhang (JOO yuwen-JAHNG)

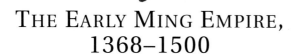

THE EARLY MING EMPIRE, 1368–1500

After the fall of the Yuan to the Ming in 1368, the intense need for technological advances in warfare waned, while population growth reduced the need for mechanization in agriculture and some manufacturing. Eastern Eurasia became a wealthy and culturally brilliant region. But the fact that Ming China had no technologically innovative, ambitious rivals on its northern frontier contributed to a slowdown in technological change.

Ming China on a Mongol Foundation

During the chaotic last decades of the Yuan Empire, Zhu Yuanzhang, who had been a monk, a soldier, and a bandit, vanquished his rivals in rebellion. In 1368 he established the **Ming Empire** and ruled as Hongwu (r. 1368–1398). Zhu said that his dedication to rebellion was inspired by the deaths of his parents and other family members from famine and disease, which he blamed on Mongol misrule. He also drew encouragement from radical Buddhist beliefs in the coming of a new age of salvation. As Emperor Hongwu, he oversaw the establishment of a distinct, highly centralized, militarily formidable empire.

In many ways the change from Yuan to Ming was more ideological than structural. The Ming were strong in their nationalist passions, and partly to symbolize their rejection of the Mongols, they established their imperial capital at Nanjing° ("southern capital") on the Yangzi River, rather than at Beijing ("northern capital") (see Map 14.1). The Ming were aggressive in their attempts to intimidate the remaining Mongols and the other peoples of Central and Southeast Asia. In these wars, they used Confucianism to depict the Ming emperor as the champion of civilization and virtue, justified in making war on uncivilized "barbarians."

The reaction against the Mongols had a vivid impact on early Ming policies regarding trade and money. Hongwu moved to choke off the close relations with Central Asia and the Middle East that had been part of the Mongol trade system. He imposed strict limits on imports and closed much of the border to foreigners. He also attempted to eradicate paper money and to force all tax and commercial payments to be made in silver.

When these extreme measures proved unhealthy for the economy, they were changed, but they are evidence of the vigorous early Ming rejection of Yuan practices.

Nevertheless, in its basic outlines the Ming government resembled that of the Yuan. Ming rulers employed Mongols who could translate communications between the Ming court and the Mongol powers remaining in Central Asia and Mongolia. They retained the provincial structure. In a continuation of Mongol social legislation, the Ming observed hereditary professional categories. The Ming also retained Muslims for making calendars and running their new observatory at Nanjing (a replica of Khubilai's observatory at Beijing), and they continued to use the calendar promulgated by the Mongols.

Ming continuities with the Yuan were even more evident after an imperial prince staged a coup d'état and then ruled as **Yongle°** from 1403 to 1424. He returned the capital to Beijing, enlarging and improving the imperial complex that Khubilai had built. It was mainly during the Yongle reign that the central part of this complex—the **Forbidden City**—took on its present character, with moats, outer vermilion walls, golden roofs, and alabaster bridges. Yongle intended this combination fortress, religious site, bureaucratic center, and imperial residential park to overshadow the imperial architecture at Nanjing, and today it is the most imposing traditional architectural complex that survives.

Economic revitalization was another consideration Yongle restored commercial links with the Middle East. Because the hostile Mongols still controlled much of the territory through which the land routes passed, Yongle sought to establish a connection by sea. In their first half-century the Ming emperors also pursued the Mongol program of aggression against Southeast Asia, and Annam became a Ming province. Control of Annam and access to Southeast Asia also helped inspire the expeditions of the trusted imperial eunuch **Zheng He°**, from 1405 to 1433.

The Chinese and many of the peoples of Southeast Asia had been exchanging seafaring knowledge for many centuries. Tens of thousands of Chinese descendants had settled throughout Southeast Asia, in the regions ringing the Indian Ocean, almost certainly in some parts of coastal Australia, and possibly in some sites in eastern Africa. From one point of view, Zheng He was merely retracing the routes that the Chinese had been exploring for centuries. The difference was that his expeditions were sponsored by the emperor, at great cost. In any event, he was a superb sea captain who believed that his exploits were measurably increasing the glory of Emperor Yongle, whom he served unflinchingly.

Nanjing (nahn-JING)

Yongle (yoong-LAW)   **Zheng He** (JEHNG HUH)

Forbidden Spaces   The general shape of the imperial complex at Beijing and the set of artificial lakes at its northwest corner were built under the Mongol ruler Khubilai Khan in the late 1200s. It was during the Yongle period (1403–1424) of the Ming, however, that the architectural style was set. In addition to the gold-tiled roofs and the vermilion walls, the Forbidden City is noted for its marble-paved courtyards and three large central palaces, all set on a north-south axis that was part of a spatial pattern that the Forbidden City's planners believed would give it supernatural protection. (Reproduced by permission of the Commercial Press [Hong Kong] Limited, from *The Forbidden City*)

Zheng He was a Muslim. His father and grandfather had made the pilgrimage to Mecca, so Zheng He had a good knowledge of the Middle East. His religion also made him an effective ambassador to the states of the Indian subcontinent, which was the destination of his first three voyages. On subsequent journeys similar ships reached Hormuz, sailed along the southern coast of the Arabian peninsula and the northeast coast of Africa, and reached as far south, perhaps, as the Strait of Madagascar (see Map 14.1).

An important objective of Zheng He's early voyages was to visit Chinese merchant communities in Southeast Asia, affirm their allegiance to the Ming Empire, and demand taxes from them. When a community on Sumatra resisted, Zheng He's marines slaughtered the men of the community to set an example. The Ming court also hoped to advertise the reversal of Hongwu policies opposing foreign trade and to establish lucrative commercial relationships with the Middle East and possibly with Africa.

A great increase in long-distance trade with these regions did not result. The primary achievement was to introduce the Ming Empire to new countries and to sign them on as tributary states. Zheng He's expeditions added as many as fifty new tributaries. The result was sporadic embassies to Beijing from rulers in India, the Middle East, Africa, and Southeast Asia. An early ruler of Brunei° died in Beijing during such a visit and was buried at the Chinese capital with great pomp and ceremony. Many of the expeditions also brought exotic animals—

Brunei (broo-NIE)

the most beloved by the Chinese court was the giraffe—
that lived for a time in the Ming imperial zoo.

Historians have long been intrigued by the extraordinary adventure in Chinese seafaring that began under the command of Zheng He in 1405 and continued sporadically until the 1430s, after both Yongle and Zheng He were dead. The feat itself was remarkable, involving ships of unprecedented size and a very well documented survey of nearly the entire Indian Ocean, long before voyages of a similar scale were undertaken by Europeans. Many historians consider Zheng He's expeditions as an early form of exploration that could have opened a period of Chinese military and colonial domination of a large part of the globe. Having accomplished long-distance navigation far in advance of the Europeans, why did the Chinese not develop seafaring for commercial and military gain?

Much of the answer requires setting aside superficial similarities to the European voyages and instead looking at the fundamental characteristics of the Zheng He expeditions. The designs of the enormous junks and of the compasses that Zheng He used were not new, and neither were his navigation techniques or geograhical concepts. Most dated from the Song period. Any empire based in China since the eleventh century that for any reason wanted to spread its reputation through the sponsorship of such voyages could have done so. But neither the Song nor the Yuan had considered it worth the trouble.

The expectation that the voyages would create new commercial opportunities or awe overseas Chinese and foreign nations into immediate submission to Yongle was not realized. In the meantime, Japanese piracy along the coast intensified, and the Mongol threat in the north and west grew. The human and financial demands of fortifying the north, remodeling and strengthening Beijing, and outfitting military expeditions against the Mongols were more than enough for a government that had outgrown its initial enthusiasm for world dominion.

Perhaps the Zheng He voyages are best seen as what people at the time understood them to be: the personal project of Emperor Yongle. This ruler, who had wrested control from a branch of the imperial family in 1403, always felt that he had to prove his worthiness. In Beijing he accomplished most of the intense building that now represents the Forbidden City. He sponsored gigantic encyclopedia projects designed to collect and organize all known knowledge and literature. And he prosecuted effective campaigns against the peoples of Mongolia and northeastern Asia. His nearest model for what he wished to achieve in the voyages west may well have been Khubilai Khan, who also hoped to use enormous fleets of large ships to demand the submission of Japan and

How to Navigate   The navigational techniques that Zheng He and his crew used were well established and tested, as his manual shows. Ships were precisely guided by reference to the Pole Star, and the routes to India, the Middle East, and East Africa were well known. The manual underscores that Zheng He's mission was not to explore but to carry out political and if possible economic mandates.   (From *Wubei zhi* [records of military preparations], 1621)

Southeast Asia. Indeed, Yongle's self-image was so like that of Khubilai that his political enemies spread the rumor that Yongle was a Mongol.

It is important to remember that the cessation of the voyages did not represent a Chinese turning-away from the sea. Zheng He's phenomenal fleet was only one episode in the saga of Chinese seafaring, which continued to be wide ranging and vigorous after Zheng He's voyages ceased. The question to be answered is not about Chinese involvement with the sea but about the Ming emperors' lack of interest in centralizing the organization of such voyages, funding them with government money, and turning them to military uses. The Ming empire was a large, complex, and constantly challenged land-based empire, and the Ming emperors saw little reason to attempt to impose and sustain rule over distant and far-flung sea-based colonies. It is true that before the year 1500 Europeans were engaged in sea-based exploration that brought them to East Asia. But the Zheng He voyages were not the same phenomenon, and it would be a mistake to think that the cessation of the voyages was a major miscalculation by the Ming emperors.

Technology and Population

The economy of Ming China fueled the enrichment of East Asia—and attracted ambitious Europeans. But Ming advances showed less dependence on technological innovation than had been evident in the Song. Innovation continued in all areas of the Ming economy but became less frequent and less important, particularly in agriculture. Agricultural productivity peaked by about the mid-1400s and remained level for more than a century. The slowdown in innovation is apparent in comparisons of Ming China to Song China, or Ming China to its contemporary economies in East Asia.

The slowing of technological development seems to have occurred first in mining and metallurgy, during the Yuan period. The Mongol conquest brought peace to China, and peace removed the pressure to constantly manufacture weapons. Especially striking is the apparent loss of the knowledge required to make high-quality bronze and steel. When instruments were cast for Khubilai's observatory at Beijing, the work was done by Central Asian and Middle Eastern technicians. The failure in China to preserve Song knowledge of high-temperature metallurgy has not been fully explained.

At roughly the time that Chinese metallurgy began to stagnate, Japan made dramatic advances and quickly surpassed China in the production of swords demanding steel of extremely high quality. It appears that copper, iron, and steel had become very expensive commodities in China (remember that the early Ming government preferred metal coins to paper money)—so expensive that farm implements and well-caps made of these materials became prohibitive to manufacture. Shipbuilding also declined sharply, particularly after the death of Emperor Yongle in 1424. There were fewer advances in printing, timekeeping, or agricultural technology. Innovations in the mechanization of weaving seem to have continued through the fifteenth century but were rare after 1500.

The slowing of technological development might be partly due to a significant shift in the career patterns of educated men. During the Yuan period, when few posts in the government were open to Chinese, many wealthy families had turned to commercial pursuits, investing in trading ventures and agriculture. The Ming government reactivated the old examination system, employed large numbers of educated men in government, and deprived the economy of the participation of some of its best educated, most ambitious men.

The Ming economy also may have suffered from a labor glut, which lowered the incentives for mechanization. At the end of the Yuan period in 1368, the population was perhaps as low as 60 million. By 1400 it rebounded to nearly 100 million. This growth constituted a boom to which the economy may have adjusted awkwardly. The rapid growth in population shifted economic importance away from commercial agriculture, where innovation had been rewarded in the Song period, to the production of staples—primarily wheat, millet and barley in the north and rice in the south. Staple crops, though necessary to sustain farming families and feed the rest of the population, did not offer the profit margins of specialized commercial crops and did not provide farmers with money to pay for capital improvements.

Also, the materials necessary for the building of machines had become scarce. The Ming government attempted to limit the mining of metals, partly to reinforce the value of metal coins and partly to control and tax the industry. Iron and bronze were difficult for farmers to obtain. Wood was becoming expensive because of the deforestation of southern and central China during the Ming period, when trees were cut to provide houses and coffins for the expanding population. Farmers who could not acquire plows had little need for draft animals, harnesses, or crops that required deep planting.

In warfare, the Ming faced few technological challenges. The Mongols whom the Ming confronted in the north fought on horseback with simple weapons. The Ming fought back with technology that was nearly as old: arrows, scattershot mortars, and explosive canisters. The Ming used a small number of cannon, but selectively. They were not under pressure to innovate and advance in the technologies of warfare, as the Song had been (see Environment and Technology: From Gunpowder to Guns).

The Ming state, unlike the Song, did not encourage the rapid dissemination and application of technology. Fear of **technology transfer**—whether from the state to the people or from China to foreign nations—seems evident in much of the behavior of the Ming government. Encyclopedias of practical knowledge were produced in the early Ming period, but chapters on gunpowder and guns were censored. Ming shipyards and ports were closed to avoid contact with Japanese pirates and

From Gunpowder to Guns

The word *gunpowder* suggests a substance invented for the gun, but in fact gunpowder had a variety of uses long before guns appeared. Gunpowder was used in China and Korea to do the excavation necessary for mining, canal building, and irrigation. Alchemists in China used formulas related to gunpowder to construct noxious gas pellets that they believed would not only paralyze enemies but also expel evil spirits. Certainly, the devices reduced disease-carrying insects, a critical aid to the colonization of malarial regions in China and Southeast Asia. And gunpowder was used in the Mongol Empire for fireworks displays on ceremonial occasions, delighting European visitors to Karakorum who saw them for the first time.

China is often credited with the invention of gunpowder. But anecdotal evidence in Chinese records gives credit for its introduction to a Sogdian Buddhist monk of the 500s and thus suggests that gunpowder was a Central Asian invention. The monk described the wondrous alchemical transforma-tion of elements produced by a combination of charcoal and saltpeter. In this connection he also mentioned sulfur. Naphtha distillation, too, seems to have been a skill first developed in Central Asia, for some of the earliest devices for distilling naphtha have been found in the Gandhara region (in modern Pakistan).

By the eleventh century, the Chinese had made and used flamethrowers powered by the slow igniting of naphtha, sulfur, or gunpowder in a long tube. They used these weapons not only to intimidate and injure foot soldiers and horses but also to set fire to thatched roofs in hostile villages and, occasionally, the rigging of enemy ships.

During their war against the Mongols, the Song learned to enrich saltpeter to increase the amount of nitrate in gunpowder and thereby produce forceful explosions that could destroy bridges and buildings. Launched from catapults, canisters filled with the explosive material could rupture fortifications and inflict mass casualties. Ships could be set afire or sunk by explosives hurled from a distance.

The Song also seem to have been the first to experiment with the construction of metal gun barrels from which to fire projectiles propelled by the explosion of gunpowder. The earliest of these gun barrels were broad and squat and were carried on special wagons to their emplacements. From the mouths of the barrels projected saltpeter mixed with scatter-shot minerals to be ignited by the firing of the gun. The Chinese and then the Koreans also learned to use gunpowder to shoot masses of arrows—sometimes flaming arrows—at enemy fortifications. But it was the Mongols who used Song expertise to devise cannon.

In 1280, in the aftermath of the conquest of the Southern Song, the Yuan Empire produced a device featuring a projectile that completely filled the mouth of the cannon and thus concentrated the explosive force. The Yuan used cast bronze for the barrel and iron for the cannonball. The new weapon could be aimed better and shot farther than the earlier devices of the Song. Its ability to smash through brick, wood, and flesh without suffering destruction itself was unprecedented.

Knowledge of the cannon and cannonball moved westward across Eurasia. By the end of the thirteenth century, more accurate, more mobile cannon were being produced in the Middle East. By 1327, small, squat cannon called "bombards" were being produced and used in Europe.

Launching Flaming Arrows Song soldiers used gunpowder to launch flaming arrows. (British Library)

Everyday Law in Ming China

When used carefully, legal documents can provide insights into daily life. Court documents, collections of legal cases, and guidebooks for judges and lawyers can all be valuable. In Ming China, law was a well-developed profession with an extensive printed literature. The following are two cases from a text illustrating when domestic complaints have gone far enough to justify legal action.

You are old and your son is dead. The candle of your life flickers, and is about to go out. By the intervention of friends a young man is engaged to care for you. How were you to know that, after he has lived with you for three years, when you have cared for him as if he were your son, he takes it into his head to betray your trust? He becomes wild and stubborn, wants to take your money and grain and run off. If you let him have his way, he will leave. But if you scold him and make him stay, he will hate you.

Sue!

You have been adopted by a childless man, and helped him build up the family property. Later, your father takes a concubine, and she has a son. The concubine wants to gain control of the property, so she has turned your father against you. One day for no reason he beat you, pulled your hair, bit your elbow to the bone, knocked out your front teeth. The woman beat you with a club, wounding you all over. Still not satisfied, the woman actually accuses you to the authorities.

Sue!

What principles of fairness seem to be behind these cases? How do you imagine these issues were addressed before it became the custom to go to court? Do you think it is important that these passages come from a training book for lawyers?

Source: Adapted from translated passages in John D. Langlois, Jr., "Ming Law," in *The Cambridge History of China*, vol. 8, *The Ming Dynasty*, 1368–1644, part 2, ed. Denis Twitchett and Frederick W. Mote (New York: Cambridge University Press, 1998), 206.

prevent Chinese from migrating to Southeast Asia. Guns and cannon, known from contacts with the Middle East and later with Europeans, were not manufactured or used on any significant scale. Advanced printing techniques were not developed. When printed editions of rare books from the Tang or Song periods were desired, they were purchased from Korea. When superior steel was needed, it was purchased from Japan. New crops, such as sweet potatoes, were available but not adopted.

The technological disparities between China and Europe that were to attract the attention of historians looking at the later Ming period were foreshadowed by the early Ming technology gap with Korea and Japan. For the first time Korea moved ahead of China in the design and production of firearms and ships and in the sciences of weather prediction and calendar making. And for the first time Japan surpassed China in mining and metallurgy and in the manufacture of novel household goods. Nevertheless, it is important to remember that the issue is not "advancement" or "development." Ming China lagged in technological innovation, but it led the world in the generation of massive wealth, and in Korea and Japan this wealth fueled innovation by energetic merchants who hoped to tap into the China markets.

The Ming Achievement

The early Ming period—the late 1300s and the 1400s—was a time of cultural brilliance. The distinctive Ming achievements in literature, the decorative arts, and painting sprang from both the wealth and the consumerism of the time. The period was creative, but also contentious. Ming legal records show the enthusiasm of landed families—and lawyers—for resolving complex personal disputes in court (see Society and Culture: Everyday Law in Ming China).

The interest in plain writing that had been encouraged during the Yuan period came to fruition in some of the world's earliest novels. One of the most famous, *Water Margin*, was based on the raucous drum-song performances of the Yuan period (and was loosely related

Ceramics Manufacture Ming porcelain factories perfected a style of assembly-line manufacture. The techniques were well established in central coastal China, and woodblock-printed technical books such as this one made the information widely available to technicians, investors, managers, and officials. This combination of industrial organization and printed information was later emulated in Korea, Japan, and Europe. (From *Tiangong Kaiwu*)

Ming Ware Before the Ming, the most prized porcelain in China was celadon ware, normally in a single shade of green or light blue. Patterned porcelain also existed, but it was the early Ming that refined the painting of cobalt blues on white porcelain. Ming designs were celebrated throughout East Asia and highly prized in the Middle East. Despite the great variety of patterns and colors in Ming porcelain, the blue-and-white combination remains the primary image of Ming ware. (Victoria & Albert Museum)

to Chinese opera). A group of dashing Chinese bandits struggle against Mongol rule, much as Robin Hood and his merry men resist Norman rule in the English legends of an earlier century. The fictional work distorts many of the original stories on which it is based, and it is clear that many authors were involved in its final commission to paper and print.

One of the early Ming authors of *Water Margin*, Luo Guanzhong°, is believed to be the author of *Romance of the Three Kingdoms*. Based on a much older series of story cycles, the saga in some ways resembles the Arthurian stories. It describes the attempts of an upright but doomed war leader and his talented followers to restore the Han Empire of ancient times and resist the power of the cynical but brilliant villain, Cao Cao. *Romance of the Three Kingdoms* and *Water Margin* expressed much of the militant but joyous pro-China sentiment of the early Ming and remain among the most appreciated fictional works in China.

Perhaps the best-known accomplishments of the early Ming were advances in porcelain making. The great imperial ceramic works at Jingdezhen° was a constant site not only of technological improvement but also of the organization and rationalization of labor. Ming patterns—most famous is the blue-on-white widely recognized as "Ming ware"—were stimulated in the 1400s by motifs from India, Central Asia, and the Middle East. Ming porcelain was among the most prized commercial products of Eurasia, and Ming industrial organization seems to have responded effectively to increased international demand.

Luo Guanzhong (LAW GWAHB-JOONG)

Jingdezhen (JING-deh-JUHN)

Other Ming goods for which demand was great were furniture, lacquered screens, and silk, all of which were eagerly transported by both Chinese and foreign merchants to distant markets in Southeast Asia and the Pacific, India, the Middle East, and East Africa.

CENTRALIZATION AND MILITARISM IN EAST ASIA, 1200–1500

As in western Eurasia, in eastern Eurasia areas at the margins of the Mongol advance were more likely to centralize their government and develop a sense of local solidarity. The experiences of East Asian countries apart from China were various. The Mongols conquered Korea after a difficult war of resistance, and Korean elites were drawn into close association with the leaders of the Yuan Empire. Japan managed to escape Mongol conquest.

Korea, like China, emerged from the Mongol period with significant social and economic disadvantages but with a revitalized interest in its vernacular language and its history. Korean merchants continued to develop international connections established in the Mongol period, and Korean armies proved effective in the struggle to establish a new kingdom and in the campaigns to ward off piracy. Japan and Annam, in contrast, were shaped to a certain extent by pressure from the Mongols but did not suffer the economic depletion of conquered territories. They responded to the fall of the Yuan Empire with more effective, ambitious, and expansive regimes.

Korea from the Mongols to the Yi, 1231–1500

During the 1200s, the battle against the Southern Song led the Mongols to seek greater control of the coasts of East Asia. They hoped to find new launching sites for naval expeditions against the south and for strategic points to choke off Song sea trade. Korea offered such possibilities.

When the Mongols attacked in 1231, the leader of a prominent Korean family assumed the role of military commander and protector of the king (not unlike the shoguns of Japan). Under this leader, Korean forces waged a defensive war against the Mongol invaders for over twenty years, until the countryside and the Korean armies were exhausted. Korea's losses in the war were heavy. One of the most important wooden buildings in

East Asia, the nine-story pagoda at Hwangnyong-sa°, was destroyed, and the wooden printing blocks of the *Tripitaka*°—a ninth-century masterpiece of printing art—were burned. In 1258 the Korean military commander was killed by his own underlings. Soon afterward, the Koryo° king surrendered to the Mongols, and his family was joined by marriage to the family of the Great Khan.

By the middle 1300s the Koryo kings were mostly Mongol by descent and were comfortable with the Mongolian language, dress, and customs. Many lived in Beijing, and travel by the kings, princes, their families, and their entourages between China and Korea was steady. In this way, the Mongols exposed Korea to direct influence from the most current philosophical and artistic styles of Yuan China, such as neo-Confucianism, Chan Buddhism (in Korea, called *Sŏn*), and celadon ceramics.

The capacity of the Mongol Empire to facilitate the sharing of information among distant cultures strongly influenced Korea. Since the tenth century Korea had been somewhat isolated. Under the Mongols, the growing of cotton began in southern Korea and gunpowder arrived for the first time. The arts of astronomical observation and mathematics were introduced to Korea as a unified science of calendar making, eclipse prediction, and vector calculation. The direct influence of Central Asia is evident in Korean celestial clocks built for the royal observatory at Seoul. A superficial resemblance to Chinese celestial clocks is apparent, but the mechanics and astronomical orientation are Islamic in inspiration. The Mongol conquest opened new avenues of advancement to Korean scholars willing to learn Mongolian, to Korean landowners willing to open their lands to falconry and to grazing, and to Korean merchants able to capitalize on the new royal traffic to Beijing. In this and other ways, the Mongols encouraged the rise of a new landed and educated class in Korea.

Koryo attachment to the Mongol imperial family became so strong that when the Yuan Empire fell in 1368, Koryo decided to remain loyal to the Mongols and had to be forced to recognize the new Ming Empire in China. But within a generation, Koryo collapsed and was succeeded by the **Yi**° kingdom in 1392.

Korea's new royal family, the Yi, was anxious to reestablish a local identity. Like Russia and China after the Mongols, the Yi regime in Korea publicly rejected the period of Mongol domination. But much of Yi government administration adopted Mongol practices and institutions. Mongol-style land surveys, techniques in the administration of military garrisons, and taxation in kind were all continued.

Hwanghnyong-sa (hwahng-NEEYAHNG-sah)
Tripitaka (tri-PIH-tah-kah) **Koryo** (KAW-ree-oh) **Yi** (YEE)

Like the Ming Empire, the Yi kingdom revived the study of the Confucian classics. This scholarly activity required the Korean elites to retain their knowledge of Chinese, and it also showed the dedication of the state to the promotion of reading and study. The revival of interest in the Confucian classics may have been the primary factor leading to a key technological breakthrough in printing technology.

Koreans began using Chinese woodblock printing in the 700s. This technology was well suited to China, where a large number of literate men wanted copies of a comparatively small number of texts. But in Korea, comparatively few men could read, and those who could were interested in a wide range of texts. Movable wooden or ceramic type had been used in Korea since the early thirteenth century and may have been invented there. But texts printed from this movable type were frequently inaccurate and difficult to read. In the 1400s Yi printers, working directly with the king, developed a reliable device to anchor the pieces of type to the printing plate: they replaced the old beeswax adhesive with solid copper frames. The legibility of the printed page improved, and high-volume, accurate reproduction of many pages in rapid succession became possible. In combination with the creation in Korea of the phonetic *han'gul*° writing system, this printing technology laid the foundation for a very high rate of literacy in Korea.

Displaying their willingness to adapt and shape Eurasian knowledge imported by the Mongols, the Yi Koreans used the astronomical arts of the Koryo period to develop a meteorological science of their own. Redesigned and newly invented instruments to measure wind speed and rainfall, the first of their kind, augmented the astronomical clock and armillary spheres of the royal observatory at Seoul. A local calendar based on minute comparisons with the calendrical systems of China and the Islamic world was perfected. Interest in commercial agriculture also sparked improvements in the production and use of fertilizer, the transplanting of seedlings in rice paddies, and the engineering of reservoirs (of which there were thousands in Yi times), all disseminated through the powerful new publishing abilities of the Yi government.

Yi agriculture was so well developed that the growing of cash crops became common (this is roughly the reverse of what was happening in Ming China). **Cotton,** introduced under the Mongols, was the primary cash crop. It was so highly valued by the state that it was accepted as payment for taxes. Demand was stimulated by the need of the large and frequently mobilized Yi army for cotton uniforms. Cotton also displaced traditional

Movable Type The improvement of cast bronze tiles, each showing a single character, made it no longer necessary to cast or carve whole pages. Individual tiles could be moved from page frame to page frame. In Korea, where this set was cast, movable type that was more stable in the frame and gave a more pleasing appearance was produced, and all parts of East Asia eventually adopted this form of printing for cheap, popular books. In the mid-1400s Korea also experimented with a fully phonetic form of writing, which in combination with movable type allowed Koreans unprecedented levels of literacy and access to printed works. (Courtesy, Yushin Yoo)

fabrics in the clothing worn by the Korean civil elite. Artisans built cotton gins and spinning wheels, often powered by water, to produce this profitable cloth. In mechanizing the processing of cotton, Korea advanced more rapidly than China. Soon, Korea was exporting considerable amounts of cotton to both China and Japan.

Koreans were innovators in military technology. Yi military campaigns were directed both against the northern part of the country, where Jurchens and other northeastern peoples threatened Yi control of the Yalu River, and also against the coasts, where pirates previously had operated at will and driven harassed farmers inland. Although both the Yuan and the Ming withheld the formula for destructive gunpowder from the Korean government, Korean officials acquired the information by subterfuge. By the later 1300s they had mounted cannon on their patrol ships and used gunpowder-driven

---

han'gul (HAHN-goor)

arrow launchers against enemy personnel and to propel flaming arrows into the rigging of enemy ships. In combination with Koreans' skill in armoring ships, these techniques made the Yi navy, though small, a formidable defense force.

Political Transformation in Japan, 1274–1500

Once Korea was conquered in the mid-thirteenth century, Japan was the Mongols' likely next stop. It was easily accessible by sea from Korea's southern tip, and from Japan's islands the coast of southern China might be controlled. But, as the Mongols were stopped in the west by the Mamluks (see Chapter 13), so they were stopped in the east by the Japanese.

The Mongols launched their first naval expedition against Japan in 1274. The invading force was diverse and imposing. It included not only the horses and riders of the Mongols but also light catapults and incendiary and explosive projectiles manufactured by the Chinese. Some captains of the fleet, and many archers, were Koreans. Additional warriors were drawn from the Jurchens and other peoples from northeastern Asia, many of whom were excellent archers and experienced sailors. In numbers—perhaps thirty thousand combatants—and in technical outfitting, the expedition presented a clear threat to the independence of Japan. But it was not equal to the weather of Hakata° Bay on the north side of Kyushu° Island (see Map 14.2). Although the Mongol forces were able to land and inflict stunning damage on mounted Japanese warriors, a storm prevented them from establishing a base on the beach. The Mongols returned to their ships and sailed back to Korea.

The appearance of the Mongol invasion force with its superior military technology made a deep impression on the leaders of Japan and hastened social and political changes already under way. At the time Japan was organized under the Kamakura° Shogunate (established in 1185), although another powerful family actually exercised control. The military leader—the shogun—distributed land and privileges to his followers, who paid him tribute and supplied him with soldiers. Based on the balancing of power among regional warlords, this system was fairly stable, but it was also decentralized. Lords in the north and east of Japan's main island were remote from those in the south and west; little united them beyond their declared devotion to the emperor and the shogun. The Mongol threat served to pull them together because it was alien, terrifying, and prolonged.

Hakata (HAH-kah-tah)   Kyushu (KYOO-shoo)
kamakura (kah-mah-KOO-rah)

Map 14.2   Korea and Japan, 1200–1500   The proximity of Korea and of northern China to Japan gave the Mongols the opportunity for launching their enormous fleets. They were defeated by the warriors of the Kamakura Shogunate, which controlled most of the three islands (Honshu, Shikoku, and Kyushu) of central Japan.

After the initial foray in 1274, Khubilai sent envoys to Japan demanding submission. Japanese leaders executed the ambassadors and began preparations to defend against a new attack. In the past, ambitious local military commanders had frequently ignored the civil code that limited their power. Now, in response to the Mongol attack, the shogun took steps to centralize his military government and strengthen the position of mid-level military officials. The influence of warlords from the south and west of Honshu (Japan's main island) and from the island of Kyushu, which was closest to the expected point of attack, rose.

Japanese military planners attempted to imitate what they had observed of Mongol war tactics. Efforts were made to retrain Japanese warriors and outfit them for defense against the advanced weaponry of the attackers. Farm laborers were drafted from all over the country to construct defensive fortifications at Hakata and other points along the Honshu and Kyushu coasts. This effort demanded, for the first time, a national system to move resources toward western points rather than toward the imperial or shogunal centers to the east.

The Mongols attacked again in 1281. They came in a sea force greater than any ever before amassed. They brought 140,000 warriors, including Mongols, Chinese, Koreans, and Jurchens, as well as thousands of horses, in hundreds of ships. Since the first Mongol attack, however, the Japanese had built a wall cutting off Hakata Bay from the mainland. The wall deprived the Mongol forces of a reliable landing point. As Mongol ships lingered offshore, Japanese swordsmen rowed out to board them. With their supremely strong and sharp steel swords, they hacked the startled invaders to pieces. After a standoff lasting months, a typhoon struck and sent perhaps half of the Mongol ships to the bottom of the sea. The remainder of the fleet returned to the mainland, never again to harass Japan. The Japanese gave thanks to the "wind of the Gods"—**kamikaze°**—for driving away the Mongols.

The well-founded belief that the Mongols still posed a threat continued to influence Japanese development. On his deathbed in 1294 Khubilai was indeed planning a third expedition to Japan. His successors did not carry through with it, but the shoguns did not know that the Mongols had given up the idea of conquering Japan. They continued to make plans for coastal defense well into the fourteenth century. This planning helped to consolidate the social position of Japan's warrior elite. It also stimulated the development of a national infrastructure for trade and communication. But the Kamakura Shogunate was structured around the idea that finances would be regionally collected and regionally dispersed. The costs of a more centralized system of roads and defenses strained the small central treasury.

At least one member of the imperial family—which for centuries had lived in seclusion without exercising real political power—saw opportunities in the weakening of the shoguns. Between 1333 and 1338 the emperor Go-Daigo tried to reclaim power from the shoguns, igniting a civil war that destroyed the Kamakura system. In 1338 a new shogunate, the **Ashikaga°,** was established. The new government, not threatened by Mongols, was based at the imperial center of Kyoto.

Political authority was more relaxed in the Ashikaga Shogunate than in the Kamakura, and provincial warlords enjoyed renewed independence. Around their imposing castles, they sponsored the development of market towns, religious institutions, and schools. The application of technologies imported in earlier periods,

kamikazi (KUM-i-kuh-zee)   **Ashikaga** (ah-shee-KAH-gah)

Painting by Sesshu   Sesshu Toyo (1420–1506) is renowned as the creator of a distinctive style in ink painting that contrasted with the Chinese styles that predominated earlier in Japan. He owed much of his training to the development of Japanese commerce in the period of the Ashikaga Shogunate. As a youth he traveled to China, where he first learned his techniques. As he developed his style, a market for his art developed among the merchant communities of the Ashikaga period, and spread to other urban elites.   (Collection of the Tokyo National Museum)

including water wheels, improved plows, and Champa rice, increased the productivity of the land.

The growing wealth and relative peace of the period stimulated artistic creativity, most of which reflected the Zen Buddhist beliefs of the warrior elite. In the simple elegance of the architecture and gardens, in the contemplative landscapes of artists such as Sesshu Toyo, and in the eerie, stylized performances of the No theater, the unified aesthetic code of Zen became established in the Ashikaga era.

Despite the technological advancement, artistic productivity, and rapid urbanization of this period, the progressive aggrandizement of the warlords and their followers led to regional military hostilities. By the later 1400s these conflicts were so severe that they resulted in the near destruction of the warlords. In the aftermath of the great Onin War in 1477, Kyoto was devastated and the Ashikaga Shogunate remained a central government only in name. Ambitious but low-ranking warriors began to scramble for control of the provinces. They were aided by the revival of trade with continental Asia.

After the fall of the Yuan Empire, trade among China, Korea, and the islands of Japan and Okinawa resumed. Japan benefited from the development of firearms in China and Korea by exporting copper, sulfur, and other raw materials. The folding fan, invented in Japan during the period of isolation, and swords, for which Japan quickly became famous, became desireable items in Korea and China. From China, Japan imported primarily books and porcelain. This trade, in combination with Japan's volatile political environment, produced energetic partnerships between warlords and local merchants. All of them worked to strengthen their own towns and treasuries through exploitation of the overseas trade and, sometimes, through piracy.

The Emergence of Vietnam, 1200–1500

The states of Annam (in what is now northern Vietnam) and **Champa** (in what is now southern Vietnam) had an uneasy relationship in the centuries before the Mongol invasions. Annam (once called Dai Viet) had established close relations with empires based in China and had been subject to the Tang Empire. Chinese political ideas, social philosophies, dress, religion, and language heavily influenced its official culture. Champa, in contrast, had a close relationship with the trading networks of the Indian Ocean, and its official culture was marked by a strong influence from Indian religion, language, architecture, and dress. In the Song period, when Annam was not formally subject to China and was less threatening to its southern neighbor, Champa had entered into the trade and tribute relationship with China that distributed the fast-ripening Champa rice throughout East Asia.

The Mongols exacted submission and tribute from both Annam and Champa, but after the fall of the Yuan the old conflicts between Annam and Champa resurfaced. By 1400 they were at war with each other. Taking advantage of Annam's concentration on its southern border, Ming troops occupied Hanoi and installed a puppet government. The puppet government lasted almost thirty years, then was destroyed in a war for Annamese independence. Annam returned to the tributary status it had held in the Song Empire.

But as was the case with Lithuania, the Ottomans, Egypt, and Korea, Annam's struggle against a greater empire inspired expansionist dreams of its own when the Ming were distracted by Mongol challenges in the mid-1400s. In a series of ruthless campaigns, Annamese armies defeated the forces of Champa. By 1500 the conquest was complete. Champa disappeared, and the ancestor of the modern state of Vietnam was born.

The new state, still called Annam, reinforced its centralization with Confucian bureaucratic government and an examination system. But it differed from Chinese practices in two important ways. The Vietnamese legal code preserved the tradition of group landowning and decision making within the villages. It also preserved women's property rights. Both developments probably had roots in an early rural culture based on the growing of rice in wet paddies, but by this time the Annamese considered them distinctive features of their own culture.

CONCLUSION

The effects of the Mongol period in eastern Eurasia differed from region to region. Within different societies, some groups prospered while others suffered.

In China, the Mongols destroyed the empires that had divided the region. They consolidated China as a geographical entity, and they standardized Chinese elite. China was enriched by new access to scientific, commercial, and cultural influences from Central Asia and the Middle East.

Though merchants, artists, and some officials flourished under the Yuan, the farming majority suffered. By the time the Mongol rulers realized that they were destroying the basis of the wealth they hoped to tax, the damage was done. The country was engulfed in a growing number of rebellions, infighting among Mongol princes, and floods.

But the impact of the Yuan Empire was not as fleeting as the empire itself. The Ming Empire pursued many projects inspired by the Mongols, including completion of the Forbidden City and conquests in Southeast Asia. They also showed the indirect influence of the period of Mongol domination, as they sponsored cultural and commercial measures intended to limit or purge foreign influences, and restore what they saw as the classical civilization of China.

With the Ming established in 1368, the population began a rapid recovery. For decades this increased tax revenues, fed hungry labor markets, and allowed the recovery of profitable farm land. The rapid reversal of the isolationist economic policies of the Hongwu period stimulated Ming industries, particularly procelain, which brought tremendous prosperity to China's ports, water transport systems, and industrial centers. Demand grew, labor remained cheap, credit was ample, and the currency was stable.

The concentrations of wealth created huge markets into which merchants from all parts of China tapped, as well as ambitious and technologically innovative manufacturers in Korea and Japan. A powerful economic engine was operating—it simply happened that its mechanisms did not promote technological innovation in China itself.

The close connections forged between Korea and China in the period of Mongol domination clearly aided in their commercial growth. Innovations in printing as well as in the Korean script helped accelerate the spread of knowledge. It also strengthened Yi programs to establish an extensive literature on Korean history. Koreans used sciences to which they had unusual access under the Mongols to develop very precise methods of minimizing their vulnerability to floods and droughts while maximizing their use of cash crops. The growth of the Yi state, and its many military enterprises, stimulated all industries associated with cotton, mining, and forestry.

Japan's decentralized system of military rule, the shogunate, was challenged by the prolonged threat of Mongol invasion. The threat reinforced the status of the warrior elites, and altered the regional balances of power. When the Mongol threat ended, Japan experienced a strong economic stimulus from the reestablishment of trade relations with China, stimulating advances in metallurgy and ceramics. The wealth of the Ashikaga period resulted not only from overseas trade but also from increasing productivity of the land. This wealth accelerated urbanization and produced a brilliant period in the arts.

In Vietnam, the period of Mongol attacks in the late 1200s threatened both Annam and Champa. Ming China subjugated Annam in the late 1300s, but this fueled a strong movement for ending Chinese interference. When the Ming became distracted by their problems with the remaining Mongol powers in the north, Annam quickly threw off Ming control and proceeded to obliterate Champa as an indepdent state. This laid the foundations of modern Vietnam—one of several cases of peripherally challenged states, throughout Eurasia, that experienced a period of expansoin, independence, and increased national consciousness after the period of Mongol domination had passed.

■ Key Terms

Yuan Empire	Forbidden City
lama	Zheng He
Khubilai Khan	technology transfer
Beijing	Yi
cottage industries	cotton
Manchuria	*kamikaze*
Ming Empire	Ashikaga Shogunate
Yongle	Champa

■ Suggested Reading

See Chapter 13 for works on the general history of the Mongols. For China under the Mongols see Morris Rossabi's *Khubilai Khan: His Life and Times* (1988). On the effects of the Mongol period on economy and technology in Yuan and Ming China see Mark Elvin, *The Pattern of the Chinese Past* (1973); Joel Mokyr, *The Lever of Riches: Technological Creativity and Economic Progress* (1990); and Joseph Needham, *Science in Traditional China* (1981). Also see the important interpretation of Ming economic achievement in Andre Gunder Frank, *ReORIENT: Global Economy in the Asian Age* (1998).

Scholarly studies in English on the early Ming period are not so well developed as studies on some other periods of Chinese history, but the publication of *The Cambridge History of China, vol. 8, The Ming Dynasty 1368–1644, part 2,* ed. Denis Twitchett and Frederick W. Mote (1998) improves the situation. See also Albert Chan, *The Glory and Fall of the Ming Dynasty* (1982), and Edward L. Farmer, *Early Ming Government: The Evolution of Dual Capitals* (1976).

On early Ming literature see Lo Kuan-chung, *Three Kingdoms: A Historical Novel Attributed to Luo Guanzhong,* translated and annotated by Moss Roberts (1991); Pearl Buck's translation of *Water Margin*, entitled *All Men Are Brothers,* 2 vols. (1933), and a later translation by J. H. Jackson, *Water Margin, Written by Shih Nai-an* (1937); Richard Gregg Irwin, *The Evolution of a Chinese Novel: Shui-hu-chuan* (1953); Ellen Widmer, *The Margins of Utopia: Shui-hu hou-chuan and the Literature of Ming Loyalism* (1987); and Shelley HsÜeh-lun Chang, *History and Legend: Ideas and Images in the Ming Historical Novels* (1990).

On Ming painting see James Cahill, *Parting at the Shore: Chinese Painting of the Early and Middle Ming Dynasty* (1978). See also selected essays in Paul S. Ropp, ed., *Heritage of China* (1990).

The Zheng He expeditions are extensively discussed in secondary works. A classic interpretation is Joseph R. Levenson, ed., *European Expansion and the Counter-Example of Asia, 1300–1600* (1967). More recent scholarship is available in Philip Snow, *The Star Raft* (1988), and a full and lively account is Louise Levathes, *When China Ruled the Seas* (1993).

For a general history of Korea in this period see Andrew C. Nahm, *Introduction to Korean History and Culture* (1993); Ki-Baik Lee, *A New History of Korea* (1984); and William E. Henthorn, *Korea: The Mongol Invasions* (1963). On a more specialized topic see Joseph Needham et al., *The Hall of Heavenly Records: Korean Astronomical Instruments and Clocks, 1380–1780* (1986).

For narrative histories of Japan, see also John W. Hall and Toyoda Takeshi, eds., *Japan in the Muromachi Age* (1977), and H. Paul Varley, trans., *The Onin War: History of Its Origins and Background with a Selective Translation of the Chronicle of Onin* (1967). On the Mongol invasion see Yamada Nakaba, *Ghenko, the Mongol Invasion of Japan, with an Introduction by Lord Armstrong* (1916), and the novel *Fûtô* by Inoue Yasushi, translated by James T. Araki as *Wind and Waves* (1989). On the No theater and Zen aesthetics there is a great deal of writing. Perhaps most direct and charming are Donald Keene, *No: The Classical Theatre of Japan* (1966), and Ueda Makoto, trans., *The Old Pine Tree and Other Noh Plays* (1962).

15

TROPICAL AFRICA AND ASIA,
1200–1500

Tropical Lands and Peoples • New Islamic Empires • Indian Ocean Trade •
Social and Cultural Change
ENVIRONMENT AND TECHNOLOGY: The Indian Ocean Dhow
SOCIETY AND CULTURE: Personal Styles of Rule in India and Mali

East African Pastoralists   Herding large and small livestock has long
been a way of life in drier parts of the tropics.

ultan Abu Bakr° customarily offered his personal hospitality to all distinguished visitors arriving at his city of Mogadishu, an Indian Ocean port on the northeast coast of Africa. In 1331 he provided food and lodging for Muhammad ibn Abdullah ibn Battuta° (1304–1369), a young Muslim scholar from Morocco, who had set out to explore the Islamic world. Having already completed a pilgrimage to Mecca and traveled throughout the Middle East, Ibn Battuta was touring the trading cities of the Red Sea and East Africa. Subsequent travels took him to Central Asia and India, China and Southeast Asia, Muslim Spain, and sub-Saharan West Africa. Logging some 75,000 miles (120,000 kilometers) in his twenty-nine years of travel, Ibn Battuta became the most widely traveled man of his times. For this reason his journal, which describes where he went and what he saw, is a valuable historical source for these lands.

Other Muslim princes and merchants welcomed Ibn Battuta as graciously as did the ruler of Mogadishu. Hospitality was a noble virtue among Muslims, who ignored visitors' physical and cultural differences. Although the Moroccan traveler noted that Sultan Abu Bakr had skin darker than his own and spoke a different native language (Somali), that was of little consequence. They were brothers in faith when they prayed together at Friday services in the Mogadishu mosque, where the sultan greeted his foreign guest in Arabic, the common language of the Islamic world: "You are heartily welcome, and you have honored our land and given us pleasure." When Sultan Abu Bakr and his jurists heard and decided cases after the mosque service, they used the law code familiar in all the lands of Islam.

Islam was not the only thing that united Africa and southern Asia. The most basic links among the diverse peoples of these regions were products of the tropical enviornment itself. A network of land and sea trade routes joined their lands. Older than Islam, these routes were important for spreading beliefs and technologies as well as goods. Ibn Battuta made his

way down the coast of East Africa in merchants' ships and joined their camel caravans across the Sahara to West Africa. His path to India followed overland trade routes, and a merchant ship carried him on to China.

As you read this chapter, ask yourself the following questions:

- How did environmental differences shape cultural differences in tropical Africa and Asia?
- How did cultural and ecological differences promote trade in specialized goods from one place to another?
- How did trade and other contacts promote state growth and the spread of Islam?

TROPICAL LANDS AND PEOPLES

To obtain food, the people who inhabited the tropical regions of Africa and Asia used methods that generations of experimentation had proved successful, whether at the desert's edge, in grasslands, or in tropical rain forests. Much of their success lay in learning how to blend human activities with the natural order, but their ability to modify the environment to suit their needs was also evident in irrigation works and mining.

The Tropical Environment

Because of the angle of earth's axis, the sun's rays warm the **tropics** year-round. The equator marks the center of the tropical zone, and the Tropic of Cancer and Tropic of Capricorn mark its outer limits. As Map 15.1 shows, Africa lies almost entirely within the tropics, as do southern Arabia, most of India, and all of the Southeast Asian mainland and islands.

Lacking the hot and cold seasons of temperate lands, the Afro-Asian tropics have their own cycle of rainy and dry seasons caused by changes in wind patterns across the surrounding oceans. Winds from a permanent high-pressure air mass over the South Atlantic deliver heavy rainfall to the western coast of Africa during much of the year. However, in December and January

---

Abu Bakr (a-BOO BAK-uhr)   **Ibn Battuta** (IB-uhn ba-TOO-tuh)

CHRONOLOGY

	Tropical Africa	Tropical Asia
1200		1206 Delhi Sultanate founded in India
	1230s Mali Empire founded	
1300	1270 Solomonic dynasty in Ethiopia founded	1298 Delhi Sultanate annexes Gujarat
	1324–1325 Mansa Musa's pilgrimage to Mecca	
1400	1400s Great Zimbabwe at its peak	1398 Timur sacks Delhi, Delhi Sultanate declines
	1433 Tuareg retake Timbuktu, Mali declines	
1500		1500 Port of Malacca at its peak

large high-pressure zones over northern Africa and Arabia produce a southward movement of dry air that limits the inland penetration of the moist ocean winds.

In the lands around the Indian Ocean the rainy and dry seasons reflect the influence of alternating winds known as **monsoons**. A gigantic high-pressure zone over the Himalaya° Mountains that is at its peak from December to March produces a strong southward air movement (the northeast monsoon) in the western Indian Ocean. This is southern Asia's dry season. Between April and August a low-pressure zone over India creates a northward movement of air from across the ocean (the southwest monsoon) that brings southern Asia its heaviest rains. This is the wet season.

Along with geographical features, these wind and rain patterns are responsible for the variations in tropical lands, from desert to rain forest. Where rainfall is exceptionally abundant, as in the broad belt along the equator in coastal West Africa and west-central Africa, the natural vegetation is dense tropical rain forest. Rain forests also characterize Southeast Asia and parts of coastal India. Somewhat lighter rains produce other tropical forests. The English word *jungle* comes from an Indian word for the tangled undergrowth in the tropical forests that once covered most of India.

Although heavy rainfall is common in some of the tropics, other parts rarely see rain at all. Stretching clear across the width of northern Africa is the world's largest desert, the Sahara. This arid zone continues eastward across northwest India. Another desert zone occupies southwestern Africa. The lands between the deserts and the rain forests that are favored with moderate amounts of moisture during the rainy seasons form the majority of tropical India and Africa. These lands and range from fairly wet woodlands to the much drier grasslands characteristic of much of East Africa.

Other variations in tropical climate result from altitude. Thin atmospheres at high altitudes can hold less of the tropical heat than can atmospheres at lower elevations. The volcanic mountains of eastern Africa rise to such heights that some are covered with snow all or part of the year. The Himalayas that form the northern frontier of India are also snowcapped and so high that they block the movement of cold air into the northern India plains, giving this region a more tropical climate than its latitude would suggest. The many plateaus of inland Africa and the Deccan° Plateau of central India also make these regions somewhat cooler than the coastal plains.

The mighty rivers that rise in these mountains and plateaus redistribute water far from where it falls. Heavy rains in the highlands of Central Africa and Ethiopia supply the Nile's annual floods that make Egypt bloom in the desert. On its long route to the Atlantic, the Niger River of West Africa arcs northward to the Sahara's edge, providing waters to the trading cities along its banks. In like fashion, the Indus River provides nourishing waters from the Himalayas to arid northwest India. The Ganges° and its tributaries provide valuable moisture to northeastern India during the dry season. Mainland Southeast Asia's great rivers, such as the Mekong, are similarly valuable.

Himalaya (him-uh-LAY-uh)

Deccan (de-KAN)   Ganges (GAN-jeez)

Map 15.1   Africa and the Indian Ocean Basin: Physical Characteristics   Seasonal wind patterns control rainfall in the tropics and produce the different tropical vegetation zones to which human societies have adapted over thousands of years. The wind patterns also dominated sea travel in the Indian Ocean.

Human Ecosystems

Thinkers in temperate lands once imagined that, because of the absence of a harsh winter season, surviving in the tropics was as easy as picking wild fruit off a tree. In fact, mastering the tropics' many different environments was a long and difficult struggle. A careful observer touring the tropics in 1200 would have noticed how much the differences in societies could be attributed to their particular ecosystems—that is, to how human groups made use of the plants, animals, and other resources of their physical environments. Tropical peoples' success in adapting to their natural worlds was fundamental to all their other achievements.

Long before 1200, most tropical Africans and Asians had taken up raising domesticated plants and animals as the best way to feed themselves. But people in some environments found it preferable to rely primarily on wild food that they obtained by hunting, fishing, and gather-

ing. This was true of Pygmy° hunters in the dense forests of Central Africa. Their small size itself was a physical adaptation that permitted them to pursue their prey through dense undergrowth. Hunting also was a way of life in the upper altitudes of the Himalayas and in some desert environments. A Portuguese expedition led by Vasco da Gama visited the arid coast of southwestern Africa in 1497 and recorded the presence there of a healthy group of people who lived off both land and sea creatures, feeding themselves on "the flesh of seals, whales, and gazelles, and the roots of wild plants."

Fishing was a highly skilled and successful form of food gathering everywhere in the region, along all the major lakes and rivers as well as in the oceans, though it might be combined with farming. The ocean fishermen of East Africa and Southeast Asia were particularly distinguished, as were those of coastal India. The boating

Pygmy (PIG-mee)

skills of fishermen often led to their playing an important role in ocean trade.

In areas too arid for agriculture, tending herds of domesticated animals was common. Knowledge of local waterholes and observation of the scattered rains enabled pastoralists, unencumbered by bulky personal possessions and elaborate dwellings, to find adequate grazing for their animals in all but the severest droughts. They fed themselves with milk from their herds and with grain and vegetables obtained from farmers in exchange for hides and meat. The world's largest concentration of pastoralists was in the arid and semiarid lands of northeastern Africa and Arabia. Like Ibn Battuta's host at Mogadishu, some Somali were urban dwellers, but most grazed their herds of goats and camels in the desert hinterland of the Horn of Africa. The western Sahara sustained herds of sheep and camels belonging to the Tuareg°, whose intimate knowledge of the desert also made them invaluable as guides to caravans, such as the one **Ibn Battuta** joined on the two-month journey across the desert. Along the Sahara's southern edge the cattle-herding Fulani° people gradually extended their range during this period, and by 1500 they were found throughout the western and central Sudan. A few weeks after encountering the hunter-gatherers of southern Africa, Vasco da Gama's expedition bartered for meat with a pastoral people possessing fat cattle and sheep.

Although food gathering and animal husbandry continued, farming was the dominant way of life for most tropical peoples between 1200 and 1500. The density of agricultural populations was closely tied to the adequacy of rainfall and soils. South and Southeast Asia were generally much better watered than tropical Africa, and the farmers on the Asian plains practiced intensive cultivation. Their high yields supported dense populations. In 1200 there were probably over 100 million people living in South and Southeast Asia, more than four-fifths of them on the fertile Indian mainland. This was three times the number of people living in all of Africa at that time and nearly twice as many as in Europe, though still a little less than the population of China.

Because of India's lush vegetation, one Middle Eastern writer of the time identified it as "the most agreeable abode on earth . . . its delightful plains resemble the garden of Paradise."[1] Rice cultivation was particularly important in places such as the fertile Ganges plain of northeast India, mainland Southeast Asia, and southern China. In drier areas tropical farmers grew grains (such as wheat, sorghum, millet, and ensete) and legumes (such as peas and beans), whose ripening cycle

matched the pattern of the rainy and dry seasons. A variety of tubers and tree crops were characteristic of farming in rain-forest clearings.

By the year 1200 human migrations had spread many useful domesticated plants and animals around the tropics. Bantu-speaking farmers (see Chapter 8) had introduced grains and tubers from West Africa throughout the southern half of the continent. Bananas, brought to southern Africa centuries earlier by mariners from Southeast Asia, had become the staple food for people farming the rich soils around the Great Lakes of East Africa. Yams and cocoyams of Asian origin had spread across equatorial Africa. Asian cattle breeds grazed contentedly in pastures throughout Africa, and coffee of Ethiopian origin would shortly become a common drink in the Middle East.

The spread of farming did not always create permanent changes in the natural environment. In most parts of sub-Saharan Africa and many parts of Southeast Asia until quite recent times, the basic form of cultivation was extensive rather than intensive. Instead of enriching fields with manure and vegetable compost so they could be cultivated year after year, farmers abandoned fields every few years when the natural fertility of the soil was exhausted, and they cleared new fields. Ashes from the brush, grasses, and tree limbs that were cut down and burned gave the new fields a significant boost in fertility. Even though a great deal of work was needed to clear the fields initially, modern research suggests that such shifting cultivation was an efficient use of labor in areas where soils were not naturally rich in nutrients.

Water Systems and Irrigation

In parts of the tropics environmental necessity and population pressure led to the adoption of more intensive forms of agriculture. A rare area of intensive cultivation in sub-Saharan Africa was the inland delta of the Niger River, where large crops of rice were grown using the river's naturally fertilizing annual floods. The rice was probably sold to the trading cities along the Niger bend.

One of the great challenges of the tropical environment in parts of Asia was the uneven distribution of rainfall during the year. Unlike pastoralists who could move their herds to the water, farmers had to find ways of moving the water to their crops. Farmers met the challenge by conserving some of the monsoon rainfall for use during the drier parts of the year. Farming communities in Vietnam, Java, Malaya, and Burma constructed terraced hillsides with special water-control systems for growing rice. Water-storage dams and irrigation canals were also

---

Tuareg (TWAH-reg)   **Fulani** (foo-LAH-nee)

becoming common in both north and south India. For example, during these centuries villagers in southeast India built a series of stone and earthen dams across rivers to store water for gradual release through elaborate irrigation canals. Over many generations these canals were extended to irrigate more and more land. Although these dams and channels covered large areas, they were relatively simple structures that local people could keep working by routine maintenance.

As had been true since the days of the first river-valley civilizations (see Chapter 2), the largest irrigation systems in the tropics were government public works projects. Under the government of the **Delhi° Sultanate** (1206–1526) northern India acquired extensive new water-control systems. Ibn Battuta commented appreciatively on a large reservoir, constructed under one ruler in the first quarter of the thirteenth century, that supplied the city of Delhi with water. Enterprising farmers planted sugar cane, cucumbers, and melons along the reservoir's rim as the water level fell during the dry season. In the fourteenth century the Delhi Sultan built in the Ganges plain a network of irrigation canals that were not surpassed in size until the nineteenth century. These irrigation systems made it possible to grow crops throughout the year.

Since the tenth century the Indian Ocean island of Ceylon (modern Sri Lanka°) had been home to the greatest concentration of irrigation reservoirs and canals in the world. These facilities enabled the powerful Sinhalese° kingdom in arid northern Ceylon to support a large population. There was another impressive waterworks in Southeast Asia, where a system of reservoirs and canals served Cambodia's capital city Angkor°.

Yet such complex systems were vulnerable to disruption. Between 1250 and 1400 the irrigation complex in Ceylon fell into ruin when invaders from South India disrupted the Sinhalese government. The population of Ceylon then suffered from the effects of malaria, a tropical disease spread by mosquitoes breeding in the irrigation canals. The great Cambodian system fell into ruin in the fifteenth century when the government that maintained it collapsed. Neither system was ever rebuilt.

The vulnerability of complex irrigation systems built by powerful governments suggests an instructive contrast. Although village-based irrigation systems could be damaged by invasion and natural calamity, they usually bounced back because they were the product of local initiative, not centralized direction, and they depended on simpler technologies.

Delhi (DEL-ee)   **Sri Lanka** (sree LAHNG-kuh)
Sinhalese (sin-huh-LEEZ)   **Angkor** (ANG-kor)

Mineral Resources

Metalworking was another way in which people made use of natural resources. Skilled metalworkers furnished their customers with tools, weapons, and decorative objects. The mining and processing of metals was also important for long-distance trade.

Iron was the most abundant of the metals worked in the tropics. People in most parts of the tropical world produced sufficient quantities of iron tools and implements to satisfy their own needs. The iron hoes, axes, and knives that enabled farmers to clear and cultivate their fields seem to have been used between 1200 and 1500 to open up the rain forests of coastal West Africa and Southeast Asia for farming. Iron-tipped spears and arrows improved hunting success. Needles were used in sewing clothes, nails in building. The skill of Indian metalsmiths was renowned, especially in making strong and beautiful swords. So great was the skill of African iron smelters and blacksmiths that they were believed to possess magical powers.

Also of special importance in Africa were copper and its alloys. In the Copperbelt of southeastern Africa, copper mining was in full production in the fourteenth and fifteenth centuries. The refined metal was cast into large X-shaped ingots (metal castings). Local coppersmiths worked these ingots into wire and decorative objects. Copper mining was also important in the western Sudan, where Ibn Battuta described a mining town that produced two sizes of copper bars that were used as a currency in place of coins. Some coppersmiths in West Africa during these centuries skillfully cast copper and brass (an alloy of copper and zinc) statues and heads that are considered among the masterpieces of world art. These works were made by the "lost-wax" method, in which molten metal melts a thin layer of wax sandwiched between clay forms, replacing the "lost" wax with hard metal.

Africans also possessed an international reputation for their production of gold, which was exported in quantity across the Sahara and into the Indian Ocean and Red Sea trades. Gold was mined and collected from stream beds along the upper Niger River and farther south in modern Ghana°. In the hills south of the Zambezi° River (in modern Zimbabwe°) archaeologists have discovered thousands of mine shafts, dating from 1200, that were sunk up to a 100 feet (30 meters) into the ground to get at gold ores. Although panning for gold remained important in the streams descending from the mountains of

Ghana (GAH-nuh)   **Zambezi** (zam-BEE-zee)
Zimbabwe (zim-BAHB-way)

King and Queen of Ife   This copper-alloy work shows the royal couple of the Yoruba kingdom of Ife, the oldest and most sacred of the Yoruba kingdoms of southwestern Nigeria. The casting dates to the period between 1100 and 1500, except for the reconstruction of the male's face, the original of which shattered in 1957 when the road builder who found it accidentally struck it with his pick.   (Andre Held, Switzerland)

northern India, the gold and silver mines in India seem to have been exhausted by this period. For that reason, Indians imported from Southeast Asia and Africa considerable quantities of gold for jewelry and temple decoration.

Metalworking and food-producing systems were important to tropical peoples for two reasons. First, most people made a successful livelihood through such skilled exploitation of their environment. Second, the labors and skills of such ordinary people made possible the rise of powerful states and profitable commercial systems. When considering the better-documented lives of rulers and merchants described later in this chapter, ask yourself: Could the caravans have crossed the Sahara without the skilled guidance of desert pastoralists? Could the trade of the Indian Ocean have reached its full importance were it not for the seafaring skills of the coastal fishermen? Could the city-based empires of Delhi and Mali have endured without the food taxed from rural farmers? Could the long-distance trade routes have prospered without the precious metals, spices, and grains produced by such ordinary folks?

New Islamic Empires

The empires of Mali in West Africa and Delhi in northern India were the two largest and richest tropical states of the period between 1200 and 1500. Both utilized Islamic administrative and military systems introduced from the Islamic heartland, but in other ways these two Muslim sultanates were very different. **Mali** was founded by an indigenous African dynasty that had earlier adopted Islam through the peaceful influence of Muslim merchants and scholars. In contrast, the Delhi Sultanate of northern India was founded and ruled by invading Turkish and Afghan Muslims. Mali depended heavily for its wealth on its participation in the trans-Saharan trade, but long-distance trade played only a minor role in Delhi's wealth.

Mali in the Western Sudan

The consolidation of the Middle East and North Africa under Muslim rule during the seventh and eighth centuries (see Chapter 9) greatly increased the volume of trade along the routes that crossed the Sahara. In the centuries that followed, the faith of Muhammad gradually spread to the lands south of the desert, which the Arabs called the *bilad al-sudan*°, "land of the blacks."

The role of force in spreading Islam south of the Sahara was limited. Muslim Berbers invading out of the desert in 1076 caused the collapse of Ghana, the empire that preceded Mali in the western Sudan (see Chapter 8), but their conquest did little to spread Islam. To the east, the Muslim attacks that destroyed the Christian Nubian

---

bilad al-sudan (bih-LAD uhs–soo-DAN)

Map of the Western Sudan (1375) A Jewish geographer on the Mediterranean island of Majorca drew this lavish map in 1375, incorporating all that was known in Europe about the rest of the world. This portion of the Catalan Atlas shows a North African trader approaching the king of Mali, who holds a gold nugget in one hand and a golden scepter in the other. A caption identifies the black ruler as Mansa Musa, "the richest and noblest king in all the land." (Bibliothèque Nationale de France)

kingdoms on the upper Nile in the late thirteenth century opened that area to Muslim influences, but Christian Ethiopia successfully withstood Muslim advances. Instead, the usual pattern for the spread of Islam south of the Sahara was through gradual and peaceful conversion. The expansion of commercial contacts in the western Sudan and on the East African coast greatly promoted the process of conversion. Most Africans found meaning and benefit in the teachings of Islam and found it suited their interests. The first sub-Saharan African state to adopt the new faith was Takrur° in the far western Sudan, whose rulers accepted Islam about 1030.

Shortly after the year 1200 Takrur expanded in importance under King Sumanguru°. Then in about 1240 Sundiata°, the upstart leader of the Malinke° people, handed Sumanguru a major defeat. Even though both leaders were Muslims, the Malinke legends recall their battles as the clash of two powerful magicians, suggesting how much old and new beliefs mingled. Legends say that Sumanguru was able to appear and disappear at will, assume dozens of shapes, and catch arrows in mid-

flight. Sundiata defeated Sumanguru's much larger forces through superior military maneuvers and by successfully wounding his adversary with a special arrow that robbed him of his magical powers. This victory was followed by others that created Sundiata's Mali empire (see Map 15.2).

Mali, like Ghana before it, depended on a well-developed agricultural base and control of the lucrative regional and trans-Saharan trade routes. But Mali differed from Ghana in two ways. First, it was much larger. Mali controlled not only the core trading area of the upper Niger but the gold fields of the Niger headwaters to the southwest as well. Second, its rulers were Muslims, who fostered the spread of Islam among the political and trading elites of the empire. Control of the important gold and copper trades and contacts with North African Muslim traders gave Mali and its rulers unprecedented prosperity.

Under the Mali ruler **Mansa Kankan Musa**° (r. 1312–1337), the empire's reputation for wealth spread far and wide. Mansa Musa's pilgrimage to Mecca in 1324–1325, in fulfillment of his personal duty as a Muslim, also

---

Takrur (TAHK-roor) Sumanguru (soo-muhn-GOO-roo)
Sundiata (soon-JAH-tuh) Malinke (muh-LING-kay)

Mansa Kankan Musa (MAHN-suh KAHN-kahn MOO-suh)

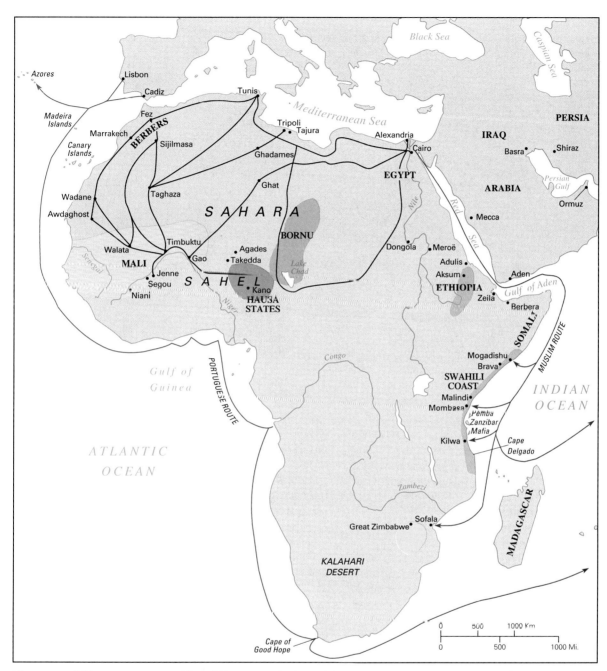

Map 15.2   Africa, 1200–1500   Many African states had beneficial links to the trade that crossed the Sahara and the Indian Ocean. Before 1500, sub-Saharan Africa's external ties were primarily with the Islamic world.

became an occasion for him to display the exceptional wealth of his empire. As befitted a powerful ruler, he traveled with a large entourage. Besides his senior wife and 500 of her ladies in waiting and their slaves, one account says there were also 60,000 porters and a vast caravan of camels carrying supplies and provisions. Even more lavish was the gold that Mansa Musa is reported to have taken along. For purchases and gifts he took 80 packages of gold each weighing 122 ounces (3.8 kilograms). In addition, 500 slaves each carried a golden

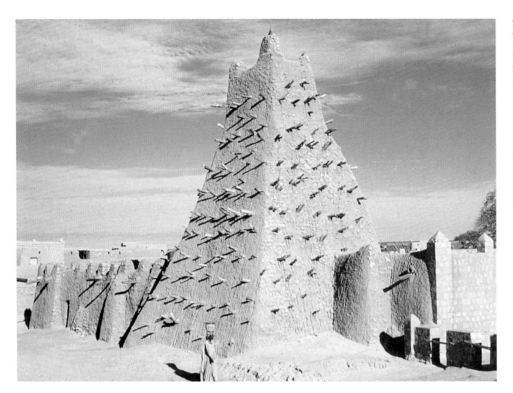

Sankore Mosque, Timbuktu
The wall and tower at the left and center represent traditional styles of construction in clay in a region where building stone is rare. At its peak in the four-teenth through the sixteenth centuries, Timbuktu was a major emporium for trade at the southern edge of the Sahara and a center of Islamic religion and education. (Aldona Sabalis/Photo Researchers, Inc.)

staff. When the entourage passed through Cairo, Mansa Musa was so lavish with his gifts that the value of gold was depressed for years.

Mansa Musa returned from his pilgrimage eager to promote the religious and cultural influence of Islam in his empire. He built new mosques and opened Quranic schools in the cities along the Niger bend. When Ibn Battuta visited Mali from 1352 to 1354, during the reign of Mansa Musa's successor Mansa Suleiman° (r. 1341–1360), the practice of Islam in the empire met with his approval. He lauded Malians for their faithful recitation of prayers and for their zeal in teaching children the Quran.

Ibn Battuta also had high praise for Mali's government. He reported that "complete and general safety" prevailed in the vast territories ruled by Suleiman and that foreign travelers had no reason to fear being robbed by thieves or having their goods confiscated if they died. (For Ibn Battuta's account of the sultan's court and his subjects' respect see Society and Culture: Personal Styles of Rule in India and Mali.)

Two centuries after Sundiata founded the empire, Mali began to disintegrate. When Mansa Suleiman's suc-cessors proved to be less able rulers, rebellions broke out among the diverse peoples who had been subjected to Malinke rule. Avid for Mali's wealth, other groups at-tacked from without. The desert Tuareg retook their city of Timbuktu° in 1433. By 1500 the rulers of Mali had do-minion over little more than the Malinke heartland.

The cities of the upper Niger survived Mali's col-lapse, but some of the western Sudan's former trade and intellectual life moved east to other African states in the central Sudan. Shortly after 1450 the rulers of several of the Hausa city-states adopted Islam as their official reli-gion. The Hausa states were also able to increase their importance as manufacturing and trading centers, be-coming famous for their cotton textiles and leatherwork-ing. Also expanding in the late fifteenth century was the central Sudanic state of Kanem-Bornu°. It was de-scended from the ancient kingdom of Kanem, whose rulers had accepted Islam in about 1085. At its peak about 1250, Kanem had absorbed the state of Bornu south and west of Lake Chad and gained control of im-portant trade routes crossing the Sahara. As Kanem-Bornu's armies conquered new territories in the late fifteenth century, they also spread the rule of Islam.

Mansa Suleiman (MAHN-suh SOO-lay-mahn)

Timbuktu (tim-buk-TOO)   **Kanem-Bornu** (KAH-nuhm–BOR-noo)

Personal Styles of Rule in India and Mali

Ibn Battuta wrote vividly of the powerful men who ruled the Muslim states he visited. His account of Sultan Muhammad ibn Tughluq of Delhi reflects the familiarity he acquired during a long stay in India in the 1340s.

Muhammad is a man who, above all others, is fond of making presents and shedding blood. There may always be seen at his gate some poor person becoming rich, or some living one condemned to death. His generous and brave actions, and his cruel and violent deeds, have obtained notoriety among the people. In spite of this, he is the most humble of men, and the one who exhibits the greatest equity. The ceremonies of religion are dear to his ears, and he is very severe in respect of prayer and the punishment which follows its neglect. . . . When drought prevailed . . . the Sultan gave orders that provisions for six months should be supplied to all the inhabitants of Delhi from the royal granaries . . . .

One of the most serious charges against this Sultan is that he forced all the inhabitants of Delhi to leave their homes. [After] the people of Delhi wrote letters full of insults and invectives against [him,] the Sultan . . . decided to ruin Delhi, so he purchased all the houses and inns from the inhabitants, paid them the price, and then ordered them to remove to Daulatabad . . . .

The greater part of the inhabitants departed, but [h]is slaves found two men in the streets: one was paralyzed, the other blind. They were brought before the sovereign, who ordered the paralytic to be shot away from a *manjanik* [catapult], and the blind man to be dragged from Delhi to Daulatabad, a journey of forty days' distance. The poor wretch fell to pieces during the journey, and only one of his legs reached Daulatabad.

In contrast, Ibn Battuta's describes Mansa Suleiman of Mali, whom he visited in 1353, in remote and impersonal terms that accord with African political traditions.

On certain days the sultan holds audiences in the palace yard, where there is a platform under a tree . . . carpeted with silk, [over which] is raised the umbrella, . . . surmounted by a bird in gold, about the size of a falcon. The sultan comes out of a door in a corner of the palace, carrying a bow in his hand and a quiver on his back. On his head he has a golden skullcap, bound with a gold band which has narrow ends shaped like knives, more than a span in length. His usual dress is a velvety red tunic, made of the European fabrics called mutanfas. The sultan is preceded by his musicians, who carry gold and silver [two-stringed guitars], and behind him come three hundred armed slaves. He walks in a leisurely fashion, affecting a very slow movement, and even stops and looks round the assembly, then ascends [the platform] in the sedate manner of a preacher ascending a mosque-pulpit. As he takes his seat, the drums, trumpets, and bugles are sounded. Three slaves go at a run to summon the sovereign's deputy and the military commanders, who enter and sit down . . . .

The blacks are of all people the most submissive to their king and the most abject in their behavior before him. They swear by his name, saying *Mansa Suleiman ki* [by Mansa Suleiman's law]. If he summons any of them while he is holding an audience in his pavilion, the person summoned takes off his clothes and puts on worn garments, removes his turban and dons a dirty skullcap and enters with his garments and trousers raised knee-high. He goes forward in an attitude of humility and dejection, and knocks the ground hard with his elbows, then stands with bowed head and bent back listening to what he says. If anyone addresses the king and receives a reply from him, he uncovers his back and throws dust over his head and back, for all the world like a bather splashing himself with water. I used to wonder how it was that they did not blind themselves.

How can the kind and cruel sides of Sultan Muhammad be reconciled? What role would Islam have played in his generosity? Could cruelty have brought any benefits to the ruler of a conquest state? How did Mansa Suleiman's ritual appearances serve to enhance his majesty? What attitudes toward Suleiman do his subjects' actions suggest? How different were the ruling styles of Muhammad and Suleiman?

Source: The first excerpt is from Henry M. Elliot, *The History of India as Told by Its Own Historians* (London: Trübner and Co., 1869–1871) 3:609–614. The second excerpt is adapted from H. A. R. Gibb, ed., *Selections from the Travels of Ibn Battuta in Asia and Africa* (London: Cambridge University Press, 1929), pp. 326–327. Copyright © 1929. Reprinted with permission of the Cambridge University Press.

The Delhi Sultanate in India

The arrival of Islam in India was more violent than in West Africa. Having long ago lost the defensive unity of the Gupta Empire (see Chapter 7), the divided states of northwest India were subject to raids by Afghan warlords from the early eleventh century. Motivated by a wish to spread their Islamic faith and by a desire for plunder, the raiders looted Hindu and Buddhist temples of their gold and jewels, kidnapped women for their harems, and slew Indian defenders by the thousands.

In the last decades of the twelfth century a new Turkish dynasty, armed with powerful crossbows, mounted a furious assault that succeeded in capturing the important northern Indian cities of Lahore and Delhi. The Muslim warriors could fire crossbows from the backs of their galloping horses thanks to the use of iron stirrups. One partisan Muslim chronicler recorded, "The city [Delhi] and its vicinity was freed from idols and idol-worship, and in the sanctuaries of the images of the [Hindu] Gods, mosques were raised by the worshippers of one God."[2] The invaders' strength was bolstered by a ready supply of Turkish adventurers from Central Asia eager to follow individual leaders and by the unifying force of their common religious faith. Although Indians fought back bravely, their small states, often at war with one another, were unable to present an effective united front.

Between 1206 and 1236 the Muslim invaders extended their rule over the Hindu princes and chiefs in much of northern India. Sultan Iltutmish° (r. 1211–1236) consolidated the conquest of northern India in a series of military expeditions that made his empire the largest state in India (see Map 15.3). He also secured official recognition of the Delhi Sultanate as a Muslim state by the caliph of Baghdad. Although the looting and destruction of temples, enslavement, and massacres continued, especially on the frontiers of the empire, the incorporation of north India into the Islamic world marked the beginning of the Muslim invaders' transformation from brutal conquerors to somewhat more benign rulers. Hindus whose land came under the control of foreign Muslim military officials were accorded special measures of protection that freed them from persecution in return for the payment of a special tax. Yet Hindus never forgot the intolerance and destruction of their first contacts with the invaders.

To the astonishment of his ministers, Iltutmish passed over his weak and pleasure-seeking sons and designated as his heir his beloved and talented daughter Raziya°. When they questioned the unprecedented idea of a woman ruling a Muslim state, he said, "My sons are devoted to the pleasures of youth: no one of them is qualified to be king. . . . There is no one more competent to guide the State than my daughter." In fact, his wish was not immediately carried out after his death, but after seven months of rule by her inept brother—whose great delight was riding his elephant through the bazaar, showering the crowds with coins—the ministers relented and put Raziya on the throne.

A chronicler of the time who knew her explained why the reign of this able ruler lasted less than four years (r. 1236–1240):

> Sultan Raziya was a great monarch. She was wise, just, and generous, a benefactor to her kingdom, a dispenser of justice, the protector of her subjects, and the leader of her armies. She was endowed with all the qualities befitting a king, but that she was not born of the right sex, and so in the estimation of men all these virtues were worthless. May God have mercy upon her![3]

Doing her best to prove herself a proper king, Raziya dressed like a man and rode at the head of her troops atop an elephant. Nothing, however, could overcome the prejudices of the Turkish chiefs against a woman ruler. In the end, she was imprisoned and later killed by a robber while trying to escape.

After a half-century of stagnation and rebellion, the ruthless but efficient policies of Sultan Ala-ud-din Khalji° (r. 1296–1316) increased his control over the empire's outlying provinces. Successful frontier raids and high taxes kept his treasury full, wage and price controls in Delhi kept down the cost of maintaining a large army, and a network of spies stifled intrigue. When a Mongol threat from the northeast eased, Ala-ud-din's forces extended the sultanate's southern flank, seizing the rich trading state of **Gujarat**° in 1298. Then troops drove into south India and briefly held the southern tip of the Indian peninsula.

At the time of Ibn Battuta's visit, Delhi's ruler was Sultan Muhammad ibn Tughluq° (r. 1325–1351), who received his visitor at his palace's celebrated Hall of a Thousand Pillars. The world traveler praised the sultan's piety and generosity—traditional Muslim virtues—but also recounted his cruelties (see Society and Culture: Personal Styles of Rule in India and Mali). In keeping with these complexities, the sultan resumed against independent Indian states a policy of aggressive expansion that enlarged the sultanate to its greatest extent. He bal-

---

Iltutmish (il-TOOT-mish) Raziya (rah-ZEE-uh)

Ala-ud-din Khalji (uh-LAH–uh-DEEN KAL-jee)
Gujarat (goo-juh-RAHT) Tughlug (toog-LOOK)

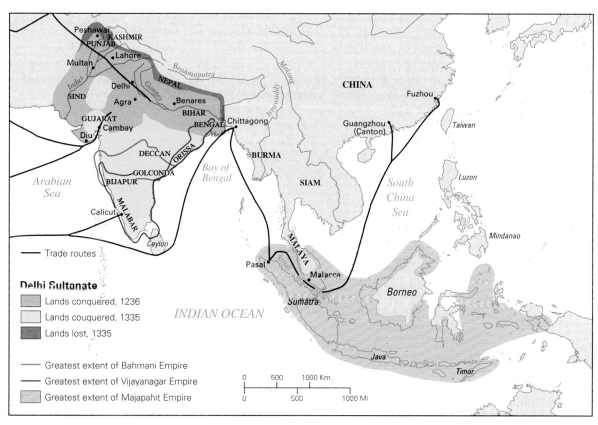

Map 15.3   South and Southeast Asia, 1200–1500   The rise of new empires and the expansion of maritime trade reshaped the lives of many tropical Asians.

anced that policy with one of religious toleration intended to win the loyalty of Hindus and other non-Muslims. He even attended Hindu religious festivals. However, his successor Firuz Shah° (r. 1351–1388) alienated powerful Hindus by taxing the Brahmins, preferring to cultivate good relations with the Muslim elite. Muslim chroniclers praised him for constructing forty mosques, thirty colleges, and a hundred hospitals.

A small minority in a giant land, the Turkish rulers relied on terror to keep their subjects submissive, on harsh military reprisals to put down rebellion, and on pillage and high taxes to sustain the ruling elite in luxury and power. Even under its most enlightened rulers, the Delhi Sultanate was probably more a burden than a benefit to most of its subjects. Although this criticism could be made of most large states of this time (including Mali), the sultanate's rulers never lost the disadvantage of their foreign origins and their practice of a religion alien to most of their subjects. Over time their hostility to any Hindu participation moderated as some Hindus

were incorporated into the administration. Some members of the ruling elite also married women from prominent Hindu families, though the brides had to become Muslims.

Personal and religious rivalries within the Muslim elite, as well as the discontent of the Hindus, threatened the Delhi Sultanate with disintegration whenever it showed weakness and finally hastened its end. In the mid-fourteenth century Muslim nobles challenged the sultan's dominion and successfully established the Bahmani° kingdom (1347–1482), which controlled the Deccan Plateau. To defend themselves against the southward push of Bahmani armies, the Hindu states of South India united to form the Vijayanagar° Empire (1336–1565), which at its height controlled the rich trading ports on both coasts of south India and held Ceylon as a tributary state.

The conflict between Vijayanagar and the Bahmani was as much a struggle among different elites as it was a conflict between Muslims and Hindus, since both states

---

Firuz Shah (fuh-ROOZ shah)   **Bahmani** (bah MAHN-ee)   **Vijayanagar** (vee-juh-yah-NAH-gar)

pursued policies that turned a blind eye to religious differences when doing so favored their interests. Bahmani rulers sought to balance devotion to Muslim domination, on the one hand, with the practical importance of incorporating the leaders of the majority Hindu population into the government, marrying Hindu wives, and appointing Brahmins to high offices, on the other. Vijayanagar rulers hired Muslim cavalry specialists and archers to strengthen their military forces, and they formed an alliance with the Muslim-ruled state of Gujarat.

By 1351, when all of South India was independent of Delhi's rule, much of north India was also in rebellion. In the northeast, Bengal successfully broke away from the sultanate in 1338, becoming a center of the mystical Sufi tradition of Islam (see Chapter 9). In the west, Gujarat regained its independence by 1390. The weakening of Delhi's central authority revived Mongol interests in the area. In 1398 the Turko-Mongol leader Timur (see Chapter 13) seized the opportunity to invade and captured the city of Delhi. When his armies withdrew the next year, dragging vast quantities of pillage and tens of thousands of captives behind them, the largest city in southern Asia lay empty and in ruins. The Delhi Sultanate never recovered.

For all its shortcomings, the Delhi Sultanate was important in the development of centralized political authority in India. It established a bureaucracy headed by the sultan, who was aided by a prime minister and provincial governors. There were efforts to improve food production, promote trade and economic growth, and establish a common currency. Despite the many conflicts that Muslim conquest and rule provoked, Islam gradually acquired a permanent place in South Asia. Yet the mixture of indigenous political traditions with these Islamic practices served to distinguish the Delhi Sultanate, like Mali, from the states in the Middle East, where Islam had first flourished.

INDIAN OCEAN TRADE

Food producers sustained tropical Africa and Asia. Sultans and kings directed its political affairs. Merchants were a third force uniting the tropics. Their maritime network stretched across the Indian Ocean from the Islamic heartlands of Iran and Arabia to Southeast Asia. Connecting routes extended to Europe, Africa, and China. The world's richest maritime trading network at this time, the Indian Ocean routes also facilitated the spread of Islam.

Monsoon Mariners

Between 1200 and 1500 the volume of trade in the Indian Ocean increased, stimulated by the prosperity of Islamic and Mongol empires in Asia, of Latin Europe, as well as of Africa and Southeast Asia. The demand for luxuries for the wealthy—precious metals and jewels, rare spices, fine textiles, and other manufactures—rose. The construction of larger ships made shipments of bulk cargoes of ordinary cotton textiles, pepper, food grains (rice, wheat, barley), timber, horses, and other goods profitable. And when the collapse of the Mongol Empire in the fourteenth century disrupted overland trade routes across Central Asia, the Indian Ocean routes assumed greater strategic importance in tying together the peoples of Eurasia and Africa.

Some goods were transported from one end of this trading network to the other, but few ships or crews made a complete circuit. Instead the Indian Ocean trade was divided into the two legs: from the Middle East across the Arabian Sea to India and from India across the Bay of Bengal to Southeast Asia (see Map 15.4).

The characteristic cargo and passenger ship of the Arabian Sea was the **dhow**° (see Environment and Technology: The Indian Ocean Dhow). Large numbers of these ships were constructed in Malabar coastal ports of southwestern India. They grew from an average capacity of 100 tons in 1200 to 400 tons in 1500. On a typical expedition a dhow might sail west from India to Arabia and Africa on the northeast monsoon winds (December to March) and return on the southwest monsoons (April to August). Small dhows kept the coast in sight. Relying on the stars to guide them, skilled pilots steered large vessels by the quicker route straight across the water. A large dhow could sail from the Red Sea to mainland Southeast Asia in from two to four months, but few did so. Eastbound cargoes and passengers from dhows reaching India were likely to be transferred to junks, which dominated the eastern half of the Indian Ocean and the South China Sea.

The largest, most technologically advanced, and most seaworthy vessels of this time, junks had been developed in China and spread with Chinese influence. They were built from heavy spruce or fir planks held together with enormous nails. The space below the deck was divided into watertight compartments to minimize flooding in case of damage to the ship's hull. According to Ibn Battuta, the largest junks had twelve sails made of bamboo and carried a crew of a thousand men, of whom

---

dhow (dow)

Map 15.4   Arteries of Trade and Travel in the Islamic World, to 1500   Ibn Battuta's journeys across Africa and Asia made use of land and sea routes along which Muslim traders and the Islamic faith had long traveled.

four hundred were soldiers. A large junk might have up to a hundred passenger cabins and could carry a cargo of over 1,000 tons. Chinese junks dominated China's foreign shipping to Southeast Asia and India, but not all of the junks that plied these waters were under Chinese control. During the fifteenth century, vessels of this type also were built in Bengal and Southeast Asia and were sailed by local crews.

The trade of the Indian Ocean was decentralized and cooperative. Commercial interests, not political authorities, united the several distinct regions that participated in it (see Map 15.4). The **Swahili° Coast** supplied gold from inland areas of eastern Africa. Ports around the Arabian peninsula supplied horses and goods from the northern parts of the Middle East, the Mediterranean, and eastern Europe. At the center of the Indian Ocean trade, merchants in the cities of coastal India received goods from east and west, sold some locally, passed others along, and added vast quantities of Indian goods to the trade. The Strait of Malacca°, between the

eastern end of the Indian Ocean and the South China Sea, was the meeting point of trade from Southeast Asia, China, and the Indian Ocean. In each region certain ports functioned as giant emporia for the trade, consolidating goods from smaller ports and inland areas for transport across the seas. The operation of this complex trading system can best be understood by looking at some of these regions and their emporia in greater detail.

Africa: The Swahili Coast and Zimbabwe

Trade expanded steadily along the East African coast from about 1250, giving rise to between thirty and forty separate city-states by 1500. Archaeological excavations reveal that after 1200 many mud and thatch African fishing villages were rebuilt with new masonry buildings, sometimes three or four stories high. Archaeology also reveals the growing presence of imported glass beads, Chinese porcelain, and other exotic goods. The people of the coast and island shared a common culture and and a common language, African in

Swahili (swah-HEE-lee)   **Malacca** (meh-LAK-eh)

The Indian Ocean Dhow

The sailing vessels that crossed the Indian Ocean shared the diversity of that trading area. The name by which we know them, *dhow*, comes from the Swahili language of the East African coast. The planks of teak from which their hulls were constructed were hewn from the tropical forests of south India and Southeast Asia. Their pilots, who navigated by stars at night, used the ancient technique that Arabs had used to find their way across the desert. Some pilots used a magnetic compass, which originated in China.

Dhows came in various sizes and designs, but they all had two distinctive features in common. The first was hull construction. The hulls of dhows consisted of planks that were sewn together, not nailed. Cord made of fiber from the husk of coconuts or other materials was passed through rows of holes drilled in the planks. Because cord is weaker than nails, outsiders considered this shipbuilding technique strange. Marco Polo fancifully suggested that it indicated sailors' fear that large ocean magnets would pull any nails out of their ships. More probable explanations are that pliant sewn hulls were cheaper to build than rigid nailed hulls and were less likley to be damaged if the ships ran aground on coral reefs.

The second distinctive feature of dhows was their triangular (lateen) sails made of palm leaves or cotton. The sails were suspended from tall masts and could be turned to catch the wind.

The sewn hull and lateen sails were technologies developed centuries earlier, but there were two innovations between 1200 and 1500. First, a rudder positioned at the stern (rear end) of the ship replaced the large side oar that formerly had controlled steering. Second, shipbuilders increased the size of dhows to accommodate bulkier cargoes.

Dhow This modern model shows the vessel's main features. (National Maritime Museum, London)

grammar and vocabulary but enriched with many Arabic and Persian terms and written in Arabic script. In time these people became known as "Swahili," from the Arabic name *sawahil° al-sudan*, meaning "shores of the blacks."

Until shortly before Ibn Battuta's visit in 1331 the northern city of Mogadishu had been the Swahili Coast's most important commercial center, but in the fourteenth century the southern city of Kilwa surpassed it in importance. After visiting Kilwa, Ibn Battuta declared it "one of the most beautiful and well-constructed towns in

---

sawahil (suh-WAH-hil)

the world." He noted that its dark-skinned inhabitants were devout and pious Muslims, and he took special pains to praise their ruler as a man rich in the traditional Muslim virtues of humility and generosity.

Oral traditions associate the Swahili Coast's commercial expansion with the arrival of Arab and Iranian merchants, but what had attracted them? In Kilwa's case the answer is gold. By the late fifteenth century the city was exporting a ton of gold a year. The gold was mined by inland Africans much farther south. Much of it came from or passed through a powerful state on the plateau south of the Zambezi River, whose capital city is known

Royal Enclosure, Great Zimbabwe   Inside these oval stone walls the rulers of the trading state of Great Zimbabwe lived. Forced to enter the enclosure through a narrow corridor between two high walls, visitors were meant to be awestruck.   (Courtesy of the Department of Information, Rhodesia)

as **Great Zimbabwe.** At its peak in about 1400, the city which occupied 193 acres (78 hectares) may have had 18,000 inhabitants.

Between about 1250 and 1450, local African craftsmen built stone structures for Great Zimbabwe's rulers, priests, and wealthy citizens. The largest structure, a walled enclosure the size and shape of a large football stadium, served as the king's court. Its drystone walls were up to 17 feet (5 meters) thick and 32 feet (10 meters) high. Inside the walls were many buildings, including a large conical stone tower. The stone ruins of Great Zimbabwe are one of the most famous historical sites in sub-Saharan Africa.

Like Mali, the Great Zimbabwe state rested on a mixed farming and cattle-herding economy, but depended on long-distance trade for its wealth. It first prospered in a regional trade based on copper ingots from the upper Zambezi Valley, salt, and local manufactures. The great expansion in the export of gold into the Indian Ocean in the fourteenth and fifteenth centuries brought Zimbabwe to the peak of its political and economic power. However, historians suspect that the city's residents depleted nearby forests for firewood while

their cattle overgrazed surrounding grasslands. The result was an ecological crisis that hastened the empire's decline in the fifteenth century.

Arabia: Aden and the Red Sea

The city of **Aden°** had a double advantage in the Indian Ocean trade. Most of the rest of Arabia was desert, but monsoon winds brought Aden enough rainfall to supply drinking water to a large population and to grow grain for export. In addition, Aden's location (see Map 15.2) made it a convenient stopover for trade with India, the Persian Gulf, East Africa, and Egypt. Aden's merchants sorted out the goods from one place and sent them on to another: cotton cloth and beads from India, spices from Southeast Asia, horses from Arabia and Ethiopia, pearls from the Red Sea, luxurious manufactures from Cairo, slaves, gold, and ivory from Ethiopia, and grain, opium, and dyes from Aden's own hinterland.

Aden (AY-den)

Ibn Battuta sailed from Mecca through the Red Sea to Aden in 1331, probably wedged in among bales of trade goods. He commented at length on the great wealth of Aden's leading merchants, telling a story about the slave of one merchant who paid the fabulous sum of 400 dinars for a ram in order to keep the slave of another merchant from buying it. Instead of punishing the slave for this extravagance, the master freed him as a reward for outdoing his rival. Ninety years later a Chinese Muslim visitor, Ma Huan, found "the country . . . rich, and the people numerous," living in stone residences several stories high.

Common commercial interests generally promoted good relations among the different religions and cultures of this region. For example, in the mid-thirteenth century a wealthy Jew from Aden named Yosef settled in Christian Ethiopia, where he acted as an adviser. South Arabia had been trading with neighboring parts of Africa since before the times of King Solomon of Israel. The dynasty that ruled Ethiopia after 1270 claimed descent from Solomon and from the South Arabian princess Sheba. Solomonic Ethiopia's consolidation was associated with a great increase in trade through the Red Sea port of Zeila°, including slaves, amber, and animal pelts, which went to Aden and on to other destinations.

Nevertheless, some religious and political conflict occurred. In the fourteenth century the Sunni Muslim king of Yemen sent materials for the building of a large mosque in Zeila, but the local Somalis (who were Shi'ite Muslims) threw the stones into the sea. The result was a year-long embargo of Zeila ships in Aden. In the late fifteenth century Ethiopia's territorial expansion and efforts to increase control over the trade provoked conflicts with Muslims who ruled the coastal states of the Red Sea.

India: Gujarat and the Malabar Coast

The state of Gujarat in western India prospered as its ports shared in the expanding trade of the Arabian Sea and the rise of the Delhi Sultanate. Blessed with a rich agricultural hinterland and a long coastline, Gujarat attracted new trade after the Mongol capture of Baghdad in 1258 disrupted the northern land routes. Gujarat's forcible incorporation into the Delhi Sultanate in 1298 had mixed results. The state suffered from the violence of the initial conquest and from subsequent military crackdowns, but it also prospered from increased trade with Delhi's wealthy ruling class. Independent again after 1390, the Muslim rulers of Gujarat extended their control over neighboring Hindu states and regained their preeminent position in the Indian Ocean trade.

The state derived much of its wealth from its export of cotton textiles and indigo to the Middle East and Europe, largely in return for gold and silver. Gujaratis also dominated the trade from India to the Swahili Coast, selling cotton cloth, carnelian beads, and foodstuffs in exchange for ebony, slaves, ivory, and gold. During the fifteenth century traders expanded their trade from Gujarat eastward to the Strait of Malacca. These Gujarati merchants helped spread the Islamic faith among East Indian traders, some of whom even imported specially carved gravestones from Gujarat.

Unlike Kilwa and Aden, Gujarat was important for its manufactures as well as its commerce. According to the thirteenth-century Venetian traveler Marco Polo, Gujarat's leatherworkers dressed enough skins in a year to fill several ships to Arabia and other places and also made beautiful sleeping mats for export to the Middle East "in red and blue leather, exquisitely inlaid with figures of birds and beasts, and skilfully embroidered with gold and silver wire," as well as leather cushions embroidered in gold. Later observers considered the Gujarati city of Cambay the equal of cities in Flanders and northern Italy (see Chapter 16) in the size, skill, and diversity of its textile industries. Gujarat's cotton, linen, and silk cloth, as well as its carpets and quilts, found a large market in Europe, Africa, the Middle East, and Southeast Asia. Cambay also was famous for its polished gemstones, gold jewelry, carved ivory, stone beads, and both natural and artificial pearls. At the height of its prosperity in the fifteenth century, this substantial city's well-laid-out streets and open places boasted with fine stone houses with tiled roofs. Although most of Gujarat's overseas trade was in the hands of its Muslim residents, members of its Hindu merchant caste profited so much from related commercial activities that their wealth and luxurious lives were the envy of other Indians.

Gujarat's importance in trade and manufacturing was duplicated farther south in the cities of the Malabar Coast. Calicut° and other coastal cities prospered from their commerce in locally made cotton textiles and locally grown grains and spices, and as clearing-houses for the long-distance trade of the Indian Ocean. The Malabar Coast was united under a loose federation of its Hindu rulers, presided over by the Zamorin° (ruler) of Calicut. As in eastern Africa and Arabia, rulers were generally tolerant of other religious and ethnic groups who were important to commercial profits. Most trading activity lay in the hands of Muslims, many originally from Iran and Arabia, who intermarried with local Indian Muslims. Jewish merchants also operated from Malabar's trading cities.

Zeila (ZEYE-luh)

Calicut (KAL-ih-cut)   **Zamorin** (ZAH-much-ruhn)

Southeast Asia: The Rise of Malacca

At the eastern end of the Indian Ocean, the principal passage into the South China Sea was through the Strait of Malacca between the Malay Peninsula and the island of Sumatra (see Map 15.3). As trade increased in the fourteenth and fifteenth centuries, this commercial choke point became the object of considerable political rivalry. The mainland kingdom of Siam gained control of most of the upper Malay Peninsula, while the Java-based kingdom of Majapahit° extended its dominion over the lower Malay Peninsula and much of Sumatra. Majapahit, however, was not strong enough to suppress a nest of Chinese pirates who had gained control of the Sumatran city of Palembang° and preyed on ships sailing through the strait. In 1407 a fleet sent by the Chinese government smashed the pirates' power and took their chief back to China for trial.

Weakened by internal struggles, Majapahit was unable to take advantage of China's intervention. The chief beneficiary of the safer commerce was the newer port of **Malacca** (or Melaka), which dominated the narrowest part of the strait. Under the leadership of a prince from Palembang, Malacca had quickly grown from an obscure fishing village into an important port by means of a series of astute alliances. Nominally subject to the king of Siam, Malacca also secured an alliance with China that was sealed by the visit of the imperial fleet in 1407. The conversion of an early ruler from Hinduism to Islam helped promote trade with the Gujarati and other Muslim merchants who dominated so much of the Indian Ocean commerce. Merchants also appreciated Malacca's security and low taxes.

Besides serving as the meeting point for traders from India and China, Malacca also served as an emporium for Southeast Asian trade: rubies and musk from Burma, tin from Malaya, gold from Sumatra, as well as cloves and nutmeg from the Moluccas (or Spice Islands as Europeans later dubbed them) to the east. Shortly after 1500, when Malacca was at its height, one resident counted eighty-four languages spoken among the merchants gathered there, who came from as far away as Turkey, Ethiopia, and the Swahili Coast. Four officials administered the large foreign merchant communities: one official for the very numerous Gujaratis, one for other Indians and Burmese, one for Southeast Asians, and one for the Chinese and Japanese. Malacca's wealth and its cosmopolitan residents set the standard for luxury in Malaya for centuries to come.

Majapahit (mah-jah-PAH-hit)
Palembang (pah-lem-BONG)

SOCIAL AND CULTURAL CHANGE

State growth, commercial expansion, and the spread of Islam between 1200 and 1500 led to many changes in the social and cultural life of tropical peoples. The political and commercial elites at the top of society grew in size and power. To serve their needs, the number of slaves increased considerably. There were also changes in the lives of women in different social classes. The spread of Islamic practices and beliefs in many parts of the African and Asian tropics was a major aspect of social and cultural change, evident from the fact that the words *Sahara, Sudan, Swahili,* and *monsoon* are all Arabic in origin. Even so, traditional religious and social customs remained important.

Architecture, Learning, and Religion

As in other periods of history, social and cultural changes were more obvious in the cities than in rural areas. Some urban change was physical. As Ibn Battuta and other travelers observed, wealthy merchants and ruling elites spent lavishly on new mansions, palaces, and places of worship. In architecture, as well as in education and religious practice, the spread of Islam was a major force for change in many tropical societies.

Most of the places of worship that survive from this period exhibit fascinating blends of older traditions and new influences. African Muslims produced strikingly rendered Middle Eastern mosque designs in local building materials: sun-baked clay and wood in the western Sudan; coral stone on the Swahili Coast. Many mosques in Gujarat were influenced by the styles of Hindu temple architecture and even incorporated pieces of older structures. The congregational mosque at Cambay, built in 1325 with courtyard, cloisters, and porches typical of Islamic mosques, was assembled primarily out of pillars, porches, and arches taken from sacked Hindu and Jain° temples of earlier generations. The congregational mosque erected at the Gujarati capital of Ahmadabad° in 1423 was the culmination of a mature Hindu-Muslim architecture. It had an open courtyard typical of mosques everywhere, but the surrounding verandas incorporated many typical Gujarati details and architectural conventions.

Jain (jine)
Ahmadabad (AH-muhd-ah-bahd)

Church of Saint George, Ethiopia King Lalibela, who ruled the Christian kingdom of Ethiopia between about 1180 and 1220, had a series of churches carved out of solid volcanic rock to adorn his kingdom's new capital (also named Lalibela). The church of Saint George, excavated to a depth of 40 feet (13 meters) and hollowed out inside, has the shape of a Greek cross. (S. Sassoon/ Robert Harding Picture Library)

Even more unusual than these Islamic architectural amalgams were the Christian churches of King Lalibela° of Ethiopia, constructed during the first third of the thirteenth century. As part of his new capital, Lalibela directed Ethiopian sculptors to carve eleven churches out of solid rock, each commemorating a sacred Christian site in Jerusalem. These unique structures carried on an old Ethiopian tradition of rock sculpture, though on a far grander scale.

Mosques, churches, and temples were centers of education as well as prayer. Muslims promoted literacy among their sons (and sometimes their daughters) so that they could read the religion's classic texts. Ibn Battuta reported seeing several boys in Mali who had been placed in chains until they completed memorizing passages of the Quran. In sub-Saharan Africa the spread of Islam was associated with the spread of literacy, which had previously been confined largely to Christian Ethiopia. Initially literacy was in Arabic, but in time Arabic characters were used to write local languages.

India already had a long literate heritage, so the impact of Islam on literacy there was less dramatic. Arabic spread among Indian scholars along with Persian (the language of Iran), which was considered more refined. Many new works of prose and poetry were written in **Urdu°**, a Persian-influenced literary form of Hindi written in Arabic characters. Muslims also introduced papermaking in India, a second-century Chinese invention that had spread through the Indian Ocean trade routes. Paper facilitated the distribution of written texts in India, even though they still had to be copied by hand.

Although most of the education was concerned with basic literacy and the recitation of the Quran, advanced Muslim scholars studied Islamic law, theology, and administration, as well as classical Greek works of mathematics, medicine, and science. By the sixteenth century in the West African city **Timbuktu,** there were over 150 Quranic schools, and advanced classes were held in the mosques and homes of the leading clerics. So great was the demand for books that they were the most profitable item to bring from North Africa to Timbuktu. At his death in 1536 one West African scholar, al-Hajj Ahmed of Timbuktu, possessed some seven hundred volumes, an unusually large library for that time. In Southeast Asia, Malacca became a center of Islamic learning from which scholars spread Islam throughout the region. Other im-

---

Lalibela (LAH-lee-BEL-uh)

Urdu (ER-doo)

portant centers of learning developed in Muslim India, particularly in Delhi, the capital.

These changes in architecture and education were results of the spread of Islam as a religion. Even where Islam entered as the result of conquest, as in India, conversions were rarely forced. Example and persuasion seem to have been far more effective. The communities of Muslim merchants throughout the region, along with the large number of Muslim warriors and administrators who moved into India during these centuries, attracted interest in their religion. Many Muslims were active missionaries for their faith and worked hard to persuade others of its superiority.

Muslim domination of long-distance trade and markets was particularly important in fostering the adoption of Islam. Many commercial transactions took place between people of different religions, but trust was most easily established among individuals who shared the common code of morality and law that Islam provided. For this reason many local merchants were attracted to Islam. From the major trading centers along the Swahili Coast, in the Sudan, in coastal India, and in Southeast Asia, Islam's influence spread along regional trade routes.

Another important way in which Islam spread was through marriage. Most of the foreign Muslims who settled in tropical Africa and Asia were single men. They often married local women, whom they required to be (or become) Muslims and to raise their children in the Islamic faith. Since Islam permitted a man to have up to four legal wives and many men took concubines as well, some wealthy men had dozens of children. In large elite Muslim households the many servants, both free and enslaved, were also required to be Muslims. Although such conversions were not fully voluntary, individuals could still find personal fulfillment in the Islamic faith.

In parts of southern Asia the upheavals of this period also promoted the spread of Islam. In India, Islamic invasions practically destroyed the last strongholds of long-declining Buddhism. In 1196 the great Buddhist center of study at Nalanda° in Bihar° was overrun, its manuscripts were burned, and thousands of its monks were killed or driven into exile in Nepal and Tibet. Buddhism became a minor faith in the land of its birth (see Chapter 8), while Islam, swelled by substantial immigration, emerged as India's second most important religion. Hinduism was still India's dominant faith in 1500, but in most of maritime Southeast Asia the combined impact of Mongol invasion and the peaceful expansion of Mus-

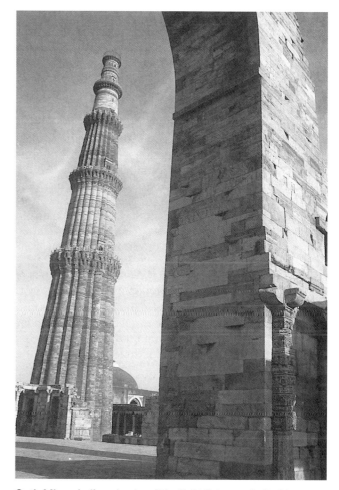

Qutb Minar, India   A ruler of the Delhi Sultanate built this unusually tall minaret and mosque near Delhi in the early thirteenth century to display the power of Islam. Five times a day the muezzin climbed the 240-foot (73-meter) tower of red sandstone and white marble to call Muslims to prayer.   (Jean-Louis Nou)

lim merchants led to the displacement of Hinduism by Islam.

Some peoples outside the cities were attracted to Islam in this period. The seed of Islamic belief was planted among the pastoral Fulani of West Africa and Somali of northeastern Africa, as well as among pastoralists in northwest India. Low-caste rural Bengalis also began to adopt Islam, perhaps because they saw more hope in the universalism of Islam than in the fixed inequalities of the Hindu hierarchy. Yet the spread of Islam was not a simple process by which one set of beliefs was replaced by new ones. Islam too was changed by the cultures of the regions it penetrated, developing African, Indian, and Indonesian varieties.

Nalanda (nuh-LAN-duh)   **Bihar** (bee-HAHR)

Social and Gender Distinctions

The political, commercial, and religious changes of these centuries significantly affected class structure and the status of at least some women. The gap between the elites and the masses widened. It is not clear that the poor became poorer—the 50 percent of the harvest that peasants in India paid in tax to the Delhi Sultanate may have been no more than what they formerly had paid to local lords—but the rich surely became richer and more numerous as a result of conquests and commerce.

A growth in slavery accompanied the rising prosperity of the elites. Many slaves were the product of wars of expansion by the powerful new states. The campaigns of conquest and pillage in India, according to Islamic sources, reduced hundreds of thousands of Hindu "infidels" to slavery. The courts of the ruling elites of Delhi overflowed with slaves. Sultan Ala ud-Din owned 50,000; Firuz Shah had 180,000, including 12,000 skilled artisans. Sultan Tughluq sent 100 male slaves and 100 female slaves as a gift to the emperor of China in return for a similar gift. His successor prohibited any more exports of slaves, perhaps because of reduced supplies in the smaller empire.

In Africa, the growth of powerful states also had led to an increase in domestic slavery, as well as to a rising export trade in slaves. As Ibn Battuta reported, Mali and Bornu sent slaves across the Sahara to North Africa, including beautiful maidens and eunuchs (castrated males). The expanding Ethiopian Empire regularly sent captives for sale to Aden traders at Zeila. According to modern estimates, about 2.5 million enslaved Africans were sent across the Sahara and the Red Sea between 1200 and 1500. Some slaves were also shipped from the Swahili Coast to India, where Africans played conspicuous roles in the navies, armies, and administrations of some Indian states, especially in the fifteenth century. A few African slaves even found their way to China, where a Chinese source dating from about 1225 says rich families preferred gatekeepers whose bodies were "black as lacquer."

The status of slaves varied enormously, depending on their skill and sex. Relatively few in this period were used as field hands because "free" labor was so abundant and cheap. Most slaves were trained for special purposes. In some places, skilled trades and military service were dominated by hereditary castes of slaves, some of whom were rich and powerful. Indeed, the earliest rulers of the Delhi Sultanate were military slaves, though their status had long ceased to be a disadvantage. A slave general in the western Sudan named Askia Muhammad seized control of the Songhai Empire (Mali's successor) in 1493. Less fortunate were slaves who did hard menial work, such as the men and women who mined copper in Mali.

In all wealthy households there was a tremendous demand for slaves to be employed as servants. Ibn Battuta observed large numbers at the sultan of Mali's palace. Some servants were males, including the eunuchs who guarded the harems of wealthy Muslims, but most household slaves were females. Female slaves were also in great demand as entertainers and concubines. Having a concubine from every part of the world was a rich man's ambition in some Muslim circles. One of Firuz Shah's nobles was said to have two thousand harem slaves, including women from Turkey and China.

Sultan Ala ud-Din's campaigns against Gujarat at the end of the thirteenth century yielded a booty of twenty thousand maidens in addition to innumerable younger children of both sexes. The supply of captives became so great that the lowest grade of horse sold for five times as much as an ordinary female slave destined for service, although beautiful young virgins destined for the harems of powerful nobles commanded far higher prices. Some decades later when Ibn Battuta was given ten girls captured from among the "infidels," he commented: "Female captives [in Delhi] are very cheap because they are dirty and do not know civilized ways. Even the educated ones are cheap." It would seem fairer to say that such slaves were cheap because the large numbers offered for sale had made them so.

How much the status of tropical women—whether slave or free—changed during this period is a subject needing more study. No one has yet offered a general opinion about Africa. Based on a reading of contemporary Hindu legal digests and commentaries, some authors speculate that the position of Hindu women may have improved somewhat compared to earlier periods, but in the absence of detailed information it is impossible to be sure. Hindu women continued to suffer from social and religious disabilities, but some restrictions on their lives may have been relaxed—or, at the very least, not expanded. For example, the ancient practice of sati°—that is, of an upper-caste widow throwing herself on her husband's funeral pyre—remained a meritorious act strongly approved by social custom. But Ibn Battuta leaves no doubt that, in his observation at least, sati was strictly optional. Since the Hindu commentaries devote considerable attention to the rights of widows without sons to inherit their husbands' estates, one may conclude that sati was exceptional.

It remained the custom for Indian girls to be given in marriage before the age of puberty, although the consummation of the marriage was not to take place until

---

sati (suh-TEE)

the young woman was ready. Wives were expected to observe far stricter rules of fidelity and chastity than were their husbands and could be abandoned for many serious breaches. But women often were punished by lighter penalties than men for offenses against law and custom.

A female's status was largely determined by the status of her male master—father, husband, or owner. Women usually were not permitted to play the kind of active roles in commerce, administration, or religion that would have given them scope for personal achievements. Even so, women possessed considerable skills within those areas of activity that social norms allotted to them.

Besides child rearing, one of the most widespread female skills was food preparation. So far historians have paid little attention to the development of culinary skills, but preparing meals that were healthful and tasty required much training and practice, especially given the limited range of foods available in most places. One kitchen skill that has received greater attention is brewing, perhaps because men were the principal consumers. In many parts of Africa women commonly made beer from grains or bananas. These mildly alcoholic beverages, taken in moderation, were a nutritious source of vitamins and minerals. Socially they were an important part of male rituals of hospitality and relaxation that promoted social harmony.

Women's activities were not confined to the hearth, however. Throughout tropical Africa and Asia women did much of the farm work. They also toted home heavy loads of food, firewood, and water for cooking balanced on their heads. Other common female activities included making clay pots for cooking and storage and making clothing. In India the spinning wheel, introduced by the Muslim invaders, greatly reduced the cost of making yarn for weaving. Spinning was a woman's activity done in the home; the weavers were generally men. Marketing was a common activity among women, especially in West Africa, where they sold their agricultural surplus and pottery and other craftwork.

It is difficult to judge how the spread of Islam affected the status of women. Women of some social classes found their status improved by becoming part of a Muslim household. The rare exception, such as Sultan Raziya, might even command supreme authority. Of course, many other women were incorporated into Muslim households as servants, concubines, and slaves.

Yet not all places that adopted Islam accepted all the social customs of the Arab world. In Mali's capital Ibn Battuta was appalled that Muslim women both free and slave did not completely cover their bodies and veil their faces when appearing in public. He considered their nakedness an offense to women's (and men's) modesty.

Indian Woman Spinning, ca. 1500   This drawing of a Muslim woman by an Indian artist shows the influence of Persian styles. The spinning of cotton fiber into thread—women's work—was made much easier by the spinning wheel, which the Muslim invaders introduced. Men then wove the threads into the cotton textiles for which India was celebrated.   (British Library, Oriental and Indian Office Library, Or 3299, f. 151)

In another part of Mali he berated a Muslim merchant from Morocco for permitting his wife to sit on a couch and chat with a male friend of hers. The husband replied, "The association of women with men is agreeable to us and part of good manners, to which no suspicion attaches." Ibn Battuta's shock at this "laxity" and his refusal to ever visit the merchant again reveal the patriarchal precepts that were dear to most elite Muslims. So does the fate of Sultan Raziya of Delhi.

CONCLUSION

With nearly 40 percent of the world's population and over a quarter of its habitable land, tropical Africa and Asia was a large and diverse place. In the centuries between 1200 and 1500 commercial, political, and cultural expansion drew the region's peoples closer together. The Indian Ocean became the world's most important and richest trading area. The Delhi Sultanate brought the greatest political unity to India since the decline of the Guptas. Mali extended the political and trading role pioneered by Ghana in the western Sudan. The growth of trade and empires was closely connected with the enlargement of Islam's presence in the tropical world along with the introduction of greater diversity into Islamic practice.

But if change was an important theme of this period, so too was social and cultural stability. Most tropical Africans and Asians never ventured far outside the rural communities where their families had lived for generations. Their lives followed the familiar pattern of the seasons, the cycle of religious rituals and festivals, and the stages from childhood to elder status. Custom and necessity defined occupations. Most people engaged in food production by farming, herding, and fishing; some specialized in crafts or religious leadership. Based on the accumulated wisdom about how best to deal with their environment, such village communities were remarkably hardy. They might be ravaged by natural disaster or pillaged by advancing armies, but over time most recovered. Empires and kingdoms rose and fell in these centuries, but the villages endured.

In comparison, social, political, and environmental changes taking place in the Latin West, described in the next chapter, were in many ways more profound and disruptive. And, after 1500, changes there had great implications for tropical peoples.

Key Terms

tropics	dhow
Ibn Battuta	Swahili Coast
monsoon	Great Zimbabwe
Delhi Sultanate	Aden
Mali	Malacca
Mansa Kankan Musa	Urdu
Gujarat	Timbuktu

Suggested Reading

The trading links among the lands around the Indian Ocean have attracted the attention of recent scholars. A fine place to begin is Patricia Risso, *Merchants and Faith: Muslim Commerce and Culture in the Indian Ocean* (1995). More ambitious and perhaps more inclinded to overreach the evidence is Janet Abu-Lughod, *Before European Hegemony: The World System, A.D. 1250–1350* (1989), which may usefully be read with K. N. Chaudhuri, *Asia Before Europe: Economy and Civilization of the Indian Ocean from the Rise of Islam to 1750* (1991). Students will find clear summaries of Islam's influences in tropical Asia and Africa in Ira Lapidus, *A History of Islamic Societies* (1988), part II, and of commercial relations in Philip D. Curtin, *Cross-Cultural Trade in World History* (1984).

Greater detail about tropical lands is found in regional studies. For Southeast Asia see Nicholas Tarling, ed., *The Cambridge History of Southeast Asia*, vol. 1 (1992); John F. Cady, *Southeast Asia: Its Historical Development* (1964); and G. Coedes, *The Indianized States of Southeast Asia*, ed. Walter F. Vella (1968). India is covered comprehensively by R. C. Majumdar, ed., *The History and Culture of the Indian People*, vol. 4, *The Delhi Sultanate*, 2d ed. (1967); with brevity by Stanley Wolpert, *A New History of India*, 6th ed. (1999); and from an intriguing perspective by David Ludden, *A Peasant History of South India* (1985). For advanced topics see Tapan Raychaudhuri and Irfan Habib, eds., *The Cambridge Economic History of India*, vol. 1, *c. 1200–c. 1750* (1982).

Africa in this period is well served by the later parts of Graham Connah's *African Civilizations: Precolonial Cities and States in Tropical Africa: An Archaeological Perspective* (1987) and in greater depth by the relevant chapters in D. T. Niane, ed., *UNESCO General History of Africa*, vol. 4, *Africa from the Twelfth to the Sixteenth Century* (1984), and in Roland Oliver, ed., *The Cambridge History of Africa*, vol. 3, *c. 1050 to c. 1600* (1977).

For accounts of slavery and the slave trade see Salim Kidwai, "Sultans, Eunuchs and Domestics: New Forms of Bondage in Medieval India," in *Chains of Servitude: Bondage and Slavery in India*, ed. Utsa Patnaik and Manjari Dingwaney (1985), and the first two chapters of Paul E. Lovejoy, *Transformations in Slavery: A History of Slavery in Africa* (1983).

Three volumes of Ibn Battuta's writings have been translated by H. A. R. Gibb, *The Travels of Ibn Battuta*, A.D. 1325–1354 (1958–1971). Ross E. Dunn, *The Adventures of Ibn Battuta: A Muslim of the 14th Century* (1986), provides a modern retelling of his travels with commentary. For annotated selections see Said Hamdun and Noël King, *Ibn Battuta in Black Africa* (1995).

The most accessible survey of Indian Ocean sea travel is George F. Hourani, *Arab Seafaring*, expanded ed. (1995). For a Muslim Chinese traveler's observations see Ma Huan, *Ying-yai Shenglan, "The Overall Survey of the Ocean's Shore" [1433]*, trans. and ed. J. V. G. Mills (1970). Another valuable contemporary account of trade and navigation in the Indian Ocean is G. R. Tibbetts, *Arab Navigation in the Indian Ocean Before the Coming of the Portuguese, Being a Translation of the Kitab al-Fawa'id . . . of Ahmad b. Majid al-Najdi* (1981).

Notes

1. Tarikh-i-Wassaf, in Henry M. Elliot, *The History of India as Told by Its Own Historians*, ed. John Dowson (London: Trübner and Co., 1869–1871), 2:28.
2. Hasan Nizami, Taju-l Ma-asir, ibid., 2:219.
3. Minhaju-s Siraj, Tabakat-i Nasiri, ibid., 2:332–333.

THE LATIN WEST,

1200–1500

Making Wine   In this Flemish tapestry, workers use a mechanical press and foot stomping to crush grapes for wealthy vineyard owners.

n the summer of 1454, the man who in four years would become pope was pessimistic about the future of Latin Christendom. Aeneas Sylvius Piccolomini° was trying to stir up support for a crusade to halt the Muslim advances that were engulfing southeastern Europe. Just a year earlier, the Ottoman Turks had captured the Greek Christian city of Constantinople and showed no sign of stopping. But he doubted anyone could persuade the rulers of the Christian Europe to take up arms together, for, he lamented, "Christendom has no head whom all will obey—neither the pope nor the emperor receives his due."

Another problem was that Christian European states were more inclined to fight with each other than to join a common front against the Turks. French and English armies had been battling for over a century. The German emperor presided over dozens of states that were virtually independent of his control. The Spanish and Italians were divided into numerous kingdoms and principalities that often turned to war. With only slight exaggeration Aeneas Sylvius moaned, "Every city has its own king, and there are as many princes as there are households."

This lack of unity, he believed, was due to Europeans being so preoccupied with personal welfare and material gain that they would never sacrifice themselves to stop the Turkish armies. Both pessimism about human nature and materialism had increased during the previous century, after a devastating plague had carried off a third of western Europe's population.

Yet despite all these divisions, disasters, and wars, historians now see the period from 1200 to 1500 (Europe's later Middle Ages) as a time of unusual progress. The avarice and greed Aeneas Sylvius lamented were the dark side of the material prosperity that was most evident in the cities with their splendid architecture, institutions of higher learning, and cultural achievements. Frequent wars caused havoc and destruction, but in the long run they promoted the development of more powerful weapons and more unified monarchies.

A European fifty years later would have known that the Turks did not overrun Europe, that a truce in the Anglo-French conflict would hold, and that explorers sent by Portugal and a newly united Spain would extend Europe's reach to other continents. In 1454 Aeneas Sylvius knew only what had been, and the conflicts and calamities of the past made him shudder.

Although their contemporary Muslim and Byzantine neighbors commonly called western Europeans "Franks," western Europeans ordinarily referred to themselves as "Latins." That term underscored their allegiance to the Latin rite of Christianity (and to its patriarch, the pope) as well as the use of the Latin language by their literate members. The **Latin West** deserves special attention because its achievements during this period had profound implications for the future of the world. The region was emerging from the economic and cultural shadow of its Islamic neighbors and, despite grave disruptions caused by plague and warfare, boldly setting out to extend its dominance. Some common elements promoted the Latin West's remarkable resurgence: competition, the pursuit of success, and the effective use of borrowed technology and learning.

As you read this chapter, ask yourself the following questions:

- How well did inhabitants of the Latin West deal with their natural environment?
- How did warfare help rulers in the Latin West acquire the skills, weapons, and determination that enabled them to challenge other parts of the world?
- How did superior technology in the Latin West promote excellence in business, learning, and architecture?
- How much did the region's achievements depend on its own people and how much on things borrowed from Muslim and Byzantine neighbors?

Aeneas Sylvius Piccolomini (uh-NEE-uhs SIL-vee-uhs pee-kuh-lo-MEE-nee)

CHRONOLOGY

	Technology and Environment	Culture	Politics and Society
1200	**1200s** Use of crossbows and longbows becomes widespread; windmills in increased use	**1210s** Religious orders founded: Teutonic Knights, Franciscans, Dominicans **1225–1274** Thomas Aquinas, monk and philosopher **1265–1321** Dante Alighieri, poet **ca. 1267–1337** Giotto, painter	**1200s** Champagne fairs flourish **1204** Fourth Crusade launched **1215** Magna Carta issued
1300	**1300** First mechanical clocks in the West **1315–1317** Great Famine **1347–1351** Black Death **ca. 1350** Growing deforestation	**1300–1500** Rise of universities **1304–1374** Francesco Petrarch, humanist writer **1313–1375** Giovanni Boccaccio, humanist writer **ca. 1340–1400** Geoffrey Chaucer, poet **1389–1464** Cosimo de' Medici, banker **ca. 1390–1441** Jan van Eyck, painter	**1337** Start of Hundred Years War **1381** Wat Tyler's Rebellion
1400	**1400s** Large cannon in use in warfare; hand-held firearms become prominent **ca. 1450** First printing with movable type in the West **1454** Gutenberg Bible printed	**1449–1492** Lorenzo de' Medici, art patron **1452–1519** Leonardo da Vinci, artist **ca. 1466–1536** Erasmus of Rotterdam, humanist **1472–1564** Michelangelo, artist **1492** Expulsion of Jews from Spain	**1415** Portuguese take Ceuta **1431** Joan of Arc burned as witch **1453** End of Hundred Years War; Turks take Constantinople **1469** Marriage of Ferdinand of Aragon and Isabella of Castile **1492** Fall of Muslim state of Granada

RURAL GROWTH AND CRISIS

Between 1200 and 1500 the Latin West brought more land under cultivation, adopted new farming techniques, and made greater use of machinery and mechanical forms of energy. Yet for most rural Europeans—more than nine out of ten people were rural—this period was a time of calamity and struggle. Most rural men and women worked hard for meager returns and suffered mightily from the effects of famine, epidemics, warfare, and social exploitation. After the devastation caused from 1347 to 1351 by the plague known as the Black Death, social changes speeded up by peasant revolts released many persons from serfdom and brought some improvements to rural life.

Peasants, Population, and Plague

In 1200 most western Europeans were serfs, obliged to till the soil on large estates owned by the nobility and the church (see Chapter 10). In return for the use of a portion of their lord's land, serfs had to give their lord a share of their harvests and perform numerous labor

Rural French Peasants   Many scenes of peasant life in winter are visible in this small painting by the Flemish Limbourg brothers from the 1410s. Above the snow-covered beehives one man chops firewood, while another drives a donkey loaded with firewood to a little village. At the lower right a woman, blowing on her frozen fingers, heads past the huddled sheep and hungry birds to join other women warming themselves in the cottage (whose outer wall the artists have cut away). (Musée Conde, Chantilly, France/Art Resource, NY)

services for him. Lords and serfs were not motivated to introduce extensive improvements in farming practices because each side knew it would get only part of the larger harvest such efforts would bring.

As a consequence of the inefficiency of farming practices and their obligations to landowners, peasants received meager returns for their hard work. Despite the existence of numerous religious holidays, peasant culti-

vators labored some 54 hours a week in their fields. More than half of that labor was in support of the local nobility. Each noble household typically rested on the labors of from fifteen to thirty peasant families. The standard of life in the lord's stone castle or manor house stood in sharp contrast to the peasant's one-room thatched cottage containing little furniture and no luxuries.

Scenes of rural life show both men and women at work in the fields, although there is no reason to believe that equality of labor meant equality of decision making at home. In the peasant's hut as elsewhere in medieval Europe, women were subordinate to men. The influential theologian Thomas Aquinas° (1225–1274) spoke for his age when he argued that, although both men and women were created in God's image, there was a sense in which "the image of God is found in man, and not in woman: for man is the beginning and end of woman; as God is the beginning and end of every creature."[1]

Rural poverty was not simply the product of inefficient farming methods and social inequality. It also resulted from the rapid growth of Europe's population. In 1200 China's population may have surpassed Europe's by two to one; by 1300 the population of each was about 80 million. China's population fell because of the Mongol conquest (see Chapter 14). Why Europe's more than doubled between 1100 and 1445 is uncertain. Some historians believe that the reviving economy may have stimulated the increase. Others argue that warmer-than-usual temperatures reduced the number of deaths from starvation and exposure while the absence of severe epidemics lessened deaths from disease.

Whatever the causes, more people required more productive ways of farming and new agricultural settlements. One new technique gaining widespread acceptance in northern Europe increased the amount of farmland available for producing crops. Instead of following the custom of leaving half of their land fallow (uncultivated) every year to regain its fertility, some farmers tried a new **three-field system.** They grew crops on two-thirds of their land each year and planted the third field in oats. The oats stored nitrogen and rejuvenated the soil, and it could be used to feed plow horses. In much of Europe, however, farmers continued to let half of their land lie fallow and to use oxen (less efficient but cheaper than horses) to pull their plows.

Population growth also led to the foundation of new agricultural settlements. In the twelfth and thirteenth centuries large numbers of Germans migrated into the fertile lands east of the Elbe River and into the eastern Baltic states. Knights belonging to Latin Christian religious orders slaughtered or drove away native inhabi-

Aquinas (uh-KWY-nuhs)

tants who had not yet adopted Christianity. For example, during the thirteenth century, the Order of Teutonic Knights conquered, resettled, and administered a vast area along the eastern Baltic that later became Prussia (see Map 16.3 on page 412). Other Latin Christians founded new settlements on lands conquered from the Muslims and Byzantines in southern Europe and on Celtic lands in the British Isles.

By draining swamps and clearing forests, people also brought new land under cultivation within the existing boundaries of the Latin West. But as population continued to rise, some people had to farm lands that had poor soils or were vulnerable to flooding, frost, or drought. The result was a decline in average crop yields after 1250 and an increase in the number of people living at the edge of starvation, vulnerable to even slight changes in the food supply resulting from bad weather or the disruptions of war. According to one historian, "By 1300, almost every child born in western Europe faced the probability of extreme hunger at least once or twice during his expected 30 to 35 years of life."[2] One unusually cold spell led to the Great Famine of 1315–1317, during which starvation was widespread in Europe.

In time the cumulative effect of such crises might have reduced the population to a size that existing agricultural methods could more readily support. However, what actually eased population pressure was not famine but the **Black Death.** This terrible plague seems to have originated in India and then struck Mongol armies attacking the city of Kaffa° on the Black Sea in 1346 (see Chapter 13). A year later Genoese° traders in Kaffa carried the disease back to Italy and southern France. During the next two years the Black Death spread across Europe, in some places carrying off two-thirds of the population. Overall the epidemic may have killed one of every three western Europeans by the time it subsided.

The plague's symptoms were ghastly to behold. Victims developed boils the size of eggs in their groins and armpits, black blotches on their skin, foul body odors, and severe pain. In most cases, death came within a few days. To prevent the plague from spreading, town officials closed their gates to people from infected areas and burned the victims' possessions. Such measures helped to spare some communities but could not halt the advance of the disease across Europe (see Map 16.1). It is now known that the Black Death was the bubonic plague, a disease that was spread not just from person to person but also by the bites of fleas that infested the fur of certain rats. But even if medieval Europeans had been aware of that route of infection, they could have done little to eliminate the rats, which thrived on urban refuse.

The plague left its mark not only physically but psychologically, bringing home to people how sudden and unexpected death could be. In response to the plague some people became more religious, giving money to the church or hitting themselves with iron-tipped whips to atone for their sins. Others chose to enjoy life while they still had it, spending their money on fancy clothes, feasts, and drinking. Whatever their mood, most people soon resumed their daily routines. Life went on.

Although population gradually rebounded from the losses caused by the Black Death, recovery was slow and uneven because of periodic returns of plague. By 1400 Europe's population had regained only the levels of 1200. Not until after 1500 did it rise above its preplague levels. Meanwhile, China was recovering from its thirteenth-century losses (see Chapter 14).

Social Rebellion

In addition to its demographic and psychological effects, the Black Death set off social changes in western Europe. Skilled and manual laborers who survived demanded higher pay for their services. At first authorities tried to freeze wages at the old levels. Seeing such repressive measures as a plot by the rich, peasants rose up against wealthy nobles and churchmen. During a widespread revolt in France in 1358, known as the Jacquerie, peasants looted castles and killed dozens of persons. Urban unrest also took place. In a large revolt led by Wat Tyler in 1381, English peasants invaded London, calling for an end to all forms of serfdom and to most kinds of manorial dues. Angry demonstrators murdered the archbishop of Canterbury and many royal officials. Authorities put down these rebellions with even greater bloodshed and cruelty, but they could not stave off the higher wages and other social changes the rebels demanded.

Serfdom practically disappeared in western Europe as peasants bought their freedom or ran away. Many free persons who got higher wages from the landowners saved their money and bought their own land in depopulated areas. Many large English landowners who could no longer afford to hire enough fieldworkers to farm their lands began pasturing sheep for their wool. Others grew less labor-intensive crops or made greater use of draft animals and labor-saving tools. Because the plague had not killed wild and domesticated animals, more meat was available for each survivor and more leather for shoes. Thus the welfare of the rural masses generally improved after the Black Death, though the gap between rich and poor remained wide.

In urban areas employers had to raise wages to attract enough workers to replace those killed by the

---

Kaffa (KAH-fah)   **Genoese** (JEN-oh-eez)

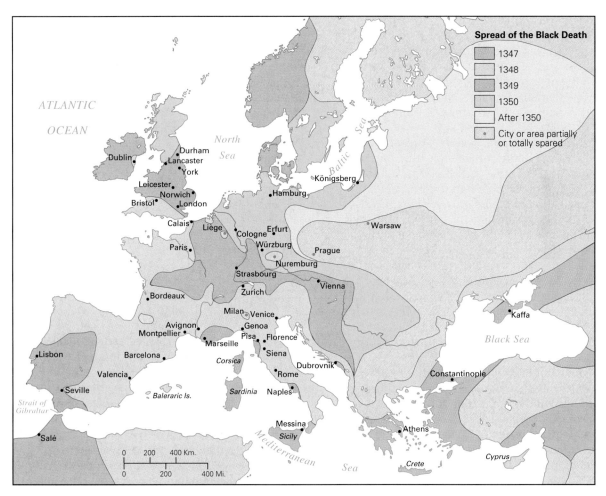

Map 16.1 The Black Death in Fourteenth-Century Europe Spreading out of southwestern China along the routes opened by Mongol expansion, the plague reached the Black Sea port of Kaffa in 1346. This map documents its deadly progress year by year from there into the Mediterranean and north and east across the face of Europe.

plague. Guilds (see below) found it necessary to reduce the period of apprenticeship. Competition within crafts also became more common. Although the overall economy shrank with the decline in population, per capita production actually rose.

Mills and Mines

Despite calamities and conflicts, the use of mechanical energy, mining, and metallurgy grew so much in the centuries before 1500 that some historians have spoken of an "industrial revolution" in medieval Europe. That may be too strong a term, but the landscape fairly bristled with mechanical devices. Mills powered by water or wind were used to grind grain and flour, saw logs into lumber, crush olives, tan leather, make paper, or perform other useful tasks.

England's many rivers had some 5,600 functioning watermills in 1086. After the year 1200 such mills spread rapidly across the western European mainland. By the early fourteenth century entrepreneurs had crammed 68 watermills into a one-mile section of the Seine° River in Paris. A mill's **water wheel** could be turned by the flow of a river beneath it or by the weight of water falling over the top of the wheel. For maximum efficiency, dams were built to ensure a steady flow of water throughout the year. Some watermills in France and England were designed to harness the power of ocean tides.

Seine (sen)

Watermills on the Seine River in Paris
Sacks of grain were brought to these mills under the bridge called the Grand Pont to be ground into flour. The water wheels were turned by the river flowing under them. Gears translated the vertical motion of the wheels into the horizontal motion of the millstones. (Bibliothèque Nationale de France)

Windmills also were common, especially in dry lands like Spain, where the flow of rivers was too irregular for efficient watermills, and in northern Europe, where the power of the wind could be tapped even in winter when ice made water wheels useless. Neither type of mill was a new invention nor unique to Europe. Water wheels and windmills had long been common in the Islamic world, but people in the medieval Latin West used such devices to harness the power of nature on a much larger scale than did people elsewhere.

Mills were expensive to build, but nature furnished the energy to run them for free. Over time, mills returned great profits to their owners. Some mills were built by individuals or monasteries, but most were built by groups of investors. The ability of mill owners to grow rich by using wind or water power to grind grain often aroused the jealousy of their neighbors. In his *Canterbury Tales* the English poet Geoffrey Chaucer (c. 1340–1400) captured millers' unsavory reputation (not always deserved) by portraying a miller as "a master-hand at stealing grain" by pushing down on the balance scale with his thumb.[3]

Waterpower also made possible such a great expansion of iron making that some historians say Europe's real Iron Age was in the later Middle Ages, not in antiquity. Water powered the stamping mills that broke up the iron, the trip hammers that pounded it, and the bellows (first documented in the West in 1323) that raised temperatures to the point where the iron was liquid enough to be poured into molds. Blast furnaces capable of producing high-quality iron are documented from 1380. The finished products included everything from armor to nails, from horseshoes to agricultural tools.

The demand for iron stimulated iron mining in many parts of Europe. In addition, new silver, lead, and copper mines in Austria and Hungary supplied metal for coins and church bells, cannon and statues. Techniques of deep mining developed in Central Europe were introduced farther west in the latter part of the fifteenth century. A building boom led to more stone quarrying in France during the eleventh, twelfth, and thirteenth centuries than during all of the millennia of ancient Egypt.

The rapid growth of industry produced significant changes in the landscape. Towns grew outward and new ones were founded, dams and canals changed the flow of rivers, and the countryside was scarred by quarry pits and mines tunneled into hillsides. Pollution sometimes became a serious problem. Urban tanneries (factories that cured and processed leather) dumped acidic wastewater back into streams, where it mixed with human waste and the runoff from slaughterhouses. The first recorded antipollution law was passed by the English Parliament in 1388, although enforcement was difficult.

One of the most dramatic environmental changes during these centuries was deforestation. Trees were cut to provide timber for buildings and for ships. Tanneries stripped bark to make acid for tanning leather. Many forests were cleared to make room for farming. The use of wood for fuel, especially by the glass and iron industries, was also a great consumer of forests. Charcoal—used to produce the high temperatures that the glass, iron, and other industries required—was made by controlled burning of oak or other hardwood. It is estimated that a single iron furnace could consume all the trees within five-eighths of a mile (1 kilometer) in just 40 days. As a consequence of all these demands, many once-dense forests in western Europe were greatly depleted in the later Middle Ages, except for those that powerful landowners protected as hunting preserves.

Map 16.2 Trade and Manufacturing in Later Medieval Europe The economic revival of European cities was associated with great expansion of commerce. Notice the concentration of wool and linen textile manufacturing in northern Italy, the Netherlands, and England; the importance of trade in various kinds of foodstuffs; and the slave-exporting markets in Cairo, Kiev, and Rostov.

URBAN REVIVAL

In the tenth century not a single town in the Latin West could compare in wealth and comfort—still less in size—with the cities in the Byzantine Empire and the Islamic caliphates. Yet by the later Middle Ages wealthy commercial centers stood all along the Mediterranean, Baltic, and Atlantic, as well as on major rivers draining into these bodies of water (see Map 16.2). The greatest cities in the East were still larger, but those in the West were undergoing greater commercial, cultural, and administrative changes. Their prosperity was visible in impressive new churches, guild halls, and residences. This urban revival is a measure of the Latin West's recovery from the economic decline that had followed the collapse of the Roman Empire (see Chapter 10) as well as an illustration of how the West's rise was aided by its ties to other parts of the world.

Trading Cities

Most urban growth in the Latin West after 1200 was due to the continuing growth of trade and manufacturing. The greatest part of the trade was between cities and their hinterlands, but long-distance trade also stimulated urban revival. Cities in northern Italy in particular benefited from maritime trade with the bustling port cities of the eastern Mediterranean and, through them, with the great markets of the Indian Ocean and East Asia. In northern Europe commercial cities in the County of Flanders (roughly today's Belgium) and around the Baltic Sea profited from growing regional networks and from overland and sea routes to the Mediterranean.

Two events in the thirteenth century strengthened Italian trade with the eastern Mediterranean. One was the Venetian-inspired assault in 1204 against the city of Constantinople, which dominated the passage between the Mediterranean and Black Seas. Misleadingly named the "Fourth Crusade," this assault by Latin Christians on Greek Christians had little to do with the religious differences between them and much to do with Venice's desire to gain better access to the rich trade of the East. By crippling Byzantine power, Venetians were able to seize the strategic island of Crete in the eastern Mediterranean and expand their trading colonies around the Black Sea. The other boon to Italian trade was the westward expansion of the Mongol Empire, which opened trade routes from the Mediterranean to China (see Chapter 13).

To take advantage of that trade, the young Marco Polo set out from Venice in 1271 on the long trek across Central Asia. After reaching the Mongol court, the talented Marco spent many years serving the emperor Khubilai Khan as an ambassador and as the governor of a Chinese province. Marco later authored a fabulous account of these adventures and of the treacherous return voyage through the Indian Ocean that finally brought him back to Venice in 1295, after an absence of twenty-four years. Yet even in relatively prosperous Venice, few who had not seen for themselves could believe that Asian lands could be so wealthy.

When the disintegration of the Mongol Empire in the fourteenth century halted direct European contact with distant Asian markets, Venetian merchants purchased eastern silks and spices brought by other middlemen to Constantinople, Beirut, and Alexandria. Three times a year galleys (ships powered by some sixty oarsmen each) sailed in convoys of two or three from Venice, bringing back some 2,000 tons of goods. Other merchants began to explore new overland or sea routes.

Venice was not the only Latin city whose trade expanded in the thirteenth century. The sea trade of Genoa on the west coast of northern Italy probably equaled that of Venice. Genoese merchants built up colonies on the shores of the eastern Mediterranean and around the Black Sea as well as in the western Mediterranean. In northern Europe an association of trading cities known as the **Hanseatic° League** conducted extensive trade in the Baltic, including the newly conquered coasts of Prussia, and as far east as Novgorod in Russia and westward across the North Sea to London.

By the late thirteenth century, Genoese galleys from the Mediterranean and Hanseatic ships from the Baltic were converging on a third area, the trading and manufacturing cities in Flanders. In the Flemish towns of Bruges°, Ghent°, and Ypres° skilled artisans turned raw wool from English sheep into a fine cloth that was softer and smoother than the coarse "homespuns" from simple village looms. Dyed in vivid hues, these Flemish textiles appealed to wealthy Europeans who formerly had imported their fine textiles from Asia.

Along the overland route connecting Flanders and northern Italy important trading fairs developed in the Champagne° region of Burgundy. The Champagne fairs began as regional markets, meeting once or twice a year, where manufactured goods, livestock, and farm produce were exchanged. When Champagne came under the control of the king of France at the end of the twelfth

---

Hanseatic (han-see-AT-ik)   **Bruges** (broozh)
Ghent (gent [hard *g* as in *get*])   **Ypres** (EE-pruh)
Champagne (sham-PAIN)

Flemish Weavers, Ypres The spread of textile weaving gave employment to many people in the Netherlands. The city of Ypres in Flanders (now northern Belgium) was an important textile center in the thirteenth century. This drawing from a fourteenth-century manuscript shows a man and a woman weaving cloth on a horizontal loom, while a child makes thread on a spinning wheel. (Stedelijke Openbare Bibliotheek, Ypres)

century, royal guarantees of safe conduct to all merchants turned the regional markets into international fairs. A century later fifteen Italian cities had permanent consulates in Champagne to represent the interests of their citizens. The fairs were also important for currency exchange and other financial transactions. During the fourteenth century the volume of trade grew so large that it became cheaper to send Flemish woolens to Italy by sea rather than overland on pack animals. As a consequence, the fairs of Champagne lost some of their international trade but remained important regional markets.

Textile manufacturing also spread beyond Flanders. In the late thirteenth century the English monarchy raised taxes on the export of raw wool, making it more profitable to turn wool into cloth in England rather than in Flanders. Flemish textile specialists crossed the English Channel and introduced the spinning wheel and other devices to England. As a consequence the number of sacks of raw wool exported annually from England fell from 35,000 at the beginning of the fourteenth century

to 8,000 in the mid-fifteenth, while exports of English wool cloth rose from 4,000 pieces just before 1350 to 54,000 a century later.

Florence was also developing as a wool-making center. Local banking families financed the production of much of the high-quality cloth that in the past Florence had bought from the Flemish cities. In 1338, Florence manufactured 80,000 pieces of cloth, while importing only 10,000. These changes in the textile industry show how competition promoted the spread of manufacturing and encouraged new specialties.

The growing textile industries made extensive use of windmills and water wheels. The power of wind and water was channeled through gears, pulleys, and belts to drive all sorts of machinery. The thriving textile industry in Flanders, for example, used mills to clean and thicken woven cloth by beating it in water, a process known as fulling. Another application of mill power was in papermaking. Although papermaking had been common in China and the Muslim world for centuries before it spread to southern Europe in the thirteenth century,

Westerners were the first to use machines to do the heavy work in its manufacturing.

In the fifteenth century Venice surpassed its European rivals in the volume of its trade in the Mediterranean as well as across the Alps into Central Europe. Its skilled craftspeople also manufactured luxury goods once obtainable only from eastern sources, notably silk and cotton textiles, glassware and mirrors, jewelry, and paper. At the same time exports of Italian and northern European woolens to the eastern Mediterranean were also on the rise. In the space of a few centuries western European cities had used the eastern trade to increase their prosperity and then reduce their dependence on eastern goods.

Civic Life

Trading cities in Europe offered people more social freedom than rural places. Most northern Italian and German cities were independent states, much like the port cities of the Indian Ocean basin (see Chapter 15). Other European cities held special royal charters that exempted them from the authority of local nobles. Because of their autonomy, they were able to adapt to changing market conditions more quickly than were cities in China and the Islamic world that were controlled by imperial authorities. Social mobility was also easier in the Latin West because anyone who lived in a chartered city for over a year might claim freedom. Thus cities became a refuge for all sorts of ambitious individuals, whose labor and talent added to their wealth.

Cities were also home to most of Europe's Jews. The largest population of Jews was in Spain, where earlier Arab rulers had made them welcome. Many commercial cities elsewhere welcomed Jews for their manufacturing and business skills. Despite the official protection they received from some Christian princes and kings, Jews were subject to violent religious persecutions or expulsions in times of crisis, such as during the Black Death (see Society and Culture: Blaming the Black Death on the Jews, Strasbourg, 1349). In 1492 the Spanish monarchs expelled all Jews in the name of religious and ethnic purity. In all of the medieval West only the papal city of Rome left its Jews undisturbed throughout the centuries before 1500.

Opportunities for individual enterprise in European cities came with many restrictions. Within most towns and cities powerful associations known as guilds dominated civic life. A **guild** was an association of craft specialists, such as silversmiths, or of merchants who worked in a particular trade. Each guild regulated the

Jewish Procession, 1517   This delegation of wealthy Jews paid their respects to the newly elected Pope Martin V and sought the papacy's continued support of their community's traditional rights and privileges. Pope Martin granted their wishes and, as was common, the pope's personal physician was a Jew. (Bibliothèque Nationale de France)

business practices of its members and the prices they charged. Guilds also trained apprentices and promoted members' interests with the city government. By denying membership to outsiders and all Jews, guilds perpetuated the interests of the families that already were members. Guilds also perpetuated male dominance of most skilled jobs.

Nevertheless, despite serious restrictions, in a few places women were able to join guilds either on their own or as the wives, widows, or daughters of male guild members. Large numbers of poor women also toiled in nonguild jobs in urban textile industries and in the food and beverage trades, generally receiving lower wages than their male counterparts.

Blaming the Black Death on the Jews, Strasbourg, 1349

Prejudice against Jews was common in the Latin West. This selection is from the official chronicles of the upper-Rhineland towns.

In the year 1349 there occurred the greatest epidemic that ever happened. Death went from one end of the earth to the other, on that side and this side of the [Mediterranean] sea. . . . This epidemic also came to Strasbourg in the summer of [that] year, and . . . about sixteen thousand people died.

In the matter of this plague the Jews throughout the world were reviled and accused in all lands of having caused it through the poison which they are said to have put into the water and the wells—that is what they were accused of—and for this reason the Jews were burnt all the way from the Mediterranean into Germany, but not in Avignon, for the pope protected them there.

. . . The deputies of the city of Strasbourg were asked what they were going to do with their Jews. They answered and said that they knew no evil of them. [The town-council was deposed. A new council gave in to the mob and arrested the Jews.]

On Saturday—that was St. Valentine's Day—they burnt the Jews on a wooden platform in their cemetery. There were about two thousand people of them. Those who wanted to baptize themselves were spared. Many small children were taken out of the fire and baptized against the will of their fathers and mothers. And everything that was owed to the Jews was cancelled, and the Jews had to surrender all pledges and notes that they had taken for debts. The council, however, took the cash that the Jews possessed and divided it among the working-men proportionately. The money was indeed the thing that killed the Jews. If they had been poor and if the feudal lords had not been in debt to them, they would not have been burnt.

To what extent was the massacre of the Strasbourg Jews due to fear of the plague, to prejudice, and to greed? Why did some officials try to protect them?

Source: Jacob R. Marcus, ed., *The Jew in the Medieval World: A Source Book, 315–1791* (1938; reprint, Westport, CT: Greenwood, 1975), 45–47. Reprinted with permission of the Hebrew Union College Press, Cincinnati.

For many women marriage to wealthy men could be a means of social advancement. One of Chaucer's *Canterbury Tales* concerns a woman from Bath, a city in southern England, who became wealthy by marrying a succession of old men for their money (and then two other husbands for love), "aside from other company in youth." She was also a skilled weaver, Chaucer says: "In making cloth she showed so great a bent, / She bettered those of Ypres and of Ghent."

By the fifteenth century, the growth of commerce had given rise to a new class of wealthy merchant-bankers. They operated on a vast scale and specialized in money changing, loans, and investments made on behalf of other parties. Merchants great and small used their services, but the merchant-bankers also handled the financial transactions of ecclesiastical and secular officials. They arranged for the transmission to the pope of funds known as Peter's pence, a collection taken up annually in every church in the Latin West. They also ad-vanced large sums of money to the princes and kings of Europe to support their wars and lavish courts. Some merchant-bankers even developed their own news services, gathering information on any topic that could affect their businesses.

Florence pioneered new banking services. Its financiers invented checking accounts, organized private shareholding companies (the forerunners of modern corporations), and improved bookkeeping techniques. In the fifteenth century, the Medici° family of Florence operated banks in Italy, Flanders, and London. Medicis also controlled the government of Florence and were important patrons of the arts. By 1500 the greatest banking family in western Europe was the Fuggers° of Augsburg, who had ten times the Medici bank's lending capital. Starting out as cloth merchants under Jacob "the Rich"

Medici (MED-ih-chee)   **Fuggers** (FOOG-uhrz)

(1459–1525), the family branched into many other activities, including the trade in Hungarian copper, essential for casting cannon.

Most money lenders were Jews because Latin Christians generally considered charging interest (usury) sinful. Christian bankers had to devise ways to profit from loans indirectly in order to get around the Latin Church's condemnation of usury. Some borrowers agreed to repay a loan in another currency at a rate of exchange favorable to the lender. Others added to the borrowed sum a "gift" in thanks to the lender. For example, in 1501 church officials agreed to repay a loan of 6,000 gold ducats in five months to the Fuggers along with a "gift" of 400 ducats, amounting to an effective interest rate of 16 percent a year. In fact, the return was much smaller since the church failed to repay the loan on time.

Despite the money to be made by some, for most residents of western European cities poverty and squalor was the norm. Even for the wealthy, European cities generally lacked civic amenities, such as public baths and water supply systems, that had existed in the cities of Western antiquity and still survived in cities of the Islamic Middle East.

Strasbourg Cathedral   Only one of the two spires originally planned for this Gothic cathedral was completed when work ceased in 1439. But the Strasbourg Cathedral was still the tallest masonry structure of medieval Europe. This engraving is from 1630. (Courtesy of the Trustees of the British Museum)

Gothic Cathedrals

Among the skilled people in greatest demand in the thriving cities of late medieval Europe were master builders and associated craftsmen. The finest and most expensive buildings these craftsmen designed and erected were **Gothic cathedrals**. Cities competed with one another in the magnificence of their guild halls, town halls, and other structures (see Environment and Technology: The Clock). But it was these new cathedrals, which made their appearance in about 1140 in France, that were the architectural wonders of their times.

One distinctive feature of the new cathedrals was the pointed, or Gothic, arch, which replaced the older round, or Roman, arch. Another was the external (flying) buttresses that stabilized the high, thin stone columns below the arches. Using this method of construction, master builders were able to push the Gothic cathedrals to great heights and to fill the outside walls with giant windows depicting religious scenes in brilliantly colored stained glass. During the next four centuries, interior heights went ever higher, towers and spires pierced the heavens, and walls became dazzling curtains of stained glass.

Cathedrals were designed and built by men with little or no formal education and limited understanding of the mathematical principles of modern civil engineering. Master masons sometimes miscalculated, and parts of some overly ambitious cathedrals collapsed. The record-high choir vault of Beauvais Cathedral, for instance—154 feet (47 meters) in height—came tumbling down in 1284. But practical experience was the greatest teacher, and as builders constantly invented novel solutions to the problems they encountered, success rose from the rubble of their mistakes. The cathedral spire in Strasbourg reached 466 feet (142 meters) into the air—as high as a 40-story building. The heights achieved by Gothic cathedrals were unsurpassed until the twentieth century.

The Clock

Clocks were a prominent feature of the Latin West in the late medieval period. The Song-era Chinese had built elaborate mechanical clocks centuries earlier (see Chapter 11), but the West was the first part of the world where clocks became a regular part of urban life. Whether mounted in a church steeple or placed on a bridge or tower, mechanical clocks proclaimed Western people's delight with mechanical objects, concern with precision, and display of civic wealth.

The word *clock* comes from a word for bell. The first mechanical clocks that appeared around 1300 in western Europe were simply bells with an automatic mechanical device to strike the correct number of hours. The most elaborate Chinese clock had been powered by falling water, but this was impractical in cold weather. The levers, pulleys, and gears of European clocks were powered by a weight hanging from a rope wound around a cylinder. An "escapement" lever regulated the slow, steady unwinding.

Enthusiasm for building expensive clocks came from various parts of the community. For some time, monks had been using devices to mark the times for prayer. Employers welcomed chiming clocks to regulate the hours of their employees. Universities used them to mark the beginning and end of classes. Prosperous merchants readily donated money to build a splendid clock that would display their city's wealth. The city of Strasbourg, for example, built a clock in the 1350s that included statues of the Virgin, the Christ Child, and the three Magi, a mechanical rooster, the signs of the zodiac, a perpetual calendar, and an astrolabe—and it could play hymns too!

By the 1370s and 1380s clocks were common enough for their measured hours to displace the older system that varied the length of the hour in proportion to the length of the day. Previously, for example, the London hour had varied from 38 minutes in winter to 82 minutes in summer. By 1500 clocks had numbered faces with hour and minute hands. Small clocks for indoor use were also in vogue. Though not very accurate by today's standards, these clocks were still a great step forward. Some historians consider the clock the most important of the many technological advances of the later Middle Ages because it fostered so many changes during the following centuries.

Early Clock This weight-driven clock dates from 1454. (Bodleian Library Oxford, Ms. Laud Misc. 570, 25v.)

LEARNING, LITERATURE, AND THE RENAISSANCE

Throughout the Middle Ages people in the Latin West lived amid reminders of the achievements of the Roman Empire. They wrote and worshiped in a version of its language, traveled its roads, and obeyed some of its laws. Even the vestments and robes of medieval popes, kings, and emperors were modeled on the regalia of Roman officials. Yet early medieval Europeans lost touch with much of the learning of Greco-Roman antiquity. More vivid was the biblical world they heard about in the Hebrew and Christian scriptures.

Intellectuals in the Latin West struggled to recover the learning and values of of the Greco-Roman classical past. A small revival of learning associated with the court of Charlemagne in the ninth century was followed by a larger *renaissance* (rebirth) in the twelfth century. Many growing cities became centers of intellectual and artistic life. One expression of this cultural revival was found in the universities established across the Latin West after 1200. In the mid-fourteenth century the pace of intellectual and artistic life quickened in what is often called the **Renaissance,** which began in northern Italy and later spread to northern Europe. Some Italian authors saw the Italian Renaissance as a sharp break with an age of darkness. A more balanced view might reveal this era as the high noon of a day that had been dawning for several centuries.

Universities and Scholarship

Before 1100 Byzantine and Islamic scholarship generally surpassed scholarship in Latin Europe. When southern Italy was wrested from the Byzantines and Sicily and Toledo from the Muslims in the eleventh century, many manuscripts of Greek and Arabic works came into Western hands and were translated into Latin for readers eager for new ideas. The manuscripts included works of ancient philosophy by Plato and Aristotle° and Greek treatises on medicine, mathematics, and geography that were previously unknown to medieval Latin Christians. In addition, some scientific and philosophical writings by medieval Muslims came into the Latin West. The works of the Iranian philosopher Ibn Sina° (980–1037),

known in the West as Avicenna°, were particularly influential. The Jewish scholarly community contributed significantly to the translation and explication of Arabic and other manuscripts.

As in the early Middle Ages (see Chapter 10), Christian monasteries were important centers of learning, and the church was an important advocate of scholarship. Joining the older monastic schools after 1200 were new institutions of higher education: independent colleges. The thirteenth century saw the foundation of two new religious orders, the Dominicans and the Franciscans, some of whose most talented members would have distinguished careers as university professors.

The colleges established in Paris and Oxford in the late twelfth and thirteenth centuries may have been modeled after similarly endowed places of study long known in the Islamic world—madrasas, which provided subsidized housing for poor students and paid the salaries of their teachers. The Latin West, however, was the first part of the world to establish modern **universities,** degree-granting corporations specializing in multidisciplinary research and advanced teaching. Between 1300 and 1500 the twenty oldest universities in the Latin West were joined by some sixty others. Some of the first universities were started by students; others were founded as guilds to which all the professors of a city belonged. These teaching guilds, like the guilds overseeing manufacturing and commerce, set the standards for membership in their profession, trained apprentices and masters, and defended their professional interests.

Universities set the curriculum of study for each discipline and instituted comprehensive final examinations for degrees. After passing exams at the end of their apprenticeship, students received a first diploma known as a "license" to teach. More advanced students, who completed longer training and defended a masterwork of scholarship, became "masters" and "doctors." The colleges of Paris were gradually absorbed into the city's university, but the colleges of Oxford and Cambridge remained independent, self-governing organizations.

Universally recognized degrees, well-trained professors, and exciting new texts promoted the rapid spread of universities in late medieval Europe. Because all university courses were taught in Latin, students and masters could move freely across political and linguistic lines, seeking out the university that offered the courses they wanted and that had the most interesting professors. Universities offered a variety of programs of study but generally were identified with a particular specialty.

Aristotle (AR-ih-stah-tahl)   **Ibn Sina** (IB-uhn SEE-nah)

Avicenna (av-uh-SEN-uh)

Bologna° was famous for the study of law; Montpellier and Salerno specialized in medicine; Paris and Oxford were best known for theology.

The prominence of theology partly reflected the fact that many students were destined for ecclesiastical careers, but theology was also seen as "queen of the sciences"—the central discipline that encompassed all knowledge. For this reason thirteenth-century theologians sought to synthesize the newly rediscovered philosophical works of Aristotle, as well as the commentaries by Avicenna, with the revealed truth of the Bible. Their daring efforts to synthesize reason and faith were known as **scholasticism°**.

The most notable scholastic work was the *Summa Theologica°*, issued between 1267 and 1273 by Thomas Aquinas, a brilliant Dominican priest who was a professor of theology at the University of Paris. Although Aquinas's exposition of Christian belief organized on Aristotelian principles was later accepted as a masterly demonstration of the reasonableness of Christianity, scholasticism upset many traditional thinkers. Some church authorities even tried to ban Aristotle from the curriculum. There also was much rivalry between the leading Dominican and Franciscan theological scholars over the next two centuries. However, the considerable freedom of medieval universities from both secular and religious authorities enabled the new ideas of accredited scholars eventually to prevail over the fears of church administrators.

Humanists and Printers

The intellectual achievements of the later Middle Ages were not confined to the universities. Talented writers of this era made important contributions to literature and literary scholarship. A new technology in the fifteenth century helped bring works of literature and scholarship to a larger audience.

Dante Alighieri° (1265–1321) completed a long, elegant poem, the *Divine Comedy*, shortly before his death. This supreme expression of medieval preoccupations tells the allegorical story of Dante's journey through the nine circles of hell and the seven terraces of purgatory, followed by his entry into Paradise. His guide through hell and purgatory is the Roman poet Virgil. His guide through Paradise is Beatrice, a woman whom he had loved from afar since childhood and whose death inspired him to write the poem.

The *Divine Comedy* foreshadows some of the literary fashions of the later Italian Renaissance. Like Dante, later Italian writers made use of Greco-Roman classical themes and mythology and sometimes chose to write not in Latin but in the vernacular languages spoken in their regions, in order to reach a broader audience (Dante used the vernacular spoken in Tuscany°.)

The English poet Geoffrey Chaucer was another vernacular writer of this era. Many of his works show the influence of Dante, but he is most famous for the *Canterbury Tales*, the lengthy poem written in the last dozen years of his life. These often humorous and earthy tales, told by fictional pilgrims on their way to the shrine of Thomas à Becket in Canterbury, are cited several times in this chapter because they present a marvelous cross-section of medieval people and attitudes.

Dante also influenced a literary movement that began in his native Florence in the mid-fourteenth century. The writers of the fourteenth and fifteenth centuries who championed the traditions pioneered by Dante are **humanists**. The term refers to their interest in grammar, rhetoric, poetry, history, and moral philosophy (ethics)—subjects known collectively as the humanities, an ancient discipline. With the brash exaggeration characteristic of new intellectual fashions, humanist writers such as the poet Francesco Petrarch° (1304–1374) and the poet and storyteller Giovanni Boccaccio° (1313–1375) proclaimed a revival of respect for the classical Greco-Roman tradition, which, they claimed, for centuries had lain buried under the rubble of the Middle Ages.

This idea of a rebirth of learning long dead too readily dismisses the efforts of scholars at the monasteries and universities who for centuries had been recovering all sorts of Greco-Roman learning and the writers such as Dante (whom the humanists revered) who anticipated humanist interests by a generation. Yet it is hard to exaggerate the beneficial influences of the humanists on their own times and later, as educators, advisers, and reformers. The humanists' greatest influence was in reforming secondary education. They introduced a curriculum centered on the languages and literature of Greco-Roman antiquity, which they felt provided intellectual discipline, moral lessons, and refined tastes. This curriculum dominated European secondary schools well into the twentieth century. Humanist influence in

---

Bologna (buh-LOHN-yuh)   scholasticism (skoh-LAS-tih-sizm)
Summa Theologica (SOOM-uh thee-uh-LOH-jih-kuh)
Dante Alighieri (DAHN-tay ah-lee-GYEH-ree)

Tuscany (TUS-kuh-nee)
Franceso Petrarch (fran-CHES-koh PAY-trahrk)
Giovanni Boccaccio (jo-VAH-nee boh-KAH-chee-oh)

the universities was less and came mostly after 1500. Despite the humanists' influence, theology, law, medicine, and branches of philosophy other than ethics remained prominent in university education during this period.

Though some humanists followed Dante in composing literary works in vernacular languages, many tried to duplicate the elegance of classical Latin and (to a lesser extent) Greek, which they revered as the pinnacle of learning, beauty, and wisdom. Boccaccio is most famous for his vernacular writings, which resemble Dante's, and especially for the *Decameron*, an earthy work that has much in common with Chaucer's boisterous tales. Under Petrarch's influence, however, Bocaccio turned to writing in classical Latin.

As humanist scholars of the fifteenth century mastered Latin and Greek, they turned their language skills to restoring the original texts of Greco-Roman writers and of the Bible. By comparing many different manuscripts, they eliminated errors introduced by generations of copyists. To aid in this task, Pope Nicholas V (r. 1447–1455) created the Vatican Library, buying scrolls of Greco-Roman writings and paying to have accurate copies and translations made. Working independently, the respected Dutch scholar Erasmus° of Rotterdam (ca. 1466–1536) produced a critical edition of the New Testament in Greek. Erasmus was able to correct many errors and mistranslations in the Latin text that had been in general use throughout the Middle Ages. In later years, this humanist priest and theologian also wrote—in classical Latin—influential moral guides including the *Enchiridion militis christiani* (*The Manual of the Christian Knight*, 1503) and *The Education of a Christian Prince* (1515).

The influence of the humanists was enhanced after 1450 because new printing technology increased the availability of their critical editions of ancient texts, literary works, and moral guides. The Chinese were the first to use carved wood blocks for printing (see Chapter 14), and block-printed playing cards from China were circulating in Europe before 1450. Then, around 1450, three technical improvements revolutionized printing: (1) movable pieces of type consisting of individual letters, (2) new ink suitable for printing on paper, and (3) the **printing press,** a mechanical device that pressed inked type onto sheets of paper.

The man who did most to perfect printing was Johann Gutenberg° (ca. 1394–1468) of Mainz. The Gutenberg Bible of 1454, the first book in the West printed from

A French Printshop, 1537   A workman operates the "press," quite literally a screw device that presses the paper to the inked type. Other employees examine the printed sheets, each of which holds four pages. When folded, the sheets make a book. (Giraudon/Art Resource, NY)

movable type, was a beautiful and finely crafted work that bore witness to the printer's years of diligent experimentation. As printing spread to Italy and France, humanists worked closely with printers. Erasmus worked for years as an editor and proofreader for the great Italian scholar-printer Aldo Manuzio (1449–1515) in Venice. Manuzio's press published many critical editions of classical Latin and Greek texts.

By 1500 at least 10 million printed works had issued forth from presses in 238 towns in western Europe. Though the days of mass-produced paperbacks were still in the future, the printers and humanists had launched a revolution that was already having an effect on students, scholars, and a growing number of literate people who could gain access to ancient texts as well as to unorthodox political and religious tracts.

Erasmus (uh-RAZ-muhs)
Johann Gutenberg (yoh-HAHN GOO-ten-burg)

The Medici Family   This detail of a mural painting of 1459 by Benozzo Gozzoli depicts the arrival of the Magi at the birthplace of the Christ Child, but the principal figures in this detail are important members of the wealthy Medici family of Florence and their entourage in costumes of their day. The African bowman on the left is an interesting detail, showing how common African servants and slaves became in southern Europe during the Renaissance. (Florence, Palazzo Medici-Riccardi)

Renaissance Artists

The fourteenth and fifteenth centuries were as distinguished for their masterpieces of painting, sculpture, and architecture as they were for their scholarship. Although artists continued to depict biblical subjects, the spread of Greco-Roman learning led many artists, especially in Italy, to portray Greco-Roman deities and mythical tales. Another popular trend was depicting the scenes of daily life.

However, neither daily life nor classical images were entirely new subjects. Renaissance art, like Renaissance scholarship, owed a major debt to earlier generations. The Florentine painter Giotto° (ca. 1267–1337) had a formidable influence on the major Italian painters of the fifteenth century who credited him with singlehandedly reviving the "lost art of painting." In his religious scenes Giotto replaced the stiff, staring figures of the Byzantine style, which were intended to overawe viewers, with more natural and human portraits with whose emotions of grief and love viewers could identify. Rather than floating on backgrounds of gold leaf, his saints inhabit earthly landscapes.

Another important contribution to the early Italian Renaissance was a new painting technology from north of the Alps. The Flemish painter Jan van Eyck° (ca. 1390–1441) mixed his pigments with linseed oil in place of the diluted egg yolk of earlier centuries. Oil paints were slower drying and more versatile, and they gave pictures a superior luster. Van Eyck's use of the technique for his own masterfully realistic paintings on religious and domestic themes was quickly copied by talented painters of the Italian Renaissance.

The great Italian Leonardo da Vinci° (1452–1519), for example, used oil paints for his famous *Mona Lisa*. Renaissance artists like Leonardo were masters of many media. His other works include the fresco (painting in wet plaster) *The Last Supper*, bronze sculptures, as well as imaginative designs for airplanes, submarines, and tanks. Leonardo's younger contemporary Michelangelo° (1472–1564) painted frescoes of biblical scenes on the ceiling of the Sistine Chapel in the Vatican, sculpted statues of David and Moses, and designed the dome for a new Saint Peter's Basilica.

The patronage of wealthy and educated merchants and prelates did much to foster an artistic blossoming in the cities of northern Italy and Flanders. The Florentine

Giotto (JAW-toh)

Jan van Eyck (yahn vahn-IKE)
Leonardo da Vinci (lay-own-AHR-doh dah-VIN-chee)
Michelangelo (my-kuhl-AN-juh-low)

banker Cosimo de' Medici (1389–1464), for example, spent immense sums on paintings, sculpture, and public buildings. His grandson Lorenzo (1449–1492), known as "the Magnificent," was even more lavish. The church was also an important source of artistic commissions. Seeking to restore Rome as the capital of the Latin Church, the papacy° launched a building program culminating in the construction of the new Saint Peter's Basilica and a residence for the pope.

These scholarly and artistic achievements exemplify the innovation and striving for excellence of the Late Middle Ages. The new literary themes and artistic styles of this period had lasting influence on Western culture. But the innovations in the organization of universities, in printing, and in oil painting had wider implications, for they were later adopted by cultures all over the world.

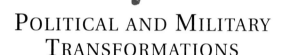

POLITICAL AND MILITARY TRANSFORMATIONS

Stronger and more unified states and armies developed in western Europe in parallel with the economic and cultural revivals. In no case were transformations smooth and steady, and the political changes unfolded somewhat differently in each state (see Map 16.3). During and after the prolonged struggle of the Hundred Years War, French and English monarchs forged closer ties with the nobility, the church and the merchants. The consolidation of Spain and Portugal was linked to crusades against Muslim states. In Italy and Germany, however, political power remained in the hands of small states and loose alliances.

Monarchs, Nobles, and the Church

Thirteenth-century states still shared many features of early medieval state (see Chapter 10). Hereditary monarchs occupied the peak of the political pyramid, but their powers were limited by modest treasuries and the rights possessed by others. Below them came the powerful noblemen who controlled vast estates and whose advice and consent was often required on important matters of state. The church, jealous of its traditional rights and independence, was another powerful body within each kingdom. Towns, too, had acquired many rights and privileges. Indeed, the towns in Flanders, the Hanseatic League, and Italy were nearly independent from royal interference. The power within kingdoms, however, was far from balanced and clearly defined, as some examples will illustrate.

In theory nobles were vassals of the reigning monarchs and were obliged to furnish them with armored knights in time of war. In practice vassals sought to limit the monarch's power and protect their own rights and privileges. The nobles' privileged economic and social position rested on the large estates that had been granted to their ancestors in return for supporting and training knights in armor to serve in a royal army.

In the year 1200 knights were still the backbone of western European fighting forces, but two changes in weaponry were bringing into question their central military role and thus the system of estates that supported them. The first involved the humble arrow. Improved crossbows could shoot metal-tipped arrows with such force that they could pierce helmets and light body armor. Professional crossbowmen, hired for wages, became increasingly common and much feared. Indeed, a church council in 1139 outlawed the crossbow as being too deadly for use against Christians. The ban was largely ignored. The second innovation in military technology that weakened the feudal system was the firearm. This Chinese invention, using gunpowder to shoot stone or metal projectiles (see Environment and Technology: Explosive Power in Chapter 14), further transformed the medieval army.

The church also resisted royal control. In 1302 the outraged Pope Boniface VIII (r. 1294–1303) went so far as to assert that divine law made the papacy superior to "every human creature," including monarchs. This theoretical claim of superiority was challenged by force. Issuing his own claim of superiority, King Philip "the Fair" of France (r. 1285–1314) sent an army to arrest the pope. After this treatment hastened Pope Boniface's death, Philip engineered the election of a French pope who established a new papal residence at Avignon° in southern France in 1309.

With the support of the French monarchy, a succession of popes residing in Avignon improved church discipline—but at the price of compromising the papacy's neutrality in the eyes of other rulers. Papal authority was further eroded by the **Great Western Schism** (1378–1415), a period when rival papal claimants at Avignon and Rome vied for the loyalties of Latin Christians. The conflict was eventually resolved by returning the papal residence to its traditional location, the city of Rome. The papacy regained its independence, but the long crisis broke the pope's ability to challenge the rising power of the larger monarchies.

papacy (PAY-puh-see)

Avignon (ah-vee-NYON)

Latin Christendom

- In 1000 C.E.
- Added, 1000–1200
- Lost 1000–1200 (Regained 1200–1500)
- Added 1200–1500
- Lost, 1200–1500

—— English holdings, 1360

—— Boundary of the Holy Roman Empire

Map 16.3 Europe in 1453 This year marked the end of the Hundred Years War between France and England and the fall of the Byzantine capital city of Constantinople to the Ottoman Turks. Muslim advances into southeastern Europe were offset by the Latin Christian reconquests of Islamic holdings in southern Italy and the Iberian Peninsula and by the conversion of Lithuania.

King Philip gained an important advantage at the beginning of his dispute with Pope Boniface when he persuaded a large council of French nobles to grant him the right to collect a new tax, which sustained the monarchy for some time. Earlier, by adroitly using the support of the towns, the saintly King Louis IX of France (r. 1226–1270) had been able to issue ordinances that applied throughout his kingdom without first obtaining the nobles' consent. But later kings' efforts to extend royal authority sparked prolonged resistance by the most powerful vassals.

In 1200, in the smaller kingdom of England, royal power was already well centralized as a result of consolidation that had taken place after the Norman conquest of 1066. The Anglo-Norman kings also extended their realm by assaults on their Celtic neighbors. Between 1200 and 1400 they incorporated Wales and reasserted control over most of Ireland. Nevertheless, English royal power was far from absolute. In the span of just three years the ambitions of King John (r. 1199–1216) were severely set back. First he was compelled to acknowledge the pope as his overlord (1213). Then he lost his bid to reassert claims to Aquitaine in southern France (1214). Finally he was forced to sign Magna Carta ("Great Charter," 1215), which affirmed that monarchs were subject to established law, confirmed the independence of the church and the city of London, and guaranteed nobles' hereditary rights.

Separate from the challenges to royal authority presented by the church and the nobles were the alliances and conflicts generated by the hereditary nature of monarchial rule. Monarchs and their vassals both entered into strategic marriages with a view to increasing their lands and their wealth. Such marriages showed scant regard for the emotions of the wedded parties or for "national" interests. Besides unhappiness for the parties involved, these marriages often led to conflicts over far-flung inheritances. Although these dynastic struggles and shifting boundaries make European politics seem chaotic in comparison with the empires of Asia, some important changes were emerging from them. Aided by the changing technology of war, monarchs were strengthening their authority and creating more stable (but not entirely fixed) state boundaries within which the nations of western Europe would in time develop. Nobles lost autonomy and dominance on the battlefield but retained their social position and important political roles.

The Hundred Years War

A key example of the transformation in politics and fighting methods was the long conflict between the king of France and his vassals known as the **Hundred Years War** (1337–1453). These vassals included the kings of England (for lands that belonged to their Norman ancestors), the counts of prosperous and independent-minded Flanders in the north, the dukes of Brittany, and the dukes of Burgundy. In typical fashion, the conflict grew out of a marriage alliance.

The marriage of Princess Isabella of France to King Edward II of England (r. 1307–1327) was meant to ensure that this powerful vassal remained loyal to the French monarchy. However, none of Isabella's three brothers, who served in turn as kings of France, produced a male heir, so Isabella's son, King Edward III of England (r. 1327–1377), laid claim to the French throne in 1337. After French courts instead awarded the throne to a more distant (and more French) cousin, Edward decided to fight for his rights. Other vassals joined in a series of battles for the French throne that persisted until 1453.

The new military technology shaped the conflict. Early in the war French cavalry was reinforced by hired Italian crossbowmen, but arrows from another late medieval innovation, the English longbow, nearly annihilated the French force. Adopted from the Welsh, the 6-foot (108-meter) longbow could shoot farther and more rapidly than the crossbow. Although arrows from longbows could not pierce armor, in concentrated volleys they often found gaps in the knights' defenses or struck their less-well-protected horses. To defend against these weapons, armor became heavier and more encompassing, making it harder for a knight to move. A knight who was pulled off his steed by a foot soldier armed with a pike (hooked pole) was usually unable to get up to defend himself.

In later stages of the Hundred Years War firearms became more prominent. At first cannon were more likely to spook the horses with their smoke and noise than hit these rapidly moving targets. Then as cannon grew larger, they proved quite effective in blasting holes through the heavy walls of medieval castles and towns. The first use of such artillery against the French, in the Battle of Agincourt (1415), gave the English an important victory.

The English gains that followed were halted by a young French peasant woman, Joan of Arc. Believing she was instructed by God to save France, she donned a knight's armor and rallied the French troops that defeated the English in 1429 just as they seemed close to conquering France. Shortly after this victory, Joan had the misfortune to fall into English hands. She was tried by English churchmen for being a witch and was burned at the stake in 1431.

In the final battles of the Hundred Years War, French forces used large cannon to demolish the walls of once-secure castles held by the English and their allies. The truce that ended the struggle in 1453 left the French monarchy in firm control.

New Monarchies in France and England

To contemporaries the advantage in the Hundred Years War seemed to shift first to one side and then to the other, but in retrospect the war can be seen as a watershed that helped produce **new monarchies** in France and England. These monarchies differed from their medieval predecessors in having greater centralization of power, more fixed "national" boundaries, and stronger representative institutions.

Barred from their efforts to add France to their domains, English monarchs after 1453 directed their efforts to consolidating control over territory within the British Isles, though the Scots strongly defended their independence. With the English defeated, the French monarchs also turned to consolidating their control over powerful noble families, especially when these happened to be headed by women. First, Mary of Burgundy (1457–1482) was forced to surrender most of her family's vast holdings to the king of France. Then in 1491, Anne of Brittany was compelled to marry the king of France, a step that led to the eventual incorporation of her duchy° into France.

Nobles' resistance was undermined by changes in military technology. The smaller and more mobile cannon developed in the late fifteenth century proved very effective in battles and against castle walls. And improvements in hand-held firearms—by the late fifteenth century they could pierce even the heaviest armor—led to the final rout of the armored knight. These changes in military hardware meant that armies depended less on knights and more on bowmen, pikemen, musketeers, and specialized artillery units.

Because payment for the new armed forces came from the royal treasury, the new monarchies needed a way to finance their standing armies. Some funds came from nobles who were willing to convert their obligations to monarchs into money payments and to cough up taxes for wars they supported. For example, in 1439 and 1445 Charles VII of France (r. 1422–1461) won from his vassals the right to levy a new tax on land. The tax not only enabled him to pay the costs of the current war with England but provided the financial base of the French monarchy for the next 350 years.

Taxes on merchants were another source of new revenue. King Edward III was the first English ruler to tax the wool trade, which provided most of the funds for fighting the Hundred Years War. Some Christian princes and kings taxed Jewish merchants or extorted large contributions from wealthy towns in return for their protection. Individual merchants sometimes curried royal favor with loans, even though such debts could be difficult or dangerous to collect. For example, the wealthy fifteenth-century French merchant Jacques Coeur° gained many social and financial benefits for himself and his family by lending money to important members of the French court, but he was ruined when his jealous debtors accused him of murder and had his fortune confiscated.

A third source of revenue was the church. The clergy in a kingdom often agreed to make a voluntary contribution to support a war. English and French monarchs gained further control of church funds in the fifteenth century by winning the right to appoint important church officials in their realms. In so doing, the monarchs were not abandoning the church. Indeed, they often used state power to enforce religious orthodoxy in their realms more vigorously than the popes had ever been able to do. But, as reformers complained, the church's spiritual mission was often subordinated to political and economic concerns.

As a result of these complex dynastic and military struggles, political power in England and France had shifted by the end of the fifteenth century in favor of the monarchs and away from the nobility and the church. But the shift was only partial. Nobles retained their social position and their roles as government officials and military officers. Moreover, in both England and France in 1500 monarchs had to deal with representative institutions that had not existed in 1200. The English Parliament had become a permanent check on royal power: the House of Lords contained all the great nobles and English church officials; the House of Commons represented the towns and the leading citizens of the counties. In France a similar representative body known as the Estates General represented the church, the nobles, and the towns, though its rights were not so well entrenched as the English Parliament's.

Iberian Unification

The growth of Spain and Portugal into strong, centralized states was also shaped by struggles between kings and vassals, dynastic marriages and mergers, and warfare. But Spain and Portugal's **reconquest of Iberia** from Muslim rule was also a crusade to expand the boundaries of Latin Christianity. Such religious zeal did not rule out personal gain. The Christian Iberian knights who gradually pushed the borders of their kingdoms southward knew that to the victors would go

---

duchy (DUTCH-ee)

Coeur (cur)

the spoils. The spoils included irrigated farmland capable of producing an abundance of food, rich cities of glittering Moorish architecture, and ports offering access to the Mediterranean and the South Atlantic. Victorious Christian knights were often rewarded with a grant over the land and people in a newly conquered territory. Serving God, growing rich, and living off the labor of others became a way of life for the Iberian nobility.

The reconquest advanced in waves over several centuries; there were long pauses to consolidate the conquered territory and unify the Christian kingdoms. Toledo was taken in 1085 and made into a Christian outpost. The Atlantic port of Lisbon fell in 1147 with the aid of English crusaders on their way to capture the Holy Land. It became the new capital of Portugal and the kingdom's leading city, displacing the older capital of Oporto, whose name (meaning "the port") is the root of the word *Portugal*. The reconquest quickened in the thirteenth century. A Christian victory in 1212 broke the back of Muslim power in Iberia. During the next few decades Portuguese and Castilian forces captured the beautiful and prosperous cities of Cordova (1236) and Seville (1248) and in 1249 drove the Muslims from the southwestern corner of Iberia, known as Algarve° ("the west" in Arabic). Only the small kingdom of Granada hugging the Mediterranean coast remained in Muslim hands.

By incorporating Algarve in 1249, Portugal attained its modern territorial limits and turned to settling and revitalizing its newly acquired lands. The resettlement of peasants in these lands south of Lisbon did much to weaken serfdom in Portugal. After a long pause to colonize, Christianize, and consolidate this land, Portugal took the Christian reconquest to North Africa. In 1415, Portuguese knights seized the port city of Ceuta° in Morocco, where they learned more of the caravan trade in gold and slaves from south of the Sahara (see Chapter 15). During the next few decades Portuguese mariners sailed down the Atlantic coast of Africa in an effort to gain access to this rich trade and to make contact with African Christian allies (see Chapter 17).

Although it took the other Iberian kingdoms much longer to complete the reconquest, the struggle served to bring them together and to keep their Christian religious zealotry at a high pitch. The marriage of Princess Isabella of Castile and Prince Ferdinand of Aragon in 1469 led to the permanent union of their kingdoms into Spain a decade later when they inherited their respective thrones. Their conquest of Granada in 1492 secured the final piece of Muslim territory in Iberia for the new kingdom.

The year 1492 was also memorable because of Ferdinand and Isabella's sponsorship of the voyage from

Seville led by Christopher Columbus to the riches of the Indian Ocean (see Chapter 17). But a third event that year was as momentous an extension of the Spanish crusading mentality. Less than three months after Granada's fall, the monarchs ordered all Jews to be expelled from their kingdoms, and efforts to force the remaining Muslims to convert or leave led to a Muslim revolt at the end of 1499 that was not put down until 1501. The Spanish rulers expelled the last Muslims in 1502. Portugal also ordered the expulsion of all Jews from its kingdom in 1496, including 100,000 who had fled from Spain.

CONCLUSION

From an ecological perspective the later medieval history of the Latin West is a story of triumphs and disasters. Westerners excelled in harnessing the inanimate forces of nature with their windmills, water wheels, and sails. They mined and refined the mineral wealth of the earth, although localized pollution and deforestation were among the results. But their inability to improve food production and distribution as rapidly as their population grew created a demographic crisis that became a demographic calamity when the Black Death swept through Europe in the mid-fourteenth century.

From a regional perspective the centuries from 1200 to 1500 witnessed the coming together of the basic features of the modern West. States were of moderate size but had exceptional military capacity honed by frequent wars with one another. The ruling class, convinced that economic strength and political strength were inseparable, promoted the welfare of the urban populations that specialized in trade, manufacturing, and finance—and taxed their profits. Autonomous universities fostered intellectual excellence, and printing diffused the latest advances in knowledge. Art and architecture reached peaks of design and execution that set the standard for subsequent centuries. Perhaps most fundamentally, later medieval western Europe was a society fascinated by tools and techniques. In commerce, warfare, industry, and navigation, new inventions and improved versions of old ones underpinned the region's continuing dynamism.

From a global perspective these centuries marked the Latin West's change from a region dependent on cultural and commercial flows from the East to a region poised to export its culture and impose its power on other parts of the world. It is one of history's great ironies that many of the tools that the Latin West used to challenge Eastern supremacy had originally been borrowed from the East. Medieval Europe's mills, printing,

---

Algarve (ahl-GAHRV)   Ceuta (say-OO-tuh)

firearms, and navigational devices owed much to Eastern designs, just as its agriculture, alphabet, and numerals had in earlier times. Western European success depended as much on strong motives for expansion as on adequate means. Long before the first voyages overseas, population pressure, religious zeal, economic motives, and intellectual curiosity had expanded the territory and resources of the Latin West. From the late eleventh century onward such expansion of frontiers was notable in the English conquest of Celtic lands, in the establishment of crusader and commercial outposts in the eastern Mediterranean and Black Seas, in the massive German settlement east of the Elbe River, and in the reconquest of southern Iberia from the Muslims. The early voyages into the Atlantic were an extension of similar motives in a new direction.

■ Key Terms

Latin West	universities
three-field system	scholasticism
Black Death	humanists (Renaissance)
water wheel	printing press
Hanseatic League	Great Western Schism
guild	Hundred Years War
Gothic cathedrals	new monarchies
Renaissance (European)	reconquest of Iberia

■ Suggested Reading

A fine guide to the Latin West (including its ties to eastern Europe, Africa, and the Middle East) is Robert Fossier, ed., *The Cambridge Illustrated History of the Middle Ages*, vol. 3, *1250–1520* (1986). Denys Hay, *Europe in the Fourteenth and Fifteenth Centuries*, 2d ed. (1989), is comprehensive and up-to-date. For the West's economic revival and growth see Robert S. Lopez, *The Commercial Revolution of the Middle Ages, 950–1350* (1976), and Harry A. Miskimin, *The Economy of Early Renaissance Europe, 1300–1460* (1975).

For fascinating primary sources see James Bruce Ross and Mary Martin McLaughlin, eds., *The Portable Medieval Reader* (1977) and *The Portable Renaissance Reader* (1977). *The Notebooks of Leonardo da Vinci*, ed. Pamela Taylor (1960), show this versatile genius at work.

Technological change is surveyed by Arnold Pacey, *The Maze of Ingenuity: Ideas and Idealism in the Development of Technology* (1974); Jean Gimpel, *The Medieval Machine: The Industrial Revolution of the Middle Ages* (1977); and William H. McNeill, *The Pursuit of Power: Technology, Armed Force, and Society Since A.D. 1000* (1982). For a key aspect of the environment see Roland Bechmann, *Trees and Man: The Forest in the Middle Ages* (1990).

Charles Homer Haskins, *The Rise of the Universities* (1923; reprint, 1957), is a brief, lighthearted introduction; more detailed and scholarly is Olef Pedersen, *The First Universities: Studium Generale and the Origins of University Education in Europe* (1998). Johan Huizinga, *The Waning of the Middle Ages* (1924), is the classic account of the "mind" of the fifteenth century. A multitude of works deal with the Renaissance but few in any broad historical context. Lisa Jardine, *Worldly Goods: A New History of the Renaissance* (1996), is well illustrated and balanced; see also John R. Hale, *The Civilization of Europe in the Renaissance* (1995).

For social history see Georges Duby, *Rural Economy and Country Life in the Medieval West* (1990), for the earlier centuries. George Huppert, *After the Black Death: A Social History of Early Modern Europe* (1986), takes the analysis past 1500. Brief lives of individuals are found in Eileen Power, *Medieval People*, new ed. (1997), and Frances Gies and Joseph Gies, *Women in the Middle Ages* (1978). More systematic are the essays in Mary Erler and Maryanne Kowaleski, eds., *Women and Power in the Middle Ages* (1988). Vita Sackville-West, *Saint Joan of Arc* (1926; reprint, 1991), is a readable introduction to this extraordinary person.

Key events in the Anglo-French dynastic conflict are examined by Christopher Alland, *The Hundred Years War: England and France at War, ca. 1300–ca. 1450* (1988). Joseph F. O'Callaghan, *A History of Medieval Spain* (1975), provides the best one-volume coverage; for more detail see Jocelyn N. Hillgarth, *The Spanish Kingdoms*, 2 vols. (1976, 1978). Barbara W. Tuchman, *A Distant Mirror: The Calamitous 14th Century* (1978), gives a popular account of the crises of that era. P. Ziegler, *The Black Death* (1969), supplies a thorough introduction.

The Latin West's expansion is well treated by Robert Bartlett, *The Making of Europe: Conquest, Colonization, and Cultural Change* (1993); J. R. S. Phillips, *The Medieval Expansion of Europe*, new ed. (1998); and P. E. Russell, *Portugal, Spain and the African Atlantic, 1343–1492* (1998).

Francis C. Oakley, *The Western Church in the Later Middle Ages* (1985), is a reliable summary of modern scholarship. Kenneth R. Stow, *Alienated Minority: The Jews of Medieval Latin Europe* (1992), provides a fine survey up through the fourteenth century. For pioneering essays on the Latin West's external ties see Khalil I. Semaan, ed., *Islam and the Medieval West: Aspects of Intercultural Relations* (1980).

■ Notes

1. Quoted in Marina Warner, *Alone of All Her Sex: The Myth and Cult of the Virgin Mary* (New York: Random House, 1983), 179.
2. Harry Miskimin, *The Economy of the Early Renaissance, 1300–1460* (Englewood Cliffs, NJ: Prentice-Hall, 1969), 26–27.
3. Quotations here and later in the chapter are from Geoffrey Chaucer, *The Canterbury Tales*, trans. Nevill Coghill (New York: Penguin Books, 1952), 25, 29, 32.

17

THE MARITIME REVOLUTION,
to 1550

Global Maritime Expansion Before 1450 • Iberian Expansion, 1400–1550 •
Encounters with Europe, 1450–1550
ENVIRONMENT AND TECHNOLOGY: Vasco da Gama's Fleet
SOCIETY AND CULTURE: European Male Sexual Dominance Overseas

Columbus Prepares to Cross the Atlantic, 1492   This later representation shows Columbus
with the ships, soldiers, priests, and seamen that were part of Spain's enterprise.

n 1511 the young Ferdinand Magellan sailed from Europe around the southern tip of Africa and eastward across the Indian Ocean as a member of the first Portuguese expedition to explore the East Indies (maritime Southeast Asia). Eight years later, this time in the service of Spain, he headed an expedition that sought to demonstrate the feasibility of reaching the East Indies by sailing westward from Europe. By the middle of 1521 Magellan's expedition had achieved its goal by sailing across the Atlantic, rounding the southern tip of South America, and crossing the Pacific Ocean—but at a high price.

One of the five ships that had set out from Spain in 1519 was wrecked on a reef, and the captain of another deserted and sailed back to Spain. The passage across the vast Pacific took much longer than anticipated, resulting in the deaths of dozens of sailors due to starvation and disease. In the Philippines, Magellan himself was killed on April 27, 1521, while aiding a local king who had promised to become a Christian. Magellan's successor met the same fate a few days later.

To consolidate their dwindling resources, the expedition's survivors burned the least seaworthy of their remaining three ships and transferred the men and supplies from that ship to the smaller *Victoria*, which continued westward across the Indian Ocean, around Africa, and back to Europe. Magellan's flagship, the *Trinidad*, tried unsuccessfully to recross the Pacific to Central America. The *Victoria*'s return to Spain on September 8, 1522, was a crowning example of Europeans' new ability and determination to make themselves masters of the oceans. A century of daring and dangerous voyages backed by the Portuguese crown had opened new routes through the South Atlantic to Africa, Brazil, and the rich trade of the Indian Ocean. Rival voyages sponsored by Spain since 1492 had opened new contacts with the American continents. Now the unexpectedly broad Pacific Ocean had been crossed as well. A maritime revolution was under way that would change the course of history.

That new maritime skill marked the end of an era in which the flow of historical influences tended to move from east to west. Before 1500, most overland and maritime expansion had come from Asia, as had the most useful technologies and the most influential systems of belief. Asia also had been home to the most powerful states and the richest trading networks. The Iberians set out on their voyages of exploration to reach Eastern markets, and their success began a new era in which the West gradually became the world's center of power, wealth, and innovation.

The maritime revolution created many new contacts, alliances, and conflicts. Some ended tragically for individuals like Magellan. Some were disastrous for entire populations: Amerindians, for instance, suffered conquest, colonization, and a rapid decline in numbers. Sometimes the results were mixed: Asians and Africans found both risks and opportunities in their new relations with the visitors from Europe.

As you read this chapter, ask yourself the following questions:

- Why did Portugal and Spain undertake voyages of exploration?
- Why do the voyages of Magellan and other Iberians mark a turning point in world history?
- What were the consequences for the different peoples of the world of the new contacts resulting from these voyages?

GLOBAL MARITIME EXPANSION BEFORE 1450

Since ancient times travel across the salt waters of the world's seas and oceans had been one of the great challenges to people's technological ingenuity. Ships had to be sturdy enough to survive heavy winds and waves, and pilots had to learn how to cross featureless expanses of water to their destination. In time ships, sails, and navigational techniques perfected in the more protected seas were tried on the vast, open oceans.

However complex the solutions and dangerous the voyages, the rewards of sea travel made it all worthwhile. For ships could move goods and people more quickly and cheaply than any form of overland travel then possible. Because of its challenges and rewards, sea travel attracted adventurers. To cross the unknown waters, find new lands, and open up new trade or settlements was an

CHRONOLOGY

	Pacific Ocean	Atlantic Ocean	Indian Ocean
Pre 1400	**400–1300** Polynesian settlement of Pacific islands	**770–1200** Viking voyages **1300s** Settlement of Madeira, Azores, Canaries **Early 1300s** Mali voyages	
1400 to 1500		**1418–1460** Voyages of Henry the Navigator **1440s** Slaves from West Africa **1482** Portuguese at Gold Coast and Kongo **1486** Portuguese at Benin **1488** Bartolomeu Dias reaches Indian Ocean **1492** Columbus reaches Caribbean **1493** Columbus returns to Caribbean (second voyage) **1498** Columbus reaches mainland of South America (third voyage) **1492–1500** Spanish conquer Hispaniola	**1405–1433** Voyages of Zheng He **1497–1498** Vasco da Gama reaches India
1500 to 1550	 **1519–1522** Magellan expedition	**1500** Cabral reaches Brazil **1513** Ponce de León explores Florida **1519–1520** Cortés conquers Aztec Empire **1531–1533** Pizarro conquers Inca Empire	**1505** Portuguese bombard Swahili Coast cities **1510** Portuguese take Goa **1511** Portuguese take Malacca **1515** Portuguese take Hormuz **1535** Portuguese take Diu **1538** Portuguese defeat Ottoman fleet **1539** Portuguese aid Ethiopia

exciting prospect. For these reasons some men on every continent had long turned their attention to the sea.

By 1450 much had been accomplished and much remained undone. Daring mariners had discovered and settled most of the islands of the Pacific, the Atlantic, and the Indian Oceans. The greatest success was the trading system that united the peoples around the Indian Ocean. But no individual had yet crossed the Pacific in either direction. Even the narrower Atlantic was a barrier that kept the peoples of the Americas, Europe, and Africa in ignorance of each other's existence. The inhabitants of Australia were likewise completely cut off from contact with the rest of humanity. All this was about to change.

The Pacific Ocean

The vast distances Polynesian peoples voyaged out of sight of land across the Pacific Ocean are one of the most impressive feats in maritime history before 1450 (see Map 17.1). Though they left no written records, it is now clear that over several thousand years intrepid mariners from the Malay° Peninsula of Southeast Asia explored and settled the island chains of the East Indies and moved onto New Guinea and the smaller islands of Melanesia°. Beginning some time before the

Malay (May-LAY)   **Melanesia** (mel-uh-NEE-zhuh)

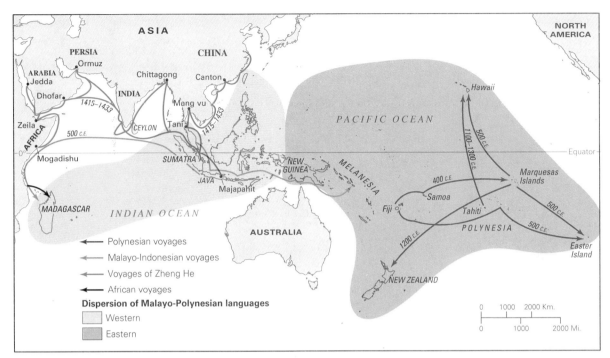

Map 17.1   Exploration and Settlement in the Indian and Pacific Oceans Before 1500   Over many centuries mariners originating in Southeast Asia gradually colonized the islands of the Pacific and Indian Oceans. The Chinese voyages led by Zheng He in the fifteenth century were lavish official expeditions.

Common Era (C.E.), a new wave of expansion from the area of Fiji brought the first humans to the islands of the central Pacific known as Polynesia. The easternmost of the Marquesas° Islands were reached about 400 C.E.; Easter Island, 2,200 miles (3,540 kilometers) off the coast of South America, was settled a century later. From the Marquesas Polynesian sailors sailed to the Hawaiian Islands as early as 500 C.E. They settled New Zealand about 1200. Then between 1100 and 1300, new voyages northward from Tahiti to Hawaii brought more Polynesian settlers across the more than 2,000 nautical miles (4,000 kilometers) to Hawaii.

Until recent decades some historians argued that Polynesians could have reached the eastern Pacific islands only by accident because they lacked navigational devices to plot their way. Others wondered how Polynesians could have overcome the difficulties, illustrated by Magellan's flagship, *Trinidad*, of sailing eastward across the Pacific. In 1947 one energetic amateur historian of the sea, Thor Heyerdahl°, argued that Easter Island and Hawaii were actually settled from the Americas. He

sought to prove his theory by sailing his balsawood raft *Kon Tiki* westward from Peru.

Although some Amerindian voyagers did use ocean currents to travel northward from Peru to Mexico between 300 and 900 C.E., there is now considerable evidence that the settlement of the islands of the eastern Pacific was the result of planned expansion by Polynesian mariners. The first piece of evidence is the fact that the languages of these islanders are all closely related to the languages of the western Pacific and ultimately to those of Malaya. The second is the finding that accidental voyages could not have brought sufficient numbers of men and women for founding a new colony along with all the plants and domesticated animals that were basic to other Polynesian islands.

In 1976 a Polynesian crew led by Ben Finney used traditional navigational methods to sail an ocean canoe from Hawaii south to Tahiti. The *Hokulea* was a 62-foot-long (19-meter-long) double canoe patterned after old oceangoing canoes that sometimes were as long as 120 feet (37 meters). Not only did the *Hokulea* prove seaworthy, but, powered by an inverted triangular sail and steered by paddles (not by a rudder), it was able to sail across the winds at a sharp enough angle to make the dif-

---

Marquesas (mar-KAY-suhs)   Heyerdahl (HIGH-uhr-dahl)

Polynesian Canoes   Pacific Ocean mariners sailing canoes such as these, shown in an eighteenth-century painting, made epic voyages of exploration and settlement. A large platform connects two canoes at the left, providing more room for the members of the expedition, and a sail supplements the paddlers. ("Tereoboo, King of Owyhee, bringing presents to Captain Cook," D. L. Ref. p. xx 2f. 35. Courtesy, The Dixon Library, State Library of New South Wales)

ficult voyage, just as ancient mariners must have done. Perhaps even more remarkable, the *Hokulea*'s crew was able to navigate to their destination using only their observation of the currents, stars, and evidence of land.

The Indian Ocean

While Polynesian mariners were settling Pacific islands, other Malayo-Indonesians were sailing westward across the Indian Ocean and colonizing the large island of Madagascar off the southeastern coast of Africa. These voyages continued through the fifteenth century. To this day the inhabitants of Madagascar speak Malayo-Polynesian languages. However, part of the island's population is descended from Africans who had crossed the 600 miles (1,000 kilometers) from the mainland to Madagascar, most likely in the centuries just before 1500.

Other peoples had been using the Indian Ocean for trade since ancient times. The landmasses of Southeast Asia and eastern Africa that enclose the Indian Ocean's sides, and the Indian subcontinent that juts into its middle, provided coasts that seafarers might safely follow and coves for protection. Moreover, seasonal winds known as monsoons are so predictable and steady that navigation using sailing vessels called dhows° was less difficult and dangerous in ancient times than elsewhere.

The rise of medieval Islam gave Indian Ocean trade an important boost. The great Muslim cities of the Middle East provided a demand for valuable commodities. Even more important were the networks of Muslim traders that tied the region together. Muslim traders shared a common language, ethic, and law and actively spread their religion to distant trading cities. By 1400 there were Muslim trading communities all around the Indian Ocean.

The Indian Ocean traders operated largely independently of the empires and states that they served, but in East Asia imperial China's rulers were growing more and more interested in these wealthy ports of trade. In 1368 the Ming dynasty overthrew Mongol rule and began expansionist policies to reestablish China's predominance and prestige abroad.

Having restored Chinese dominance in East Asia, the Ming next moved to establish direct contacts with

dhow (dow)

Chinese Junk   This modern drawing shows how much larger one of Zheng He's ships was than one of Vasco da Gama's vessels. Watertight interior bulkheads made junks the most seaworthy large ships of the fifteenth century. Sails made of pleated bamboo matting hung from the junk's masts and a stern rudder provided steering. European ships of exploration, though smaller, were faster and more maneuverable. (Dugald Stermer)

the peoples around the Indian Ocean. In choosing to send out seven imperial fleets between 1405 and 1433, the Ming may have been motivated partly by curiosity. The fact that most of the ports the fleets visited were important in the Indian Ocean trade suggests that enhancing China's commerce was also a motive. Yet because the expeditions were far larger than needed for exploration or promoting trade, their main purpose probably was to inspire awe of Ming power and achievements.

The Ming expeditions into the Indian Ocean basin were launched on a scale that reflected imperial China's resources and importance. The first consisted of sixty-two specially built "treasure ships," large Chinese junks each about 300 feet long by 150 feet wide (90 by 45 meters). There were also at least a hundred smaller vessels, most of which were larger than the flagship in which Columbus later sailed across the Atlantic. Each treasure ship had nine masts, twelve sails, many decks, and a carrying capacity of 3,000 tons (six times the capacity of Columbus's entire fleet). One expedition carried over 27,000 individuals, including infantry and cavalry troops. The ships would have been armed with small cannon, but in most Chinese sea battles arrows from highly accurate crossbows dominated the fighting.

At the command of the expeditions was Admiral **Zheng He**° (1371–1435). A Chinese Muslim with ancestral connections to the Persian Gulf, Zheng was a fitting emissary to the increasingly Muslim-dominated Indian Ocean basin. The expeditions carried other Arabic-speaking Chinese as interpreters.

One of these interpreters kept a journal recording the customs, dress, and beliefs of the people visited, along with the trade, towns, and animals of their countries. Among his observations were these: exotic animals such as the black panther of Malaya and the tapir of Sumatra; beliefs in legendary "corpse headed barbarians" whose heads left their bodies at night and caused infants to die; the division of coastal Indians into five classes, which correspond to the four Hindu varna and a separate Muslim class; the fact that traders in the rich Indian trading port of Calicut° could perform error-free calculations by counting on their fingers and toes rather than using the Chinese abacus. After his return, the interpreter went on tour in China, telling of these exotic places and "how far the majestic virtue of [China's] imperial dynasty extended."[1]

Zheng He (jung huh)   **Calicut** (KAL-ih-kut)

The Chinese "treasure ships" carried rich silks, precious metals, and other valuable goods intended as gifts for distant rulers. In return those rulers sent back gifts of equal or greater value to the Chinese emperor. Although the main purpose of these exchanges was diplomatic, they also stimulated trade between China and its southern neighbors. For that reason they were welcomed by Chinese merchants and manufacturers. Yet commercial profits could not have offset the huge cost of the fleets.

Interest in new contacts was not confined to the Chinese side. In 1415–1416 at least three trading cities on the Swahili° Coast of East Africa sent delegations to China. The delegates from one of them, Malindi, presented the emperor of China with a giraffe, creating quite a stir among the normally reserved imperial officials. Such African delegations may have encouraged more contacts, for the next three of Zheng's voyages were extended to the African coast. Unfortunately no documents record how Africans and Chinese reacted to each other during these historic meetings between 1417 and 1433. It appears that China's lavish gifts stimulated the Swahili market for silk and porcelain. An increase in Chinese imports of pepper from southern Asian lands also resulted from these expeditions.

Had the Ming court wished to promote trade for the profit of its merchants, Chinese fleets might have continued to play a dominant role in Indian Ocean trade. But some high Chinese officials opposed increased contact with peoples whom they regarded as barbarians with no real contribution to make to China. Such opposition caused a suspension in the voyages from 1424 to 1431, and after the final expedition of 1432 to 1433, no new fleets were sent out. Later Ming emperors focused their attention on internal matters in their vast empire. China's withdrawal left a power vacuum in the Indian Ocean.

The Atlantic Ocean

The greatest mariners of the Atlantic in the early Middle Ages were the Vikings. These northern European raiders and pirates used their small, open ships to attack coastal European settlements for several centuries. They also discovered and settled one island after another in the North Atlantic during these warmer than usual centuries. Like the Polynesians, the Vikings had neither maps nor navigational devices, but they managed to find their way wonderfully well using their knowledge of the heavens and the seas.

The Vikings first settled Iceland in 770. From there some moved on to Greenland in 982, and by accident one group sighted North America in 986. Fifteen years later Leif Ericsson established a short-lived Viking settlement on the island of Newfoundland, which he called Vinland. When a colder climate returned after 1200, the northern settlements in Greenland went into decline, and Vinland became only a mysterious place mentioned in Norse sagas.

Some southern Europeans also used the maritime skills they had acquired in the Mediterranean and coastal Atlantic to explore the Atlantic. In 1291 two Vivaldo brothers from Genoa set out to sail through the South Atlantic and around Africa to India. They were never heard of again. Other Genoese and Portuguese expeditions into the Atlantic in the fourteenth century discovered (and settled) the islands of Madeira°, the Azores°, and the Canaries.

There is also written evidence of African voyages of exploration in the Atlantic in this period. The celebrated Syrian geographer al-Umari (1301–1349) relates that when Mansa Kankan Musa°, the ruler of the West African empire of Mali, passed through Egypt on his lavish pilgrimage to Mecca in 1324, he told of voyages to cross the Atlantic undertaken by his predecessor, Mansa Muhammad. Muhammad had sent out four hundred vessels with men and supplies, telling them, "Do not return until you have reached the other side of the ocean or if you have exhausted your food or water." After a long time one canoe returned, reporting the others had been swept away by a "violent current in the middle of the sea." Muhammad himself then set out at the head of a second, even larger, expedition, from which no one returned.

In addition to sailing up the Pacific coast, early Amerindian voyagers from South America also colonized the West Indies. By the year 1000 Amerindians known as the **Arawak**° had moved up from the small islands of the Lesser Antilles (Barbados, Martinique, Guadaloupe) and into the Greater Antilles (Cuba, Hispaniola, Jamaica, and Puerto Rico) as well as into the Bahamas (see Map 17.2). Their route was followed in later centuries by the Carib, who by the late fifteenth century had overrun most Arawak settlements in the Lesser Antilles and were raiding parts of the Greater Antilles. From the West Indies Arawak and Carib also undertook voyages to the North American mainland.

Swahili (swah-HEE-lee)

Madeira (muh-DEER-uh)   Azores (A-zorz)
Mansa Kankan Musa (MAHN-suh KAHN-kahn MOO-suh)
Arawak (AR-uh-wahk)

Map 17.2 Middle America to 1533 Early Amerindian voyages from South America brought new settlers to the West Indies and western Mexico. The arrival of Europeans in 1492 soon led to the conquest and depopulation of Amerindians.

EUROPEAN EXPANSION, 1400–1550

The preceding survey shows that maritime expansion occurred in many parts of the world before 1450. The epic sea voyages sponsored by the Iberian kingdoms of Portugal and Spain are of special interest because they began a maritime revolution that profoundly altered the course of world history. The Portuguese and Spanish expeditions ended the isolation of the Americas and increased global interaction. The influence in world affairs of the Iberians and other Europeans who followed them overseas rose steadily in the centuries after 1500.

Iberian overseas expansion was the product of two related phenomena. First, Iberian rulers had strong economic, religious, and political motives to expand their contacts and increase their dominance. Second, improvements in their maritime and military technologies gave them the means to master treacherous and unfamiliar ocean environments, seize control of existing maritime trade routes, and conquer new lands.

Background to European Expansion

Why did Iberian kingdoms decide to sponsor voyages of exploration in the fifteenth century? Part of the answer lies in the individual ambitions and adventurous personalities of these states' leaders. Another part of the answer can be found in long-term tendencies in Europe and the Mediterranean. In many ways these voyages continued four trends evident in the Latin West since about the year 1000: (1) the revival of urban life and trade, (2) a struggle with Islamic powers for dominance of the Mediterranean that mixed religious motives with the desire for trade with distant lands, (3) growing intellectual curiosity about the outside world, and (4) a peculiarly European alliance between merchants and rulers.

The city-states of northern Italy took the lead in all of these developments. By 1450 they had well established trade links to northern Europe, the Indian Ocean, and the Black Sea, and their merchant princes had also sponsored an intellectual and artistic Renaissance. But there were two reasons why Italian states did not take the lead in exploring the Atlantic, even after the expansion of the Ottoman Empire disrupted their trade to the East and led other Christian Europeans to launch new religious wars against the Ottomans in 1396 and 1444. The first was that the trading states of Venice and Genoa preferred to continue the system of alliances with the Muslims that had given their merchants privileged access to the lucrative trade from the East. The second was that the ships of the Mediterranean were ill suited to the more violent weather of the Atlantic. However, many individual Italians played leading roles in the Atlantic explorations.

In contrast, the special history and geography of the Iberian kingdoms led them in a different direction. Part of that special history was centuries of anti-Muslim warfare that dated back to the eighth century when Muslim forces overran most of Iberia. By about 1250 the Iberian kingdoms of Portugal, Castile, and Aragon had conquered all the Muslim lands in Iberia except the southern kingdom of Granada. United by a dynastic marriage in 1469, Castile and Aragon conquered Granada in 1492. These territories were gradually amalgamated into Spain, sixteenth-century Europe's most powerful state.

Christian militancy continued to be an important motive for both Portugal and Spain in their overseas ventures. But the Iberian rulers and their adventurous subjects were also seeking material returns. With only a modest share of the Mediterranean trade, they were much more willing than the Italians to take risks to find new routes through the Atlantic to the rich trades of Africa and Asia. Moreover, both were participants in the shipbuilding changes and the gunpowder revolution that were under way in Atlantic Europe. Though not centers of Renaissance learning, both were especially open to new geographical knowledge. Finally, both states were blessed with exceptional leaders.

Portuguese Voyages

Portugal's decision to invest significant resources in new exploration rested on well-established Atlantic fishing and a history of anti-Muslim warfare. When the Muslim government of Morocco in northwestern Africa showed weakness in the fifteenth century, the Portuguese went on the attack, beginning with the city of Ceuta° in 1415. This assault combined aspects of a religious crusade, a plundering expedition, and a military tournament in which young Portuguese knights displayed their bravery. The capture of this rich North African city, whose splendid homes, they reported, made those of Portugal look like pigsties, also made the Portuguese better informed about the caravans that brought gold and slaves to Ceuta from the African states south of the Sahara. Despite the capture of several more ports along Morocco's Atlantic coast, the Portuguese were unable to push inland and gain access to the gold trade. So they sought more direct contact with the gold producers by sailing down the African coast.

The attack on Ceuta was led by the young Prince Henry (1394–1460), third son of the king of Portugal. Because he devoted the rest of his life to promoting exploration of the South Atlantic, he is known as **Henry the Navigator.** His official biographer emphasized Henry's mixed motives for exploration—converting Africans to Christianity, making contact with existing Christian rulers in Africa, and launching joint crusades with them against the Ottomans. Prince Henry also wished to discover new places and hoped that such new contacts would be profitable. His initial explorations were concerned with Africa. Only later did reaching India become an explicit goal of Portuguese explorers.

Despite being called "the Navigator," Prince Henry himself never ventured much farther from home than North Africa. Instead, he founded a sort of research institute at Sagres° for studying navigation and collecting information about the lands beyond Muslim North Africa. His staff drew on the pioneering efforts of Italian merchants, especially the Genoese, who had learned some of the secrets of the trans-Saharan trade, and of fourteenth-century Jewish cartographers who used information from Arab and European sources to produce remarkably accurate sea charts and maps of distant places. Henry also oversaw the collection of new geographical information from sailors and travelers and sent out ships to explore the Atlantic. His ships established permanent contact with the islands of Madeira in 1418 and the Azores in 1439.

Ceuta (say-OO-tuh)   **Sagres** (SAH-gresh)

Map 17.3 European Exploration, 1420–1542   Portuguese and Spanish explorers showed the possibility and practicality of intercontinental maritime trade. Before 1540 European trade with Africa and Asia was much more important than that with the Americas, but after the Spanish conquest of the Aztec and Inca Empires transatlantic trade began to increase. Notice the Tordesillas line, which in theory separated the Spanish and Portuguese spheres of activity.

Henry also devoted his resources to solving the technical problems faced by mariners sailing in unknown waters and open seas. His staff studied and improved navigational instruments that had come into Europe from China and the Islamic world. These instruments included the magnetic compass, first developed in China, and the astrolabe, an instrument of Arab or Greek invention that enabled mariners to determine their location at sea by measuring the position of the sun or the stars in the night sky. Even with such instruments, however, voyages still depended most on the skill and experience of the navigators.

Another achievement of Portuguese mariners was the design of vessels appropriate for the voyages of exploration. The galleys in use in the Mediterranean were powered by large numbers of oarsmen and were impractical for long ocean voyages. The square sails of the three-masted European ships of the North Atlantic were propelled by friendly winds but could not sail at much of an angle against the wind. The voyages of exploration made use of a new vessel, the **caravel**°. Caravels were small, only one-fifth the size of the largest European ships of their day and of the large Chinese junks. Their size permitted them to enter shallow coastal waters and explore upriver, but they were strong enough to weather ocean storms. When equipped with lateen sails, caravels had great maneuverability and could sail deeply into the wind; when sporting square Atlantic sails, they had great speed. The addition of small cannon made them good fighting ships as well. The caravels' economy, speed, agility, and power justified a contemporary's claim that they were "the best ships that sailed the seas."[2]

To conquer the seas, pioneering captains had to overcome crew's fears that the South Atlantic waters were boiling hot and contained ocean currents that would prevent any ship entering them from ever returning home. It took Prince Henry fourteen years—from 1420 to 1434—to coax an expedition to venture beyond southern Morocco (see Map 17.3). The crew's fears proved unfounded, but the next stretch of coast, 800 miles (1,300 kilometers) of desert, offered little of interest to the explorers. Finally in 1444 the mariners reached the Senegal River and the well-watered and -populated lands below the Sahara beginning at what they named "Cape Verde" (Green Cape) because of its vegetation.

In the years that followed, Henry's explorers made an important addition to the maritime revolution by learning how to return speedily to Portugal. Instead of battling the prevailing northeast trade winds and currents back up the coast, they discovered that by sailing

caravel (KAR-uh-vel)

Astrolabe   This ancient navigational instrument was critical to the fifteenth-century voyages of exploration because it enabled mariners to find their locations at sea from the angle of the sun above the horizon. This unusually elaborate Italian example is from about 1500. (Museum fur Kunst und Gewerbe, Hamburg)

northwest into the Atlantic to the latitude of the Azores, ships could pick up prevailing westerly winds that would blow them back to Portugal. The knowledge that ocean winds tend to form large circular patterns helped explorers discover many other ocean routes.

To pay for the research, the ships, and the expeditions during the many decades before the voyages became profitable, Prince Henry drew partly on the income of the Order of Christ, a military religious order of which he was the governor. The Order of Christ had inherited the properties and crusading traditions of the Order of Knights Templar, which had disbanded in 1314. The Order of Christ received the exclusive right to promote Christianity in all the lands that were discovered, and the Portuguese emblazoned their ships' sails with the crusaders' red cross.

The first financial return from the voyages came from selling into slavery Africans captured by the Portuguese in raids on the northwest coast of Africa and the Canary Islands during the 1440s. The total number of Africans captured or purchased on voyages exceeded eighty thousand by the end of the century and rose steadily thereafter. However, the gold trade quickly became more important than the slave trade as the Portuguese made contact with the trading networks that

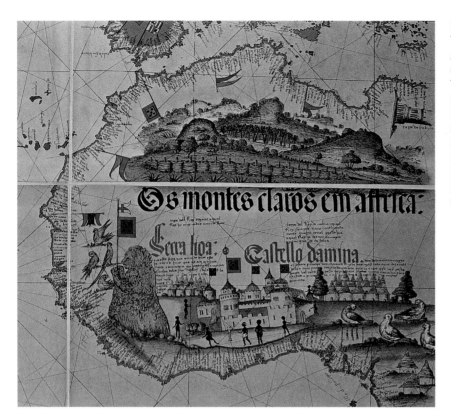

Portuguese Map of Western Africa, 1502
This map shows in great detail a section of African coastline that Portuguese explorers charted and named in the fifteenth century. The cartographer illustrated the African interior, which was almost completely unknown to Europeans, with drawings of birds and views of coastal sights: Sierra Leone (*Serra lioa*), named for a mountain shaped like a lion, and the Portuguese Castle of the Mine (*Castello damina*) on the Gold Coast. (From the American Geographical Society Collection, University of Wisconsin–Milwaukee Library)

flourished in West Africa and reached across the Sahara. By 1457 enough African gold was coming back to Portugal for the kingdom to issue a new gold coin called the *cruzado* (crusade), another reminder of how deeply the Portuguese entwined religious and secular motives.

By the time of Prince Henry's death in 1460, his explorers had established a secure base of operations in the uninhabited Cape Verde Islands, explored 600 miles (950 kilometers) of coast beyond Cape Verde, as far as what they named Sierra Leone° (Lion Mountain). From there they knew the coast of Africa curved sharply toward the east. It had taken the Portuguese four decades to cover the 1,500 miles (2,400 kilometers) from Lisbon to Sierra Leone; it took only three decades to explore the remaining 4,000 miles (6,400 kilometers) to the southern tip of the African continent.

The Portuguese crown continued to sponsor voyages of exploration, but speedier progress resulted from the growing participation of private commercial interests. In 1469 a prominent Lisbon merchant named Fernão Gomes purchased from the Crown the privilege of exploring 350 miles (550 kilometers) of new coast a year for five years in return for a monopoly on the trade he

developed there. During the period of his contract, Gomes discovered the uninhabited island of São Tomé° on the equator; in the next century it became a major source of sugar produced with African slave labor. He also explored what later Europeans called the **Gold Coast,** which became the headquarters of Portugal's West African trade.

The final thrust down the African coast was spurred along by the expectation of finding a passage around Africa to the rich trade of the Indian Ocean. **Bartolomeu Dias** was the first Portuguese explorer to round the southern tip of Africa (in 1488) and enter the Indian Ocean. In 1497–1498 a Portuguese expedition led by **Vasco da Gama** sailed around Africa and reached India (see Environment and Technology: Vasco da Gama's Fleet). In 1500 ships in an expedition under Pedro Alvares Cabral°, while swinging wide to the west in the South Atlantic to catch the winds that would sweep them around southern Africa and on to India, came on the eastern coast of South America, laying the basis for Portugal's later claim to Brazil. The gamble that Prince Henry had begun eight decades earlier was about to pay off handsomely.

Sierra Leone (see- ER-uh lee-OWN

São Tomé (sow toh-MAY)   Cabral (kah-BRAHL)

Vasco da Gama's Fleet

The four small ships that sailed from Lisbon in June 1497 for India may seem a puny fleet compared to the sixty-two Chinese vessels that Zheng He had led into the Indian Ocean ninety-five years earlier. But given the fact that China had a hundred times as many people as Portugal, Vasco da Gama's fleet represented at least as great a commitment of resources. In any event, the Portuguese expedition had a far greater impact on the course of history. Having achieved its aim of inspiring awe at China's greatness, the Chinese throne sent out no more expeditions after 1432. Although da Gama's ships seemed more odd than awesome to Indian Ocean observers, that modest fleet began a revolution in global relations.

Portugal spared no expense in ensuring that the fleet would make it to India and back. Craftsmen built extra strength into the hulls to withstand storms at the tip of Africa as powerful as the ones Dias had encountered in 1488. Also, small enough to be able to navigate any shallow harbors and rivers they might encounter, the ships were crammed with specially strengthened casks and barrels of water, wine, oil, flour, meat, and vegetables far in excess of what was required even on a voyage that would take the better part of a year to reach India. Arms and ammunition were also in abundance.

Three of da Gama's ships were rigged with square sails on two masts for speed and a lateen sail on the third mast. The fourth vessel was a caravel with lateen sails. Each ship carried three sets of sails and plenty of extra rigging so as to be able to repair any damages due to storms. The crusaders' red crosses on the sails signaled one of the expedition's motives.

The captains and crew—Portugal's most talented and experienced—received extra pay and other rewards for their service. Yet there was no expectation that the unprecedented sums spent on this expedition would bring any immediate return. According to a contemporary chronicle, the only immediate return the Portuguese monarch received was "the knowledge that some part of Ethiopia and the beginning of Lower India had been discovered." However, the scale and care of the preparations suggest that the Portuguese expected the expedition to open up profitable trade to the Indian Ocean. And so it did.

Vasco da Gama's Flagship
This vessel carried the Portuguese captain on his second expedition to India in 1505. (The Pierpont Morgan Library/Art Resource, NY)

Spanish Voyages

Portugal's century-long efforts to explore the South Atlantic are a testimony to planning and persistence. Spain's early discoveries owed more to haste and blind luck. Throughout most of the fifteenth century, the Spanish kingdoms had been preoccupied with internal affairs: completion of the reconquest of southern Iberia; amalgamation of the various dynasties; the conversion or expulsion of religious minorities. Only in the last decade of the century were Spanish monarchs ready to turn again to overseas exploration, by which time the Portuguese had already found a new route to the Indian Ocean.

The leader of their overseas mission would be **Christopher Columbus** (1451–1506), a Genoese mariner. His three voyages between 1492 and 1498 would reveal the existence of vast lands across the Atlantic, whose existence and whose inhabitants were entirely new to the "old world" peoples of Eurasia and Africa. But Columbus was frustrated rather than fulfilled by his momentous discovery, for his intention had been to find a new route to the Indian Ocean even shorter than the one the Portuguese were pioneering.

As a younger man Columbus had gained considerable experience of the South Atlantic while participating in Portuguese explorations along the African coast, but he had become convinced there was a shorter way to reach the riches of the East than the route around Africa. By his reckoning (based on a serious misreading of a ninth-century Arab authority), the Canaries were a mere 2,400 nautical miles (4,450 kilometers) from Japan. The actual distance was five times as far.

It was not easy for Columbus to find a sponsor willing to underwrite the costs of testing his theory that one could reach Asia by sailing west. Portuguese authorities twice rejected his plan, first in 1485 following a careful study and again in 1488 after Dias had established the feasibility of a route around Africa. Columbus received a more sympathetic hearing in 1486 from Castile's able ruler, Queen Isabella, but no commitment of support. After a four-year study a Castilian commission appointed by Isabella concluded that a westward sea route to the Indies rested on many questionable geographical assumptions, but Columbus's persistence finally won over the queen and her husband, King Ferdinand of Aragon. In 1492 they agreed to fund a modest expedition. Their elation at expelling the Muslims from Granada may have put them in a favorable mood.

Columbus recorded in his log that he and his mostly Spanish crew of ninety men "departed Friday the third day of August of the year 1492," toward "the regions of India." Their mission, the royal contract stated, was "to discover and acquire certain islands and mainland in the Ocean Sea." He carried letters of introduction from the Spanish sovereigns to Eastern rulers, including one to the "Grand Khan" (meaning the Chinese emperor). Also on board was a Jewish convert to Christianity whose knowledge of Arabic was expected to facilitate communication with the peoples of eastern Asia. The expedition traveled in three small ships, the *Santa María*, and two caravels, the *Santa Clara* (nicknamed the *Niña*), and a third vessel now known only by its nickname, the *Pinta*.

The expedition began well. Other attempts to explore the Atlantic west of the Azores had been impeded by unfavorable headwinds. But on earlier voyages along the African coast, Columbus had learned that he could find west-blowing winds in the latitudes of the Canaries, which is why he chose that southern route. After reaching the Canaries, he had the *Niña*'s lateen sails replaced with square sails, for he knew that from then on speed would be more important than maneuverability.

In October 1492 the expedition reached the islands of the Caribbean. Columbus insisted on calling the inhabitants "Indians" because he believed that the islands were part of the East Indies. A second voyage to the Caribbean in 1493 did nothing to change his mind. Even when, two months after Vasco da Gama reached India in 1498, Columbus first sighted the mainland of South America on a third voyage, he stubbornly insisted it was part of Asia. But by then other Europeans were convinced he had discovered islands and continents previously unknown to the Old World. Amerigo Vespucci's explorations, first on behalf of Spain and then for Portugal, led mapmakers to name the new continents "America" after him, rather than "Columbia" after Columbus.

To prevent disputes arising from their efforts to exploit their new discoveries and to spread Christianity among the people there, Spain and Portugal agreed to split the world between them. The Treaty of Tordesillas°, negotiated by the pope in 1494, drew an imaginary line down the middle of the North Atlantic Ocean. Lands east of the line in Africa and southern Asia could be claimed by Portugal; lands to the west in the Americas were reserved for Spain. Cabral's discovery of Brazil, however, gave Portugal a valid claim to the part of South America that bulged east of the line.

But if the Tordesillas line were extended around the earth, where would Spain's and Portugal's spheres of influence divide in the East? Given Europeans' ignorance of the earth's true size in 1494, it was not clear whether the Moluccas°, whose valuable spices had been a goal of the Iberian voyages, were on Portugal's or Spain's side of the line. The missing information concerned the size

---

Tordesillas (tor-duh-SEE-yuhs) **Moluccas** (muh-LOO-kuhz)

of the Pacific Ocean. By chance, in 1513 a Spanish adventurer named Vasco Núñez de Balboa° crossed the isthmus (a narrow neck of land) of Panama from the east and sighted the Pacific Ocean on the other side. And the 1519 expedition of **Ferdinand Magellan** (ca. 1480–1521) was designed to complete Columbus's interrupted westward voyage by sailing around the Americas and across the Pacific, whose vast size no European then guessed. The Moluccas turned out to lie well within Portugal's sphere, as Spain formally acknowledged in 1529.

Magellan's voyage laid the basis for Spanish colonization of the Philippine Islands after 1564. Nor did Magellan's death prevent him from being considered the first person to encircle the globe, for a decade earlier he had sailed from Europe to the East Indies as part of an expedition sponsored by his native Portugal. His two voyages took him across the Tordesillas line, through the separate spheres claimed by Portugal and Spain—at least until other Europeans began demanding a share. Of course, in the year 1500 European claims were largely theoretical. Portugal and Spain had only modest settlements overseas.

Although Columbus failed to find a new route to the East, the consequences of his voyages for European expansion were momentous. Those who followed in his wake laid the basis for Spain's large colonial empires in the Americas and for the empires of other European nations. In turn, these empires promoted, among the four Atlantic continents, the growth of a major new trading network whose importance rivaled and eventually surpassed that of the Indian Ocean network. The more immediately important consequence was Portugal's entry into the Indian Ocean, which quickly led to a major European presence and profit. Both the eastward and the westward voyages of exploration marked a tremendous expansion of Europe's role in world history.

ENCOUNTERS WITH EUROPE, 1450–1550

European actions alone did not determine the consequences of the new contacts that Iberian mariners had opened. The ways in which Africans, Asians, and Amerindians perceived their new visitors and interacted with them also influenced their future relations. Some welcomed the Europeans as potential allies; others

viewed them as rivals or enemies. In general, Africans and Asians had little difficulty in recognizing the benefits and dangers that European contacts might bring. However, the long isolation of the Amerindians from the rest of the world added to the strangeness of their encounter with the Spanish and made them more vulnerable to the unfamiliar diseases that these explorers inadvertently introduced.

Western Africa

Many Africans along the West African coast were eager for trade with the Portuguese. It would give them new markets for their exports and access to imports cheaper than those that reached them through the middlemen of the overland routes to the Mediterranean. This reaction was evident along the Gold Coast of West Africa, first visited by the Portuguese in 1471. Miners in the hinterland had long sold their gold to African traders, who took it to the trading cities along the southern edge of the Sahara, where it was sold to traders who had crossed the desert from North Africa. Recognizing that they might get more favorable terms from the new sea visitors, coastal Africans were ready to negotiate with the royal representative of Portugal who arrived in 1482 seeking permission to erect a trading fort.

The Portuguese noble in charge and his officers (likely including the young Christopher Columbus, who had entered Portuguese service in 1476) were eager to make a proper impression. They dressed in their best clothes, erected and decorated a reception platform, celebrated a Catholic Mass, and signaled the start of negotiations with trumpets, tambourines, and drums. The African king, Caramansa, staged his entrance with equal ceremony, arriving with a large retinue of attendants and musicians. Through an African interpreter, the two leaders exchanged flowery speeches pledging goodwill and mutual benefit. Caramansa then gave his permission for a small trading fort to be built, assured, he said, by the appearance of these royal delegates that they were honorable persons, unlike the "few, foul, and vile" Portuguese visitors of the previous decade.

Neither side made a show of force, but the Africans' upper hand was evident in Caramansa's warning that if the Portuguese failed to be peaceful and honest traders, he and his people would simply move away, depriving their post of food and trade. Trade at the post of Saint George of the Mine (later called Elmina) enriched both sides. From there the Portuguese crown was soon purchasing gold equal to one-tenth of the world's production at the time. In return, Africans received large quantities of goods that Portuguese ships brought from Asia, Europe, and other parts of Africa.

Balboa (bal-BOH-uh)

Afro–Portuguese Ivory A skilled ivory carver from the kingdom of Benin probably made this saltcellar. Intended for a European market, it depicts a Portuguese ship on the cover and Portuguese nobles around the base. However European the subject, the craftsmanship is typical of Benin. (Courtesy of the Trustees of the British Museum)

Early contacts generally involved a mixture of commercial, military, and religious interests. Some African rulers were quick to appreciate that the European firearms could be a useful addition to their spears and arrows in conflicts with their enemies. Because African religions did not presume to have a monopoly on religious knowledge, coastal rulers were also willing to test the value of Christian practices, which the Portuguese eagerly promoted. The rulers of Benin and Kongo, the two largest coastal kingdoms, invited Portuguese missionaries and soldiers to accompany them into battle to test the Christians' religion along with their muskets.

After a century of aggressive expansion, the kingdom of Benin in the Niger Delta was near the peak of its power when it first encountered the Portuguese. Its oba (king) presided over an elaborate bureaucracy from a spacious palace in his large capital city, also known as Benin. In response to a Portuguese visit in 1486, the oba sent an ambassador to Portugal to learn more about the homeland of these strangers. Then he established a royal monopoly on trade with the Portuguese, selling pepper and ivory tusks (to be taken back to Portugal) as well as stone beads, textiles, and prisoners of war (to be resold at Elmina). In return, the Portuguese merchants provided Benin with copper and brass, fine textiles, glass beads, and a horse for the king's royal procession. In the early sixteenth century, as the demand for slaves for the Portuguese sugar plantations on the nearby island of São Tomé grew, the oba first raised the price of slaves and then imposed restrictions that limited their sale.

Portuguese efforts to persuade the king and nobles of Benin to accept the Catholic faith ultimately failed. Early kings showed some interest, but after 1538 the rulers declined to receive further missionaries. They also closed the market in male slaves for the rest of the sixteenth century. Exactly why Benin chose to limit its contacts with the Portuguese is uncertain, but the rulers clearly had the power to control how much interaction they wanted.

Farther south, on the lower Congo River, relations between the kingdom of Kongo and the Portuguese began similarly but had a quite different outcome. Like the oba of Benin, the *manikongo*° (king of Kongo) sent delegates to Portugal, established a royal monopoly on trade with the Portuguese, and expressed interest in missionary teachings. Deeply impressed with the new religion, the royal family made Catholicism the kingdom's official faith. But Kongo, lacking ivory and pepper, had less to trade than Benin. So to acquire the goods brought by Portugal and to pay the costs of the missionaries, it had to sell more and more slaves.

Soon the manikongo began to lose his royal monopoly over the slave trade. In 1526 the Christian manikongo, Afonso I (r. 1506–ca. 1540), wrote to his royal "brother," the king of Portugal, begging for his help in stopping the trade because unauthorized Kongolese were kidnapping and selling people, even members of good families. Afonso's appeal that contacts be limited to "some priests and a few people to teach in the schools, and no other goods except wine and flour for the holy sacrament" received no reply. Other subjects took advantage of the manikongo's weakness to rebel against his authority. Indeed, after 1540 the major part of the slave trade from this part of Africa moved farther south.

---

manikongo (mah-NEE-KONG-goh)

Eastern Africa

Different still were the reactions of the Muslim rulers of the trading coastal states of eastern Africa. As Vasco da Gama's fleet sailed up the coast in 1498, most rulers gave the Portuguese a cool reception, suspicious of the intentions of these visitors who painted crusaders' crosses on their sails. But the ruler of one of the cities, Malindi, saw in the Portuguese an ally who could help him expand their trading position and provided da Gama with a pilot to guide him to India. The suspicions of most rulers were justified seven years later when a Portuguese war fleet bombarded and looted most of the coastal cities of eastern Africa in the name of Christ and commerce, though they spared Malindi.

Another eastern African state that saw potential benefit in an alliance with the Portuguese was Christian Ethiopia. In the fourteenth and early fifteenth centuries, Ethiopia faced increasing conflicts with Muslim states along the Red Sea. Emboldened by the rise of the Ottoman Turks, who had conquered Egypt in 1517 and launched a major fleet in the Indian Ocean to counter the Portuguese, the talented warlord of the Muslim state of Adal launched a furious assault on Ethiopia. Adal's decisive victory in 1529 reduced the Christian kingdom to a precarious state. At that point Ethiopia's contacts with the Portuguese became crucial.

For decades, delegations from Portugal and Ethiopia had been exploring a possible alliance between their states based on their mutual adherence to Christianity. A key figure was Queen Helena of Ethiopia, who acted as regent for her young sons after her husband's death in 1478. In 1509 Helena sent a letter to "our very dear and well-beloved brother," the king of Portugal, along with a gift of two tiny crucifixes said to be made of wood from the cross on which Christ had died in Jerusalem. In her letter she proposed an alliance of her land army and Portugal's fleet against the Turks. No such alliance was completed by the time Helena died in 1522. But as Ethiopia's situation grew increasingly desperate, renewed appeals for help were made.

Finally a small Portuguese force commanded by Vasco da Gama's son Christopher reached Ethiopia in 1539, at a time when what was left of the empire was being held together by another woman ruler. With Portuguese help the queen rallied the Ethiopians to renew their struggle. Christopher da Gama was captured and tortured to death, but the Muslim forces lost heart when their leader was mortally wounded in a later battle. Portuguese aid helped the Ethiopian kingdom save itself from extinction, but a permanent alliance faltered because Ethiopian rulers refused to transfer their Christian affiliation from the patriarch of Alexandria to the Latin patriarch of Rome (the pope) as the Portuguese wanted.

As these examples illustrate, African encounters with the Portuguese before 1550 varied considerably, as much because of the strategies and leadership of particular African states as because of Portuguese policies. Africans and Portuguese might become royal brothers, bitter opponents, or partners in a mutually profitable trade, but Europeans remained a minor presence in most of Africa in 1550. By then the Portuguese had become far more interested in the Indian Ocean trade.

Indian Ocean States

Vasco da Gama's arrival on the Malabar Coast of India in May 1498 did not make a great impression on the citizens of Calicut. After more than ten months at sea, many members of the crew were in ill health. And da Gama's four small ships were far less imposing than the Chinese fleets of gigantic junks that had called at Calicut sixty-five years earlier and no larger than many of the dhows that filled the harbor of this rich and important trading city. The *samorin* (ruler) of Calicut and his Muslim officials showed mild interest in the Portuguese as new trading partners, but the gifts da Gama had brought for the samorin evoked derisive laughter. Twelve pieces of fairly ordinary striped cloth, four scarlet hoods, six hats, and six wash basins seemed inferior goods to those accustomed to the luxuries of the Indian Ocean trade. When da Gama tried to defend his gifts as those of an explorer, not a rich merchant, the samorin cut him short, asking whether he had come to discover men or stones: "If he had come to discover men, as he said, why had he brought nothing?"

Coastal rulers soon discovered that the Portuguese had no intention of remaining poor competitors in the rich trade of the Indian Ocean. Upon da Gama's return to Portugal in 1499 the jubilant King Manuel styled himself "Lord of the Conquest, Navigation, and Commerce of Ethiopia, Arabia, Persia, and India," setting forth the ambitious scope of his plans. Previously the Indian Ocean had been an open sea, used by merchants (and pirates) of all the surrounding coasts. Now the Portuguese crown intended to make it Portugal's sea, the private property of the Portuguese alone, which others might use only on Portuguese terms.

The ability of little Portugal to assert control over the Indian Ocean stemmed from the superiority of its ships and weapons over the smaller and lightly armed merchant dhows. In 1505 the Portuguese fleet of 81 ships and some 7,000 men bombarded Swahili Coast cities. Next on the list were Indian ports. Goa, on the west coast of India, fell to a well-armed fleet in 1510, becoming the base from which the Portuguese menaced the trading

Portuguese in India   In the sixteenth century Portuguese men moved to the Indian Ocean basin to work as administrators and traders. This Indo-Portuguese drawing from about 1540 shows a Portuguese man speaking to an Indian woman, perhaps making a proposal of marriage. (Ms. 1889, c. 97, Biblioteca Casanateunse Rome. Photo: Humberto Nicoletti Serra)

cities of Gujarat° to the north and Calicut and other Malabar Coast cities to the south. The port of Hormuz, controlling the entry to the Persian Gulf, was taken in 1515. Aden, at the entrance to the Red Sea, with its intricate natural defenses was able to preserve its independence. The addition of the Gujarati port of Diu in 1535 consolidated Portuguese dominance of the western Indian Ocean.

Meanwhile, Portuguese explorers had been reconnoitering the Bay of Bengal and the waters farther east. The independent city of Malacca° on the strait between the Malay Peninsula and Sumatra became the focus of their attention. During the fifteenth century Malacca had become the main entrepôt° (a place where goods are stored or deposited and from which they are distributed) for the trade from China and Japan, from India, and from the Southeast Asian mainland and the Moluccas. Among the city's more than 100,000 residents an early Portuguese counted eighty-four different languages, including those of merchants from as far west as Cairo, Ethiopia, and the Swahili Coast of East Africa. Many non-Muslim residents supported letting the Portuguese join this cosmopolitan trading community, perhaps to offset the growing solidarity of Muslim traders. In

1511, however, the Portuguese seized this strategic trading center with a force of a thousand fighting men, including three hundred recruited in southern India.

Force was not always necessary. On the China coast local officials and merchants interested in profitable new trade with the Portuguese persuaded the imperial government to allow the Portuguese to establish a trading post at Macao° in 1557. Operating from Macao, Portuguese ships nearly monopolized the trade between China and Japan.

In the Indian Ocean the Portuguese used their control of the major port cities to enforce an even larger trading monopoly. They required all spices to be carried in Portuguese ships, as well as all goods on the major ocean routes such as between Goa and Macao. In addition, the Portuguese also tried to control and tax other Indian Ocean trade by requiring all merchant ships entering and leaving one of their ports to carry a Portuguese passport and to pay customs duties. Portuguese patrols seized vessels that attempted to avoid these monopolies, confiscated their cargoes, and either killed the captain and crew or sentenced them to forced labor.

Reactions to this power grab varied. Like the emperors of China, the Mughal° emperors of India largely ignored Portugal's maritime intrusions, seeing their interests as maintaining control over their vast land possessions. The Ottomans responded more aggressively. From 1501 to 1509 they supported Egypt's fleet of fifteen thousand men against the Christian intruders. Then, having absorbed Egypt into their empire, the Ottomans sent another large expedition against the Portuguese in 1538. Both expeditions failed because the Ottoman galleys were no match for the faster, better-armed Portuguese vessels in the open ocean. However, the Ottomans retained the advantage in the Red Sea and Persian Gulf, where they had many ports of supply.

The smaller trading states of the region were even less capable of challenging Portuguese domination head on, since their mutual rivalry impeded the formation of any common front. Some chose to cooperate with the Portuguese as the best way to maintain their prosperity and security. Others engaged in evasion and resistance. Two examples illustrate the range of responses among Indian Ocean peoples.

The merchants of Calicut put up some of the most sustained local resistance. In retaliation the Portuguese embargoed all trade with Aden, Calicut's principal trading partner, and centered their trade on the port of Cochin, which had once been a dependency of Calicut. Some Calicut merchants became adept at evading the

---

Gujarat (goo-juh-RAHT)   Malacca (muh-LAH-kuh)
entrepôt (ON-truh-poh)

Macao (muh-COW)   Mughal (MOO-gahl)

patrol, but the price of resistance was the shrinking of Calicut's importance as Cochin gradually became the major pepper-exporting port on the Malabar Coast.

The traders and rulers of the state of Gujarat farther north had less success in keeping the Portuguese at bay. At first they resisted Portuguese attempts at monopoly and in 1509 joined Egypt's failed effort to sweep the Portuguese from the Arabian Sea. But in 1535, finding his state at a military disadvantage due to Mughal attacks, the ruler of Gujarat made the fateful decision to allow the Portuguese to build a fort at Diu in return for their support. Once established, the Portuguese gradually extended their control, so that by midcentury they were licensing and taxing all Gujarati ships. Even after the Mughals (who were Muslims) took control of Gujarat in 1572, the Mughal emperor Akbar permitted the Portuguese to continue their maritime monopoly in return for allowing one pilgrim ship a year to sail to Mecca without paying the Portuguese any fee.

The Portuguese never gained complete control of the Indian Ocean trade, but their domination of key ports and the main trade routes during the sixteenth century brought them considerable profit, which they sent back to Europe in the form of spices and other luxury goods. The effects were dramatic. The Portuguese sold the large quantities of pepper that they exported for less than the price charged by Venice and Genoa for pepper obtained through Egyptian middlemen, thus breaking the Italian cities' monopoly.

In Asia the consequences were equally startling. Asian and East African traders were at the mercy of Portuguese warships, but their individual responses affected their fates. Some were devastated. Others prospered by meeting the Portuguese demands or evading their patrols. Because the Portuguese were ocean-based, they had little impact on the Asian and African mainland, in sharp contrast to what was occurring in the Americas.

The Americas

In the Americas the Spanish established a vast *territorial* empire, in contrast to the *trading* empires the Portuguese created in Africa and Asia. This outcome had little to do with differences between the two Iberian kingdoms, except for the fact that the Spanish kingdoms had somewhat greater resources to draw on. The Spanish and Portuguese monarchies had similar motives for expansion and used identical ships and weapons. Rather, the isolation of the Amerindian peoples made their responses to outside contacts different from the responses of peoples in Africa and the Indian Ocean cities. In dealing with the small communities

in the Caribbean, the first European settlers resorted to conquest and plunder rather than trade. This practice was later extended to the more powerful Amerindian kingdoms on the American mainland. The spread of deadly new diseases among the Amerindians after 1518 weakened their ability to resist.

The first Amerindians to encounter Columbus were the Arawak of Hispaniola (modern Haiti and the Dominican Republic) in the Greater Antilles and the Bahamas to the north (see Map 17.2). They cultivated maize (corn), cassava (a tuber), sweet potatoes, and hot peppers, as well as cotton and tobacco, and they met their other material needs from the sea and wild plants. Although they were skilled at mining and working gold, the Arawak did not trade gold over long distances as Africans did, and they had no iron. The Arawak at first extended a cautious welcome to the Spanish but were unprepared to sell them large quantities of gold. Instead, they told Columbus exaggerated stories about gold in other places to persuade him to move on.

When Columbus made his second trip to Hispaniola, in 1493, he brought with him several hundred settlers from southern Iberia who hoped to make their fortune and missionaries who were eager to persuade the Indians to accept Christianity. The settlers stole gold

Arawak Women Making Tortillas   This sixteenth-century woodcut depicts techniques of food preparation in the West Indies. The woman at the left grinds cornmeal on a *metate*. The woman in the center pats cornmeal dough flat and fries the tortillas. The third woman serves tortillas with a bowl of stew. (Courtesy of the John Carter Brown Library at Brown University)

European Male Sexual Dominance Overseas

European expansion and colonization were overwhelmingly the work of men. Missionaries chose to remain celibate; other men did not, as these two letters make clear. The first letter, dated 1495, is from Michele de Cuneo, an officer on Columbus's second voyage across the Atlantic.

While I was in the boat I captured a very beautiful Carib woman, whom the said Lord Admiral [Columbus] gave to me, and with whom, having taken her into my cabin, she being naked according to their custom, I conceived desire to take pleasure. I wanted to put my desire into execution but she did not want it and treated me with her finger nails in such a manner that I wished I had never begun. But seeing that, (to tell you the end of it all), I took a rope and thrashed her well, for which she raised such unheard of screams that you would not have believed your ears. Finally we came to an agreement in such manner that I can tell you that she seemed to have been brought up in a school of harlots.

The second letter, dated 1550, is from an Italian Jesuit missionary in India to Ignatius Loyola, the founder of the Society of Jesus (the Jesuits), in Rome.

Your reverence must know that the sin of licentiousness is so widespread in these regions [India] that no check is placed upon it, which leads to great inconveniences, and to great disrespect of the sacraments. I say this of the Portuguese, who have adopted the vices and customs of the land without reserve, including the evil custom of buying droves of slaves, male and female, just as if they were sheep, large and small. There are countless men who buy droves of girls and sleep with all of them, and subsequently sell them. There are innumerable married settlers who have four, eight, or ten female slaves and sleep with them, as is common knowledge. This is carried to such excess that there was one man in Malacca who had twenty-four women of various races, all of whom were his slaves, and all of whom he enjoyed. I quote this city because it is a thing that everybody knows. Most men, as soon as they can afford to buy a female slave, almost invariably use her as a girl-friend (*amiga*), besides many other dishonesties, in my poor understanding.

What circumstances made it nearly impossible for the women in question to resist the European men's advances? What phrases in the letters suggest that the writers attribute some responsibility for these encounters to the sexual license of the women involved? Are such inferences credible?

Source: The first letter is reprinted from Samuel Eliot Morison, trans. and ed., *Journals and Other Documents in the Life and Voyages of Christopher Columbus* (New York: Heritage Press, 1963), 212. The second letter is from C. R. Boxer, *The Portuguese Seaborne Empire, 1415–1825* (New York: Knopf, 1969). Copyright © 1969 by C. R. Boxer. Reprinted by permission of Alfred A. Knopf, Inc.

---

ornaments, confiscated food, and raped women (see Society and Culture: European Male Sexual Dominance Overseas), provoking the Hispaniola Arawak to war in 1495. In this and later conflicts, horses and body armor gave the Spaniards a great advantage. Tens of thousands of Arawak were slaughtered. Those who survived were forced to pay a heavy tax in gold, spun cotton, and food. Any who failed to meet the quotas were condemned to forced labor. Meanwhile, the cattle, pigs, and goats introduced by the settlers devoured the Arawak's food crops, causing deaths from famine and disease. A governor appointed by the Spanish crown in 1502 forced the Arawak remaining on Hispaniola to be laborers under the control of Spanish settlers.

The actions of the Spanish in the Antilles were reflections of Spanish actions and motives during the wars against the Muslims in Spain in the previous centuries: seeking to serve God by defeating nonbelievers and placing them under Christian control—and becoming rich in the process. Individual **conquistadors**° (conquerors) extended that pattern around the Caribbean. Some attacked the Bahamas to get gold and labor as

---

conquistador (kon-KEY-stuh-dor)

Coronation of Emperor Moctezuma
This painting by an unnamed Aztec artist depicts the Aztec ruler's coronation. Moctezuma, his nose pierced by a bone, receives the crown from a prince in the palace at Tenochtitlan. (Oronz)

both became scarce on Hispaniola. Many Arawak from the Bahamas were taken to Hispaniola as slaves. Juan Ponce de León (1460–1521), who had participated in the conquest of Muslim Spain and the seizure of Hispaniola, conquered the island of Borinquen (Puerto Rico) in 1508 and then in 1513 explored southeastern Florida.

An ambitious and ruthless nobleman, **Hernán Cortés°** (1485–1547), led the most audacious expedition to the mainland. Cortés left Cuba in 1519 with six hundred fighting men and most of the island's stock of weapons to assault the Mexican mainland in search of slaves and to establish trade. But when the expedition learned of the rich Aztec Empire in central Mexico, Cortés brought to the American mainland, on a massive scale, the exploitation and conquest that had begun in the Greater Antilles.

The Aztecs themselves had conquered their vast empire only during the pervious century, and many of the Amerindians they had subjugated were far from loyal subjects. Many resented the tribute they had to pay the Aztecs, the forced labor, and the large-scale human sacrifices to the Aztec gods. Many subject people saw the Spaniards as powerful human allies against the Aztecs and gave them their support. Like the Caribbean people, the Amerindians of Mexico had no precedent by which to judge these strange visitors.

Later accounts suggest that some believed Cortés to be the legendary ruler Quetzalcoatl°, whose return to earth had been prophesied, and treated him with great deference. Another consequence of millennia of isolation was far more significant: the lack of acquired immunity to the diseases of the Old World. Smallpox was the most deadly of the early epidemics that accompanied the Spanish conquistadores. It appeared for the first time on the island of Hispaniola late in 1518. An infected member of the Cortés expedition then transmitted smallpox to Mexico in 1519, where it spread with deadly efficiency.

From his glorious capital city Tenochtitlan°, the Aztec emperor **Moctezuma° II** (r. 1502–1520) sent messengers to greet Cortés and figure out whether he was god or man, friend or foe. Cortés advanced steadily toward the capital, Tenochtitlan, overcoming Aztec opposition with cavalry charges and steel swords and gaining the support of thousands of Amerindian allies from among the unhappy subjects of the Aztecs. When the Spaniards were near, the emperor went out in a great procession, dressed in all his finery, to welcome Cortés with gifts and flower garlands.

Cortés (kor-TEZ)

Quetzalcoatl (ket-zahl-COH-ah-tal)
Tenochtitlan (teh-noch-TIT-lan)
Moctezuma (mock-teh-ZOO-ma)

Despite Cortés's initial promise that he came in friendship, Moctezuma quickly found himself a prisoner in his own palace. His treasury was looted, its gold melted down. Soon a battle was raging in and about the capital between the Spaniards (helped by their new Amerindian allies) and the Aztecs and their supporters. Briefly the Aztecs gained the upper hand. They destroyed half of the Spanish force and four thousand of the Spaniards' Amerindian allies, and they sacrificed to their gods fifty-three Spanish prisoners and four horses, displaying their severed heads in rows on pikes. Reinforced by troops from Cuba, Cortés was able to regain the advantage by means of Spanish cannon and clever battle strategies. The capture of Tenochtitlan in 1520 was also greatly facilitated by the spread of smallpox, which weakened and killed more of the city's defenders than died in the fighting. One source remembered that the disease "spread over the people as a great destruction." The bodies of the afficted were covered with oozing sores, and large numbers soon died. It is likely that many Amerindians as well as Europeans saw the devastating spread of this disease as due to supernatural forces.

After the capital fell, the conquistadores took over other parts of Mexico. Then some Spaniards began eyeing the vast Inca Empire, stretching nearly 3,000 miles (5,000 kilometers) south from the equator and containing half of the population in South America. The Inca had conquered the inhabitants of the Andes Mountains and the Pacific coast of South America during the previous century, and their rule was not fully accepted by all of the peoples whom they had defeated.

With the vast Pacific Ocean on one side of their realm and the sparsely inhabited Amazon forests on the other, it is not surprising that Inca rulers believed they controlled most of the world worth controlling. Theirs was a great empire with highly productive agriculture, exquisite stone cities (such as the capital, Cuzco), and rich gold and silver mines. The power of the Inca emperor was sustained by beliefs that he was descended from the Sun God and by an efficient system of roads and messengers that kept him informed about major events in the empire. Yet all was not well.

At the end of the 1520s, before even a whisper of news about the Spanish reached them, smallpox claimed countless Amerindian lives, perhaps including the Inca emperor in 1530. Even more devastating was the threat awaiting the empire from **Francisco Pizarro°** (ca. 1478–1541) and his motley band of 180 men, 37 horses, and two cannon.

With limited education and some military experience, Pizarro had come to the Americas in 1502 at the age of twenty-five to seek his fortune. He had participated in the conquest of Hispaniola and in Balboa's expedition across the isthmus of Panama. By 1520 Pizarro was a wealthy landowner and official in Panama, yet he gambled his fortune on more adventures, exploring the Pacific coast to a point south of the equator, where he learned of the riches of the Inca. With a license from the king of Spain, he set out from Panama in 1531 to conquer them.

In November 1532 Pizarro arranged to meet the new Inca emperor, **Atahualpa°** (r. 1531–1533), near the Andean city of Cajamarca°. With supreme boldness and brutality, Pizarro's small band of armed men seized Atahualpa off a rich litter borne by eighty nobles as it passed through an enclosed courtyard. Though surrounded by an Inca army of at least forty thousand, the Spaniards were able to use their cannon to create confusion while their swords sliced the emperor's lightly armed retainers and servants to pieces by the thousands. The strategy to replicate the earlier Spanish conquest of Mexico was working.

Noting the glee with which the Spaniards seized gold, silver, and emeralds, the captive Atahualpa offered them what he thought would satisfy even the greediest among them in exchange for his freedom: a roomful of gold and silver. But when the ransom of 13,400 pounds (6,000 kilograms) of gold and 26,000 pounds (12,000 kilograms) of silver was paid, the Spaniards gave Atahualpa a choice: he could be burned at the stake as a heathen or baptized as a Christian and then strangled. He chose the latter. His death and the Spanish occupation broke the unity of the Inca Empire.

In 1533 the Spaniards took Cuzco and from there set out to conquer and loot the rest of the empire. The defeat of a final rebellion in 1536 spelled the end of Inca rule. Five years later Pizarro himself met a violent death at the hands of Spanish rivals, but the conquest of the mainland continued. Incited by the fabulous wealth of the Aztecs and Inca, conquistadores extended Spanish conquest and exploration in South and North America, dreaming of new treasuries to loot.

Patterns of Dominance

Within fifty years of Columbus's first landing in 1492, the Spanish had located and occupied all of the major population centers of the Americas, and the penetration of the more thinly populated areas was well under way. In no

---

Pizarro (pih-ZAHR-oh)

Atahualpa (ah-tuh-WAHL-puh)
Cajamarca (kah-hah-MAHR-kah)

other part of the world was European dominance so complete. Why did the peoples of the Americas suffer a fate so different from that of peoples in Africa and Asia? Why were the Spanish able to erect a vast land empire in the Americas so quickly? Three factors seem crucial.

First, long isolation from the rest of humanity made the inhabitants of the Americas vulnerable to new diseases. The unfamiliar illnesses first devastated the native inhabitants of the Caribbean islands and then spread to the mainland. Contemporaries estimated that between 25 and 50 percent of those infected with smallpox died. Repeated epidemics inhibited Amerindians' ability to regain control. Because evidence is very limited, estimates of the size of the population before Columbus's arrival vary widely, but there is no disputing the fact that the Amerindian population fell sharply during the sixteenth century. The Americas became a "widowed land," open to resettlement from across the Atlantic.

A second major factor was Spain's superior military technology. Steel swords, protective armor, and horses gave the Spaniards an advantage over their Amerindian opponents in many battles. Though few in number, muskets and cannon also gave the Spaniards a significant psychological edge. However, it should not be forgotten that the Spanish conquests depended heavily on large numbers of Amerindian allies armed with weapons the same as those of the people they defeated. But perhaps the Spaniards' most decisive military advantage came from the no-holds-barred fighting techniques they had developed during a long history of warfare at home.

The third factor in Spain's conquest of the New World was patterns previously established in the Spanish reconquest of Granada in 1492. The reconquest provided precedents for forced labor, forced conversion, and the incorporation of conquered lands into a new empire.

The same three factors help explain the quite different outcomes elsewhere. Because of centuries of contacts before 1500, Europeans, Africans, and Asians shared the same Old World diseases. Only small numbers of very isolated peoples in Africa and Asia suffered the demographic calamity that undercut Amerindians' ability to retain control of their lands. The Iberians enjoyed a military advantage at sea, as the conquest of the Indian Ocean trade routes showed, but on land they had no decisive advantage against more numerous indigenous people who were not weakened by disease. Everywhere, Iberian religious zeal to conquer non-Christians went hand in hand with a desire for riches. In Iberia and America conquest brought wealth. But in Africa and Asia, where existing trading networks were already well established, Iberian desire for wealth from trade restrained or negated the impulse to conquer.

CONCLUSION

Historians agree that the century between 1450 and 1550 was a major turning point in world history. It was the beginning of an age to which they have given various names: the "Vasco da Gama epoch," the "Columbian era," the "age of Magellan," or simply the "modern period." During those years European explorers opened new long-distance trade routes across the world's three major oceans, for the first time establishing regular contact among all the continents. By 1550 those who followed them had broadened trading contacts with sub-Saharan Africa, gained mastery of the rich trade routes of the Indian Ocean, and conquered a vast land empire in the Americas.

As dramatic and momentous as these events were, they were not completely unprecedented. The riches of the Indian Ocean trade that brought a gleam to the eye of many Europeans had been developed over many centuries by the trading peoples who inhabited the surrounding lands. European conquests of the Americas were no more rapid or brutal than the earlier Mongol conquests of Eurasia. Even the crossing of the Pacific had been done before, though in stages.

What gave this maritime revolution unprecedented importance had more to do with what happened after 1550 than with what happened earlier. Europeans' overseas empires would endure longer than the Mongols' and would continue to expand for three-and-a-half centuries after 1550. Unlike the Chinese, the Europeans did not turn their backs on the world after an initial burst of exploration. Not content with dominance in the Indian Ocean trade, Europeans opened in the Atlantic a maritime network that grew to rival the Indian Ocean network in the wealth of its trade. They also pioneered regular trade across the Pacific. The maritime expansion begun in the period from 1450 to 1550 marked the beginning of a new age of growing global interaction.

■ Key Terms

Zheng He	Christopher Columbus
Arawak	Ferdinand Magellan
Henry the Navigator	conquistadors
caravel	Hernán Cortés
Gold Coast	Moctezuma
Bartolomeu Dias	Francisco Pizarro
Vasco da Gama	Atahualpa

■ Suggested Reading

There is no single survey of the different expansions covered by this chapter, but the selections edited by Joseph R. Levenson, *European Expansion and the Counter Example of Asia, 1300–1600* (1967), remain a good introduction to Chinese expansion and Western impressions of China. Janet Abu-Lughod, *Before European Hegemony: The World System, A.D. 1250–1350* (1989), is a stimulating speculative reassessment of the importance of the Mongols and the Indian Ocean trade in the creation of the modern world system; she summarizes her thesis in the American Historical Association (AHA) booklet *The World System in the Thirteenth Century: Dead-End or Precursor?* (1993).

The Chinese account of Zheng He's voyages is Ma Huan, *Ying-yai Sheng-lan: "The Overall Survey of the Ocean's Shores"* [1433], ed. and trans. J. V. G. Mills (1970). A reliable guide to Polynesian expansion is Jesse D. Jennings, ed., *The Prehistory of Polynesia* (1979), especially the excellent chapter "Voyaging," by Ben R. Finney, which encapsulates his *Voyage of Rediscovery: A Cultural Odyssey Through Polynesia* (1994). The medieval background to European intercontinental voyages is summarized by Felipe Fernandez-Armesto, *Before Columbus: Exploration and Colonization from the Mediterranean to the Atlantic, 1229–1492* (1987).

A simple introduction to the technologies of European expansion is Carlo M. Cipolla, *Guns, Sails, and Empires: Technological Innovation and the Early Phases of European Expansion, 1400–1700* (1965; reprint, 1985). More advanced is Roger C. Smith, *Vanguard of Empire: Ships of Exploration in the Age of Columbus* (1993).

The European exploration is well documented and the subject of intense historical investigation. Clear general accounts based on the contemporary records are Boies Penrose, *Travel and Discovery in the Age of the Renaissance, 1420–1620* (1952); J. H. Parry, *The Age of Reconnaissance: Discovery, Exploration, and Settlement, 1450–1650* (1963); and G. V. Scammell, *The World Encompassed: The First European Maritime Empires, c. 800–1650* (1981).

An excellent general introduction to Portuguese exploration is C. R. Boxer, *The Portuguese Seaborne Empire, 1415–1825* (1969). More detail can be found in Bailey W. Diffie and George D. Winius, *Foundations of the Portuguese Empire, 1415–1580* (1977); A. J. R. Russell-Wood, *The Portuguese Empire: A World on the Move* (1998); and Luc Cuyvers, *Into the Rising Sun: The Journey of Vasco da Gama and the Discovery of the Modern World* (1998). John William Blake, ed., *Europeans in West Africa, 1450–1560* (1942), is an excellent two-volume collection of contemporary Portuguese, Castilian, and English sources. Elaine Sanceau, *The Life of Prester John: A Chronicle of Portuguese Exploration* (1941), is a very readable account of Portuguese relations with Ethiopia. *The Summa Oriental of Tomé Pires: An Account of the East, from the Red Sea to Japan, Written in Malacca and India in 1512–1515*, trans. Armando Cortesão (1944), provides a detailed firsthand account of the Indian Ocean during the Portuguese's first two decades there.

The other Iberian kingdoms' expansion is well summarized by J. H. Parry, *The Spanish Seaborne Empire* (1967). Samuel Eliot Morison's *Admiral of the Ocean Sea: A Life of Christopher Columbus* (1942) is a fine scholarly celebration of the epic mariner, also available in an abridged version as *Christopher Columbus, Mariner* (1955). More focused on the shortcomings of Columbus and his Spanish peers is Tzvetan Todorov, *The Conquest of America*, trans. Richard Howard (1985). Marvin Lunenfeld, ed., *1492: Discovery, Invasion, Encounter* (1991), critically examines contemporary sources and interpretations. William D. Phillips and Carla Rhan Phillips, *The Worlds of Christopher Columbus* (1992), examines the mariner and his times in terms of modern concerns. Peggy K. Liss, *Isabel the Queen: Life and Times* (1992), is a sympathetic examination of Queen Isabella of Castile. Detailed individual biographies of each of the individuals in Pizarro's band are the subject of James Lockhart's *Men of Cajamarca: A Social and Biographical Study of the First Conquerors of Peru* (1972). A firsthand account of Magellan's expedition is Antonio Pigafetta, *Magellan's Voyage: A Narrative Account of the First Circumnavigation*, available in a two-volume edition (1969) that includes a facsimile reprint of the manuscript.

The trans-Atlantic encounters of Europe and the Americas are described by J. H. Elliott, *The Old World and the New, 1492–1650* (1970). Alfred W. Crosby, *The Columbian Voyages, the Columbian Exchange, and Their Historians* (1987), available as an AHA booklet, provides a brief overview of the first encounters in the Americas and their long-term consequences. The early chapters of Mark A. Burkholder and Lyman L. Johnson, *Colonial Latin America*, 2d ed. (1994), give a clear and balanced account of the Spanish conquest.

The perceptions of the peoples European explorers encountered are not usually so well documented. John Thornton, *Africa and Africans in the Making of the Atlantic World, 1400–1800*, 2d ed. (1998), examines Africans' encounters with Europeans, importance in the Atlantic economy, and impact in the New World. *The Broken Spears: The Aztec Account of the Conquest of Mexico*, ed. Miguel Leon-Portilla (1962), presents Amerindian chronicles in a readable package, as does Nathan Wachtel, *The Vision of the Vanquished: The Spanish Conquest of Peru Through Indian Eyes* (1977). Anthony Reid, *Southeast Asia in the Age of Commerce, 1450–1680*, 2 vols. (1988, 1993), deals with events in that region.

■ Notes

1. Ma Huan, *Ying-yai Sheng-lan: "The Overall Survey of the Ocean's Shores,"* ed. Feng Ch'eng-Chün, trans. J. V. G. Mills (Cambridge, England: Cambridge University Press, 1970), 180.
2. Alvise da Cadamosto in *The Voyages of Cadamosto and Other Documents*, ed. and trans. G. R. Crone (London: Hakluyt Society, 1937), 2.

THE GLOBE ENCOMPASSED,

1500–1750

CHAPTER 18
THE TRANSFORMATION OF EUROPE, 1500–1750

CHAPTER 19
THE DIVERSITY OF AMERICAN COLONIAL SOCIETIES, 1530–1770

CHAPTER 20
THE ATLANTIC SYSTEM AND AFRICA, 1550–1800

CHAPTER 21
SOUTHWEST ASIA AND THE INDIAN OCEAN, 1500–1750

CHAPTER 22
EASTERN EURASIA, 1500–1800

uropean voyages of exploration greatly expanded global commercial, cultural, and biological exchanges between 1500 and 1750. Europeans built new commercial empires that grew stronger with each passing century. The Portuguese had begun the mastery of the seas by opening trade with sub-Saharan Africa and seizing control of maritime trading networks in the Indian Ocean. Then European colonization in the Americas stimulated the growth of a new Atlantic economy. From its colonial base in Mexico, Spain also pioneered new trade routes across the Pacific to the Philippines and China. In time, the Dutch, French, and English expanded these profitable maritime trading networks.

Commerce and colonization led to new interregional demographic and cultural exchanges. The introduction of unfamiliar diseases caused severe population losses in the Americas. To meet the resulting acute labor shortage, Europeans introduced enslaved Africans in ever-growing numbers. Europeans and Africans brought new languages, religious practices, music, and forms of personal adornment to the New World. Some Europeans who spent time overseas adopted new ways and developed new tastes that they later brought back with them when they returned to Europe.

In Asia and Africa, most important changes continued to come from internal causes rather than European expansion. The Islamic world saw the growth of regional empires in the Middle East, South Asia, and West Africa and continued its expansion into sub-Saharan Africa, southeastern Europe, and southern

Asia. Secure from external penetration, China experienced military expansion and population growth, and the expansion of educational institutions reinforced traditional values among China's upper classes. In Japan, a strong new national government promoted economic development and stemmed foreign influence, and the development of an indigenous merchant class widened the gap between popular and elite cultures.

Some of the farthest-reaching cultural changes in this period occurred in Europe. Reformers challenged established religious and political institutions, and new scientific discoveries and humanist concerns raised questions about traditional Western values and beliefs.

Important ecological changes occurred in areas of rising population and economic activity. The spread of new plants and animals around the world enhanced food supplies and altered landscapes. Forests were cut down to meet the increasing need for farmland, lumber, and fuel. But the most significant environmental changes resulted from the growing mastery of the winds and currents that propelled European ships across the world's oceans. Europeans' leadership in navigational technology went hand in hand with their emerging dominance in military technology. Lacking an expanding economic base, the great Islamic empires and China fell behind the smaller European nations in military strength. After 1750, the consequences of this widening technological and economic gap were to become momentous.

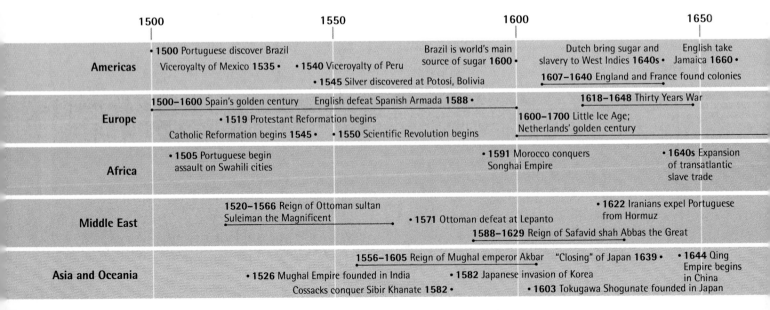

	1500	1550	1600	1650
Americas	• **1500** Portuguese discover Brazil Viceroyalty of Mexico **1535** •	• **1540** Viceroyalty of Peru • **1545** Silver discovered at Potosí, Bolivia	Brazil is world's main source of sugar **1600** •	Dutch bring sugar and slavery to West Indies **1640s** • **1607–1640** England and France found colonies	English take Jamaica **1660** •
Europe	**1500–1600** Spain's golden century • **1519** Protestant Reformation begins Catholic Reformation begins **1545** •	English defeat Spanish Armada **1588** • • **1550** Scientific Revolution begins	**1600–1700** Little Ice Age; Netherlands' golden century	**1618–1648** Thirty Years War
Africa	• **1505** Portuguese begin assault on Swahili cities		• **1591** Morocco conquers Songhai Empire	• **1640s** Expansion of transatlantic slave trade
Middle East	**1520–1566** Reign of Ottoman sultan Suleiman the Magnificent	• **1571** Ottoman defeat at Lepanto **1588–1629** Reign of Safavid shah Abbas the Great	• **1622** Iranians expel Portuguese from Hormuz	
Asia and Oceania	**1556–1605** Reign of Mughal emperor Akbar • **1526** Mughal Empire founded in India Cossacks conquer Sibir Khanate **1582** •	• **1582** Japanese invasion of Korea • **1603** Tokugawa Shogunate founded in Japan	"Closing" of Japan **1639** •	• **1644** Qing Empire begins in China

ARCTIC OCEAN

St. Petersburg

England

Netherlands

EUROPE

R u s s i a n   E m p i r e

ASIA

Spain

Ottoman Empire

Korea

Japan

Safavid Empire

China

MIDDLE EAST

Mughal Empire

Calcutta

Songhai

AFRICA

PACIFIC OCEAN

Asante

Dahomey

Swahili Coast

East Indies

INDIAN OCEAN

SOUTH ATLANTIC OCEAN

AUSTRALIA

| 0 | 1000 | 2000 | 3000 Km. |
| 0 | 1000 | 2000 | 3000 Mi. |

1700   **1750**   **1800**

• **1664** English take New Netherland from Dutch

1756–1763 French and Indian War; British take Canada

West Indies are world's main source of sugar **1700** •

• **1718** French found New Orleans

1780–1782 Revolt of Tupac Armaru in Peru

1667–1697 Wars of Louis XIV

• **1712** Peter the Great founds St. Petersburg

1700–1800 The Enlightenment

1701–1714 War of the Spanish Succession

• **1755** Lisbon earthquake

• **1680s** Rise of Asante kingdom

• **1720s** Rise of kingdom of Dahomey

1750–1800 Growing slave trade reduces population

• **1683** Last Ottoman siege of Vienna

1718–1730 Tulip Period of Ottoman Empire; Ottoman military decline

Fall of Safavid Empire **1722** •

1736–1747 Nadir Shah reunites Iran

• **1689** Treaty of Nerchinsk

• **1792** Russian ships reach Japanese coast

• **1691** British found trading post at Calcutta

• **1755** Qing conquest of Turkestan

1736–1799 Reign of Qing emperor Qianlong

18

THE TRANSFORMATION OF EUROPE,

1500–1750

Religious and Political Innovations • Building State Power • Urban Society
and Commercial Technology • Rural Society and the Environment •
The Realm of Ideas

ENVIRONMENT AND TECHNOLOGY: Mapping the World

SOCIETY AND CULTURE: Witchcraft

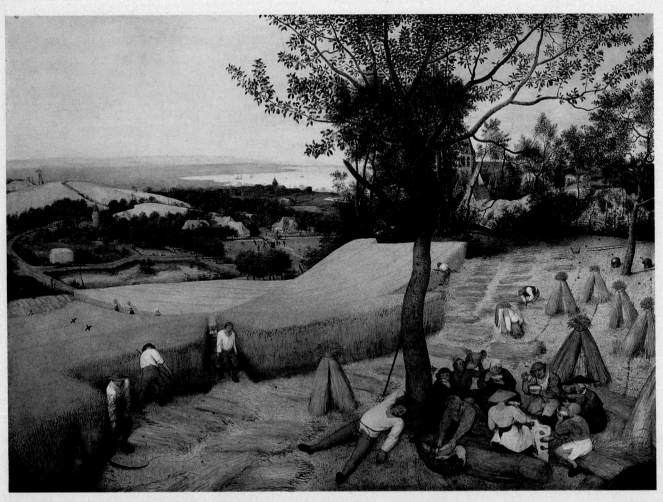

The Harvesters, 1565, by Pieter Bruegel, the Elder
A successful wheat harvest was necessary to feed bread- and pasta-eating Europe.

I n the winter of 1697–1698 Tsar° Peter I, the young ruler of Russia, traveled in disguise through the Netherlands and England, eager to discover how western European societies were becoming so powerful and wealthy. A practical man, Peter paid special attention to ships and weapons, even working for a time as a ship's carpenter in the Netherlands. With great insight, he perceived that western European success owed as much to trade and toleration as to technology. Trade generated the money to spend on weapons, while toleration attracted talented persons fleeing persecution.

Upon his return to Russia, Peter resolved to "open a window onto Europe," to reform features of his vast empire that he believed were backward. He ended the servile status of women and personally trimmed his noblemen's long beards to conform to Western styles. Peter also put the skilled technical advisers he brought back with him to work on modernizing Russia's industry and military forces. His reformed armies soon gained success against Sweden for possession of a port on the Baltic Sea and against the Ottoman Turks for access to the warm waters of the Black Sea. Then Peter turned to redesigning Russia's government on a German model. He built a new palace like King Louis XIV's and copied the French king's rituals of absolute royal power.

As Peter's actions imply, by the end of the seventeenth century, western European achievements in state administration, warfare, business, and ideas were setting standards that others wished to imitate. Along with maritime expansion (examined in Chapter 17), these internal transformations promoted Western global ascendancy. Yet such achievements did not come smoothly. Warfare, poverty, persecution, and environmental degradation were also widespread in Europe between 1500 and 1750.

As you read this chapter, ask yourself the following questions:

- Was Tsar Peter right in thinking that military, economic, and political changes were moving western Europe ahead of other parts of the world?

- What were the immediate and long-term consequences of those changes and others in European religious and scientific ideas?

- How did the many conflicts and rapid changes of this period affect ordinary men and women in Europe?

RELIGIOUS AND POLITICAL INNOVATIONS

Two bitter struggles in the early sixteenth century marked the end of Europe's medieval era and the beginning of the early modern period. One was the Reformation, a movement that introduced many religious reforms but shattered the ideal of Latin Christian unity. The other was an unsuccessful attempt to unite Christian Europe politically in order to block the inroads of the Muslim armies of the Ottoman Empire.

Instead of achieving unity, early modern Europe was plagued by division and persistent warfare among its national monarchies. Yet such disunity helped foster Europe's growing strength in the world. Competition and conflict promoted technological, administrative, social, and economic changes that propelled western Europe ahead of the more unified and peaceful empires of China and India and even ahead of the militarily aggressive Ottoman Empire.

Religious Reformation, 1517–1563

In 1500 the **papacy**, the central government of Latin Christianity, was simultaneously gaining stature and suffering from corruption and dissent. Economic prosperity produced larger donations and tax receipts, allowing popes to fund ambitious construction projects in Rome, their capital city. During the sixteenth century Rome gained fifty-four new churches and other buildings that showcased the artistic **Renaissance** then under way. However, the church's wealth and power also attracted some ambitious men, some of whose personal lives became the source of scandal.

The jewel of the new building projects was the magnificent new Saint Peter's Basilica in Rome. The unprecedented size and splendor of this church were intended to glorify the Christian faith, display the skill of Renaissance artists and builders, and enhance the standing of

---

tsar (zahr)

Martin Luther This detail of a painting by Lucas Cranach (1547) shows the Reformer preaching in his hometown church at Wittenberg. (Church of St. Marien, Wittenberg, Germany/The Bridgeman Art Library, New York and London)

the papacy. Such a project required refined tastes and vast sums of money.

The skillful overseer of the design and financing of the new Saint Peter's was Pope Leo X (r. 1513–1521), a member of the wealthy Medici° family of Florence, famous for its patronage of the arts. Pope Leo's artistic taste was superb and his personal life free from scandal, but he was more a man of action than a spiritual leader. One technique that he used to raise funds for the basilica was to authorize an **indulgence**—a forgiveness of the punishment due for past sins, granted by church authorities as a reward for a pious act such as making a pilgrimage, saying a particular prayer, or making a donation to a religious cause.

Medici (MED-ih-chee)

In one German state where the new indulgence was being preached lived a young professor of sacred scripture named Martin Luther (1483–1546), whose personal religious quest had led him to forsake money and marriage for a life of prayer and self-denial in a monastery. Luther had found consolation in the passage in Saint Paul's Epistle to the Romans that argued that salvation came not by "doing certain things" but from religious faith. Thus Luther was very upset by the indulgence preachers, who he thought emphasized the act of giving money more than the faith behind the act. He wrote to Pope Leo, asking him to stop the abuses and challenged the preachers to a debate on the theology of indulgences.

This theological dispute quickly escalated into a contest between two strong-minded men. Largely ignoring Luther's theological objections, Pope Leo regarded his letter as a challenge to papal power and acted to silence him. During a debate in 1519 a papal representative led Luther into open disagreement with some church doctrines, for which the papacy condemned him. Blocked in his effort to reform the church from within, Luther burned the papal bull (document) of condemnation, rejecting the pope's authority and beginning the movement known as the **Protestant Reformation.**

Accusing those whom he called "Romanists" (Roman Catholics) of relying on "good works," Luther insisted that the only way to salvation was through faith in Jesus Christ. He further declared that Christian belief must be based on the word of God in the Bible and on Christian tradition, not on the authority of the pope, as Catholics held. Eventually his conclusions led him to abandon his monastic prayers and penances and to marry a former nun.

Today Roman Catholics and most Lutherans have resolved their differences on many theological issues. But in the sixteenth century, stubbornness on both sides made reconciliation impossible.

Inspired by Luther, others raised their voices to denounce the ostentation and corruption of church leaders and to call for a return to authentic Christian practices and beliefs. John Calvin (1509–1564), a well-educated Frenchman who turned from the study of law to theology after experiencing a religious conversion, became a highly influential Protestant leader. As a young man in 1535, Calvin published *The Institutes of the Christian Religion*, a masterful synthesis of Christian teachings. Much of the *Institutes* was traditional medieval theology, but in two respects Calvin's teaching differed from that of Roman Catholics and Lutherans. First, while agreeing with Luther's emphasis on faith over works, Calvin denied that even human faith could merit salvation. Salvation, said Calvin, was God's free gift to those

CHRONOLOGY

	Politics and Culture	Environment and Technology	Warfare
1500	**1500s** Spain's golden century **1519** Protestant Reformation begins **1540s** Scientific Revolution begins **1545** Catholic Reformation begins	**Mid-1500s** Improved windmills and increasing land drainage in Holland	**1526–1571** Ottoman wars **1546–1555** German Wars of Religion **1562–1598** French Wars of Religion **1566–1648** Netherlands Revolt
	Late 1500s Witchhunts increase	**1590s** Dutch develop flyboats; Little Ice Age begins	
1600	**1600s** Holland's golden century	**1600s** Depletion of forests growing **1609** Galileo's astronomical telescope	**1618–1648** Thirty Years War **1642–1648** English Civil War **1652–1678** Anglo-Dutch Wars **1667–1697** Wars of Louis XIV **1683–1697** Ottoman wars
1700	**1700s** The Enlightenment begins	**1682** Canal du Midi completed	**1700–1721** Great Northern War **1701–1714** War of the Spanish Succession
		1750 English mine nearly 5 million tons of coal a year **1755** Lisbon earthquake	

God "predestined" for it. Second, Calvin went further than Luther in curtailing the power of ordained clergymen and in simplifying religious rituals. Calvinist congregations elected their own governing committees and in time created regional and national synods (councils) to regulate doctrinal issues. Calvinists also displayed simplicity in dress, life, and worship. In an age of ornate garments, they wore simple black clothes, avoided ostentatious living, and worshiped in churches devoid of statues, most musical instruments, stained-glass windows, incense, and vestments.

The Reformers appealed to religious sentiments, but political and social agendas also inspired many who joined them. Part of the appeal of Lutheranism to German-speakers was in reaction to the power of Italians in the Catholic Church. Peasants and urban laborers sometimes defied their masters by adopting a different faith. Neither tradition had a special attraction for women, since both Protestants and Roman Catholics believed in male dominance in the church and the family. Most Protestants, however, rejected the medieval tradition of celibate priests and nuns and advocated Christian marriage for all adults.

Shaken by the intensity of the Protestant Reformers' appeal, the Catholic Church undertook its own reforms. A council that met at the city of Trent, in northern Italy, in three sessions between 1545 and 1563 issued decrees reforming the education, discipline, and practices of the Roman Catholic clergy. The council also reaffirmed the supremacy of the pope and clarified Catholic beliefs (including those concerning indulgences) in light of Protestant challenges. Also important to this **Catholic Reformation** were the activities of a new religious order—the Society of Jesus, or "Jesuits," that Ignatius of Loyola (1491–1556), a Spanish nobleman, founded in 1534. Well-educated Jesuits helped stem the Protestant tide and win back some adherents by their teaching and preaching (see Map 18.1). Other Jesuits became important missionaries overseas (see Chapters 19 and 22).

Given the complexity of the issues and the intensity of the emotions that the Protestant Reformation stirred, it is not surprising that violence often flared up. Both

Map 18.1 Religious Reformation in Europe The Reformation brought greater religious freedom but also led to religious conflict and persecution. In many places the Reformation accelerated the trend toward state control of religion and added religious differences to the motives for wars among Europeans.

Predominant Religion in 1555

- Lutheran
- Calvinist (Reformed)
- Church of England
- Roman Catholic
- ▲ Huguenot centers
- → Spread of Calvinism

0   150   300 Mi.
0   150   300 Km.

sides persecuted and sometimes executed those of differing views. Bitter "wars of religion," fought over a mixture of religious and secular issues, continued in parts of western Europe until 1648.

The Failure of Empire, 1519–1556

Meanwhile, there was also trouble in another great medieval institution, the **Holy Roman Empire,** a loose federation of Germanic states and principalities. The threat that the Ottoman Turks posed by their advances into southeastern Europe stirred interest in a pan-European coalition to stop the Muslim advances. Hope centered on a young man named Charles (1500–1557), descended from the powerful **Habsburg°** family of Austria and the rulers of Burgundy on his father's side and from the rulers of Spain on his mother's. After the death of his maternal grandfather in 1516, Charles inherited the Spanish thrones of Castile and Aragon along with their extensive European and American possessions. At the death of his paternal grandfather in 1519, the young king inherited the Austrian Habsburg possessions and also secured election as Emperor Charles V, ruler of the Holy Roman Empire, which the Habsburgs had headed for three generations (see Map 18.2).

A Latin Christian coalition led by Charles eventually halted the Ottomans at the gates of Vienna in 1529, but did not end Ottoman attacks, which continued on and off until 1697. Charles's efforts to forge his several possessions into Europe's strongest state met strong resistance. King Francis I of France, who had lost to Charles in the election for Holy Roman Emperor, openly supported the Muslim Turks to weaken his rival. Nor were the heads of the many states within the Holy Roman Empire eager to share their powers and revenues with the emperor. Luther's Reformation played into their hands. In the imperial Diet (assembly) many German princes, swayed partly by Luther's appeals to German nationalism, also opposed Charles, a French-speaking emperor who defended the papacy. Some Lutheran princes enriched themselves by seizing the church's lands within their states in the name of reform. The new kingdom of Prussia (created in 1701) came into being in lands that a Lutheran prince had seized from a Catholic religious order in 1525.

After decades of bitter squabbles turned to open warfare in 1546 (the German Wars of Religion), Charles V finally gave up his efforts at unification, abdicated control of his various possessions to different heirs, and retired to a monastery. To his son Philip went the throne of Spain, Europe's most powerful state then in the midst of its golden age. Administration of the war-torn Holy Roman Empire went to his brother Ferdinand, who ended the lost war against Lutheranism and the German princes. By the Peace of Augsburg (1555), he recognized the princes' right to choose whether Catholicism or Lutheranism would prevail in their particular states, and he allowed them to keep church lands they had seized before 1552.

Thus two institutions that had symbolized Western unity during the Middle Ages—the papacy and the Holy Roman Empire—were seriously weakened by the mid-sixteenth century. Luther emerged from a monastery to break the papacy; Charles retired to a monastery, broken by opposition to an effective pan-European empire. Both the papacy and the Holy Roman Empire continued to exist, but national kingdoms assumed much of the religious and political leadership in western Europe. Indeed, the collapse of religious and imperial unity was partly the work of ambitious monarchs eager to enhance their own power by bringing all other institutions under their control and preventing the emergence of any imperial superpower.

Royal Centralization, 1500–1750

Talented rulers and their able ministers guided the rise of these European kingdoms. When the system of monarchical succession worked best, it brought to the throne a creative, energetic young person who gained experience and won loyalty over many decades. By good fortune the leading states produced many such talented, hard-working, and long-lived rulers. Spain had only six rulers in the two centuries from 1556 to 1759, and France had but five between 1574 and 1774 (see Table 18.1). The long reigns of the Tudor monarchs Henry VIII and his Protestant daughter Elizabeth I helped stabilize sixteenth-century England, but their Stuart successors were twice overthrown by revolution during the next century.

Successful monarchs depended heavily on their chief advisers, who also eased the transition between rulers. Cardinal Jiménez° guided the nineteen-year-old Charles V's entry to the throne of Spain. Cardinal Richelieu° oversaw the policies of the young Louis XIII in France, and Richelieu's successor Cardinal Mazarin° guided the youthful Louis XIV, who came to the throne at the age of five. By the seventeenth century, kings were beginning to draw on the talents of successful businessmen, such as Jean Baptiste Colbert° (1619–1683), Louis

---

Habsburg (HABZ-berg)

Jiménez (he-MEH-nes)   Richelieu (ree-shuh-LYOO)
Mazarin (MAZ-uh-rin, maz-uh-RAN)   Colbert (kohl-BEAR)

Map. 18.2 The European Empire of Charles V Charles was Europe's most powerful ruler from 1519 to 1556, but he failed to unify the Christian West. In addition to being the elected head of the Holy Roman Empire, he was the hereditary ruler of the Spanish realms of Castile and Aragon and the possessions of the Austrian Habsburgs in Central Europe. The map does not show his extensive holdings in the Americas and Asia.

Table 18.1   Rulers in Early Modern Western Europe

Spain	France	England/Great Britain
Habsburg Dynasty	**Valois Dynasty**	**Tudor Dynasty**
Charles I (1516–1556) (Holy Roman-Emperor Charles V)	Francis I (1515–1547)	Henry VIII (1509–1547)
Philip II (1556–1598)	Henry II (1547–1559)	Edward VI (1547–1553)
	Francis II (1559–1560)	Mary I (1553–1558)
	Charles IX (1560–1574)	Elizabeth I (1558–1603)
	Henry III (1574–1589)	
	Bourbon Dynasty	**Stuart Dynasty**
Philip III (1598–1621)	Henry IV (1589–1610)[a]	James I (1603–1625)
Philip IV (1621–1665)	Louis XIII (1610–1643)	Charles I (1625–1649)[a, b]
Charles II (1665–1700)	Louis XIV (1643–1715)	(Puritan Republic, 1649–1660)
		Charles II (1660–1685)
		James II (1685–1688)[b]
		William III (1689–1702)
		and Mary II (1689–1694)
Bourbon Dynasty		Anne (1702–1714)
Philip V (1700–1746)		
		Hanoverian Dynasty
	Louis XV (1715–1774)	George I (1714–1727)
Ferdinand VI (1746–1759)		George II (1727–1760)

[a]Died a violent death.   [b]Was overthrown.

XIV's able minister of finance. In Great Britain, Robert Walpole, the powerful prime minister from 1721 to 1742, dominated the early Hanoverian kings.

Able monarchs and their advisers worked to enhance royal authority by limiting the autonomy of the church. Well before the Reformation, rulers in Spain, Portugal, and France had gained control over church appointments and had used church revenues to enhance royal power. This absorption of the church into the state helps explain why religious uniformity became a hot political issue. Following the pattern used by his predecessors to suppress Jewish and Muslim practices, King Philip II of Spain used an ecclesiastical court, the Spanish Inquisition, to bring into line those who resisted his authority. It was the one institution common to his three Spanish kingdoms. Suspected Protestants, as well as critics of the king, found themselves accused of heresy, an offense punishable by death. Even those who were acquitted of the charge learned not to oppose the king again.

In France, Prince Henry of Navarre switched his faith from Calvinist to Catholic after gaining the military advantage in the French Wars of Religion (1562–1598), so that, as King Henry IV (the first of the Bourbon kings), he

would share the faith of the majority of his subjects. His son and grandson, Kings Louis XIII and Louis XIV (see Table 18.1), were as devoted to French Catholic religious uniformity as their counterparts in Spain. In 1685 Louis XIV even revoked the Edict of Nantes°, by which his grandfather had granted religious freedom to his Protestant supporters in 1598.

Elsewhere, the Protestant Reformation made it easier for monarchs to increase their control of the church. The church in England lost its remaining autonomy after the pope turned down King Henry VIII's petition for an annulment of his marriage to Katharine of Aragon. Distressed that Katharine had not furnished him with a male heir, Henry had the English archbishop of Canterbury annul the marriage in 1533. The breach with Rome was sealed the next year when Parliament made the English monarch head of the Church of England.

Henry used his authority to disband monasteries and convents. He gave some of their landholdings to his powerful allies and sold others to pay for his new navy. In other respects religion changed little under Henry and his successors, despite growing pressures from English

Nantes (nahnt)

Calvinists known as Puritans to "purify" the Anglican church of Catholic practices and beliefs. In 1603, the first Stuart king, James I, dismissed a Puritan petition to eliminate bishops with the statement "No bishops, no king"—a reminder of the essential role that bishops played in royal administration.

In addition to gaining control of the church, western European kings and queens enhanced their powers by promoting national institutions. In 1500 many of the separate provinces of Spain and France had their own laws and institutions, reflecting their piecemeal acquisition by inheritance and conquest. By 1750 there was more uniformity in law and administration. Seventeenth-century French kings took two steps to decrease local power. They appointed *intendants*°, new royal officials to enforce their orders in the provinces. They also used the army to tear down the fortifications behind which powerful nobles and towns had often asserted their independence.

The growth of a common language, especially among the elites, further strengthened national unity. In Spain the Castilian dialect gained currency. In France people increasingly imitated the speech of Paris. The Protestant emphasis on reading the Bible in vernacular languages (instead of in Latin) speeded up the replacement of many dialects with standardized national languages. Luther's magnificent translation of the Bible into the High German of Saxony laid the basis for modern German. The biblical translation prepared under the direction of King James I did the same for English, as did Calvin's translation for French. Important new secular literatures also helped to standardize national languages. These included the English plays of William Shakespeare (1564–1616), the French satires of François Rabelais° (1483–1553), the Spanish novel *Don Quixote* by Miguel de Cervantes° (1547–1616), and *The Lusiads*, an epic poem celebrating overseas exploration, by the Portuguese poet Luís de Camões° (1524?–1580).

Absolutism and Constitutionalism

The absence of any constitutional check on a ruler's power is called **absolutism.** Many seventeenth- and eighteenth-century European monarchs admired absolutism and tried to put it into practice. But monarchs trying to concentrate power in their own hands had to confront the representative assemblies that traditionally had to approve important royal actions such as making war and levying new taxes. As we have seen, the princes in the imperial Diet of the Holy Roman Empire effectively resisted Charles V. In contrast, French kings succeeded in circumventing the Estates General. In England, Parliament checked royal power and established **constitutionalism,** a system of government that subjects the ruler's power to limits specified by law and custom.

In France the Estates General represented the traditional rights of three groups: the clergy, the nobility, and the towns (that is, townspeople with wealth and high status). The Estates General was able to assert itself during the sixteenth-century French Wars of Religion, when the monarchy was weak. But, except in 1614 when Queen Marie de Medici was ruling in the name of her young son, the Bourbon kings refused to call it into session. Unable to impose new taxes without summoning the Estates General, Louis XIV turned to his astute finance minister, Colbert, who devised new, efficient tax collection methods that tripled the amount of money reaching the royal treasury. To increase the tax base, Colbert also promoted economic development both in France and overseas. When Louis XIV's wars (1667–1697) and high living strained the treasury to the breaking point, the king raised additional sums by selling high offices, again bypassing the Estates General.

Louis XIV's gigantic new palace at Versailles° symbolized the French monarch's triumph over the traditional rights of the nobility. Capable of housing ten thousand people and surrounded by elaborately landscaped grounds and parks, the palace can be seen as a sort of theme park of royal absolutism. Required to spend much of their time at elaborate ceremonies and banquets centered on the king, the nobles who lived at Versailles were kept away from the real politics of the kingdom. According to one of them, the duke of Saint-Simon°, "no one was so clever in devising petty distractions" as the king. So successful was Versailles in taming the nobles that not only Tsar Peter in Russia but other kings, princes, and even a powerful German archbishop built imitations of it.

As eager as his French counterparts to promote royal absolutism, King Charles I of England (see Table 18.1) ruled for eleven years without summoning Parliament, his kingdom's representative body. To raise money, he coerced "loans" from wealthy subjects and twisted tax laws to new uses. Then in 1640, a rebellion in Scotland forced him to summon the members of Parliament to approve new taxes to pay for an army. Noblemen and churchmen sat in the House of Lords. Representatives

---

intendants (in-TEN-dants)   **Rabelais** (RAB-uh-lay)
Cervantes (ser-VAHN-tees)   **Camões** (kuh-MOINSH)

Versailles (vuhr-SIGH)   **Saint-Simon** (san see-MON)

Versailles, 1722   This painting by P.-D. Martin shows the east expanse of buildings and courtyards that make up the palace complex built by King Louis XIV.   (Giraudon/Art Resource, NY)

from the towns and counties sat in the House of Commons. Before authorizing new taxes, Parliament insisted on strict guarantees that the king would never again ignore its traditional rights. These King Charles refused to grant. When he ordered the arrest of his leading critics in the House of Commons in 1642, he plunged the kingdom into civil war.

Defending Parliament's traditional rights were the rich commoners and the well-organized religious Puritans, who had not given up on their plans to cleanse the English church of Catholic traits. Supporting the king were most of the established nobility and the conservative northern parts of the kingdom. When Charles refused to compromise even after being defeated on the battlefield, a "Rump" Parliament purged of his supporters ordered him executed in 1649 and replaced the monarchy with a Puritan Republic under the Puritan general Oliver Cromwell.

Cromwell expanded England's power overseas and imposed firm control over Ireland and Scotland, but he was as unwilling as the Stuart kings to share power with Parliament. After his death the Stuart line was restored in 1660, and for a time it was unclear which side had won the English Civil War.

However, when King James II refused to respect Parliament's rights and had his heir baptized a Roman Catholic, Parliament offered the throne to his Protestant daughter Mary and her Dutch husband, Prince William of Orange. Their triumphal arrival in England forced James into exile in the bloodless Glorious Revolution of 1688. This time, there was no doubt about the outcome. The Bill of Rights of 1689 specified that Parliament had to be called "frequently" and had to consent to changes in laws and to the raising of an army in peacetime. Another law reaffirmed the official status of the Church of England but gave religious toleration to Puritans.

BUILDING STATE POWER

The growing power of early modern European rulers, whether absolutist or constitutional, would have been of modest global significance if they had not achieved notable success in two other important areas. One was developing some of the world's most powerful armed forces. The other was ensuring sufficient economic growth to support the heavy costs of royal administration and warfare.

War and Diplomacy

Warfare was almost constant in early modern Europe (see the Chronology at the beginning of the chapter). These struggles for dominance first produced a dramatic change in the size, skill, and weapons of armed forces and then an advance in diplomacy. The military revolution began in the Late Middle Ages when firearms became the preferred weapons of war: cannon replaced catapults as siege weapons, muskets displaced lances and crossbows, and gun-toting commoners on foot supplanted aristocratic knights on horseback.

The numbers of men in arms increased steadily throughout the early modern period. Spanish armies doubled in size from about 150,000 in the 1550s to 300,000 in the 1630s. French forces, about half the size of the Spanish in the 1630s, grew to 400,000 by the early eighteenth century. Even smaller European states built up impressive armies. Sweden, with under a million people, had one of the finest and best-armed military forces in seventeenth-century Europe. Prussia, with fewer than 2 million inhabitants in 1700, devoted so many resources to building a splendid army that it became one of Europe's major powers. Only England did not maintain a standing army in peacetime, but the Royal Navy protected the island nation from invasion.

Large armies required effective command structures. Long before the development of modern field communications systems, European armies, in the words of a modern historian, "evolved . . . the equivalent of a central nervous system, capable of activating technologically differentiated claws and teeth."[1] New signaling techniques improved control of battlefield maneuvers. Better discipline was achieved by frequent marching drills, which trained troops to obey orders instantly and gave them a close sense of comradeship. First developed in the Netherlands during a long struggle for independence from Spain, the drilling techniques were quickly imitated by the best armies in Europe.

Military victories by the giant armies were not assured, however. New fortifications able to withstand cannon bombardments made cities harder to capture, and battles between evenly matched armies often ended in stalemates, as in the Thirty Years War (1618–1648). Victory in war increasingly depended on naval superiority. Warships were redesigned to accommodate several tiers of cannon that had the power to blow holes in the thick sides of enemy ships. Improved four-wheel carriages made cannon easier to pull back and reload.

The rapid changes in naval warfare are evident in two fleets used by Philip II of Spain. In 1571 a combined Spanish and Italian fleet of 200 ships met an even larger Ottoman force off Lepanto on the Greek coast. Both fleets consisted principally of oar-powered galleys, which had only light armaments. To attack, one galley rammed another so that armed men could climb aboard for hand-to-hand combat. Four hours after the battle began, the remains of 200 Ottoman galleys littered the sea's surface, and the waters were red with the blood of 30,000 slain men. The Christian coalition's victory resulted from the valor of Spanish troops and the superior firepower of a handful of specially built Venetian ships.

A very different Spanish fleet, the Catholic Armada, sailed from Lisbon in 1588 hoping to repeat the Lepanto success over the Protestant enemies of the north. The complex mission of these 130 heavily armed ships was to replace the Protestant ruler of England, Queen Elizabeth, with a Roman Catholic, then put down the rebellion in the Netherlands, and finally intervene on the Catholic side in the French Wars of Religion. But history did not repeat itself. The English could fire more rapidly because of their new cannon carriages, and their smaller, quicker ships successfully evaded the ram-and-board technique, which the Spanish retained from their Mediterranean victory. Moreover, a chance storm, celebrated by the English as a providential "Protestant wind," scattered and sank many Spanish ships that had survived the sea battles, thus dooming Philip's other plans for the armada.

The armada's defeat signaled the end of Spain's military dominance in Europe. By the time of the Thirty Years War, France had recovered from its Wars of Religion to become Europe's most powerful state. With twice the population of Spain at their command, France's forceful kings of the Bourbon dynasty could field Europe's largest armies, whether to squelch domestic unrest, extend France's boundaries, or intervene in the affairs of neighboring states.

After emerging from its own civil conflicts in 1689, England became France's major rival. By then England ruled a North American empire as well as Ireland, and in 1707 England merged with Scotland to become Great

Austrian Siege of Belgrade, 1688   The Ottoman Turks, in control of the Balkan Peninsula since the early sixteenth century, again assaulted the city of Vienna in 1683. Revitalized Austrian Habsburg armies successfully defended their capital and then took the offensive against the Muslim invaders, retaking Hungary and capturing the city of Belgrade, south of the Danube River. Although the Turks soon regained Belgrade, the annexation of Hungary doubled the size of the Austrian Empire and altered the balance of power in southeastern Europe.   (Giraudon/Art Resource, NY)

Britain. England's rise as a sea power had begun in the time of King Henry VIII, who spent heavily on ships and promoted a domestic iron-smelting industry to supply cannon. Queen Elizabeth's victorious fleet of 1588 was considerably improved by the copying of innovative ship designs from the Dutch in the second half of the seventeenth century. The Royal Navy grew in numbers, surpassing the French fleet by the early eighteenth century.

In a series of eighteenth-century wars, beginning with the War of the Spanish Succession (1701–1714), the combination of Britain's naval strength and the land armies of its Austrian and Prussian allies was able to block French expansionist efforts and prevent the Bourbons from uniting the thrones of France and Spain. This defeat of the French monarchy's empire-building efforts illustrated the principle of **balance of power** in international relations: the major European states formed temporary alliances to prevent any one state from becoming too powerful.

Russia emerged as a major power in Europe after Peter the Great's modernized armies defeated Sweden in the Great Northern War (1700–1721). During the next two centuries, though adhering to four different branches of Christianity, the great powers of Europe—Catholic France, Anglican Britain, Catholic Austria, Lutheran Prussia, and Orthodox Russia (see Map 18.3)—maintained an effective balance of power in Europe by shifting their alliances for geopolitical rather than religious reasons.

Politics and the Economy

To pay the extremely heavy military costs of their wars, European rulers had to increase their revenues. The most successful of them after 1600 promoted mutually beneficial alliances with the rising commercial elites. Both parties understood that trade thrived where government taxation and regulation were not excessive, where courts enforced contracts and collected debts, and where military power stood ready to protect overseas expansion by force when necessary.

Spain, sixteenth-century Europe's mightiest state, illustrates how the financial drains of an aggressive military policy and the failure to promote economic development

Map. 18.3 Europe in 1740 By the middle of the eighteenth century the great powers of Europe were France, the Austrian Empire, Great Britain, Prussia, and Russia. Spain, the Holy Roman Empire, and the Ottoman Empire were far weaker in 1740 than they had been two centuries earlier.

could lead to decline. Expensive wars against the Ottomans, northern European Protestants, and rebellious Dutch subjects caused the treasury of King Philip II to default on its debts four times. Moreover, the Spanish rulers' concerns for religious uniformity and traditional aristocratic privilege further undermined the country's economy. In the name of religious uniformity they expelled Jewish merchants, persecuted Protestant dissenters, and forced tens of thousands of skilled farmers and artisans into exile because of their Muslim ancestry. While exempting the landed aristocracy from taxation, Spanish rulers imposed high sales taxes that discouraged manufacturing.

For a time, vast imports of silver and gold bullion from Spain's American colonies filled the government treasury. These bullion shipments also contributed to severe inflation (rising prices), worst in Spain but bad throughout the rest of western Europe as well. A Spanish saying captured the problem: American silver was like rain on the roof—it poured down and washed away. Huge debts for foreign wars drained bullion from Spain to its creditors. More wealth flowed out to purchase manufactured goods and even food in the seventeenth century.

The rise of the Netherlands as an economic power stemmed from opposite policies. The Spanish crown had acquired these resource-poor but commercially successful provinces as part of Charles V's inheritance. But King Philip II's decision to impose Spain's ruinously heavy sales tax and enforce Catholic orthodoxy drove the Dutch to revolt in 1566 and again in 1572. Those measures would have discouraged business and driven away the Calvinists, Jews, and others who were essential to Dutch prosperity. The Dutch fought with skill and ingenuity, raising and training an army and a navy that were among the most effective in Europe. By 1609 Spain was forced to agree to a truce that recognized the autonomy of the northern part of the Netherlands. In 1648, after eight decades of warfare, the independence of these seven United Provinces of the Free Netherlands (to give their full name) became final.

Rather than being ruined by the long war, the United Netherlands emerged in the seventeenth century as the dominant commercial power in Europe and the world's greatest trading nation. During this golden century the wealth of the Netherlands multiplied instead of flowing away. This economic success owed much to a decentralized government. During the long struggle against Spain, the provinces united around the prince of Orange, their sovereign, who served as commander-in-chief of the armed forces. But in economic matters each province was free to pursue its own interests. The maritime province of Holland grew rich by favoring commercial interests.

Holland's many towns and cities were filled with skilled craftsmen. Factories and workshops turned out goods of exceptional quality at a moderate price and on a vast scale. The textile industry concentrated on the highly profitable finishing and printing of cloth, transforming into fine textiles the cloth spun and woven by low-paid workers. Other factories refined West Indian sugar, brewed beer from Baltic grain, cut Virginia tobacco, and made imitations of Chinese ceramics. Holland's printers published books in many languages, free from the censorship imposed by political and religious authorities in neighboring countries. For a small province, barely above sea level, lacking timber and other natural resources, this was a remarkable achievement.

Amsterdam, Holland's major city, was seventeenth-century Europe's financial center and major port. From there Dutch ships dominated the sea trade of Europe, carrying over 80 percent of the trade to Spain from northern Europe, even while Spain and the Netherlands were at war. The Dutch dominance of Atlantic and Indian Ocean trade was such that, by one estimate, they conducted more than half of all the oceangoing commercial shipping in the world (for details see Chapters 20 and 21).

After 1650 the Dutch faced growing competition from the English, who were developing their own close association of business and government. In a series of wars (1652–1678) England used its naval might to break Dutch dominance in overseas trade and to extend England's colonial empire. With government support, the English merchant fleet doubled between 1660 and 1700, and foreign trade rose by 50 percent. As a result, state revenue from customs duties tripled. During the eighteenth century Britain's trading position strengthened still more.

The debts run up by the Anglo-Dutch Wars helped persuade the English monarchy to greatly enlarge the government's role in managing the economy. The outcome has been called a "financial revolution." The government increased revenues by taxing the formerly exempt landed estates of the aristocrats and by collecting taxes directly. Previously private individuals known as tax farmers had advanced the government a fixed sum of money; in return they could keep whatever money they were able to collect from taxpayers. To secure cash quickly for warfare and other emergencies and to reduce the burden of debts from earlier wars, England also followed the Dutch lead in creating a central bank, from which the government was able to obtain long-term loans at low rates.

The French government was also developing its national economy, especially under Colbert. He streamlined tax collection, promoted French manufacturing

Port of Amsterdam   Ships, barges and boats of all types are visible in this busy seventeenth-century scene. The large building in the center is the Admiralty House, which housed the headquarters of the Dutch East India Company.   (Mansell Collection/Time Inc.)

and shipping by imposing taxes on foreign goods, and improved transportation within France itself. Yet the power of the wealthy aristocrats kept the French government from following England's lead in taxing wealthy landowners, collecting taxes directly, and securing low-cost loans. Nor did France succeed in managing its debt as efficiently as England. (The role of governments in promoting overseas trade is discussed in Chapter 20.)

URBAN SOCIETY AND COMMERCIAL TECHNOLOGY

Just as palaces were early modern Europe's centers of political power, cities were its economic power centers. The urban growth under way since the eleventh century was accelerating and spreading. In 1500, Paris was the only northern European city with over 100,000 inhabitants. By 1700, both Paris and London had populations over 500,000, Amsterdam had burgeoned from a fishing

village to a metropolis of some 200,000, and twenty other European cities contained over 60,000 people.

The cities' growth depended primarily on the prosperous merchants who managed the great expansion of regional and overseas commerce. Improved business techniques and manufacturing technologies also added to the cities' prosperity, but wealth was unevenly distributed.

Urban Social Classes

In about 1580 the mayor of the French city of Bordeaux° asked a group of visiting Amerindian chiefs what impressed them most about European cities. The chiefs are said to have expressed astonishment at the disparity between the fat, well-fed people and the poor, half-starved men and women in rags. Why, the visitors wondered, did the poor not grab the rich by the throat or set fire to their homes? The contrasts of wealth in European cities were indeed startling, and social tension often ran high.[2]

Bordeaux (bor-DOH)

The French called the well-off who dominated the cities **bourgeoisie**° (town dwellers). Their wealth came from manufacturing, finance, and especially trade, both regional and overseas.

Grain for bread was brought by carts and barges from the surrounding countryside or, in the largest cities of western Europe, transported by special fleets from the eastern Baltic lands. Other fleets brought wine from southern to northern Europe. Parisians downed 100,000 barrels of wine a year at the end of the seventeenth century. The poor also consumed large amounts of beer. In 1750 Parisian breweries made 23 million quarts (22 million liters) for local consumption, another stimulus to the grain trade. In the seventeenth and eighteenth centuries wealthier urban classes could buy exotic luxuries imported from the far corners of the earth—Caribbean and Brazilian sugar and rum, Mexican chocolate, Virginian tobacco, North American furs, East Indian cotton textiles and spices, and Chinese tea.

As related above, the rise of the bourgeoisie was aided by mutually beneficial alliances with monarchs who saw economic growth as the best means of increasing state revenues. Unlike the old nobility, who shunned productive labor, members of the bourgeoisie devoted long hours to their businesses and poured their profits into new business ventures or other investments rather than spending them. Even so, they still had enough money to live comfortably in large houses with many servants.

Like merchants in the Islamic world, Europe's merchants relied on family and ethnic networks. In addition to families of local origin, many northern European cities contained merchant colonies from Venice, Florence, Genoa, and other Italian cities. In Amsterdam and Hamburg lived Jewish merchants who had fled religious persecution in Iberia. Other Jewish communities expanded out of eastern Europe into the German states, especially after the Thirty Years War. Armenian merchants from Iran were moving into the Mediterranean and became important in Russia in the seventeenth century.

Europe's cities were home not only to the well-off bourgeoisie, but also to craftworkers and many poor people. From 10 to 20 percent of the city dwellers were so poor they were exempt from taxation. This number included only the "deserving poor," whom officials considered permanent residents. Cities contained large numbers of "unworthy poor"—recent migrants from impoverished rural areas, peddlers traveling from place to place, and beggars (many with horrible deformities and sores) who tried to survive on charity. There were also criminals, usually organized in gangs, ranging from youthful pickpockets to highway robbers.

Some people managed to improve their lot in life and others slipped lower, but most followed the careers of their parents.

In contrast to the arranged marriages common in much of the rest of the world, young men and women in early modern Europe generally chose their own spouses and after marriage set up their own households instead of living with their parents. The sons and daughters of craftworkers and the poor had to delay marriage until they could afford to live on their own. Young men had to serve a long apprenticeship to learn a trade. Young women had to work—helping their parents, as domestic servants, or in some other capacity—to save money for the dowry they were expected to bring into the marriage. A dowry was the money and household goods—the amount varied by social class—that enabled a young couple to begin marriage independent of their parents. The typical groom in early modern Europe could not hope to marry before his late twenties, and his bride would be a few years younger—in contrast to the rest of the world, where people usually married in their teens.

Marriage also came late in bourgeois families. One reason for the delay was to allow men to finish their education. Bourgeois parents did not formally arrange their children's marriages, but the fact that nearly all found spouses within their social class strongly suggests that parents promoted marriages that forged business alliances with other families.

Bourgeois parents were very concerned that their children have the education and training necessary for success. They promoted the establishment of municipal schools to provide a solid education, including Latin and perhaps Greek, for their sons, who were then sent abroad to learn modern languages or to a university to earn a law degree. Legal training was useful for conducting business and was a prerequisite for obtaining government judgeships and treasury positions. Daughters were less likely to be groomed for a business career, but wives often helped their husbands as bookkeepers and sometimes inherited businesses.

Besides enabling young people to be independent of their parents, the late age of marriage in early modern Europe also held down the birthrate and thus limited family size. Even so, about one-tenth of the births in a city were to unmarried women, often servants, who generally left their infants on the doorsteps of churches, convents, or rich families. Despite efforts to raise such abandoned children, many perished. Delayed marriage

---

bourgeoisie (boor-zwah-ZEE)

The Fishwife, 1572 Women were essential partners in most Dutch family businesses. This scene by the Dutch artist Adriaen van Ostade shows a woman preparing fish for retail sale. (Rijksmuseum-Stichting)

also had links to the existence of public brothels, where young men could satisfy their lusts in cheap and impersonal encounters with unfortunate young women, often newly arrived from impoverished rural villages. Nevertheless, rape was a common occurrence, usually perpetrated by gangs of young men who attacked young women rumored to be free with their favors. Some historians believe that such gang rapes reflect poor young men's jealousy at older men's easier access to women.

Commercial Techniques and Technology

The expansion of trade in early modern Europe prompted the development of new techniques to manage far-flung business enterprises and invest the profits they produced. As elsewhere in the world, most businesses in Europe operated with family-owned funds or money borrowed from private moneylenders. But a key change in Europe was the rise of large financial institutions to serve the interests of big business and big government. In the seventeenth century, private Dutch banks developed such a reputation for security that wealthy individuals and governments from all over western Europe entrusted them with their money. To make a

profit, the banks invested these funds in real estate, local industries, loans to governments, and overseas trade.

Another commercial innovation was the **joint-stock company,** which sold shares to individuals. Often backed by a government charter, such companies offered a way to raise large sums for overseas enterprises while spreading the risks (and profits) among many investors (the operation of chartered joint-stock companies in the overseas trade is examined in Chapter 20). After the initial offerings, investors could buy and sell shares in specialized financial markets called **stock exchanges,** an Italian innovation transferred to the cities of northwestern Europe in the sixteenth century. The greatest stock market in the seventeenth and eighteenth centuries was the Amsterdam Exchange, founded in 1530. Large insurance companies also emerged in this period, and insuring long voyages against loss became a standard practice after 1700 (see Chapter 20).

Changes in technology also facilitated economic growth. As in the case of military developments, this was more an age of technological refinement and multiplication than innovation. For example, water wheels—a traditional source of mechanical energy for mills and factories—gradually increased in size. In the Dutch province of Holland, improved systems of gears made it possible to adapt windmills for new uses, such as driving a saw. Information about new devices was spread by means of printed manuals on machinery, metallurgy, agriculture, and other technical subjects.

Improvements in water transport expanded Europe's superb natural network of seas and navigable rivers for moving bulk items such as grain, wine, and timber. The Dutch built numerous canals to drain the lowlands for agriculture and for transport. Other canals, with elaborate systems of locks to cross hills, were built in France, Germany, Italy, and England. One of the most important was the 150–mile (240–kilometer) Canal du Midi in France, built by the French government between 1661 and 1682 to link the Atlantic and the Mediterranean.

The expansion of maritime trade led to new designs for merchant ships. In this, too, the Dutch played a dominant role. Using timber imported from northern Europe, shipyards in Dutch ports built ships for their own vast fleets and for export. Especially successful was the *fluit,* or "flyboat," a large-capacity cargo ship developed in the 1590s. It was inexpensive to build and required only a small crew. Another successful type of merchant ship, the heavily armed "East Indiaman," helped the Dutch establish their supremacy in the Indian Ocean. The Dutch also excelled at mapmaking (see Environment and Technology: Mapping the World).

Mapping the World

In 1602 the Jesuit missionary Matteo Ricci in China printed an elaborate map of the world. Working from maps produced in Europe and incorporating the latest knowledge gathered by European maritime explorers, Ricci introduced two changes to make the map more appealing to his Chinese hosts. He labeled it in Chinese characters, and he split his map down the middle of the Atlantic so that China lay in the center. This version pleased Chinese elites, who considered China the "Middle Kingdom" surrounded by lesser states. A copy of Ricci's map in six large panels adorned the emperor's Beijing palace.

The stunningly beautiful maps and globes of sixteenth-century Europe were the most complete, detailed, and useful representations of the earth that any society had ever produced. The best mapmaker of the century was Gerhard Kremer, who is remembered as Mercator (the merchant) because his maps were so useful to European ocean traders. By incorporating the latest discoveries and scientific measurements, Mercator could depict the outlines of the major continents in painstaking detail, even if their interiors were still largely unknown to outsiders.

To represent the spherical globe on a flat map, Mercator drew the lines of longitude as parallel lines. Because such lines actually meet at the poles, Mercator's projection greatly exaggerated the size of every landmass and body of water distant from the equator. However, Mercator's rendering offered a very practical advantage: sailors could plot their course by drawing a straight line between their point of departure and their destination. Because of this useful feature the Mercator projection of the world remained in common use until quite recently. To some extent, its popularity came from the exaggerated size this projection gave to Europe. Like the Chinese, Europeans liked to think of themselves as at the center of things. Europeans also understood their true geographical position better than people in any other part of the world.

Dutch World Map, 1641
It is easy to see why the Chinese would not have liked to see their empire at the far right edge of this widely printed map. Besides the distortions caused by the Mercator projection, geographical ignorance exaggerates the size of North America and Antarctica.   (Courtesy of the Trustees British Museum)

RURAL SOCIETY AND THE ENVIRONMENT

For all its new political, military, and commercial strengths, early modern Europe rested on a fragile agrarian base. The techniques and efficiency of European agriculture had improved little since 1300. Bad years brought famine; good ones provided only small surpluses. Social tensions and conflicts multiplied as warfare, environmental deterioration, and adverse economic conditions worsened the circumstances of most rural Europeans between 1500 and 1750.

The Struggle for Food

Under the pressure of social and environmental change and inflation, the condition of the average person in western Europe seems to have worsened sharply during the century after 1530. Peasants in England were reduced to a diet of black bread and little else. Elsewhere people starved. Wars and other human-engineered calamities were partly to blame. In Spain the old nobility was responsible for the consolidation of landownership and the impoverishment of the peasantry. By 1600 only 3 percent of the population controlled 97 percent of the land. When Spanish landowners decided that they could increase their incomes by turning cropland into pastures for their sheep, food production and population declined.

Rural Europeans also felt the adverse effects of a century of relatively cool climate that began in the 1590s. During this **Little Ice Age,** average temperatures fell only a few degrees, but the effects were startling. Glaciers in the Alps grew much larger. Rivers and canals important to commerce froze solid from bank to bank. In some places during the coldest years, the growing season shrank by two months. As a result, food crops ripened more slowly during cooler summers and were often damaged by early fall frosts. In spring late frosts withered the tender shoots of newly planted crops.

People could survive a smaller-than-average harvest in one year with reserves left from the year before. But when one cold year followed another, the consequences were devastating. Records show that when average summer temperatures in northern Europe were 2.7°F (1.5°C) lower in 1674 and 1675 and again in 1694 and 1695, deaths due to malnutrition and cold increased sharply.

The cold spell of 1694–1695 caused a famine in Finland that carried off between a quarter and a third of the population.

By 1700, new crops from the Americas were helping the rural poor avoid starvation. At first eaten only in desperate times, potatoes and maize (corn) became staples for the rural poor in the eighteenth century because they yielded more abundant food from small garden plots. Potatoes sustained life in northeastern and Central Europe and in Ireland. Peasants along the Mediterranean who could not afford to eat the wheat they raised for urban markets grew maize for their own consumption.

Deforestation

Another threat to rural life came from **deforestation.** Early modern Europeans cut down their great hardwood forests to provide timbers for ships, lumber for buildings, wagons, and barrels, fuel for heating and cooking, and charcoal for smelting ores and other industrial processes. Each of the three hundred ironworks in England in the late seventeenth century consumed a thousand loads of oak a year. Wood shortages resulting from such high consumption led to increased imports of timber and charcoal from more heavily forested Scandinavian countries and Russia. Sweden used its vast forest resources to become a major iron producer in the seventeenth century. After 1716 Russia was Europe's largest producer of iron.

Because of this consumption of wood for Europe's rising population and expanding economy, forest depletion emerged as a serious issue in the seventeenth and eighteenth centuries. The shortages were particularly acute in England, where one early-seventeenth-century observer lamented: "within man's memory, it was held impossible to have any want of wood in England. But . . . at present, through the great consuming of wood . . . and the neglect of planting of woods, there is a great scarcity of wood throughout the whole kingdom."[3] Shortages in England drove the price of ordinary firewood up five times faster than other prices between the late fifteenth and the mid-seventeenth centuries.

High wood prices encouraged the use of coal as an alternative fuel. England's coal mining increased twelvefold from 210,000 tons in 1550 to 2.5 million tons in 1700. From 1709, coke—coal refined to remove impurities—gradually replaced charcoal in the smelting of iron. These new demands drove English coal production to nearly 5 million tons a year by 1750.

France was much more forested than England, but increasing consumption there caused Colbert to predict that "France will perish for lack of wood." By the late

Winter in Flanders, 1565   This January scene by the Flemish artist Pieter Bruegel, the Elder, shows many everyday activities. At left, men return from trapping hares, and the women under the sign singe the bristles off a slaughtered pig. On the frozen ponds, people skate and play hockey and curling. An old woman carries a load of faggots across the bridge. A February scene that Bruegel painted as part of this series shows the snow all melted. A few decades later, however, winters became longer and colder.   (Kunsthistorisches Museum, Vienna/The Bridgeman Art Library, New York and London)

eighteenth century, deforestation was becoming an issue even in Sweden and Russia. New laws in France and England designed to protect the forests were largely inspired by fears of shortages for naval vessels, whose keels required high-quality timbers of exceptional size and particular curvature. Although wood consumption remained high, rising prices encouraged some individuals to plant trees for future harvest.

Everywhere in Europe the rural poor felt the depletion of the forests most strongly. For centuries they had depended on woodlands for abundant supplies of wild nuts and berries, free firewood and building materials, and wild game. Many poor men and women flocked to the cities in hopes of finding better jobs, but most were disappointed. As we have seen, begging, theft, and prostitution were the result.

Peasantry and Gentry

The bright side of rural life in western Europe was the remarkable personal freedom of the peasantry in comparison with people of similar status in many other parts of the world. Serfdom, which bound men and women to land owned by a local lord, declined sharply after the great plague of the mid-fourteenth century. Most remaining serfs in western Europe gained their freedom by 1600. By that date slavery in southern Iberia, which had been sustained by large numbers of captives from Africa, had also come to an end. Coincidentally, the disappearance of serfdom in western Europe was paralleled by the introduction of serfdom in much of early modern eastern Europe.

Legal freedom in western Europe did little to make the peasants' lives safe and secure. Peasants with surplus crops to sell benefited from the higher prices brought about by inflation, but the broader trend was for peasants to fall deeper and deeper into debt until they lost their land. This transformation of rural ownership was accelerated by the desire of many successful members of the bourgeoisie to use their wealth to raise their social status. Retiring from their professions and buying country estates gained them admission to the ranks of gentry. These new owners of rural estates affected the lifestyle of the old aristocracy and sometimes received the aristocracy's exemption from taxation, but they did not have titles of nobility.

The gentry loaned money to impoverished peasants and to members of the nobility and in time increased their ownership of land. Some families sought aristocratic husbands for their daughters. The old nobility found such alliances attractive because of the large dowries that rich merchants provided. In France a family could gain the exemption from taxation by living in gentility for three generations. The same family could gain noble status more quickly by purchasing a title. French kings sold so many new patents of nobility that people came to distinguish the new *noblesse de robe*° (dress nobility) from the medieval *noblesse d'épée*° (sword nobility).

Rural misery in early modern Europe provoked many rebellions. For example, in 1525 peasant rebels in the Alps attacked both nobles and clergy as representatives of the privileged and landowning classes. They had no love for merchants either, whom they denounced for lending at interest and charging high prices. Rebellions multiplied as rural conditions worsened. In southwestern France alone some 450 uprisings occurred between 1590 and 1715, many of them set off by food shortages and tax increases. The exemption of the wealthy from taxation was a frequent souce of complaint. A rebellion in southern France in 1670 began when a mob of townswomen attacked the tax collector. It quickly spread to the country, where peasant leaders cried, "Death to the people's oppressors!" Authorities dealt severely with such revolts and executed or maimed their leaders.

In 1750 most Europeans still lived in general wretchedness. Modest improvements in food production in some places were overwhelmed by population growth. Even in the prosperous Dutch towns half of the population lived in acute poverty. Some rural poor in the eighteenth century worked at home spinning yarn and weaving cloth from materials supplied by entrepreneurs. So many single women supported themselves by spinning yarn that *spinster* became the normal English word for an unmarried woman.

---

noblesse de robe (no-BLES deh ROHB)
noblesse d'épée (no-BLES day-PAY)

THE REALM OF IDEAS

New ideas and old beliefs pulled early modern Europeans in several different directions, even after the Reformation controversies subsided. The hold of biblical and traditional folk beliefs on the thinking of most people showed itself in widespread new fears about witches and the power of the Devil. The Renaissance helped sharpen the influence of writings from Greco-Roman antiquity on educated people. A few thinkers broke new scientific ground in deciphering the motion of the planets and constructing mathematical models of the force of gravitation. In time, the new scientific ideas encouraged some to reevaluate traditional social and political systems, with important implications for the period after 1750.

Traditional Thinking and Witch-Hunts

Prevailing European ideas about the natural world blended two distinct traditions. The older was made up of stories and beliefs from local folk cultures and pre-Christian religions, which had not lost their hold on the minds of most Europeans. On to this tradition was grafted the biblical traditions of the Christian and Jewish scriptures, heard by all in church and read by growing numbers in vernacular translations. In the minds of most people ideas of magic and folk spirits mixed with Christian teachings about miracles, saints, and devils.

Like people in other parts of the world, most early modern Europeans believed that natural events could have supernatural causes. When crops failed or domestic animals died unexpectedly, many people blamed unseen spirits. People also attributed human triumphs and tragedies to supernatural causes. When an earthquake destroyed much of Lisbon, Portugal's capital city, in November 1755, for example, both educated and uneducated saw the event as a punishment sent by God. A Jesuit charged it "scandalous to pretend that the earthquake was just a natural event." An English Protestant leader agreed, comparing Lisbon's fate with that of Sodom, the city that God destroyed because of the sinfulness of its citizens, according to the Hebrew Bible.

Nowhere was the belief in unseen forces more evident than in the extraordinary series of **witch-hunts** that swept across northern Europe in the late sixteenth and seventeenth centuries. It is estimated that secular and church authorities tried over a hundred thousand people—some three-fourths of them women—for prac-

Witchcraft

The elderly widow whose account follows was fairly typical of the kind of person accused of witchcraft in the Holy Roman Empire. Her confession, given in 1587, mentions activities commonly associated with witches: fornicating with devils, murdering children, desecrating the Blessed Sacrament, causing destructive storms, and night flying—though on a pitchfork, not a broomstick.

The herein mentioned, malefic and miserable woman, Walpurga Hausmännin, now imprisoned and in chains, has, upon kindly questioning and also torture, . . . confessed her witchcraft and admitted the following. When one-and-thirty years ago, she became a widow, she cut corn for Hans Schlumperger, of this place, together with his former servant, Bis im Pfarrhof, by name. Him she enticed with lewd speeches and gestures and they convened that they should, on an appointed night, meet in her, Walpurga's, dwelling, there to indulge in lustful intercourse. So when Walpurga in expectation of this, sat awaiting him at night in her chamber, meditating upon evil and fleshy thoughts, it was not the said bondsman who appeared unto her, but the Evil One in the latter's guise and raiment and indulged in fornication with her. . . . After the act of fornication she saw and felt the cloven foot of her whoremonger, and that his hand was not natural, but as if made of wood. She was greatly affrighted thereat and called upon the name of Jesus, whereupon the Devil left her and vanished.

On the ensuing night the Evil Spirit visited her again in the same shape and whored with her. . . . Further, the above-mentioned Walpurga confesses that she oft and much rode on a pitchfork by night with her paramour, but not far on account of her duties [as a midwife].

Since she surrendered to the Devil, she had seemingly oft received the Blessed Sacrament of the true Body and Blood of Jesus Christ, apparently by the mouth, but had not partaken of it, but (which once more is terrible to relate) had always taken it out of her mouth again and delivered it up to Federlin, her paramour. At their nightly gatherings she had oft with her other playfellows trodden under foot the Holy and Blessed Sacrament and the image of the Holy Cross. . . .

He also compelled her to do away with and to kill young infants at birth, even before they had been taken to Holy Baptism. This she did whenever possible. . . . She had used the said little bones to manufacture hail; this she was wont to do once or twice a year. . . .

After all this, the Judges and Jury of the Court of this Town of Dillingen . . . at last unanimously gave the verdict that the aforesaid Walpurga Hausmännin be punished and dispatched from life to death by burning at the stake as being a maleficent and well-known witch and sorceress, convicted according to the context of Common Law and the Criminal Code of the Emperor Charles V and the Holy Roman Empire. All her goods and chattels and estate left after her to go to the Treasury of our Most High Prince and Lord. The aforesaid Walpurga to be led, seated on a cart, to which she is tied, to the place of her execution, and her body first to be torn five times with red-hot irons. . . . But since for nineteen years she was a licensed and pledged midwife of the city of Dillingen, yet has acted so vilely, her right hand with which she did such knavish tricks is to be cut off at the place of execution. Neither are her ashes after burning to remain lying on the ground, but are thereafter to be carried to the nearest flowing water and thrown thereinto.

Under what circumstances did the widow confess to these deeds? Why was she so brutally executed?

Source: The Fugger News-Letters, ed. Victor von Klarwill, trans. Pauline de Chary (London: John Lane, The Bodley Head Ltd., 1924); reissued as *News and Rumor in Renaissance Europe: The Fugger Newsletters*, trans. Pauline de Chary (New York: Putnam, 1959), 137–139, 142–143.

ticing witchcraft. Some were acquitted, some recanted, but over half were executed. The trial records make it clear that both the accusers and the accused believed that it was possible for angry and jealous individuals to use evil magic and the power of the Devil to cause people and domestic animals to sicken and die or cause crops to wither in the fields. Torture and badgering questions persuaded many accused witches to confess to casting spells and to describe in vivid detail their encounters with the Devil and their attendance at nighttime assemblies of witches (see Society and Culture: Witchcraft).

Modern historians have sought other explanations for these witch-hunts. The fact that many of the accused were older women, especially widows, may reflect the widespread belief that women not directly under the control of fathers or husbands were likely to turn to evil. The fear of people rebelling against those in authority was well founded.

Modern research, however, also stresses that at least some of those accused in early modern Europe may really have tried to use witchcraft and the powers of the Devil to harm their enemies. The Reformation had focused attention on the Devil and may have helped revive older fears of witchcraft. In parts of the world where belief in witchcraft is still strong, witch-hunts often arise at times of social stress, and people who are marginalized by poverty and by the suspicions of others often relish the celebrity that public confession brings. Self-confessed "witches" may even find release from the guilt they feel for wishing evil on their neighbors.

No single reason can explain the rise in witchcraft accusations and fears in early modern Europe, but, for both the accusers and the accused, there are plausible connections between the witch-hunts and rising social tensions, rural poverty, and environmental strains. Far from being a bizarre aberration, witch-hunts reflected the larger social climate of early modern Europe.

The Scientific Revolution

Ideas about the natural world were influenced by folk and Christian traditions and by writings from Greco-Roman antiquity that had been revived during the Renaissance. Among intellectuals prevailing ideas were based on the physics of Aristotle. The Greek philosopher taught that everything on earth was reducible to four elements. The surface of the earth was composed of the two heavy elements, earth and water. The atmosphere was made up of two lighter elements, air and fire, which floated above the ground. Higher still were the sun, moon, planets, and stars, which, according to Aristotelian physics, were so light and pure that they floated in crystalline spheres. This division between the ponderous, heavy earth and the airy, celestial bodies accorded perfectly with the common-sense perception that all heavenly bodies revolved around the earth.

The prevailing conception of the universe was also influenced by the mathematical tradition derived from the ancient Greek mathematician Pythagoras, who proved the validity of the famous theorem that still bears his name: In a right triangle, the squares of the hy-potenuse is equal to the sum of the squares of the other two sides ($a^2 + b^2 = c^2$). Pythagoreans attributed to mystical properties the ability of simple mathematical equations to describe physical objects. They attached special significance to the simplest (to them perfect) geometrical shapes: the circle (a point rotated around another point) and the sphere (a circle rotated on its axis). They believed that celestial objects were perfect spheres orbiting the earth in perfectly circular orbits.

In the sixteenth century, however, the careful observations and mathematical calculations of some daring and imaginative European investigators began to challenge these prevailing conceptions of the physical world. These pioneers of the **Scientific Revolution** demonstrated that the workings of the universe could be explained by natural causes.

Over the centuries, observers of the nighttime skies had plotted the movements of the heavenly bodies, and mathematicians had worked to fit these observations into the prevailing theories of circular orbits. To make all the evidence fit, they had come up with eighty different spheres and some ingenious theories to explain the many seemingly irregular movements. Pondering these complications, a Polish monk and mathematician named Nicholas Copernicus (1473–1543) came up with a mathematically simpler solution: switching the center of the different orbits from the earth to the sun would reduce the number of spheres that were needed.

Copernicus did not challenge the idea that the sun, moon, and planets were light, perfect spheres, or that they moved in circular orbits. But his placement of the sun, not the earth, at the center of things began a revolution in understanding about the structure of the heavens and about the central place of humans in the universe. To escape the anticipated controversies, Copernicus delayed the publication of his heliocentric (sun-centered) theory until after his death in 1543.

Other astronomers, including the Danish Tycho Brahe (1546–1601) and his German assistant Johannes Kepler (1571–1630), strengthened and improved on Copernicus's model, showing that planets actually move in elliptical, not circular orbits. The most brilliant of the Copernicans was the Italian Galileo Galilei° (1564–1642). In 1609 Galileo built a telescope through which he took a closer look at the heavens. Able to magnify distant objects thirty times beyond the powers of the naked eye, Galileo saw that heavenly bodies were not the perfectly smooth spheres of the Aristotelians. The moon, he re-

Galileo Galilei (gal-uh-LAY-oh gal-uh-LAY-ee)

ported in *The Starry Messenger* (1610), had mountains and valleys; the sun had spots; other planets had their own moons. In other words, the earth was not alone in being heavy and changeable.

At first, the Copernican universe found more critics than supporters because it so directly challenged not just popular ideas but the intellectual synthesis of classical and biblical authorities. How, demanded Aristotle's defenders, could the heavy earth move without producing vibrations that would shake the planet apart? Is the Bible wrong, asked the theologians, when the Book of Joshua says that, by God's command, "the sun [not the earth] stood still . . . for about a whole day" to give the ancient Israelites victory in their conquest of Palestine? If Aristotle's physics was wrong, worried other traditionalists, would not the theological synthesis built on other parts of his philosophy be open to question?

Intellectual and religious leaders encouraged political authorities to suppress the new ideas. Most Protestant leaders, following the lead of Martin Luther, condemned the heliocentric universe as contrary to the Bible. Catholic authorities waited longer to act. After all, both Copernicus and Galileo were Roman Catholics Copernicus had dedicated his book to the pope, and another pope, Gregory XIII, in 1582 had used the latest astronomical findings to issue a new and more accurate calendar (still used today). Galileo ingeniously argued that the conflict between scripture and science was only apparent: the word of God revealed in the Bible was expressed in the imperfect language of ordinary people, but in nature God's truth was revealed more perfectly in a language that could be learned by careful observation and scientific reasoning.

Unfortunately, Galileo also ridiculed those who were slow to accept his findings, charging that Copernican ideas were "mocked and hooted at by an infinite multitude . . . of fools." Smarting under Galileo's stinging sarcasm, some Jesuits and other critics got his ideas condemned by the Roman Inquisition in 1616, which put *The Starry Messenger* on the Index of Forbidden Books and prohibited Galileo from publishing further on the subject. (In 1992 the Catholic Church officially retracted its condemnation of Galileo.)

Despite official opposition, printed books spread the new scientific ideas among scholars across Europe. In England, Robert Boyle (1627–1691) used experimental methods and a trial-and-error approach to examine the inner workings of chemistry. He and fellow members of the Royal Society were enthusiastic missionaries of mechanical science and fierce opponents of the Aristotelians.

Galileo in 1624   This engraving by Ottavio Leone shows the Italian scientist in full vigor at age sixty, before he was hounded by the Roman Inquisition.   (British Museum)

Meanwhile, English mathematician Isaac Newton (1642–1727) was carrying Galileo's demonstration that the heavens and earth share a common physics to its logical conclusion. Newton formulated a set of mathematical laws that all physical objects obeyed. It was the force of gravity—not angels—that governed the elliptical orbits of heavenly bodies. It was gravitation (and the resistance of air) that caused cannonballs to fall back to earth. From 1703 until his death Newton served as president of the Royal Society, using his prestige to promote the new science that came to bear his name.

As the condemnation of Galileo demonstrates, many religious and intellectual leaders viewed the new science with suspicion or outright hostility. Yet the principal pioneers of the Scientific Revolution were all convinced that scientific discoveries and revealed religion were not in conflict. At the peak of his fame Newton promoted a series of lectures devoted to proving the validity of Christianity. However, by showing that the Aristotelians and biblical writers held ideas about the natural world that were naive and unfactual, these pioneers opened the door to others who used reason to challenge a broader range of unquestioned traditions and superstitions. The world of ideas was forever changed.

The Early Enlightenment

Advances in scientific thought had few practical applications until long after 1750. But they inspired governments and private groups in many countries to reexamine the reasonableness of everything from agricultural methods to laws, religion, and social hierarchies. The belief that human reason could discover the laws that governed social behavior and were just as scientific as the laws that governed physics energized a movement known as the **Enlightenment.** Like the Scientific Revolution, this movement was the work of a few "enlightened" individuals who often faced bitter opposition from the political, intellectual, and religious establishment. Leading Enlightenment thinkers became accustomed to having their books burned or banned and spent long periods in exile to escape being imprisoned themselves.

Influences besides the Scientific Revolution affected the Enlightenment. The Reformation had aroused many to champion one creed or another, but partisan bickering and bloodshed led others to doubt the superiority of any theological position and to recommend toleration of all religions. The killing of suspected witches also shocked many thoughtful people. The leading French thinker Voltaire (the pen name of François Marie Arouet, 1694–1778) declared: "No opinion is worth burning your neighbor for."

Accounts of cultures in other parts of the world also led some European thinkers to question assumptions about the superiority of European political institutions, moral standards, and religious beliefs. Reports of Amerindian life, though romanticized, led some to conclude that those whom they had called savages were in many ways nobler than European Christians. Matteo Ricci, a Jesuit missionary to China whose journals made a strong impression in Europe, contrasted the lack of territorial ambition of the Chinese with the constant warfare in the West and attributed the difference to the fact that China was wisely ruled by educated men whom he called "Philosophers."

Another influence on the "enlightened" thinkers of the eighteenth century was the English Revolution. In the wake of the Glorious Revolution of 1688 and the English Bill of Rights, the English political philosopher John Locke (1632–1704), who had lived in the Netherlands during the period of Oliver Cromwell's Puritan Republic, published his influential *Second Treatise of Civil Government* (1690). Locke disputed the prevailing idea that government was sacred and that kings ruled by divine right. He argued that rulers derived their power from the consent of the governed, who surrendered some of their rights to the state so that they might better preserve their lives, liberty, and property. Locke challenged the continental monarchs' often-repeated claim that they held absolute authority over their subjects. He believed that absolute monarchy was incompatible with civil society, and he wrote that monarchs, like everyone else, were subject to the law that laid the basis for the compact that brought civil society into existence. If monarchs overstepped the law, Locke argued, citizens had not only the right but the duty to rebel. The consequences of this idea are considered in Chapter 23.

Although many circumstances shaped "enlightened" thinking, the new scientific methods and discoveries provided the clearest model for changing European society. Voltaire posed the issues in these terms: "it would be very peculiar that all nature, all the planets, should obey eternal laws" but a human being, "in contempt of these laws, could act as he pleased solely according to his caprice." The English poet Alexander Pope (1688–1774) made a similar point in verse: "Nature and Nature's laws lay hidden in night; /God said, 'Let Newton be' and all was light."

The Enlightenment was more a frame of mind than a coherent movement. Individuals who embraced it drew inspiration from different sources and promoted different agendas. By 1750 its proponents were clearer about what they disliked than about what new institutions should be created. Some "enlightened" thinkers thought society could be made to function with the mechanical orderliness of planets spinning in their orbits. Nearly all were optimistic that—at least in the long run—human beliefs and institutions could be improved. This belief in progress would help foster political and social revolutions after 1750, as Chapter 23 recounts.

Despite the enthusiasm the Enlightenment aroused in some circles, it was decidedly unpopular with many absolutist rulers and with most clergymen. Europe in 1750 was neither enlightened nor scientific. It was a place where political and religious divisions, growing literacy, and the printing press made possible the survival of the new ideas that profoundly changed life in future centuries.

CONCLUSION

Historians use the word *revolution* to describe many different changes taking place in Europe between 1500 and 1750. The inflation of the sixteenth century has been called a price revolution, the expansion of trade a commercial revolution, the reform of state spending a financial revolution, the changes in weapons and warfare a military revolution. We have also encountered a scientific revolution and the religious revolution of the Reformation.

These important changes in early modern European government, economy, society, and thought were parts of a dynamic process that began in the later Middle Ages and led to even bigger industrial and political revolutions before the eighteenth century was over. Yet the years from 1500 to 1750 were not simply—perhaps not even primarily—an age of progress for Europe. For many, the ferocious competition of European armies, merchants, and ideas was a wrenching experience. The growth of powerful states extracted a terrible price in death, destruction, and misery. The Reformation brought greater individual choice in religion but widespread religious persecution as well. Individual women rose or fell with their social class, but few gained equality with men. The expanding economy benefited members of the emerging merchant elite and their political allies, but most Europeans became worse off as prices rose faster than wages. New scientific and enlightened ideas ignited new controversies long before they yielded any tangible benefits.

The historical significance of this period of European history is clearest when viewed in a global context. What stands out are the powerful and efficient European armies, economies, and governments, which were envied, and sometimes imitated, by other people such as Tsar Peter the Great. Seen from a global perspective, the balance of political and economic power shifted slowly but inexorably in the Europeans' favor from 1500 to 1750. In 1500 the Ottomans threatened Europe. By 1750, as the remaining chapters of Part Five detail, Europeans had brought the world's seas and a growing part of its land and people under their control. No single group of Europeans accomplished this. The Dutch eclipsed the pioneering Portuguese and Spanish; then the English and French bested the Dutch. Competition, too, was a factor in the European success.

Other changes in Europe during this period had no great overseas significance yet. The more representative

and financially stable government begun in Britain, the new ideas of the Scientific Revolution and the Enlightenment, and the innovations in agriculture and manufacturing were still of minor importance. Their full effects in furthering Europeans' global dominion were felt after 1750, as Parts Six and Seven will explore.

■ Key Terms

papacy	balance of power
Renaissance (Europe)	bourgeoisie
indulgence	joint-stock company
Protestant Reformation	stock exchange
Catholic Reformation	Little Ice Age
Holy Roman Empire	deforestation
Habsburg	witch-hunt
absolutism	Scientific Revolution
constitutionalism	Enlightenment

■ Suggested Reading

Overviews of this period include Euan Cameron, *Early Modern Europe* (1999), and H. G. Koenigsberger, *Early Modern Europe: Fifteen Hundred to Seventeen Eighty-Nine* (1987). Global perspectives can be found in Fernand Braudel, *Civilization and Capitalism, 15th–18th Century*, trans. Siân Reynolds, 3 vols. (1979), and Immanuel Wallerstein, *The Modern World-System*, vol. 2, *Mercantilism and the Consolidation of the European World-Economy, 1600–1750* (1980).

Excellent introductions to social and economic life are George Huppert, *After the Black Death: A Social History of Early Modern Europe* (1986), and Carlo M. Cipolla, *Before the Industrial Revolution: European Society and Economy, 1000–1700*, 2d ed. (1980). Peter Burke, *Popular Culture in Early Modern Europe* (1978), offers a broad treatment of nonelite perspectives, as does Robert Jütte, *Poverty and Deviance in Early Modern Europe* (1994). For more economic detail see Robert S. DuPlessis, *Transitions to Capitalism in Early Modern Europe* (1997); Myron P. Gutmann, *Toward the Modern Economy: Early Industry in Europe, 1500–1800* (1988); and Carlo M. Cipolla, ed., *The Fontana Economic History of Europe*, vol. 2, *The Sixteenth and Seventeenth Centuries* (1974). Merry E. Wiesner summarizes a body of new research in *Women and Gender in Early Modern Europe* (1994).

Technological and environmental changes are the focus of Geoffrey Parker, *Military Revolution: Military Innovation and the Rise of the West, 1500–1800*, 2d ed. (1996); William H. McNeill, *The Pursuit of Power: Technology, Armed Force, and Society Since A.D. 1000* (1982); Robert Greenhalgh Albion, *Forests and Sea Power: The Timber Problem of the Royal Navy, 1652–1862*

(1965); Emmanuel Le Roy Ladurie, *Times of Feast, Times of Famine: A History of Climate Since the Year 1000*, trans. Barbara Bray (1971); and Jean M. Grove, *The Little Ice Age* (1988). Robert C. Allen, *Enclosure and the Yeoman: The Agricultural Development of the South Midlands, 1450–1850* (1992), focuses on England.

Steven Stapin, *The Scientific Revolution* (1998), and Hugh Kearney, *Science and Change, 1500–1700* (1971) are accessible introductions. Thomas S. Kuhn, *The Structure of Scientific Revolution*, 3d ed. (1996), and A. R. Hall, *The Scientific Revolution, 1500–1800: The Formation of the Modern Scientific Attitude*, 2d ed. (1962), are classic studies. Carolyn Merchant, *The Death of Nature: Women, Ecology and the Scientific Revolution* (1980), tries to combine several broad perspectives. *The Sciences in Enlightened Europe*, ed. W. Clark, J. Golinski, and S. Schaffer (1999), examines particular topics in a sophisticated way. Dorinda Outram, *The Enlightenment* (1995), provides a recent summary of research.

An excellent place to begin examining the complex subject of witchcraft is Brian Levack, *The Witch-Hunt in Early Modern Europe*, 2d ed. (1995). Anne Llewellyn Barstow, *Witchcraft: A New History of the European Witch Hunts* (1994), offers a postmodern interpretation; other up-to-date perspectives can be found in J. Barry, M. Hester, and G. Roberts, eds., *Witchcraft in Early Modern Europe: Studies in Culture and Belief* (1998), and Carlo Ginzburg, *The Night Battles: Witchcraft and Agrarian Cults in the Sixteenth and Seventeenth Centuries*, trans. John and Anne Tedechi (1983). Cross-cultural perspectives are presented by Lucy Mair, *Witchcraft* (1969), and Geoffrey Parrinder, *Witchcraft: European and African* (1963).

Good single-country surveys are J. A. Sharpe, *Early Modern England: A Social History*, 2d ed. (1997); Emmanuel Le Roy Ladurie, *The Royal French State, 1460–1610* (1994) and *The Ancien Régime: A History of France, 1610–1774* (1998); Jonathan Israel, *The Dutch Republic: Its Rise, Greatness and Fall, 1477–1806* (1995); and James Casey, *Early Modern Spain: A Social History* (1999).

■ Notes

1. William H. McNeill, *The Pursuit of Power: Technology, Armed Force, and Society Since* A.D. *1000* (Chicago: University of Chicago Press, 1982), 124.
2. Michel de Montaigne, *Essais*, ch. 31, "Des Cannibales."
3. Quoted by Carlo M. Cipolla, "Introduction," *The Fontana Economic History of Europe*, vol. 2, *The Sixteenth and Seventeenth Centuries* (Glasgow: Collins/Fontana Books, 1974), 11–12.

19

THE DIVERSITY OF AMERICAN COLONIAL SOCIETIES,

1530–1770

The Columbian Exchange • Spanish America and Brazil • English and
French Colonies in North America • Colonial Expansion and Conflict
ENVIRONMENT AND TECHNOLOGY: The Silver Refinery at Potosí, Bolivia, 1700
SOCIETY AND CULTURE: Colonial Wealth and the Exploitation of Indigenous Peoples

Vista de una Máquina, para cerník Tabáco enla R.¹ Fabrica de Sigarr.ˢ

VIVA EL REY.

Tobacco Factory Machinery in Colonial Mexico City   The tobacco factory in eighteenth-century Mexico City
used a horse-driven mechanical shredder to produce snuff and cigarette tobacco.

*S*hulush Homa—an eighteenth-century Choctaw leader called "Red Shoes" by the English—faced a dilemma. For years he had befriended the French who had moved into the lower Mississippi Valley, protecting their outlying settlements from other indigenous groups and producing a steady flow of deerskins for trade. In return, he received guns and gifts as well as honors previously given only to chiefs. Though born a commoner, he had parlayed his skillful politicking with the French—and the shrewd distribution of the gifts he received—to enhance his position in Choctaw society. Then his fortunes turned. In the course of yet another war between England and France, the English cut off French shipping. Faced with followers unhappy over his sudden inability to supply French guns, Red Shoes decided to make a deal with the English. Unfortunately, the new tactic backfired. His former allies, the French, put a price on his head, which was soon collected. His murder in 1747 launched a Choctaw civil war, a conflict that left French settlements unprotected and the Choctaw people weakened.

The story of Red Shoes reveals a number of themes from the period of European colonization of the Americas. First, although the wars, epidemics, and territorial loss associated with European settlement threatened Amerindians, many adapted the new technologies and new political possibilities to their own purposes and thrived—at least for a time. In the end, though, the best that they could achieve was a holding action. The people of the Old World were coming to dominate the people of the New.

Second, after centuries of isolation, the Americas were being drawn into global events, influenced by the political and economic demands of Europe. The influx of Europeans and Africans resulted in a vast biological and cultural transformation, as the introduction of new plants, animals, diseases, peoples, and technologies fundamentally altered the natural environment of the Western Hemisphere. This was not a one-way transfer, however. The technologies and resources of the New World contributed to profound changes in the Old. Staple crops introduced from the Americas provided highly nutritious foods that helped fuel a population spurt in Europe, Asia, and Africa. As we saw in Chapter 18, riches and products funneled from the Americas changed economic, social, and political relations in Europe.

Third, the fluidity of the Choctaw's political situation reflects the complexity of colonial society, where Amerindians, Europeans, and Africans all contributed to the creation of new cultures. Although similar processes took place throughout the Americas, the particulars varied from place to place, creating a diverse range of cultures. The society that arose in each colony reflected the colony's mix of native peoples, its connections to the slave trade, and the characteristics of the European society establishing the colony. As the colonies matured, new concepts of identity developed, and those living in the Americas began to see themselves as unique.

As you read this chapter, ask yourself the following questions:

- How did the development of European colonies in the Americas alter the natural environment?
- What were the most important differences in the colonial political institutions and economies created by Spain, Portugal, England, and France?
- How important was forced labor to the European colonies?

THE COLUMBIAN EXCHANGE

The term **Columbian Exchange** refers to the transfer of peoples, animals, plants, and diseases between the New and Old Worlds. The European invasion and settlement of the Western Hemisphere opened a long era of biological and technological transfers that altered American environments. Within a century of first settlement, the domesticated livestock and major agricultural crops of the Old World (the known world before Columbus's voyage) had spread over much of the Americas, and the New World's useful staple crops had enriched the agricultures of Europe, Asia, and Africa. Old World diseases

CHRONOLOGY

	Spanish America	Brazil	British America	French America
1500	**1518** Smallpox arrives in Caribbean **1535** Creation of Viceroyalty of New Spain **1540s** Creation of Viceroyalty of Peru **1542** New Laws outlaw Amerindian enslavement **1545** Silver discovered at Potosí, Bolivia	**1540–1600** Era of Amerindian slavery **After 1540** Sugar begins to dominate the economy		**1524–1554** Jacques Cartier's voyages to explore Newfoundland and Gulf of St. Lawrence
1600	**1625** Population of Potosí reaches 120,000	**By 1620** African slave trade provides majority of plantation workers	**1583** Unsuccessful effort to establish colony on Newfoundland **1607** Jamestown founded **1620** Plymouth founded **1660** Slave population in Virginia begins period of rapid growth **1664** English take New York from Dutch	**1608** Quebec founded
1700	**1700** Last Habsburg ruler of Spain dies **1713** First Bourbon ruler of Spain crowned	**1750–1777** Reforms of marquis de Pombal	**1756–1763** French and Indian War	**1699** Louisiana founded **1760** English take Canada

that entered the Americas with European immigrants and African slaves devastated indigenous populations. These dramatic population changes weakened native peoples' capacity for resistance and facilitated the transfer of plants, animals, and related technologies. As a result, the colonies of Spain, Portugal, England, and France became vast arenas of cultural and social experimentation.

Demographic Changes

Because of their long isolation from other continents (see Chapter 17), the peoples of the New World lacked immunity to diseases introduced from the Old World. As a result, death rates among Amerindian peoples during the epidemics of the early colonial period were very high. The

lack of reliable data has frustrated efforts to measure the deadly impact of these diseases. Scholars disagree about the size of the precontact population but generally agree that, after contact, Old World diseases overwhelmed native populations. According to one estimate, in the century that followed the triumph of Hernán Cortés in 1521, the population of central Mexico fell from a high somewhere between 13 million and 25 million to approximately 700,000. In this same period nearly 75 percent of the Maya population disappeared. In the region of the Inca Empire, population fell from about 9 million to approximately 600,000. Brazil's native population was similarly ravaged, falling from 2.5 million to under a million within a century of the arrival of the Portuguese. The most conservative estimates of population loss begin with smaller precontact populations but accept that epidemics had a catastrophic effect.

Smallpox, which arrived in the Caribbean in 1518, was the most deadly of the early epidemics. In Mexico and Central America, 50 percent or more of the Amerindian population died during the first wave of smallpox epidemics. The disease then spread to South America with equally devastating effects. Measles arrived in the New World in the 1530s and was followed by diphtheria, typhus, influenza, and, perhaps, pulmonary plague. Mortality was often greatest when two or more diseases struck at the same time. Between 1520 and 1521 influenza in combination with other ailments attacked the Cakchiquel of Guatemala. Their chronicle recalls:

> Great was the stench of the dead. After our fathers and grandfathers succumbed, half the people fled to the fields. The dogs and vultures devoured the bodies. . . . So it was that we became orphans, oh my sons! . . . We were born to die![1]

By the mid-seventeenth century, malaria and yellow fever were also present in tropical regions. The deadliest form of malaria arrived with the African slave trade. It ravaged the already reduced native populations and afflicted European immigrants as well. Most scholars believe that yellow fever was also brought from Africa, but new research suggests that the disease was present before the conquest in the tropical low country near present-day Veracruz on the Gulf of Mexico. Whatever its origins, yellow fever killed Europeans in the Caribbean Basin and in other tropical regions nearly as efficiently as smallpox had earlier extinguished Amerindians. Syphilis is the only significant disease believed to have been transferred from the Americas to Europe.

The development of English and French colonies in North America in the seventeenth century led to similar patterns of contagion and mortality. In 1616 and 1617 epidemics nearly exterminated many of New England's indigenous groups. French fur traders transmitted measles, smallpox, and other diseases as far as Hudson Bay and the Great Lakes. Although there is very little evidence that Europeans consciously used disease as a tool of empire, the deadly results of contact clearly undermined the ability of native peoples to resist settlement.

Transfer of Plants and Animals

Even as epidemics swept through the indigenous population, the New and the Old Worlds were participating in a vast exchange of plants and animals that radically altered diet and lifestyles in both regions. All the staples of southern European agriculture—such as wheat, olives,

The Columbian Exchange   After the conquest, the introduction of plants and animals from the Old World dramatically altered the American environment. Here an Amerindian woman is seen milking a cow. Livestock sometimes destroyed the fields of native peoples, but cattle, sheep, pigs, and goats also provided food, leather, and wool.   (From Martinez Compañon, *Trujillo del Perú*, V.II, E 79. Photo: Imaging services, Harvard College Library)

grapes, and garden vegetables—were being grown in the Americas in a remarkably short time after contact. African and Asian crops—such as rice, bananas, coconuts, breadfruit, and sugar cane—were soon introduced as well. Native peoples remained loyal to their traditional staples but added many Old World plants to their diet. Citrus fruits, melons, figs, and sugar as well as onions, radishes, and salad greens all found a place in Amerindian cuisines.

In return the Americas offered the Old World an abundance of useful plants. The New World staples—

maize, potatoes, and manioc—revolutionized agriculture and diet in parts of Europe, Africa, and Asia (see Environment and Technology: Amerindian Foods in Africa, in Chapter 20). Many experts assert that the rapid growth of world population after 1700 resulted in large measure from the spread of these useful crops, which provided more calories per acre than any of the Old World staples except rice. Beans, squash, tomatoes, sweet potatoes, peanuts, chilies, and chocolate also gained widespread acceptance in the Old World. The New World also provided the Old with plants that provided dyes, medicinal plants, varieties of cotton, and tobacco.

The introduction of European livestock had a dramatic impact on New World environments and cultures. Faced with few natural predators, cattle, pigs, horses, and sheep, as well as pests like rats and rabbits, multiplied rapidly in the open spaces of the Americas. On the vast plains of present-day southern Brazil, Uruguay, and Argentina, herds of wild cattle and horses exceeded 50 million by 1700. Large herds of both animals also appeared in northern Mexico and what became the southwest of the United States.

Where Old World livestock spread most rapidly, environmental changes were most dramatic. Many priests and colonial officials noted the destructive impact of marauding livestock on Amerindian agriculturists. The first viceroy of Mexico, Antonio de Mendoza, wrote to the Spanish king, "May your Lordship realize that if cattle are allowed, the Indians will be destroyed." Sheep, which grazed grasses close to the ground, were also an environmental threat. Yet the viceroy's stark choice misrepresented the complex response of indigenous peoples to these new animals.

Wild cattle on the plains of South America, northern Mexico, and Texas provided indigenous peoples with abundant supplies of meat and hides. In the present-day southwestern United States, the Navajo became sheepherders and expert weavers of woolen cloth. Even in the centers of European settlement, individual Amerindians turned European animals to their own advantage by becoming muleteers, cowboys, and sheepherders.

No animal had a more striking effect on the cultures of native peoples than the horse, which increased the efficiency of hunters and the military capacity of warriors on the plains. The horse permitted the Apache, Sioux, Blackfoot, Comanche, Assiniboine, and others to hunt more efficiently the vast herds of buffalo in North America. The horse also revolutionized the cultures of the Araucanian (or Mapuche) and Pampas peoples in South America.

SPANISH AMERICA AND BRAZIL

The frontiers of conquest and settlement expanded rapidly. Within one hundred years of Columbus's first voyage to the Western Hemisphere, the Spanish Empire in America included most of the islands of the Caribbean, Mexico, the American southwest, Central America, the Caribbean and Pacific coasts of South America, the Andean highlands, and the vast plains of the Rio de la Plata region (a region that includes the modern nations of Argentina, Uruguay, and Paraguay). Portuguese settlement in the New World developed more slowly. But before the end of the sixteenth century, Portugal occupied most of the Brazilian coast.

Early settlers from Spain and Portugal sought to create colonial societies based on the institutions and customs of their homelands. They viewed society as a vertical arrangement of estates (classes of society), as uniformly Catholic, and as an arrangement of patriarchal extended-family networks. And they moved quickly to establish in the new colonies the religious, social, and administrative institutions that were familiar to them.

Despite the imposition of foreign institutions and the massive loss of life caused by epidemics in the sixteenth century, indigenous peoples exercised a powerful influence on the development of colonial societies. Aztec and Inca elite families sought to protect their traditional privileges and rights through marriage or less formal alliances with the Spanish settlers. They also often used colonial courts to defend their claims to land. In Spanish and Portuguese colonies, indigenous military allies and laborers proved crucial to the development of European settlements. Nearly everywhere, Amerindian religious beliefs and practices survived beneath the surface of an imposed Christianity. Amerindian languages, cuisines, medical practices, and agricultural techniques also survived the conquest and influenced the development of Latin American culture.

The African slave trade added a third cultural stream to colonial Latin American society. At first, African slaves were concentrated in plantation regions of Brazil and the Caribbean (see Chapter 20), but by the end of the colonial era, Africans and their descendants were living throughout Latin America, enriching colonial societies with their traditional agricultural practices, music, religious beliefs, cuisine, and social customs.

State and Church   The Spanish crown moved quickly to curb the independent power of the conquistadors and to establish royal authority over both the defeated native populations and the rising tide of European settlers. Created in 1524, the **Council of the Indies** in Spain supervised all government, ecclesiastical, and commercial activity in the Spanish colonies. Geography and technology, however, limited the Council's real power. Local officials could not be controlled too closely, because a ship needed more than two hundred days to make a roundtrip voyage from Spain to Veracruz, Mexico, and additional months of travel were required to reach Lima, Peru.

As a result of these difficulties of communication, the viceroy of New Spain and the viceroy of Peru, the highest-ranking Spanish officials in the colonies, enjoyed broad power. But the two viceroyalties in their jurisdiction were also vast territories with geographic obstacles to communication. Created in 1535, the Viceroyalty of New Spain, with its capital in Mexico City, included Mexico and the southwest of what is now the United States, Central America, and the islands of the Caribbean. The Viceroyalty of Peru, with its capital in Lima, was formed in the 1540s to govern Spanish South America (see Map 19.1). Each viceroyalty was divided into a number of judicial and administrative districts. Until the seventeenth century, almost all of the officials appointed to high positions in Spain's colonial bureaucracy were born in Spain. Eventually, economic mismanagement in Spain forced the Crown to sell appointments to these positions, and, as a result, local-born members of the colonial elite gained many offices.

In the sixteenth century Portugal concentrated its resources and energies on Asia and Africa. Because early settlers found neither mineral wealth nor rich native empires in Brazil, the Portuguese king hesitated to set up expensive mechanisms of colonial government in the New World. Seeking to promote settlement but limit costs, the king in effect sublet administrative responsibilities in Brazil to court favorites by granting twelve hereditary captaincies in the 1530s. After mismanagement and inadequate investment doomed this experiment, the king appointed a governor-general in 1549 and made Salvador, in the northern province of Bahia, Brazil's capital. In 1720 the first viceroy of Brazil was named.

The government institutions of the Spanish and Portuguese colonies had a more uniform character and were much more extensive and costly than those later established in North America by France and Great Britain. Taxes paid by the silver and gold mines of Spanish America and in Brazil by the sugar plantations and after 1690 by gold mines funded large and intrusive colonial bureaucracies. These institutions made the colonies more responsive to the initiatives of Spain and Portugal, but they also thwarted local economic initiative and political experimentation.

The Catholic Church became the primary agent for the introduction and transmission of Christian belief as well as European language and culture in both Spanish America and Brazil. It undertook the conversion of Amerindians, ministered to the spiritual needs of European settlers and their children, and promoted intellectual life through the introduction of the printing press and formal education.

Spain and Portugal justified their American conquests by assuming an obligation to convert native populations to Christianity. This religious objective was sometimes forgotten, and some members of the clergy were themselves exploiters of native populations. Nevertheless, the effort to convert America's native peoples expanded Christianity on a scale similar to its earlier expansion in Europe at the time of Constantine in the fourth century. In Mexico alone hundreds of thousands of conversions and baptisms were achieved within a few years of the conquest.

The Catholic clergy sought to achieve their evangelical ends by first converting members of the Amerindian elites, in the hope that they could persuade others to follow their example. Franciscan missionaries in Mexico hoped to train members of the indigenous elite for the clergy. These idealistic efforts had to be abandoned when church authorities discovered that many converts were secretly observing old beliefs and rituals. The trial and punishment of two converted Aztec nobles for heresy in the 1530s highlighted this problem. Three decades later, Spanish clergy resorted to torture, executions, and the destruction of native manuscripts to eradicate traditional beliefs and rituals among the Maya. Repelled by these events, the church hierarchy ended both the violent repression of native religious practice and efforts to recruit an Amerindian clergy.

Despite its failures, the Catholic clergy did provide native peoples with some protections against the abuse and exploitation of Spanish settlers. The priest **Bartolomé de Las Casas** (1474–1566) was the most influential defender of the Amerindians in the early colonial

Map. 19.1   Colonial Latin America in the Eighteenth Century
Spain and Portugal controlled most of the Western Hemisphere in the eighteenth century. In the sixteenth century they had created new administrative jurisdictions—viceroyalties—to defend their respective colonies against European rivals. Taxes assessed on colonial products helped pay for this extension of governmental authority.

NEW
FRANCE

ENGLISH COLONIES
(Independence declared, 1776)

*ATLANTIC
OCEAN*

Colorado

Effective frontier
of Spanish settlement

Silver

Silver

COAHUILA

Gulf of Mexico

FLORIDA
(Ceded to England, 1763–1783)

Havana

Sugar cane
Beef
Tobacco

HAITI [SAINT DOMINGUE]
(Ceded to France, 1697)

VICEROYALTY OF NEW SPAIN
(1535)

Silver

BAJIO LEÓN

Guadalajara   Silver

Veracruz

Mexico City

Silver

Sugar cane
Indigo

Beef

Sugar cane

PUERTO RICO

Cacao

Sugar cane

Sugar
cane
Cochineal

**BRITISH
HONDURAS**

SANTO DOMINGO

Sugar cane

JAMAICA
(Conquered by England, 1655)

Guatemala

Silver

Cochineal
Cacao
Indigo

*Caribbean
Sea*

Sugar cane

Pearls

Caracas

Cacao

GUIANA

Gold

Bogotá

**VICEROYALTY OF
NEW GRANADA**
(Separated from
Viceroyalty of Peru,
1717, 1739)

Quito

Amazon

Forest
products

*PACIFIC
OCEAN*

**VICEROYALTY
OF PERU**
(1590s)

Sugar cane

ANDES

**VICEROYALTY
OF BRAZIL**
(1720)

Pernambuco

Lima

Cuzco

Sugar
cane

Sugar
cane

Bahia

Sugar
cane

La Paz

Cacao

Chuquisaca
(La Plata; Sucre)

Potosí

Silver

Paraná

Diamonds
Gold

Yerba
Tobacco

São Paulo

Rio de Janeiro
(Capital, 1763)

**VICEROYALTY OF
LA PLATA**
(Separated from
Viceroyalty of Peru,
1776)

Wheat

ANDES

Beef and
hides

**AUDIENCIA
OF CHILE**
(Retained by
Viceroyalty of Peru,
1776)

Santiago

Buenos Aires

Montevideo

Beef
and
hides

Claimed but
not settled by Spain

Spanish colonies

Viceroyalty of New Spain

Viceroyalty of New Granada

Viceroyalty of Peru and Audiencia of Chile

Viceroyalty of La Plata

Portuguese colonies

Viceroyalty of Brazil

0   500   1000 Km.

0   500   1000 Mi.

*Islas Malvinas
(Falkland Islands)*

Cape Horn

Saint Martín de Porres (1579–1639) Martín de Porres was the illegitimate son of a Spanish nobleman and his black servant. Eventually recognized by his father, he entered the Dominican Order in Lima, Peru. Known for his generosity, he experienced visions and gained the ability to heal the sick. As was common in colonial religious art, the artist celebrates Martín de Porres's spirituality while representing him doing the type of work assumed most suitable for a person of mixed descent. (Mint Museum of Art, Charlotte, NC)

1542—reform legislation that outlawed the enslavement of Amerindians and limited other forms of forced labor.

European clergy arrived in the colonies with the intention of transmitting Catholic Christian belief and ritual without alteration. But the large size of Amerindian populations and their geographic dispersal over a vast landscape thwarted this objective. Linguistic and cultural differences among native peoples also inhibited missionary efforts. These problems frustrated Catholic missionaries and sometimes led to repression and cruelty. But the limited success of evangelization permitted the appearance of what must be seen as an Amerindian Christianity that blended Catholic Christian beliefs with important elements of traditional native cosmology and ritual. Most commonly, indigenous beliefs and rituals came to be embedded in the celebration of saints' days or Catholic rituals associated with the Virgin Mary. The Catholic clergy and most European settlers viewed this evolving mixture as the work of the Devil or as evidence of Amerindian inferiority. Instead it was one component of the process of cultural borrowing and innovation that contributed to a distinct and original Latin American culture.

The terrible loss of Amerindian population caused by epidemics and growing signs of resistance to conversion led the Catholic Church to redirect most of its resources from native regions in the countryside to growing colonial cities and towns with large European populations after 1600. One important outcome of this altered mission was the founding of universities and secondary schools and the stimulation of urban intellectual life. Over time, the church became the richest institution in the Spanish colonies, controlling ranches, plantations, and vineyards as well as serving as the society's banker.

Colonial Economies

The silver mines of Peru and Mexico and the sugar plantations of Brazil dominated the economic development of colonial Latin America. The mineral wealth of the New World fueled the early development of European capitalism and funded Europe's greatly expanded trade with Asia. Profits produced in these economic centers also promoted the growth of colonial cities, concentrated scarce investment capital and labor resources, and stimulated the development of livestock raising and agriculture in neighboring rural areas (see Map 19.1). Once established, this colonial dependence on mineral and agricultural exports left an enduring social and economic legacy in Latin America.

period. He arrived in Hispaniola in 1502 as a settler and initially lived off the forced labor and appropriated goods of Amerindians. Deeply moved by the deaths of so many Amerindians and by the misdeeds of the Spanish, Las Casas gave up this way of life and entered the Dominican Order, later becoming the first bishop of Chiapas, in southern Mexico. For the remainder of his long life Las Casas served as the most important advocate for native peoples, writing a number of books that detailed their mistreatment by the Spanish. His most important achievement was the enactment of the New Laws of

Gold worth millions of pesos was extracted from mines in Latin America, but silver mines in the Spanish colonies generated the most wealth and therefore exercised the greatest economic influence. The first important silver strikes occurred in Mexico in the 1530s and 1540s. In 1545 the single richest silver deposit in the Americas was discovered at **Potosí°,** in what is now Bolivia, and until 1680 the silver production of Bolivia and Peru dominated the Spanish colonial economy. After this date Mexican silver production greatly surpassed that of the Andean region.

A large labor force was needed to mine silver. The metal was extracted from deep shafts, and the refining process was complex. Silver mines supported farming, livestock raising, and even textile production, which, in turn, promoted urbanization and the elaboration of regional commercial relations. Silver mining also greatly altered the environment.

At first, silver was extracted from ore by smelting: the ore was crushed in giant stamping mills then packed with charcoal in a furnace and fired. Within a short time this wasteful use of forest resources for fuel destroyed forests near the mining centers. Faced with rising fuel costs, Mexican miners developed an efficient method of chemical extraction that relied on mixing mercury with the silver ore (see Environment and Technology: The Silver Refinery at Potosí, Bolivia, 1700). But this process, too, had severe environmental costs. Mercury was a poison, and its use contaminated the environment and sickened the Amerindian work force. Silver yields and profits increased with mercury amalgamation, but the environmental costs were high.

From the time of Columbus indigenous populations had been compelled to provide labor for European settlers in the Americas. Until the 1540s in Spanish colonies, Amerindian peoples were divided among the settlers and were forced to provide them with labor or with textiles, food, or other goods. This form of forced labor was called the **encomienda°.** As epidemics and mistreatment led to the decline in Amerindian population, reforms such as the New Laws sought to eliminate the encomienda. The discovery of silver in both Peru and Mexico, however, led to new forms of compulsory labor. In the mining region of Mexico, Amerindian populations had been greatly reduced by epidemic diseases. Therefore, from early in the colonial period, Mexican silver miners relied on free-wage laborers. Peru's Amerindian population survived in larger numbers, allowing the Spanish to impose a form of labor called the mita°.

Rural Blacksmiths in Colonial Peru   In colonial Latin America husbands, wives, and older children commonly worked together whether in agriculture or in urban occupations. Because few artisans earned enough to hire help, they often relied on their familes for assistance. In this illustration from Peru a rural blacksmith works alongside his wife.   (From Martinez Compañon, Trujillo del Perú, v.ll, E 105. Photo: Imaging Services, Harvard College Library)

Under this system, one seventh of adult male Amerindians were compelled to work for six months each year in mines, or on farms and in textile factories. The most dangerous working conditions existed in the silver mines where workers were forced to carry heavy bags of ore up fragile ladders to the surface.

This colonial institution was a corrupted version of the Inca-era mit'a (see Chapter 12), which had been both a labor tax that supported elites and a reciprocal labor obligation that allowed kin groups to produce surpluses of essential goods that provided for the elderly and incapacitated. In the Spanish mita, few Amerindian workers

---

Potosí (poh-toh-SEE)   encomienda (in-co-mee-EN-dah)
mita (MEE-tah)

The Silver Refinery at Potosí, Bolivia, 1700

The silver refineries of Spanish America were among the largest and most heavily capitalized industrial enterprises in the Western Hemisphere during the colonial period. By the middle of the seventeenth century the mines of Potosí, Bolivia, had attracted a population of more than 120,000.

The accompanying illustration shows a typical refinery (*ingenio*). Aqueducts carried water from large reservoirs on nearby mountainsides to the refineries. The water wheel shown on the right drove two sets of vertical stamps that crushed ore. Each iron-shod stamp was about the size and weight of a telephone pole. Crushed ore was sorted, dried, and mixed with mercury and other catalysts to extract the silver. The amalgam was then separated by a combination of washing and heating. The end result was a nearly pure ingot of silver that was later assayed and taxed at the mint.

Silver production carried a high environmental cost. Forests were cut to provide fuel and the timbers needed to shore up mine shafts and construct stamping mills and other machinery. Unwanted base metals produced in the refining process poisoned the soil. In addition, the need for tens of thousands of horses, mules, and oxen to drive machinery and transport material led to overgrazing and widespread erosion.

A Bolivian Silver Refinery, 1700   The silver refineries of Spanish America were among the largest industrial establishments in the Western Hemisphere.   (Courtesy, Fundacao Biblioteca Nacional, Rio de Janeiro)

could survive on their wages. Wives and children were commonly forced to join the workforce to help meet expenses (see Society and Culture: Colonial Wealth and the Exploitation of Indigenous Peoples). Even those who remained behind in the village were forced to send food and cash to support mita workers.

As the Amerindian population fell with each new epidemic, some of Peru's villages were forced to shorten the period between mita obligations. Instead of serving every seven years, many men were forced to return to mines after only a year or two. Unwilling to accept mita service and the other tax burdens imposed on Amerindian villages, large numbers of Amerindians abandoned traditional agriculture and moved permanently to Spanish mines and farms as wage laborers. The long-term result of these individual decisions weakened Amerindian village life and promoted the assimilation of Amerindians into Spanish-speaking Catholic colonial society.

Before the settlement of Brazil the Portuguese had already developed sugar plantations that depended on slave labor on the Atlantic islands of Madeira, the Azores, the Cape Verdes, and São Tomé. Because of the success of these early experiences, they were able to quickly transfer this profitable form of agriculture to Brazil. After 1550, sugar production expanded rapidly in the northern provinces of Pernambuco and Bahia. By the seventeenth century, sugar dominated the Brazilian economy.

The sugar plantations of colonial Brazil always depended on slave labor. At first the Portuguese sugar planters enslaved Amerindians captured in war or seized from their villages. They used Amerindian men as field hands, although in this indigenous culture women had primary responsibility for agriculture. Any effort to resist or flee led to harsh punishments. Thousands of Amerindian slaves died during the epidemics that raged across Brazil in the sixteenth and seventeenth centuries. This terrible loss of Amerindian life and the rising profits of the sugar planters led to the development of an internal slave trade dominated by settlers from the southern region of São Paulo. To supply the rising labor needs of the sugar plantations of the northeast, slave raiders pushed into the interior, even attacking Amerindian populations in neighboring Spanish colonies. Many of the most prominent slavers were the sons of Portuguese fathers and Amerindian mothers.

Amerindian slaves remained an important source of labor and slave raiding a significant business in frontier regions into the eighteenth century. But sugar planters eventually came to rely more on African than Amerindian slaves. Although African slaves at first cost much more than Amerindian slaves, planters found them to be more productive and more resistant to disease. As profits from the plantations increased, imports of African slaves rose from an average of 2,000 per year in the late sixteenth century to approximately 7,000 per year a century later, outstripping the immigration of free Portuguese settlers. Between 1650 and 1750, for example, more than three African slaves arrived in Brazil for every free immigrant from Europe.

Within Spanish America, the mining centers of Mexico and Peru eventually exercised global economic influence. American silver increased the European money supply, promoting commercial expansion and, later, industrialization. Large amounts of silver also flowed across the Pacific to the Spanish colony of the Philippines, where it was exchanged for Asian spices, silks, and pottery. Spain tried to limit this trade, but the desire for Asian goods in the colonies was so strong that there was large-scale trade in contraband goods.

The rich mines of Peru, Bolivia, and Mexico stimulated urban population growth as well as commercial links with distant agricultural and textile producers. The population of the city of Potosí, high in the Andes, reached 120,000 inhabitants by 1625. This rich mining town became the center of a vast regional market that depended on Chilean wheat, Argentine livestock, and Ecuadorian textiles.

The sugar plantations of Brazil played a similar role in integrating the economy of the south Atlantic region. The ports of Bahia and Rio de Janeiro in Brazil exchanged sugar, tobacco, and reexported slaves from Brazil for yerba (Paraguayan tea), hides, livestock, and silver produced in neighboring Spanish colonies. Portugal's increasing openness to British trade also allowed Brazil to become a conduit for an illegal trade between Spanish colonies and Europe. At the end of the seventeenth century the discovery of gold in Brazil helped overcome this large region's currency shortage and promoted further economic integration.

Both Spain and Portugal attempted to control the trade of their American colonies. Spain's efforts were more ambitious, granting first Seville and then Cádiz monopoly trade rights. Similar monopoly privileges were then awarded to the merchant guilds of Lima, Peru, and Mexico City. Because ships returning to Spain with silver and gold were often attacked by foreign naval forces and pirates, Spain came to rely on convoys escorted by warships to supply the colonies and return with silver and gold. By 1650, Portugal had instituted a similar system of monopoly trade and fleets. The combination of monopoly commerce and convoy systems

Colonial Wealth and the Exploitation of Indigenous Peoples

The conditions imposed on indigenous peoples in the Spanish colonies generated contentious debates from the early sixteenth century to the end of the colonial period. Two Spanish naval officers who accompanied a French scientific expedition to South America in the mid-eighteenth century wrote the following description.

Without having to assume anything that cannot be proved absolutely or exaggerating to stretch the truth, we can agree indisputably that all the wealth produced in the Indies [Spain's American colonies], even what is consumed there, stems from the toil of the Indians. From close observation one sees that Indians work the silver and gold mines, cultivate the fields, and raise the livestock. In a word, there is no heavy labor that the Indians do not perform. They are so badly recompensed for their work that if one wanted to find out what the Spaniards paid them, he would discover it to be nothing except consistently cruel punishment, worse than that meted out in the galleys.... The gold and silver which the Spaniards acquire at the expense of the natives' sweat and toil never falls into the hands of the Indians.

[T]hose who contribute most are the ones who enjoy its fruits least and are the most poorly paid for the most arduous tasks....

There are two ways to remedy the abuse perpetrated on the free and mita Indians [the mita was a forced labor system]. The most reasonable and just method would be to eliminate the mita entirely and have free labor work the haciendas, mines, obrajes [textile mills] and everything else....

In the second place it would be fitting to prohibit completely all physical punishment of the Indians in the haciendas and obrajes under severe penalties.

How important were Amerindians to the economy of the Spanish Empire? How did these two visitors judge the treatment of Amerindian peoples? What remedies did these authors suggest?

Source: Jorge Juan and Antonio de Ulloa, *Discourse and Political Reflections on the Kingdom of Peru,* ed. John J. Tepaske and Besse A. Clement (Norman: University of Oklahoma Press, 1978), 126–148.

---

protected shipping and facilitated the collection of taxes, but these measures also slowed the flow of European goods to the colonies and kept prices high. Frustrated by these restraints, colonial populations established illegal commercial relations with the English, French, and Dutch. By the middle of the seventeenth century a majority of European imports were arriving in Latin America illegally.

Society in Colonial Latin America

With the exception of a few early viceroys, few members of Spain's great noble families came to the New World. *Hidalgos°*—lesser nobles—were well represented, as were Spanish merchants, artisans, miners, priests, and lawyers. Small numbers of criminals, beggars, and prosti-

tutes also found their way to the colonies. This flow of immigrants from Spain was never large, and Spanish settlers were always a tiny minority in a colonial society numerically dominated by Amerindians and rapidly growing populations of Africans, **creoles** (whites born in America to European parents), and people of mixed ancestry.

Conquistadors and early settlers who received from the Crown grants of labor and tribute goods (encomienda) from Amerindian communities as rewards for service to Spain dominated colonial society in early Spanish America. These *encomenderos* sought to create a hereditary social and political class comparable to the nobles of Europe. But their systematic abuse of Amerindian communities and the catastrophic loss of Amerindian life during the epidemics of the sixteenth century undermined their position. They also confronted the growing power of colonial viceroys, judges, and bishops appointed by the king.

By the end of the sixteenth century, the elite of Spanish America included both European immigrants and

---

hidalgos (ee-DAHL-goes)

creoles. Europeans dominated the highest levels of the church and government as well as commerce. Creoles commonly controlled colonial agriculture and mining. Wealthy creole families with extensive holdings in land and mines often sought to increase their family prestige by arranging for their daughters to marry successful Spanish merchants and officials. Often richer in reputation than in wealth, immigrants from Spain welcomed the opportunity to forge these connections. Although tensions between Spaniards and creoles were inevitable, most elite families had members from both groups.

Before the Europeans arrived in the Americas, the native peoples were members of a large number of distinct cultural and linguistic groups. Cultural diversity and class distinctions were present even in the highly centralized Aztec and Inca empires. The loss of life provoked by the European conquest undermined this rich social and cultural complexity, and the imposition of Catholic Christianity further eroded ethnic boundaries among native peoples. Colonial administrators and settlers broadly applied the racial label "Indian," which facilitated the imposition of special taxes and labor obligations while at the same time erasing long-standing class and ethnic differences.

Indigenous Amerindian elites survived only briefly in the Spanish colonies and Brazil. Some of the conquistadors and early settlers married or established less formal relations with elite Amerindian women, but fewer of these alliances occurred after European women began to arrive. By 1600 the descendants of the most powerful Amerindian families were indistinguishable from the descendants of the village leaders who had been subordinate to them. Both groups of hereditary leaders, however, had proved indispensable to the first Spanish colonists, helping the Spaniards to organize draft labor and collect taxes. Some descendants of both groups prospered in the colonial period as ranchers, muleteers, and merchants; many others lived in the same materially deprived conditions as Amerindian commoners.

Thousands of blacks participated in the conquest and settlement of Spanish America. The majority were European-born Catholic slaves who came to the New World with their masters. Some free blacks immigrated voluntarily. More than four hundred blacks, most of them slaves, participated in the conquest of Peru and Chile. In the fluid social environment of the conquest era, many slaves gained their freedom. Some simply fled from their masters. Juan Valiente escaped his master in Mexico, participated in Francisco Pizarro's conquest of the Inca Empire, and later became one of the most prominent early settlers of Chile, where he was granted Amerindian laborers in an encomienda.

The status of the black population of colonial Latin America declined with the opening of a direct slave trade with Africa (for details, see Chapter 20). Africans were culturally different from the Afro-Iberian slaves and freedmen who accompanied the conquerors. Afro-Iberians commonly had deep roots in Spain or Portugal, their language was Spanish or Portuguese, and their religion was Catholicism. African slaves were different in language, religious belief, and cultural practice, and these differences were viewed by settlers as signs of inferiority, ultimately serving as a justification for slavery. By 1600 anyone with black ancestry was barred from positions in church and government as well as from many skilled crafts.

The rich mosaic of African identities was retained in colonial Latin America. Many cultural groups struggled in slavery to retain their languages, religious beliefs, and marriage customs. But, in regions with large slave majorities, these cultural and linguistic barriers often divided slaves and made resistance more difficult. Over time, elements from many African traditions blended and mixed with European (and in some cases Amerindian) language and beliefs to forge distinct local cultures. The rapid growth of an American-born slave population accelerated this process of cultural change.

Slave resistance took many forms, including sabotage, malingering, running away, and rebellion. Although many slave rebellions occurred, colonial authorities were always able to reestablish control. Groups of runaway slaves, however, were sometimes able to defend themselves for years. In both Spanish America and Brazil communities of runaways (called *quilombos*° in Brazil and *palenques*° in Spanish colonies) were common. The largest quilombo was Palmares, where thousands of slaves defended themselves against Brazilian authorities for sixty years until they were finally overrun in 1694.

Slaves were skilled artisans, musicians, servants, artists, cowboys, and even soldiers. However, the vast majority worked in agriculture. Conditions for slaves were worst on the sugar plantations of Brazil and the Caribbean, where harsh discipline, brutal punishments, and backbreaking labor were common. Because planters preferred to buy male slaves, there was always a gender imbalance on plantations. As a result, neither the traditional marriage and family patterns of Africa nor those of Europe developed. The disease environment of the tropics, as well as the poor housing, diet, hygiene, and medical care offered to slaves, also weakened slave families.

---

quilombos (key-LOM-bos)   *palenques* (pah-LEN-kays)

Painting of Castas This is an example of a common genre of colonial Spanish American painting. In the eighteenth century there was increased interest in ethnic mixing, and wealthy colonials as well as some Europeans commissioned sets of paintings that showed mixed families. Commonly the paintings also indicated what the artist believed was an appropriate class setting. In this painting a richly dressed Spaniard is depicted with his Amerindian wife dressed in European clothing. Notice that the painter has the mestiza daughter look to her European father for guidance. (Private Collection. Photographer: Camilo Garza/Fotocam, Monterrey, Mexico)

The colonial development of Brazil was distinguished from that of Spanish America by the absence of rich and powerful indigenous civilizations such as those of the Aztecs and Inca and by lower levels of European immigration. Nevertheless, Portuguese immigrants came to exercise the same domination in Brazil as the Spanish exercised in their colonies. The growth of cities and the creation of imperial institutions eventually duplicated in outline the social structures found in Spanish America, but with an important difference. By the early seventeenth century, Africans and their American-born descendants were the largest racial group in Brazil. As a result, Brazilian colonial society (unlike Spanish Mexico and Peru) was influenced more by African culture than by Amerindian culture.

Both Spanish and Portuguese law provided for manumission, the granting of freedom to individual slaves. The majority of those gaining their liberty had saved money and purchased their own freedom. This was easiest to do in cities, where slave artisans and market women had the opportunity to earn and save money. Only a tiny minority of owners freed slaves without demanding compensation. Household servants were the most likely beneficiaries of this form of manumission. Only about 1 percent of the slave population gained freedom each year through manumission. However, because slave women received the majority of manumissions and because children born subsequently were considered free, the free colored population grew rapidly.

Within a century of settlement, groups of mixed descent were in the majority in many regions. There were few marriages between Amerindian women and European men, but less formal relationships were common. Few European or creole fathers recognized their mixed offspring, who were called **mestizos°**. Nevertheless, this rapidly expanding group came to occupy a middle position in colonial society, dominating urban artisan trades and small-scale agriculture and ranching. In frontier regions many members of the elite were mestizos, some proudly asserting their descent from the Amerindian elite. The African slave trade also led to the appearance of new American ethnicities. Individuals of mixed European and African descent—called **mulattoes**—came to occupy intermediate position in the tropics similar to the social position of mestizos in Mesoamerica and the Andean region. In Spanish Mexico and Peru and in Brazil, mixtures of Amerindians and Africans were also common.

All these mixed-descent groups were called *castas°* in Spanish America. Castas dominated small-scale retailing and construction trades in cities. In the countryside, many small ranchers and farmers as well as wage laborers were castas. Members of these mixed groups who gained high status or significant wealth generally spoke Spanish or Portuguese, observed the requirements of Catholicism, and, whenever possible, lived the life of Europeans in their residence, dress, and diet.

mestizo (mess-TEE-zoh)   castas (CAZ-tahs)

ENGLISH AND FRENCH COLONIES IN NORTH AMERICA

The North American colonial empires of England and France and the colonies of Spain and Portugal had many characteristics in common (see Map 19.1). The governments of England and France hoped to find easily extracted forms of wealth or great indigenous empires like those of the Aztecs or Inca. Like the Spanish and Portuguese, English and French settlers responded to native peoples with a mixture of diplomacy and violence. African slaves proved crucial to the development of all four colonial economies.

Important differences, however, distinguished North American colonial development from the Latin American model. The English and French colonies were developed nearly a century after Cortés's conquest of Mexico and initial Portuguese settlement in Brazil. The intervening period witnessed significant economic and demographic growth in Europe. It also witnessed the Protestant Reformation, which helped to propel English and French settlement in the Americas. By the time England and France secured a foothold in the Americas, the regions of the world were also more interconnected commercially. Distracted by ventures elsewhere and by increasing military confrontation in Europe, neither England nor France imitated the large and expensive colonial bureaucracies established by Spain and Portugal. As a result, private companies and individual proprietors played a much larger role in the development of English and French colonies. Particularly in the English colonies, this practice led to greater regional variety in economic activity, political institutions and culture, and social structure than was evident in the colonies of Spain and Portugal.

Early English Experiments

England's first efforts to gain a foothold in the Americas produced more failures than successes. The first attempt was made by a group of West Country gentry and merchants led by Sir Humphrey Gilbert. Their effort in 1583 to establish a colony in Newfoundland, off the coast of Canada, quickly failed. After Gilbert's death in 1584, his half-brother Sir Walter Raleigh organized private financing for a new colonization scheme. A year later, 108 men attempted a settlement on Roanoke Island, off the coast of present-day North Carolina. Afflicted with poor leadership, undersupplied, and threatened by Amerindian groups, the colony was abandoned within a year. Another effort to settle Roanoke was made in 1587. Because the Spanish Armada was threatening England, no relief expedition was sent to Roanoke until 1590. When help finally arrived, there was no sign of the 117 men, women, and children who had attempted settlement. Raleigh's colonial experiment was abandoned.

In the seventeenth century, England renewed its effort to establish colonies in North America. England continued to rely on private capital to finance settlement and continued to hope that the colonies would become sources of high-value products such as silk, citrus, and wine. New efforts to establish American colonies were influenced also by English experience in colonizing Ireland after 1566. In Ireland land had been confiscated, cleared of its native population, and offered for sale to English investors. The city of London, English guilds, and wealthy private investors all purchased Irish "plantations" and then recruited "settlers." By 1650 investors had sent nearly 150,000 English and Scottish immigrants to Ireland. Indeed, Ireland attracted six times as many colonists in the early seventeenth century as did New England.

The South

London investors, organized as the privately funded Virginia Company, took up the challenge of colonizing Virginia in 1606. A year later 144 settlers disembarked at Jamestown, an island 30 miles (48 kilometers) up the James River in the Chesapeake Bay region. Additional settlers arrived in 1609. The investors and settlers hoped for immediate profits, but these unrealistic dreams were soon dashed. Although the location was easily defended, it was a swampy and unhealthy place; nearly 80 percent of all settlers in Jamestown in the first fifteen years died from disease or Amerindian attacks. There was no mineral wealth, no passage to Asia, and no docile and exploitable native population. By concentrating their energies on the illusion of easy wealth, settlers failed to grow enough food and were saved on more than one occasion by the generosity of neighboring Amerindian peoples.

In 1624 the English crown was forced to dissolve the Virginia Company because of its mismanagement of the colony. Freed from the company's commitment to Jamestown's unhealthy environment, colonists pushed deeper into the interior, developing a sustainable economy based on furs, timber, and, increasingly, tobacco. The profits from tobacco soon attracted new immigrants and new capital. Along the shoreline of Chesapeake Bay and the rivers that fed it, settlers spread out, developing plantations and farms. Colonial Virginia's population remained dispersed. In Latin America, large and powerful cities dominated by viceroys and royal courts and networks of secondary towns flourished. In contrast, in colonial Virginia no city of any significant size developed.

Colonists in Latin America had developed systems of forced labor to develop the region's resources. Encomienda, mita, and slavery were all imposed on indigenous peoples, and later the African slave trade compelled the migration of millions of additional forced laborers to the colonies of Spain and Portugal. The English settlement of the Chesapeake Bay region added a new system of compulsory labor to the American landscape: **indentured servants.** Ethnically indistinguishable from free settlers, indentured servants eventually accounted for approximately 80 percent of all English immigrants to Virginia and the neighboring colony of Maryland. Young men and women unable to pay for their transportation to the New World accepted indentures (contracts) that bound them to a term ranging from four to seven years of labor in return for passage, a small parcel of land, and some tools and clothes. During the seventeenth century, approximately fifteen hundred indentured servants, mostly male, arrived each year (see Chapter 20 for details on the indentured labor system). Planters were less likely to lose money if they purchased the cheaper limited contracts of indentured servants instead of purchasing African slaves during the period when both groups suffered high mortality rates. As life expectancy in the colony improved, planters began to purchase more slaves. They calculated that greater profits could be secured by paying the higher initial cost of slaves owned for life than by purchasing the contracts of indentured servants bound for short periods of time. As a result, Virginia's slave population grew rapidly from 950 in 1660 to 120,000 by 1756.

By the 1660s many of the elements of the mature colony were in place in Virginia. Colonial government was administered by a Crown-appointed governor and his council, as well as by representatives of towns meeting together as the **House of Burgesses.** When these representatives began to meet alone as a deliberative body, they initiated a form of democratic representation that distinguished the English colonies of North America from the colonies of other European powers. Ironically, this expansion in colonial liberties and political rights occurred along with the dramatic increase in the colony's slave population. The intertwined evolution of American freedom and American slavery gave England's southern colonies a unique and conflicted political character that endured even after independence.

At the same time, the English colonists were expanding settlements to the South. The Carolinas at first prospered from the profits of the fur trade. Fur traders pushed into the interior, eventually threatening the French trading networks based in New Orleans and Mobile. Native peoples eventually provided over a hundred thousand deerskins annually to this profitable commerce. The environmental and cultural costs of the fur trade were little appreciated at the time. As Amerindian peoples hunted more intensely, the natural balance of animals and plants was disrupted in southern forests. The profits of the fur trade altered Amerindian culture as well, leading villages to place less emphasis on subsistence hunting and fishing and traditional agriculture. Deepening dependencies on European products, including firearms, metal tools, textiles and alcohol, further altered Amerindian life.

Although increasingly brought into the commerce and culture of the Carolina colony, indigenous peoples were being weakened by epidemics, alcoholism, and a rising tide of ethnic conflicts generated by competition for hunting grounds. Conflicts among indigenous peoples—now armed with firearms—became more deadly. Many Amerindians captured in these wars were sold as slaves to local colonists, who used them as agricultural workers or exported them to the sugar plantations of the Caribbean islands. Dissatisfied with the terms of trade imposed by fur traders and angered by this slave trade, Amerindians launched attacks on English settlements in the early 1700s. Their defeat by colonial military forces led inevitably to new seizures of Amerindian land by European settlers.

The northern part of the Carolinas had been settled from Virginia and followed that colony's mixed economy of tobacco and forest products. Slavery expanded slowly in this region. Charleston and the interior of South Carolina followed a different path. Settled first by planters from the Caribbean Island of Barbados in 1670, this colony soon developed an economy based on plantations and slavery in imitation of the colonies of the Caribbean and Brazil. In 1729 North and South Carolina became separate colonies.

Despite an unhealthy climate, the prosperous rice and indigo plantations near Charleston attracted a diverse array of immigrants and an increasing flow of African slaves. African slaves were present from the founding of Charleston. They were instrumental in introducing irrigated rice agriculture along the coastal lowlands and in developing indigo (a plant that produced a blue dye) plantations at higher elevations away from the coast. Slaves were often given significant responsibilities. As one planter sending two slaves and their families to a frontier region put it: "[They] are likely young people, well acquainted with Rice & every kind of plantation business, and in short [are] capable of the management of a plantation themselves."[2]

As profits from rice and indigo rose, the importation of African slaves created a black majority in South Carolina. African languages and Gullah (a dialect with African and English roots), as well as African religious beliefs and diet, strongly influenced this unique colonial culture. African slaves were more likely than American-born slaves to rebel or run away. In South Carolina's largest slave uprising, the Stono Rebellion of 1739, Africans played a major role. After a group of about twenty slaves, many of them African Catholics who sought to flee south to Spanish Florida, seized firearms, about a hundred slaves from nearby plantations joined them. The colonial militia soon defeated the rebels and executed many of them, but the rebellion shocked slave owners throughout England's southern colonies and led to greater repression.

Colonial South Carolina was the most hierarchical society in British North America. Planters controlled the economy and political life. The richest maintained households both in the countryside and in Charleston, the largest city in the southern colonies. Small farmers, cattlemen, artisans, merchants, and fur traders held an intermediate but clearly subordinate social position. Native peoples remained influential participants in colonial society through commercial contacts and alliances, but they were increasingly marginalized. As had occurred in colonial Latin America, the growth of a large mixed population blurred racial and cultural boundaries. On the frontier, the children of white men and Indian women held an important place in the fur trade. In the plantation regions and Charleston, the offspring of white men and black women often held preferred positions within the slave work force or, if they had been freed, as carpenters, blacksmiths, or in other skilled trades.

New England

The colonization of New England by two separate groups of Protestant dissenters, Pilgrims and Puritans, put the settlement of this region on a different course. The **Pilgrims,** who came first, wished to break completely with the Church of England, which they believed was still essentially Catholic. Unwilling to confront the power of the established church and the monarch, they sought an opportunity to pursue their spiritual ends in a new land. As a result, in 1620 approximately one hundred settlers—men, women, and children—established the colony of Plymouth on the coast of present-day Massachusetts. Although nearly half of the settlers died during the first winter, the colony survived. Plymouth benefited from strong leadership and the discipline and cooperative nature of the settlers. Nevertheless, this experiment in creating a church-directed community failed. The religious enthusiasm and purpose that at first sustained the Pilgrims was dissipated by new immigrants who did not share the founders' religious beliefs, and by geographic dispersal to new towns. In 1691, Plymouth was absorbed into the larger Massachusetts Bay Colony of the Puritans.

The **Puritans** wished to "purify" the Church of England, not break with it. They wanted to abolish its hierarchy of bishops and priests, free it from governmental interference, and limit membership to people who shared their beliefs. Subjected to increased discrimination in England for their efforts to transform the church, large numbers of Puritans began emigrating from England in 1630.

The Puritan leaders of the Massachusetts Bay Company—the joint-stock company that had received a royal charter to finance the Massachusetts Bay Colony—carried with them from England to Massachusetts the company charter, which spelled out company rights and obligations as well as the direction of company government. By bringing the charter with them, they limited Crown efforts to control them; the Crown could revoke but not alter the terms of the charter. By 1643, more than 20,000 Puritans had settled in the Bay Colony.

Immigration to Massachusetts differed from immigration to the Chesapeake and to South Carolina. Most newcomers to Massachusetts arrived with their families. Whereas 84 percent of Virginia's population in 1625 was male, Massachusetts had a normal gender balance in its population almost from the beginning. It was also the healthiest of England's colonies. The result was a rapid natural increase in population. The population of Massachusetts quickly became more "American" than the population of the colonies to the south or in the Caribbean, whose survival depended on a steady flow of new English immigrants to counter the high mortality rates. Massachusetts also was more homogeneous and less hierarchical than the southern colonies.

Political institutions evolved out of the terms of the company charter. A governor was elected, along with a council of magistrates drawn from the board of directors of the Massachusetts Bay Company. Disagreements between this council and elected representatives of the towns led, by 1650, to the creation of a lower legislative house that selected its own speaker and began to develop procedures and rules similar to those of the House of Commons in England. The result was greater autonomy and greater local political involvement than in the colonies of Latin America.

Economically, Massachusetts differed dramatically from the southern colonies. Agriculture met basic needs, but poor soils and harsh climate offered no opportunity to develop cash crops like tobacco or rice. To pay for imported tools, textiles, and other essentials, the colonists needed to discover some profit-making niche in the growing Atlantic market. Fur, timber and other forest products, and fish provided the initial economic foundation, but New England's economic well-being soon depended on providing commercial and shipping services in a dynamic and far-flung commercial arena that included the southern colonies, the smaller Caribbean islands, Africa, and Europe.

In Spanish and Portuguese America, heavily capitalized monopolies (companies or individuals given exclusive economic privileges) dominated international trade. In New England, by contrast, merchants survived by discovering smaller but more sustainable profits in diversified trade across the Atlantic. The colony's commercial success rested on market intelligence, flexibility, and streamlined organization. The success of this development strategy is demonstrated by urban population growth. With 16,000 inhabitants in 1740, Boston, capital of Massachusetts Bay Colony, was the largest city in British North America. This coincided with the decline of New England's once-large indigenous population, which had been dramatically reduced by a combination of epidemics and brutal military campaigns.

Lacking a profitable agricultural export like tobacco, New England did not develop the extreme social stratification of the southern plantation colonies. Slaves and indentured servants were present, but in very small numbers. New England was ruled by the richest colonists and shared the racial attitudes of the southern colonies, but it also was the colonial society with fewest differences in wealth and status and with the most uniformly British and Protestant population in the Americas.

The Middle Atlantic Region

Much of the future success of English-speaking America was rooted in the rapid economic development and remarkable cultural diversity that appeared in the Middle Atlantic colonies—diversity that grew in part from non-European origins. In 1624 the Dutch West India Company established the colony of New Netherland and located its capital on Manhattan Island. The colony was poorly managed and underfinanced from the start, but its location commanded the potentially profitable and strategically important Hudson River. Dutch merchants established with the **Iroquois Confederacy**—an alliance among the Mohawk, Oneida, Onondaga, Cayuga, and Seneca peoples—and with other native peoples alliances and trading relationships that gave them access to the rich fur trade of Canada. When confronted by an English military expedition in 1664, the Dutch surrendered without a fight. James, duke of York and later King James II of England, became proprietor of the colony, which was renamed New York.

New York was characterized by tumultuous politics and corrupt public administration. The colony's success was guaranteed in large measure by the development of New York City as a commercial and shipping center. Located at the mouth of the Hudson River, the city played an essential role in connecting the region's grain farmers to the booming markets of the Caribbean and southern Europe. By the early eighteenth century, New York Colony had a diverse population that included (in addition to English colonists) Dutch, German, and Swedish settlers as well as a large slave community.

Pennsylvania began as a proprietary colony and as a refuge for Quakers, a persecuted religious minority. In 1682 William Penn secured an enormous grant of territory (nearly the size of England) because the English king Charles II was indebted to Penn's father. As proprietor (owner) of the land, Penn had sole right to establish a government, subject only to the requirement that he provide for an assembly of freemen.

Penn quickly lost control of the colony's political life, but the colony enjoyed remarkable success. By 1700 Pennsylvania had a population of more than 21,000, and Philadelphia, its capital, soon passed Boston to become the largest city in the British colonies. Healthy climate, excellent land, relatively peaceful relations with native peoples (prompted by Penn's emphasis on negotiation rather than warfare), and access through Philadelphia to good markets led to rapid economic and demographic growth in the colony.

Both Pennsylvania and South Carolina were grain-exporting colonies, but they were very different societies. South Carolina's rice plantations required large numbers of slaves. In Pennsylvania, free workers, including a large number of German families, produced the bulk of the colony's grain crops on family farms. As a result, Pennsylvania's economic expansion in the late seventeenth century occurred without reproducing South Carolina's hierarchical and repressive social order. By the early eighteenth century, however, the prosperous city of Philadelphia did have a large population of black slaves and freedmen. Many were servants in the homes of wealthy merchants, but the fast-growing economy offered many opportunities in skilled trades as well.

The Home of Sir William Johnson, British Superintendent for Indian Affairs, Northern District   As the colonial era drew to a close, the British attempted to limit the cost of colonial defense by negotiating land settlements between native peoples and settlers. These agreements were doomed by the growing tide of western migration. William Johnson (1715–1774) maintained a fragile peace along the northern frontier by building strong personal relations with influential leaders of the Mohawk and other members of the Iroquois Confederacy. His home in present-day Johnstown, New York, shows the mixed nature of the frontier—the relative opulence of the main house offset by the two defensive blockhouses built for protection.   ("Johnson Hall," by E. L. Henry. Courtesy, Albany Institute of History and Art)

French America

Patterns of French settlement more closely resembled those of Spain and Portugal than of England. The French were committed to missionary activity among Amerindian peoples and emphasized the extraction of natural resources—furs rather than minerals. The navigator and promoter Jacques Cartier first stirred France's interest in North America. In three voyages between 1524 and 1542, he explored the region of Newfoundland and the Gulf of St. Lawrence. A contemporary of Cortés and Pizarro, Cartier also hoped to find mineral wealth, but the stones he brought back to France turned out to be quartz and iron pyrite, "fool's gold."

The French waited more than fifty years before establishing settlements in North America. Coming to Canada after spending years in the West Indies, Samuel de Champlain founded the colony of **New France** at Quebec°, on the banks of the St. Lawrence River, in 1608. This location provided ready access to Amerindian trade routes, but it also compelled French settlers to take sides in the region's ongoing warfare. Champlain allied New France with the Huron and Algonkian peoples, traditional enemies of the powerful Iroquois Confederacy. Although French firearms and armor at first tipped the balance of power to France's native allies, the members of the Iroquois Confederacy proved to be resourceful and persistent enemies.

The European market for fur, especially beaver, fueled French settlement. Young Frenchmen were sent to live among native peoples to master their languages and customs. These **coureurs de bois°**, or runners of the woods, often began families with indigenous women,

Quebec (kwuh-BEC)   coureurs de bois (koo-RUHR day BWA)

Canadian Fur Trader   The fur trade provided the economic foundation of early Canadian settlement. The trade depended on a mix of native and European skills and resources. The fur trader's canoe was developed from native technology to carry large loads over great distances.   (Hudson's Bay Company Archives, Provincial Archives of Manitoba)

and they and their children, who were called *métis*°, helped to direct the fur trade, guiding French expansion to the west and south. Amerindians actively participated in this trade because they quickly came to depend on the goods they received in exchange for furs—firearms, metal tools and utensils, textiles, and alcohol. This change in the material culture of the native peoples led to overhunting, which rapidly transformed the environment and led to the depletion of beaver and deer populations. It also increased competition among native peoples for hunting grounds, thus promoting warfare.

The proliferation of firearms made indigenous warfare more deadly. The Iroquois Confederacy responded to the increased military strength of France's Algonkian allies by forging commercial and military links with Dutch and later English settlements in the Hudson River Valley. Well armed by the Dutch and English, the Iroquois Confederacy nearly eradicated the Huron in 1649 and in-

métis (may-TEES)

flicted a series of humiliating defeats on the French. At the high point of their power in the early 1680s, Iroquois hunters and military forces gained control of much of the Great Lakes region and the Ohio River Valley. A large French military expedition and a relentless attack focused on Iroquois villages and agriculture finally checked Iroquois power in 1701.

Spain had effectively limited the spread of firearms in its colonies. But the fur trade, together with the growing military rivalry between Algonkian and Iroquois peoples and their respective French and English allies, led to the rapid spread of firearms in North America. Use of firearms in hunting and warfare moved west and south, reaching indigenous plains cultures that previously had adopted the horse introduced by the Spanish. This intersection of horse and gun frontiers in the early eighteenth century dramatically increased the military power and hunting efficiency of the Sioux, Comanche, Cheyenne, and other indigenous peoples, and slowed the pace of European settlement in the North American west.

In French Canada, the Jesuits led the effort to convert native peoples to Christianity. Building on earlier evangelical efforts in Brazil and Paraguay, French Catholic missionaries mastered native languages, created boarding schools for young boys and girls, and set up model agricultural communities for converted Amerindians. The Jesuits' greatest successes coincided with a destructive wave of epidemics and renewed warfare among native peoples in the 1630s. Eventually, churches were established throughout Huron and Algonkian territories. Nevertheless, local culture persisted. In 1688 a French nun who had devoted her life to instructing Amerindian girls expressed the frustration of many missionaries with the resilience of indigenous culture:

> We have observed that of a hundred that have passed through our hands we have scarcely civilized one. . . . When we are least expecting it, they clamber over our wall and go off to run with their kinsmen in the woods, finding more to please them there than in all the amenities of our French house.[3]

As epidemics undermined conversion efforts in mission settlements and evidence of indigenous resistance to conversion mounted, the church redirected some of its resources from the evangelical effort to the larger French settlements, founding schools, hospitals, and churches.

Responsibility for finding settlers and supervising the colonial economy was first granted to a monopoly company chartered in France. Even though the fur trade flourished, population growth was slow. Founded at about the same time as French Canada, Virginia had twenty times as many European residents as Canada by

1627. After the establishment of royal authority in the 1660s, Canada's French population increased but remained at only 7,000 in 1673. Although improved fiscal management and more effective colonial government did promote a limited agricultural expansion, the fur trade remained important. It is clear that Canada's small settler population and the fur trade's dependence on the voluntary participation of Amerindians allowed indigenous peoples to retain greater independence and more control over their traditional lands than was possible in the colonies of Spain, Portugal, or England. Unlike these colonial regimes, which sought to transform ancient ways of life or force the transfer of native lands, the French were compelled to treat indigenous peoples as allies and trading partners. This permitted indigenous peoples to more gradually adapt to new religious, technological, and market realities.

Despite Canada's small population, limited resources, and increasing vulnerability to attack by the English and their indigenous allies, the French aggressively expanded to the west and south. Louisiana was founded in 1699, but by 1708 there were fewer than 300 soldiers, settlers, and slaves in the territory. Like Canada, Louisiana depended on the fur trade, exporting more than 50,000 deerskins in 1726. And also as in Canada, Amerindians, driven by a desire for European goods, eagerly embraced this trade. In 1753 a French official reported a Choctaw leader as saying, "[The French] were the first . . . who made [us] subject to the different needs that [we] can no longer now do without."[4]

France's North American colonies were threatened by a series of wars fought by France and England and by the population growth and increasing prosperity of neighboring English colonies. The "French and Indian War" (also known as the Seven Years War, 1756–1763), however, proved to be the final contest for North American empire (see Map 19.2). England committed a larger military force to the struggle and, despite early defeats,

Map. 19.2 European Claims in North America, 1755–1763   The results of the French and Indian War dramatically altered the map of North America. France's losses precipitated conflicts between Amerindian peoples and the rapidly expanding population of the British colonies.

took the French capital of Quebec in 1759. Although resistance continued briefly, French forces in Canada surrendered in 1760. The peace agreement forced France to yield Canada to the English and cede Louisiana to Spain. The differences between French and English colonial realities were suggested by the petition of one Canadian indigenous leader to a British officer after the French surrender. "[W]e learn that our lands are to be given away not only to trade thereon but also to them in full title to various [English] individuals. . . . We have always been a free nation, and now we will become slaves, which would be very difficult to accept after having enjoyed our liberty so long."[5] With the loss of Canada the French concentrated their efforts on their sugar-producing colonies in the Caribbean (see Chapter 20).

COLONIAL EXPANSION AND CONFLICT

In the last decades of the seventeenth century, all of the European colonies in the Americas began to experience a long period of economic and demographic expansion. The imperial powers responded by strengthening their administrative and economic controls in the colonies. They also sought to force colonial populations to pay a larger share of the costs of administration and defense. These efforts at reform and restructuring coincided with a series of imperial wars fought along Atlantic trade routes and in the Americas. France's loss of its North American colonies was one of the most important results of these struggles. Equally significant, colonial populations throughout the Americas became more aware of separate national identities and more aggressive in asserting local interests against the will of distant monarchs.

Imperial Reform in Spanish America and Brazil

Spain's Habsburg dynasty ended when the Spanish king Charles II died without an heir in 1700 (see Table 18.1). After thirteen years of conflict involving the major European powers and factions within Spain, Philip of Bourbon, grandson of Louis XIV of France, gained the Spanish throne. Under Philip V and his Bourbon heirs, Spain's colonial administration and tax collection were reorganized. Spain's reliance on convoys protected by naval vessels was abolished, more colonial ports were permitted to trade with Spain, and intercolonial trade was expanded. Spain also created new commercial monopolies to produce tobacco, some alcoholic beverages, and chocolate. Also, the Spanish navy was strengthened, and trade in contraband was more effectively policed.

For most of the Spanish Empire, the eighteenth century was a period of remarkable economic expansion associated with population growth. Amerindian populations began to recover from the early epidemics, the flow of Spanish immigrants increased, and the slave trade to the plantation colonies was expanded. Mining, the heart of the Spanish colonial economy, increased as silver production in Mexico and Peru rose steadily into the 1780s. Agricultural exports also expanded: tobacco, dyes, hides, chocolate, cotton, and sugar joined the flow of goods to Europe.

But these reforms carried unforeseen consequences that threatened the survival of the Spanish Empire. Despite expanded silver production, the economic growth of the eighteenth century was led by the previously minor agricultural and grazing economies of Cuba, the Rio de la Plata region, Venezuela, Chile, and Central America. These export economies were less able than the mining economies of Mexico and Peru to weather breaks in trade caused by imperial wars. Each such disruption forced landowning elites in Cuba and the other regions to turn to alternative, often illegal, trade with English, French, or Dutch merchants. By the 1790s, the wealthiest and most influential sectors of Spain's colonial society had come to view the Spanish Empire as an impediment to prosperity and growth.

Bourbon political and fiscal reforms also contributed to a growing sense of colonial grievance by limiting creoles' access to colonial offices and by imposing new taxes and monopolies on colonial production. Consumer and producer resentment, for example, led to rioting when the Spanish established monopolies on tobacco, cacao (chocolate), and brandy. Because these reforms produced a more intrusive and expensive colonial government that interfered with established business practices, many colonists saw these changes as an abuse of the informal constitution that had long governed the empire. Only in the Bourbon effort to expand colonial militias in the face of English threats did creoles find opportunity for improved status and greater responsibility.

In addition to tax rebellions and urban riots, colonial policies also provoked Amerindian uprisings. Most spectacular was the rebellion initiated in 1780 by the Peruvian Amerindian leader José Gabriel Condorcanqui. Once in rebellion, he took the name of his Inca ancestor

Market in Rio de Janeiro   In many of the cities of colonial Latin America female slaves and black free women dominated retail markets. In this scene from late colonial Brazil, Afro-Brazilian women sell a variety of foods and crafts.   (Sir Henry Chamberlain, *Views and Costumes of the City and Neighborhoods of Rio de Janeiro*, London, 1822)

Tupac Amaru°, who had been executed as a rebel in 1572. **Tupac Amaru II** was well connected in Spanish colonial society. He had been educated by the Jesuits and was actively involved in trade with the silver mines at Potosí. Despite these connections, he still resented the abuse of Amerindian villagers.

Historians still debate the objectives of this rebellion. Tupac Amaru's own pronouncements did not clearly state whether he sought to end local injustices or overthrow Spanish rule. It appears that a local Spanish judge who challenged Tupac Amaru's hereditary rights provided the initial provocation, but that Tupac Amaru was ultimately driven by the conviction that colonial authorities were oppressing the indigenous people. As thousands joined him, he dared to contemplate the overthrow of Spanish rule.

Amerindian communities suffering under the mita and tribute obligations provided the majority of Tupac Amaru's army. He also received some support from creoles, mestizos, and slaves. After his capture, he was brutally executed, as were his wife and fifteen other

Tupac Amaru (TOO-pack a-MAH-roo)

family members and allies. Even after his execution Amerindian rebels continued the struggle for more than two years. By the time Spanish authority was firmly reestablished, more than a hundred thousand lives had been lost and enormous amounts of property destroyed.

Brazil experienced a similar period of expansion and reform after 1700. Portugal created new administrative positions and gave monopoly companies exclusive rights to little-developed regions. Here, too, a more intrusive colonial government led to rebellions and plots, including open warfare in 1707 between "sons of the soil" and "outsiders" in São Paulo. The most aggresive period of reform occurred during the ministry of the marquis of Pombal (1750–1777). The Pombal reforms were made possible by an economic expansion fueled by the discovery of gold in the 1690s and diamonds after 1720 as well as by the development of markets for coffee and cotton. This new wealth paid for the importation of nearly 2 million African slaves. In Spanish America, a reinvigorated Crown sought to eliminate contraband trade. Portugal, however, had fallen into the economic orbit of England, and Brazil's new prosperity fueled a new wave of English imports.

Reform and Reorganization in British North America

England's efforts to reform and reorganize its North American colonies began earlier than the Bourbon initiative in Spanish America. After the period of Cromwell's Puritan Republic, the restored Stuart king, Charles II, undertook an ambitious campaign to establish greater Crown control over the colonies. Between 1651 and 1673 a series of Navigation Acts sought to severely limit colonial trading and colonial production that competed directly with English manufacturers. James II also attempted to increase royal control over colonial political life. Royal governments replaced orginal colonial charters as in Massachusetts and proprietorships as in the Carolinas. Because the New England colonies were viewed as centers of smuggling, the king temporarily suspended their elected assemblies. At the same time, he appointed colonial governors and granted them new fiscal and legislative powers.

James II's overthrow in the Glorious Revolution of 1688 ended this confrontation, but not before colonists were provoked to resist and, in some cases, rebel. They overthrew the governors of New York and Massachusetts and removed the Catholic proprietor of Maryland. William and Mary restored relative peace, but these conflicts alerted the colonists to the potential for aggression by the English government. Colonial politics would remain confrontational until the American Revolution.

During the eighteenth century the English colonies experienced renewed economic growth and attracted a new wave of European immigration, but social divisions were increasingly evident. The colonial population in 1770 was more urban, more clearly divided by class and race, and more vulnerable to economic downturns. Crises were provoked when imperial wars with France and Spain disrupted trade in the Atlantic, increased tax burdens, forced military mobilizations, and provoked frontier conflicts with the Amerindians. On the eve of the American Revolution, England defeated France and weakened Spain. The cost, however, was great. Administrative, military, and tax policies imposed to gain empirewide victory alienated much of the American colonial population.

CONCLUSION

The New World colonial empires of Spain, Portugal, France, and England had many characteristics in common. All subjugated Amerindian peoples and introduced large numbers of enslaved Africans. Within all four empires, forests were cut down, virgin soils were turned with the plow, and Old World animals and plants were introduced. Colonists in all four applied the technologies of the Old World to the resources of the New, producing wealth and exploiting the commercial possibilities of the emerging Atlantic market.

Each of the New World empires also reflected the distinctive cultural and institutional heritages of its colonizing power. Mineral wealth allowed Spain to develop the most centralized empire. Political and economic power was concentrated in the great capital cities of Mexico City and Lima. Portugal and France pursued objectives similar to Spain's in their colonies. However, neither Brazil's agricultural economy nor France's Canadian fur trade produced the financial resources that made possible the centralized control achieved by Spain. Nevertheless, all three of these Catholic powers were able to impose and enforce significant levels of religious and cultural uniformity, relative to the British.

Greater cultural and religious diversity characterized British North America. Colonists were drawn to British North America from throughout the British Isles and included participants in all of Britain's numerous religious traditions. They were joined by German, Swedish, French Huguenot, and Dutch immigrants. British colonial government varied somewhat from colony to colony and was more responsive to local interests. Thus colonists in British North America were better able than colonists in the areas controlled by Spain, Portugal, and France to respond to changing economic and political circumstances. Most important, the British colonies attracted many more European immigrants than did the other New World colonies. Between 1580 and 1760, French colonies received 60,000 immigrants, Brazil 523,000, and the Spanish colonies 678,000. Within a shorter period—between 1600 and 1760—the British settlements welcomed 746,000. Population in British North America—free and slave combined—then reached an extraordinary 2.5 million by 1775.

By the eighteenth century, colonial societies across the Americas had matured as wealth increased, populations grew, and contacts with the rest of the world became more common (see Chapter 20). Colonial elites were more confident of their ability to define and defend local interests. Colonists were in general increasingly aware of their unique and distinctive cultural identities and willing to defend American experience and practice in the face of European presumptions of superiority. Moreover, influential groups in all the colonies were drawn toward the liberating ideas of Europe's Enlightenment. In the open and less inhibited spaces of the Western Hemisphere, these ideas (as Chapter 23 examines) soon provided a potent intellectual basis for opposing the continuation of empire.

■ Key Terms

Columbian Exchange

Council of the Indies

Bartolomé de Las Casas

Potosí

encomienda

creoles

mestizo

mulatto

indentured servant

House of Burgesses

Pilgrims

Puritans

Iroquois Confederacy

New France

coureurs de bois

Tupac Amaru II

■ Suggested Reading

Alfred W. Crosby, Jr., is justifiably the best-known student of the Columbian Exchange. See his *The Columbian Exchange: Biological and Cultural Consequences of 1492* (1972) and *Ecological Imperialism* (1986). William H. McNeill, *Plagues and People* (1976), puts the discussion of the American exchange in a world history context. Elinor G. K. Melville, *A Plague of Sheep: Environmental Consequences of the Spanish Conquest of Mexico* (1994), is the most important recent contribution to this field.

Colonial Latin America, 2d ed. (1994), by Mark A. Burkholder and Lyman L. Johnson, provides a good introduction to colonial Latin American history. *Early Latin America* (1983) by James Lockhart and Stuart B. Schwartz and *Spain and Portugal in the New World, 1492–1700* (1984) by Lyle N. McAlister are both useful introductions as well.

The specialized historical literature on the American colonial empires is extensive and deep. A sampling of useful works follows. For the early colonial period see Inga Clendinnen, *Ambivalent Conquests* (1987); James Lockhart, *The Nahuas After the Conquest* (1992); and John Hemming, *Red Gold: The Conquest of the Brazilian Indians* (1978). Nancy M. Farriss, *Maya Society Under Spanish Rule: The Collective Enterprise of Survival* (1984), is also one of the most important books on colonial Spanish America. For the Catholic Church see William Taylor, *Magistrates of the Sacred: Priests and Parishioners in Eighteenth-Century Mexico* (1996). Lyman L. Johnson and Sonya Lipsett-Rivera, *The Faces of Honor* (1999), provides a good introduction to the culture of honor. For the place of women see Asunción Lavrin, ed., *Sexuality and Marriage in Colonial Latin America* (1989). On issues of class R. Douglas Cope, *The Limits of Racial Domination* (1994), is recommended. On the slave trade, Herbert S. Klein, *The Middle Passage* (1978), and Philip D. Curtin, *The Atlantic Slave Trade: A Census* (1969), are indispensable. Frederick P. Bowser, *The African Slave in Colonial Peru, 1524–1650* (1973); Mary C. Karasch, *Slave Life and Culture in Rio de Janeiro, 1808–1850* (1986); and Stuart B. Schwartz, *Sugar Plantations in the Formation of Brazilian Society: Bahia, 1550–1835* (1985), are excellent introductions to the African experience in two very different Latin American societies.

Among the useful general studies of the British colonies are Charles M. Andrews, *The Colonial Period of American History: The Settlements,* 3 vols. (1934–1937); David Hackett Fischer, *Albion's Seed: Four British Folkways in America* (1989); and Gary B. Nash, *Red, White, and Black: The Peoples of Early America,* 2d ed. (1982). On the economy see John J. McCusker and Russell R. Menard, *The Economy of British America, 1607–1789* (1979). For slavery see David Brion Davis, *The Problem of Slavery in Western Culture* (1966); Allan Kulikoff, *Tobacco and Slaves: The Development of Southern Cultures in the Chesapeake, 1680–1800* (1986); and Peter H. Wood, *Black Majority: Negroes in Colonial South Carolina from 1670 Through the Stono Rebellion* (1974). Two very useful works on the relations between Europeans and Indians are James Merrill, *The Indians' New World: Catawbas and Their Neighbors from European Contact Through the Era of Removal* (1989); and Daniel H. Usner, Jr., *Indians, Settlers, and Slaves in a Frontier Exchange Economy: The Lower Mississippi Valley Before 1783* (1992).

For late colonial politics see Gary B. Nash, *Urban Crucible: Social Change, Political Consciousness, and the Origins of the American Revolution* (1979); Bernard Bailyn, *The Origins of American Politics* (1986); Jack P. Greene, *The Quest for Power: The Lower Houses of Assembly in the Southern Royal Colonies* (1963); and Richard Bushman, *King and People in Provincial Massachusetts* (1985). On immigration see Bernard Bailyn, *The Peopling of British North America* (1986).

On French North America, William J. Eccles, *France in America,* rev. ed. (1990), is an excellent overview; see also his *The Canadian Frontier, 1534–1760* (1969). G. F. G. Stanley, *New France, 1701–1760* (1968), is also an important resource. R. Cole Harris, *The Seigneurial System in Canada: A Geographical Study* (1966), provides an excellent analysis of the topic. Harold Innis, *The Fur Trade in Canada: An Introduction to Canadian Economic History* (1927), remains indispensable. Also of value are Cornelius Jaenen, *The Role of the Church in New France* (1976), and Alison L. Prentice, *Canadian Women: A History* (1988).

■ Notes

1. Quoted in Alfred W. Crosby, Jr., *The Columbian Exchange: Biological and Cultural Consequences of 1492* (Westport, CT: Greenwood, 1972), 58.
2. Quoted ibid.
3. Quoted in R. Douglas Francis, Richard Jones, and Donald B. Smith, *Origins: Canadian History to Confederation* (Toronto: Holt, Rinehart, and Winston of Canada, 1992), 52.
4. Quoted in Daniel H. Usner, Jr., *Indians, Settlers and Slaves in a Frontier Exchange Economy: The Lower Mississippi Valley Before 1783,* Institute of Early American History and Culture Series (Chapel Hill: University of North Carolina Press, 1992), 96.
5. Quoted in Cornelius J. Jaenen, "French and Native Peoples in New France," in J. M. Bumsted, *Interpreting Canada's Past,* vol. 1, 2d ed. (Toronto: Oxford University Press, 1993), 73.

20

THE ATLANTIC SYSTEM AND AFRICA,

1550–1800

Plantations in the West Indies • **Plantation Life in the Eighteenth Century** •
Creating the Atlantic Economy • **Africa, the Atlantic, and Islam**
ENVIRONMENT AND TECHNOLOGY: Amerindian Foods in Africa
SOCIETY AND CULTURE: A Maroon Village in French Guiana, 1748

Caribbean Sugar Mill   The wind mill crushes sugar cane whose juice
is boiled down in the smoking building next door.

As the ship bearing a cargo of slaves from West Africa neared the West Indian island of Barbados in 1757, the English crew gave a joyful shout, glad that this leg of their trading tour around the Atlantic was over. Since leaving England, some of their number had died of African tropical diseases, and one crewman had been flogged to death for insubordination. The survivors, thankful to put the risk of disease and slave insurrection behind them, looked forward to returning to England.

However, one of the slaves on board, Olaudah Equiano°, recorded in his biography that the sight of Barbados filled the shackled Africans with apprehension. Although fortunate to have survived long weeks of suffocating heat and loathsome smells packed side by side in the cargo hold, the captive African men, women, and children feared they were going to be eaten by the white people who rushed to inspect them after the ship anchored in the harbor of Bridgetown. To ease the new arrivals' panic, local sugar planters sent veteran slaves on board to assure them in several African languages that they would not be eaten. Instead, most were destined to work on the island's sugar plantations. After landing, Equiano relates, he and his companions were relieved to discover that most of the island's inhabitants were Africans. The eleven-year-old Equiano found many of his own Igbo° people there.

After examining the slaves for physical defects, the local merchants divided them into "parcels" of several slaves each and penned them in a yard, in Equiano's words, "like so many sheep in a fold without regard to sex or age." A few days later they were sold to the planters, not by auction but in a terrifying "scramble." At the beat of a drum, buyers rushed into the yard and seized the parcel of slaves they wanted. "In this manner," Equiano commented, "without scruple, are relations and friends separated, most of them never to see each other again."

Olaudah Equiano (oh-LAU-duh ay-kwee-AHN-oh)
Igbo (EE-boh)

By the 1750s, Barbados was past its prime as a sugar colony, so Equiano and some companions were shipped to the colony of Virginia. There for a time he was put to work weeding; he later worked on a ship. In 1766 at the age of twenty-one, Equiano was able to buy his freedom with money he earned in private trading. He worked as a seaman and then resided in England, where he married and joined the campaign against the slave trade.

The slave trade and the plantations in the West Indies, Virginia, and elsewhere in the Americas were crucial pieces of a new **Atlantic system.** This network of trading links moved not only goods and wealth but also people and cultures around the Atlantic world.

As you read this chapter, ask yourself the following questions:

- How did participation in the Atlantic system affect Europe, Africa, and the Americas?
- How and why did European businessmen, with the help of their governments, put this trading system together?
- How and why did the West Indies and other places in the Americas become centers of African population and culture?
- How did sub-Saharan Africa's expanding contacts in the Atlantic compare with its contacts with the Islamic world?

PLANTATIONS IN THE WEST INDIES

The West Indies was the first place in the Americas reached by Columbus and the first part of the Americas where native populations collapsed. It took a long time to repopulate these islands from abroad and forge new economic links between them and other parts of the Atlantic. But after 1650, sugar plantations, African slaves, and European capital made these islands a major center of the Atlantic economy.

Colonization Before 1650

Spanish settlers introduced sugar-cane cultivation into the West Indies shortly after 1500, but soon these colonies fell into neglect as attention shifted to colonizing the American mainland. After 1600 the West Indies revived as a focus of colonization, this time by northern Europeans interested in growing tobacco and other crops. In the 1620s and 1630s English colonization societies founded small European settlements on Montserrat°, Barbados°, Trinidad°, and other Caribbean islands, while the French colonized Martinique°, Guadeloupe°, and some other islands. Because of greater support from their government, the English colonies prospered first, largely by growing tobacco for export.

This New World leaf, long used by Amerindians for recreation and medicine, was finding a new market among seventeenth-century Europeans. Despite the opposition of individuals like King James I of England, who condemned tobacco smoke as "dangerous to the eye, hateful to the nose, harmful to the brain, and dangerous to the lungs," the habit spread. By 1614 tobacco was reportedly being sold in seven thousand shops in and around London, and some English businessmen were dreaming of a tobacco trade as valuable as Spain's silver fleets.

Turning such pipe dreams into reality was not easy. Diseases, hurricanes, and attacks by the Carib and the Spanish scourged the early French and English West Indies colonists. They also suffered from shortages of supplies from Europe and shortages of labor sufficient to clear and plant virgin land with tobacco. Two changes improved the colonies' prospects. One was the formation of **chartered companies.** To promote national claims without government expense, France and England gave groups of private investors monopolies over trade to their West Indies colonies in exchange for the payment of an annual fee. The other change was that the companies began to provide free passage to the colonies for poor Europeans. These indentured servants paid off their debt by working three or four years for the established colonists (see Chapter 19).

Under this system the French and English population on several tobacco islands grew rapidly in the 1630s and 1640s. By the middle of the century, however, the Caribbean colonies were in crisis because of stiff competition from milder Virginia-grown tobacco, also cultivated by indentured servants. The cultivation of sugar cane, introduced in the 1640s by Dutch investors expelled from Brazil, provided the Caribbean colonies a way out of this crisis. In the process their labor force changed from mostly European to mostly African.

The Portuguese had introduced sugar cultivation into Brazil from islands along the African coast after 1550 and had soon introduced enslaved African labor as well (see Chapter 19). By 1600 Brazil was the Atlantic world's greatest sugar producer. Some Dutch merchants invested in Brazilian sugar plantations so that they might profit from transporting the sugar across the Atlantic and distributing it in Europe. However, in the first half of the seventeenth century the Dutch were fighting for their independence from the Spanish crown, which then ruled Portugal and Brazil. As part of that struggle, the Dutch government chartered the **Dutch West India Company** in 1621 to carry the conflict to Spain's overseas possessions.

Not just a disguised form of the Dutch navy, the Dutch West India Company was a private trading company. Its investors expected the company's profits to cover its expenses and pay them dividends. After the capture of a Spanish treasure fleet in 1628, the company used some of the windfall to pay its stockholders a huge dividend and the rest to finance an assault on Brazil's valuable sugar-producing areas. By 1635 the Dutch company controlled 1,000 miles (1,600 kilometers) of northeastern Brazil's coast. Over the next fifteen years the new Dutch owners improved the efficiency of the Brazilian sugar industry, and the company prospered by supplying the plantations with enslaved Africans and European goods and carrying the sugar back to Europe.

Like its assault on Brazil, the Dutch West India Company's entry into the African slave trade combined economic and political motives. It seized the important West African trading station of Elmina from the Portuguese in 1638 and took their port of Luanda° on the Angolan coast in 1641. From these coasts the Dutch shipped slaves to Brazil and the West Indies. Although the Portuguese were able to drive the Dutch out of Angola after a few years, Elmina remained the Dutch West India Company's headquarters in West Africa.

Once free of Spanish rule in 1640, the Portuguese crown turned its attention to reconquering Brazil. By 1654 Portuguese armies had driven the last of the Dutch sugar planters from Brazil. Some of the expelled planters transplanted their capital and knowledge of sugar production to small colonies, which the Dutch had founded earlier as trading bases with Spanish colonies; others in-

---

Montserrat (mont-suh-RAHT) **Barbados** (bahr-BAY-dohs)
Trinidad (TRIN-ah-dad) **Martinique** (mahr-tee-NEEK)
Guadeloupe (gwah-duh-LOOP)

Luanda (loo-AHN-duh)

CHRONOLOGY

	West Indies	Atlantic	Africa
1500	**ca. 1500** Spanish settlers introduce sugar-cane cultivation	**1530** Amsterdam Exchange opens	**1500–1700** Gold trade predominates
1600	**1620s and 1630s** English and French colonies in Caribbean **1640s** Dutch bring sugar plantation system from Brazil **1655** English take Jamaica **1670s** French occupy western half of Hispaniola	**1621** Dutch West India Company chartered **1660s** English Navigation Acts **1672** Royal African Company chartered **1698** French *Exclusif*	**1591** Morocco conquers Songhai **1638** Dutch take Elmina **1680s** Rise of Asante
1700	**1700** West Indies surpass Brazil in sugar production **1760** Tacky's rebellion in Jamaica **1795** Jamaican Maroon rebellion	**1700 to present** Atlantic system flourishing	**1700–1830** Slave trade predominates **1720s** Rise of Dahomey **1730** Oyo makes Dahomey pay tribute

troduced the Brazilian system into English and French Caribbean islands. This was a momentous turning point in the history of the Atlantic economy.

Sugar and Slaves The Dutch infusion of expertise and money revived the French colonies of Guadeloupe and Martinique, but the English colony of Barbados best illustrates the dramatic transformation that sugar brought to the seventeenth-century Caribbean. In 1640 Barbados's economy depended largely on tobacco, mostly grown by European settlers, both free and indentured. By the 1680s sugar had become the colony's principal crop, and enslaved Africans were three times as numerous as Europeans. Exporting up to 15,000 tons of sugar a year, Barbados had become the wealthiest and most populous of England's American colonies. By 1700, the West Indies had surpassed Brazil as the world's principal source of sugar.

The expansion of sugar plantations in the West Indies required a sharp increase in the volume of the slave trade from Africa (see Figure 20.1). During the first half of the seventeenth century about 10,000 slaves a year had arrived from Africa. Most were destined for Brazil and the mainland Spanish colonies. In the second half of the century the trade averaged 20,000 slaves a year. More than half were intended for the English, French, and Dutch West Indies and most of the rest for Brazil. A century later the volume of the Atlantic slave trade was three times larger.

The shift in favor of African slaves was a product of many factors. Recent scholarship has cast doubt on the once-common assertion that Africans were more suited than Europeans to field labor, since newly arrived Africans and Europeans both died in large numbers in the American tropics. Africans' slightly higher survival rate was not decisive because mortality was about the same among later generations of blacks and whites born in the West Indies and acclimated to its diseases.

The West Indian historian Eric Williams also refuted the idea that the rise of African slave labor was primarily motivated by prejudice. Citing the West Indian colonies' prior use of enslaved Amerindians and indentured Europeans, along with European convicts and prisoners of war, he argued, "Slavery was not born of racism: rather, racism was the consequence of slavery."[1] Williams suggested the shift was due to the lower cost of African labor.

Yet slaves were far from cheap. Cash-short tobacco planters in the seventeenth century preferred indentured

Figure 20.1 Transatlantic Slave Trade from Africa, 1551–1850

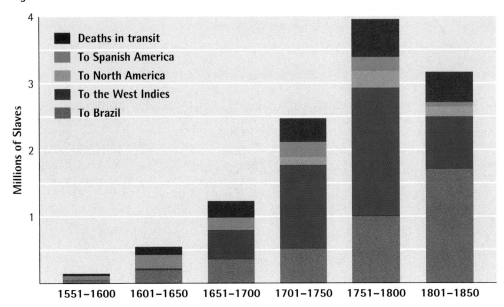

Source: Philip D. Curtin, *The Atlantic Slave Trade: A Census* (Madison: University of Wisconsin Press, 1969), tables 33, 34, 65; Paul E. Lovejoy, "The Volume of the Atlantic Slave Trade: A Synthesis," *Journal of African History* 23 (1982): 473–501; David Eltis, *Economic Growth and the Ending of the Transatlantic Slave Trade* (New York: Oxford University Press, 1987), table A8.

Europeans because they cost half as much as African slaves. Poor European men and women were willing to work for little in order to get to the Americas, where they could acquire their own land cheaply at the end of their term of service. However, as the cultivation of sugar spread after 1750, rich speculators drove the price of land in the West Indies up so high that end-of-term indentured servants could not afford to buy it. As a result, poor Europeans chose to indenture themselves in the mainland North American colonies, where cheap land was still available. Rather than raise wages to attract European laborers, Caribbean sugar planters switched to slaves.

Rising sugar prices helped the West Indian sugar planters afford the higher cost of African slaves. The fact that the average slave lived seven years, while the typical indentured labor contract was for only three or four years, also made slaves a better investment. The planters could rely on the Dutch and other traders to supply them with enough new slaves to meet the demands of the expanding plantations. Rising demand for slaves (see Figure 20.1) drove their sale price up steadily during the eighteenth century. These high labor costs were one more factor favoring large plantations over smaller operations.

PLANTATION LIFE IN THE EIGHTEENTH CENTURY

To find more land for sugar plantations, France and England founded new Caribbean colonies. In 1655 the English had wrested the island of Jamaica from the Spanish (see Map 19.1). The French seized the western half of the large Spanish island of Hispaniola in the 1670s. During the eighteenth century this new French colony of Saint Domingue° (present-day Haiti) became the greatest producer of sugar in the Atlantic world, while Jamaica surpassed Barbados as England's most important sugar colony. The technological, environmental, and social transformation of these island colonies illustrates the power of the new Atlantic system.

Saint Domingue (san doh-MANGH)

Plantation Scene, Antigua, British West Indies   Even in this romanticized painting the slave's simple earthen huts contrast sharply with the planter's elegant great house on the rising ground on the left. Notice the large church in the center background and the women performing domestic tasks.   (West India Committee)

Technology and Environment

The cultivation of sugar cane was fairly straightforward. From fourteen to eighteen months after planting, the canes were ready to be cut. The roots continued to produce new shoots that could be harvested about every nine months. Only simple tools were needed: spades for planting, hoes to control the weeds, and sharp machetes to cut the canes. What made the sugar plantation a complex investment was that it had to be a factory as well as a farm. Freshly cut canes needed to be crushed within a few hours to extract the sugary sap. Thus, for maximum efficiency, each plantation needed its own expensive crushing and processing equipment.

At the heart of the sugar works was the mill where canes were crushed between sets of heavy rollers. Small mills could be turned by animal or human power, but larger, more efficient mills needed more sophisticated sources of power. Eighteenth-century Barbados went in heavily for windmills, and the French sugar islands and Jamaica used costly water-powered mills often fed by elaborate aqueducts.

From the mill, lead-lined wooden troughs carried the cane juice to a series of large copper kettles in the boiling shed, where the excess water boiled off, leaving a thick syrup. Workers poured the syrup into conical molds in the drying shed. The sugar crystals that formed in the molds were packed in wooden barrels for shipment to Europe. The dark molasses that drained off was made into rum in yet another building, or it was barreled for export.

To make their operation more efficient and profitable, investors gradually increased the size of the typical West Indian plantation from around 100 acres (40 hectares) in the seventeenth century to at least twice that size in the eighteenth century. Some plantations were even larger. In 1774 Jamaica's 680 sugar plantations averaged 441 acres (178 hectares) each; some spread over 2,000 acres (800 hectares). Jamaica specialized so heavily in sugar production that the island had to import most of its food. Saint Domingue had a comparable number of plantations of smaller average size but generally higher productivity. The French colony was also more diverse in its economy. Although sugar production was paramount, some planters raised provisions for local consumption of crops such as coffee and cacao for export.

In some ways the mature sugar plantation was environmentally responsible. The crushing mill was powered by water, wind, or animal power, not fossil fuels. The boilers were largely fueled by burning the crushed canes, and the fields were fertilized by manure of the cattle. In two respects, however, the plantation was very damaging to the environment: soil exhaustion and deforestation.

Repeated cultivation of a single crop removes from the soil more nutrients than animal fertilizer and fallow periods can restore. Instead of rotating sugar with other crops in order to restore the nutrients naturally, planters found it more profitable to clear new lands when yields declined too much in the old fields. When land close to the sea was exhausted, planters moved on to new islands. Many of the English who first settled Jamaica were from Barbados, and the pioneer planters on Saint Domingue came from older French sugar colonies. In the second half of the eighteenth century Jamaican sugar production began to fall behind that of Saint Domingue, which still had access to virgin land. Thus the plantations of this period were not a stable form of agriculture but one that gradually laid waste to the landscape.

Deforestation, the second form of environmental damage, continued a trend begun in the sixteenth century. The Spanish had cut down some forests in the Caribbean to make pastures for the cattle they introduced. Sugar cultivation rapidly accelerated land clearing. Forests near the coast were the first to disappear, and by the end of the eighteenth century only land in the interior of the islands retained dense forests.

Other changes, combined with soil exhaustion and deforestation, profoundly altered the ecology balance of the West Indies. By the eighteenth century nearly all of the domesticated animals and cultivated plants in the Caribbean were ones that Europeans had introduced. The Spanish had brought cattle, pigs, and horses, all of which multiplied so rapidly that no new imports had been necessary after 1503. They had also introduced new plants. Of these, bananas and plantain from the Canary Islands were a valuable addition to the food supply, and sugar and rice formed the basis of plantation agriculture, along with native tobacco. Other food crops arrived with the slaves from Africa, including okra, black-eyed peas, yams, grains such as millet and sorghum, and mangoes. Many of these new animals and plants were useful additions to the islands, but they crowded out indigenous species.

The most tragic and dramatic transformation in the West Indies occurred in the human population. Chapter 17 detailed how the indigenous Arawak peoples of the large islands were wiped out by disease and abuse within fifty years of Columbus's first voyage. As the plantation economy spread, the Carib surviving on the smaller islands were also pushed to the point of extinction. Far earlier and more completely than in any mainland colony, the West Indies were repeopled from across the Atlantic—first from Europe and then from Africa.

Slaves' Lives

During the eighteenth century, West Indian plantation colonies were the world's most polarized societies. On most islands 90 percent or more of the inhabitants were slaves. Power resided in the hands of a **plantocracy,** a small number of very rich men who owned most of the slaves and most of the land as well. Between the slaves and the masters might be found only a few others—a few estate managers and government officials and, in the French islands, some small farmers, both white and black. Thus it is only a slight simplification to describe eighteenth-century Caribbean society as being made up of a large, abject class of slaves and a small, powerful class of masters.

The profitability of a Caribbean plantation depended on extracting as much work as possible from the slaves. Their long workday might stretch to eighteen hours or more when the cane harvest and milling were in full swing. Sugar plantations achieved exceptional productivity through the use of force and the threat of force. As Table 20.1 shows, on a typical Jamaican plantation about 80 percent of the slaves actively engaged in productive tasks; the only exceptions were infants, the seriously ill, and the very old. Everyone on the plantation, except those disabled by age or infirmity, had an assigned task.

Table 20.1 also illustrates how slave labor was organized by age, sex, and ability. As in other Caribbean colonies, only 2 or 3 percent of the slaves served as house servants. About 70 percent of the able-bodied slaves worked in the fields, generally in one of three labor gangs. A "great gang," made up of the strongest slaves in the prime of life, did the heaviest work, such as breaking up the soil at the beginning of the planting season. A second gang of youths, elders, and less fit slaves did somewhat lighter work. A "grass gang," composed of children under the supervision of an elderly slave, was responsible for weeding and other simple work, such as collecting grass for the animals. Women formed the majority of the field laborers, even in the great gang. Nursing mothers took their babies with them to the fields. Slaves too old for field labor tended the toddlers.

Because slave ships brought twice as many males as females from Africa, men outnumbered women on Caribbean plantations. As Table 20.1 shows, a little over half of the adult males were employed in nongang work. Some tended the livestock, including the mules and oxen that did the heavy carrying work; others were skilled tradesmen, such as blacksmiths and carpenters. The most important artisan slave was the head boiler, who oversaw the delicate process of reducing the cane sap to crystallized sugar and molasses.

Table 20.1   Slave Occupations on a Jamaican Sugar Plantation, 1788

Occupations and Conditions	Men	Women	Boys and Girls	Total
Field laborers	62	78		140
Tradesmen	29			29
Field drivers	4			4
Field cooks		4		4
Mule-, cattle-, and stablemen	12			12
Watchmen	18			18
Nurse		1		1
Midwife		1		1
Domestics and gardeners		5	3	8
Grass-gang			20	20
Total employed	**125**	**89**	**23**	**237**
Infants			23	23
Invalids (18 with yaws)				32
Absent on roads				5
Superannuated [elderly]				7
Overall total				**304**

Source: Adapted from "Edward Long to William Pitt," in Michael Craton, James Walvin, and David Wright, eds., *Slavery, Abolition, and Emancipation* (London: Longman, 1976), 103. Used by permission of Pearson Education Limited.

Punishment for Slaves   In addition to whipping and other cruel punishments, slave owners devised other ways to shame and intimidate slaves into obedience. This metal face mask prevented the wearer from eating or drinking   (By permission of the Syndics of Cambridge University Library)

Skilled slaves received rewards of food and clothing or time off for good work, but the most common reason for working hard was to escape punishment. A slave gang was headed by a privileged male slave, appropriately called the **"driver,"** whose job was to ensure that the gang completed its work. Since production quotas were high, slaves toiled in the fields from sunup to sunset, except for meal breaks. Those who fell behind due to fatigue or illness soon felt the sting of the whip. Openly rebellious slaves, who refused to work, disobeyed orders, or tried to escape, were punished with flogging, confinement in irons, or mutilation. On a Virginia plantation Equiano was shocked to see a woman slave being punished with an "iron muzzle" that "locked her mouth so fast that she could scarcely speak, and could not eat nor drink."

Even though slaves did not work in the fields on Sunday, it was no day of rest, for they had to farm their own provisioning grounds, maintain their dwellings, and do other chores, such as washing and mending their rough clothes. Sunday markets, where slaves sold small amounts of produce or animals they had raised to get a little spending money, were common in the British West Indies.

Except for occasional holidays—including the Christmas-week revels in the British West Indies—there was little time for recreation and relaxation. Slaves might sing in the fields, but singing was simply a way to distract themselves from their fatigue and the monotony of the work. There was certainly no time for schooling, and no willingness to educate slaves, beyond skills useful to the plantation.

Time for family life was also inadequate. Although the large proportion of young adults in plantation colonies ought to have led to a high rate of natural increase, the opposite occurred. Poor nutrition and overwork lowered fertility. A woman who did become pregnant found it difficult to carry a child to term while continuing heavy fieldwork or to ensure her infant's survival. As a result of these conditions, along with disease and accidents from dangerous mill equipment, deaths heavily outnumbered births on West Indian plantations (see Table 20.2). Life expectancy for slaves in nineteenth-century Brazil was only 23 years of age for males and 25.5 years for females. The figures were probably similar for the eighteenth-century Caribbean. A callous opinion, common among slave owners in the Caribbean and in parts of Brazil, held that it was cheaper to import a youthful new slave from Africa than to raise one to the same age on a plantation.

The harsh conditions of plantation life played a major role in shortening slaves' lives, but the greatest killer was disease. The very young were carried off by dysentery caused by contaminated food and water. Slaves newly arrived from Africa went through the period of adjustment to a new environment, known as **seasoning,** during which one-third on average died of unfamiliar diseases. Slaves also suffered from diseases brought with them, including malaria. On the plantation profiled in Table 20.1, for example, more than half of the slaves incapacitated by illness had yaws, a painful and debilitating skin disease common in Africa. As a consequence, only slave populations in the healthier temperate zones of North America experienced natural increase; those in tropical Brazil and the Caribbean had a negative rate of growth.

Such high mortality greatly added to the volume of the Atlantic slave trade, since plantations had to purchase new slaves every year or two just to replace those who died (see Table 20.2). The additional imports of slaves to permit the expansion of the sugar plantations meant that the majority of slaves were African-born on most West Indian plantations. As a result, African religious beliefs, patterns of speech, styles of dress and adornment, and music were prominent parts of West Indian life.

Given the harsh conditions of their lives, it is not surprising that slaves in the West Indies often sought to regain the freedom into which most had been born. Individual slaves often ran away, hoping to elude the men and dogs who would track them. Sometimes large groups of plantation slaves rose in rebellion against their bondage and abuse. For example, a large rebellion in Jamaica in 1760 was led by a slave named Tacky, who had been a chief on the Gold Coast of Africa. One night his followers broke into a fort and armed themselves. Joined by slaves from other nearby plantations, they stormed several plantations, setting them on fire and killing the planter families. Tacky died in the fighting that followed, and three other rebel leaders stoically endured cruel deaths by torture that were meant to deter others from rebellion.

Because they believed rebellions were usually led by slaves with the strongest African heritage, European planters tried to curtail African cultural traditions. They required slaves to learn the colonial language and discouraged the use of African languages by deliberately mixing slaves from different parts of Africa. In French and Portuguese colonies, slaves were encouraged to adopt Catholic religious practices, though African deities and beliefs also survived. In the British West Indies, where only Quaker slave owners encouraged Christianity among their slaves before 1800, African herbal medicine remained strong, as did African beliefs concerning nature spirits and witchcraft.

Table 20.2 Birth and Death on a Jamaican Sugar Plantation, 1779–1785

Year	Born			Died		
	Males	Females	Purchased	Males	Females	Proportion of Deaths
1779	5	2	6	7	5	1 in 26
1780	4	3	—	3	2	1 in 62
1781	2	3	—	4	2	1 in 52
1782	1	3	9	4	5	1 in 35
1783	3	3	—	8	10	1 in 17
1784	2	1	12	9	10	1 in 17
1785	2	3	—	0	3	1 in 99
Total	19	18	27	35	37	
	Born 37			Died 72		

Source: From "Edward Long to William Pitt," in Michael Craton, James Walvin, and David Wright, eds., *Slavery, Abolition, and Emancipation* (London: Longman, 1976), 105. Used by permission of Pearson Education Limited.

Free Whites and Free Blacks

The lives of the small minority of free people were very different from the lives of slaves. In the French colony of Saint Domingue, which had nearly half of the slaves in the Caribbean in the eighteenth century, free people fell into three distinct groups. First, at the top of free society were the wealthy owners of large sugar plantations (the *grand blancs°*, or "great whites"), who dominated the economy and society of the island. Second came less-well-off Europeans (*petits blancs°*, or "little whites"). Most of them raised provisions for local consumption and crops such as coffee, indigo, and cotton for export, relying on their own and slave labor. Third came the free blacks. Though nearly as numerous as the free whites and engaged in similar occupations, they ranked below whites socially. A few free blacks became wealthy enough to own their own slaves.

The dominance of the plantocracy was even greater in British colonies. Whereas sugar constituted about half of Saint Domingue's exports, in Jamaica the figure was over 80 percent. Such concentration on sugar cane left much less room for small cultivators, white or black, and confined most landholding to a few larger owners. Three-quarters of the farmland in Jamaica at mid-century belonged to individuals who owned 1,000 acres (400 hectares) or more.

One source estimated that a planter had to invest nearly £20,000 ($100,000) to acquire even a medium-size Jamaican plantation of 600 acres (240 hectares) in 1774. A third of this money went for land on which to grow sugar and food crops, pasture animals, and cut timber and firewood. A quarter of the expense was for the sugar works and other equipment. The largest expense was to purchase 200 slaves at about £40 ($200) each. In comparison, the wage of an English rural laborer at this time was about £10 ($50) a year (one-fourth the price of a slave), and the annual incomes in 1760 of the ten wealthiest noble families in Britain averaged only £20,000 each.

Reputedly the richest Englishmen of this time, West Indian planters often translated their wealth into political power and social prestige. The richest planters put their plantations under the direction of managers and lived in Britain, often on rural estates that once had been the preserve of country gentlemen. Between 1730 and 1775 seventy of these absentee planters secured election to the British Parliament, where they formed an influential voting bloc. Those who resided in the West Indies had political power as well, for the British plantocracy controlled the colonial assemblies.

The Unknown Maroon of Saint-Domingue This modern sculpture by Albert Mangonès celebrates the brave but perilous life of a run-away slave, who is shown drinking water from a seashell. (Albert Mangonès, "The Unknown Maroon of Saint-Domingue." From Richard Price, *Maroon Societies*, Johns Hopkins University Press. Reproduced with permission.)

Most Europeans in plantation colonies were single males. Many of them took advantage of slave women for sexual favors or took slave mistresses. A slave owner who fathered a child by a female slave often gave both mother and child their freedom. In some colonies such **manumission** (a legal grant of freedom to an individual slave) produced a significant free black population. By the late eighteenth century, free blacks were more numerous than slaves in most of the Spanish colonies. They were almost 30 percent of the black population of Brazil, and they existed in significant numbers in the French colonies. Free blacks were far less common in the British colonies and the United States, where manumission was rare.

As in Brazil (see Chapter 19), escaped slaves constituted another part of the free black population. In the Caribbean runaways were known as **maroons,** Maroon communities were especially numerous in the mountainous interiors of Jamaica and Hispaniola as well as in the island parts of the Guianas° (see Society and Culture:

---

grands blancs (grawn blawnk)   *petits blancs* (pay-TEE blawnk)

Guianas (guy-AHN-uhs)

A Maroon Village in French Guiana). The Jamaican Maroons, after withstanding several attacks by the colony's militia, signed a treaty in 1739 that recognized their independence in return for their cooperation in stopping new runaways and suppressing slave revolts. Similar treaties with the large maroon population in the Dutch colony of Surinam (Dutch Guiana) recognized their possession of large inland regions.

CREATING THE ATLANTIC ECONOMY

At once archaic in their cruel system of slavery and oddly modern in their specialization in a single product, the West Indian plantation colonies were the bittersweet fruits of a new Atlantic trading system. Changes in the type and number of ships crossing the Atlantic illustrate the rise of this new system. The Atlantic trade of the sixteenth century calls to mind the treasure fleet, an annual convoy of from twenty to sixty ships laden with silver and gold bullion from Spanish America. Two different vessels typify the far more numerous Atlantic voyages of the late seventeenth and eighteenth centuries. One was the sugar ship, returning to Europe from the West Indies or Brazil crammed with barrels of brown sugar destined for further refinement. At the end of the seventeenth century an average of 266 sugar ships sailed every year just from the small island of Barbados. The second type of vessel was the slave ship. At the trade's peak between 1760 and 1800, some 300 ships, crammed with an average of 250 African captives each, crossed the Atlantic to the Americas each year.

Many separate pieces went into the creation of the new Atlantic economy. Besides the plantation system itself, three other elements merit further investigation: new economic institutions, new partnerships between private investors and governments in Europe, and new working relationships between European and African merchants. The new trading system is a prime example of how European capitalist relationships were reshaping the world.

Capitalism and Mercantilism

The Spanish and Portuguese voyages of exploration in the fifteenth and sixteenth centuries were government ventures, and both countries tried to keep their overseas trade and colonies royal monopolies (see Chapters 17

and 18). Monopoly control, however, proved both expensive and inefficient. The success of the Atlantic economy in the seventeenth and eighteenth centuries owed much to private enterprise, which made trading venues more efficient and profitable. European private investors were attracted by the profits they could make from an established and growing trading and colonial system, but their successful participation in the Atlantic economy depended on new institutions and a significant measure of government protection that reduced the likelihood of catastrophic loss.

Two European innovations enabled private investors to fund the rapid growth of the Atlantic economy. One was the ability to manage large financial resources through mechanisms that modern historians have labeled **capitalism.** The essence of early modern capitalism was a system of large financial institutions—banks, stock exchanges, and chartered trading companies—that enabled wealthy investors to reduce risks and increase profits. Originally developed for business dealings within Europe, the capitalist system expanded overseas in the seventeenth century, when slow economic growth in Europe led many investors to seek greater profits abroad.

Banks were a central capitalist institution. By the early seventeenth century, Dutch banks had developed such a reputation for security that individuals and governments from all over western Europe entrusted them with large sums of money. To make a profit, the banks invested these funds in real estate, local industries, loans to governments, and overseas trade.

Individuals seeking returns higher than the low rate of interest paid by banks could purchase shares in a joint-stock company, a sixteenth-century forerunner of the modern corporation. Shares were bought and sold in specialized financial markets called stock exchanges. The Amsterdam Exchange, founded in 1530, became the greatest stock market in the seventeenth and eighteenth centuries. To reduce risks in overseas trading, merchants and trading companies bought insurance on their ships and cargoes from specialized companies that agreed to cover losses.

The capitalism of these centuries was buttressed by **mercantilism,** policies adopted by European states to promote their citizens' overseas trade and accumulate capital in the form of precious metals. Mercantilist policies strongly discouraged citizens from trading with foreign merchants and used armed force when necessary to secure exclusive relations.

Chartered companies were one of the first examples of mercantilist capitalism. A charter issued by the government of the Netherlands in 1602 gave the Dutch East India Company a legal monopoly over all Dutch trade in the Indian Ocean. This privilege encouraged private in-

A Maroon Village in French Guiana, 1748

Runaway slaves, called maroons, *were common in planta-tion colonies. Colonial officials regularly tried to recapture them and destroy their villages. In 1748 a captured maroon youth named Louis gave the following testimony to officials in French Guiana in South America.*

He declared and admitted that he has been a maroon for about eighteen moons [lunar months] with Rémy, his fa-ther, and other Negroes belonging to [M. Gourgues]; that Rémy having displeased the said M. Gourgues and having been whipped by him, had planned this marronage having first gotten together a supply of . . . cassava and bananas for the trip . . . ; that after an unknown number of weeks, a cer-tain André [guided them] to the maroon village . . . ; that in the said village there are twenty-seven houses and three open sheds . . . ; that the said houses belong to and are in-habited by twenty-nine strong male Negroes . . . , twenty-two female Negroes . . . , nine Negro boys, and twelve Negro girls, making in all seventy-two slaves. . . .

[Louis further declared that the captain of the village,] Bernard, nicknamed Couacou, . . . takes care of wounds [with herbal medicines,] baptizes with holy water and recites daily prayer. . . . That no member of the troop has died during the past two years.

That the captain's orders are obeyed perfectly; it is in his yard that prayers are recited in the morning and evening, as they are on well-run plantations; those who are sick recite their prayers in their houses.

That André either whips or has whipped those who de-serve punishment. . . . That André and some of his trusted followers make sorties from time to time to recruit new members in the area. . . . That no whites ever entered the vil-lage, nor any Negroes other than the ones who are re-cruited . . . and who promise never to betray them nor to run away, under penalty of being hunted down and killed. . . .

That whenever land has to be cleared, everyone works to-gether, and that once a large area has been burned, everyone is allotted a plot according to the needs of the family to plant and maintain. That the wild pigs that they kill fre-quently are divided among them, as is other large game, even fish that they dry when there are large numbers of them. . . .

That . . . they maintain and repair their arms themselves, keeping them in good condition at all times, but that when having hunted a great deal they are without powder and shot, . . . they use tiny stones, which . . . are found in abun-dance in the area. . . .

That the women spin cotton when the weather is bad and work in the fields in good weather. That [men] weave cotton cloth, which serves to make skirts for the women and loin-cloths for the men; that this cotton material is woven piece by piece and then assembled and decorated with Siamese cotton thread. . . .

That they get salt from the ashes of the Maracoupy palm. That they make a beverage out of sweet potatoes, yams, ba-nanas, and various grains, in addition to their [cassava beer].

That they store all their belongings in [baskets, and they all] are equipped with axes and machetes and that there are spares . . . and that they have no tools other than a few files, gimlets, and hammers; that they have no saws or adzes [wood-working axes]. That they had at the said Negro village two Negro drums, which they played on certain holidays.

What is the significance of the maroons employing African forms of communal ownership, herbal medicine, brewing, cloth making, and musical instruments? How much did they rely on tools, weapons, beliefs, and practices that they acquired from the French?

Source: Richard Price, ed., *Maroon Societies: Rebel Slave Communities in the Americas,* 2d ed. (Baltimore: Johns Hopkins University Press, 1979), 313–318. Reprinted by permission of the Johns Hopkins University Press.

vestors to buy shares in the company. They were amply rewarded when Dutch East India Company captured control of the long-distance trade routes in the Indian Ocean from the Portuguese (see Chapter 21). As we have seen, a sister firm, the Dutch West India Company, was chartered in 1621 to engage in the Atlantic trade and to seize sugar-producing areas in Brazil and African slaving ports from the Portuguese.

Such successes inspired other governments to set up their own chartered companies. In 1672, a royal char-ter placed all English trade with West Africa in the hands of a new **Royal African Company,** which established its headquarters at Cape Coast Castle, just east of Elmina on the Gold Coast. The French government also played an active role in chartering companies and promoting overseas trade and colonization. Jean Baptiste Colbert°, King Louis XIV's minister of finance from 1661 to 1683, chartered French East India and French West India companies to reduce French colonies' dependence on Dutch and English traders.

French and English governments also used military force in pursuit of commercial dominance, especially to break the trading advantage of the Dutch in the Americas. Restrictions on Dutch access to French and English colonies provoked a series of wars with the Netherlands between 1652 and 1678 (see Chapter 18), during which the larger English and French navies defeated the Dutch and drove the Dutch West India Company into bankruptcy.

With Dutch competition in the Atlantic reduced, the French and English governments moved to revoke the monopoly privileges of their chartered companies. England opened trade in Africa to any English subject in 1698 on the grounds that ending monopolies would be "highly beneficial and advantageous to this kingdom." It was hoped that such competition would also cut the cost of slaves to West Indian planters, though the demand for slaves soon drove the prices up again.

Such new mercantilist policies fostered competition among a nation's own citizens, while using high tariffs and restrictions to exclude foreigners. In the 1660s England had passed a series of Navigation Acts that confined trade with its colonies to English ships and cargoes. The French called their mercantilist legislation, first codified in 1698, the *Exclusif*°, highlighting its exclusionary intentions. Other mercantilist laws defended manufacturing and processing interests in Europe against competition from colonies, imposing prohibitively high taxes on any manufactured goods and refined sugar imported from the colonies.

As a result of such mercantilist measures, the Atlantic became Britain, France, and Portugal's most important overseas trading area in the eighteenth century. Britain's imports from its West Indian colonies in this period accounted for over one-fifth of the value of total British imports. The French West Indian colonies played an even larger role in France's overseas trade. Only the Dutch, closed out of much of the American trade, found Asian trade of greater importance (see Chapter 21). Profits from the Atlantic economy, in turn, promoted further economic expansion and increased the revenues of European governments.

Colbert (kohl-BEAR)
Exclusif (ek-skloo-SEEF)

The Great Circuit and the Middle Passage

At the heart of the Atlantic system was a great clockwise network of trade routes known as the **Great Circuit** (see Map 20.1). It began in Europe, ran south to Africa, turned west across the Atlantic Ocean to the Americas, and then swept back to Europe. Like Asian sailors in the Indian Ocean, Atlantic mariners depended on the prevailing winds and currents to propel their ships. What drove the ships as much as the winds and currents was the desire for the profits that each leg of the circuit was expected to produce.

The first leg, from Europe to Africa, carried European manufactures—notably metal bars, hardware, and guns—as well as great quantities of cotton textiles brought from India. Some of these goods were traded for West African gold, timber, and other products, which were taken back to Europe. More goods went to purchase slaves, who were transported across the Atlantic to the plantation colonies in the part of the Great Circuit known as the **Middle Passage.** On the third leg, plantation goods from the colonies returned to Europe. Each leg of the circuit carried goods from where they were abundant and relatively cheap to where they were scarce and therefore more valuable. Thus, in theory, each leg of the Great Circuit could earn much more than its costs, and a ship that completed all three legs could return a handsome profit to its owners. In practice, shipwrecks, deaths, piracy, and other risks could turn profit into loss.

The three-sided Great Circuit is only the simplest model of Atlantic trade. Many other trading voyages supplemented the basic circuit. Cargo ships made long voyages from Europe to the Indian Ocean, passed southward through the Atlantic with quantities of African gold and American silver, and returned with the cotton textiles necessary to the African trade. Other sea routes brought to the West Indies manufactured goods from Europe or foodstuffs and lumber from New England. In addition, some Rhode Island and Massachusetts merchants participated in a "Triangular Trade" that carried rum to West Africa, slaves to the West Indies, and molasses and rum back to New England. There was also a considerable two-way trade between Brazil and Angola, which exchanged Brazilian liquor and other goods for slaves. On another route, Brazil and Portugal exchanged sugar and gold for European imports.

Map. 20.1 The Atlantic Economy By 1700 the volume of maritime exchanges among the Atlantic continents had begun to rival the trade of the Indian Ocean basin. Notice the trade in consumer products, slave labor, precious metals, and other goods. A silver trade to East Asia laid the basis for a Pacific Ocean economy.

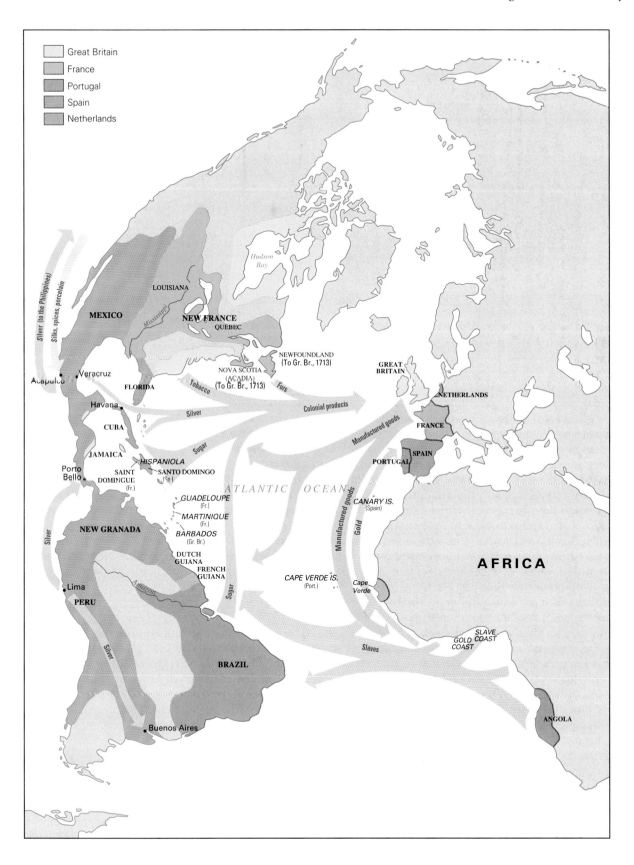

Great Britain
France
Portugal
Spain
Netherlands

Silver (to the Philippines)

Silks, spices, porcelain

Hudson Bay

LOUISIANA

Mississippi

MEXICO

NEW FRANCE

QUEBEC

NEWFOUNDLAND
(To Gr. Br., 1713)

GREAT BRITAIN

Veracruz

Acapulco

NOVA SCOTIA
(ACADIA)
(To Gr. Br., 1713)

Tobacco

Furs

NETHERLANDS

FLORIDA

Havana

Silver

Colonial products

FRANCE

Manufactured goods

CUBA

Sugar

PORTUGAL

SPAIN

JAMAICA

HISPANIOLA

SANTO DOMINGO
(Sp.)

Porto Bello

SAINT DOMINGUE
(Fr.)

A T L A N T I C   O C E A N

CANARY IS.
(Spain)

Silver

GUADELOUPE
(Fr.)

Manufactured goods

Gold

MARTINIQUE
(Fr.)

NEW GRANADA

BARBADOS
(Gr. Br.)

AFRICA

DUTCH
GUIANA

FRENCH
GUIANA

CAPE VERDE IS.
(Port.)

Cape Verde

Amazon

Sugar

Lima

PERU

SLAVE
COAST

Silver

GOLD
COAST

Slaves

BRAZIL

ANGOLA

Buenos Aires

Slave Ship This model of the English vessel *Brookes* shows the specially built section of the hold where enslaved Africans were packed together during the Middle Passage. Girls, boys, and women were confined separately. (Wilberforce House Museum, Hull, Humberside, UK/The Bridgeman Art Library, London and New York)

European interests dominated the Atlantic system. The manufacturers who supplied the trade goods and the investors who provided the capital were all based in Europe, but so too were the principal consumers of the plantation products. Before the seventeenth century, sugar had been rare and fairly expensive in western Europe. By 1700 annual consumption of sugar in England had risen to about 4 pounds (nearly 2 kilograms) per person. Rising western European prosperity and declining sugar prices promoted additional consumption, starting with the upper classes and working its way down the social ladder. People spooned sugar into popular new beverages imported from overseas—tea, coffee, and chocolate—to overcome the beverages' natural bitterness. By 1750 annual sugar consumption in Britain had doubled, and it doubled again to about 18 pounds (8 kilograms) per person by the early nineteenth century (well below the American average of about 100 pounds [45 kilograms] a year in 1960).

The flow of sugar to Europe depended on another key component of the Atlantic trading system: the flow of slaves from Africa (see Map 20.2). The rising volume of the Middle Passage also measures the Atlantic system's expansion. During the first 150 years after the European discovery of the Americas, some 800,000 Africans had begun the journey across the Atlantic. During the boom in sugar production between 1650 and 1800, the slave trade amounted to nearly 7,500,000. Of the survivors, over half landed in the West Indies and nearly a third in

Brazil. Plantations in North America imported another 5 percent, and the rest went to other parts of Spanish America (see Figure 20.1).

In these peak decades, the transportation of slaves from Africa was a highly specialized trade, although it regularly attracted some amateur traders hoping to make a quick profit. Most slaves were carried in ships that had been specially built or modified for the slave trade by the construction between the ships' decks of additional platforms on which the human cargo was packed as tightly as possible.

Seventeenth-century mercantilist policies placed much of the Atlantic slave trade in the hands of chartered companies. During their existence the Dutch West India Company and the English Royal African Company each carried about 100,000 slaves across the Atlantic. In the eighteenth century, private English traders from Liverpool and Bristol controlled about 40 percent of the slave trade. The French, operating out of Nantes and Bordeaux, handled about half as much, but the Dutch hung on to only 6 percent. The Portuguese supplying Brazil and other places had nearly 30 percent of the Atlantic slave trade, in contrast to the 3 percent carried in North American ships.

To make a profit, European slave traders had to buy slaves in Africa for less than the cost of the goods they traded in return. Then they had to deliver as many healthy slaves as possible across the Atlantic for resale in the plantation colonies. The treacherous voyage to the

Map. 20.2   The African Slave Trade, 1500–1800   After 1500 a vast new trade in slaves from sub-Saharan Africa to the Americas joined the ongoing slave trade to the Islamic states of North Africa, the Middle East, and India. The West Indies were the major destination of the Atlantic slave trade, followed by Brazil.

Americas lasted from six to ten weeks. Some ships completed it with all of their slaves alive, but large, even catastrophic, losses of life were common. On average between 1650 and 1800, about one slave in every six perished during the Middle Passage (see Figure 20.1).

Some deaths resulted from the efforts of the captives to escape. On his voyage Equiano witnessed two of his Igbo countrymen, who were chained together, jump into the sea, "preferring death to such a life of misery." To inhibit such attempts, African men were confined below deck during most of the voyage, and special netting was installed around the outside of the ship. Some slaves fell into deep psychological depression, known to contemporaries as "fixed melancholy," from which many perished. Others, including Equiano, refused to eat, so forced feeding was used to keep slaves alive. When opportunities presented themselves (nearness to land,

illness among the crew), some cargoes of enslaved Africans tried to overpower their captors. Such "mutinies" were rarely successful and were put down with brutality that occasioned further losses of life.

Other deaths during the Middle Passage were due to the ill treatment slaves received. Although it was in the interests of the captain and crew to deliver their slave cargo in good condition, whippings, beatings, and even executions were used to maintain order and force the captives to take nourishment. Moreover, the dangers and brutalities of the slave trade were so notorious that many ordinary seamen shunned such work. As a consequence, cruel and brutal characters abounded among the officers and crews on slave ships.

Although examples of unspeakable cruelties are common in the records, most deaths in the Middle Passage were the result of disease rather than abuse, just as on the plantations. Dysentery spread by contaminated food and water caused many deaths. Others died of contagious diseases such as smallpox carried by persons whose infections were not detected during the medical examinations of slaves prior to boarding. Such maladies spread quickly in the crowded and unsanitary confines of the ships, claiming the lives of many slaves already physically weakened and mentally traumatized by their ordeals.

Crew members who were in close contact with the slaves were equally exposed to the epidemics and regularly suffered heavy losses. Moreover, sailors often fell victim to tropical diseases, such as malaria, to which Africans had acquired resistance. It is a measure of the callousness of the age, as well as the cheapness of European labor, that over the course of a Great Circuit voyage the proportion of crew deaths could be as high as the slave deaths on the Middle Passage.

AFRICA, THE ATLANTIC, AND ISLAM

The Atlantic system took a terrible toll in African lives both during the Middle Passage and under the harsh conditions of plantation slavery. Many other Africans died while being marched to African coastal ports for sale overseas. The overall effects on Africa of these losses and of other aspects of the slave trade have been the subject of considerable historical debate. It is clear that the trade's impact depended on the intensity and terms of different African regions' involvement.

Any assessment of the Atlantic system's effects in Africa must also take into consideration the fact that some Africans profited from the trade by capturing and selling slaves. They chained the slaves together or bound them to forked sticks for the march to the coast, then bartered them to the European slavers for trade goods. The effects on the enslaver were different from the effects on the enslaved. Finally, a broader understanding of the Atlantic system's effects in sub-Saharan Africa comes from comparisons with the effects of Islamic contacts.

The Gold Coast and the Slave Coast

As Chapter 17 showed, early European visitors to Africa's Atlantic coast were interested more in trading than in colonizing or controlling the continent. As the Africa trade mushroomed after 1650, this pattern continued. African kings and merchants sold slaves and other goods at many new coastal sites, but the growing slave trade did not lead to any substantial European colonization.

The transition to slave trading was not sudden. Even as slaves were becoming Atlantic Africa's most valuable export, nonslave goods such as gold, ivory, and timber remained a significant part of the total trade. For example, during its eight decades of operation from 1672 to 1752, the English Royal African Company made 40 percent of its profits from dealings in gold, ivory, and forest products. In some parts of West Africa, such nonslave exports remained predominant even at the peak of the trade.

African merchants were very discriminating about what merchandise they received in return for slaves or other goods. A European ship that arrived with goods of low quality or not suited to local tastes found it hard to purchase a cargo at a profitable price. European guidebooks to the African trade carefully noted the color and shape of beads, the pattern of textiles, the type of guns, and the sort of metals that were in demand on each section of the coast. In the early eighteenth century, the people of Sierra Leone had a strong preference for large iron kettles, brass pans were preferred on the Gold Coast, and iron and copper bars were in demand in the Niger Delta, where smiths turned them into useful objects (see Map 20.3).

Although preferences for merchandise varied, Africans' greatest demands were for textiles, hardware, and guns. Of the goods the Royal African Company traded in West Africa in the 1680s, over 60 percent were Indian and European textiles, 30 percent hardware and weaponry. Beads and other jewelry formed 3 percent. The rest consisted of cowrie shells that were used as money. In the eighteenth century, tobacco and rum from the Americas became welcome imports.

Both Europeans and Africans naturally attempted to drive the best bargain for themselves and sometimes engaged in deceitful practices. The strength of the African bargaining position, however, may be inferred from the fact that as the demand for slaves rose, so too did their price in Africa. In the course of the eighteenth century the goods needed to purchase a slave on the Gold Coast doubled and in some places tripled or quadrupled.

West Africans' trading strengths were reinforced by African governments on the Gold and Slave Coasts that made Europeans observe African trading customs and prevented them from taking control of African territory. Rivalry among European nations, each of which established its own trading "castles" along the Gold Coast, also reduced Europeans' bargaining strength. In 1700 the head of the Dutch East India Company in West Africa,

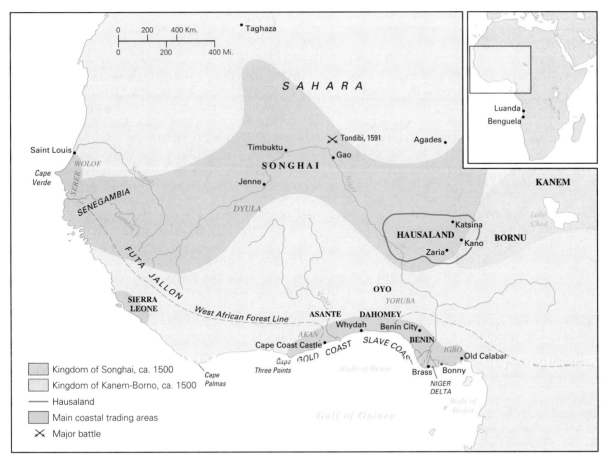

Map. 20.3   West African States and Trade, 1500–1800   The Atlantic and the trans-Saharan trade brought West Africans new goods and promoted the rise of powerful states and trading communities. The Moroccan invasion of Songhai and Portuguese colonization of the Angolan ports of Luanda and Benguela showed the political dangers of such relations.

Willem Bosman°, bemoaned the fact that, to stay competitive against the other European traders, his company had to include large quantities of muskets and gunpowder in the goods it exchanged, thereby adding to Africans' military power.

Bosman also related that before being allowed to buy slaves at Whydah on the Slave Coast his agents first had to pay the king a substantial customs duty and buy at a premium price whatever slaves the king had to sell. By African standards, Whydah was a rather small kingdom controlling only that port and its immediate hinterland. In 1727 it was annexed by the larger kingdom of Dahomey°, which maintained a strong trading position with Europeans at the coast. Dahomey's rise in the 1720s

depended heavily on the firearms that the slave trade supplied for its well-trained armies of men and women.

In the cases of two of Dahomey's neighbors, the connections between state growth and the Atlantic trade were more complex. One was the inland Oyo° kingdom to the northeast. Oyo cavalry overran Dahomey in 1730 and forced it to pay an annual tribute to keep its independence. The other was the newer kingdom of Asante°, west of Dahomey along the Gold Coast, which expanded rapidly after 1680. Both Oyo and Asante participated in the Atlantic trade, but neither kingdom was so dependent on it as Dahomey. Overseas trade formed a relatively modest part of the economies of these large and populous states and was balanced by their extensive overland trade with their northern neighbors and with

Willem Bosman (VIL-uhm boos-MAHN)
Dahomey (dah-HOH-mee)

Oyo (aw-YOH)   **Asante** (uh-SHAN-tee)

states across the Sahara. Like the great medieval empires of the western Sudan, Oyo and Asante were stimulated by external trade but not controlled by it.

How did African kings and merchants obtain slaves for sale? Bosman dismissed misconceptions prevailing in Europe in his day. "Not a few in our country," he wrote to a friend in 1700, "fondly imagine that parents here sell their children, men their wives, and one brother the other. But those who think so, do deceive themselves; for this never happens on any other account but that of necessity, or some great crime; but most of the slaves that are offered to us are prisoners of war, which are sold by the victors as their booty."[2] Other accounts agree that prisoners taken in war were the greatest source of slaves for the Atlantic trade, but it is difficult to say how often capturing slaves for export was the main cause of warfare. "Here and there," conclude two respected historians of Africa, "there are indications that captives taken in the later and more peripheral stages of these wars were exported overseas, but it would seem that the main impetus of conquest was only incidentally concerned with the slave-trade in any external direction."[3]

An early-nineteenth-century king of Asante had a similar view: "I cannot make war to catch slaves in the bush, like a thief. My ancestors never did so. But if I fight a king, and kill him when he is insolent, then certainly I must have his gold, and his slaves, and his people are mine too. Do not the white kings act like this?"[4] English rulers had indeed sentenced seventeenth-century Scottish and Irish prisoners to forced labor in the West Indies. One may imagine that the African and the European prisoners did not share their kings' view that such actions were legitimate.

The Bight of Biafra and Angola

In the eighteenth century the slave trade expanded eastward to the Bight (bay) of Biafra. In contrast to the Gold and Slave Coasts, where strong kingdoms predominated, the densely populated interior of the Bight of Biafra contained no large states. Even so, the powerful merchant princes of the coastal ports still made European traders give them rich presents. Because of the absence of sizable states, there were no large-scale wars and consequently few prisoners of war. Instead, kidnapping was the major source of slaves, as Equiano's autobiography indicates. In about 1756, while their parents were away working in the fields, the eleven-year-old Equiano and his younger sister were snatched from their yard by two men and a woman. After passing through many hands, Equiano finally reached a coastal port, where, he relates,

he was astonished at the sight of the slave ship and alarmed at his first sight of "white men with horrible looks, red faces, and loose hair." By then he had become separated from his sister, whose fate he never learned.

As Equiano discovered on his way to the coast, some inland African merchants were experienced in procuring debtors, victims of kidnapping, and convicted criminals and shepherding them through a network of markets to the coast. The largest inland traders of the Bight of Biafra were the Aro of Arochukwu, who used their control of a famous religious oracle to enhance their prestige. The Aro cemented their business links with powerful inland families and the coastal merchants through gifts and marriage alliances.

As the volume of the Atlantic trade along the Bight of Biafra expanded in the late eighteenth century, some inland markets evolved into giant fairs with different sections specializing in slaves and imported goods. An English ship's doctor reported that in the 1780s slaves were "bought by the black traders at fairs, which are held for that purpose, at a distance of upwards of two hundred miles from the sea coast." He reported seeing from twelve hundred to fifteen hundred enslaved men and women arriving at the coast from a single fair.[5]

The local context of the Atlantic trade was different south of the Congo estuary at Angola, the greatest source of slaves for the Atlantic trade (see Map 20.2). This was also the one place along the Atlantic coast where a single European nation, Portugal, controlled a significant amount of territory. Except when overrun by the Dutch for a time in the seventeenth century, Portuguese residents of the main coastal ports of Luanda and Benguela° served as middlemen between the caravans that arrived from the far interior and the ships that crossed from Brazil. From the coastal cities Afro-Portuguese traders guided large caravans of trade goods inland to exchange for slaves at special markets. Some markets met in the shadow of Portuguese frontier forts; powerful African kings controlled others.

Many of the slaves sold at these markets were prisoners of war captured by expanding African states. By the late eighteenth century, slaves sold from Angolan ports were prisoners of wars fought from as far as 600 to 800 miles (1,000 to 1,300 kilometers) inland. Many were victims of wars of expansion fought by the giant federation of Lunda kingdoms. As elsewhere in Africa, such prisoners usually seem to have been a byproduct of African wars rather than the purpose for which the wars were fought.

Benguela (ben-GWAY-luh)

Queen Nzinga of Angola, 1622   This formidable African woman went to great lengths to maintain her royal dignity when negotiating a treaty for her brother with the Portuguese governor of Luanda. To avoid having to stand in his presence, she had one of her women bend herself into a human seat. Nzinga later ruled in her own name and revolted against the Portuguese with the aid of Dutch and African allies.   (Jean-Loup Charmet)

Recent research has linked other enslavement with environmental crises in the hinterland of Angola.[6] During the eighteenth century these southern grasslands periodically suffered severe droughts, which drove famished refugees to better-watered areas. Powerful African leaders gained control of such refugees in return for supplying them with food and water. These leaders built up their followings by assimilating refugee children, along with adult women, who were valued as food producers and for reproduction. However, they often sold into the Atlantic trade the adult make refugees, who were more likely than the women and children to escape or challenge the ruler's authority. Rising Angolan leaders parceled out the Indian textiles, weapons, and alcohol they received in return for such slaves as gifts to attract new followers and to cement the loyalty of their established allies.

The most successful of these inland Angolan leaders became heads of powerful new states that stabilized areas devastated by war and drought and repopulated them with the refugees and prisoners they retained. The slave frontier then moved farther inland. This cruel system worked to the benefit of a few African rulers and merchants at the expense of the many thousands of Africans who were sent to death or perpetual bondage in the Americas.

Although the organization of the Atlantic trade in Africa varied, it was based on a partnership between European and African elites. To obtain foreign textiles, metals, and weapons, African rulers and merchants sold slaves and many other products. Most of the exported slaves were prisoners taken in wars associated with African state growth. But strong African states also helped offset the Europeans' economic advantage and hindered them from taking control of African territory. Even in the absence of strong states, powerful African merchant communities everywhere dominated the movement of goods and people. The Africans who gained from these exchanges were the rich and powerful few. Many more Africans were losers in these exchanges.

Comparing European and Islamic Contacts

The growing European influence in Atlantic Africa has a parallel in the continuing Islamic influence along the southern border of the Sahara and in eastern Africa. There are striking similarities and differences in the political, commercial, and cultural impacts of these two external influences on sub-Saharan Africa between 1500 and 1800.

Despite all their commercial expansion in the centuries before 1800, Europeans had acquired control of little African territory. Their trading posts along the Gold and Slave Coasts were largely dependent on the goodwill of local African rulers. Only on islands and in Angola did the Atlantic trade lead to significant European colonies. Ironically, the largest European colony in Africa before 1800, the Dutch East India Company's Cape Colony at the southern tip of the continent, was tied to the Indian Ocean trade, not to the Atlantic trade. The Cape Colony did not export slaves; rather the 25,750 slaves in its population were mostly derived from persons *imported* from Madagascar, South Asia, and the East Indies.

Muslim territorial dominance was more extensive. Arab conquests in the seventh century permanently brought North Africa into the Muslim world. Muslim practices and traders spread south of the Sahara, but Arab and North African Muslims had little success in extending their territorial dominance southward before 1500. During the sixteenth century, all of North Africa except Morocco was annexed to the new Ottoman Islamic empire, while Ethiopia lost extensive territory to other Muslim conquerors (see Chapter 17).

In the 1580s Morocco began a southward expansion aimed at gaining control of the Saharan trade. To that end it sent a military expedition of 4,000 men and 10,000 camels from Marrakesh to attack the indigenously ruled Muslim empire of Songhai° in the western Sudan. Half of the men perished on their way across the desert. The remainder, armed with 2,500 muskets, succeeded in besting Songhai's army of 40,000 cavalry and foot soldiers in 1591, reducing the empire to a shadow of its former self. Although Morocco was never able to annex the western Sudan, for the next two centuries the occupying troops extracted a massive tribute of slaves and goods from the local population and collected tolls from passing merchants.

Morocco's destruction of Songhai weakened the trans-Saharan trade in the western Sudan. Caravans continued to cross the desert bringing textiles, hardware, and weapons, but much of the trade shifted eastward to the central Sudan. Except for the absence of alcohol (which was prohibited to Muslims), these goods were similar to those in the Atlantic trade. There was also a continuation of the salt trade southward from Saharan mines. Communities of Dyula° traders in the western Sudan and Hausa traders in the central Sudan distributed these imports and local goods throughout West Africa. They also collected goods for shipment northward, including gold, caffeine-rich kola nuts from Asante and other parts of the forest (a stimulant allowed by Muslim law), African textiles and leather goods, as well as slaves.

Fewer slaves crossed the Sahara than crossed the Atlantic, but their numbers were substantial. It is estimated that between 1600 and 1800 about 850,000 slaves trudged across the desert's various routes (see Map 20.2). A nearly equal number of slaves from sub-Saharan Africa entered the Islamic Middle East and India by way of the Red Sea and the Indian Ocean.

The tasks that African slaves performed in the Islamic world were very different from their tasks in the Americas. In the late seventeenth and eighteenth centuries, Morocco's rulers employed an army of 150,000 slaves obtained from the south to keep them in power. Other slaves worked for Moroccans on sugar plantations, as servants, and as artisans. In contrast to the makeup of the Atlantic slave trade, the majority of the slaves crossing the desert were women, intended to serve wealthy households as concubines and servants. The trans-Saharan slave trade also included a much higher proportion of children than did the Atlantic trade, including eunuchs meant for eventual service as harem guards. It is estimated that only one in ten of these boys survived the surgical removal of their genitals.

The central Sudanese kingdom of Bornu illustrates some aspects of trans-Saharan contacts. This ancient Muslim state had grown and expanded in the sixteenth century as the result of guns imported from the Ottoman Empire. Bornu retained many captives from its wars, or sold them as slaves to the north in return for the firearms and horses that underpinned the kingdom's military power. Bornu's king, Mai Ali, conspicuously displayed his kingdom's new power and wealth while on four pilgrimages to Mecca between 1642 and 1667. On the last, an enormous entourage of slaves—said to number fifteen thousand—accompanied him.

Like Christians, Muslims of this period saw no moral impediment to owning and trading in slaves. Indeed, Is-

---

Songhai (song-GAH-ee)

Dyula (JOO-lah)

lam recognized the *jihad* (holy war) as a means by which their religion could be spread and considered enslaving "pagans" to be a meritorious act because it brought them into the faith. Although Islam forbade the enslavement of Muslims, some Muslim states south of the Sahara did not strictly observe that law. Ahmad Baba, a Muslim scholar of Timbuktu, in a 1614 treatise on slavery lamented that the enslavement of free Muslims was much practiced, notably by Muslim Hausa rulers.

A West African named Ayuba Suleiman Diallo° may serve as a revealing example of an enslaved Muslim. In 1730 his father, a prominent Muslim scholar, sent Ayuba to sell two slaves to an English ship on the Gambia River so as to buy paper and other necessities. On his way home a few days later, other Africans kidnapped Ayuba, shaved his head to make him appear to have been a war captive, and sold him to the same English ship. A planter from Maryland purchased Ayuba. Soon after, an English scholar, impressed by Ayuba's knowledge of Arabic and his elevated social origins, bought his freedom and arranged for him to return home.[7]

Because of sub-Saharan Africa's long and deep exposure to Islam, Muslim cultural influences were much greater than European ones before 1800. The Arabic language, long dominant in North Africa, continued to expand as a means of communication among scholars and merchants south of the Sahara. The Islamic religion also increased the number of its adherents south of the desert, reaching well beyond the urban centers that had been its medieval strength.

In contrast, African conversion to Christianity was limited to coastal Angola and the immediate vicinity of small European trading posts. The use of European languages was also largely confined to the trading coasts. Still it is notable that some African merchants sent their sons to Europe to learn European ways. One of these young men, Philip Quaque°, was educated in England and ordained as a priest in the Church of England and became the official chaplain of the Cape Coast Castle from 1766 until his death in 1816. Not only men of Quaque's stature but many African merchants learned to write a European language. A leading trader of Old Calabar on the Bight of Biafra kept a diary in pidgin English in the late eighteenth century.

The interesting details of the lives of elite and culturally sophisticated individuals such as Ayuba Suleiman and Philip Quaque must not distract us from the grim, sordid details of this era of slave trading. It is easy to re-

---

Ayuba Suleiman Diallo (ah-YOO-bah SOO-lay-mahn JAH-loh)
Quaque (KWAH-kay)

Ayuba Suleiman Diallo (1701–??)   Known as Job ben Solomon to the Maryland planter who owned him as a slave from 1731 to 1735, this Muslim from the West African state of Bondu was able to regain his freedom and return to Africa. Notice the booklet of Quranic verses around his neck.   (British Library)

joice in Ayuba's return to Africa while forgetting the unrecorded fates of the two persons whom he sold into slavery. In admiring Quaque's achievement of a position second only to the British governor on the Gold Coast, we should not overlook that his principal duties were to tend the spiritual needs of the slave traders, not the slaves. Unfortunately, surviving records tell us much less about the large number of Africans who suffered than about the small number who prospered from the European and Muslim trades.

Despite uncertainty over many details, it is still possible to assess some of the effects of the Atlantic and Islamic trades on sub-Saharan Africa. One key issue is how the European and Islamic slave trades affected Africa's population. Most scholars who have looked deeply into the question agree on two points: (1) the effect of slave exports could not have been large when measured against the population of the entire continent, but (2) losses in regions that contributed heavily to the slave trade were severe. The lands behind the Slave Coast are thought to have been acutely affected. The large slave

Amerindian Foods in Africa

The migration of European plants and animals across the Atlantic to the New World was one side of the Columbian Exchange (see Chapter 19). The Andean potato, for example, became a staple crop of the poor in Europe, and cassava (a Brazilian plant cultivated for its edible roots) and maize (corn) moved across the Atlantic to Africa.

Maize was a high-yielding grain that could produce much more food per acre than many grains indigenous to Africa. The varieties of maize that spread to Africa were not modern high-bred "sweet corn" but starchier types found in white and yellow corn meal. Cassava—not well known to modern North Americans except perhaps in the form of tapioca—became the most important New World food in Africa. Truly a marvel, cassava had the highest yield of calories per acre of any staple food and thrived even in poor soils and during droughts. Both the leaves and the root could be eaten. Ground into meal, the root could be made into a bread that would keep for up to six months, or it could be fermented into a beverage.

Cassava Plant   Both the leaves and the starchy root of the cassava plant could be eaten. (Engraving from André Thevet, *Les Singularitez de la Franc Antarctique*. Paris: Maurice de la Porte, 1557). Courtesy of the James Bell Library, University of Minnesota)

Cassava and maize were probably introduced accidentally into Africa by Portuguese ships from Brazil that discarded leftover supplies after reaching Angola. It did not take long for local Africans to recognize the food value of these new crops, especially in drought-prone areas. As the principal farmers in Central Africa, women must have played an important role in learning how to cultivate, harvest, and prepare these foods. By the eighteenth century, Lunda rulers hundreds of miles from the Angolan coast were actively promoting the cultivation of maize and cassava on their royal estates in order to provide a more secure food supply.

Some historians of Africa believe that in the inland areas these Amerindian food crops provided the nutritional base for a population increase that partially offset losses due to the Atlantic slave trade. By supplementing the range of food crops available and by enabling populations to increase in once lightly settled or famine-prone areas, cassava and maize, along with peanuts and other New World legumes, permanently altered Africans' environmental prospects.

---

trade may also have caused serious depopulation in Angola. To some extent, however, losses from famine in this region may have been reduced by the increasing cultivation of high-yielding food plants from the Americas (see Environment and Technology: Amerindian Foods in Africa).

Although both foreign Muslims and Europeans obtained slaves from sub-Saharan Africa, there was a significant difference in the numbers they obtained and thus in the overall effects of the two slave trades. Between 1550 and 1800 some 8 million Africans were exported into the Atlantic trade, four times as many as were taken from sub-Saharan Africa to North Africa and the Middle East. The families of all those sent abroad suffered from their individual loss, but the ability of the population to replenish its numbers through natural increase depended on the proportion of women lost to these slave trades. The much higher proportion of women in the Muslim slave trade would have multiplied its lasting effects on sub-Saharan African populations.

It is impossible to assess with precision the complex effects of the goods received in sub-Saharan Africa from these trades. Africans were very particular about what they received, so it is unlikely that they could have been consistently cheated. Some researchers have suggested that imports of textiles and metals undermined African weavers and metalworkers, but most economic historians calculate that on a per capita basis the volume of these imports was too small to have idled many African artisans. Imports supplemented rather than replaced local production. The goods received in sub-Saharan Africa were intended for consumption and thus did not serve to develop the economy. Likewise, the sugar, tea, and chocolate Europeans consumed did little to promote economic development in Europe. However, both African and European merchants profited from trading these consumer goods. Because they directed the whole Atlantic system, Europeans gained far more wealth than Africans.

Historians disagree in their assessment of how deeply European capitalism dominated Africa before 1800, but Europeans clearly had much less political and economic impact in Africa than in the West Indies or in other parts of the Americas. Still, it is significant that Western capitalism was expanding rapidly in the seventeenth century, while the Ottoman Empire, the dominant state of the Middle East, was entering a period of economic and political decline (see Chapter 27). The tide of influence in Africa was thus running in the Europeans' direction.

CONCLUSION

The new Atlantic trading system had great importance and momentous implications for world history. In the first phase of their expansion Europeans had conquered and colonized the Americas and captured major Indian Ocean trade routes. The development of the Atlantic system showed Europeans' ability to move beyond the conquest and capture of existing systems to create a major new trading system that could transform a region almost beyond recognition.

The West Indies felt the transforming power of capitalism more profoundly than did any other place outside Europe in this period. The establishment of sugar plantation societies was not just a matter of replacing native vegetation with alien plants and native peoples with Europeans and Africans. More fundamentally it made these once-isolated islands part of a dynamic trading system controlled from Europe. To be sure, the West Indies was not the only place affected. Parts of northern Brazil were touched as deeply by the sugar revolution, and other parts of the Americas were yielding to the power of European colonization and capitalism.

Africa played an essential role in the Atlantic system, importing trade goods and exporting slaves to the Americas. Africa, however, was less dominated by the Atlantic system than were Europe's American colonies. Africans remained in control of their continent and interacted culturally and politically with the Islamic world more than with the Atlantic.

Historians have seen the Atlantic system as a model of the kind of highly interactive economy that became global in later centuries. For that reason the Atlantic system was a milestone in a much larger historical process, but not a monument to be admired. Its transformations were destructive as well as creative, producing victims as well as victors. Yet one cannot ignore that the system's awesome power came from its ability to create wealth. As the next chapter describes, southern Asia and the Indian Ocean basin were also beginning to feel the effects of Europeans' rising power.

■ Key Terms

Atlantic system	maroon
chartered company	capitalism
Dutch West India Company	mercantilism
plantocracy	Royal African Company
driver	Great Circuit
seasoning	Middle Passage
manumission	

■ Suggested Reading

The global context of early modern capitalism is examined by Immanuel Wallerstein, *The Modern World-System*, 3 vols. (1974–1989); by Fernand Braudel, *Civilization and Capitalism, 15th–18th Century*, 3 vols. (1982–1984); and in two volumes of scholarly papers edited by James D. Tracy: *The Rise of Merchant Empires* (1990) and *The Political Economy of Merchant Empires* (1991). Especially relevant are the chapters in *The Rise of Merchant Empires* by Herbert S. Klein, summarizing scholarship on the Middle Passage, and by Ralph A. Austen, on the trans-Saharan caravan trade between 1500 and 1800.

The best general introductions to the Atlantic system are Philip D. Curtin, *The Rise and Fall of the Plantation Complex* (1990), and Herbert S. Klein, *The Atlantic Slave Trade* (1999) and David

Ellis, *The Rise of African Slavery in the Americas* (2000). Recent scholarly articles on subjects considered in this chapter are available in *The Atlantic Slave Trade: Effects on Economies, Societies, and Peoples in Africa, the Americas and Europe*, ed. Joseph E. Inikori and Stanley L. Engerman (1992); in *Slavery and the Rise of the Atlantic System*, ed. Barbara L. Solow (1991); and in *Africans in Bondage: Studies in Slavery and the Slave Trade*, ed. Paul Lovejoy (1986). Pieter Emmer has edited a valuable collection of articles on *The Dutch in the Atlantic Economy, 1580–1880: Trade, Slavery, and Emancipation* (1998).

Edward Reynolds, *Stand the Storm: A History of the Atlantic Slave Trade* (1993), provides a brief overview of research on that subject. A useful collection of primary and secondary sources is David Northrup, ed., *The Atlantic Slave Trade* (1994). Hugh Thomas's *The Slave Trade: The Story of the Atlantic Slave Trade, 1440–1870* (1999), and Basil Davidson's *The Atlantic Slave Trade*, rev. ed. (1980), are other useful historical narratives.

The cultural connections among African communities on both sides of the Atlantic are explored by John Thornton, *Africa and Africans in the Making of the Atlantic World, 1400–1800*, 2d ed. (1998), and Margaret E. Crahan and Franklin W. Knight, eds., *Africa and the Caribbean: The Legacies of a Link* (1979). See also the collection edited by Richard Price, *Maroon Societies: Rebel Slave Communities in the Americas*, 2d ed. (1979).

Herbert S. Klein's *African Slavery in Latin America and the Caribbean* (1986) is an exceptionally fine synthesis of recent research on New World slavery, including North American slave systems. The larger context of Caribbean history is skillfully surveyed by Eric Williams, *From Columbus to Castro: The History of the Caribbean* (1984), and more simply surveyed by William Claypole and John Robottom, *Caribbean Story*, vol. 1, *Foundations*, 2d ed. (1990). Michael Craton, James Walvin, and David Wright, eds., *Slavery, Abolition, and Emancipation* (1976), is a valuable collection of primary sources about slavery in the British West Indies.

Roland Oliver and Anthony Atmore, *The African Middle Ages, 1400–1800* (1981), summarize African history in this period. Students can pursue specific topics in more detail in Richard Gray, ed., *The Cambridge History of Africa*, vol. 4 (1975), and B. A. Ogot, ed., *UNESCO General History of Africa*, vol. 5 (1992).

For recent research on slavery and the African, Atlantic, and Muslim slave trades with Africa see Paul Lovejoy, *Transformations in Slavery: A History of Slavery in Africa* (1983); Claire C. Robertson and Martin A. Klein, eds., *Women and Slavery in Africa* (1983); and Patrick Manning, *Slavery and African Life: Occidental, Oriental, and African Slave Trades* (1990). Case studies are found in J. E. Inikori, ed., *Forced Migration: The Impact of the Export Slave Trade on African Societies* (1982). *The Interesting Narrative of the Life of Olaudah Equiano* (1789) exists in several old and modern editions, and a critical edition of the portion relevant to the slave trade is reprinted in Philip D. Curtin, ed., *Africa Remembered: Narratives by West Africans from the Era of the Slave Trade* (1968, 1997), along with other African voices.

Those interested in Islam's cultural and commercial contacts with sub-Saharan Africa will find useful information in James L. A. Webb, Jr., *Desert Frontier: Ecological and Economic Change along the Western Sahel, 1600–1850* (1995); Elizabeth Savage, ed., *The Human Commodity: Perspectives on the Trans-Saharan Slave Trade* (1992); and J. Spencer Trimingham, *The Influence of Islam upon Africa* (1968).

■ Notes

1. Eric Williams, *Capitalism and Slavery* (Charlotte: University of North Carolina Press, 1944), 7.
2. Willem Bosman, *A New and Accurate Description of Guinea, etc.* (London, 1705), quoted in David Northrup, ed., *The Atlantic Slave Trade* (Lexington, MA: D. C. Heath, 1994), 72.
3. Roland Oliver and Anthony Atmore, *The African Middle Ages, 1400–1800* (Cambridge, England: Cambridge University Press, 1981), 100.
4. King Osei Bonsu, quoted in Northrup, ed., *The Atlantic Slave Trade*, 93.
5. Alexander Falconbridge, *Account of the Slave Trade on the Coast of Africa* (London: J. Phillips, 1788), 12.
6. Joseph C. Miller, "The Significance of Drought, Disease, and Famine in the Agriculturally Marginal Zones of West-Central Africa," *Journal of African History* 23 (1982) 17–61.
7. In Philip D. Curtin, ed., *Africa Remembered: Narratives by West Africans from the Era of the Slave Trade* (Madison: University of Wisconsin Press, 1968).

21

SOUTHWEST ASIA AND THE INDIAN OCEAN,

1500–1750

The Ottoman Empire, to 1750 • The Safavid Empire, 1502–1722 •
The Mughal Empire, 1526–1761 • Trade Empires in the Indian Ocean, 1600–1729
ENVIRONMENT AND TECHNOLOGY: Metal Currency and Inflation
SOCIETY AND CULTURE: Indian Merchants in Russia

Ottoman Astronomers   Instruments shown include an astrolabe, a quadrant, and an hourglass.

Anthony Jenkinson, merchant-adventurer for the Muscovy Company, founded in 1555 to develop trade with Russia, was the first Englishman to set foot in Iran. Eight years after the first English ship dropped anchor at Archangel on the White Sea in Russia's frigid north, Jenkinson made his way through Russia, down the Volga River, and across the Caspian Sea. The local ruler he met when he disembarked in 1561 in northwestern Iran was an object of wonder, "richly apparelled with long garments of silk, and cloth of gold, embroidered with pearls of stone; upon his head was a *tolipane* [headdress shaped like a tulip] with a sharp end pointing upwards half a yard long, of rich cloth of gold, wrapped about with a piece of India silk of twenty yards long, wrought in gold richly enameled, and set with precious stones; his earrings had pendants of gold a handful long, with two rubies of great value, set in the ends thereof."

Moving on to Qazvin°, Iran's capital, Jenkinson met the shah, whom the English referred to as the "Great Sophie" (apparently from Safavi°, the name of the ruling family). "In lighting from my horse at the Court gate, before my feet touched the ground, a pair of the Sophie's own shoes . . . were put upon my feet, for without the same shoes I might not be suffered to tread upon his holy ground."[1] After presenting a letter from Queen Elizabeth in Latin, English, Hebrew, and Italian but finding no one capable of reading it, he managed nevertheless to propose trade between England and Iran. The shah rejected the idea, since diverting Iranian silk from the markets of the Ottoman sultans, with whom he was negotiating a truce after a half-century of intermittent war, would have been undiplomatic.

Though Central Asia's bazaars were only meagerly supplied with goods, as Jenkinson and later merchants discovered, the idea of bypassing the Ottomans in the eastern Mediterranean and trading directly with Iran through Russia remained tempting. By the same token, the Ottomans were tempted by the idea of outflanking Safavid Iran. In 1569, an Ottoman army tried unsuccessfully to dig a 40-mile (64-kilometer) canal between the Don River, which opened into the Black Sea, and the Volga, which flowed into the Caspian. Their objective was to enable Ottoman ships to reach the Caspian and attack Iran from the north.

The Ottomans' foe was Russia, then ruled by Tsar Ivan IV (r. 1533–1584), known as Ivan the Terrible or Awesome. Ivan transformed his principality from a second-rate power into the sultan's primary competitor in Central Asia. In the river-crossed steppe, where Turkic nomads had long enjoyed uncontested sway, Slavic Christian Cossacks from the region of the Don and Dnieper Rivers used armed wagon trains and river craft fitted with small cannon to push southward and establish a Russian presence.

A contest for trade with or control of Central Asia was natural after the centrality conferred on the region by three centuries of Mongol and Turkic conquest, highlighted by the campaigns of Genghis Khan and Timur. But as we shall see, changes in the organization of trade were sapping the vitality of the Silk Road. Wealth and power were shifting to European seaborne empires linking the Atlantic with the Indian Ocean. Though the Ottomans were a formidable naval power in the Mediterranean, neither they nor the Safavid shahs in Iran nor the Mughal emperors of India deployed more than a token navy in the southern seas.

As you read this chapter, ask yourself the following questions:

- What were the advantages and disadvantages of a land as opposed to a maritime empire?
- What role did religion play in political alliances and rivalries and in the formation of states?
- How did trading patterns change between 1500 and 1750?

THE OTTOMAN EMPIRE, TO 1750

The most long-lived of the post-Mongol Muslim empires was the **Ottoman Empire,** founded around 1300. By extending Islamic conquests into eastern Europe, starting in the late fourteenth century, and by taking Syria and Egypt from the Mamluk rulers in the early

---

Qazvin (kaz-VEEN)   **Safavi** (SAH-fah-vee)

CHRONOLOGY

	Ottoman Empire	Safavid Empire	Mughal Empire	Europeans in the Indian Ocean States
1500		**1502–1524** Shah Ismail establishes Safavid rule in Iran		**1511** Portuguese seize Malacca from local Malay ruler
	1514 Selim I defeats Safavid shah at Chaldiran; conquers Egypt and Syria (1516–1517)	**1514** Defeat by Ottomans at Chaldiran limits Safavid growth		
	1520–1566 Reign of Suleiman the Magnificent; peak of Ottoman Empire			
	1529 First Ottoman siege of Vienna		**1526** Babur defeats last sultan of Delhi at Panipat	
			1539 Death of Nanak, founder of Sikh religion	
	1571 Ottoman naval defeat at Lepanto	**1587–1629** Reign of Shah Abbas the Great; peak of Safavid Empire	**1556–1605** Akbar rules in Agra; peak of Mughal Empire	**1565** Spanish establish their first fort in the Philippines
1600				**1600** English East India Company founded
				1602 Dutch East India Company founded
	1610 End of Anatolian revolts	**1622** Iranians oust Portuguese from Hormuz after 108 years		**1606** Dutch reach Australia
				1641 Dutch seize Malacca from Portuguese
			1658–1707 Aurangzeb imposes conservative Islamic regime	**1650** Omani Arabs capture Musqat from Portuguese
			1690 British found city of Calcutta	
1700				**1698** Omani Arabs seize Mombasa from Portuguese
	1718–1730 Tulip Period; military decline apparent to Austria and Russia	**1722** Afghan invaders topple last Safavid shah		
		1736–1747 Nadir Shah temporarily reunites Iran; invades India (1739)	**1739** Iranians under Nadir Shah sack Delhi	**1742** Expansion of French Power in India

sixteenth, the Ottomans seemed to recreate the might of the original Islamic caliphate, the empire established by the Muslim Arab conquests in the seventh century. However, the empire was actually more similar to the new centralized monarchs of France and Spain (see Chapter 18) than to any medieval model.

Enduring more than five centuries, until 1922, the Ottoman Empire survived several periods of wrenching change, some caused by internal problems, others by the growing power of European adversaries. These periods of change reveal the problems faced by huge, land-based empires around the world.

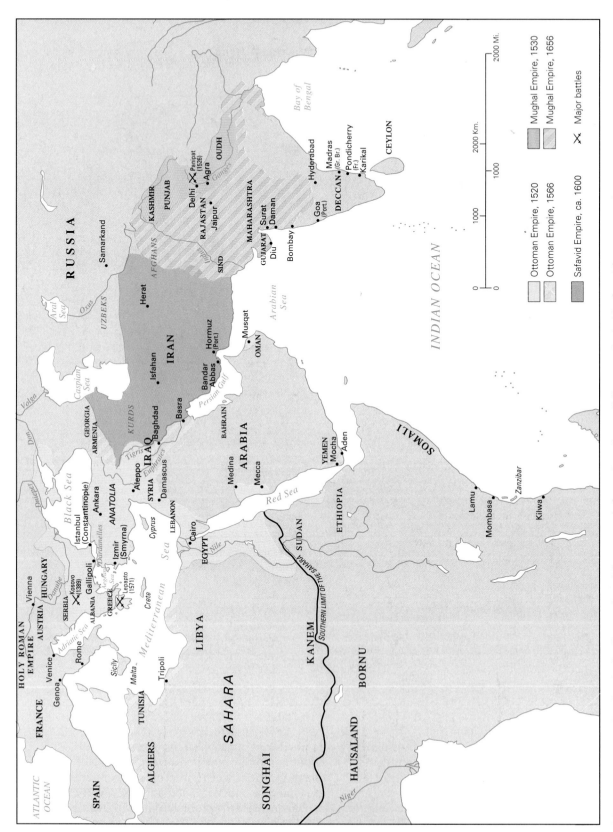

Map 21.1 Muslim Empires in the Sixteenth and Seventeenth Centuries Iran, a Shi'ite state flanked by Sunni Ottomans on the west and Sunni Mughals on the east, had the least exposure to European influences. Ottoman expansion across the southern Mediterranean Sea intensified European fears of Islam. The areas of strongest Mughal control dictated that Islam's spread into southeast Asia would be heavily influenced by merchants and religious figures from Gujarat instead of from eastern India.

Aya Sofya Mosque in Istanbul   Orginally a Byzantine cathedral, Aya Sofya (in Greek, Hagia Sophia) was transformed into a mosque after 1453, and four minarets were added. It then became a model for subsequent Ottoman mosques. To the right behind it is the Bosporus strait dividing Europe and Asia, to the left the Golden Horn inlet separating the old city of Istanbul from the newer parts. The gate to the Ottoman sultan's palace is to the right of the mosque. The pointed tower to the left of the dome is part of the palace.   (Robert Frerck/Woodfin Camp & Associates)

Expansion and Frontiers

The Ottoman Empire grew from a tiny state in northwestern Anatolia established around 1300 on the strength of Turkish nomad warriors and a few Christian converts to Islam (see Map 21.1). The empire grew because of three factors: (1) the shrewdness of its founder Osman (from which the name "Ottoman" comes) and his descendants, (2) control of a strategic link between Europe and Asia at Gallipoli° on the Dardanelles strait, and (3) the creation of an army that took advantage of the traditional skills of the Turkish cavalryman and the new military possibilities presented by gunpowder.

At first, Ottoman armies concentrated on Christian enemies in Greece and the Balkans, in 1389 conquering a strong Serbian kingdom at the Battle of Kosovo° (in present-day Yugoslavia). Much of southeastern Europe and Anatolia was under the control of the sultans by 1402, when Bayazid° I, "the Thunderbolt," confronted Timur's challenge from Central Asia. After Timur defeated and captured Bayazid at the Battle of Ankara (1402), a generation of civil war followed, until Mehmed° I reunified the sultanate.

During a century and a half of fighting for territory both east and west of Constantinople, the sultans had repeatedly eyed the heavily fortified capital of the slowly dying Byzantine Empire. In 1453, Sultan Mehmed II, "the Conqueror," laid siege to Constantinople. His forces used enormous cannon to bash in the city's walls, dragged warships over a high hill from the Bosporus strait to the city's inner harbor to get around its sea defenses, and finally penetrated the city's land walls through a series of direct infantry assaults. The fall of Constantinople—henceforth commonly known as Istanbul—brought to an end over eleven hundred years of Byzantine rule and made the Ottomans seem invincible.

In 1514, at the Battle of Chaldiran (in Armenia), Selim° I, "the Inexorable," ended a potential threat on his eastern frontier from the new and expansive realm of the Safavid shah in Iran (see below). Although further wars were to be fought with Iran, the general border between the Ottomans and their eastern neighbors was essentially established at this time, leaving Iraq a contested and repeatedly ravaged frontier province.

When Selim conquered the Mamluk Sultanate of Egypt and Syria in 1516 and 1517, the Red Sea became the Ottomans' southern frontier. As for the Ottomans'

Gallipoli (gah-LIP-po-lee)   Kosovo (KO-so-vo)
Bayazid (BAY-yan-zeed)   Mehmed (MEH-met)

Selim (seh-LEEM)

western frontier, the rulers of the major port cities of Algeria and Tunisia, some of them Greek or Italian converts to Islam, voluntarily joined the empire in the early sixteenth century, thereby greatly strengthening its Mediterranean fleets.

The sultan who presided over the greatest Ottoman assault on Christian Europe was **Suleiman° the Magnificent** (r. 1520–1566), known to his subjects as Suleiman Kanuni, "the Lawgiver." The son of Selim I, Suleiman seemed unstoppable as he conquered Belgrade in 1521, expelled the Knights of the Hospital of St. John from the island of Rhodes the following year, and laid siege to Vienna in 1529. Vienna was saved by the lateness of the season and the need to retreat before the onset of winter more than by military action. In later centuries, Ottoman historians looked back on the reign of Suleiman as the period when the imperial system worked to perfection and spoke of it as the golden age of Ottoman greatness.

While Ottoman armies pressed deeper and deeper into eastern Europe, the sultans also sought to control the Mediterranean. Between 1453 and 1502, the Ottomans fought the opening rounds of a two-century war with Venice, the most powerful of Italy's commercial city-states. From the Fourth Crusade of 1204 onward, Venice had assembled a profitable maritime empire that included major islands such as Crete and Cyprus along with strategic coastal strongpoints in Greece. Venice thereby became more than just a trading nation. Its island sugar plantations, exploiting cheap slave labor, competed favorably with Egypt in the international trade of the fifteenth century. With their rivals the Genoese, trading through the strategic island of Chios, the Venetians stifled Ottoman maritime activities in the Aegean Sea.

The initial fighting left Venice in control of its lucrative islands for another century. But it also left Venice a reduced military power compelled to pay tribute to the Ottomans. The Ottomans, like the Chinese, were willing to let other nations carry trade to and from their ports—they preferred trade of this sort—so long as those other nations acknowledged Ottoman authority. It never occurred to them that a sea empire held together by flimsy ships could truly rival a great land empire fielding an army of a hundred thousand men.

In the south, Muslims of the Red Sea and Indian Ocean region were accustomed to trading by way of Egypt and Syria. In the early sixteenth century, merchants from southern India and Sumatra sent emissaries to Istanbul requesting naval support against the Portuguese. The Ottomans responded vigorously to Portuguese threats close to their territories, such as at Aden at the southern entrance to the Red Sea, but their efforts farther afield were insufficient to stifle growing Portuguese domination.

Eastern luxury products still flowed to Ottoman markets. Portuguese power was territorially limited to fortified coastal points, such as Hormuz at the entrance to the Persian Gulf, Goa in western India, and Malacca in Malaya (see Chapter 17). Why commit major resources to subduing an enemy whose main threat was a demand that merchant vessels, mostly belonging to non-Ottoman Muslims, buy protection from Portuguese attack? The Ottomans did send a small naval force to Indonesia, but they never formulated a consistent or aggressive policy with regard to political and economic developments in the Indian Ocean.

Central Institutions

Heirs of the military traditions of Central Asia, the Ottoman army originally consisted of lightly armored mounted warriors skilled at shooting a short bow made of compressed layers of bone, wood, and leather. The conquest of Christian territories in the Balkans in the late fourteenth century, however, gave the Ottomans access to a new military resource: Christian prisoners of war induced to serve as military slaves.

Slave soldiery had a long history in Islamic lands. The Mamluk Sultanate of Egypt and Syria was built on that practice. The Mamluks, however, acquired their new blood from slave markets in Central Asia. Enslaving Christian prisoners, an action of questionable legality in Islamic law, was an Ottoman innovation. Converted to Islam, these "new troops," called *yeni cheri* in Turkish and "**Janissary**"° in English, gave the Ottomans unusual military flexibility.

Christians by upbringing, the Janissaries had no misgivings about fighting against Turks and Muslims when the sultans wished to expand in western Asia. Since horseback riding and bowmanship were not part of their cultural backgrounds, they readily accepted the idea of fighting on foot and learning to use guns, which at that time were still too heavy and awkward for a horseman to load and fire. The Janissaries lived in barracks and trained all year round. Up to the middle of the sixteenth century, they were barred both from holding jobs and from marrying.

The process of selection for Janissary training changed early in the fifteenth century. The new system, called the **devshirme°** (literally "selection"), imposed a regular levy of male children on Christian villages in the Balkans and occasionally elsewhere. Devshirme children were placed with Turkish families to learn their language and then were sent to the sultan's palace in Istanbul for an education that included instruction in Islam, military training, and, for the most talented, what we might call liberal arts. This regime, sophisticated for its time, produced not only the Janissary soldiers but also, from among the chosen few who received special training in the inner service of the palace, senior military commanders and heads of government departments up to the rank of grand vizier.

The Ottoman Empire became cosmopolitan in character. The sophisticated court language, Osmanli° (the Turkish form of *Ottoman*), shared basic grammar and vocabulary with the Turkish spoken by Anatolia's nomads and villagers, but Arabic and Persian elements made it as distinct from that language as the Latin of educated Europeans was from the various Latin-derived Romance languages. Everyone who served in the military or the bureaucracy and conversed in Osmanli was considered to belong to the *askeri*°, or "military," class. Members of this class were exempt from taxes and owed their well-being to the sultan. The mass of the population, whether Muslims, Christians, or Jews—Jews flooded into Ottoman territory after their expulsion from Spain in 1492 (see Chapter 17)—constituted the *raya*°, literally "flock of sheep."

By the beginning of the reign of Sultan Suleiman the Magnificent, the Ottoman Empire was the most powerful and best-organized state in either Europe or the Islamic world. Its military was balanced between mounted archers, primarily Turks supported by grants of land in return for their military service, and Janissaries, Turkified Albanians, Serbs, and Macedonians paid from the central treasury and trained in the most advanced weaponry. The galley-equipped navy was manned by Greek, Turkish, Algerian, and Tunisian sailors, usually under the command of an admiral from one of the North African ports.

The balance of the Ottoman land forces brought success to Ottoman arms in recurrent wars with the Safavids, who were much slower to adopt firearms, and in the inexorable conquest of the Balkans. Expansion by sea was less dramatic. A major expedition against Malta that would have given the Ottomans a foothold in the western Mediterranean failed in 1565. Combined Christian forces also achieved a massive naval victory at the Battle of Lepanto, off Greece, in 1571. But Ottoman resources were so extensive that in a year's time they had replaced all of the galleys sunk in that battle.

Under the land-grant system, resident cavalrymen administered most rural areas in Anatolia and the

Ottoman Glassmakers on Parade Celebrations of the circumcisions of the sultan's sons featured parades organized by the craft guilds of Istanbul. This float features glassmaking, a common craft in Islamic realms. The most elaborate glasswork included oil lamps for mosques and colored glass for the small stained-glass windows below mosque domes. (Topkapi Saray Museum)

Balkans. They maintained order, collected taxes, and reported for each summer's campaign with their horses, retainers, and supplies, all paid for from the taxes they collected. When not campaigning, they stayed at home. Some historians maintain that these cavalrymen, who did not own their land, had little interest in encouraging production or introducing new technologies, but since a militarily able son often succeeded his father, the grant holders did have some interest in productivity.

The Ottoman conception of the world saw the sultan providing justice for his "flock of sheep" (raya) and the military protecting them. In return, the raya paid the taxes that supported both the sultan and the military. In reality, the sultan's government, like most large territorial governments in premodern times, remained comparatively isolated from the lives of most subjects. Arab, Turkish, and Balkan townsfolk depended on local notables and religious leaders to represent them before Ottoman provincial governors and their staffs. Islam was the ruling religion and gradually became the majority religion in Balkan regions such as Albania and Bosnia that had large numbers of converts. Thus the law of Islam (the Shari'a°), as interpreted by local *ulama*° (religious

---

Osmanli (os-MAHN-lee) *askeri* (AS-keh-ree) *raya* (RAH-yah)

Shari'a (sha-REE-ah) *ulama* (oo-leh-MAH)

Metal Currency and Inflation

Inflation occurs when the quantity of goods and services available for purchase remains stable while the quantity of money in circulation increases. With more money in their pockets, people are willing to pay more to get what they want. Prices go up, and what people think of as the value of money goes down.

Today, with paper money and electronic banking, governments try to control inflation by regulating the printing of money or by other means. Prior to the nineteenth century, money consisted of silver and gold coins, and governments did not keep track of how much money was in circulation. As long as the annual production of gold and silver mines was quite small, inflation was not a worry. In the sixteenth and seventeenth centuries, however, precious metal poured into Spain from silver and gold mines in the New World, but there was no increase in the availability of goods and services. The resulting inflation triggered a "price revolution" in Europe—a general tripling of prices between 1500 and 1650. In Paris in 1650, the price of wheat and hay was fifteen times higher than the price had been in 1500.

This wave of inflation worked its way east, contributing to social disorder in the Ottoman Empire. European traders had more money available than Ottoman merchants and could outbid them for scarce commodities. Lacking silver and gold mines,

the Ottoman government reduced the amount of precious metal in Ottoman coins. This made the problem worse. Hit hardest were people who had fixed incomes. Cavalrymen holding land grants worth a set amount each year were unable to equip themselves for military campaigns. Students living on fixed scholarships went begging.

Safavid Iran needed silver and gold to pay for imports from Mughal India, which imported few Iranian goods. Iranians sold silk to the Ottoman Empire for silver and gold, worsening the Ottoman situation, and then passed the precious metal on to India. Everyday life in Iran depended on barter or locally minted copper coinage, both more resistant to inflation. Copper for coins was sometimes imported from China.

Though no one then grasped the connection between silver production in Mexico and the trade balance between Iran and India, the world of the sixteenth and seventeenth centuries was becoming more closely linked economically than it had ever been before.

Set of Coin Dies   The lower die, called the anvil die, was set in a piece of wood. A blank disk of gold, silver, or copper was placed on top of it. The hammer die was placed on top of the blank and struck with a hammer to force the coin's image onto it.   (Courtesy, Israel Museum, Jerusalem)

---

scholars), conditioned urban institutions and social life. Local customs prevailed among non-Muslims and in many rural areas; and non-Muslims looked to their own religious leaders for guidance in family and spiritual matters.

Crisis of the Military State, 1585–1650

As military technology evolved, cannon and lighter-weight firearms played an ever-larger role on the battlefield. Accordingly, the size of the Janissary corps—and its cost to the government—grew steadily, and the role of the Turkish cavalry, which continued to disdain firearms even as they became lighter and easier to use, diminished. To fill state coffers and pay the Janissaries, in the mid-sixteenth century the sultan started reducing the number of landholding cavalrymen. Revenues previously spent on their living expenses and military equipment went directly into the imperial treasury. Some of the displaced cavalrymen, armed and unhappy, became a restive element in rural Anatolia.

At about the same time, in the late sixteenth century, inflation caused a flood of cheap silver from the New World (see Environment and Technology: Metal Currency and Inflation) affected many of the remaining landholders restricted by law to collecting a fixed amount of taxes. Their purchasing power declined so much that they were unable to report for military service. This delinquency, however, played into the hands of the sultan's government, which wanted to reduce the cavalry and increase the Janissary corps and thus made no reforms to allow landholders to keep their land grants. As land was returned to the state, more and more cavalrymen joined the ranks of dispossessed troopers. Students and professors in *madrasas* (religious colleges) similarly found it impossible to live on fixed stipends from madrasa endowments.

Constrained by religious law from fundamentally changing the tax system, the government levied emergency surtaxes to obtain enough funds to pay the Janissaries and bureaucrats. For additional military strength, particularly in its wars with Iran, the government reinforced the Janissary ranks with partially trained, salaried soldiers hired for the duration of a campaign. Once the summer campaign season was over, however, these soldiers found themselves out of work and short on cash.

This complicated situation resulted in revolts that devastated Anatolia between 1590 and 1610. Former landholding cavalrymen, short-term soldiers released at the end of the campaign season, peasants overburdened by emergency taxes, and even impoverished students of religion formed bands of marauders. Anatolia experienced the worst of the rebellions and suffered greatly from emigration and the loss of agricultural production. But an increase in banditry, made worse by the government's inability to stem the spread of muskets among the general public, beset other parts of the empire as well.

In the meantime, the Janissaries took advantage of their growing influence to gain relief from prohibitions on their marrying and engaging in business. Janissaries who involved themselves in commerce lessened the burden on the state budget, and married Janissaries who enrolled sons or relatives in the corps made it possible in the seventeenth century for the government to save state funds by abolishing the devshirme system with its traveling selection officers. These savings, however, were more than offset by the increase in the total number of Janissaries and in their steady deterioration as a military force, which necessitated the hiring of more and more supplemental troops.

Economic Change and Growing Weakness, 1650–1750

A very different Ottoman Empire emerged from this period of crisis. The sultan once had led armies. Now he mostly resided in his palace and had little experience of the real world. This manner of living resulted from a gradually developed policy of keeping the sultan's male relatives confined to the palace to prevent them from plotting coups or meddling in politics. The sultan's mother and the chief eunuch overseeing the private quarters of the palace thus became important arbiters of royal favor, and even of succession to the sultanate, and the affairs of government were overseen more and more by the chief administrators—the grand viziers. (Ottoman historians draw special attention to the negative influence of women in the palace after the time of Suleiman, but to some degree they are reflecting traditional male, and Muslim, fears about women in politics.)

The devshirme had been discontinued, and the Janissaries had taken advantage of their increased power and privileges to make membership in their corps hereditary. Together with several other newly prominent infantry regiments, they involved themselves in crafts and trading, both in Istanbul and in provincial capitals such as Cairo, Aleppo, and Baghdad. This activity took a toll on their military skills, but they continued to be a powerful faction in urban politics that the sultans could neither ignore nor reform.

Land grants in return for military service also disappeared. Tax farming arose in their place. Tax farmers paid specific taxes, such as customs duties, in advance in return for the privilege of collecting a greater amount from the actual taxpayers. In one instance, two tax farmers advanced the government 18 million akches (small silver coins) for the customs duties of the Aegean port of Izmir°, and collected a total of 19,169,203 akches for a profit of 6.5 percent.

Rural administration, already disrupted by the rebellions, suffered from the transition to tax farms. The former landholders had been military men who readily kept order on their lands in order to maintain their incomes. Tax farmers were less likely to live on the land, and their tax collection rights could vary from year to year. The imperial government, therefore, faced greater administrative burdens and came to rely heavily on powerful provincial governors or on wealthy men who purchased lifelong tax collection rights that prompted them to behave more or less like private landowners.

Rural disorder and decline in administrative control sometimes opened the way for new economic opportunities. The port of Izmir, known to Europeans by the ancient name "Smyrna," had a population of around 2,000 in 1580. By 1650 the population had increased almost twentyfold to between 30,000 and 40,000. Along with refugees from the Anatolian uprisings and from European pirate attacks along the coast came European merchants and large colonies of Armenians, Greeks, and Jews. A French traveler in 1621 wrote: "At present, Izmir

Izmir (IZ-meer)

has a great traffic in wool, beeswax, cotton, and silk, which the Armenians bring there instead of going to Aleppo . . . because they do not pay as many dues.[2]

Izmir was able to transform itself between 1580 and 1650 from a small Muslim Turkish town into a multiethnic, multireligious, multilinguistic entrepôt because of the Ottoman government's inability to control trade and the slowly growing dominance of European traders in the Indian Ocean. Spices from the East, though still traded in Aleppo and other long-established Ottoman centers, were not to be found in Izmir. Aside from Iranian silk brought in by caravan, European traders at Izmir purchased local agricultural products—dried fruits, sesame seeds, nuts, and olive oil. As a consequence local farmers who previously had grown grain for subsistence shifted their plantings more and more to cotton and other cash crops, including, after its introduction in the 1590s, tobacco, which quickly became popular in the Ottoman Empire despite government prohibitions. In this way the agricultural economy of western Anatolia, the Balkans, and the Mediterranean coast—the Ottoman lands most accessible to Europe (see Map 21.1)—became enmeshed in the seventeenth century in a growing European commercial network.

At the same time, Ottoman military power slowly ebbed. The ill-trained Janissaries sometimes resorted to hiring substitutes to go on campaign, and the sultans relied on partially trained seasonal recruits and on armies raised by the governors of frontier provinces. By the middle of the eighteenth century, it was obvious to the Ottomans' Austrian and Russian opponents that the empire was in decline. On the eastern front, however, Ottoman exhaustion after many wars was matched by the demise in 1722 of their perennial adversary, the Safavid state of Iran.

The Ottoman Empire lacked both the wealth and the inclination to match European economic advances. Overland trade from the east dwindled as political disorder in Safavid Iran cut deeply into Iranian silk production (see below). Coffee, an Arabian product that rose from obscurity in the fifteenth century to become the rage first in the Ottoman Empire and then in Europe, was grown in the highlands of Yemen and exported by way of Egypt. By 1770, however, Muslim merchants trading in the Yemeni port of Mocha° (literally "the coffee place") were charged 15 percent in duties and fees. But European traders, benefiting from trade agreements with the Ottoman Empire going back to the time of Mehmed the Conqueror, paid little more than 3 percent.

Such trade agreements led to European domination of Ottoman import and export trade by sea. Neverthe-less, the Europeans did not control strategic ports in the Mediterranean comparable to Malacca in the Indian Ocean and Hormuz on the Persian Gulf, so their economic power stopped short of colonial settlement and direct political administration in Ottoman territories.

A few astute Ottoman statesmen observed the growing disarray of the empire and advised the sultans to reestablish the land-grant and devshirme systems of Suleiman's reign. But to most people the downward course of imperial power was far from evident, much less the reasons behind it. Ottoman historians named the period between 1718 and 1730 the "**Tulip Period**" because of the craze for high-priced tulip bulbs that swept Ottoman ruling circles. The craze replicated a Dutch tulip mania that had begun in the mid-sixteenth century, when the flower was introduced into Holland from Istanbul, and peaked in 1636 with particularly rare bulbs going for 2,500 florins apiece—the value of twenty-two oxen. Far from seeing Europe as the enemy that eventually would dismantle the weakening Ottoman Empire, the Istanbul elite experimented with European clothing and furniture styles and purchased printed books from the empire's first (and short-lived) press.

In 1730, however, the gala soirees, at which guests watched turtles with candles on their backs wander in the dark through massive tulip beds, gave way to a conservative Janissary revolt with strong religious overtones. Sultan Ahmed III abdicated, and the leader of the revolt, Patrona Halil°, an Albanian former seaman and stoker of the public baths, swaggered around the capital for several months dictating government policies before he was seized and executed.

The Patrona Halil rebellion confirmed the perceptions of a few that the Ottoman Empire was facing severe difficulties. But decay at the center spelled benefit elsewhere. In the provinces, ambitious and competent governors, wealthy landholders, urban notables, and nomad chieftains were well placed to take advantage of the central government's weakness. By the middle of the eighteenth century, groups of Mamluks had regained a dominant position in Egypt, and Janissary commanders had become virtually independent rulers in Baghdad. In central Arabia, Muhammad ibn Abd al-Wahhab's conservative Sunni movement had begun its remarkable rise beyond the reach of Ottoman power. Although no region declared full independence, the sultan's power was slipping away to the advantage of a broad array of lower officials and upstart chieftains in all parts of the empire, and the Ottoman economy was reorienting itself toward Europe.

Mocha (MOH-kuh)

Patrona Halil (pa-TROH-nuh ha-LEEL)

Safavid Shah with Attendants and Musicians This painting by Ali-Quli Jubbadar, a European convert to Islam working for the Safavid armory, reflects Western influences. Notice the use of light and shadow to model faces and the costume of the attendant to the shah's right. The shah's waterpipe indicates the spread of tobacco, a New World crop, to the Middle East. (Courtesy of Oriental Institute, Academy of Sciences, Leningrad. Reproduced from *Album of Persian and Indian Miniatures* [Moscow, 1962], ill. no. 98)

THE SAFAVID EMPIRE, 1502–1722

The **Safavid Empire** of Iran (see Map 21.1) resembled its long-time Ottoman foe in many ways: it initially relied militarily on cavalry paid through land grants; its population spoke several different languages; it was oriented inward away from the sea; and urban notables, nomadic chieftains, and religious scholars served as intermediaries between the people and the government. It also had distinct qualities that to this day set Iran off from its neighbors: it derived part of its legitimacy from the pre-Islamic dynasties of ancient Iran, and it adopted the Shi'ite form of Islam.

The Rise of the Safavids

Timur had been a great conqueror. But his children and grandchildren contented themselves with modest realms in Afghanistan and Central Asia, while a number of would-be rulers vied for control elsewhere. In Iran itself, the ultimate victor in a complicated struggle for power among Turkish chieftains was Ismail°, a boy of Kurdish, Iranian, and Greek ancestry, the hereditary leader of a militant Sufi brotherhood named "Safaviya" for his ancestor Safi al-Din. In 1502, at the age of sixteen, Ismail proclaimed himself shah of Iran. At around the same time, he declared that from that time forward his realm would be devoted to **Shi'ite Islam,** which revered the family of Muhammad's son-in-law Ali, and he called on all his subjects to abandon their Sunni beliefs.

Most of the members of the Safavi brotherhood were Turkish-speakers from nomadic groups known as *qizilbash*°, or "redheads," because of their distinctive turbans. They believed that Ismail was practically a god incarnate, and they fought ferociously on his behalf. If Ismail wished his state to be Shi'ite, his word was law to the qizilbash. The Iranian subject population, however, was not so easily persuaded. Neighboring lands received Sunni refugees from Safavid rule. Their preaching and intriguing helped stoke the fires that kept Ismail (d. 1524) and his son Tahmasp° (d. 1576) engaged in war after war. It took a century and a series of brutal persecutions to make Iran an overwhelmingly Shi'ite land. The transformation also required the importation of Arab Shi'ite scholars from Lebanon and Bahrain to institute Shi'ite religious education at a high level.

Although Ismail's reasons for compelling Iran's conversion to Shi'ism are unknown, the effect of this radical act was to create a deep chasm between Iran and its neighbors, all of which were Sunni. Iran became a truly separate country for the first time since its incorporation into the Islamic caliphate in the seventh century.

Ismail (IS-ma-eel)

qizilbash (KIH-zil-bahsh)   **Tahmasp** (tah-MAHSP)

Society and Religion

The imposition of Shi'ite belief made permanent the split between Iran and its neighbors, but differences between them had long been in the making. Persian, written in the Arabic script from the tenth century onward, had emerged as the second language of Islam. By 1500, an immense library of legal and theological writings; epic, lyric, and mystic poetry; histories; and drama and fiction had come into being. Iranian scholars and writers normally read Arabic as well as Persian and sprinkled their writings with Arabic phrases, but their Arab counterparts were much less inclined to learn Persian. Even handwriting styles differed, Iranians preferring highly cursive forms of the Arabic script.

This divergence between the two language areas had intensified after the Mongols destroyed Baghdad, the capital of the Islamic caliphate, in 1258 and diminished the importance of Arabic-speaking Iraq. Syria and Egypt had become the heartland of the Arab world while Iran developed largely on its own, having more extensive contacts with India—where Muslim rulers favored the Persian language—than with the Arabs.

In the heyday of the Islamic caliphate in the seventh through ninth centuries, cultural styles had radiated in all directions from Baghdad. In the post-Mongol period—a time of immense artistic creativity and innovation in Iran, Afghanistan, and Central Asia—styles in the East went their own separate ways. Painted and molded tiles and tile mosaics, often in vivid turquoise blue, became the standard exterior decoration of mosques in Iran but never were used in Syria and Egypt. Persian poets raised morally instructive and mystical-allegorical verse to peaks of perfection that had no reflection in Arabic poetry, generally considered to be in a state of decline.

The Turks, who steadily came to dominate the political scene from Bengal to Algeria, generally preferred Persian as a vehicle for literary or religious expression. The Mamluks in Egypt and Syria showed greatest respect for Arabic. The Turkish language, which had a vigorous tradition of folk poetry, developed only slowly, primarily in the Ottoman Empire, as a language of literature and administration. Ironically, Ismail Safavi was a noted religious poet in the Turkish language of his qizilbash followers, and his mortal adversary, the Ottoman Selim I (r. 1512–1520), was known for the elegance of his Persian poetry.

To be sure, Islam itself provided a tradition that crossed ethnic and linguistic borders. Mosque architecture differed, but Iranians, Arabs, and Turks, as well as Muslims in India, all had mosques. They also had madrasas that trained the ulama to sustain and interpret the Shari'a as the all-encompassing law of Islam. Yet local understandings of the common tradition differed substantially.

All Sufi orders had distinctive rituals and concepts of mystical union with God. These orders also were present in pre-Safavid Iran, but Iran stood out as the land where Sufism most often fused with militant political objectives. The Safavi Order was not the first to deploy armies and use the point of a sword to promote love of God. The Safavid shahs were unique, however, in eventually banning, somewhat ineffectively, all Sufi orders from their domain.

Even prior to Shah Ismail's imposition of Shi'ism, therefore, Iran had become a distinctive society. Nevertheless, the impact of Shi'ism was significant. Shi'ite doctrine says that all temporal rulers, regardless of title, are temporary stand-ins for the **"Hidden Imam"**: the twelfth descendant of Ali, who was the prophet Muhammad's cousin and son-in-law. Shi'ites believe that leadership of the Muslim community rests solely with divinely appointed Imams from Ali's family, that the twelfth descendant (the Hidden Imam) disappeared as a child in the ninth century, and that the Shi'ite community will lack a proper religious authority until he returns. Some Shi'ite scholars concluded that the faithful should calmly accept the world as it was and wait quietly for the Hidden Imam's return. Others maintained that they themselves should play a stronger role in political affairs because they were best qualified to know the Hidden Imam's wishes. These two positions, which still play a role in Iranian Shi'ism, tended to enhance the self-image of the ulama as independent of imperial authority and stood in the way of religious scholars becoming subordinate government functionaries, as happened with many Ottoman ulama.

Shi'ism also affected the psychological life of the people. Commemoration of the martyrdom of Imam Husayn (d. 680), Ali's son and the third Imam, during the first two weeks of every lunar year regularized an emotional outpouring with no parallel in Sunni lands. Day after day for two weeks (as they do today) preachers recited the woeful tale to crowds of weeping believers, and elaborate street processions, often organized by craft guilds, paraded chanting and self-flagellating men past crowds of reverent onlookers. Passion plays in which Husayn and his family are mercilessly killed by the agents of the caliph became a unique form of Iranian public theater.

Of course, Shi'ites elsewhere observed some of the same rites of mourning for Imam Husayn, particularly in the Shi'ite pilgrimage cities of Karbala and Najaf° in

Najaf (NAH-jaf)

Ottoman Iraq. But the impact of these rites on society as a whole was especially great in Iran, where 90 percent of the population was Shi'ite. Over time, the subjects of the Safavid shahs came to feel more than ever a people apart, even though many of them had been Shi'ite for only two or three generations.

A Tale of Two Cities: Isfahan and Istanbul

Isfahan° became Iran's capital in 1598 by decree of **Shah Abbas I** (r. 1587–1629). Outwardly, Istanbul and Isfahan looked quite different. Built on seven hills on the south side of the narrow Golden Horn inlet, Istanbul boasted a skyline punctuated by the gray stone domes and thin, pointed minarets of the great imperial mosques. Their design was inspired by Hagia Sophia, the Byzantine cathedral converted to a mosque and renamed Aya Sofya after 1453 (see page 525). The mosques surrounding the royal plaza in Isfahan, in contrast, had unobtrusive minarets and brightly tiled domes that rose to gentle peaks. High walls surrounded the sultan's palace in Istanbul. Shah Abbas in Isfahan focused his capital on the giant royal plaza, which was large enough for his army to play polo, and he used an airy palace overlooking the plaza to receive dignitaries and review his troops. This public image contributed to Shah Abbas being called "the Great."

The harbor of Istanbul, the primary Ottoman seaport, teemed with sailing ships and smaller craft, many of them belonging to a colony of European merchants perched on a hilltop on the north side of the Golden Horn. Isfahan, far from the sea, was only occasionally visited by Europeans. Most of its trade was in the hands of Jews, Hindus, and especially a colony of Armenian Christians brought in by Shah Abbas and settled in a suburb of the city.

Beneath these superficial differences, the two capitals had much in common. Wheeled vehicles were scarce in hilly Istanbul and nonexistent in Isfahan, which was within the broad zone where camels supplanted wheeled transport after the rise of the Arab caravan cities in the pre-Islamic centuries. In size and layout both cities were built for walking and, aside from the royal plaza in Isfahan, lacked the open spaces common in contemporary European cities. Away from the major mosque complexes, streets were narrow and irregular. Houses crowded against each other in dead-end lanes. Open areas were interior courtyards where residents could enjoy their privacy. Artisans and merchants organized themselves into guilds that had strong social and religious as well as economic bonds. The shops of each guild adjoined each other in the markets.

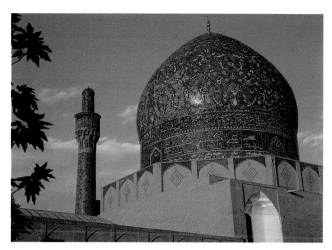

Masjid i Shah (Royal Mosque) in Isfahan   This masterpiece of Safavid architecture reflects several highlights of Iranian craftsmanship. The tile mosaics include different styles of Arabic calligraphy: a cursive version with long uprights in a band around the dome; below that, a partially squared-off script between the window grills; and below that, and on the minaret, completely orthogonal words set within polygons. The flowery pattern on the dome recalls the designs of Persian carpets. Notice the difference between this minaret and the Ottoman minarets in the illustration on page 525.   (Walter H. Hodge/Peter Arnold, Inc.)

Women were seldom seen in public, even in Istanbul's mazelike covered market or in Isfahan's long, serpentine bazaar. At home, the women's quarters—called *anderun*°, or "interior," in Iran and *harem*, or "forbidden area," in Istanbul—were separate from the public rooms where the men of the family received visitors. In both areas, low cushions, charcoal braziers for warmth, carpets, and small tables constituted most of the furnishings. In Iran and the Arab provinces, shelves and niches for books could be cut into the thick, mud-brick walls. Residences in Istanbul were usually built of wood. Glazed tile in geometric or floral patterns covered the walls of wealthy men's reception areas.

The private side of family life has left few traces, but it is apparent that women's society—consisting of wives, children, female servants, and sometimes one or more eunuchs—was not entirely cut off from the outside world. Ottoman court records reveal that women, using male agents, were very active in the urban real estate market. Often they were selling inherited shares of their father's estate, but some both bought and sold real estate on a regular basis and even established religious

---

Isfahan (is-fah-HAHN)

anderun (an-deh-ROON)

Istanbul Family on the Way to a Bath House Public baths, an important feature of Islamic cities, set different hours for men and women. Young boys, such as the lad in the turban shown here, went with their mothers and sisters. Notice that the children wear the same styles as the adults. (Osterreichische Nationalbibliothek)

endowments for pious purposes. The fact that Islamic law, unlike some European codes, permitted a wife to retain her property after marriage gave some women a stake in the general economy and a degree of independence from their spouses. Women also appeared in other types of court cases, where they often testified for themselves, for Islamic courts did not recognize the role of attorney. Although comparable Safavid court records do not survive, historians assume that a parallel situation prevailed in Iran.

European travelers commented on the veiling of women outside the home, but miniature paintings indicate that ordinary female garb consisted of a long, ample dress with a scarf or long shawl pulled tight over the forehead to conceal the hair. Lightweight trousers, either close-fitting or baggy, were often worn under the dress. This mode of dress was not far different from that of men. Poor men wore light trousers, a long shirt, a jacket, and a hat or turban. Wealthier men wore over their trousers ankle-length caftans, often closely fitted around the chest. The norm for both sexes was complete coverage of arms, legs, and hair.

Public life was almost entirely the domain of men. Poetry and art, both somewhat more elegantly developed in Isfahan than in Istanbul, were as likely to extol the charms of beardless boys as pretty women. Despite religious disapproval of homosexuality, attachments

to adolescent boys were neither unusual nor hidden. Women who appeared in public—aside from non-Muslims, the aged, and the very poor—were likely to be slaves. Miniature paintings frequently depict female dancers, musicians, and even acrobats in attitudes and costumes that range from decorous to decidedly erotic.

Despite social similarities, the overall flavors of Isfahan and Istanbul were not the same. Isfahan had its prosperous Armenian quarter across the river from the city's center, but it was not a truly cosmopolitan capital, just as the peoples of the Safavid realm were not remarkably diverse. Like other rulers of extensive land empires, Shah Abbas located his capital toward the center of his domain within comparatively easy reach of any threatened frontier. Istanbul, in contrast, was a great seaport and crossroads located on the straits separating the sultan's European and Asian possessions. People of all sorts lived or spent time in Istanbul—Venetians, Genoese, Arabs, Turks, Greeks, Armenians, Albanians, Serbs, Jews, Bulgarians, and more. In this respect Istanbul conveyed the cosmopolitan character of major seaports from London to Canton (Guangzhou) and belied the fact that its prosperity rested on the vast reach of the sultan's territories rather than on the voyages of its merchants.

Economic Crisis and Political Collapse

The silk fabrics of northern Iran, monopolized by the shahs, were the mainstay of the Safavid Empire's foreign trade. However, the manufacture that eventually became most powerfully associated with Iran was the deep-pile carpet made by knotting colored yarns around stretched warp threads. Different cities produced distinctive carpet designs. Women and girls did much of the actual knotting work.

Carpets with geometrical or arabesque designs appear in Timurid miniature paintings, but no knotted "Persian rug" survives from the pre-Safavid era. One of the earliest dated carpets was produced in 1522 to adorn the tomb of Shaikh Safi al-Din, the fourteenth-century founder of the Safavi Order. This use indicates the high value accorded these products within Iran. One German visitor to Isfahan remarked: "The most striking adornment of the banqueting hall was to my mind the carpets laid out over all three rostra in a most extravagant fashion, mostly woolen rugs from Kirman with animal patterns and woven of the finest wool."[3]

Overall, Iran's manufacturing sector was neither large nor notably productive. Most of the shah's subjects, whether Iranians, Turks, Kurds, or Arabs, lived by subsistence farming or herding. Neither area of activity recorded significant technological advances during the Safavid period. Large sections of the country were granted to the qizilbash nomads in return for their furnishing mounted warriors for the army. These lands were held by the groups in common, however, and were not subdivided into individual landholdings as in the Ottoman Empire. Thus many people in rural areas lived according to the will of a nomad chieftain who had little interest in building the agricultural economy.

The Safavids, like the Ottomans, had difficulty finding the money to pay troops armed with firearms. This crisis occurred somewhat later in Iran because of its greater distance from Europe. By the end of the sixteenth century, it was evident that a more systematic adoption of cannon and firearms in the Safavid Empire would be needed to hold off the Ottomans and the Uzbeks° (Turkish rulers who had succeeded the Timurids on Iran's Central Asian frontier; see Map 21.1). Like the Ottoman cavalry a century earlier, however, the warriors furnished by the nomad leaders were not inclined to trade in their bows for firearms. Shah Abbas responded by establishing a slave corps of year-round soldiers and arming them with guns.

The Christian converts to Islam who initially provided the manpower for the new corps were mostly captives taken in raids on Georgia in the Caucasus°. Some became powerful members of the court. They formed a counterweight to the nomad chiefs just as the Janissaries had earlier challenged the landholding Turkish cavalry in the Ottoman Empire. Under the strong hand of Shah Abbas, the inevitable rivalries and intrigues between the factions were kept under control. His successors were less fortunate.

In the late sixteenth century, the inflation caused by cheap silver spread into Iran; then overland trade through Safavid territory declined because of mismanagement of the silk monopoly after Shah Abbas's death in 1629. As a result, the country faced the unsolvable problem of finding money to pay the army and bureaucracy. Trying to unseat the nomads from their lands to regain control of taxes was more difficult and more disruptive militarily than the piecemeal dismantlement of the land-grant system in the Ottoman Empire. The nomads were still a cohesive military force, and pressure from the center simply caused them to withdraw to their mountain pastures until the pressure subsided. By 1722, the government had become so weak and commanded so little support from the nomadic groups that an army of marauding Afghans was able to capture Isfahan and effectively end Safavid rule.

Despite Iran's long coastline, the Safavids never possessed a navy. The Portuguese seized the strategic Persian Gulf island of Hormuz in 1517 and were expelled only in 1622, when the English ferried Iranian soldiers to the attack. Land-oriented rulers, the shahs relied on the English and Dutch for naval support and never considered competing with them at sea. Nadir Shah, a general who emerged from the confusion of the Safavid fall to reunify Iran briefly between 1736 and 1747, purchased some naval vessels from the English and used them in the Persian Gulf. But his navy decayed after his death, and Iran did not have a navy again until the twentieth century.

THE MUGHAL EMPIRE, 1526–1761

What distinguished the Indian empire of the Mughal° sultans from the empires of the Ottomans and Safavids was the fact that India was a land of Hindus ruled by a Muslim minority. To be sure, the Ottoman provinces in the Balkans, except for Albania and Bosnia, remained mostly Christian, but the remainder of the Ottoman Empire was overwhelmingly Muslim with small Christian and Jewish minorities. The Ottoman sultans made much of their control of Mecca and Medina and resulting supervision of the annual pilgrimage caravans just as the Safavids fostered pilgrimages to a shrine in Mashhad in northeastern Iran for their overwhelmingly Shi'ite subjects.

India, in contrast, was far from the Islamic homelands (see Map 21.1). Muslim dominion in India was the result of repeated military campaigns from the early eleventh century onward, and the Mughals had to contend with the Hindus' long-standing resentment of the destruction of their culture by Muslims. The Balkan peoples had struggled to maintain their separate identities in relation to the Byzantines, the crusaders, and one another before arrival of the Turks. The peoples of the Indian subcontinent, in contrast, had used centuries of freedom from foreign intrusion to forge a distinctive Hindu civilization that could not easily accommodate the world-view of Islam. Thus the challenge facing the Mughals was not just conquering and organizing a large territorial state but also finding a formula for Hindu-Muslim coexistence.

Uzbeks (UHZ-bex)   **Caucasus** (CAW-kuh-suhs)

Mughal (MOH-guhl)

New Year Celebration at the Court of Shah Jahan (r. 1628–1658) The Pre-Islamic Iranian tradition of celebrating the New Year (in Persian *No Ruz,* "New Day") on March 21, the vernal equinox, spread with Islamic rule. The dancing girls are a characteristically Indian aspect of the celebration. (The Royal Collection © Her Majesty Queen Elizabeth II)

Political Foundations

Babur° (1483–1530), the founder of the **Mughal Empire,** was a Muslim descendant of Timur. Though *Mughal* is Persian for "Mongol," the Timurids were of Turkic rather than Mongol origin. Timur's marriage to a descendant of Genghis Khan had earned him the Mongol designation "son-in-law," but he and his descendants, like the Ottomans, could never claim the mantle of Genghisid political legitimacy that came naturally to lesser rulers in Central Asia and in the Crimea north of the Black Sea.

Invading from Central Asia, Babur defeated the last Muslim sultan of Delhi at the Battle of Panipat in 1526. But even though this victory marked the birth of a brilliant and powerful state in India, Babur's descendants continued to think of Central Asia as their true home, from time to time expressing intentions of recapturing Samarkand and referring to its Uzbek ruler—a genuine descendant of Genghis Khan—as a governor rather than an independent sovereign.

India proved to be the primary theater of Mughal accomplishment, however. Babur's grandson **Akbar** (r. 1556–1605), a brilliant but mercurial man whose lifelong illiteracy betrayed his upbringing in the wilds of Afghanistan, established the central administration of the expanding state. Under him and his three successors—the last of whom died in 1707—all but the southern tip of India fell under Mughal rule, administered first from Agra and then from Delhi°.

Akbar granted land revenues to military officers and government officials in return for their service. Ranks, called *mansabs°,* some high and some low, entitled their holders to revenue assignments. As in the other Islamic empires, revenue grants were not considered hereditary, and the central government kept careful track of their issuance.

With a population of 100 million, a thriving trading economy based on cotton cloth, and a generally efficient administration, India under Akbar was probably the most prosperous empire of the sixteenth century (see Society and Culture: Indian Merchants in Russia). He and his successors faced few external threats and experienced generally peaceful conditions in their northern Indian heartland. Nevertheless, they were capable of squandering immense amounts of blood and treasure to subdue Hindu kings and rebels in the Deccan region or Afghans on their western frontier (see Map 21.1).

Foreign trade boomed at the port of Surat in the northwest, which also served as an embarkation point for pilgrims on their way to Mecca. Like the Safavids, the Mughals had no navy or merchant ships. The government saw the Europeans—now primarily Dutch and English, the Portuguese having lost most of their Indian ports—less as enemies than as shipmasters whose naval support could be procured as needed in return for trading privileges. It never questioned the wisdom of selling Indian cottons for European coin—no one understood how cheap silver had become in Europe—and shipping them off to European customers in English and Dutch vessels.

Babur (BAH-bur)

Delhi (DEL-ee) *mansabs* (MAN-sabz)

Indian Merchants in Russia

Overland commerce through Central Asia continued throughout this period. Few traders from eastern lands reached western Europe, but trading missions from India visited Russia, and a small but important colony of Indian merchants developed in Astrakhan, at the mouth of the Volga River, where they dealt primarily in cotton and silk cloth.

In 1675, Indian merchants in Moscow informed Russian officials that:

In the Indian state the highest demand for Russian goods is for high-priced sables—10, 20, 30 roubles a pair, good, red broad cloth and green broad cloth, red leather, walrus teeth, coral, large middle sized and small mirrors, gold and silver velvet and Turkish velvet.... And the Indian rulers love Borzoi dogs. (p. 91)

One Indian merchant of Astrakhan, Marwar Bara, wrote in 1735:

Previously there were favorable conditions for trade from India to Russia and merchants comfortably went [abroad]. Each year about two hundred exported . . . goods, and then when disturbances occurred in Persia and passage became difficult because of robbers the number of merchants declined year by year. Now exceedingly few came, less than eighty. (p. 128)

Nevertheless, in 1777 the Russian governor of Astrakhan complained:

It is not a secret that they, the Indians, having trade with Russian subjects, attempt, in exchange for Russian money and for goods, to receive Russian silver money, and especially heavy silver of the best kind with the portrait of Peter the Great.... Silver is in short supply in Russia and is aggravated by these noncitizens, the Indians. (p. 111)

How do the circumstances of Indian traders in Russia compare with those of Europeans in India? How do the goods exchanged between India and Russia compare with goods exchanged across the Indian Ocean?

Source: Stephen Frederic Dale, *Indian Merchants and Eurasian Trade, 1600–1750* (Cambridge: Cambridge University Press, 1994)

Hindus and Muslims

India had not been dominated by a single ruler since the time of Harsha Vardhana (r. 606–647). Hindus were horrified by Muslim destruction of Hindu cultural monuments, the expansion of Muslim territory, and the practice, until Akbar's time, of enslaving prisoners of war and compelling them to convert to Islam. But Hindu efforts to oppose Muslim rule were piecemeal rather than concerted. The Mughal state, in contrast, inherited traditions of unified imperial rule both from the Islamic caliphate and from the more recent examples of Genghis Khan and Timur.

Those Mongol-based traditions did not necessarily mean religious intolerance. Seventy percent of the *mansabdars°* (officials holding land revenues) appointed under Akbar were Muslim soldiers born outside India, but 15 percent were Hindus. Most of the Hindu appointees were warriors from the north called **Rajputs°**, one of whom rose to be a powerful revenue minister. Their status as mansabdars was a manifestation of the policy of religious accommodation adopted by Akbar and his successors.

Akbar was the most illustrious ruler of his dynasty. He differed from his Ottoman and Safavid counterparts—Suleiman the Magnificent and Shah Abbas the Great—in his striving for social harmony and not just for more territory and revenue. He succeeded to the throne at the age of thirteen, and his actions at first were dominated by a regent and then by his strong-minded childhood nurse. At the age of twenty, he took command of the government. He married a Rajput princess, whose name is not recorded, and welcomed her father and brother to the court in Agra.

mansabdars (man-sab-DAHRZ)

Rajputs (RAHJ-putz)

Other rulers might have used such a marriage as a means of humiliating a subject group. But Akbar signaled by this marriage his desire for reconciliation and even intermarriage between Muslims and Hindus. A year later he rescinded the head tax that Muslim rulers traditionally levied on tolerated non-Muslims. This measure was more symbolic than real because the tax had not been regularly collected, but the gesture helped cement the allegiance of the Rajputs.

Akbar longed for an heir. Much to his relief, his Rajput wife gave birth to a son in 1569, ensuring that future rulers would have both Muslim and Hindu ancestry.

Akbar ruled that in legal disputes between two Hindus, decisions would be made according to village custom or Hindu law as interpreted by local Hindu scholars. Shari'a law was in force for Muslims. Akbar made himself the legal court of last resort in a 1579 declaration that he was God's infallible earthly representative. Thus appeals could be made to Akbar personally, a possibility not usually present in Islamic jurisprudence.

Akbar also made himself the center of a new "Divine Faith" incorporating Muslim, Hindu, Zoroastrian, Sikh°, and Christian beliefs. He was strongly attracted by Sufi ideas, which permeated the religious rituals he instituted at his court. To promote serious consideration of his religious principles, he oversaw, from a catwalk high above the audience, debates among scholars of all religions assembled in his octagonal private audience chamber. When courtiers uttered the Muslim exclamation "Allahu Akbar"—"God is great"—they also understood it in its second grammatical meaning: "God is Akbar." Akbar's religious views did not survive him, but the court culture he fostered, reflecting a mixture of Muslim and Hindu traditions, flourished until his zealous great-grandson Aurangzeb° (r. 1658–1707) reinstituted many restrictions on Hindus.

Mughal and Rajput miniature paintings reveled in precise portraits of political figures and depictions of scantily clad women, even though they brought frowns to the faces of pious Muslims, who deplored the representation of human beings in art. Most of the leading painters were Hindus. In poetry, in addition to the florid style of Persian verse favored at court, a new taste developed for poetry and prose in the popular language of the Delhi region. The Turkish word *ordu,* meaning "army," led to the modern descendant of this language being called *Urdu* in Pakistan (in India it is called *Hindi*).

Akbar's policy of toleration does not explain the pattern of conversion to Islam in Mughal India. Some scholars maintain that most converts came from members of the lowest Hindu social groups, or castes, who hoped to improve their lot in life, but there is little data to confirm this theory. Others argue that Sufi brotherhoods, which developed strongly in India, led the way in converting people to Islam, but this proposition has not been proved. The most heavily Muslim regions were in the valley of the Indus River and east Bengal. The Indus center dates from the establishment of Muslim rule there as early as the eighth century.

A careful study of local records and traditions from east Bengal indicates that the eastward movement of the delta of the Ganges River and the spread of rice cultivation into forest clearings played the primary role in conversions to Islam there. Mansabdars (mostly Muslims) with land grants in east Bengal contracted with local entrepreneurs to collect a labor force, cut down the forest, and establish rice paddies. Some of the entrepreneurs were Hindus, but most were non-Sufi Muslim religious figures. Like the Hindus, those Muslims used religion, represented by the construction of mosques and shrines, as a cement to maintain their farming communities. Most natives of the region were accustomed to worshiping local forest deities rather than the main Hindu gods. So the shift to Islam represented a move to a more sophisticated, literate culture appropriate to their new status as farmers producing for the commercial rice market. Gradual religious change of this kind often produced Muslim communities whose social customs differed little from those in neighboring Hindu communities. In east Bengal, common Muslim social institutions, such as madrasas, the ulama, and law courts, were little in evidence.

Another change in Indian religious life in the Mughal period was the appearance of **Sikhism** in the Punjab region of northwest India. Nanak (1469–1539), the religion's first *guru* (spiritual teacher), stressed meditation as a means of seeking enlightenment and drew from both Muslim and Hindu imagery in his teachings. His followers formed a single community without differences of caste. However, after Aurangzeb ordered the ninth guru beheaded in 1675 for refusing to convert to Islam, the tenth and final guru dedicated himself to avenging his father's death and reorganized his followers into "the army of the pure," a religious order dedicated to defending Sikh beliefs. These devotees signaled their faith by leaving their hair uncut; carrying a comb, a steel bracelet, and a sword or dagger; and wearing military-style breeches. By the eighteenth century, the Mughals were encountering fierce opposition from the Sikhs as well as from Hindu guerrilla forces in the rugged and ravine-scarred province of Maharashtra on India's west coast.

Sikh (sick) **Aurangzeb** (ow-rang-ZEB)

Central Decay and Regional Challenges 1707–1761

Mughal power did not long survive Aurangzeb's death in 1707. Some historians consider the land-grant system a central element in the rapid decline of imperial authority, but other factors were at play as well. Aurangzeb's additions to Mughal territory in southern India were not all well integrated into the imperial structure, and a number of strong regional powers arose to challenge Mughal military supremacy. The Marathas proved a formidable enemy as they carved out a swath of territory across India's middle, and Sikhs, Hindu Rajputs, and Muslim Afghans exerted intense pressure from the northwest. A climax came in 1739 when Nadir Shah, the warlord who had seized power in Iran after the fall of the Safavids, invaded the subcontinent and sacked Delhi, which Akbar's grandson had rebuilt and beautified as the Mughal capital some decades before. The "peacock throne," the priceless, jewel-encrusted symbol of Mughal gandeur, was carried off to Iran as part of the booty. Another throne was found for the later Mughals to sit on; but their empire, which survived in name to 1857, was finished.

In 1723, Nizam al-Mulk°, the powerful vizier of the Mughal sultan, gave up on the central government and established his own nearly independent state at Hyderabad in the eastern Deccan. Other officials bearing the title *nawab*°, Anglicized as "nabob," became similarly independent in Bengal and Oudh° in the northeast, as did the Marathas farther west. In the northwest, simultaneous Iranian and Mughal weakness allowed the Afghans to establish an independent kingdom.

Some of these regional powers, and the smaller princely states that arose on former Mughal territory, were prosperous and benefited from the removal of the sultan's heavy hand. Linguistic and religious communities, freed from the religious intolerance instituted during the reign of Aurangzeb, similarly enjoyed greater opportunity for political expression. However, this disintegration of central power favored the intrusion of European adventurers.

Joseph François Dupleix° took over the presidency of the French stronghold of Pondicherry° in 1741 and began a new phase of European involvement in India. He captured the English trading center of Madras and used his small contingent of European and European-trained Indian troops to become a power broker in southern India. Though offered the title *nawab,* Dupleix preferred to

operate behind the scenes, using Indian princes as puppets. His career ended in 1754 when he was called home. Deeply involved in wars in Europe, the French government was unwilling to pursue further adventures in India. Dupleix's departure opened the way for the British, whose ventures in India are described in Chapter 26.

TRADE EMPIRES IN THE INDIAN OCEAN, 1600–1729

It is no coincidence that the Mughal, Safavid, and Ottoman Empires declined simultaneously in the seventeenth and eighteenth centuries. Complex changes in military technology and in the world economy, along with the increasing difficulty of basing an extensive land empire on military forces paid through land grants, affected them all adversely. The opposite was true for sea faring countries intent on turning trade networks into maritime empires. Improvements in ship design, navigation accuracy, and the use of cannon gave an ever-increasing edge to European powers competing with local seafaring peoples. Moreover, the development of joint-stock companies in which many merchants pooled their capital provided a flexible and efficient financial instrument for exploiting new possibilities. The English East India Company was founded in 1600, the Dutch East India Company in 1602.

Although the Ottomans, Safavids, and the Mughals did not seriously contest the growth of Portuguese and then Dutch, English, and French maritime power, the majority of non-European shipbuilders, captains, sailors, and traders were Muslim. Groups of Armenian, Jewish, and Hindu traders were also active, but they remained almost as aloof from the Europeans as the Muslims did. The presence in every port of Muslims following the same legal traditions and practicing their faith in similar ways cemented the Muslims' trading network. Islam, from its very outset in the life and preachings of Muhammad (570–632), was always congenial to trade and traders. Unlike Hinduism, it was a proselytizing religion, a factor that encouraged the growth of coastal Muslim communities as local non-Muslims were drawn into Muslim commercial activities, converted, and intermarried with Muslims from abroad.

Although European missionaries, particularly the Jesuits, tried to extend Christianity into Asia and Africa

---

Nizam al-Mulk (nee-ZAHM al-MULK)   *nawab* (NAH-wab)
Oudh (OW-ad)   Dupleix (doo-PLAY)
Pondicherry (pon-dir-CHEH-ree)

Map 21.2   European Colonization in the Indian Ocean to 1750   Since Portuguese explorers were the first Europeans to reach India by rounding Africa, Portugal gained a strong foothold in both areas. Rival Spain was barred from colonizing the region by the Treaty of Tordesillas in 1494, which limited Spanish efforts to lands west of a line drawn through the mid-Atlantic Ocean. The line carried around the globe provided justification of Spanish colonization in the Philippines. French, British, and Dutch colonies date from after 1600 when joint stock companies provided a new stimulus for overseas commerce.

(see Chapters 17 and 22), most Europeans, the Portuguese excepted, were less inclined than the Muslims were to treat local converts or the offspring of mixed marriages as full members of their communities. As a consequence, Islam spread extensively into East Africa and Southeast Asia during precisely the time of rapid European commercial expansion. Even without the support of the Muslim land empires, Islam became a source of resistance to growing European domination.

Muslims in the East Indies

Historians disagree about the chronology and manner of Islam's spread in Southeast Asia. Arab traders were well known in southern China as early as the eighth century, so Muslims probably reached the East Indies at a similarly early date. Nevertheless, the dominance of Indian cultural influences in the area for several centuries thereafter indicates that early Muslim visitors had little impact on local beliefs. Clearer indications of conversion and the formation of Muslim communities date from roughly the fourteenth century. The strongest overseas linkage is to the port of Cambay in India (see Map 21.2) rather than to the Arab world. Islam took root first in port cities and in some royal courts and spread inland slowly, possibly transmitted by itinerant Sufis.

Although appeals to the Ottoman sultan for support against the Europeans ultimately proved of little use, Islam as a political ideology strengthened resistance to Portuguese, Spanish, and Dutch intruders. When the Spaniards conquered the Philippines during the decades following the establishment of their first fort in 1565 (see Chapter 17), they encountered Muslims on the southern island of Mindanao° and the nearby Sulu archipelago. They called them "Moros," the Spanish term for their old enemies, the Muslims of North Africa. In the ensuing Moro wars, the Spaniards portrayed the Moros as greedy pirates who raided non-Muslim territories for slaves. In fact, they were political, religious, and commercial competitors whose perseverance enabled them to establish the Sulu Empire based in the southern Philippines, one of the strongest states in Southeast Asia from 1768 to 1848.

Other local kingdoms that looked on Islam as a force to counter the aggressive Christianity of the Europeans included the actively proselytizing Brunei° Sultanate in northern Borneo and the **Acheh° Sultanate** in northern Sumatra. At its peak in the early seventeenth century, Acheh succeeded Malacca as the main center of Islamic expansion in Southeast Asia. It prospered from trade in pepper and cotton cloth from Gujarat in India. Acheh declined after the Dutch seized Malacca from Portugal in 1641.

How well Islam was understood in these Muslim kingdoms is open to question. In Acheh, for example, a series of women ruled between 1641 and 1699. This practice came to an end when local Muslim scholars obtained a ruling from scholars in Mecca and Medina that Islam did not approve of female rulers. This ruling became a turning point after which scholarly understandings of Islam gained greater prominence in the East Indies.

Historians have theorized that the first propagators of Islam in Southeast Asia were merchants, Sufi preachers, or both. The scholarly vision of Islam, however, took root in the sixteenth century by way of pilgrims returning from years of study in Mecca and Medina. Islam was the primary force in the dissemination of writing in the region. Some of the returning pilgrims wrote in Arabic, others in Malay or Javanese. As Islam continued to spread, *adat,* a form of Islam rooted in pre-Muslim religious and social practices, retained its preeminence in rural areas over practices centered on the Shari'a, the religious law. But the royal courts in the port cities began to heed the views of the pilgrim teachers, as in their condemnation of female rulers. Though different in many ways, both varieties of Islam provided believers with a firm basis of identification in the face of the growing European presence. Christian missionaries gained most of their converts in regions that had not yet converted to Islam, such as the northern Philippines.

Muslims in East Africa

The East African ports that the Portuguese began to visit in the fifteenth century were governed by Muslim rulers but were not linked politically (see Map 21.2). People living in the millet and rice lands of the Swahili Coast—from the Arabic *sawahil°* meaning "coasts"—had little contact with those in the dry hinterlands. Throughout this period, the East African lakes region and the highlands of Kenya witnessed unprecedented migration and relocation of peoples because of drought conditions that persisted from the late sixteenth through most of the seventeenth century.

Cooperation among the trading ports of Kilwa, Mombasa, and Malindi was hindered by the thick bush country that separated the cultivated tracts of coastal

Mindanao (min-duh-NOW)   Brunei (BROO-nie)
Acheh (AH-cheh)

sawahil (suh-WAH-hil)

Portuguese Fort Guarding Musqat Harbor   Musqat in Oman and Aden in Yemen, the best harbors in southern Arabia, were targets for imperial navies trying to establish dominance in the Indian Ocean. Mosqat's harbor is small and circular with one narrow entrance overlooked by this fortress. The palace of the sultan of Oman is still located at the opposite end of the harbor.
(Robert Harding Picture Library)

land and by the fact that the ports competed with one another in the export of ivory; ambergris° (a whale byproduct used in perfumes); and forest products such as beeswax, copal tree resin, and wood (Kilwa also exported gold). In the eighteenth century, slave trading, primarily to Arabian ports but also to India, increased in importance. Because Europeans—the only peoples who kept consistent records of slave-trading activities—played a minor role in this slave trade, few records have survived to indicate its extent. Perhaps the best estimate is that 2.1 million slaves were exported between 1500 and 1890, a little over 12.5 percent of the total traffic in African slaves during that period (see Chapter 20).

The Portuguese conquered all of the coastal ports from Mozambique northward except Malindi, with whose ruler Portugal cooperated. A Portuguese description of the ruler indicates some of the cloth and metal goods that Malindi imported, as well as some local manufactures:

> The King wore a robe of damask trimmed with green satin and a rich [cap]. He was seated on two cushioned chairs of bronze, beneath a rough sunshade of crimson satin attached to a pole. An old man, who attended him as a page, carried a short sword in a silver sheath. There were many players on [horns], and two trumpets of ivory richly carved and of the size of a man, which were blown through a hole in the side, and made sweet harmony with the [horns].[4]

Initially, the Portuguese favored the port of Malindi, which caused the decline of Kilwa and Mombasa. Repeatedly plagued by local rebellion, Portuguese power suffered severe blows when the Arabs of **Oman** in southeastern Arabia captured their south Arabian stronghold at Musqat (1650) and then went on in support of African resistance to seize Mombasa (1698), which had become the Portuguese capital in East Africa. The Portuguese briefly retook Mombasa but lost control permanently in 1729. From then on, the Portuguese had to content themselves with Mozambique in Africa and a few remaining ports in India (Goa) and farther east (Macao and Timor).

The Omanis created a maritime empire of their own, but one that worked in greater cooperation with the African populations. The Bantu language of the coast, broadened by the absorption of Arabic, Persian, and Portuguese loanwords, developed into **Swahili°,** which was spoken throughout the region. Arabs and other Muslims who settled in the region intermarried with local families, giving rise to a mixed population that played an important role in developing a distinctive Swahili culture.

Islam also spread in the southern Sudan in this period, particularly in the dry areas away from the Nile River. This growth coincided with a waning of Ethiopian power as a result of Portugal's stifling of trade in the Red Sea. Yet no significant contact developed between the emerging Muslim Swahili culture and that of the Muslims in the Sudan, to the north.

---

ambergris (AM-ber-grees)

Swahili (swah-HEE-lee)

The Coming of the Dutch

The Dutch played a major role in driving the Portuguese from their possessions in the East Indies. They were better organized than the Portuguese through the Dutch East India Company (see Chapter 20). Just as the Portuguese had tried to dominate the trade in spices, so the Dutch concentrated at first on the spice-producing islands of Southeast Asia. The Portuguese had seized Malacca, a strategic town on the narrow strait at the end of the Malay Peninsula, from a local Malay ruler in 1511 (see Chapter 17). The Dutch took it away from them in 1641, leaving Portugal little foothold in the East Indies except the islands of Ambon° and Timor (see Map 21.2).

Although the United Netherlands was one of the least autocratic countries of Europe, the governors-general appointed by the Dutch East India Company deployed almost unlimited powers in their efforts to maintain their trade monopoly. They could even order the execution of their own employees for "smuggling" –that is, trading on their own. Under strong governors-general, the Dutch fought a series of wars against Acheh and other local kingdoms on Sumatra and Java. In 1628 and 1629, their new capital at **Batavia,** now the city of Jakarta on Java, was besieged by a fleet of fifty ships belonging to the sultan of Mataram°, a Javanese kingdom. The Dutch held out with difficulty and eventually prevailed when the sultan was unable to get effective help from the English.

Suppressing local rulers, however, was not enough to control the spice trade once other European countries adopted Dutch methods, became more knowledgeable about where goods might be acquired, and started to send more ships to Southeast Asia. In the course of the eighteenth century, therefore, the Dutch gradually turned from being a middleman for Southeast Asian producers and European buyers to being a producer of crops in areas they controlled, notably in Java. Javanese teak forests yielded high-quality lumber, and coffee, transplanted from Yemen, grew well in the hilly regions of western Java. In this new phase of colonial export production, Batavia developed from being the headquarters town of a far-flung enterprise to being the administrative capital of a conquered land.

Beyond the East Indies, the Dutch utilized their discovery of a band of powerful eastward-blowing winds (called the "Roaring Forties" because they blow throughout the year between 40 and 50 degrees south latitude) to reach Australia in 1606. In 1642 and 1643 Abel Tasman became the first European to set foot on Tasmania and New Zealand and to sail around Australia, signaling European involvement in that region (see Chapter 26).

Ambon (am-BOHN)   Mataram (MAH-tah-ram)

CONCLUSION

That a major shift in world economic and political alignments was well under way by the late seventeenth century was scarcely perceivable in those parts of Asia and Africa ruled by the Ottoman and Mughal sultans and the Safavid shahs. They focused their efforts on conquering more and more land, sometimes at the expense of Christian Europe or Hindu India, but also at one another's expense since the Sunni-Shi'ite division justified Iranian attacks on its neighbors and vice versa.

To be sure, more and more trade was being carried in European vessels, particularly after the advent of joint-stock companies in 1600; and Europeans had enclaves in a handful of port cities and islands. But the age-old tradition of Asia was that imperial wealth came from control of broad expanses of agricultural land. Except in the case of state monopolies, such as Iranian silk, governments did not greatly concern themselves with what farmers planted. They relied mostly on land taxes, usually indirectly collected via holders of land-grants or tax farmers, rather than on customs duties or control of markets to fill the government coffers.

With ever-increasing military expenditures, these taxes fell short of the rulers' needs. Few people realized, however, that this was a problem basic to the entire economic system rather than a temporary revenue shortfall. Imperial courtiers pursued their luxurious ways, poetry and the arts continued to flourish, and the quality of manufacturing and craft production remained generally high. Eighteenth century European observers, luxuriating in the prosperity gained from their ever increasing control of the Indian Ocean, marvelled no less at the riches and industry of these eastern lands than at the fundamental weakness of their political and military systems.

■ Key Terms

Ottoman Empire	Mughal Empire
Suleiman the Magnificent	Akbar
Janissary	*mansabs*
devshirme	Rajputs
Tulip Period	Sikhism
Safavid Empire	Acheh Sultanate
Shi'ite Islam	Oman
Hidden Imam	Swahili
Shah Abbas I	Batavia

■ Suggested Reading

The best comprehensive and comparative account of the post-Mongol Islamic land empires, with an emphasis on social history, is Ira Lapidus, *A History of Islamic Societies* (1988). For a work of similar scope concentrating on intellectual history see Marshall G. S. Hodgson, *The Venture of Islam*, vol. 3, *The Gunpowder Empires and Modern Times* (1974).

Ottoman origins are well covered in Cemal Kafadar, *Between Two Worlds* (1995). On the Ottoman Empire, the standard political history is Stanford J. Shaw, *History of the Ottoman Empire and Modern Turkey*, vol. 1, *Empire of the Ghazis: The Rise and Decline of the Ottoman Empire, 1280–1808* (1976). Jason Goodwin, *Lords of the Horizons: A History of the Ottoman Empire* (1999), offers a more readable and journalistic account. For a collection of articles on nonpolitical matters see Halil Inalcik and Donald Quataert, eds., *An Economic and Social History of the Ottoman Empire, 1300—1914* (1994).

The world's foremost Ottoman historian, Halil Inalcik, analyzes the history and structure of the empire in *The Ottoman Empire: The Classical Age, 1300–1600* (1989). For a sociological analysis of change in the seventeenth century see Karen Barkey, *Bandits and Bureaucrats* (1994).

Among the specialized studies of cities and regions that give a good sense of some of the major changes in Ottoman society and economy after the sixteenth century are Daniel Goffman, *Izmir and the Levantine World, 1550–1650* (1990); Abraham Marcus, *The Middle East on the Eve of Modernity: Aleppo in the Eighteenth Century* (1989); and Bruce McGowan, *Economic Life in the Ottoman Empire: Taxation, Trade, and the Struggle for Land, 1600–1800* (1981).

Questions relating to religious minorities in the Ottoman Empire are best covered by the articles in Benjamin Braude and Bernard Lewis, eds., *Christians and Jews in the Ottoman Empire: The Functioning of a Plural Society* (1982). The role of women in the governance of the empire is skillfully treated by Leslie Pierce, *The Imperial Harem: Women and Sovereignty in the Ottoman Empire* (1993). Ralph S. Hattox, *Coffee and Coffeehouses: The Origins of a Social Beverage in the Medieval Near East* (1988), is an excellent contribution to Ottoman social history.

The most comprehensive treatment of the history of Safavid Iran is in the articles in Peter Jackson and Laurence Lockhart, eds., *The Cambridge History of Iran*, vol. 6, *The Timurid and Safavid Periods* (1986). The articles by Hans Roemer in this volume provide the best political narratives of the pre-Safavid and Safavid periods. Roger Savory's important article on the structure of the Safavid state is available in a more extensive form in his *Iran Under the Safavids* (1980).

For the artistic side of Safavid history, abundantly illustrated, see Anthony Welch, *Shah Abbas and the Arts of Isfahan* (1973). Said Amir Arjomand, *The Shadow of God and the Hidden Imam: Religion, Political Order, and Societal Change in Shiite Iran from the Beginning to 1890* (1984), contains the best analysis of the complicated relationship between Shi'ism and monarchy. Safavid economic history is not well developed, but useful studies have been published by Ann K. S. Lambton, *Landlord and Peasant in Persia: A Study of Land Tenure and Land Revenue Administration*, rev. ed. (1991), and Mehdi Keyvani, *Artisans and Guild Life in the Later Safavid Period: Contribution to the Social-Economic History of Persia* (1982).

A highly readable work that situates the Mughal Empire within the overall history of the subcontinent is Stanley Wolpert, *A New History of India*, 4th ed. (1993). For a broad treatment of the entire development of Islamic society in India with emphasis on the Mughal period see S. M. Ikram, *History of Muslim Civilization in India and Pakistan* (1989). Wheeler Thackston has made a lively translation of Babur's autobiography in *The Baburnama: Memoirs of Babur, Prince and Emperor* (1996). For a comprehensive history of the Mughals see John F. Richards, *The Mughal Empire* (1993). Irfan Habib has edited an extensive collection of articles on the Mughal Empire in its prime entitled *Akbar and His India* (1997). For the history of the Sikhs see W. H. McLeod *The Sikhs: History, Religion, and Society* (1989). Two specialized works on the economic and trading history of India are Ashin Das Gupta and M. N. Pearson, eds., *India and the Indian Ocean, 1500–1800* (1987), and Stephen Frederic Dale, *Indian Merchants and Eurasian Trade, 1600–1750* (1994).

The history of East Africa in this period is not well documented, but B. A. Ogot, ed., *UNESCO General History of Africa*, vol. 5, *Africa from the Sixteenth to the Eighteenth Century* (1992), provides a useful collection of articles. See also Tom Spear *The Swahili*, (1984) and James de Vere Allen, *Swahili Origins* (1993).

For a brief, general introduction to the relations between the Muslim land empires and the development of Indian Ocean trade see Patricia Risso, *Merchants and Faith: Muslim Commerce and Culture in the Indian Ocean* (1995). Esmond Bradley Martin and Chryssee Perry Martin have written a popular and well-illustrated work on the western Indian Ocean entitled *Cargoes of the East: The Ports, Trade and Culture of the Arabian Seas and Western Indian Ocean* (1978). C. R. Boxer, *The Dutch Seaborne Empire, 1600–1800* (1973), is a classic account of all aspects of Dutch maritime expansion.

■ Notes

1. Quoted in Sarah Searight, *The British in the Middle East* (New York: Atheneum 1970), 36.
2. Daniel Goffman, *Izmir and the Levantine World, 1550–1650* (Seattle: University of Washington Press, 1990), 52.
3. Quoted in Peter Jackson and Laurence Lockhart, eds., *The Cambridge History of Iran*, vol. 6, *The Timurid and Safavid Periods* (New York: Cambridge University Press, 1986), 703.
4. Esmond Bradley Martin and Chryssee Perry Martin, *Cargoes of the East: The Ports, Trade and Culture of the Arabian Seas and Western Indian Ocean* (1978), 17.

22

EASTERN EURASIA,
1500–1800

New Patterns of Contact in Eurasia • The Triumph of the Russian Empire •
The Late Ming and Early Qing Empires, 1500–1800 • Decentralization and
Innovation in Tokugawa Japan, to 1800

ENVIRONMENT AND TECHNOLOGY: Women and Tokugawa Technology

SOCIETY AND CULTURE: Style and Conversion: Christian Rivalries in Beijing

Russian Ambassadors to Holland Display Their Furs, 1500s Representatives from Muscovy impressed
the court of the German prince Maximillian II of Regensburg with their sable coats and caps.

*I*n the 1650s, two enormous and expanding empires battled for control of Siberia, the Amur° River basin, and the Pacific coast of northern Asia. Hardy Russian scouts, mostly Cossacks, came east across the tundra, hoping to stake an early claim to the great Amur waterway. They built wooden forts on its northern bank, but they were countered by Manchu agents of the Qing° Empire based in China, which hoped to secure Qing territories north of Korea and to secure the same stretch of Pacific coast the Russians sought. The Manchus built wooden forts on the southern bank of the Amur.

Neither empire sent large forces into the Amur territories, and the contest was mostly a struggle for the goodwill of the local Evenk and Dagur peoples. The Qing emperor emphasized the importance of treading lightly in the struggle and well understood the principles of espionage:

> Upon reaching the lands of the Evenks and the Dagurs you will send to announce that you have come to hunt deer. Meanwhile, keep a careful record of the distance and go, while hunting, along the northern bank of the Amur until you come by the shortest route to the town of Russian settlement at Albazin. Thoroughly reconnoitre its location and situation. I don't think the Russians will take a chance on attacking you. If they offer you food, accept it and show your gratitude. If they do attack you, don't fight back. In that case, lead your people and withdraw into our own territories. For I have a plan of my own.[1]

That delicacy gives a false impression of the intensity of the struggle between these two great empires. The contest was partly for dominance in the new northeast Asian economy of furs, timber, and metals concentrated in Siberia, Manchuria, and Yakutsk. But even without the attraction of those specific resources, the Amur River would have been critical in the interplay of the two empires, because each had an overriding need to protect itself against the other. The kingdoms of Europe, and even Europe's emerging sea-based empires, were small in territory and weak in economic influence in comparison with these titanic Eurasian empires.

Where the Russian and Qing Empires faced each other—in Central Asia, in Mongolia, and in Northeast Asia—they had to expend great resources conquering and defending lands that in the long run yielded very little profit. But for either to have flinched would have meant disaster at the hands of the other.

In 1689, the Qing and Russian Empires formalized their stand-off with a treaty establishing a border and a set of customs regulations. Russia was denied access to the Pacific coast east of the Amur, but the Russians exploited a more northerly route to explore the North Pacific and colonize the northwestern coast of North America. The Russian and Qing Empires still sought ways around each other but apparently were evenly matched. Only the intrusion of the smaller, product-poor empires of Europe eventually upset the balance and permitted one of the Eurasian giants to outflank the other.

The Russian and Qing Empires were part of a regional power system in which size, agriculture, and infrastructure for overland communication and transport were of the greatest importance. In their struggle to maintain their power when challenged by the new empires of Europe, the Russian and Qing Empires faced common problems and experienced similar outcomes. The response of Japan was spectacularly different. That small, relatively remote nation had been a minor player in Asian affairs but was able to withstand economic and political changes more effectively than Asia's greatest empires.

As you read this chapter, ask yourself the following questions:

- What did the Russian and Qing Empires have in common? How do their similarities explain the tensions between them?

- What were the Russian and Qing attitudes toward Europe in the times of Peter the Great and Emperor Kangxi? What were the long-term consequences of these attitudes?

- What explains the comparative speed of Japanese economic and technological development in the 1700s?

Amur (AH-moor)   Qing (ching)

CHRONOLOGY

	Russia	China and Central Asia	Korea and Japan
1500			
	1547 Ivan IV tsar		
	1582 Cossacks conquer Khanate of Sibir		1582 Japanese invasion of Korea
1600		1601 Matteo Ricci active in Ming China	1600 Decisive battle begins Tokugawa Shogunate
	1613–1645 Rule of Mikhail, the first Romanov tsar	1644 Qing conquest of Beijing	1649 Closing of Japan
		1662–1722 Rule of Emperor Kangxi	
	1689–1725 Rule of Peter the Great	1689 Treaty of Nerchinsk with Russia	
		1691 Qing control of Inner Mongolia	1702 Trial of the Forty-seven Ronin
1700			
	1712 St. Petersburg becomes Russia's capital		
		1736–1795 Rule of Emperor Qianlong	
		1755 Qing conquest of Turkestan	
	1762–1796 Rule of Catherine the Great		1792 Russian ships first spotted off the coast of Japan
	1799 Alaska becomes a Russian colony		

NEW PATTERNS OF CONTACT IN EURASIA

Between 1500 and 1800 several fundamental factors transformed the routes of contact and commerce in Eurasia. During the period of Mongol domination of Eurasia in the thirteenth century, overland trade connecting Iran, southern Russia, and China had thrived. But the Ming rulers, who came to power in China in 1368, did not control Central Asia as the Mongols had done. Instead, local leaders in Central Asia fought for dominance over the trading routes and commercial centers. After 1500, no single power controlled all of Central Asia, and no unified economic policy protected and promoted trade. Large and ambitious empires based in the Middle East, in Russia, and in China competed for control of parts of Central Asia, and this competition deepened their conflicts with the remaining Mongol groups and further depressed both travel and profitable trade.

Samarkand°, Bukhara°, Kashgar° and other oasis cities that had been rich and cosmopolitan in the days when overland trade was vigorous became isolated. Their governors were often hostile to outside influences. As the 1500s passed, the transporting of many goods by caravan between East Asia and the Middle East was neither cheap nor reliable.

The troubles afflicting Central Asia in this period might have been overcome in the interests of profitable trade, but a new venue of commerce had opened: Along the southern and eastern coasts of Eurasia, merchants from Europe, the Middle East, and Asia were taking advantage of the new global trade connections. Seaborne trade was now cheaper, faster, and more reliable than overland trade. Goods once transported across the interior of Eurasia could be moved more efficiently around its edges, and many new goods were available from the sea-connected economies.

Samarkand (SAM-mar-kahnd)   **Bukhara** (boo-CAR-ruh)
Kashgar (kahsh-gar)

Ancient Asian ports that had become rich from centuries of trade found new economic stimulation from the development of European commerce. China, and later Japan, were also beneficiaries of this new trade in the old ports. And after 1700, the development of a global commercial interest in the Pacific magnified the importance of the sea and control of its main trade routes. China, Japan, and other coastal economies of East Asia participated in the trade and sought means of cushioning the effects of globalization on their own economies and societies. Russia, in contrast, had to enter a period of renewed and more militant expansion or risk being left out of the Pacific trade.

The Land-Based Empires of Eurasia

The Portuguese, Spanish, and Dutch Empires relied on the sea for contact with their colonies. As relatively small empires, they had few major strategic worries and could exercise a wide range of options in their territorial roamings and commercial and military activities. For the Ottoman, Russian, Mughal, and Ming Empires, things were very different. They were land-based empires and much larger than the sea-based empires of Europe. Their self-defense was extremely expensive, they had fewer choices than their smaller European contemporaries about where to expand and how to enrich themselves after they expanded.

Even though the commercial importance of Central Asia had declined steeply by 1500, the region remained the strategic center of gravity for the land-based Eurasian empires, because this was where each was most vulnerable to attack by an ambitious rival. Much of Central Asia, however, was arid steppes or desert, crossed by formidable mountain ranges. Maintaining garrisons in these regions was extremely expensive, for food, weapons, animals, and even building materials had to be brought in from far away. The best hope of eventually making these territories self-supporting lay in the development of agriculture and mining, which required the introduction of large-scale irrigation, crops able to thrive in cold, dry climates, extensive new roads, and large numbers of settlers or prisoners to serve as laborers. All the land-based empires achieved some success in agriculture and mining, but the costs were so steep that often there was no profit.

The challenge to make large, unprofitable areas in the land-based Eurasian empires self-supporting through environmental change strengthened two tendencies that were already strong. First, it reinforced the emphasis on agriculture as the predominant source of wealth and government tax revenues. Although these empires were interested in new industries and sea communications, they had little choice but to concentrate on agriculture. Second, it reinforced the tendency toward political centralization, which was to be important in the Russian and Qing Empires in the late 1600s. If the herculean task of environmental transformation across Central Asia and parts of northern Asia was to be achieved, imperial governments had to be in full command of the massive resources necessary for development of the infrastructure. Forced labor by the domestic population persisted in the Russian and Qing Empires after it was abandoned in Europe; in Russia serfdom became more brutal and widespread in the seventeenth and eighteenth centuries than ever before. Rulers and their advisers believed that the strategic concerns were so great that there could be no interference in policy-making from the aristocracy, low-level bureaucrats, or anyone else.

In the long run, these empires were at a disadvantage in the competition with the sea-based empires of Europe. The Europeans concentrated on the colonization of profitable areas, linked the development of commerce to the enrichment of their central governments, and enlisted the aid of joint-stock companies and other semiprivate organizations to acquire and develop territories. Between 1500 and about 1800, the land-based empires of Eurasia were the largest administrative and economic systems in the world, but they posed more of a danger to each other than they faced from any of the sea-based empires of Europe.

New Global Influences: The Society of Jesus and the East India Companies

The European entry into sea trade and communications that so challenged Russia and the Qing was not at first a project of empires or even of states. In the sixteenth and seventeenth centuries, new global organizations such as the Society of Jesus and the East India Companies created ties between Asia, Europe, and the Americas. The **Jesuits** often preceded traders, explorers, and conquerors to those regions that were newly known to Europe. One of the first Jesuits, Francis Xavier, went to India in the mid-sixteenth century looking for converts and later traveled throughout Southeast and East Asia. He spent two years in Japan and died in 1552 in China. Following Xavier, other Jesuits had a significant influence in China and presented to Europeans an intriguing picture of Asian life.

China reaped some material benefits from contact with the Jesuits. Chinese converts to Catholicism were important in introducing European techniques of crop

TROMBE DA ROTA PER CAVAR AQVA

圖 八 第

From the Jesuit Library at Beijing
Jesuits such as Matteo Ricci were willing to share books on technology and science with Chinese scholars. But without firsthand experience it was impossible for Chinese translators to convey how the devices actually worked. Here, a man walking in a wheel drives a shaft that changes the pressure inside two pumps. In the Chinese translation of the drawing, the mechanisms were all lost. (Left: From Zonca, *Trombe da Rota per Vavar Aqua* [1607]. Right: "Diagram Number Eight" from *Qi tushuo* [*Illustrations on Energy*] [1627]. Both courtesy of Joseph Needham, *Science and Civilization in China*, vol. 4)

production, irrigation, and engineering. The outstanding Jesuit of late Ming China, Matteo Ricci° (1552–1610), became expert in the Chinese language and an accomplished scholar of the Confucian classics. He and other Jesuits in China made a deep impression on the Ming elites at Beijing° and also in the wealthy, cosmopolitan cities of the Yangzi River delta and the southern China coast. Ricci himself was deeply affected by Chinese literature and philosophy. In his time and after, Jesuits remained important in transmitting to Europe knowledge of Chinese classical culture and translations of Chinese philosophical works. The high regard in which many European thinkers of the 1600s and early 1700s held the rulers of China was very much due to the activities of the Jesuits. The Society of Jesus was the most prominent transmitter of European science and technology to China, and of Chinese philosophy and literature to Europe.

European merchants arrived in East Asia by the time of the Jesuits arrival. First came the Portuguese, who after 1500 dominated the spice trade of the Moluccas and Java and the trade routes around India. The Spanish also were interested in the trade and established a small base on the island of Taiwan, off the coast of southeast China

(and not at the time part of the Ming Empire). Soon after 1600, the Dutch dislodged the Portuguese and Spanish from Taiwan. To secure their influence in East Asia and to discredit their rivals, representatives of the Dutch East India company (VOC) willingly complied with Chinese rituals by which foreigners were supposed to acknowledge the moral superiority of the emperor of China. They performed the ritual *kowtow* (in which the visitor knocked his head on the floor while crawling toward the throne) to the Ming emperor in China. The Dutch also got along well with the rulers of Japan and retained exclusive permission to live on the island of Deshima°, off Nagasaki°, after other Europeans were banned from the country. Outside Japan, however, the VOC faced a strong rival in the East India Company of England, chartered by Queen Elizabeth I in 1600.

The European trading companies and the Jesuits are examples of the global organizations that became conduits of trade and knowledge between Asia and Europe. The two-way communication that they made possible sparked enormous changes in how the opposite ends of Eurasia related to each other. But in the 1700s these organizations were viewed with suspicion by imperial authorities in Europe as well as in Asia.

Matteo Ricci (ma-TAY-o REE-chee) **Beijing** (bay-JING) **Deshima** (DUH-shee-ma) **Nagasaki** (nah-gah-SAH-kee)

The Russian Empire
- Russia in 1533
- Russia in 1598
- Russia in 1721
- Russia in 1796
- ■ Fort

PACIFIC OCEAN

Novo Arkhangelsk (Sitka)
TLINGIT

BRITISH NORTH AMERICA (CANADA)

RUSSIAN AMERICA (ALASKA)

ALEUTS
INUIT
INUIT
INUIT

Bering Strait
Bering Sea

GREENLAND

ARCTIC OCEAN

CHUKCHI

KORYAKS

Petropavlovsk
ALEUTS
Kamchatka Peninsula

Zashiversk

Okhotsk
Sea of Okhotsk

Sakalin

Novaya Zemlya
Kara Sea
Barents Sea

S I B E R I A

Zhigansk
Yakutsk
EVENKI
YAKUTS
LAMUTS

EVENKI

Amur
Nerchinsk

MANCHURIA

SWEDEN

FINLAND

Arkhangelsk

Obdorsk
SAMOYEDS
OSTYAKS

TUNGUSY
OSTYAKS

Bratsk
Krasnoyarsk
Irkutsk

St. Petersburg
Baltic Sea
Novgorod
Riga

Verkhoturye
TARTARS
Surgut

Biysk

MONGOLIA

PRUSSIA

Moscow
Smolensk
Nizhni Novgorod
Samara
POLAND
Kiev
UKRAINIANS
Saratov
COSSACKS

KAZAKS

QING EMPIRE

AUSTRIA
COSSACKS

Aral Sea

OTTOMAN EMPIRE
Black Sea
GEORGIA
Caspian Sea

TIBET

BHUTAN

AFGHANISTAN

NEPAL

BURMA

PERSIA

I N D I A

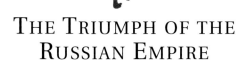

THE TRIUMPH OF THE RUSSIAN EMPIRE

The shift in intensity of exchange toward the seas and away from inland Asia presented both challenges and opportunities to the rising Russian Empire. The fragmentation of political power in Central Asia lessened the pressure on the Russian rulers to defend themselves on their southern border with Turkestan. Instead, they could turn their attention toward eastern Eurasia, including Mongolia and **Siberia,** and even to the Pacific coast. It was still necessary to maintain western and southern boundaries against the Ottoman Empire. But the rise of the European empires diminished this need somewhat, because the Europeans not only held the line against further Ottoman expansion in the Balkans but began to challenge and distract the Ottomans in the eastern Mediterranean.

The Rise of Romanov Power

After the dissolution of Mongol power in Russia, the city of Moscow became the foundation for a new state, **Muscovy°,** the territory surrounding the city of Moscow. By 1500, Muscovy was the dominant political force in the lands that had been controlled by the Kievan state. The process of unification forced by Muscovy was very difficult. By the mid-sixteenth century, Novgorod, which had been independent since the twelfth century and had maintained close connections with Sweden, was absorbed. To mark the extension of Muscovy and of his personal power, the Muscovite ruler Ivan IV ("the Terrible") assumed the title **tsar** (from "caesar") in 1547. Within a few years Ivan expanded Russia's borders far to the east through the conquest of the Khanates of Kazan and Astrakhan and the northern Caucausus region (see Map 22.1).

The westward extension of the territories ruled by Ivan IV and his successors did not progress much thereafter. Sweden and Poland, the dominant powers in north-

Map 22.1 The Expansion of Russia, 1500–1800 Sweden and Poland initially blocked Russian expansion in Europe, while the Ottoman Empire blocked the southwest. In the sixteenth century, Russia began to expand east, toward Siberia and the Pacific Ocean. By the end of the rule of Catherine the Great in 1796, Russia encompassed all of northern and northeastern Eurasia.

eastern Europe, prevented Russian expansion westward. Instead, Russia had to defend itself more strenuously on the European front. In the early seventeenth century Swedish and Polish forces briefly occupied Moscow on separate occasions, and Russian politics were rent by prolonged and deadly rivalries for the tsarship.

In the midst of this "Time of Troubles" the old line of Muscovite rulers was finally deposed, and the Russian aristocracy—the *boyar*s°—allowed one of their own, **Mikhail Romanov°,** to become tsar (r. 1613–1645). But this dynastic change did not resolve the social and political tensions resulting from boyar resistance to further centralization of political power. Equally destabilizing were attacks from Sweden, Poland, and the Ottoman Empire.

The early Romanov rulers realized that consolidation of their own authority and successful competition with neighboring powers went together. Options for Russian expansion were limited. The Ottoman Empire controlled the Balkans, and the Safavid rulers of Iran dominated southern Central Asia. Trade with Europe was blocked as well because Sweden controlled the Baltic Sea, the Ottomans the Black Sea, and Iran the access to the surviving overland routes. As we will see, the obvious direction for expansion—east—provided the Russian Empire both its greatest possibilities for conquest and its greatest conflicts with old and new powers.

Russians and Turks

Most of the peoples who defined themselves as "Russian" during the Kievan period were speakers of a language closely related to other Slavic languages, and they tended to live as farmers, hunters, builders, scribes, or merchants. Surrounding Russia to the north, east, and parts of the south were speakers of Turkic languages who tended to live as herders, caravan workers, and soldiers. Language was not a solid defining line between peoples: Turkic-speakers had lived among Russian-speakers for centuries and in many instances were indistinguishable from Russians. Nevertheless, despite instances of cooperation, suspicion between Russian and Turkic peoples remained strong. Hostility increased when the Ottoman Empire emerged as a great power in the Caucasus and in the Balkans. The Romanovs felt those two regions were critical to Russia's security and were eager to control them.

Under the Romanov dynasty, the divisions between Russians and Turks tended to be represented as conflicts

Muscovy (MUSS-koe-vee) *boyar* (BOY-ar)
Romanov (ROE-man-off or roe-MAN-off)

between Christians and "infidels" or between the civilized and the "barbaric". Despite this rhetoric, it is important to understand that the interplay of Turkic (Central Asian) Russian (Slavic) influences was what produced the Russian Empire. These cultural groups were defined not by blood ties but by the way in which they lived.

A revealing example is the **Cossacks.** Their name comes from a Turkic word for a warrior or mercenary and is related to the modern name Kazakh. The word *Cossack* in various forms seems to have first emerged in the Ukraine, where it referred to bands of people living on the steppes, herding or robbing for their livelihoods. But the Cossacks of the Ukraine were a diverse group. Many were escaped serfs from Muscovy or Lithuania; others were wandering Turks or Cumans, Poles, Hungarians, or Mongols. Who their ancestors were was irrelevant. What mattered was that they lived in close-knit bands, were superb riders and fighters, and were feared by both the villagers and the legal authorities. Poland enlisted Cossacks to be the front line against the Ottomans. The Cossacks also proved to be a danger to their Polish patrons.

The Muscovite and early Romanov rulers decided to take no chances with the Cossacks and moved to crush them as an independent political force in the Ukraine. But Russia also desired to exploit the Cossacks' extraordinary military spirit and skills. The empire reached an accommodation with them, enrolling them in special military regiments and allowing them to live in autonomous villages. In return the Cossacks performed distinctive service for Russia, not only defending against Swedish and Ottoman incursions in the west but leading campaigns for exploration, conquest, and settlement in the east.

The Cossacks were an example of the ways in which Russia combined elements considered "Turk" with those considered "Russian." They displayed the military skills of Asian horsemen but were Russian-speakers, Christians, and in most cases willing participants in the building of the Russian Empire. Although Russian rulers and churchmen often tried to draw a strong line between the realm of the Russian and the realm of the Turk, this artificial distinction was at odds with the historical realities of the Russian Empire.

Peter the Great, r. 1689–1725

Much of the rhetoric that drew distinctions between "Russians" and "Turks" was connected to the age of **Peter the Great,** who ruled Russia from 1689 to 1725 (see Chapter 18). Peter was determined to secure a warm-water port on the Black Sea, and his first priority was to build a small but formidable navy that could blockade Ottoman ports. Peter described his wars with the Ottoman Empire as a new crusade to liberate Constantinople (now Istanbul) from the Muslim sultans. He also claimed the right to function as the legal protector of Orthodox Christians living in the Balkan territories under Ottoman rule. Peter's forces seized the port of Azov in 1696, but the fortress was lost again in 1713 and Russian expansion southward was blocked for the rest of Peter's reign. The need for a Black Sea port and Russia's role as the protector of Orthodox Christians, however, were not forgotten.

Peter was more successful in his campaigns in the west. In the long and costly Great Northern War (1700–1721), Peter's modernized armies broke Swedish control of the Baltic Sea, establishing direct contacts between Russia and Europe. Previously the courts of western Europe had regarded Russia as backward, brutal, and alien. But Peter's striking intelligence, his imposing physical presence, his open admiration of European architecture, art, and military technology, and his disarming willingness to engage in physical labor while learning carpentry, shipbuilding, and architecture had made him a European celebrity and generally improved the European opinion of Russia.

Peter's victory in the Great Northern War forced the European powers to recognize Russia as a major power for the first time. Taking advantage of his new prestige in Europe, he built a new city, St. Petersburg, on land captured from Sweden. In 1712 the city became Russia's capital. Peter intended St. Petersburg to be a model to Russian elites seeking to absorb European culture and a demonstration to Europeans of Russian sophistication. Houses were to be built of stone and brick, in the baroque style then fashionable in western Europe. Nobles were ordered to wear western styles and shave their beards. Peter attempted to end the traditional seclusion of upper-class Russian women, by requiring officials, officers, and merchants to bring their wives to the social gatherings he organized in the capital.

There was also a political objective in building the new capital: Peter intended to break the power of the boyars by sharply reducing their traditional roles in government and the army. The old boyar council of Moscow was replaced by a group of advisers in St. Petersburg whom the tsar appointed. Members of the traditional nobility continued to serve as generals and admirals, but officers in Peter's modern, professional army and navy were promoted according to merit, not birth.

Peter was interested in European technology and in some of Europe's culture, but he had no intention of following the movement of the Netherlands and Britain toward political liberalization. The goal of westernization was to strengthen the Russian state and the institutions of personal power that the Russians called **autocracy.** A decree of 1716 proclaimed that the tsar "is not obliged to answer to anyone in the world for his doings, but possesses power and authority over his kingdom and land, to rule them at his will and pleasure as a Christian ruler." Under this expansive definition of his role, Peter brought the Russian Orthodox Church firmly under state control, built factories and iron and copper foundries to provide munitions and supplies for the military, and increased the burdens of taxes and forced labor on the serfs. **Serfs—** the great mass of Russian people, forced by law and custom to work the land of their overlords—could have been freed as part of Peter's reform. But there was no move to abolish serf status, because the Russian Empire was dependent on serfs for the production of basic foodstuffs. It was locked in the struggle of the Eurasian land empires, and political centralization remained critical to the strategic challenges it faced.

The Russian Drive Eastward

Long before Peter's time, Russian rulers realized that the eastern frontier was wide open to Russian expansion because no other great empire controlled the northern tier of Asia. Living there were small groups of native peoples who relied on hunting and fishing for their survival and who had not assembled the complex military organizations and weaponry of the empires to the west and south. Russian exploration of Siberia began in the time of Ivan IV and was led by a Cossack, Yermak Timofeyovich°. Yermak's troops attacked the only political power in the region, the Khanate of Sibir, and by force of their rifles destroyed the khanate in 1582. Yermak himself did not survive to return to Moscow, but Cossacks remained in the forefront of Russian campaigns to conquer and settle Siberia. Most historians believe that Cossacks founded all the major towns of Russian Siberia.

Siberian furs and timber were the first valued resources; after 1700, gold, coal, and iron also became important. From the early seventeenth century the tsar used Siberia as a penal colony for criminals and political prisoners. By the 1650s, Cossack explorers had claimed the Amur Valley for the Russian Empire, and many villages along the Amur River were rendering tribute to Russian officials. Through the 1650s, clashes occurred between

these soldiers and soldiers of the Qing Empire stationed near the river. To deprive the Russians of the goods rendered by the Amur villagers, the Qing Empire forcibly resettled native peoples westward in Qing territory.

By the late 1600s the Russian and Qing Empires also were competing for influence in Mongolia and Central Asia. The Mongol federations were attempting to maintain their independence by playing the Russians and Qing against each other. Both the Russian and the Qing rulers saw that their interests lay in a diplomatic agreement that would delineate their borders in Mongolia, Siberia, and the Amur River Valley, as well as fix trade and tariff regulations across their borders. The Treaty of Nerchinsk in 1689 was a strategic coup for both empires, and it was reinforced in the Treaty of Kiakhta in 1727.

The immediate results were two. First, Mongol groups lost the leverage they had gained by exploiting Russian and Qing competition. Thereafter, the Mongols steadily declined as a power, and the Qing Empire quickly consolidated its control over Mongolia and Central Asia. Second, with a fixed boundary and Siberia inside it, Russia could concentrate on further eastern expansion, all the way to the Pacific and, by logical extension, into North America.

The ramifications of Russia's arrival at the Pacific were apparent by the mid-1700s, as British expeditions explored not only the Hawaiian Islands but also the Alaskan coast. They were alert to the extraordinary possibilities of pelt gathering in the American northwest. Sable and fox furs were precious goods in both Europe and China, and the British looked for ways to add seal and beaver furs to the markets. Furs from the eastern part of North America had traded in Europe for a century and become the foundation of the charter companies. But to exploit the fur market in China without a ruinous overhead, traders would have to secure and process furs on the west coast of America. The economic possibilities of the fur trade in northwestern America fired the imagination of English and American entrepreneurs. But within a few decades Russia dominated Alaska, and Russian traders were active along the entire western coast of North America.

The drive to the east brought Russia control of the rich natural resources of Siberia and the strategically important Amur River and put Russia into a position to dominate the lucrative fur and shipping industries of the North Pacific. This expansion of the empire was started by the rulers of Muscovy, had its most dramatic developments under Peter, and was sustained by Peter's successors. When Catherine the Great (r. 1762–1796) died, Russian reach extended from Poland in the west to Alaska in the east, from the Barents Sea in the north to the

---

Yermak Timofeyovich (YAIR-mak tih-mo-FAY-oh-vich *or* tih-mo-fay-OH-vich)

Power and Youth   Emperor Kangxi (left) and Peter the Great (right) were contemporaries, great rulers, and rivals for control of Central and Northeast Asia. Both were child-emperors who outwitted their elders to achieve personal rule and then pursued all avenues of knowledge to strengthen their empires. But their youthful portraits show differences: Peter is depicted here while he was a student in Holland in 1697, learning engineering and shipbuilding. Kangxi, in a portrait from about 1690, preferred to be portrayed as a refined scholar. (left: The Palace Museum, Beijing; right: Collection, Countess Bobrinskoy/Michael Holford)

Caspian Sea in the south, and was still growing. Catherine ruled the world's largest land empire, the survivor of a form of Eurasian empire that had prized large territories, agriculture, logging, fishing, and furs. It shared these qualities with its old rival, the Qing Empire.

THE LATER MING AND EARLY QING EMPIRES, 1500–1800

By the time the Qing Empire was fighting Russia for control of Northeast Asia, it was in its own right a very large and growing empire. Only a half-century earlier, however, the ancestors of the Qing rulers were local chiefs trying to protect the economic enterprises of their followers in Manchuria from regulation by the **Ming Empire** based in China. Though the Ming Empire did not control Mongolia, Turkestan, or Tibet, it was a large empire with a rich and complex economy. It was militarily

and politically influential, positioned at the center of an international tributary system, mounting effective military campaigns against Vietnam and the Mongols, and defending Korea against Japanese invasion. It would have been difficult for anybody to predict that in such a short period the Ming Empire would be destroyed and the Qing would assume control of China. Was the achievement due primarily to Ming weakness or to Qing strengths?

The End of the Ming

Historians are puzzled by the Ming decline because of the brilliance of the earlier Ming period. The unusual economic and cultural achievements of the Ming period continued until 1600. Ming manufacturers had transformed the global economy with their techniques for the assembly-line production of porcelain. By the 1500s Europe knew about the high-grade blue-on-white porcelain commonly used by the elites of China. Portuguese merchants not only began importing the products to Europe but requested special designs that imitated European pitchers and bowls that otherwise would have been made of metal or wood. Many of these commissioned items featured distinctive gold fittings and designs that Chinese artisans copied from European paintings. By 1600 the Dutch were also heavily involved in this trade, and wealthy families in Europe were becoming accustomed to the fine new porcelain, which they called "china." An international market eager for Ming porcelain, as well as for silk and lacquered furniture, stimulated the commercial development of East Asia, the Indian Ocean, and Europe.

This apparent golden age, however, was beset by serious problems that by the year 1600 left the Ming Empire economically exhausted, politically deteriorating, and technologically lagging behind both its East Asian neighbors and Europe. Some of these problems were the result of natural disasters associated with climate change and disease. There is evidence of climate change in the seventeenth century. Annual temperatures dropped, reached a low point about 1645, then remained low until the early 1700s. The last decades of the Ming were a time of agricultural distress, migration of peoples out of less productive areas, and the spread of epidemic diseases. Large uprisings that speeded the end of the Ming Empire were fueled by the dissatisfaction of tenant farmers and day workers squeezed by high rents, low wages, and poor crop yields. The devastation caused by these uprisings resulted in steep declines in local populations and grinding distress for individuals who were left. Climate change also may have contributed to external pressure on the Ming, as Manchus and Mongols sought to protect their productive lands from Ming control and to acquire land along the Ming borders.

Other kinds of global change also affected China. As Europeans colonized Mexico and Central America, they exploited the new sources of silver and flooded the global trade networks with silver coins. As China became more involved in this trade in the 1500s and early 1600s, silver flowed into China in exchange for goods sold to Europe. Silver dollars from the Spanish Empire were fully accepted in the Chinese economy, and the Chinese government began to mint its own silver coins and remint foreign silver in imitation of the Spanish design.

As the amount of silver in circulation rose, its relative value fell. Nevertheless, the Ming government maintained a strict ratio in price between silver coins and copper coins. Taxes and the prices of commodities were tied to the value of silver, and most transactions required the conversion of copper coinage to silver. As silver declined in value, more and more copper was needed to make purchases and pay taxes. In a time of worsening economic and population conditions, the decline in the value of silver and consequent inflation in prices and taxes hit the rural population especially hard. The Ming government found it increasingly difficult to maintain order and eventually was overwhelmed by rebellious forces.

Environmental and economic stress do not in themselves destroy societies. Indeed both the eastern Mongols and the Manchus centralized their political systems and increased the territories under their control in the 1600s, all at the expense of the Ming Empire. The importance of global factors in the demise of the Ming must be placed in the context of the special factors operating on China.

Ming cities were culturally and commercially vibrant. Many large landowners and absentee landlords lived in the cities, as well as officials, artists, and rich merchants who had purchased ranks or prepared their sons for the examinations. The elites had created a brilliant culture in which novels, operas, poetry, porcelain, and painting were all closely interwoven. Owners of small businesses catering to the urban elites could make money through printing, tailoring, running restaurants, or selling paper, ink, ink-stones, and writing brushes. The imperial government also marketed to the urban elites by operating factories for the production of ceramics and silks. Enormous government complexes at Jingdezhen° and at Dehua° invented assembly-line techniques and produced large quantities of high-quality ceramics for sale in China and abroad. But by the end of the Ming period the factories were plagued by disorder and inefficiency. The situation became so bad during the late sixteenth and seventeeth centuries that workers held strikes with increasing frequency. During a work action at Jingdezhen in 1601, workers threw themselves into the kilns to protest working conditions.

Yet the urban and industrial sectors of later Ming society fared much better than the rural, agricultural sector. After a period of economic growth and recovery from the population decline of the thirteenth century, the rural Ming economy did not continue strong growth. After the beginning of the sixteenth century, China had knowledge, gained from European traders, of new crops from Africa and America. But they were introduced very slowly, and neither rice-growing regions in southern China nor wheat-growing regions in northern China experienced a meaningful increase in productivity during the second half of the Ming period. After 1500, economic depression in the countryside, combined with recurring epidemics in central and southern China, kept population growth in check. The Ming population—about a

---

Jingdezhen (JING-deh-JUHN) **Dehua** (duh-HUA)

hundred million—at its height probably did not much surpass that of the Song dynasty four hundred years earlier.

The Ming also were under constant pressure from the powerful Mongol federations of Central Asia. In the late 1500s large numbers of Mongols were unified again. This time, Tibetan religion was used to centralize power in the hands of a Mongol khan. To legitimize his power, the khan designated for the first time a **dalai lama°**, or universal teacher, of Tibetan Buddhism. The unification of the Mongols in the 1500s was a significant step in the reemergence of Mongolia as a regional military power around 1600. In its last decades the Ming Empire was squeezed by Mongol forces on the west and north.

In 1582 Japanese warriors invaded Korea, which was a Ming tributary state. The invasions threw East Asia into crisis. The **Manchus,** an agriculturally based people who controlled the region north of Korea, contributed troops to an international force under Ming leadership. The Koreans employed all the technological and military skill for which the Yi period was renowned. General Yi Son-sin devised and employed the covered warships, or "turtle boats," that intercepted a portion of Japanese fleet.

The effects of the Japanese invasion were lasting. The impoverished Ming had to pay a high price to bring the Manchus into the struggle. In addition, the strain of repelling the invasions hastened the Ming decline in military strength. In Korea, the factionalism afflicting the Yi court before the Japanese arrived was worsened by the devastation resulting from the invasion and the struggle for leadership after the invaders were turned back. Korea was so weakened that the Manchus soon brought the country under their sway.

For the entire later Ming period, the boundaries of the empire were critical to its health, and conditions at the boundaries are an indication of the difficulties the later Ming Empire endured. The Mongols remained strong in the north. The Manchus grew stronger in the northeast and severed the traditional relationship between China and Korea. In the southwest, there were repeated uprisings among native peoples crowded by the immigration of Chinese farmers. The Ming could not look to the seas for relief. Pirates, often of Japanese or partial Japanese ancestry, based themselves in Okinawa and in Taiwan and roamed the southeastern coast of China, frequently looting inadequately protected trading towns. Ming military resources, concentrated against the Mongols and the Manchus in the north, could not be deployed to make the coasts hospitable to Chinese traders who were not themselves connected to the pirates. Frustrated by conditions and despairing of ever making a living at home, many southern Chinese migrated to all areas of Southeast Asia, where they began to profit from the sea trading networks of the Indian Ocean.

After decades of weakening control, the Ming ruler was deposed when rebellious forces under the leadership of Li Zicheng° captured Beijing. The imperial family left the city, but a Ming general entered into an agreement with Manchu leaders, inviting them to take Beijing from the rebels. The Qing did so in the summer of 1644 but did not restore the Ming. They claimed China for their own and began a forty-year conquest of the rest of the Ming territories.

It was some years before all hope was lost for the Ming. The Ming imperial family thought they could appeal to the Catholic Church for help in resisting the invaders. On November 4, 1650, from the remote highlands of Southeast Asia, Grand Dowager Empress Wang° sent a delegation of Jesuits to Rome to ask the pope to "take pity on us sinners in God's presence and, when we die, to bestow a special absolution." Wang noted that all members of the imperial family had been converted and said that if the papacy would help repel the Manchus "ambassadors will be dispatched to perform proper ceremonies at the altars of Saints Peter and Paul." Michel Boym°, the Jesuit priest acting as Wang's envoy, did not reach Rome until 1652 and could gain no papal audience until 1656. Then, with an encouraging letter from Pope Alexander VI, Boym returned to a China nearly conquered by the Manchus, who refused to let him travel inland from Canton. By that time Wang and her family were dead. Boym himself died attempting to contact them and was buried in the highlands between China and Vietnam in 1659.[2]

Power and Trade in the Early Qing

The **Qing Empire** was ruled by a Manchu imperial family, and Manchus were the leaders of the military forces. But Manchus were a very small portion of the population, and from its beginnings the empire was dependent on diverse peoples for its achievements. Peoples of Mongol, Korean, Cossack, and Turkic descent were all important in one way or another. Some Jesuits also were helpers, particularly after the collapse of Ming resistance. But the most important population in the Qing Empire was the Chinese, particularly the millions who deserted the Ming as Qing forces entered the country. Though the Qing style

---

dalai lama (DAH-lie LAH-mah)

Li Zicheng (lee ZUH-cheng) **Wang** (wahng)
Michel Boym (mee-SHELL bwam)

Map 22.2   The Qing Empire, 1644–1783   The Qing Empire began in Manchuria and captured north China in 1644. Between 1644 and 1783 the Qing conquered all the former Ming territories and added Taiwan, the lower Amur River basin, Inner Mongolia, eastern Turkestan, and Tibet. The resulting state was more than twice the size of the Ming Empire.

of rule was multilingual and international and the Qing were keenly focused on large strategic issues relating to competition with the Russian Empire, the overwhelming majority of officials, soldiers, merchants, and farmers were Chinese.

Before the year 1700 the Qing gained south China, and for the first time the island of Taiwan was incorporated into an empire based in China (see Map 22.2). At the time, the Qing Empire was also conquering Mongolia and Central Asia. The seventeenth and eighteenth centuries in China—particularly the reigns of the Kangxi° (r. 1662–1722) and Qianlong° (r. 1736–1796) emperors—were the period of greatest economic, military, and cultural achievement.

The early Qing emperors wished to foster economic and demographic recovery in China. They repaired the

roads and waterworks, lowered transit taxes, mandated comparatively low rents and interest rates, and established economic incentives for resettlement of the areas devastated during the peasant rebellions of the late Ming period. Foreign trade was encouraged. Korean ambassadors and students were numerous in Beijing and readily absorbed the tastes of the Qing elite. Vietnam, Burma, and Nepal sent regular embassies to the Qing tribute court and carried the latest Chinese fashions back home. Overland routes of communication from Samarkand to Korea were revived, though their economic and cultural influence was a shadow of what it had been under the Mongols in the 1200s. Nevertheless, through its Central Asian conquests the Qing Empire gained access to the superior horses of Afghanistan, gained new sources of coal, iron, gold, and silver, and eventually was able to eliminate the military danger of the Mongols.

Kangxi (KAHNG-shee)   **Qianlong** (chee-YEN-loong)

Style and Conversion: Christian Rivalries in Beijing

The Treaty of Nerchinsk (1689) presented new opportunities for Russian missionaries in Beijing to continue their work of ministering to Russians in Beijing as well as spreading Orthodox Christianity in China. They failed to gain converts, largely because they did not learn Chinese. But they believed their failure was due to the interference of the Jesuits, who had arrived before them, knew Chinese, and made themselves indispensable in diplomatic communications between the Qing and Russian courts. In 1722 leaders of the Orthodox Church wrote the following comment to the new head of the Russian mission in Beijing.

It would be prudent if you kept your rank of bishop a secret, because your status might arouse opposition among our enemies—especially our main enemies, the Jesuits. They are constantly creating troubles between us and others, as well as strife among ourselves, in order to frustrate our good works. Of course it could not be otherwise, for remember that Jesus cried out to the Father, "Lord, have I not sown good seed? Where have these weeds come from?" And the Lord said, "The Devil has done this."

For their part, the Jesuits considered the Russian missionaries hopelessly unpersuasive, not only because of their limitations of language but also because of their poverty. Russians traveled overland, by caravan, to Beijing, which was very expensive. Once there, they lived on a very small allowance from the Qing court, and they were often short of food and fuel, not to mention new clothes. The relatively independent and wealthy Jesuits considered the Russian missionaries unprepared for international experience, as Matteo Ripa made clear in his report to the Vatican on the Russian mission in Beijing, probably in 1718.

I sent a present to the head of the mission, then visited him. His manners were courteous and dignified, and his dress remarkably neat. With me, he pretended to be a Roman Catholic (despite the fact he was obviously Orthodox), speaking just enough Latin to be understood. He told me that a priest who was ill and in bed could speak Latin, and so I went to visit him, but all I could get out of him was the word "intelligit, intelligit, [he understands, he understands]" over and over. The head of the mission told me that the congregation is limited to descendants of Russian prisoners of war. They cannot convert the Chinese because they don't speak Chinese, and besides they have so few priests that they have no time for any but their flock of Russians.

The truth is, their church services have no ceremony at all, and they allow men and women to worship together, which in China is considered abominable. And though the head of the mission looks elegant, the priests on his staff look very shabby. To make matters worse, the priests play in the streets in front of the mission. In China this is absolutely uncouth, and no respectable person would do it.

What do you think accounts for the tensions between the Jesuits and Russian Orthodox churchmen in China? What were they really competing for?

Source: Eric Widmer, The Russian Ecclesiastical Mission in Peking During the Eighteenth Century (Cambridge, MA: Harvard East Asian Research Center, 1976), 44, 63. © The President and Fellows of Harvard College 1976. Reproduced by permission of the Harvard University Asia Center.

Emperor Kangxi

The early Qing conquest of Beijing and north China was carried out under the leadership of a group of Manchu aristocrats who dominated the first Qing emperor based in China and were regents for his young son, who was declared emperor in 1662. This child-emperor, Kangxi, spent several years doing political battle with his regents, and in 1669 he gained real as well as formal control of the government by executing his chief regent. **Kangxi** was then sixteen. He was an intellectual prodigy who mastered classical Chinese, Manchu, and Mongolian at an early age and memorized the Chinese classics. He was a successful military commander who personally led troops in the great campaigns that brought Mongolia under Qing control by 1691. He battled with and then made peace with the Russian Empire and negotiated complex domestic political crises. His reign, lasting until his death in 1722, was marked not only by great expansion of the empire but by great stability as well.

Part of the effectiveness of Qing expansion in the Kangxi era was due to Qing willingness to incorporate ideas and technologies from different regions. Before the invasion of China, the Qing already were using the Mongol system of political organization. They also adapted a program of religious legitimation of the emperor's power that was Tibetan in origin but had been used by Mongol emperors. Many of the agricultural policies of the early Qing state were influenced by Korean and Chinese practices.

As the Qing conquest was consolidated in north China, south China, and Northeast Asia, maps in the European style—reflecting the century of Jesuit influence at the Ming court—were created as practical guides to the newly conquered regions and as symbols of Qing dominance. Kangxi considered introducing the European calendar, but protests were so strong that an anti-Jesuit backlash developed among the Confucian elites, and the plan was dropped. The emperor himself remained friendly with the Jesuits and frequently discussed scientific and philosophical issues with them (see Society and Culture: Style and Conversion: Christian Rivalries in Beijing). When he fell ill with malaria in the 1690s, he relied on Jesuit medical expertise (in this case, the use of quinine) for his recovery. He ordered the creation of illustrated books in Manchu detailing European anatomical and pharmaceutical knowlege. The Jesuits also lectured Kangxi on mathematics, astronomy, and European civilization generally.

To gain converts among the Chinese elite, the Jesuits made important compromises in their religious teaching. The most important was their toleration of Confucian ancestor worship. The matter caused great controversy between the Jesuits and their Catholic rivals in China, the Franciscans and Dominicans, and also between the Jesuits and the pope. In 1690 the disagreement reached a high pitch. Kangxi wrote to Rome supporting the Jesuit position, but the matter was dropped, inconclusively, in the early 1700s. By that time, the influx of Jesuits to China had slowed, and for the remainder of the 1700s a very small population of Jesuits remained at the Qing court.

The exchange of information between the Qing and the Europeans that Kangxi had fostered was never one-way. When the Jesuits informed the Qing court on matters of anatomy, for instance, the Qing were able to demonstrate to the Jesuits an early form of inoculation, called **variolation,** that had been used to stem the spread of smallpox after the Qing conquest of Beijing. The technique was the inspiration for the vaccines later developed by Europeans. Similarly, the enormous imperial factories that produced porcelain inspired the industrial management of practices of Josiah Wedgwood in England.

Transferring European Designs, Canton   By 1750, both Chinese and European merchants at Canton were dependent on the expansion of commerce between Europe and the Qing Empire for their fortunes. For centuries Chinese factories had produced special products in porcelain, silk, and lacquerware for European markets. By the end of the 1700s, even the trade itself was an object of commercialization: Here, a painting specially made for export shows a Canton artisan carefully transferring European designs to a glass painting that is itself specially made for export.   (V & A Picture Library)

Tea and Diplomacy

The brilliant successes of the Qing in conquest and trade excited admiration in Europe. Things Chinese—or things that looked to Europeans as if they could be Chinese—were demanded by the wealthy and the aspiring middle classes of Europe. Not only silk, porcelain, and tea were being avidly consumed, but also cloisonné jewelry, tableware and decorative items, lacquered and jeweled room dividers, painted fans, carved jade and ivory (which originated in Africa and was finished in China). Perhaps the most striking Chinese influence on the transformation of European interior life in this period was wallpaper—an adaptation of the Chinese practice of covering walls with enormous loose-hanging watercolors or calligraphy scrolls. By the mid-1700s, special workshops throughout China were producing wallpaper and other consumer items according to the specifications of European merchants. The items were shipped to Canton for export to Europe.

In political philosophy, too, the Europeans felt they had something to learn from the early Qing emperors. In the late 1770s, poems supposedly written by Emperor Qianlong were translated into French and disseminated through the intellectual circles of western Europe. These works depicted the Qing emperors as benevolent despots who campaigned against superstition and ignorance, curbed the excesses of the aristocracy, and patronized science and the arts. European intellectuals who were questioning the political systems of their own societies found the image of a practical, secular, compassionate ruler intriguing. Voltaire proclaimed the Qing emperors model philosopher-kings and advocated such rulership as a protection against the growth of aristocratic privilege. Though Jesuit interest in China was in decline by this time, the works of the Jesuits stimulated interest in the languages and civilizations of East Asia and an intensification of European efforts to establish communications with China.

The Qing were eager to expand China's economic influence but were determined to control the trade very strictly. The purposes of this regulation were to allow the imperial family to enjoy the benefits of taxation of the trade and to limit piracy on the seas and smuggling inland. The system that the Qing used for regulating trade permitted only one market point for each foreign sector. Overland trade from Central Asia was directed to Kashgar, trade from Japan was directed to a city on the eastern coast near Shanghai, and all trade from the South China Sea was directed to Canton on the southern coast. Since Europeans came to China by way of the Indian Ocean and Southeast Asia, they were included in the South China Sea sector and permitted to trade only at Canton.

This system worked well enough for European traders until the late 1700s. Britain had become an important presence in East Asia, using its bases in India and Singapore to move eastward to China. The directors of the East India Company (EIC) believed that China's technological achievements and gigantic potential markets made China the key to limitless profit. China had tea, rhubarb, porcelain, and silk to offer. Dutch merchants enriched themselves by transporting these goods to Europe for centuries, but by the early 1700s the EIC dominated the community of European "factories"—the combined residences and offices of the European merchants residing in Canton—and British families such as the Barings, Jardines, and Mathesons had established themselves as quasi-political powers.

Tea from China became enormously popular in England. It had earlier been a prized import to Russia, Central Asia, and the Middle East, all of which knew it by its northern Chinese name, *cha*, and all of which acquired it by the overland Eurasian routes of medieval and early modern times. Western Europe, however, acquired tea from sea routes first exploited by the Portuguese and Dutch and thus knew it by its name in the Fujian province of coastal China and Taiwan: *te*. From the time of its introduction to England in the mid-1600s, tea displaced chocolate and coffee as the preferred drink.

English traders, whether members of the EIC or independent businessmen, considered the potential of trade with China to be obstructed by the Qing trade system. Great fortunes were being made in the tea trade, but the English had not found a product to sell to China. They believed that China was a vast unexploited market, with hundreds of millions of potential consumers of lamp oil made from whale blubber, cotton grown in India or the American south, or guns manufactured in London or Connecticut. Particularly after the loss of the thirteen American colonies, Britain feared that its markets would diminish and believed that only the Qing trade system—the "Canton system," as the British called it—stood in the way of opening new paths for commerce.

The British government worried about Britain's massive trade deficit with China. Because the Qing Empire rarely bought anything from Britain, British silver poured into China to pay for the imported tea and other products. The Qing government, whose revenues were declining in the later 1700s while its expenses rose, needed the silver. But in Britain the imbalance of payments stirred anxiety and anger over the allegedly unfair restrictions that the Qing Empire placed on the import of foreign goods. To make matters worse, the East India Company had managed its worldwide holdings badly, and as it teetered on bankruptcy, its attempts to manipulate Parliament became increasingly intrusive. The British government attempted to limit the actions and privileges of the EIC but thought that only the opening of the China trade and increasing competition from British merchants would finally dissolve the outmoded EIC. In 1792 George Macartney was dispatched to China to open diplomatic relations with the Qing Empire and attempt to revise the trade system.

The **Macartney mission** to China, which extended into 1793, was a fiasco. Qing officials were not expecting Macartney and would not allow him to travel from Canton to Beijing. Moreover, they did not accept his credentials, and Macartney did not know how to make any headway through the Qing bureaucracy. There were prolonged disputes about rituals. Macartney was ordered to perform the kowtow, but he refused. He asked Qing officials to bow before a portrait of the king of England, and they refused. The basic issues were unresolvable. Britain wished the Qing Empire to abandon its trade system because it was benefiting only the troublesome EIC. Britain wished the Qing to open Chinese ports to a wide range of competing British firms, one of which might eventually find a product that would be popular in China and help to reverse the trade imbalance. The Qing, however, had no interest in changing the system. The EIC was not a Qing problem; the Qing were submitting British traders to no restrictions that did not also apply to all other foreign merchants; the system provided revenue to the imperial family and lessened serious piracy problems. Macartney left China humiliated by his inability to persuade the Qing to make changes. Many people at home suspected he had in fact performed the kowtow, humiliating not only himself but all of Britain.

Dutch, French, and Russian embassies soon attempted to achieve what Macartney had failed to do, When they failed also, European frustration with the Qing mounted. The great European admiration for China of the early 1700s faded, and China was considered despotic, self-satisfied, and unrealistic. Political solutions seemed impossible because the Qing court would not communicate with foreign envoys or observe the simplest rules of the diplomatic system familiar to Europeans.

There occurred here a subtle shift in the position of Russia. In the time of Peter the Great and of the Emperor Kangxi, the two great empires had faced each other in a special contest and had found a sophisticated means of resolving or at least suspending their differences. They had used a diplomatic system, relying on Jesuits as interpreters, to create treaties establishing formal borders and customs procedures. But in those times Russia and the Qing were struggling for control of Central Asia and Mongolia and had similar strengths and weaknesses. By the last decade of the eighteenth century, Russia was committed to sea exploration, colonization of overseas territories, and the creation of a European-style empire. It had moved beyond its Eurasian land empire context, and was leaning toward the European consensus that the Qing Empire was keeping in place an unreasonable and outdated trade system. The Qing emperors at the end of the 1700s did not understand the importance of this Russian shift or anticipate the ways in which it would work to destroy the status quo that the two gigantic empires had once enjoyed.

Population and Social Stress

When Macartney and his entourage visited China in 1792–1793, they were carefully guided through the most prosperous cities and the most productive farmland. They did not see evidence of the economic and environmental decline that had begun to affect China in the last decades of the 1700s. The population explosion had intensified demand for rice and wheat, for land to be opened for the planting of crops imported from Africa and the Americas, and for more thorough exploitation of land already in use.

The narratives of Marco Polo's adventures in the 1200s had already fixed in the European imagination the image of packed, affluent Chinese cities, and between the time of Marco Polo and the time of the Macartney mission the Chinese population tripled.

This growth was partly the result of the peace that the Qing enforced. In addition, foreign crops known in the late Ming but not widely exploited then were commonly used in the Qing period to supplement or replace traditional crops. For instance, in regions of northern China, years of planting wheat and barley had exhausted the soil near the surface. In these areas, the introduction of corn from America temporarily revived agricultural productivity because the roots of corn extend deep into the soil to seek their nutrients. In central and southern China, the use of sweet potatoes and other crops from Africa made possible the cultivation of land not suitable for rice or wheat. As Macartney observed, field crops were sown in neat rows by mechanical seeders—at a time when most farmers in Europe still used the broadcast method, which wasted much of the seed.

The early Qing population exploded and reached between 350 million and 400 million by the end of the 1700s. But because of the efficiency of Chinese agriculture, population growth that had driven the per capita area of arable land to one-third of what it had been a century before had not yet created general poverty.

Whatever woodlands remained in China at the beginning of the 1700s were rapidly diminishing by the end of the century. Houses could be built of brick, but erosion became a serious problem because of deforestation. As erosion advanced, the danger of flooding grew, but government corruption and general inefficiency limited efforts to prevent flooding or recover from its effects. Dams and dikes were not maintained, and silted-up river channels were not dredged. By the end of the eighteenth century the Grand Canal was nearly unusable, and the towns that bordered it were starved for commerce.

The result was localized misery in many parts of interior China by the year 1800. Environmental deterioration and the decline of agriculture prompted many people to move. They sought seasonal jobs in better-off agricultural areas, or they worked in low-status jobs such as barge puller, charcoal burner, or nightsoil carrier. Many drifted to the cities to make their way by begging, prostitution, or theft. In central and southwestern China, where farmers had been impoverished by serious flooding, rebellions became endemic. Often joining in revolt were various indigenous peoples, who were largely concentrated in the less fertile lands in the south and in the northern and western borderlands of the empire (see Map 22.3).

Map 22.3   Climate and Diversity in the Qing Empire   The Qing Empire encompassed different environmental zones, and the climate differences corresponded to population density and cultural divisions. Wetter regions to the east of the 15-inch rainfall line also contained the most densely populated 20 percent of Qing land. The drier, less densely populated 80 percent of the Empire was home to the greatest portion of peoples who spoke languages other than Chinese. Many were nomads, fishermen, hunters, or farmers who raised crops other than rice.

The Qing Empire was outgrowing the state's control. The Qing government employed about the same number of officials as the Ming even though the Qing Empire was twice the size of the Ming geographically and nearly four times its size in terms of population. To maintain local control, the Qing depended on working alliances with local elites, including gentry and aspiring official families. But this dependence undercut the government's ability to enforce tax regulations and to control standards for admission to government service. The resulting semi-privatization of governance in the late 1700s promoted a situation in which corruption was widespread, military policies were inconsistent and ineffective, banditry was growing, and government revenues were shrinking.

The Qing fell victim to some of the basic characteristics of the land-based empires. To defend itself against Russia, it had conquered a huge stretch of territory extending from Turkestan—brought under military occupation in 1755—to Northeast Asia, and the costs of maintaining it were enormous. Population growth and the need to transport food to nonagricultural areas stressed the food and grain systems. The need to invest in agriculture and in transport infrastructure limited investment in new industries and heightened government interest in taxing foreign trade. Russia was attempting to move out of that mode by turning toward European-style imperialism and industrialization. Japan, China's neighbor, was poised for an entirely different response.

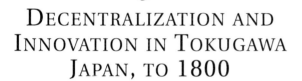

Decentralization and Innovation in Tokugawa Japan, to 1800

Like East Asia under the Qing rulers, Japan under the Tokugawa° shoguns had to deal with the transition from the intense militarization of the early 1600s to the comparative peace of the 1700s, while at the same time facing a decrease in state revenues and mounting European pressure for contact. In nearly every respect, the Japanese reaction to these problems strongly contrasted with the Qing response, with lasting consequences for Japan.

Shogunate and Economy

Japan's centralized political system had broken down in the twelfth century, when the first of the decentralized military governments—the shogunates—had been created. By 1500, civil war had brought a new warrior class to power, and the second of Japan's shogunates—the Ashikaga—was a loosely organized system of regional lords giving their loyalty to their leader, the shogun, who gave his loyalty to the secluded emperor. The extreme decentralization of the Ashikaga period fostered wars among ambitious local lords, and during the later 1500s infighting among the leaders engulfed the country.

In 1600 a new shogun, Tokugawa Ieyasu°, declared victory. Though Japan was brought under a single military government, the structure of the **Tokugawa Shogunate** had a very important influence over the development of the Japanese economy in the early modern period. The regional lords who fought for Tokugawa Ieyasu in the final battle in 1600 were understood to have an especially close relationship with the shogun. The shogun's original intention was to reward the lords who had supported him with well-developed rice lands in central Japan—relatively close to the shogunal capital—and to punish those who had not supported him by granting them remote, undeveloped lands at the northern and southern extremes of the Japanese islands.

The emperor of Japan had no political power; he remained at Kyoto°, the medieval capital. The Tokugawa shoguns built a new capital for themselves at Edo° (now Tokyo). A well-maintained road connected Kyoto and Edo, and trade and trading centers developed along this route.

The shogun was served by the regional lords, each of whom maintained a castle town, a small bureaucracy, a population of warriors—**samurai**°—and military support personnel, and often an academy. The result of this controlled decentralization was the establishment of well-spaced urban centers, between which there was frequent traffic. Because Tokugawa shoguns required the lords to visit Edo frequently, good roads, traffic, and commerce linked Edo to three of the four main islands of Japan. The shogun paid the lords in rice, and the lords paid their followers in rice. To meet their personal expenses, recipients of rice had to convert a large portion of it into cash. This transaction stimulated the development of rice exchanges at Edo and at Osaka°, where merchants speculated in rice prices.

Because of the domestic peace of the Tokugawa era, the warrior class had to adapt itself to the growing bureaucratic needs of the state. As the samurai became better educated, more attuned to the tastes of the civil elite, and more interested in conspicuous consumption, merchants dealing in silks, sake° (rice wine), fans, porcelain, lacquerware, books, and loans were well positioned to exploit the new opportunities. The state attempted—unsuccessfully—to curb the independence of the merchants when the economic well-being of the samurai was threatened, particularly when rice prices went too low or interest rates on loans were too high.

The 1600s and 1700s were centuries of high achievement in artisanship and commerce (see Environment and Technology: Women and Tokugawa Technology). Japanese skills in steel making, pottery, and lacquerware were joined by excellence in the production and decoration of porcelain, thanks in no small part to Korean experts brought back to Japan after the invasion of 1582. In the early 1600s manufacturers and merchants amassed enormous family fortunes. Several of the most important industrial and financial companies—for instance, the Mitsui° companies—had their origins in sake or beer breweries of the early Tokugawa period, then branched out into manufacturing, finance, and transport.

Wealthy industrial families usually cultivated close alliances with their regional lords and, if possible, with the shogun himself. In this way they could weaken the strict control of merchant activity that was an official part of Tokugawa policy. By the end of the 1700s, the industrial families of Tokugawa Japan held the key to modernization and the development of heavy industry, particularly in the prosperous provinces. Their political

---

Tokugawa (toe-koo-GAH-wah)   **Ieyasu** (ee-yeh-YAH-soo)
Kyoto (kee-YO-toe)   **Edo** (ED-doe)

samurai (SAH-moo-rie)   **Osaka** (OH-sah-kah)   *sake* (SAH-kay)
Mitsui (MIT-soo-ee)

Women and Tokugawa Technology

In the early modern period, the balance between available resources and demand was better in Japan than in China. In Qing China, population rapidly outstripped farmers' ability to increase agricultural output. In addition, the population of China was unevenly distributed, and when the population far exceeded the demand for labor, not everyone who needed work could find it. In such circumstances, social expectations forced many working women to relinquish skilled, specialized jobs to men and to consider themselves lucky if they were able to find low-paying, unskilled work.

In Tokugawa Japan, by contrast, women's labor remained valuable through the 1700s and became increasingly specialized. Women were regularly employed in the countryside and in the industries of the towns. In Japan as in China, they were indispensable in agricultural labor. But in Japan, because of social coherence and the comparative uniformity of the work in all regions, women's roles were well integrated with those of men, and women maintained a role in both the political and the economic life of the village. As mechanization was introduced, the value of women's work did not decline. Indeed, women's skills actually became more specialized, and mechanization became a normal part of their work.

The silk industry traditionally had been dominated by women working at home, where they oversaw the breeding and feeding of silkworms and the production of raw silk. In the Tokugawa period, these skills were mechanized—sometimes on so large a scale that the making of silk could no longer be considered a cottage industry. Nevertheless, the demand for labor remained so high that women were able to maintain their role in silk weaving.

Women also were important in mining. They were believed to have special intuition for separating desired metals from the surrounding stone, and certainly their skills at this task were very well developed. Mining was a lowly trade that was expected to attract humble workers. But as the Tokugawa economy grew, the demand for iron, copper, silver, and gold increased, and women workers remained critical to the advancement of industry, despite their low social standing. Watercolors and drawings of the period commonly depict the integration of women into the Tokugawa economic scene.

There was, however, a firm ceiling above which Tokugawa women could not rise. Although they enjoyed more economic leverage than their equally hard-working counterparts in China and Korea, they had no property rights. Moreover, despite the fact that Tokugawa women maintained their position in mechanized trades, they generally were not instructed in the most advanced techniques until after they married, because if a girl were instructed at a very young age, and then married, for the remainder of her life her skills would benefit not her own birth family but the family of her husband. Thus, when increasing complexity demanded earlier and more prolonged training in some trades, women in Japan began to lose their place in industry.

Silk Weaving by Japanese Women   Before the emergence of large factories, this sort of work could be done in the home or at a shared village site. (From Hishikawa Moronobu *Wakoku hyakujo* [1695]. Reproduced courtesy of the Harvard-Yenching Library)

Comprehensive Map of the Myriad Nations   Thanks to the "Dutch studies" scholars and to overseas contacts, many Japanese were well informed about the cultures, technologies, and political systems of various parts of the world. This combination map and ethnographic text of 1671 enthusiastically explores the differences among the many peoples living or traveling in Asia. The map of the Pacific hemisphere has the north pole on the left and south pole on the extreme right of the drawing.   (British Museum/ Fotomas Index)

influence was critical to the later transformation of Japan into an industrialized society.

The "Closing" of Japan

Like China, Japan at the end of the 1500s was a target of missionary activity by the Jesuits. But while members of the Chinese elite were open to the Jesuits so long as they accommodated Confucian values and became acquainted with Chinese culture, Japanese elite converts to Catholic Christianity were comparatively few. Missionaries could selectively gain the favor of regional lords while bypassing the shogunal court in Edo, which was consistently hostile to Christianity. This was the case with Date Masamuni°, the fierce and independent warlord of northern Honshu°, who sent his own embassy to the Vatican in 1613, by way of the Philippines (where there were significant communities of Japanese merchants and pirates) and Mexico City.

Generally, Christianity was more successful among farmers in the countryside. Jesuits had their greatest success in the southern and eastern regions of Japan. But in the late 1630s these regions were the scenes of massive uprisings by farmers impoverished by local rents and taxes. The rebellions, which were ruthlessly suppressed, were blamed on Christian influence. Hundreds of Japanese Christians were crucified as a warning to others; be-

lief in Christianity was banned by law; and in 1649 the shogunate ordered the closing of the country, making it illegal and punishable by death for foreigners to come in or for Japanese to leave.

The purpose of the closing was to prevent the spread of foreign influence in Japan, not necessarily to exclude from Japan knowledge of foreign cultures. A few Europeans, primarily the Dutch, were permitted to reside on the small island of Deshima near Nagasaki, and a few Japanese were licensed to supply their needs. Curious about Western ways, these intermediaries concentrated first on learning Dutch, so the knowledge that they acquired and that eventually spread from Nagasaki was known as "Dutch studies." It included information about European weapons technology, shipbuilding, mathematics and astronomy, anatomy and medicine, and geography. In the 1700s some Japanese theorists advocated that Japan should abandon its decentralized, agriculturally oriented system in favor of the more centralized, mercantilistic systems used by European empires.

The closing of Japan was ignored by some of the regional lords whose fortunes depended on overseas trade with Korea, Okinawa°, Taiwan, China, and Southeast Asia. The "outer" lords at the northern and southern extremes of Japan tended to be under less control by the shoguns. Many of them not only pursued overseas trade and piracy but also claimed dominion over islands between Japan

---

Date Masamuni (dah-tay mah-sah-moo-nee)   **Honshu** (hahn-shoo)   **Okinawa** (oh-kee-NAH-wah)

and Korea to the east and over islands between Japan and Taiwan to the south, including present-day Okinawa. The southern Japanese lords became wealthy and powerful by controlling sea trade—so powerful that the shogunate could no longer master them.

Elite Decline and Social Crisis

Sea trade was only one factor in the reversal of the relative fortunes of the "inner" and the "outer" lords. Population growth was putting a great strain on the well-developed lands of central Japan. In the remote provinces, where the lords had sponsored programs to settle and develop new agricultural lands, the rate of economic growth far outstripped the growth rate in centrally located domains.

Also destabilizing the Tokugawa government in the 1700s was the shogunate's inability to stabilize rice prices and halt the economic decline of the samurai. To finance their living, the samurai had to convert their rice to cash in the market. The Tokugawa government realized that the rice brokers might easily enrich themselves at the expense of the samurai if the price of rice, and the rate of interest, were not strictly controlled. Laws designed to regulate both had been passed early in the Tokugawa period, and laws requiring moneylenders to forgive samurai debts were added later. But these laws were not always enforced, sometimes because neither the lords nor the samurai wished them to be. By the early 1700s members of both groups were dependent on the willingness of merchants to provide them credit.

The Tokugawa shoguns strongly resisted the forces tending to weaken the samurai and to strengthen the merchant class. Their legitimacy rested on their ability to reward and protect the interests of the lords and samurai who had supported the Tokugawa conquest. But the Tokugawa government, like the governments of the Qing Empire, Korea, and Vietnam, accepted the Confucian idea that agriculture should be the basis of state wealth and that merchants should occupy lowly positions in society because of their reputed lack of moral character.

Governments throughout East Asia used Confucian philosophy to attempt to limit the influence and power of merchants. The Tokugawa government, however, was at a special disadvantage. Its decentralized system limited its ability to regulate merchant activities and actually stimulated the growth of commercial activities. In the first two centuries of the Tokugawa Shogunate—from 1600 to 1800—the economy grew faster than the population. Household amenities and cultural resources that in China were found only in the cities were common in the Japanese countryside. Despite official disapproval, merchants and others involved in the growing

Woodblock Print of the "Forty-Seven Ronin" Story The saga of the forty-seven ronin and the avenging of their fallen leader has fascinated the Japanese public since the event occurred in 1702. This watercolor from the Tokugawa period shows the leaders of the group pausing on the snowy banks of the Sumida River in Edo (Tokyo) before storming their enemy's residence. (Jean-Pierre Hauchecorne Collection)

economy enjoyed relative freedom and influence in eighteenth-century Japan. They produced a vivid culture of their own, fostering the development of *kabuki* theater, colorful woodblock prints and silkscreened fabrics, and restaurants.

The ideological and social crisis of Tokugawa Japan's transformation from a military to a civil society is captured in the "Forty-seven Ronin°" incident of 1702. A young regional lord was provoked by a senior minister into drawing his sword at the shogun's court. For this offense the young lord was sentenced to commit *seppuku°*, the ritual suicide of the samurai. His own followers then became *ronin*, "masterless samurai," obliged by the traditional code of the warrior to avenge their deceased master. They broke into the house of the senior minister who had provoked their own lord, and they killed him and others in his household. Then they withdrew to a temple

---

ronin (ROH-neen)   *seppuku* (SEP-poo-koo)

in Edo and petitioned the shogun to acknowledge their obligation to be loyal to their lord and avenge his death.

A legal debate began in the shogun's government. To deny the righteousness of the ronin would be to deny samurai values. But to approve their actions would create social chaos, undermine laws against murder, and deny the shogunal government itself the right to try cases of samurai violence. The shogun ruled that the ronin had to die but would be permitted to die honorably by committing *seppuku*.

This solution exposed a fatal contradiction in the structure of shogunal government. To maintain a state based on military values, the state must place the military itself outside the law. Centralization, standardization of laws, and the ability of the state to enforce law for protection of the public would be impossible. The purity of purpose of the ronin is still celebrated in Japan, but since the time of the case of 1702, Japanese writers, historians, and teachers have recognized that the self-sacrifice of the ronin for the sake of upholding civil law was necessary.

The Tokugawa Shogunate put into place a political and economic system that fostered innovation, but the government itself could not exploit it. Thus during the Tokugawa period the government remained quite traditional while other segments of society developed new methods of productivity and management.

CONCLUSION

In the early eighteenth century Eurasia was dominated by the struggle of two enormous, land-based empires to defend themselves against each other and to acquire lands that would be at least marginally profitable. Because their needs were so similar, they often competed for the same resources, from Turkestan to Northeast Asia. Russia and the Qing Empire depended on large transportation systems, intense agricultural production, and coerced labor from their domestic populations. They preserved social systems that obligated a majority of the population to work the land but withheld the right to landownership. At the center of their political structures were powerful emperors with the economic and legal resources to command armies, engineering teams, and explorers at a distance. Not surprisingly, each empire had its most brilliant period—under Peter the Great and Emperor Kangxi—when the throne was occupied by a talented, energetic, and far-sighted ruler.

There were also distinct differences between these empires. The Qing court was generally open to many kinds of foreign influences and used ideas, institutions,

and technologies from a wide range of sources. But distance and circumstance limited Qing contact with Europe. The Qing could not control which Europeans came to the Qing territories and thus encountered only merchants and missionaries. The merchants did not make much of an impression. The Jesuits were influential in philosophy, mathematics, astronomy, and other issues of concern to them. But they were not an inexhaustible resource for the Kangxi emperor, who was brilliant and inquisitive. From the Jesuits he got very little insight into the emergence of European empires, their tactics, or their goals.

Peter the Great banned the Jesuits from Russia, considering them a subversive and backward influence. St. Petersburg gave Peter a "window" into Europe, and from that vantage point his choices of what to learn from the Europeans and what to reject were unlimited. Among his choices were architecture, engineering, shipbuilding, and military technologies of all kinds. He knew how to exploit the symbolism of European emperorship, and perhaps he knew how to avoid tendencies toward liberalization represented by some Enlightenment thinkers. He understood the meaning of the new European use of the sea, and he foresaw the importance of America in the developing global economy. He set Russian rulers on a path tending toward European practices of diplomacy and imperialism and away from the static values of the huge land empires.

Russia and the Qing represent variations on an imperial pattern not shared by their neighbor Japan. Instead of pursuing centralization, standardization, and strengthening of the ruler, Japan was decentralized. Each local lord developed his own economic and political center, but there was enough connection at the level of the shogun's court for nationwide roadways and trade systems to thrive. Local lords had great incentive to develop their lands, and many turned to overseas opportunities in legitimate trade or in piracy. Despite the official policy of keeping merchants down, in practice merchants worked with the regional lords to develop local enterprises, sustain local samurai, and outfit local soldiers. Many regions of Tokugawa Japan created innovative means of financing local industry and developed unique relationships with other countries, particularly the islands of the western Pacific. In 1792, when Russian ships exploring the North Pacific turned toward the Japanese coast, the local lord used his own forces to chase them away. All local lords understood that they would be on their own as foreign incursions increased. After centuries of competition with, independence from, and often disobedience to the shogunate, they were to have a very different response to foreign challenges from either of their huge imperial neighbors.

■ Key Terms

Jesuits	Peter the Great	Qing Empire
Siberia	autocracy	Kangxi
Muscovy	serfs	variolation
tsar	Ming Empire	Macartney Mission
Mikhail Romanov	dalai lama	Tokugawa Shogunate
Cossacks	Manchus	*samurai*

■ Suggested Reading

There is a great deal of literature focused on the Jesuits' history in various countries. See these general histories: Christopher Hollis, *The Jesuits: A History* (1968), and Georg Schurhammer, *Francis Xavier: His Life, His Times*, trans. M. Joseph Costelloe, (1973–1982). For East Asia in the sixteenth and seventeenth centuries see Michael Coopers, S.J., *Rodrigues the Interpreter: An Early Jesuit in Japan and China* (1974). For China see David E. Mungello, *Curious Land: Jesuit Accommodation and the Origins of Sinology* (1985), and Jonathan D. Spence, *The Memory Palace of Matteo Ricci* (1984). For Japan see C. R. Boxer, *The Christian Century in Japan, 1549–1650* (1951). See also Cornelius Wessels, *Early Jesuit Travellers in Central Asia, 1603–1721* (1924). On European images of and interactions with China connected to the Jesuits, see the relevant portions of Jonathan D. Spence, *The Chan's Great Continent: China in Western Minds* (1998), and Joanna Waley-Cohen, *The Sextants of Beijing: Global Currents in Chinese History* (1999).

On the East India companies see John E. Wills, *Pepper, Guns, and Parleys: The Dutch East India Company and China, 1662–1681* (1974); Dianne Lewis, *Jan Compagnie in the Straits of Malacca, 1641–1795* (1995); John Keay, *The Honourable Company: A History of the English East India Company* (1991); Brian Gardner, *The East India Company* (1971); and Lucy Stuart Sutherland, *The East India Company in Eighteenth-Century Politics* (1952). On the development of global commerce in tea, coffee, and cocoa see the relevant chapters in Roy Porter and Mikulås Teich, *Drugs and Narcotics in History* (1995).

On early modern Russian history, see W. E. Brown, *A History of Eighteenth-Century Russia* (1980), and Robert O. Crummey, *Aristocrats and Servitors: The Boyar Elite in Russia, 1613–1689* (1983). On Peter the Great there is a very extensive collection of works. Among the best-known recent books are Matthew Smith Anderson, *Peter the Great* (1978); Robert K. Massie, *Peter the Great: His Life and World* (1980); and Lindsey Hughes, *Russia in the Age of Peter the Great: 1682–1725* (1998). On the effect of Peter's reforms on the serfs and on the military see Elise K. Wirtschafter, *From Serf to Russian Soldier* (1990). For Russian naval development and Russian influence in the Pacific and in America see Glynn Barratt, *Russia in Pacific Waters, 1715–1825: A Survey of the Origins of Russia's Naval Presence in the North and South Pacific* (1981), and Howard I. Kushner, *Conflict on the Northwest Coast: American-Russian Rivalry in the Pacific Northwest, 1790–1867* (1975).

For China during the transition from the Ming to Qing periods see James W. Tong, *Disorder Under Heaven: Collective Violence in the Ming Dynasty* (1991); Frederic Wakeman, *The Great Enterprise* (1985); and Lynn Struve, *Voices from the Ming-Qing Cataclysm: In Tiger's Jaws* (1993). On the history of the Manchus and of the Qing Empire see Evelyn Sakakida Rawski, *The Last Emperors* (1999), and Pamela Kyle Crossley, *The Manchus* (1997).

On Chinese society generally in this period see two classic (though slightly dated) works by Ping-ti Ho: *The Ladder of Success in Imperial China: Aspects of Social Mobility, 1368–1911* (1962), and *Studies in the Population of China 1368–1953* (1959); and see the general study by Susan Naquin and Evelyn S. Rawski, *Chinese Society in the Eighteenth Century* (1987). On the two greatest of the Qing emperors and their times see Jonathan D. Spence, *Emperor of China; Self Portrait of K'ang Hsi, 1654–1722,* (1974). For a more scholarly treatment see Lawrence D. Kessler, *K'ang-hsi and the Consolidation of Ch'ing Rule, 1661–1684* (1976); Jonathan D. Spence, *Ts'ao Yin and the K'ang-hsi Emperor: Bondservant and Master* (1966); and Harold Kahn, *Monarchy in the Emperor's Eyes: Image and Reality in the Ch'ien-lung Reign* (1971).

On the Qing trade systems see John E. Wills, *Embassies and Illusions: Dutch and Portuguese Envoys to K'ang-hsi, 1666–1687* (1984), and Craig Clunas, *Chinese Export Art and Design* (1987).

There is a great deal published on the Macartney mission, much of it originating in the diaries and memoirs of the participants. See the exhaustively detailed Alain Peyrefitte, *The Immobile Empire,* trans. Jon Rothschild (1992). For a more theoretical discussion see James L. Hevia, *Cherishing Men from Afar: Qing Guest Ritual and the Macartney Embassy of 1793* (1995).

On Japan in this period see Chie Nakane and Shinzaburo Oishi *Tokugawa Japan: The Social and Economic Antecedents of Modern Japan,* trans. Conrad Totman (1990), and Tessa Morris-Suzuki, *The Technological Transformation of Japan from the Seventeenth to the Twenty-First Century* (1994). Mary Elizabeth Berry, *Hideyoshi* (1982), is an account of the reunification of Japan at the end of the sixteenth century and the invasion of Korea. On technological advancement, capital formation, and competition in the Tokugawa period see the classic by Thomas C. Smith, *Agrarian Origins of Modern Japan* (1959); the first chapter of Albert Craig, *Choshu in the Meiji Restoration* (1961); John Whitney Hall and Marius B. Jansen, eds., *Studies in the Institutional History of Early Modern Japan* (1968); and John G. Roberts, *Mitsui: Three Centuries of Japanese Business* (1973).

■ Notes

1. Adapted from G. V. Melikhov, "Manzhou Penetration into the Basin of the Upper Amur in the 1680s," in S. L. Tikhvinshii, ed., *Manzhou Rule in China* (Moscow: Progress Publishers, 1983).
2. See Lynn Struve, *Voices from the Ming-Qing Cataclysm: In Tiger's Jaws* (New Haven, CT: Yale University Press, 1993), 235–237.

REVOLUTIONS RESHAPE THE WORLD,
1750–1870

Between 1750 and 1870, dramatic political, economic, and social changes affected nearly every part of the world. The beginnings of industrialization, the American and French Revolutions, and revolutions for independence in Latin America challenged the existing order in the West. In Africa, Asia, and the Middle East, the expansion of European commercial and military power combined with powerful internal transformations to challenge long-established institutions.

In the West, the American, French, and Haitian Revolutions unleashed forces of nationalism and social reform. At this time, the Industrial Revolution introduced technologies and patterns of work that made industrial societies wealthier, more socially fluid, and militarily more powerful than nonindustrial, traditional societies. Even while Europe's colonial empires in the Western Hemisphere were being dismantled, the Industrial Revolution was fueling European economic expansion, which undermined traditional producers in distant places such as Asia and Africa. When this economic penetration was resisted, as it was in East Asia, the industrializing nations of the West used military force to open markets.

Great Britain expanded its empire by establishing colonial rule in distant Australia, New Zealand, and India. India alone had a population larger than the combined populations of all the colonies that Europe lost in the Americas. The Atlantic slave trade was ended by an international abolitionist movement and by Great Britain's use of diplomacy and naval power. European economic influence expanded in Africa. Invigorated by this exchange, some African states created new institutions and introduced new economic sectors.

The Ottoman Empire, the Qing Empire, and Japan were deeply influenced by the expansion of Europe and the United States. Each society met the Western challenge with reform programs that preserved traditional structures while adopting elements of Western technology and organization. The Ottoman court introduced reforms in education, the military, and law and created the first constitution in an Islamic state. The Qing Empire survived the period of European expansion, but a series of military defeats and civil war seriously compromised China's centralization efforts. Japan experienced the most revolutionary change, abolishing its ancient political system and initiating radical top-down transformations.

The economic, political, and social revolutions that began in the mid-eighteenth century shook the foundations of European culture and led to the expansion of Western power across the globe. Societies throughout Asia, Africa, and Latin America responded to cross-cultural contacts. Some resisted foreign intrusion by using local culture and experience as a guide. Others adopted Western commercial policies, industrial technologies, and government institutions.

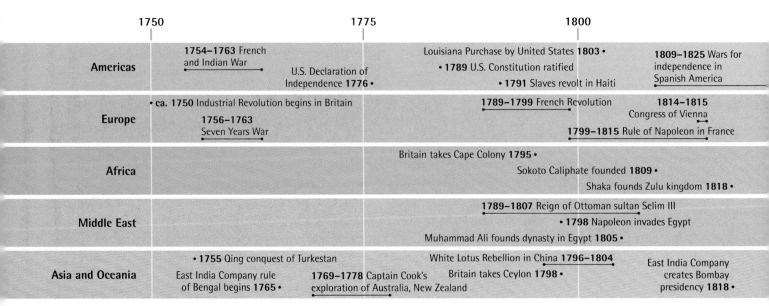

	1750	1775	1800	
Americas	1754–1763 French and Indian War	U.S. Declaration of Independence 1776 •	Louisiana Purchase by United States 1803 • • 1789 U.S. Constitution ratified • 1791 Slaves revolt in Haiti	1809–1825 Wars for independence in Spanish America
Europe	• ca. 1750 Industrial Revolution begins in Britain 1756–1763 Seven Years War		1789–1799 French Revolution 1799–1815 Rule of Napoleon in France	1814–1815 Congress of Vienna
Africa		Britain takes Cape Colony 1795 •	Sokoto Caliphate founded 1809 • Shaka founds Zulu kingdom 1818 •	
Middle East			1789–1807 Reign of Ottoman sultan Selim III • 1798 Napoleon invades Egypt Muhammad Ali founds dynasty in Egypt 1805 •	
Asia and Oceania	• 1755 Qing conquest of Turkestan East India Company rule of Bengal begins 1765 •	1769–1778 Captain Cook's exploration of Australia, New Zealand	White Lotus Rebellion in China 1796–1804 Britain takes Ceylon 1798 •	East India Company creates Bombay presidency 1818

ARCTIC OCEAN

Britain

EUROPE

France

Russian Empire

ASIA

Spain

Ottoman Empire

Japan

Algeria

MIDDLE EAST

China

Egypt

India

Burma

AFRICA

Sokoto Caliphate

PACIFIC OCEAN

Liberia

Ceylon

INDIAN OCEAN

SOUTH ATLANTIC OCEAN

AUSTRALIA

Zulu Kingdom

Cape Colony

New Zealand

| 0 | 1000 | 2000 | 3000 Km. |
| 0 | 1000 | 2000 | 3000 Mi. |

| 1825 | 1850 | 1875 |

• **1822** Independence of Brazil

• **1848** Women's Rights Convention in Seneca Falls New York

1862–1867 French invasion of Mexico

• **1867** Creation of Dominion of Canada

1861–1865 U.S. Civil War

• **1830** Revolutions of 1830

1852–1870 Rule of Napoleon III in France

• **1834** Abolition of slavery in British Empire

1853–1856 Crimean War

• **1848** Revolutions of 1848

• **1821** Republic of Liberia founded

• **1869** Jaja founds Opobo

1836–1839 Afrikaners' Great Trek

• **1826** Ottoman ruler dissolves Janissary corps

• **1860s** Beginning of Young Turk movement

1831–1847 Algerians resist French takeover

• **1869** Suez Canal opens

• **1839** Ottoman ruler Abdul Mejid launches Tanzimat reforms

• **1826** East India Company annexes Assam, northern Burma

1850–1864 Taiping Rebellion in China

1839–1842 Opium War

1857–1858 Sepoy Rebellion in India

• **1868** Meiji Restoration in Japan

23

REVOLUTIONARY CHANGES IN THE ATLANTIC WORLD, 1750–1850

Execution of Louis XVI The execution of the French king in 1793 was the most shocking and dramatic signal that the "Old Order" was about to be swept away.

On the evening of August 14, 1791, more than two hundred slaves and black freedmen met in secret in the plantation district of northern Saint Domingue° (present-day Haiti) to set the date for an armed uprising against local slave owners. Although the delegates agreed to delay the attack for a week, violence began almost immediately. During the following decade, slavery was abolished, military forces from Britain and France were defeated, and Haiti achieved independence.

This meeting was provoked by news and rumors about revolutionary events in France that had spread through the island's slave community. Events in France also had divided the island's white population into competing camps of royalists (supporters of France's King Louis XVI) and republicans (supporters of democracy). The free mixed-race population initially gained some political rights from the French Assembly but was then forced to rebel when the slave-owning elite reacted violently.

Among those planning the insurrection was a black freedman named François Dominique Toussaint. He proved to be one of the most remarkable representatives of the revolutionary era, later taking the name Toussaint L'Ouverture°. He organized the rebels into a potent military force, negotiated with the island's royalist and republican factions and with representatives of Great Britain and France, and wrote his nation's first constitution. Commonly portrayed as a fiend by slave owners throughout the Western Hemisphere, Toussaint became for slaves a towering symbol of resistance to oppression.

The Haitian slave rebellion was an important episode in the long and painful political and cultural transformation of the modern Western world. Economic expansion and the growth of trade were creating unprecedented wealth. The first stage of the Industrial Revolution (see Chapter 24) increased manufacturing productivity and led to greater global interdependence, new patterns of consumerism, and altered so-cial structures. At the same time, intellectuals were questioning the traditional place of monarchy and religion in society. An increasingly powerful class of merchants, professionals, and manufacturers created by the emerging economy provided an audience for these new intellectual currents and began to press for a larger political role.

This revolutionary era turned the Western world "upside down." The *ancien régime*°, the French term for Europe's old order, rested on medieval principles: politics dominated by powerful monarchs, intellectual and cultural life dominated by religion, and economics dominated by a hereditary agricultural elite. In the West's new order, politics was opened to vastly greater participation, science and secular inquiry took the place of religion in intellectual life, and economies were increasingly opened to competition.

This radical transformation did not take place without false starts and temporary setbacks. Imperial powers resisted the loss of colonies; monarchs and nobles struggled to retain their ancient privileges; and the church fought against the claims of science. Revolutionary steps forward were often matched by reactionary steps backward. The liberal and nationalist ideals of the eighteenth-century revolutionary movements were only imperfectly realized in Europe and the Americas in the nineteenth century. Despite setbacks, belief in national self-determination and universal suffrage, and a passion for social justice continued to animate reformers into the twentieth century.

As you read this chapter, ask yourself the following questions:

- How did imperial wars among European powers provoke revolution?
- In what ways were the revolutions, expanded literacy, and new political ideas linked?
- How did revolution in one country help to incite revolution elsewhere?
- Why were the revolutions in France and Haiti more violent than the American Revolution?

Saint Domingue (san doe-MANG)
Toussaint L'Ouverture (too-SAN loo-ver-CHORE)

ancien régime (ahn-see-EN ray-ZHEEM)

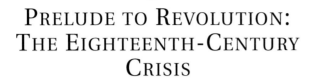

PRELUDE TO REVOLUTION: THE EIGHTEENTH-CENTURY CRISIS

In large measure, the cost of wars fought among Europe's major powers over colonies and trade precipitated the revolutionary era that began in 1775 with the American Revolution. Britain, France, and Spain were the central actors in these global struggles, but other imperial powers were affected as well. Unpopular and costly wars had been fought earlier and paid for with new taxes. But changes in the Western intellectual and political environments led to a much more critical response. Any effort to extend the power of a monarch or impose new taxes now raised questions about the rights of individuals and the authority of political institutions.

Colonial Wars and Fiscal Crises

The rivalry among European powers intensified in the early 1600s when the newly independent Netherlands began an assault on the American and Asian colonies of Spain and Portugal. The Dutch attacked Spanish treasure fleets in the Caribbean and Pacific and seized parts of Portugal's colonial empire in Brazil and Angola. Europe's other emerging sea power, Great Britain, also attacked Spanish fleets and seaports in the Americas. By the end of the seventeenth century, expanding British sea power had checked Dutch commercial and colonial ambitions and ended the Dutch monopoly of the African slave trade.

As Dutch power ebbed, Britain and France began a long struggle for political preeminence in western Europe and for territory and trade outlets in the Americas and Asia. Both the geographic scale and the expense of this conflict expanded during the eighteenth century. Nearly all of Europe's great powers were engaged in the War of the Spanish Succession (1701–1714). War between Britain and Spain, begun in 1739 over smuggling in the Americas, quickly broadened into a generalized European conflict, the War of the Austrian Succession (1740–1748). Conflict between French and English settlers in North America then helped ignite a long war that altered the colonial balance of power. When Britain finally won the Seven Years War (1756–1763), known as the French and Indian War in America, it not only gained undisputed control of North America east of the Mississippi River but also forced France to surrender most of its holdings in India.

The enormous costs of these conflicts distinguished them from earlier wars. Traditional taxes collected in traditional ways no longer covered the obligations of governments. For example, at the end of the Seven Years War in 1763, Britain's war debt had reached £137 million. Although Britain's total budget before the war had averaged only £8 million, annual interest on the war debt alone came to exceed £5 million. Even as European economies expanded because of increased trade and the early stages of the Industrial Revolution, fiscal crises overtook one European government after another. In an intellectual environment transformed by the Enlightenment, the need for new revenues provoked debate and confrontation within a vastly expanded and more critical public.

The Enlightenment and the Old Order

The complex and diverse intellectual movement called the **Enlightenment** applied the methods and questions of the Scientific Revolution of the seventeenth century to the study of human society. Dazzled by Copernicus's ability to explain the structure of the solar system and Newton's representation of the law of gravity, European intellectuals began to apply the logical tools of scientific inquiry to other questions. Some labored to systematize knowledge or organize reference materials. For example, Carolus Linnaeus° (a Swedish botanist known by the Latin form of his name) sought to categorize all living organisms, and Samuel Johnson published a comprehensive English dictionary with over forty thousand definitions. In France Denis Diderot° worked with other Enlightenment thinkers to create a compendium of human knowledge, the thirty-five-volume *Encyclopédie*.

Other thinkers pursued lines of inquiry that challenged long-established religious and political institutions. Some argued that if scientists could understand the laws of nature then surely similar forms of disciplined investigation might reveal laws of human nature. Others wondered whether society and government might be better regulated and more productive if guided by science rather than by hereditary rulers and the church. These new perspectives and the intellectual optimism that fed them were to help guide the revolutionary movements of the late eighteenth century.

The English political philosopher John Locke (1632–1704) argued in 1690 that governments were created to protect life, liberty, and property and that the people had

---

Carolus Linnaeus (kar-ROLL-uhs lin-NEE-uhs)
Denis Diderot (duh-nee DEE-duh-roe)

CHRONOLOGY

	The Americas	Europe
1750		
	1756–1763 French and Indian War	1756–1763 Seven Years War
1775	1770 Boston Massacre	
	1776 American Declaration of Independence	
	1778 United States alliance with France	
	1783 Treaty of Paris ends American Revolution	
	1791 Slaves revolt in Saint Domingue (Haiti)	1789 Storming of Bastille begins French Revolution
		1793–1794 Reign of Terror in France
		1795–1799 The Directory rules France
	1798 Toussaint L'Ouverture defeats British in Haiti	1799 Napoleon overthrows the Directory
1800		1804 Napoleon crowns himself emperor
	1804 Haitians defeat French invasion and declare independence	1814 Napoleon abdicates; Congress of Vienna opens
		1815 Napoleon defeated at Waterloo
		1830 Greece gains independence; revolution in France overthrows Charles X
		1848 Revolutions in France, Austria, Germany, Hungary, and Italy

a right to rebel when a monarch violated these natural rights. Locke's closely reasoned theory began with the assumption that individual rights were the foundation of civil government. In *The Social Contract,* published in 1762, the French-Swiss intellectual Jean-Jacques Rousseau° (1712–1778) asserted that the will of the people was sacred and that the legitimacy of the monarch depended on the consent of the people. Although both men beleived that government rested on the will of the people rather than divine will, Locke emphasized the importance of individual rights, and Rousseau envisioned the people acting collectively because of their shared historical experience.

All Enlightenment thinkers were not radicals like Rousseau. There was never a uniform program for political and social reform, and the era's intellectuals often disagreed about principles and objectives. The Enlightenment is commonly associated with hostility toward religion and monarchy, but few European intellectuals openly expressed republican or atheist sentiments. The church was most commonly attacked when it attempted to censor ideas or ban books. Critics of monarchial authority were as likely to point out violations of ancient custom as to suggest democratic alternatives. Even Voltaire, one of the Enlightenment's most critical intel-

lects and one of the era's great celebrities, believed that Europe's monarchs were likely agents of political and economic reform, and he wrote favorably of China's Qing° emperors.

Indeed, sympathetic members of the nobility and reforming European monarchs such as Charles III of Spain (r. 1759–1788), Catherine the Great of Russia (r. 1762–1796), Joseph II of Austria (r. 1780–1790), and Frederick the Great of Prussia (r. 1740–1786) actively sponsored and promoted the dissemination of new ideas, providing patronage for many intellectuals. They recognized that elements of the Enlightenment critique of the ancien régime buttressed their own efforts to expand royal authority at the expense of religious institutions, the nobility, and regional autonomy. Goals such as the development of national bureaucracies staffed by civil servants selected on merit, the creation of national legal systems, and the modernization of tax systems united many of Europe's monarchs and intellectuals. Monarchs also understood that the era's passion for science and technology held the potential of fattening national treasuries and improving economic performance (**see** Environment and Technology: The Pencil). Periodicals disseminating new technologies often gained the patronage of these reforming monarchs.

Jean-Jacques Rosseau (zhahn-zhock roo-SOE)

Qing (ching)

The Pencil

From early times, Europeans had used sharp points, lead, and other implements to sketch, make marks, and write brief notes. At the end of the seventeenth century, a source of high-quality graphite was discovered at Borrowdale in northwestern England. Borrowdale graphite gained acceptance among artists, artisans, and merchants. At first, pure graphite was simply wrapped in string. By the eighteenth century, pieces of graphite were being encased in wooden sheaths and resembled modern pencils. Widespread use of this useful tool was retarded by the limited supply of high-quality graphite from the English mines.

The English crown periodically closed the Borrowdale mines or restricted production to keep prices high and maintain adequate supplies for future needs. As a result, artisans in other European nations developed alternatives that used lower-quality graphite or, most commonly, graphite mixed with sulfur and glues.

The major breakthrough occurred in 1793 in France when war with England ruptured trade links. The government of revolutionary France responded to the shortage of graphite by assigning a thirty-nine-year-old scientist, Nicolas-Jacques Conté, to find an alternative. Conté had earlier promoted the military use of balloons and conducted experiments with hydrogen. He also had had experience using graphite alloys in the development of crucibles for melting metal.

Within a short period, Conté produced a graphite that is the basis for most lead pencils today. He succeeded by mixing finely ground graphite with potter's clay and water. The resulting paste was dried in a long mold, sealed in a ceramic box, and fired in an oven. The graphite strips were then placed in a wooden case. Although some believed the Conté pencils were inferior to the pencils made from Borrowdale

Pencils   Wartime necessity led to invention of the modern pencil in France.   (Drawing by Fred Avent for Henry Petroski. Reproduced by permission)

graphite, Conté produced a very serviceable pencil that could be produced in uniform quality and unlimited amounts.

Henry Petroski, summarizing the achievement of Conté in his *The Pencil*, wrote: "The laboratory is really the modern workshop. And modern engineering results when the scientific method is united with experience with the tools and products of craftsmen. . . . Modern engineering, in spirit if not in name, would come to play a more and more active role in turning the craft tradition into modern technology, with its base of research and development."

Source: This discussion depends on Henry Petroski, *The Pencil: A History of Design and Circumstance* (New York: Knopf, 1990); the quotation is from pp. 50–78. Drawing by Fred Avent for Henry Petroski. Reproduced by permission.

Though willing to embrace reform proposals when they served royal interests, Europe's monarchs moved quickly to suppress or ban radical ideas that promoted republicanism or directly attacked religion. However, too many channels of communication were open to permit a thoroughgoing suppression of these ideas. In fact, censorship tended to enhance intellectual reputations, and persecuted intellectuals generally found patronage in the courts of foreign rivals.

Many of the major intellectuals of the Enlightenment maintained an extensive correspondence with each other as well as with political leaders. This communication led to numerous firsthand contacts among the intellectuals of different nations and helped to create a coherent assault on what was typically called ignorance—beliefs and values associated with the ancien régime. Rousseau, for example, briefly sought refuge in Britain, where the Scottish philosopher David Hume befriended him. Similarly, Voltaire sought patronage and protection in England and later Prussia.

Women were instrumental in the dissemination of the new ideas. In England educated middle-class women purchased and discussed the books and pamphlets of the era. Some were important contributors to intellectual life as writers and commentators, raising by example and in argument the issue of the rights of women. In Paris wealthy women made their homes centers of debate, intellectual speculation, and free inquiry. Their salons brought together philosophers, social critics, artists, and members of the aristocracy and commercial elite. Unlike their contemporaries in England, the women of the Parisian salons used their social standing more to direct the conversations of men rather than to give vent to their own opinions.

The intellectual ferment of the era deeply influenced the expanding middle class in Europe and the Western Hemisphere. Members of this class were eager consumers of books and the inexpensive newspapers and journals that were widely available in the eighteenth century. This broadening of the intellectual audience overwhelmed traditional institutions of censorship. Scientific discoveries, new technologies, and controversial work on human nature and politics also were discussed in the thousands of coffeehouses and teashops opening in major cities and market towns.

Many European intellectuals were interested in the Americas. Some Europeans continued to dismiss the New World as barbaric and inferior, but others used idealized accounts of the New World to support their critiques of European society. These thinkers looked to Britain's North American colonies for confirmation of their belief that human nature unconstrained by the corrupted practices of Europe's old order would quickly produce material abundance and social justice. More than any other American, the writer and inventor **Benjamin Franklin** came to symbolize both the natural genius and the vast potential of America.

Born in 1706 in Boston, the young Franklin was apprenticed to his older brother, a printer. At seventeen he ran away to Philadelphia, where he succeeded as a printer and publisher, best known for his *Poor Richard's Almanac*. By age forty-two he was a wealthy man. He retired from active business to pursue writing, science, and public affairs. In Philadelphia, Franklin was instrumental in the creation of the organizations that later became the Philadelphia Free Library, the American Philosophical Society, and the University of Pennsylvania.

His contributions were both practical and theoretical. He was the inventor of bifocal glasses, the lightning rod, and an efficient wood-burning stove. In 1751 he published a scientific work on electricity, *Experiments and Observations on Electricity*, that established his intellectual reputation in Europe. Intellectuals heralded the book as proof that the simple and unsophisticated world of America was a particularly hospitable environment for genius.

Franklin was also an important political figure. He served Pennsylvania as a delegate to the Albany (New York) Congress in 1754, which sought to coordinate colonial defense against attacks by the French and their Amerindian allies. Later he was a Pennsylvania delegate to the Continental Congress that issued the Declaration of Independence in 1776. His service in England as colonial lobbyist and later as the Continental Congress's ambassador to Paris allowed him to cultivate his European reputation. Franklin's wide achievement, witty conversation, and careful self-promotion make him a symbol of the era. In him the Enlightenment's most radical project, the freeing of human potential from the inhibitions of inherited privilege, found its most agreeable confirmation.

As Franklin's career demonstrates, the Western Hemisphere shared in the debates of Europe. New ideas penetrated the curricula of many colonial universities and appeared in periodicals and books published in the New World. As scientific method was applied to economic and political questions, colonial writers, scholars, and artists on both sides of the Atlantic were drawn into a debate that eventually was to lead to the rejection of colonialism itself. This radicalization of the colonial intellectual community was provoked by the European monarchies' efforts to reform colonial policies. As European authorities swept away colonial institutions and long-established political practices without consultation, colonial residents had to acknowledge that their status as colonies meant perpetual subordination to European rulers. Among people compelled to recognize this structural dependence and inferiority, the idea that government authority ultimately rested on the consent of the governed was potentially explosive.

Folk Cultures and Popular Protest

While intellectuals and the reforming royal courts of Europe were embracing the rational and secular enthusiasms of the Enlightenment, most people in Western society remained loyal to competing cultural values grounded in the preindustrial past. These regionally distinct folk cultures were framed by the memory of shared local historical experience and nourished by religious practices encouraging emotional release. They emphasized the obligations that people had to each other and local, rather than national, loyalties. Though never formally articulated, these cultural traditions composed a coherent expression of the mutual rights and obligations connecting the people and their rulers. Rulers who violated the constraints of these understandings were likely to face violent opposition.

In the eighteenth century, European monarchs sought to increase their authority and to centralize power by reforming tax collection, judicial practice, and public administration. Although monarchs viewed these changes as reforms, the common people often saw them as violations of sacred customs and sometimes expressed their outrage in bread riots, tax protests, and attacks on royal officials. These violent actions were not efforts to overturn traditional authority. They were efforts to preserve custom and precedent. In Spain and the Spanish colonies, for example, protesting mobs commonly asserted the apparently contradictory slogan

"Long live the King. Death to bad government." They expressed loyalty and love of their monarch while at the same time assaulting his officials and preventing the implementation of changes to long-established customs.

Folk cultures were threatened by other kinds of reform as well. Rationalist reformers of the Enlightenment sought to bring order and discipline to the citizenry by banning or by altering in form the numerous popular cultural traditions—such as harvest festivals, religious holidays, and country fairs—that enlivened the drudgery of everyday life. These events were popular celebrations of sexuality and individuality as well as occasions where masked and costumed celebrants mocked the greed, pretension, and foolishness of government officials, the wealthy, and the clergy. Hard drinking, gambling, and blood sports like cockfighting and bearbaiting were all popular activities in this preindustrial mass culture. Because these customs were viewed as corrupt and decadent by reformers influenced by the Enlightenment,

Beer Street (1751) This engraving by William Hogarth shows an idealized London street scene where beer drinking is associated with manly strength, good humor, and prosperity. The self-satisfied corpulent figure in the left foreground has been reading a copy of the king's speech to Parliament. We can imagine him offering a running commentary to his drinking companions as he reads. (The Art Archive Limited)

governments undertook efforts to substitute civic rituals, patriotic anniversaries, and institutions of self-improvement. These challenges to custom—like the efforts at political reform—often provoked protests, rebellions, and riots.

The efforts of ordinary men and women to resist the growth of government power and the imposition of new cultural forms provide an important political undercurrent to much of the revolutionary agitation and conflict from 1750 to 1850. Spontaneous popular uprisings and protests punctuated nearly every effort at reform in the eighteenth century. But these popular actions gained revolutionary potential only when they coincided with ideological divisions and conflicts within the governing class itself. In America and France the old order was swept away when the protests and rebellions of the rural and urban poor coincided with the appearance of revolutionary leaders who followed Enlightenment ideals in the effort to create secular republican states. Likewise, a slave rebellion in Saint Domingue (Haiti) achieved revolutionary potential when it attracted the support of black freedmen and disaffected poor whites who had been radicalized by news of the French Revolution.

THE AMERICAN REVOLUTION, 1775–1800

In British North America, clumsy efforts to reform colonial tax policy to cover rising defense expenditures and to diminish the power of elected colonial legislatures outraged a populace accustomed to greater local autonomy. Once begun, the American Revolution ushered in a century-long process of political and cultural transformation in Europe and the Americas. By the end of this revolutionary century, the authority of monarchs had been swept away or limited by constitutions, and religion had lost its dominating place in Western intellectual life. Moreover, the medieval idea of a social order determined by birth had been replaced by a capitalist vision that emphasized competition and social mobility.

Frontiers and Taxes

After defeating the French in 1763, the British government faced two related problems in its North American colonies. As settlers quickly pushed into Amerindian lands west of the Appalachian Mountains and across the Ohio River, the British government saw the likelihood of armed conflict with Amerindian peoples. Already burdened with debts from the French and Indian War, Britain desperately wanted to avoid additional expenditures for frontier defense. Because of the possibility of frontier conflict and the need to hold down defense costs, Britain tried to get the colonists to shoulder more of the costs of imperial defense and colonial administration.

Every effort to impose new taxes or prevent the settlement of the trans-Appalachian frontier provoked angry protests in the colonies. The situation was made politically explosive by the confrontational and impolitic way in which a succession of weak British governments responded. Because George III (r. 1760–1820) relied upon cabinet ministers selected from among court favorites without regard to parliamentary support, the common response to colonial protests was incendiary bluster and weak enforcement. British government in the period after 1763 was a dangerous combination of qualities: both overbearing and weak.

When the British replaced the French in the Great Lakes region, they angered indigenous peoples by refusing to follow the French practice of paying rent for frontier forts and giving gifts to Amerindian allies. They also reduced the prices paid for furs. Amerindians had become accustomed to the goods they received in exchange for furs, especially firearms, gunpowder, textiles, and alcohol. To get these commodities, they had greatly intensified their hunting practices, endangering some species. Relations deteriorated quickly as settlers and white fur traders pushed across the Appalachians, adding new pressures to the natural environment.

Britain soon demonstrated that it was unable to negotiate the diplomatic and military challenges inherent in the relationship between Amerindians and settlers. Led by Pontiac, an Ottawa chief, a broad alliance of native peoples successfully drove the British military from frontier outposts and then raided deep into the settled areas of Virginia and Pennsylvania. Although this Amerindian alliance was defeated decisively within a year, the potential for renewed violence existed all along the frontier.

The British government's panicked reaction to Pontiac's challenge was the Proclamation of 1763. It sought to establish an effective western limit for settlement. The proposed boundary threw into question the claims of thousands of already established farmers without effectively protecting Amerindian land. No one was satisfied. A decade later the British government irritated the colonists even more when it attempted to slow settlement in contested regions east of the Mississippi and north of the Ohio. The Quebec Act of 1774 annexed disputed lands to the province of Quebec, thus denying eastern colonies the authority to distribute lands claimed as a result of original charters. Colonists saw the Quebec Act as punitive and tyrannical, and Amerindian peoples received no relief from the continuous assault on their land.

Frontier wars were costly and destructive but did not threaten British authority directly. The British government's campaign of fiscal reforms and new taxes, however, sparked a political confrontation that ultimately led to rebellion. New commercial regulations that increased the cost of foreign molasses and endangered colonial exports cut into New England's profitable trade with Spanish and French Caribbean sugar colonies. Britain also outlawed the colonial practice of issuing paper money, a custom made necessary by the colonies' chronic balance-of-payments deficits. These actions, which restricted trade and limited the money supply, provoked widespread anger. Colonial legislatures formally protested, and angry colonists organized boycotts of British goods.

The Stamp Act of 1765 imposed a tax, to be paid in scarce coin, on all legal documents, newspapers, pamphlets, and nearly all other types of printed material. Propertied colonists, including holders of high office and members of the colonial elite, took leading roles in the resulting protests. They used fiery political language, even calling Britain's rulers "parricides" and "tyrants." In 1765 representatives from the colonies met in New York City to protest, and women from many of the most prominent colonial families organized boycotts of British goods. Organizations such as the Sons of Liberty held public meetings, intimidated royal officials, and developed committees to enforce the boycotts. The combination of violent protest and trade boycott forced the repeal of the Stamp Act in 1766. But new taxes and duties were soon imposed, and parliament granted colonial governors new powers, even sending British troops to quell urban riots.

The result was a new round of boycotts, which cut colonial imports of British goods by two-thirds. Angry colonists also destroyed property and bullied or attacked royal officials. The mob practice of covering despised British functionaries with hot tar and feathers became a symbol of American lawlessness for the British public. Unable to control the streets, British authorities reacted by threatening traditional liberties, even dissolving the colonial legislature of Massachusetts.

The cycle of confrontation in Boston prompted the British government to dispatch a warship and two regiments of soldiers to reestablish control of Boston's streets. Conflicts soon occurred when off-duty British soldiers sought part-time employment, further enraging Boston's working class, which was suffering through a

The Tarring and Feathering of a British Official, 1774   This illustration from a British periodical shows the unfortunate John Malcomb, commissioner of customs at Boston. By the mid-1770s, British periodicals were focusing public opinion on mob violence and the breakdown of public order in the colonies. British critics of colonial political protests viewed the demand for liberty as little more than an excuse for mob violence.   (The Granger Collection, New York)

period of low wages and high unemployment. Support for a complete break with Britain grew after March 5, 1770, when a British force fired on an angry Boston crowd, killing five civilians. This "Boston Massacre," which seemed to expose the naked force on which colonial rule rested, radicalized public opinion throughout the colonies.

Parliament attempted to calm public opinion by repealing some of the taxes and duties, then stumbled into another crisis by granting the British East India Company a monopoly for importing tea to the colonies. This monopoly raised anew the constitutional issue of Parliament's right to tax the colonies. It also offended wealthy colonial merchants, who were excluded from this profitable commerce. The crisis came to a head in the already politically overheated port of Boston when tea worth £10,000 was dumped into the harbor by protesters disguised as Amerindians. Britain responded by appointing a military man, Thomas Gage, as governor of Massachusetts and by closing the port of Boston. Public order in Boston now depended on British troops, and public administration was in the hands of a general. This militarization of colonial government in Boston undermined Britain's constitutional authority and made a military test of strength inevitable.

The Course of Revolution, 1775–1783

As the crisis mounted, new governing bodies created by patriot leaders effectively deposed many British governors, judges, and customs officers. The new institutions of colonial government created laws, appointed justices, and even took control of colonial militias. Simultaneously, radical leaders organized crowds to intimidate loyalists—people who were pro-British—and to enforce the boycott of British goods.

By the time elected representatives met in Philadelphia as the Continental Congress in 1775, blood had already been shed when patriot militia met British troops at Lexington and Concord, Massachusetts (see Map 23.1). Events were propelling the colonies toward revolution. Congress assumed the powers of government, creating a currency and organizing an army. **George Washington** (1732–1799), a Virginia planter who had served in the French and Indian War, was named commander.

Popular support for independence was given a hard edge by the angry rhetoric of thousands of street-corner speakers and the inflammatory pamphlet *Common Sense*, written by Thomas Paine, a recent immigrant from England. Paine's pamphlet alone sold 120,000 copies. On July 4, 1776, Congress approved the Declaration of Independence, the document that proved to be the most enduring statement of the revolutionary era's ideology:

> We hold these truths to be self evident: That all men are created equal; that they are endowed by their creator with certain unalienable rights; that among these are life, liberty and the pursuit of happiness; that, to secure these rights, governments are instituted among men, deriving their just powers from the consent of the governed.

The Declaration's affirmation of popular sovereignty and individual rights influenced the language of revolution and popular protest around the world.

Hoping to shore up British authority, Great Britain sent an expeditionary force of 32,000 soldiers and an armada of more than 400 ships to pacify the colonies. By 1778, British land forces numbered 50,000 supported by 30,000 German mercenaries. But this military commitment proved futile. Despite the existence of a large loyalist community in the colonies, the British army found it difficult to control the countryside. Although British forces won most of the battles, Washington slowly built a competent Continental army and civilian support networks that provided supplies and financial resources.

The real problem for the British government was its inability to discover a compromise solution that would satisfy colonial grievances. Half-hearted efforts to resolve the bitter conflict over taxes failed, and a later offer to roll back the clock and reestablish the administrative arrangements of 1763 made little headway. Independence had been declared, and blood had been shed. Overconfidence and poor leadership prevented the British from finding a political solution before revolutionary institutions were in place and the armies engaged. By allowing confrontation to occur, the British government lost the opportunity to mobilize and give direction to the large numbers of loyalists and pacifists in the colonies.

Along the Canadian border, both sides solicited Amerindians as potential allies and feared them as potential enemies. For over a hundred years, members of the powerful Iroquois Confederacy—Mohawk, Oneida, Onondaga, Cayuga, Seneca, and (after 1722) Tuscarora —had protected their traditional lands with a combination of diplomacy and warfare, playing a role in all the colonial wars of the eighteenth century. Just as the American Revolution forced neighbors and families to join the rebels or remain loyal, it divided the Iroquois, who fought on both sides. The Mohawk proved to be the most valuable of British allies among the Iroquois.

The Mohawk loyalist leader **Joseph Brant** (Thayendanegea°) organized Britain's most potent fighting force along the Canadian border. Portrayed in the propaganda of the revolutionaries as a symbol of Amerindian savagery, Brant organized raids along the northern frontier that earned him the title "Monster" Brant. Actually, he was a man who moved easily between European and Amerindian cultures. Educated by missionaries, he was fluent in English and helped to translate Protestant religious tracts into Mohawk. He was tied to many of the wealthiest loyalist families through his sister, formerly the mistress of Sir William Johnson, Britain's superintendent of Indian affairs for North America. Brant had traveled to London and had had an audience with George III. He

---

Thayendanegea (ta YEHN dah NEY geh ah)

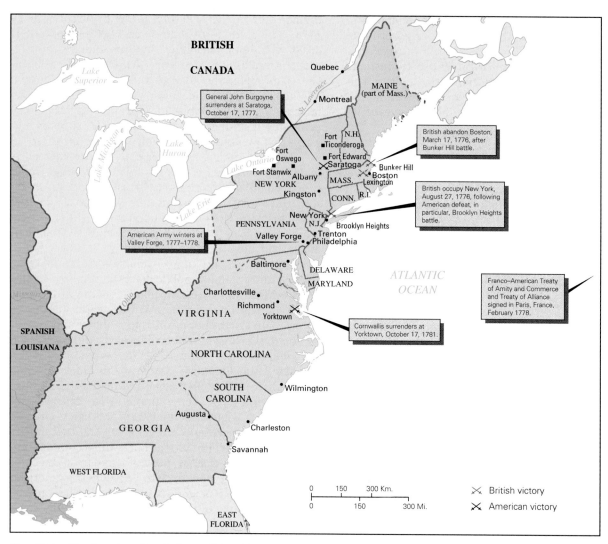

Map 23.1 The American Revolutionary War The British army won most of the major battles, and British troops held most of the major cities. Even so, the American revolutionaries eventually won a comprehensive military and political victory.

had been embraced by London's aristocratic society and initiated into one of the most exclusive secret clubs.

The defeat in late 1777 of Britain's general John Burgoyne by General Horatio Gates at Saratoga, New York, put the future of the Mohawk at risk. This victory gave heart to patriot forces that had recently suffered a string of defeats, and it led to destructive attacks on Iroquois villages. Brant's supporters fought on to the end of the war, but patriot victories along the frontier curtailed Iroquois political and military power. Brant eventually joined the loyalist exodus to Canada and led an effort to integrate the Iroquois into the market economy of the settlers. For these Americans the revolution did not mean the protection of life and property.

The British defeat at Saratoga convinced France, in 1778, to enter the war as an ally of the United States. French military help proved crucial, supplying American forces and forcing the British to defend their colonies in the Caribbean. The French contribution was most clear in the final decisive battle, fought at Yorktown, Virginia (see Map 23.1). An American army, supported by French soldiers, besieged a British army led by General Charles Cornwallis. With escape cut off by a French fleet, Cornwallis surrendered to Washington as the British military band played "The World Turned Upside-Down."

This victory effectively ended the war. The Continental Congress sent representatives to the peace conference that followed with instructions to work in tandem with the French. Believing that France was more concerned with containing British power than with guaranteeing a strong United States, America's peace delegation negotiated directly with Britain and gained a generous settlement. The Treaty of Paris (1783) granted unconditional independence and established generous boundaries for the former colonies. The United States, in return, promised to repay prewar debts due to British merchants and to allow loyalists to recover property confiscated by patriot forces. In the end, loyalists were poorly treated and thousands of them, including Brant and other Mohawk, decided to leave for Canada.

The Construction of Republican Institutions, to 1800

Even before the Declaration of Independence, most of the colonies had created new governments. After independence, ignoring the British example of an unwritten constitution, leaders in each of the new states (as the former colonies were called) summoned constitutional conventions to draft formal charters and submitted the results to voters for ratification. Europeans were fascinated by the drafting of written constitutions and by the formal ratification of these constitutions by a vote of the people. Many of these documents were quickly translated and published in Europe. Here was the social contract of Locke and Rousseau made manifest. Remembering conflicts between royal governors and colonial legislatures, the authors of state constitutions placed severe limits on executive authority but granted legislatures greater powers than in colonial times. Many states also inserted in their constitutions a bill of rights to provide further protection against government tyranny.

An effective constitution for the new national government was developed more slowly and hesitantly. The Second Continental Congress sent the Articles of Confederation—the first constitution of the United States—to the states for approval in 1777, but it was not accepted by all the states until 1781. It created a one-house legislature in which each state was granted a single vote. A simple majority of the thirteen states was sufficient to pass minor legislation, but nine votes were necessary for declaring war, imposing taxes, and coining or borrowing money. Executive power was to be exercised by committees, not by a president. Given the intended weakness of this government, it is remarkable that it successfully organized the human and material resources to defeat Great Britain.

With the coming of peace, many of the most powerful political figures in the United States began an effort to fashion a new constitution. The Confederation govern-

ment proved unable to enforce unpopular requirements of the peace treaty such as the recognition of loyalist property claims, the payment of prewar debts, and even the payment of military salaries and pensions. In September 1786 Virginia invited the other states to discuss the government's failure to deal with trade issues. This led to a call for a new convention to meet in Philadelphia nine months later. A rebellion led by Revolutionary War veterans in western Massachusetts gave the assembling delegates a sense of urgency.

The **Constitutional Convention,** which began meeting in May 1787, achieved a nonviolent second American Revolution. The delegates pushed aside the announced purpose of the convention—"to render the constitution of the federal government adequate to the exigencies of the union"—and in secret undertook to write a new constitution. George Washington was elected presiding officer. His reputation and popularity provided the solid foundation on which the delegates could contemplate an alternative political model. The real leader of the convention was James Madison of Virginia.

Debate focused on several issues: representation, electoral procedures, executive powers, and the relationship between the federal government and the states. Compromise solutions included distribution of political power among the executive, legislative, and judicial branches and the division of authority between the federal government and the states. The final compromise provided for a two-house legislature: the lower house (the House of Representatives) to be elected directly by voters and the upper house (the Senate) to be elected by state legislatures. The chief executive—the president—was to be elected indirectly by "electors" selected by ballot in the states (each state had a number of electors equal to the number of its representatives and senators).

Although the U.S. Constitution created the most democratic government of the era, only a minority of the adult population was given full rights. In some northern states where large numbers of free blacks had fought with patriot forces, there was hostility to the continuation of slavery, but southern leaders were able to protect it. Slaves were denied any participation in the political process. Slave states, however, were permitted to count three-fifths of the slave population in the calculations that determined number of congressional representatives, thus multiplying the political power of the slave-owning class in the national government. Southern delegates also gained a twenty year continuation of the slave trade to 1808 and a fugitive slave clause that required all states to return runaway slaves to their masters.

Women were powerfully affected by their participation in revolutionary politics and by the changes in the economy brought on by the break with Britain. Women had led prewar boycotts and during the war had organized relief and charitable organizations. Nevertheless, they were denied political rights in the new republic. New Jersey briefly stood as an exception. Without specifically excluding women, the framers of that state's constitution had granted the right to vote to free residents who met modest property-holding requirements. As a result, women and African-Americans who met property requirements were able to vote in New Jersey until 1807, when lawmakers eliminated this right.

THE FRENCH REVOLUTION, 1789–1815

The French Revolution undermined traditional monarchy as well as the power of the Catholic Church and the hereditary aristocracy but, unlike the American Revolution, did not create an enduring form of representative democracy. The colonial revolution in North America, however, did not confront so directly the entrenched privileges of an established church, monarchy, and aristocracy, and the American Revolution produced no symbolic drama comparable to the public beheading of the French king Louis XVI in early 1793. Among its achievements, the French Revolution expanded mass participation in political life and radicalized the democratic tradition inherited from the English and American experiences. But in the end, the passions unleashed in France by revolutionary events could not be sustained, and popular demagogues and the dictatorship of Napoleon stalled democratic reform.

French Society and Fiscal Crisis

French society was divided into three groups. The clergy, called the First Estate, numbered about 130,000 in a nation of 28 million. The Catholic Church owned about 10 percent of the nation's land and extracted substantial amounts of wealth from the economy in the form of tithes and ecclesiastical fees. Despite its substantial wealth, the church was exempted from nearly all taxes. The clergy was organized hierarchically, and members of the hereditary nobility held almost all the upper positions in the church.

The 300,000 members of the nobility, the Second Estate, controlled about 30 percent of the land and re-

tained ancient rights on much of the rest. Nobles held the vast majority of high administrative, judicial, military, and church positions. Though traditionally barred from some types of commercial activity, nobles were important participants in wholesale trade, banking, manufacturing, and mining. Like the clergy, this estate was hierarchical: important differences in wealth, power, and outlook separated the higher from the lower nobility. The nobility was also a highly permeable class: the Second Estate in the eighteenth century saw an enormous infusion of wealthy commoners who purchased administrative and judicial offices that conferred noble status.

The Third Estate included everyone else, from wealthy financier to homeless beggar. The bourgeoisie°, or middle class, grew rapidly in the eighteenth century. There were three times as many members of this class in 1774, when Louis XVI took the throne, as there had been in 1715, at the end of Louis XIV's reign. Commerce, finance, and manufacturing accounted for much of the wealth of the Third Estate. Wealthy commoners also owned nearly a third of the nation's land. This literate and socially ambitious class supported an expanding publishing industry, subsidized the fine arts, and purchased many of the extravagant new homes being built in Paris and other cities.

Peasants accounted for 80 percent of the French population. Artisans and other skilled workers, small shopkeepers and peddlers, and small landowners held a more privileged position in society. They owned some property and lived decently when crops were good and prices stable. By 1780 poor harvests had increased their cost of living and led to a decline in consumer demand for their products. They were rich enough to fear the loss of their property and status, well educated enough to be aware of the growing criticism of the king, but too poor and marginalized to influence policy.

The nation's poor were a large, growing, and troublesome sector. The poverty and vulnerability of peasant families forced younger children to seek seasonal work away from home and led many to crime and beggary. That raids by roving vagabonds threatened isolated farms was one measure of this social dislocation. In Paris and other French cities, the vile living conditions and unhealthy diet of the working poor were startling to visitors from other European nations. Urban streets swarmed with beggars and prostitutes. Paris alone had 25,000 prostitutes in 1760. The wretchedness of the French poor is perhaps best indicated by the growing

---

bourgeoisie (boor-zwah-ZEE)

problem of child abandonment. On the eve of the French Revolution at least forty thousand children a year were given up by their parents. The convenient fiction was that these children would be adopted; in reality the majority died of neglect.

Unable to afford decent housing, obtain steady employment, or protect their children, the poor periodically erupted in violent protest and rage. In the countryside violence was often the reaction when the nobility or clergy increased dues and fees. In towns and cities an increase in the price of bread often provided the spark, for bread prices largely determined the quality of life of the poor. These explosive episodes, however, were not revolutionary in character. The remedies sought were conventional and immediate rather than structural and long-term. That was to change when the Crown tried to solve its fiscal crisis.

The expenses of the War of the Austrian Succession began the crisis. Louis XV (r. 1715–1774) first tried to impose new taxes on the nobility and on other groups that in the past had enjoyed exemptions. But this effort failed in the face of widespread protest and the refusal of the Parlement of Paris, a court of appeal that heard appeals from local courts throughout France, to register the new tax. The crisis deepened when debts from the Seven Years War compelled the king to impose emergency fiscal measures. Again, the king met resistance from the Parlement of Paris. In 1768 frustrated authorities exiled the members of that Parlement and pushed through a series of unpopular fiscal measures. When the twenty-two-year-old Louis XVI assumed the throne in 1774, he attempted to gain popular support by recalling the exiled members of the Parlement of Paris, but he soon learned that provincial parlements had also come to see themselves as having a constitutional power to check any growth in monarchial authority.

In 1774 Louis's chief financial adviser warned that the government could barely afford to operate; as he put it, "the first gunshot [act of war] will drive the state to bankruptcy." Despite this warning, the French took on the heavy burden of supporting the American Revolution, delaying collapse by borrowing enormous sums and disguising the growing debt in misleading fiscal accounts. By the end of the war with Britain, more than half of France's national budget was required to service the debt alone. It soon became clear that fiscal reforms and new taxes, not new loans, were necessary.

In 1787 the desperate king called an Assembly of Notables to approve a radical and comprehensive reform of the economy and fiscal policy. Despite the fact that the members of this assembly were selected by the king's advisers from the high nobility, the judiciary, and the clergy, it proved unwilling to act as a rubber stamp for the proposed reforms or new taxes. Instead, these representatives of France's most privileged classes sought to protect their interests by questioning the competence of the king and his ministers to supervise the nation's affairs.

Protest Turns to Revolution, 1789–1792

In frustration, the king dismissed the Notables and attempted to implement some reforms on his own, but his effort was met by an increasingly hostile judiciary and by popular demonstrations. Because the king was unable to extract needed tax concessions from the French elite, he was forced to call the **Estates General,** the French national legislature, which had not met since 1614. The narrow self-interest and greed of the rich—who would not tolerate an increase in their taxes—rather than the grinding poverty of the common people, had created the conditions for political revolution.

In late 1788 and early 1789 members of the three estates came together throughout the nation to discuss grievances and elect representatives who would meet at Versailles°. The Third Estate's representatives were mostly men of property, but there was anger directed against the king's ministers and an inclination to move France toward constitutional monarchy with an elected legislature. Many nobles and members of the clergy sympathized with the reform agenda of the Third Estate, but deep internal divisions over procedural and policy issues limited the power of the First and the Second Estates.

Traditionally the three estates met separately, and a positive vote by two of the three was required for action. Tradition, however, was quickly overturned when the Third Estate refused to conduct business until the king ordered the other two estates to sit with it in a single body. During a six-week period of stalemate many parish priests from the First Estate began to meet with the commoners. When this expanded Third Estate declared itself the **National Assembly,** the king and his advisers recognized that the reformers intended to force them to accept a constitutional monarchy.

After being locked out of their meeting place, the Third Estate appropriated an indoor tennis court and pledged to write a constitution. The Oath of the Tennis Court ended Louis's vain hope that he could limit the agenda to fiscal reform. The king's effort to solve the

Versailles (vuhr-SIGH)

nation's fiscal crisis was being connected in unpredictable ways to the central ideas of the era: the people were sovereign, and the legitimacy of political institutions and individual rulers ultimately depended on their carrying out the people's will. Louis prepared for a confrontation with the National Assembly by moving military forces to Versailles. But before he could act, the people of Paris intervened.

A succession of bad harvests beginning in 1785 had propelled bread prices upward throughout France and provoked an economic depression as demand for nonessential goods collapsed. By the time the Estates General met, nearly a third of the Parisian work force was unemployed. Hunger and anger marched hand in hand through working-class neighborhoods.

When the people of Paris heard that the king was massing troops in Versailles to arrest the representatives, crowds of common people began to seize arms and mobilize. On July 14, 1789, a crowd searching for military supplies attacked the Bastille°, a medieval fortress used as a prison. The futile defense of the Bastille cost ninety-eight lives before its garrison surrendered. Enraged, the attackers hacked the commander to death and then paraded through the city with his head and that of Paris's chief magistrate stuck on pikes.

These events coincided with uprisings by peasants in the country. Peasants sacked manor houses and destroyed documents that recorded their traditional obligations. They refused to pay taxes and dues to landowners and seized common lands. Forced to recognize the fury raging through rural areas, the National Assembly voted to end traditional obligations and to reform the tax system. Having forced acceptance of their narrow agenda, the peasants ceased their revolt.

These popular uprisings strengthened the hand of the National Assembly in its dealings with the king. One manifestation of this altered relationship was passage of the **Declaration of the Rights of Man.** There were clear similarities between the language of this declaration and the U.S. Declaration of Independence. Indeed, Thomas Jefferson, who had written the American document, was U.S. ambassador to Paris and offered his opinion to those involved in the drafting of the French statement. The French declaration, however, was more sweeping in its language than the American one. Among the enumerated natural rights were "liberty, property, security, and resistance to oppression." The Declaration of the Rights of Man also guaranteed free expression of ideas, equality before the law, and representative government.

Bastille (bass-TEEL)

Parisian Stocking Mender   The poor lived very difficult lives. This woman uses a discarded wine barrel as a shop where she mends socks.   (Private collection)

While delegates debated political issues in Versailles, the economic crisis worsened in Paris. Women employed in the garment industry and in small-scale retail businesses were particularly hard hit. Because the working women of Paris faced high food prices every day as they struggled to feed their families, their anger had a hard edge. Public markets became political arenas where the urban poor met daily in angry assembly. Here the revolutionary link between the material deprivation of the French poor and the political aspirations of the French bourgeoisie was forged.

On October 5, market women organized a crowd of thousands to march the 12 miles (19 kilometers) to Versailles (see Society and Culture: The March to Versailles on page 588). Once there, they forced their way into the National Assembly to demand action from the frightened representatives: "the point is that we want bread."

Parisian Women Marching on Versailles   When the market women of Paris marched to Versailles and forced the royal family to return to Paris with them, they altered the course of the French Revolution. In this drawing the women are armed with pikes and swords and drag a cannon. Only the woman on the far left is clearly middle class, and she is pictured hesitating or turning away from the resolute actions of the poor women around her.   (Bibliothèque nationale de France)

The crowd then entered the royal apartments, killed some of the king's guards, and searched for Queen Marie Antoinette°, whom they loathed as a symbol of extravagance. Eventually, the crowd demanded that the royal family return to Paris. Preceded by the heads of two aristocrats carried on pikes and hauling away the palace's supply of flour, the triumphant crowd escorted the royal family to Paris.

With the king's ability to resist democratic change overcome by the Paris crowd, the National Assembly achieved a radically restructured French society in the next two years. It passed a new constitution that dramatically limited monarchial power and abolished the nobility as a hereditary class. Economic reforms swept away monopolies and trade barriers within France. The Legislative Assembly (the new constitution's name for the National Assembly) seized church lands to use as collateral for a new paper currency, and priests— who were to be elected—were put on the state payroll. When the government tried to force priests to take a loyalty oath, however, many Catholics joined a growing counterrevolutionary movement.

At first, many European monarchs had welcomed the weakening of the French king, but by 1791 Austria and Prussia threatened to intervene in support of the monarchy. The Legislative Assembly responded by declaring war. Although the war went badly at first for French forces, people across France responded patriotically to foreign invasions, forming huge new volunteer armies and mobilizing national resources to meet the challenge. By the end of 1792 French armies had gained the upper hand everywhere.

The Terror, 1793–1794

In this period of national crisis and foreign threat, the French Revolution entered its most radical phase. A failed effort by the king and queen to escape from Paris and find foreign allies cost the king any remaining popular support. As foreign armies crossed into France, his behavior was increasingly viewed as treasonous. On August 10, 1792, a crowd similar to the one that had marched on Versailles

---

Antoinette (ann twah-NET)

SOCIETY & CULTURE

The March to Versailles

Marie-Rose Barré, a 20-year old lace worker, participated in one of the most dramatic events of the French Revolution, the march of Parisian market women to Versailles in October 1789. The initial object of the march was to protest the high cost of bread. Once in Versailles, the crowd forced King Louis XVI and his family to return to Paris. In her testimony given shortly afterward to the Paris municipal council, Barré avoided any suggestion that she had been a leader of the march or that she had threatened the royal family.

. . . on October 5 last, at about eight o'clock in the morning, going to take back some work, she was stopped at the Pont Notre Dame by about a hundred women who told her that it was necessary to go with them to Versailles to ask for bread there. Not being able to resist this great number of women, she decided to go with them. At the hamlet at the Point-du-Jour, two young men, unknown to her, who were on foot and going their way, told them that they were running a great risk, that there were cannon mounted at the bridge at Saint-Cloud. This did not prevent them from continuing on their way. . . . At Versailles they found the King's Guards lined up in three ranks before the palace. A gentleman dressed in the uniform of the King's Guard . . . came to ask them what they wanted of the King, recommending peaceful behavior on their part. They answered that they were coming to ask him for bread. This gen-

tleman was absent for a few minutes and then returned to take four of them to introduce them to the King. The deponent was one of the four. . . .

They spoke first to M. de Saint-Priest, and then to His Majesty, whom they asked for bread. His Majesty answered them that he was suffering at least as much as they were, to see them lacking it, and that so far as he was able he had taken care to prevent them from experiencing a dearth. . . . The King promised them to have the flour escorted and said that if it depended on him, they would have bread then and there. They took leave of His Majesty and were led, by a gentleman in a blue uniform with red piping, into the apartments and courts of the palace to the ranks of the Flanders regiment, to which they called out. "Vive Le Roi!" It was then about nine o'clock. After this, they retired into a house on Rue Satory and went to bed in a stable.

Is it likely that someone pressured to join this march would have been selected to meet with the king to present the protestors' grievances? Does the king's concern for the plight of the poor ring true?

Source: Philip Dawson, ed., *The French Revolution* (Englewood Cliffs, N.J.: Prentice-Hall, Inc., 1967), pp. 66–67. Reprinted with permission of Simon & Schuster. Copyright © 1967 by Prentice-Hall, Inc., renewed 1995 by Philip Dawson.

invaded his palace in Paris and forced the king to seek protection in the Legislative Assembly. The Assembly suspended the king, ordered his imprisonment, and called for the formation of a new National Convention to be elected by the vote of all men.

Rumors of counterrevolutionary plots kept working-class neighborhoods in an uproar. In September mobs surged through the city's prisons, killing nearly half of the prisoners. Swept along by popular passion, the newly elected National Convention convicted Louis XVI of treason, sentencing him to death and proclaiming France a republic. The guillotine ended the king's life in January 1793. Invented in the spirit of the era as a more humane way to execute the condemned, this machine was to become the bloody symbol of the revolution.

The National Convention—the new legislature of the new First Republic of France—convened in September. Almost all of its members were from the middle class, and nearly all were **Jacobins**°—the most uncompromising democrats. Deep political differences, however, separated moderate Jacobins—called "Girondists°," after a region in southern France—and radicals known as "the Mountain." Members of the Mountain—so named because their seats were on the highest level in the assembly hall—were more sympathetic than the Girondists to the demands of the Parisian working class and more impatient with parliamentary procedure and constitutional constraints on government action. The Mountain

Jacobin (JAK-uh-bin) **Girondist** (juh-RON-dist)

ÉGALITÉ DE DEVOIRS   LIBERTÉ DES CULTES   EGALITÉ DE COULEURS

Playing Cards from the French Revolution   Even playing cards could be used to attack the aristocracy and Catholic Church. In this pack of cards, "Equality" and "Liberty" replaced kings and queens.   (Jean-Loup Charmet)

came to be dominated by **Maximilien Robespierre°,** a young, little-known lawyer from the provinces who had been influenced by Rousseau's ideas.

With the French economy still in crisis and Paris suffering from inflation, high unemployment, and scarcity, Robespierre used the popular press and political clubs to forge an alliance with the volatile Parisian working class. His growing strength in the streets allowed him to purge the National Convention of his enemies and to restructure the government. Executive power was placed in the hands of the newly formed Committee of Public Safety, which created special courts to seek out and punish domestic enemies.

Among the groups that lost ground were the active feminists of the Parisian middle class and the working-class women who had sought the right to bear arms in defense of the Revolution. These women had provided decisive leadership at crucial times, helping propel the Revolution toward a widened suffrage and a more democratic structure. Armed women had actively participated in every confrontation with conservative forces. It is ironic that the National Convention—the revolutionary era's most radical legislative body, one elected by universal male suffrage—chose to repress the militant feminist forces that had prepared the ground for its creation.

Faced with rebellion in the provinces and foreign invasion, Robespierre and his allies unleashed a period of repression called the Reign of Terror (1793–1794). During the Terror, approximately 40,000 people were executed or died in prison, and another 300,000 were thrown into prison. New actions against the clergy were also approved, including the provocative measure of

forcing priests to marry. Even time was subject to revolutionary change. A new republican calendar created twelve thirty-day months divided into ten-day weeks. Sunday, with its Christian meanings, disappeared from the calendar.

By the spring of 1794 the Revolution was secure from foreign and domestic enemies, but repression, now institutionalized, continued. Among the victims were some who had been Robespierre's closest political collaborators during the early stage of the Terror. The execution of these former allies prepared the way for Robespierre's own fall by undermining the sense of invulnerability that had secured the loyalty of his remaining partisans in the National Convention. After French victories eliminated the immediate foreign threat, conservatives in the Convention felt secure enough to vote for the arrest of Robespierre on July 27, 1794. Over the next two days, Robespierre and nearly a hundred of his remaining allies were executed by guillotine.

Reaction and Dictatorship, 1795–1815

Purged of Robespierre's collaborators, the Convention began to undo the radical reforms. It removed many of the emergency economic controls that had been holding down prices and protecting the working class. Gone also was toleration for violent popular demonstrations. When the Paris working class rose in protest in 1795, the Convention approved the use of overwhelming military force. Another retreat from radical objectives was signaled when the Catholic Church was permitted to regain much of its former influence. The church's confiscated wealth, however, was not returned.

Robespierre (ROBES-pee-air)

Map 23.2 Napoleon's Europe, 1810 By 1810, Great Britain was the only remaining European power at war with Napoleon. Because of the loss of the French fleet at the Battle of Trafalgar in 1805, Napoleon was unable to threaten Britain with invasion, and Britain was able to actively assist the resistance movements in Spain and Portugal, thereby helping to weaken French power.

A more conservative constitution was also ratified. It protected property, established a voting process that reduced the power of the masses, and created a new executive authority, the Directory. Once installed in power, however, the Directory proved unable to end the foreign wars or solve domestic economic problems.

After losing the election of 1797, the Directory suspended the results. The republican phase of the Revolution was clearly dead. Legitimacy was now based on coercive power rather than on elections. Two years later, **Napoleon Bonaparte** (1769–1821), a brilliant young general in the French army, seized power. Just as the American and French Revolutions had been the start of the modern democratic tradition, the military intervention that brought Napoleon to power in 1799 marked the advent of another modern form of government: popular authoritarianism.

The American and French Revolutions had resulted in part from conflicts over representation. If the people were sovereign, what institutions best expressed popular will? In the United States, the answer was to expand the electorate and institute representative government. The French Revolution had taken a different direction with the Reign of Terror. Interventions on the floor of the National Convention by market women and soldiers, the presence of common people at revolutionary tribunals and at public executions, and expanded military service were all forms of political communication that satisfied, temporarily, the French people's desire to influence their government. Napoleon tamed these forms of political expression to organize Europe's first popular dictatorship. He succeeded because his military reputation promised order to a society exhausted by a decade of crisis, turmoil, and bloodshed.

In contrast to the National Convention, Napoleon proved capable of realizing France's dream of dominating Europe and providing effective protection for persons and property at home. Negotiations with the Catholic Church led to the Concordat of 1801. This agreement gave French Catholics the right to freely practice their religion, and it recognized the French government's authority to nominate bishops and retain priests on the state payroll. In his comprehensive rewriting of French law, the Civil Code of 1804, Napoleon won the support of the peasantry and of the middle class by asserting two basic principles inherited from the moderate first stage of the French Revolution: equality in law and protection of property. Even some members of the nobility became supporters after Napoleon declared himself emperor and France an empire in 1804. However, the discrimination against women that had begun during the Terror was extended by the Napoleonic Civil Code. Women were denied basic political rights and were able to participate in the economy only with the guidance and supervision of their fathers and husbands.

While providing personal security, the Napoleonic system denied or restricted many individual rights. Free speech and free expression were limited. Criticism of the government, viewed as subversive, was proscribed, and most opposition newspapers disappeared. Spies and informers directed by the minister of police enforced these limits to political freedom. Thousands of the regime's enemies and critics were questioned or detained in the name of domestic tranquillity.

Ultimately, the Napoleonic system depended on the success of French arms and French diplomacy (see Map 23.2). From Napoleon's assumption of power until his fall, no single European state could defeat the French military. Even powerful alliances like that of Austria and Prussia were brushed aside with humiliating defeats and forced to become allies of France. Only Britain, protected by its powerful navy, remained able to thwart Napoleon's plans to dominate Europe. His effort to mobilize forces for an invasion of Britain failed in late 1805 when the British navy defeated the French and allied Spanish fleets off the coast of Spain at the Battle of Trafalgar.

Desiring to extend French power again to the Americas, Napoleon invaded Portugal in 1807 and Spain in 1808. French armies soon became tied down in a costly conflict with Spanish and Portuguese patriots who had forged an alliance with the only available European power, Great Britain. Frustrated by events on the Iberian Peninsula and faced with a faltering economy, Napoleon made the fateful decision to invade Russia. In June 1812 Napoleon began his campaign with the largest army ever assembled in Europe, approximately 600,000 men. After fighting an inconclusive battle at Borodino, Napoleon pressed on to Moscow. Five weeks after occupying Moscow, he was forced to retreat by Russian patriots who set the city on fire and by approaching armies. He ordered a retreat, but the brutal Russian winter and attacks by Russian forces destroyed his army. A broken and battered fragment of 30,000 men returned home to France.

After the debacle in Russia, Austria and Prussia deserted Napoleon and entered an alliance with England and Russia. Unable to defend Paris, Napoleon was forced to abdicate the French throne in April 1814. The allies exiled Napoleon to the island of Elba off the coast of Italy and restored the French monarchy. The next year Napoleon escaped from Elba and returned to France. But his moment had passed. He was defeated by an allied army at Waterloo, in Belgium, after only one hundred days in power. His final exile was on the distant island of St. Helena in the South Atlantic, where he died in 1821.

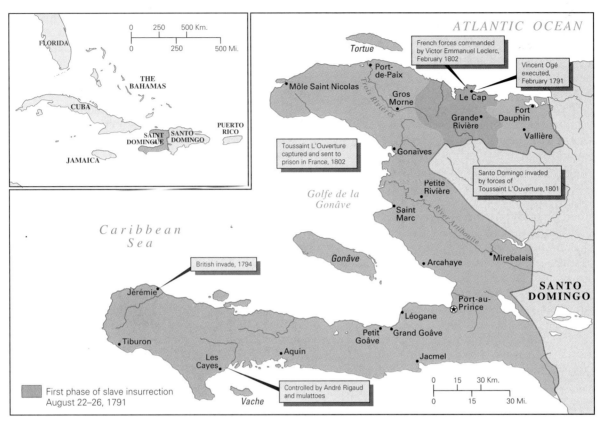

Map 23.3   The Haitian Revolution   On their way to achieving an end to slavery and gaining national independence, the Haitian revolutionaries were forced to defeat British and French military interventions as well as the local authority of the slave masters.

REVOLUTION SPREADS, CONSERVATIVES RESPOND, 1789–1850

Even as the dictatorship of Napoleon eliminated the democratic legacy of the French Revolution, revolutionary ideology was spreading and taking hold in Europe and the Americas. In Europe, the French Revolution promoted nationalism and republicanism. In the Americas, the legacies of the American and French Revolutions led to a new round of struggles for independence. News of revolutionary events in France destabilized the colonial regime in Saint Domingue (present-day Haiti), a small French colony on the western half of the island of Hispaniola, and resulted in the first successful slave rebellion. In Europe, however, the spread of revolutionary fervor was checked by reaction as monarchs formed an alliance to protect themselves from further revolutionary outbreaks.

The Haitian Revolution, 1789–1804

In 1789 the French colony of Saint Domingue was among the richest European colonies in the Americas. Its plantations produced sugar, cotton, indigo, and coffee. The colony produced two-thirds of France's tropical imports and generated nearly one-third of all French foreign trade. This impressive wealth depended on a brutal slave regime. Saint Domingue's harsh punishments and poor living conditions were notorious throughout the Caribbean. The colony's high mortality and low fertility rates created an insatiable demand for African slaves. As a result the majority of the colony's 500,000 slaves in 1790 were African-born.

In 1789, when news of the calling of France's Estates General arrived on the island, wealthy white planters sent a delegation to Paris charged with seeking more home rule and greater economic freedom for Saint Domingue. The free mixed-race population, the **gens de couleur°,** also sent representatives. These delegates were mostly drawn from the large class of slave-owning small planters and urban merchants. They focused on gaining the end to race discrimination and the achievement of political equality with whites. They did not seek freedom for slaves, because the most prosperous gens de couleur were slave owners themselves. As the French Revolution became more radical, the gens de couleur forged an alliance with sympathetic French radicals, who came to identify the colony's wealthy planters as royalists and aristocrats.

The political turmoil in France weakened the ability of colonial administrators to maintain order. The authority of colonial officials was no longer clear, and the very legitimacy of slavery was being challenged in France. In the vacuum that resulted, rich planters, poor whites, and the gens de couleur each pursued their narrow interests, engendering an increasingly bitter and confrontational struggle. Given the slaves' hatred of the brutal regime that oppressed them and the accumulated grievances of the free people of color, there was no way to limit the violence once the control of the slave owners slipped. When Vincent Ogé°, leader of the gens de couleur mission to France, returned to Saint Domingue to organize a military force, planter forces captured, tortured, and executed him. This cruelty was soon repaid in kind.

By 1791 whites, led by the planter elite, and the gens de couleur were engaged in open warfare. This breach between the two groups of slave owners gave the slaves an opening. A slave rebellion began on the plantations of the north and spread throughout the colony (see Map 23.3). Plantations were destroyed, masters and overseers killed, and crops burned. An emerging rebel leadership that combined elements of African political culture with revolutionary ideology from France mobilized and directed the rebelling slaves.

The rebellious slaves eventually gained the upper hand under the leadership of **François Dominique Toussaint L'Ouverture,** a former domestic slave, who created a more disciplined military force. Toussaint was politically strengthened in 1794 when the radical National Convention in Paris abolished slavery in all French possessions. He overcame his rivals in Saint Domingue, defeated a British expeditionary force in 1798, and then

Toussaint L'Ouverture Negotiating with the British　The former slave Toussaint L'Ouverture led the successful slave rebellion in Saint Domingue (Haiti). He then defended the revolution against British and French military intervention. Notice that in this print Toussaint seems to command the scene, directing the attention of the British officers to the document that he holds in his hand. (Biblothèque nationale de France)

led an invasion of neighboring Santo Domingo, freeing the slaves there. Toussaint continued to assert his loyalty to France but gave the French government no effective role in local affairs.

As reaction overtook revolution in France, both the abolition of slavery and Toussaint's political position were threatened. When the Directory contemplated the reestablishment of slavery, Toussaint protested,

> Do they think that men who have been able to enjoy the blessing of liberty will calmly see it snatched away? They supported their chains only so long as they did not know any condition of life more happy than slavery. But today when they have left it, if they had a thousand lives they would sacrifice them all rather than be forced into slavery again.[1]

---

gens de couleur (zhahn deh koo-LUHR)　**Ogé** (oh-ZHAY)

In 1802 Napoleon sent a large military force to Saint Domingue to reestablish both French authority and slavery (see Map 24.3). At first the French forces were successful. Toussaint was captured and sent to France, where he died in prison. Eventually, however, the loss of thousands of lives to yellow fever and the resistance of the revolutionaries turned the tide. Visible in the resistance to the French were small numbers of armed women. During the early stages of the Haitian Revolution very few slave women had taken up arms, although many had aided Toussaint's forces in support roles. But after a decade of struggle and violence, more Haitian women were politically aware and willing to join the armed resistance. In 1804 Toussaint's successors declared independence, and the free republic of Haiti joined the United States as the second independent nation in the Western Hemisphere. But independence and emancipation were achieved at a terrible price. Tens of thousands had died, the economy was destroyed, and public administration was corrupted by more than a decade of violence. Political violence and economic stagnation were to trouble Haiti throughout the nineteenth century.

The Congress of Vienna and Conservative Retrenchment, 1815–1820

From 1814 to 1815 representatives of Britain, Russia, Austria, and Prussia met as the **Congress of Vienna** to reestablish political order in Europe. While they were meeting, Napoleon escaped from Elba, then was defeated at Waterloo. The French Revolution and Napoleon's imperial ambitions had threatened the very survival of the European old order. Ancient monarchies had been overturned and dynasties replaced with interlopers. Long-established political institutions had been tossed aside, and long-recognized international borders had been ignored. The very existence of the nobility and church had been put at risk. Under the leadership of the Austrian foreign minister, Prince Klemens von Metternich° (1773–1859), the allies worked together in Vienna to create a comprehensive peace settlement that they hoped would safeguard the conservative order.

The central objective of the Congress of Vienna was to roll back the clock in France. Because the participants believed that a strong and stable France was the best guarantee of future peace, the French monarchy was reestablished and France's 1792 borders were recognized. Most of the continental European powers received some territorial gains, for Metternich sought to offset French strength with a balance of power. In addition, Austria, Russia, and Prussia formed a separate alliance to confront more actively the revolutionary and nationalist energies that the French Revolution had unleashed. In 1820 this "Holy Alliance" acted decisively to defeat liberal revolutions in Spain and Italy. By repressing republican and nationalist ideas in universities and the press, the Holy Alliance also attempted to meet the potential challenge posed by subversive ideas. Metternich's program of conservative retrenchment succeeded in the short term, but powerful ideas associated with liberalism and nationalism remained a vital part of European political life throughout the nineteenth century.

Nationalism, Reform, and Revolution, 1821–1850

Despite the power of the conservative monarchs, popular support for national self-determination and democratic reform grew throughout Europe. Greece had been under Ottoman control since the fifteenth century. In 1821, Greek patriots launched an independence movement. Metternich and other conservatives opposed Greek independence, but European artists and writers enamored with the cultural legacy of ancient Greece rallied political support for intervention. After years of struggle, Russia, France, and Great Britain forced the Ottoman Empire to recognize Greek independence in 1830.

Louis XVIII, brother of the executed Louis XVI, had been placed on the throne of France by the victorious allies in 1814. He ruled as a constitutional monarch until his death in 1824 and was followed to the throne by his brother, Charles X. Charles attempted to rule in the pre-revolutionary style of his ancestors, repudiating the constitution in 1830. Unwilling to accept this reactionary challenge, the people of Paris rose up and forced Charles to abdicate. His successor was his cousin Louis Philippe° (r. 1830–1848), who accepted the reestablished constitution and extended voting privileges.

At the same time, in both the United States and Great Britain, democratic reform movements appeared. In the United States after 1790, new states with constitutions granting voting rights to most free males joined the original thirteen states. After the War of 1812, the right to vote was expanded in the older states as well. This broadening of the franchise led in 1828 to the election of the populist president Andrew Jackson (see Chapter 25).

However, revolutionary violence in France made the British aristocracy and the conservative Tory Party fearful of expanded democracy and mass movements of any kind. In 1815 the British government passed the Corn

---

Metternich (MET-uhr-nik)

Louis Philippe (loo-EE-fee-LEEP)

The Revolution of 1830 in Belgium   After the 1830 uprising that overturned the restored monarchy in France, Belgians rose up to declare their independence from Holland. In Poland and Italy, similar uprisings, combining nationalism and a desire for self-governance, failed. This painting by Baron Gustaf Wappers romantically illustrates the popular nature of the Belgian uprising by bringing to the barricades men, women, and children drawn from both the middle and the working classes   (Musées royaux des Beaux-Arts de Belgique, Brussels)

Laws, which limited the importation of foreign grains. This law favored the profits of wealthy landowners that produced grain at the expense of the poor who were forced to pay more for their bread. When poor consumers organized to overturn these laws, the government outlawed most public meetings, using troops to crush protest in Manchester. Reacting against these policies, reformers gained the passage of laws that increased the power of the House of Commons, redistributed votes from agricultural to industrial districts, and increased the number of voters by nearly 50 percent. Although the most radical demands of these reformers, called Chartists, were defeated, new labor and economic reforms addressing the grievances of workers were passed (see Chapter 24).

Despite the achievement of Greek independence and limited political reform in France and Great Britain, conservatives continued to hold the upper hand in Europe. Finally, in 1848, the desire for democratic reform and national self-determination and the frustrations of urban workers led to upheavals across Europe. The **Revolutions of 1848** began in Paris, where members of the middle class and workers united to overthrow the regime of Louis Philippe and create the Second French Republic. Adult men were given voting rights, slavery was abolished in French colonies, the death penalty was ended, and a ten-hour workday was legislated for Paris. But Parisian workers' demand for programs to reduce unemployment and lower prices provoked conflicts with the middle class, which wanted to protect property rights. When workers rose up against the government, French troops were called out to crush them. Desiring the reestablishment of order, the French elected Louis Napoleon, nephew of the former emperor, president in December 1848. Three years later, he overturned the constitution as a result of popular plebiscite and, after ruling briefly as dictator, became Emperor Napoleon III. He remained in power until 1871.

Reformers in Hungary, Italy, Bohemia, and elsewhere pressed for greater national self-determination in 1848. When the Austrian monarchy hesitated to meet such demands, students and workers in Vienna took to the streets to force political reforms similar to those sought in Paris. With revolution spreading throughout the Austrian Empire, Metternich, the symbol of reaction, fled Vienna in disguise. Little lasting change occurred, however, because the new Austrian emperor, Franz Joseph (r. 1848–1916) was able to use Russian military assistance and loyal Austrian troops to reestablish central authority.

Middle-class reformers and workers in Berlin joined forces in an attempt to compel the Prussian king to accept a liberal constitution and seek unification of the German states. But the Constituent Assembly called to write a constitution and arrange for national integration became entangled in diplomatic conflicts with Austria and Denmark. As a result, Frederick William IV (r. 1840–1861) was able to reassert his authority, thwarting both constitutional reform and unification.

Despite their heroism on the barricades of Paris, Vienna, Rome, and Berlin, the revolutionaries of 1848 failed to gain either their nationalist or their republican objectives. Monarchs retained the support not only of aristocrats but also of professional militaries, largely recruited from among peasants who had little sympathy for urban workers. Revolutionary coalitions, in contrast, were fragile and lacked clear objectives. Workers' demands for higher wages, lower prices, and labor reform often drove their middle-class allies into the arms of the reactionaries.

CONCLUSION

This era of revolution was, in large measure, the product of a long period of costly warfare among the imperial nations of Europe. Using taxes and institutions inherited from the past, England and France found it increasingly difficult to fund distant wars in the Americas or in Asia. Royal governments attempting to impose new taxes met with angry resistance. The spread of literacy and the greater availability of books helped create a European culture more open to reform or revolutionary change of existing institutions. The ideas of Locke and Rousseau guided critics of monarchy toward a new political culture of elections and representative institutions. Each new development served as example and provocation for new revolutionary acts. French officers who took

part in the American Revolution helped ignite the French Revolution. Black freemen from Haiti traveled to France to seek their rights and returned to spread revolutionary passions. Each revolution had its own character. The revolutions in France and Haiti proved to be more violent and destructive than the American Revolution. Revolutionaries in France and Haiti, facing a more strongly entrenched and more powerful opposition and greater social inequalities, responded with greater violence.

The conservative retrenchment that followed the defeat of Napoleon succeeded in the short term. Monarchy, multinational empires, and the established church retained their hold on the loyalty of millions of Europeans and could count on the support of many of Europe's wealthiest and most powerful individuals. But liberalism and nationalism continued to stir revolutionary sentiment. The contest between adherents of the old order and partisans of change was to continue well into the nineteenth century. In the end, the nation-state, the Enlightenment legacy of rational inquiry, broadened political participation, and secular intellectual culture were to prevail. This outcome was determined in large measure by the old order's inability to satisfy the new social classes that appeared with the emerging industrial economy. The material transformation produced by industrial capitalism could not be contained in the narrow confines of a hereditary social system, nor could the rapid expansion of scientific learning be contained within the doctrines of traditional religion.

The revolutions of the late eighteenth century began the transformation of Western society, but they did not complete it. Only a minority gained full political rights. Women achieved full political rights only in the twentieth century. Democratic institutions, as in revolutionary France, often failed. Moreover, as Chapter 25 will discuss, slavery endured in the Americas past the mid-1800s, despite the revolutionary era's enthusiasm for individual liberty.

■ Key Terms

Enlightenment	Jacobins
Benjamin Franklin	Maximilien Robespierre
George Washington	Napoleon Bonaparte
Joseph Brant	*gens de couleur*
Constitutional Convention	François Dominique
Estates General	Toussaint L'Ouverture
National Assembly	Congress of Vienna
Declaration of the Rights of Man	Revolutions of 1848

■ Suggested Reading

The American Revolution has received a great amount of attention from scholars. Colin Bonwick, *The American Revolution* (1991), and Edward Countryman, *The American Revolution* (1985), provide excellent introductions. Edmund S. Morgan, *The Challenge of the American Revolution* (1976), remains a major work of interpretation. Gordon S. Wood, *The Radicalism of the American Revolution* (1992), is a brilliant examination of the ideological and cultural meanings of the Revolution. See also William Howard Adams, *The Paris Years of Thomas Jefferson* (1997). Lance Banning, *The Sacred Fire of Liberty: James Madison and the Founding of the Federal Republic* (1995), is a convincing revision of the story of Madison and his era. For the role of women in the American Revolution see Linda K. Kerber, *Women of the Republic: Intellect and Ideology in Revolutionary America* (1980), and Mary Beth Norton, *Liberty's Daughters: The Revolutionary Experience of American Women, 1750–1800* (1980). Also recommended is Norton's *Founding Mothers and Fathers: Gendered Power and the Forming of American Society* (1996). Among the many works that deal with African-Americans and Amerindians during the era, see Sylvia Frey, *Water from Rock: Black Resistance in a Revolutionary Age* (1991); Barbara Graymont, *The Iroquois in the American Revolution* (1972); and William N. Fenton, *The Great Law and the Longhouse: A Political History of the Iroquois Confederacy* (1998).

For intellectual life in the era of the French Revolution see Anne Goldgar, *Impolite Learning: Conduct and Community in the Republic of Letters, 1680–1750* (1995), and Dena Goodman, *The Republic of Letters: A Cultural History of the Enlightenment* (1994). For the "underside" of this era see *Shaping History: Ordinary People in European Politics, 1500–1700* (1998), by Wayne Te Brake, for a discussion of "folk culture." François Furet, *Interpreting the French Revolution* (1981), breaks with interpretations that emphasize class and ideological interpretations. Georges Lefebve, *The Coming of the French Revolution*, trans. R. R. Palmer (1947), presents the classic class-based analysis. George Rudé, *The Crowd in History: Popular Disturbances in France and England* (1981), remains the best introduction to the role of mass protest in the period. Lynn Hunt, *The Family Romance of the French Revolution* (1992), examines the gender content of revolutionary politics. For the role of women see Joan Landes, *Women and the Public Sphere in the Age of the French Revolution* (1988), and the recently published *The Women of Paris and Their French Revolution* (1998) by Dominique Godineau. Felix Markham, *Napoleon* (1963), and Robert B. Holtman, *The Napoleonic Revolution* (1967), provide reliable summaries of the period.

The Haitian Revolution has received less extensive coverage than the revolutions in the United States and France. C. L. R. James, *The Black Jacobins*, 2d ed. (1963), is the classic study. Anna J. Cooper, *Slavery and the French Revolutionists, 1788–1805* (1988), also provides an overview of this important topic. Carolyn E. Fick, *The Making of Haiti: The Saint Domingue Revolution from Below* (1990), is the best recent synthesis. David P. Geggus, *Slavery, War, and Revolution* (1982), examines the British role in the revolutionary period. See also David Barry Gaspar and David Patrick Geggus, eds., *A Turbulent Time: The French Revolution and the Greater Caribbean* (1997).

For the revolutions of 1830 and 1848 see Arthur J. May, *The Age of Metternich, 1814–48*, rev. ed. (1963), for a brief survey. Henry Kissinger's *A World Restored* (1957) remains among the most interesting discussions of the Congress of Vienna. Eric Hobsbawm's *The Age of Revolution* (1962) provides a clear analysis of the class issues that appeared during this era. Paul Robertson's *Revolutions of 1848: A Social History* (1960) remains a valuable introduction. See also Peter Stearns and Herrick Chapman, *European Society in Upheaval* (1991). For the development of European social reform movements see Albert Lindemann, *History of European Socialism* (1983).

For national events in Hungary see István Deák's examination of Hungary, *The Lawful Revolution: Louis Kossuth and the Hungarians, 1848–49* (1979). For Germany, see Theodore S. Hamerow, *Restoration, Revolution, and Reaction, 1815–1871* (1966). For French events see Roger Price, *A Social History of Nineteenth-Century France* (1987). Barbara Taylor, *Eve and the New Jerusalem: Socialism and Feminism in the Nineteenth Century* (1983), analyzes connections between workers' and women's rights issues in England.

■ Note

1. Quoted in C. L. R. James, *The Black Jacobins*, 2d ed., rev. (New York: Vintage Books, 1963), 196.

24

THE EARLY INDUSTRIAL REVOLUTION,

1760–1851

Causes of the Industrial Revolution • The Technological Revolution •
The Impact of the Industrial Revolution • Ideological and Political Responses
to Industrialization • Industrialization and the Nonindustrial World

ENVIRONMENT AND TECHNOLOGY: "The Annihilation of Time and Space"

SOCIETY AND CULTURE: Charles Babbage, Ada Lovelace, and the "Analytical Engine"

Opening of the Saltash Bridge over the Tamar River in England in 1859   During the celebrations,
a steam locomotive pulled a train over the bridge while a steam-powered paddle wheeler passed underneath.

n January 1840, a shipyard in Britain launched a radically new ship. The *Nemesis* had an iron hull, a flat bottom so it could navigate in shallow waters, and a steam engine to power it upriver and against the wind. The ship was heavily armed. In November it arrived off the coast of China. Though ships from Europe had been sailing to China for three hundred years, the *Nemesis* was the first steam-powered iron gunboat seen in Asian waters. A Chinese observer noted: "Iron is employed to make it strong. The hull is painted black, weaver's shuttle fashion. On each side is a wheel, which by the use of coal fire is made to revolve as fast as a running horse. . . . At the vessel's head is a Marine God, and at the head, stern, and sides are cannon, which give it a terrific appearance. Steam vessels are a wonderful invention of foreigners, and are calculated to offer delight to many."[1]

Instead of offering delight, the *Nemesis* and other steam-powered warships that soon joined it steamed up the Chinese rivers, bombarded forts and cities, and brought in troops and supplies. With this new weapon, Britain, a small island nation half a world away, was able to defeat the largest and most populated country in the world in its own heartland.

The *Nemesis* was no isolated invention. Its outstanding features—steam power and cheap iron— were part of a larger phenomenon, the **Industrial Revolution,** that involved dramatic innovations in manufacturing, mining, transportation, and communications and equally rapid changes in society and commerce. New technologies and new social and economic arrangements allowed the industrializing countries—first Britain, followed by western Europe and the United States—to unleash massive increases in production and productivity, exploit the world's natural resources as never before, and transform the environment and human life in unprecedented ways.

The distribution of this power and wealth was very uneven. The people who owned and controlled these innovations amassed wealth and power over nature and over other people. Workers and their children were harmed, for industrialization widened the gap between rich and poor.

The effect of the Industrial Revolution around the world was also very uneven. The first countries to industrialize grew in wealth and power. But in Russia and eastern Europe, we cannot speak of an industrial revolution until the end of the nineteenth century. In Egypt, India, and a few other non-Western countries, the economic and military power of the European countries soon stifled the tentative beginnings of industrialization. China and other regions without industry were easily taken advantage of. The disparity between the industrial and the nonindustrial countries that exists today dates from the early nineteenth century.

As you read this chapter, ask yourself the following questions:

- What caused the Industrial Revolution?
- What were the key innovations that increased productivity and drove industrialization?
- What was the impact of these changes on the society and environment of the industrializing countries?
- How did the Industrial Revolution affect the relations between the industrialized and the nonindustrialized parts of the world?

CAUSES OF THE INDUSTRIAL REVOLUTION

What caused the Industrial Revolution, and why did it begin in England in the late eighteenth century? These are two of the great questions of history. The basic precondition of this momentous event seems to have been economic development propelled by population growth, an agricultural revolution, the expansion of trade, and an openness to innovation.

Population

The population of Europe rose in the eighteenth century— slowly at first, faster after 1780, then even faster in the early nineteenth century. The fastest growth took place in England and Wales. Population there rose from 5.5 million in 1688 to 9 million in 1801 and to 18 million by 1851—increases never before experienced in history.

The growth of population resulted from more reliable food supplies and more widespread resistance to disease. We know that industrialization was not the cause, for the populations of China and eastern and southern Europe were also growing. We also know that the population boom did not cause industrialization. But when economic growth and population growth occurred together, they reinforced each other.

More dependable food supplies and job opportunities led people to marry at an earlier age and have more children. A high birthrate meant a large percentage of children in the general population. In the early nineteenth century some 40 percent of the population of Britain was under fifteen years of age. This high proportion of youths explains both the vitality of the British people in that period and the widespread use of child labor. People also migrated at an unprecedented rate—from the countryside to the cities, from Ireland to England, and, more generally, from Europe to the Americas. Thanks to immigration, the population of the United States rose from 4 million in 1791 to 9.6 million in 1820 to 31.5 million in 1860—faster growth than in any other part of the world at the time.

The Agricultural Revolution

Innovations in manufacturing, energy, transportation, and communications could only have taken place alongside a simultaneous revolution in farming that provided food for city dwellers and forced poorer peasants off the land. This **agricultural revolution** began long before the eighteenth century. One important aspect was the acceptance of the potato, introduced from South America centuries earlier. In the cool and humid regions of Europe, from Ireland to Russia, potatoes yielded two or three times more food per acre than grain. Maize (American corn) was grown across Europe from southwestern France to the Balkans. Turnips, legumes, and clover did not deplete the soil and could be fed to cattle, sources of milk and meat. Additional manure from cattle in turn fertilized the soil for other crops.

Only prosperous landowners with secure titles to their land could afford the risks of new methods and new crops. Rich landowners therefore "enclosed" the land—that is, consolidated their holdings—and took over the commons that in the past had been open to all. Once in control of the land, they could make their tenants drain and improve the soil, breed better livestock, and introduce crop rotation. The security of small-scale tenant farmers and sharecroppers depended on traditional methods and rural customs such as gleaning in others' fields after the harvest, pasturing their animals on common village lands, and gathering firewood in common woods. This "enclosure movement" turned tenants and sharecroppers into landless farm laborers. Many moved to the cities to seek work; others became homeless migrants and vagrants; others emigrated.

In eastern Europe, as in Britain, large estates predominated and aristocratic landowners used such improvements to increase their wealth and political influence. In western Europe, enclosure was hampered by the fact that the law gave secure property rights to numerous small farmers.

Trade and Inventiveness

In most of Europe, the increasing demand that accompanied economic growth was met by increasing production in traditional ways. Roads were improved, so stagecoaches could travel faster. Royal manufacturers trained additional craftsmen to produce fine china, silks, and carpets by hand. In rural areas much production was carried out through the putting-out system. Merchants delivered fibers, leather, and other raw materials to craftspeople (often farmers in the off-season), and picked up the finished products.

The growth of the population and food supply was accompanied by the growth of trade. Most of it was local trade in traditional goods and services. But a growing share consisted of simple goods that even middle-class people could afford: sugar, tea, cotton textiles, iron hardware, pottery. Products from other parts of the world like tea and sugar, required extensive networks of shipping and finance.

In the late eighteenth century, technology and innovation fascinated educated people throughout Europe and eastern North America. The French *Encyclopédie* contained thousands of articles and illustrations of handicrafts. The American Benjamin Franklin, like many others, experimented with electricity. The Montgolfier brothers invented a hot-air balloon. Claude Chappe created the first semaphore telegraph. French artillery officers and the American Eli Whitney proposed making guns with interchangeable parts.

Britain and Continental Europe

Economic growth was evident everywhere in the North Atlantic area, yet industrialization did not take place everywhere at once. To understand why, we must look at the peculiar role of Great Britain.

Britain enjoyed a rising standard of living during the eighteenth century, thanks to good harvests, a growing

CHRONOLOGY

	Technology	Economy, Society, and Politics
1750		
	1759 Josiah Wedgwood opens pottery factory	
	1764 Spinning jenny	
	1769 Richard Arkwright's water frame; James Watt patents steam engine	**1776** Adam Smith's *Wealth of Nations*
		1776–1783 American Revolution
	1779 First iron bridge	
	1785 Boulton and Watt sell steam engines; Samuel Crompton's mule	**1789–1799** French Revolution
	1793 Eli Whitney's cotton gin	
1800	**1800** Alessandro Volta's battery	
	1807 Robert Fulton's *Clermont*	**1804–1815** Napoleonic Wars
	1820s Construction of Erie Canal	**1820s** U.S. cotton industry begins
	1829 *Rocket,* first steam-powered locomotive	**1833** Factory Act in Britain
		1834 German Zollverein; Robert Owen's Grand National Consolidated Trade Union
	1837 Wheatstone & Cooke's telegraph	
	1838 First ships steam across the Atlantic	
	1840 *Nemesis* sails to China	
	1843 Samuel Morse's Baltimore–to–Washington telegraph	**1846** Repeal of British Corn Laws
		1847–1848 Irish famine
1850	**1851** Crystal Palace opens in London	**1848** Collapse of Chartist movement; Revolutions in Europe
		1854 First cotton mill in India

population, and a booming overseas trade. Until the mid-eighteenth century, the British were better known for their cheap imitations than for their innovations or quality products. But they put inventions into practice more quickly than other people, as the engineer John Farey told a parliamentary committee in 1829: "The prevailing talent of English and Scotch people is to apply new ideas to use and to bring such applications to perfection, but they do not imagine as much as foreigners."

Britain was the world's leading exporter of tools, guns, hardware, and other craft goods (see Map 24.1). Its mining and metal industries employed engineers willing to experiment with new ideas. It had the largest merchant marine and produced more ships, naval supplies, and navigation instruments than other countries.

Before 1790, Britain had a more fluid society than the rest of Europe. The English royal court was less ostentatious than the courts of France, Spain, or Austria. Its aristocracy was less powerful, and the lines separating the social classes were less sharply drawn. Political power was not as centralized as on the European continent, and the government employed fewer bureaucrats and officials. Members of the gentry, and even some aris-

tocrats, married into merchant families. Intermarriage among the families of petty merchants, yeoman farmers, and town craftsmen was common. Guilds, which resisted innovation, were relatively weak. Ancestry remained important, but wealth also commanded respect. A businessman with enough money could buy a landed estate, a seat in Parliament, and the social status that accompanied them.

At a time when transportation by land was very costly, Great Britain had good water transportation, thanks to its indented coastline, navigable rivers, and growing network of canals. It had a unified internal market, with none of the duties and tolls that goods had to pay every few miles in France. This encouraged specialization and trade.

Britain was highly commercial. More people there were involved in production for export and in trade and finance than in any other major country. It was especially active in overseas trade with the Americas, West Africa, the Middle East, and India. It had financial and insurance institutions able to support growing business enterprises and a patent system that offered inventors the hope of rich rewards. The example of men who be-

Map 24.1 The Industrial Revolution in Britain, ca. 1850
The first industries arose in northern and western England. These regions had abundant coal and iron-ore deposits for the iron industry and a moist climate and fast-flowing rivers, factors important for the cotton-textile industry.

came wealthy and respected for their inventions—such as Richard Arkwright, the cotton magnate, and James Watt, the steam engine designer—stimulated others.

In the eighteenth century, the economies of continental Europe underwent a dynamic expansion, thanks to the efforts of individual entrepreneurs and investors. Yet growth was still hampered by high transportation costs, misguided government regulations, and rigid social structures. The Low Countries were laced with canals, but the terrain elsewhere in Europe made canal building costly and difficult. The ruling monarchies made some attempts to import British techniques and organize factory production, but they all floundered for lack of markets or management skills. From 1789 to 1815, Europe was the scene of revolutions and wars. War created opportunities for suppliers of weapons, uni-

forms, metal goods, food, and horses. The insecurity of the times and the interruption of trade with Britain weakened the incentive to invest in new technologies.

The political revolutions swept away the restrictions of the old regimes. After 1815, when peace returned, the economies of western Europe were ready to begin industrializing. Industrialization first took hold in Belgium and northern France, as their businessmen visited Britain to observe the changes and to spy out industrial secrets. In spite of British laws forbidding the emigration of skilled workers and the export of textile machinery, many slipped through. By the 1820s, several thousand Britons were at work on the continent of Europe setting up machines, training workers in the new methods, and even starting their own businesses.

Acutely aware of Britain's head start and of the need to stimulate their own industrialization, European governments took action. They created technical schools. They eliminated internal tariff barriers, tolls, and other hindrances to trade. They encouraged the formation of joint-stock companies and banks to channel private savings into industrial investments. On the European continent, as in Britain, cotton was the first industry. The mills of France, Belgium, and Germany served local markets but could not compete abroad with the more advanced British industry. By 1830, the political climate in western Europe was as favorable to business as Britain's had been a half-century earlier.

THE TECHNOLOGICAL REVOLUTION

Five revolutionary innovations spurred industrialization: (1) mass production through the division of labor, (2) new machines and mechanization, (3) a great increase in the supply of iron, (4) the steam engine and the changes it made possible in industry and transportation, and (5) the electric telegraph.

Mass Production: Pottery

The pottery industry offers a good example of **mass production,** the making of many identical items by breaking the process into simple repetitive tasks. East Asian potters had long known how to make fine glazed porcelain, or "china." In Europe before the mid-eighteenth century only the wealthy could afford fine porcelain imported from Asia. Middle-class people used pewter tableware, and the poor ate from wooden or earthenware bowls. Several royal manufactures—Meissen in Saxony, Delft in Holland, and Sèvres in France—were founded to produce exquisite handmade products for the courts and aristocracy, but their products were much too expensive for mass consumption. Meanwhile, more and more Europeans acquired a taste for tea, cocoa, and coffee, and wanted porcelain that would not spoil the flavor of hot beverages. This demand created opportunities for inventive entrepreneurs.

Britain, like other countries, had many small pottery workshops where craftsmen made a few plates and cups at a time. Much of this activity took place in a part of the Midlands that possessed good clay, coal for firing, and lead for glazing. There **Josiah Wedgwood** opened a pottery business in 1759. Today, the name Wedgwood is associated with expensive, highly decorated china. But Wedgwood's most important contribution lay in producing ordinary porcelain cheaply, by means of the **division of labor.**

To do so, he subdivided the work into highly specialized and repetitive tasks, such as unloading the clay, mixing it, pressing flat pieces, dipping the pieces in glaze, putting handles on cups, packing kilns, and carrying things from one part of his plant to another. He substituted the use of molds for the potter's wheel wherever possible, a change that not only saved labor but created identical plates and bowls that could be stacked. Wedgwood was also interested in new technologies. He invested in toll roads and canals so that clay could be shipped economically from southwestern England to his factories in the Midlands. In 1782, to mix clay and grind flint, he purchased one of the first steam engines to be used in industry.

These were radical departures from the age-old methods of craftsmanship. But the division of labor, strict discipline, and new machinery allowed Wedgwood to lower the cost of his products while improving their quality, and to offer his wares for sale at lower prices. His factory grew far larger than his competitors' factories and employed several hundred workers. His own salesmen traveled throughout England touting his goods.

Wedgwood's interest in applying technology to manufacturing was connected with his membership in the Birmingham Lunar Society, a group of manufacturers, scientists, and inventors who met when the moon was full so they could see their way home after dark. This critical mass of creative thinkers willing to exchange ideas and discoveries encouraged the atmosphere of experimentation and innovation that characterized late-eighteenth-century England. Similar societies through-

Wedgwood's Potteries   In Staffordshire, England, Josiah Wedgwood established a factory to mass-produce beautiful and inexpensive china. The bottle-shape buildings are kilns in which thousands of pieces of china could be fired at one time. Kilns, factories, and housing were all mixed together in pottery towns, and smoke from burning coal filled the air. (Mary Evans Picture Library)

out Britain were creating a vogue for science and giving the word *progress* a new meaning: "change for the better."

Mechanization: The Cotton Industry

The cotton industry, the largest industry in this period, illustrates the role of **mechanization,** the use of machines to do work previously done by hand. Cotton cloth had long been the most common fabric in China, India, and the Middle East, where it was spun and woven by hand. The cotton plant did not grow in Europe, but the cloth was so much cooler, softer, and cleaner than wool that wealthy Europeans developed a liking for this costly import. When the powerful English woolen industry persuaded Parliament to forbid the import of cotton cloth into England, it stimulated attempts to import cotton fiber and make the cloth locally. Here was an opportunity for enterprising inventors to reduce costs with labor-saving machinery.

To turn inventions into successful businesses, inventors had to link up with entrepreneurs or become businessmen themselves. Making a working prototype often took years, even decades, and many inventions led to dead ends. History remembers the successful, but even they struggled against great odds (see Society and Culture: Charles Babbage, Ada Lovelace, and the "Analytical Engine").

Beginning in the 1760s, a series of inventions revolutionized the spinning of cotton thread. The first was the spinning jenny, invented in 1764, which drew out the cotton fibers and twisted them into thread. The jenny was simple, cheap to build, and easy for one person to operate. Early models spun six or seven threads at once, later ones up to eighty. The thread, however, was soft and irregular and could be used only in combination with linen.

In 1769 **Richard Arkwright** invented another spinning machine, the water frame, which produced thread strong enough to be used without linen. Arkwright was both a gifted inventor and a successful businessman. His machine was larger and more complex than the jenny and required a source of power such as a water wheel, hence the name "water frame." To obtain the necessary energy, he installed many machines in one building, next to a fast-flowing river. The resemblance to a flour mill gave such enterprises the name cotton mill.

In 1785 Samuel Crompton patented a machine that combined the best features of the jenny and the water frame. This device, called a mule, produced a thread that was both strong and fine enough to be used in the finer qualities of cotton called muslin. The mule could make a finer, more even thread than any human, and at a lower cost. Now British industry could undersell high-quality handmade cotton cloth from India. As a result, British cotton output increased tenfold between 1770 and 1790.

The boom in thread production and the soaring demand for cloth created bottlenecks in weaving. Inventors in England rose to the challenge. The first power loom was introduced in 1784 but was not perfected until after 1815. Other inventions of that period included carding machines, chlorine bleach, and cylindrical printing presses. By the 1830s large English textile mills powered by steam engines were turning raw cotton into printed cloth. This was a far cry from the cottage industries of the previous century.

Mechanization offered two advantages: (1) productivity for the manufacturer and (2) price for the consumer. Whereas in India it took 500 hours to spin a pound of cotton, the mule of 1790 could do so in 3 person-hours, and the self-acting mule—an improved version introduced in 1830—required only 80 minutes. Cotton mills needed very few skilled workers, and managers often hired children to tend the spinning machines. The same was true of power looms, which gradually replaced handloom weaving: the number of power looms rose from 2,400 in 1813 to 500,000 by 1850. Meanwhile, the price of cloth fell by 90 percent from 1782 to 1812 and kept on dropping.

The industrialization of Britain made cotton into America's most valuable crop. In the 1790s, most of Britain's cotton came from India, as the United States produced a mere 750 tons, mostly long-staple cotton from South Carolina. In 1793, the American Eli Whitney patented his cotton gin, a simple device that separated the bolls from the fiber and made the growing of short-staple cotton economical. This invention permitted the spread of cotton farming into Georgia, then into Alabama, Mississippi, and Louisiana, and finally as far west as Texas. By the late 1850s the southern states were producing a million tons of cotton a year, five-sixths of the world's total.

With the help of British craftsmen who introduced jennies, mules, and power looms, Americans developed a cotton industry in the 1820s. By 1840, the United States had 1,200 cotton mills, two-thirds of them in New England, powered by water rather than steam.

The Iron Industry

Iron making also was transformed during the Industrial Revolution. Throughout Eurasia and Africa, iron had been in use for thousands of years for tools, swords and other weapons, and household items such as knives, pots, hinges, and locks. In the eleventh century, during the Song period, Chinese forges had produced cast iron in large quantities. Production declined after the Song, but iron continued to be common and inexpensive in China. Wherever iron was produced, however, deforestation eventually drove up the cost of charcoal (used for smelting) and restricted output. Furthermore, iron had to be repeatedly heated and hammered to drive out impurities, a difficult and costly process. Because of limited wood supplies and the high cost of skilled labor, iron was a rare and valuable metal outside China before the eighteenth century.

A major breakthrough occurred in 1709 when Abraham Darby discovered that coke (coal from which the impurities have been cooked out) could be used in place of charcoal. The resulting metal was of lower quality than charcoal-iron but much cheaper to produce, for coal was

Charles Babbage, Ada Lovelace, and the "Analytical Engine"

In the early nineteenth century, many professions relied on tables of numbers such as logarithms, astronomical positions, and actuarial data. Calculated by hand, these tables were full of arithmetic and typographical errors. In 1820, while correcting such a table, the English mathematician Charles Babbage exclaimed: "I wish to God these calculations had been executed by steam." Babbage went on to devise a machine—he called it the "Difference Engine"—to perform calculations and print out the results as flawlessly as a power loom produced cloth. While a prototype was being built, he designed the "Analytical Engine," which could interpret instructions inserted on punched cards and could alter its calculations in response to the results of previous calculations.

One of Babbage's assistants, Ada, the countess of Lovelace, translated an article by the Italian military engineer, L. F. Menabrea, about the Analytical Engine for the magazine Taylor's Scientific Memoirs. In his autobiography, published in 1864, Babbage recalled: "The late Countess of Lovelace informed me that she had translated the memoir of Menabrea. I asked why she had not herself written an original paper on a subject with which she was so intimately acquainted? To this Lady Lovelace replied that the thought had not occurred to her. I then suggested that she should add some notes to Menabrea's memoir; an idea which was immediately adopted.... The notes of the Countess of Lovelace extend to about three times the length of the original memoir. Their author has entered fully into almost all the very difficult and abstract questions concerned with the subject.

In the notes that she added to Menabrea's article, Ada Lovelace wrote the following:

The distinctive characteristic of the Analytical Engine, and that which has rendered it possible to endow mechanism with such extensive faculties as bid fair to make this engine the executive right-hand of abstract algebra, is the introduction into it of the principle which Jacquard devised for regulating, by means of punched cards, the most complicated patterns in the fabrication of brocaded stuffs [fabrics]. . . .

The bounds of *arithmetic* were outstepped the moment the idea of applying the cards had occurred; and the Analytical Engine does not occupy common ground with mere "calculating machines." It holds a position wholly its own; and the considerations it suggests are most interesting in their nature. . . . A new, a vast, and a powerful language is developed for the future use of analysis, in which to wield its truths so that these may become of more speedy and accurate practical application for the purposes of mankind than the means hitherto in our possession have rendered possible. Thus not only the mental and the material, but the theoretical and the practical in the mathematical world, are brought into more intimate and effective connexion with each other. We are not aware of its being on record that anything partaking in the nature of what is so well designated the *Analytical Engine* has been hitherto proposed, or even thought of, as a practical possibility, any more than the idea of a thinking or of a reasoning machine.

In short, Babbage invented the computer.

The first working computers were not built until a hundred years later, but Babbage is honored as the first person to imagine such a machine. And the widely used programming language Ada is named after his friend, the countess of Lovelace.

Is "a thinking or . . . a reasoning machine" a good description of a computer? Because Babbage's Analytical Engine did not use electricity, can it really be called a computer?

Source: From Philip Morison and Emily Morison, eds., *Charles Babbage and His Calculating Engines: Selected Writings by Charles Babbage and Others* (New York: Dover, 1961), 68, 251–252. © Copyright 1961. Reprinted by permission of Dover Publications.

Crystal Palace Interior   The Crystal Palace, built for the Universal Exposition of 1851, was the largest structure in England. It was made entirely prefabricated of iron and glass and was a forerunner of the great railroad stations of the late nineteenth century and the skyscrapers of the twentieth. (Guildhall Library, Corporation of London, The Bridgeman Art Library, London and New York)

plentiful. In 1784 Henry Cort found a way to remove some of the impurities in coke-iron by puddling—stirring the molten iron with long rods. By 1790 four-fifths of Britain's iron was made with coke; other countries still used charcoal. Coke-iron was cheaper and less destructive of forests, and it allowed a great expansion in the size of individual blast furnaces, substantially reducing the cost of iron. There seemed almost no limit to the quantity of iron that could be produced with coke. Britain's iron production began rising fast, from 17,000 tons in 1740 to 3 million tons in 1844, as much as in the rest of the world put together.

In turn, there seemed no limit to the amount of iron that an industrializing society would purchase or to the novel applications for this cheap and useful material. In 1779 the iron manufacturer Abraham Darby III (grand-son of the first Abraham Darby) built a bridge of iron across the Severn River. In 1851 Londoners marveled at the **Crystal Palace,** a huge greenhouse made entirely of iron and glass and large enough to enclose the tallest trees.

The idea of interchangeable parts originated in the eighteenth century, when French army officers attempted, without success, to persuade gun makers to produce precisely identical parts. The craftsmen continued to use traditional methods to make gun parts that had to be fitted together by hand. By the mid-nineteenth century, however, interchangeable-parts manufacturing had been adopted in the manufacture of firearms, farm equipment, and sewing machines. At the Crystal Palace exhibition of 1851, Europeans called it the "American system of manufactures." In the next hundred years, the use of machinery to mass-produce consumer items was to become the hallmark of American industry.

The Steam Engine

Although the mechanization of manufacturing was very important, the most revolutionary invention of the Industrial Revolution was surely the **steam engine,** a mechanical substitute for human and animal power as well as wind and water power. By the late seventeenth century many activities were experiencing serious bottlenecks for lack of energy. In particular, deep mines filled with water faster than horses could pump it out.

Scientists understood the concept of atmospheric pressure and had created experimental devices to turn heat into motion, but they had not found a way to put those devices to practical use. Then, between 1702 and 1712, Thomas Newcomen developed the first practical steam engine, a crude and inefficient device. Its voracious appetite for fuel mattered little in coal mines, where fuel was cheap, but it was too costly for other uses.

James Watt, an instrument maker at Glasgow University in Scotland, was asked to repair the university's model Newcomen engine. Watt realized that the engine wasted fuel because the cylinder had to be alternately heated and cooled. He developed a separate condenser—a vessel into which the steam was allowed to escape after it had done its work, leaving the cylinder always hot and the condenser always cold. Watt patented his idea in 1769. He enlisted the help of the iron manufacturer Matthew Boulton to turn his invention into a commercial product. In 1785, Boulton and Watt began selling steam engines to manufacturers of iron, pottery, and cotton.

Watt's steam engine was the most celebrated invention of the eighteenth century. Because there seemed almost no limit to the amount of coal in the ground, steam-generated energy seemed an inexhaustible source of power, and steam engines could be used where animal, wind, and water power were lacking. Without the steam engine, industrialization would have been a limited phenomenon.

Inspired by the success of Watt's engine, inventors in France in 1783, in the United States in 1787, and in England in 1788 put steam engines on boats. The need to overcome great distances in the United States explains why the first commercially successful steamboat was Robert Fulton's *Clermont*, which steamed between New York City and Albany in 1807.

Soon steamboats were launched on other American rivers, especially the Ohio and the Mississippi, gateways to the midwest. In the 1820s, the Erie Canal linked the Atlantic seaboard with the Great Lakes and opened Ohio, Indiana, and Illinois to European settlement. Steamboats proliferated west of the Appalachian Mountains; by 1830 some three hundred plied the Mississippi and its tributaries. To counter the competition from New York State, Pennsylvania built a thousand miles of canals by 1840. The United States was fast becoming a nation that moved by water.

Oceangoing steam-powered ships were much more difficult to build than riverboats, for the first steam engines used so much coal that no ship could carry more than a few days' worth. The *Savannah*, which crossed the Atlantic in 1819, was a sailing ship with an auxiliary steam engine that was used for only 90 hours of its 29-day trip. But engineers soon developed more efficient engines, and in 1838 two steamers, the *Great Western* and the *Sirius*, crossed the Atlantic on steam power alone. Elsewhere, sailing ships held their own until late in the century, for world trade was growing so fast that there was enough business for ships of every kind.

On land as on water, the problem was not imagining uses for steam-powered vehicles but building ones that worked, for steam engines were too heavy and weak to pull any weight. After Watt's patent expired in 1800, inventors experimented with lighter, more powerful high-pressure engines—an idea Watt had rejected as too dangerous. In 1804, the engineer Richard Trevithick built an engine that consumed twelve times less than Newcomen's and three times less than Watt's. With it, he built several steam-powered vehicles able to travel on roads or rails.

Horses could pull heavier wagons on wooden or iron rails than on cobblestone roads. By the 1820s England had many horse-powered railways. On one of them, the Stockton and Darlington Railway, the chief engineer, George Stephenson, began using steam locomotives in 1825. Four years later, the owners of the Liverpool and Manchester Railway organized a contest between steam-powered locomotives and horse-drawn wagons. Stephenson and his son Robert easily won the contest with their locomotive *Rocket*, which pulled a 20-ton train at up to 30 miles (48 kilometers) per hour. After that triumph, a railroad-building mania that lasted for twenty years swept Britain. The first lines linked towns and mines with the nearest harbor or waterway. In the late 1830s, passenger traffic soared, and entrepreneurs built lines between the major cities and then to small towns as well. Railroads were far cheaper, faster, and more comfortable than stagecoaches, and millions of people got in the habit of traveling.

The De Witt Clinton Locomotive, 1835–1840 The De Witt Clinton was the first steam locomotive built in the United States. The high smokestack let the hot cinders cool so they would not set fire to nearby trees, an important consideration at a time when eastern North America was still covered with forests. The three passenger cars are clearly horse-carriages fitted with railroad wheels. (Corbis)

In the United States, entrepreneurs built railroads as fast and cheaply as possible with an eye to quick profits, not long-term durability. By the 1840s, 6,000 miles (10,000 kilometers) of track radiated westward from Boston, New York, Philadelphia, and Baltimore and connected these cities to one another. The boom of the 1840s was dwarfed by the mania of the 1850s, when 21,000 miles (34,000 kilometers) of new track were laid, much of it westward across the Appalachians to Memphis, St. Louis, and Chicago. After 1856, the trip from New York to Chicago, which once took three weeks by boat and on horseback, could be made in forty-eight hours. More than anything else, it was the railroads that opened up the midwest, turning the vast prairie into wheat fields and pasture for cattle to feed the industrial cities of the eastern United States.

Railways triggered the industrialization of Europe (see Map 24.2). Belgium, independent since 1830, quickly copied the British. In France and Prussia, the state planned and supervised railroad construction from the start. This delayed construction until the mid-1840s. When it began, however, it had a greater impact than in Britain, for it not only satisfied the long-standing need for transportation, but also stimulated the iron, machinery, and construction industries.

Abundant coal and iron-ore deposits determined the concentration of industries in a swath of territories running from northern France through Belgium and the Ruhr district of western Germany to Silesia in Prussia (now part of Poland). In the 1850s and 1860s, the states of Germany experienced an industrial boom, as did France and Belgium.

Borsig Ironworks in Germany in the 1840s This foundry was built to supply rails, locomotives, and other iron products to the German railroads, then under construction. (Deutsches Technikmuseum Berlin. Photo: Hans-Joachim Bartsch. Bildarchiv Preussischer Kulturbesitz)

Map 24.2   Industrialization in Europe, ca. 1850   In 1850 industrialization was in its early stages on the European continent. The first industrial regions were comparatively close to England and possessed rich coal deposits: Belgium and the Ruhr district of Germany. Politics determined the location of railroads. Notice the star-shaped French network of rail lines emanating from Paris and the lines linking the different parts of the German Confederation.

Communication over Wires

The advent of railroads coincided with the development of the **electric telegraph.** After the Italian scientist Alessandro Volta invented the battery in 1800, making it possible to produce an electric current, many inventors tried to apply electricity to communication. The first practical telegraphy systems were developed almost simultaneously in England and America. In England, Wheatstone and Cooke introduced a five-needle telegraph in 1837; it remained in use until the early twentieth century. That same year, the American Samuel Morse introduced a code of dots and dashes that could be transmitted with a single wire; in 1843, he erected a line between Washington and Baltimore.

By the late 1840s, telegraph wires were being strung throughout the eastern United States and western Europe. In 1851, the first submarine telegraph cable was laid across the English Channel from England to France; it was the beginning of a network that eventually enclosed the entire globe. The world was rapidly shrinking, to the applause of Europeans and Americans for whom speed was a clear measure of progress (see Environmental and Technology: "The Annihilation of Time and Space"). No longer were communications limited to the speed of which a ship could sail or a horse could gallop.

"The Annihilation of Time and Space"

In the 1780s it took from five to eight months to sail from England to India, and a European writing a letter to someone in India usually had to wait two years for an answer. Fifty years later, when the first steamships and telegraph lines appeared, telegraph pioneer William O'Shaughnessy, serving with the British army in India, wrote:

> The progress of science is hourly adding to the catalogue of triumphs effected by the sagacity of man over the seeming impossibilities of nature. . . . A conquest still greater than all which I have quoted would be the annihilation of time and space in the accomplishment of correspondence.

By 1870, the voyage to India had been shortened to three weeks, and correspondents could expect answers to their letters in less than two months. What O'Shaughnessy called "the annihilation of time and space" had begun.

The telegraph had an even more astonishing impact on global communications. Beginning in the 1860s, cables laid on the ocean floor allowed telegrams to be sent across oceans as readily as on land. When the first cable to India was completed in June 1870, the chairman of the Eastern Telegraph Company, John Pender, sent a telegram to Bombay and received an answer 4 minutes and 22 seconds later. The *Daily Telegraph* of London reported this astonishing news:

> Aladdin . . . must have dropped his wonderful lamp in sheer amazement and neglect, and sold his magic ring for old gold. Time itself is telegraphed out of existence. Today communicates on one hand with Yesterday, on the other, with tomorrow.

The easy, almost instantaneously communication with any country in the world that we take for granted today began in the mid-nineteenth century. Since that time, communications technologies have made the world a much smaller and more intimate place—for those who can afford them.

Source: Sir William Brooke O'Shaughnessy, "Memoranda Relative to Experiments on the Communication of Telegraphic Signals by Induced Electricity," *Journal of the Asiatic Society of Bengal* (September 1839): 720–721. Quoted in G. R. M. Garatt, *One Hundred Years of Submarine Cables* (London: HMSO, 1950), 29.

Transatlantic Steamship Race   In 1838, two ships equipped with steam engines, the *Sirius* and the *Great Western*, steamed from England to New York. Although the *Sirius* left a few days earlier, the *Great Western*—shown here arriving in New York harbor—almost caught up with it, arriving just four hours after the *Sirius*. This race inaugurated regular transatlantic steamship service.   (Courtesy of the Mariner's Museum, Newport News, VA)

Overcrowded London   The French artist Gustave Doré depicted the tenements of industrial London where workers and their families lived. This drawing shows crowded and unsanitary row houses, each one room wide, with tiny back yards, and a train steaming across a viaduct overhead.   (Prints Division, New York Public Library, Astor, Lenox, and Tilden Foundations)

THE IMPACT OF THE
INDUSTRIAL REVOLUTION

Although inventions were the most visible aspect of the Industrial Revolution, many other changes in society, politics, and the economy took place, interacting with one another. At first, the changes were quite local: smoky cities, slum neighborhoods, polluted water, child labor in mines and textile mills. By the mid-nineteenth century, the worst local effects were being alleviated. Replacing them on a national or even international scale were more complex problems: business cycles, labor conflicts, and the transformation of entire regions into industrial landscapes.

The New Industrial Cities

The most dramatic environmental changes brought about by industrialization occurred in the towns. Never before had towns grown so fast. London, one of the largest cities in Europe in 1700 with 500,000 inhabitants, grew to 959,000 by 1800, and to 2,363,000 by 1850; it was then the largest city the world had ever known. Smaller towns grew even faster. Manchester, a small town of 20,000 in 1758, reached 400,000 a century later, an eightfold increase. Liverpool grew sixfold in sixty years, from 82,000 in 1801 to 472,000 in 1861. New York City, already 100,000 strong in 1815, reached 600,000 (including Brooklyn) in 1850. These were not isolated instances. In some areas, towns merged and formed megalopolises, such as Greater London, the English Midlands, central Belgium, and the Ruhr district of Germany.

Industrialization made some people very prosperous. A great deal of this new wealth went into the building of fine homes, churches, museums, and theaters in wealthy neighborhoods in London, Berlin, and New York. Much of the beauty of London dates from the time of the Industrial Revolution. Yet, by all accounts, the industrial cities grew much too fast, and much of the growth occurred in the poorest neighborhoods.

As poor migrants streamed in from the countryside, developers built cheap, shoddy row houses for them to rent. These tenements were dangerously overcrowded. Often, several families had to live in one small room.

Sudden population growth, overcrowding, and inadequate municipal services conspired to make urban problems more serious than in earlier times. Town dwellers recently arrived from the country brought country ways with them. People threw their sewage and trash out the windows to be washed down the gutters in the streets. The poor kept pigs and chickens, the rich kept horses, and pedestrians stepped into the street at their own risk. Factories and workers' housing were mixed together. Air pollution from burning coal, a problem since the sixteenth century, got steadily worse. Londoners in particular breathed dense and noxious coal smoke. Although humans tolerated the burning of coal, it was too polluting for smelting iron or baking bread. People drank water drawn from wells and rivers contaminated by sewage and industrial runoff. The River Irwell, which ran through Manchester, was, in the words of one visitor, "considerably less a river than a flood of liquid manure."

"Every day that I live," wrote an American visitor to Manchester, "I thank Heaven that I am not a poor man with a family in England." In his poem "Milton," William Blake (1757–1827) expressed the revulsion of sensitive people at the spoliation of England's "mountains green" and "pleasant pastures":

> And did the Countenance Divine
> Shine forth upon our clouded hills?
> And was Jerusalem builded here
> Among these dark Satanic Mills?

Railroads invaded the towns. Railroad companies built their stations as close to the heart of cities as they could. On the outskirts of cities, railroad yards, sidings, and repair shops covered acres of land, surrounded by miles of warehouses and workers' housing. Farther out, far from the dangerous and polluted cities where their factories were located, newly rich industrialists created an environment halfway between country homes and townhouses: the first suburbs.

Under these conditions, diseases proliferated. To the long list of preindustrial urban diseases such as small-pox, dysentery, and tuberculosis, industrialization added new ailments. Rickets, a bone disease caused by lack of sunshine, became endemic in dark and smoky industrial cities. Steamships brought cholera from India, causing great epidemics that struck the poor neighborhoods especially hard. In the 1850s, when the average life expectancy in England was forty years, it was only twenty-four years in Manchester, and around seventeen years in Manchester's poorest neighborhoods, because of the high infant mortality. Observers of nineteenth century industrial cities documented the horrors of slum life in vivid detail. Their shocking reports led to municipal reforms, such as garbage removal, water and sewage systems, and parks and schools. These measures began to alleviate the ills of urban life after the mid-nineteenth century.

Rural Environments

Long before the Industrial Revolution began, practically no wilderness areas were left in Britain and very few in western Europe. Almost every piece of land was covered with fields, forests, or pastures shaped by human activity, or by towns; yet humans continued to alter the environment. The most serious problem was deforestation. People cut timber to build ships and houses, to heat homes, and to manufacture bricks, iron, glass, beer, bread, and many other items.

Americans transformed their environment even faster than Europeans. Land in North America seemed practically free for the taking, and, east of the Appalachian Mountains, settlers viewed forests not as a valuable resource but as a hindrance to development. In their haste to "open up the West," pioneers felled trees and burned them, built houses and abandoned them, and then moved on. The cultivation of cotton was especially harmful. Planters cut down forests, grew cotton for a few years until it depleted the soil, then moved west, abandoning the land to scrub pines. This was slash-and-burn agriculture on an industrial scale.

At that time, America seemed immune to human depredations. Americans thought of nature as an obstacle to be overcome and dominated. This mindset persisted long after the entire continent was occupied and the environment truly endangered.

Paradoxically, in some ways industrialization actually relieved pressures on the environment in Britain. Raw materials once grown on British soil (for example, wood, hay, and wool) were replaced by materials found underground (iron ore and coal) or obtained overseas (cotton). While Russia, Sweden, the United States, and other forested countries continued to smelt iron with charcoal, the British substituted coke made from coal. As the British population increased, and land grew scarcer, the cost of growing feed for horses rose, creating incentives to find new, less land-hungry means of transportation. Likewise, as iron became cheaper and wood more expensive, ships and many other things formerly made of wood began to be made of iron.

To contemporaries, the most obvious changes in rural life were brought about by the new transportation systems. In the eighteenth century, France had a national network of quality roads, which Napoleon extended into Italy and Germany. In Britain, local governments' neglect of the roads that served long-distance traffic led to the formation of private enterprises—"Turnpike Trusts"— that built numerous toll roads. For heavy goods, horse-drawn wagons were too costly even on good roads. The growing volume of heavy freight triggered canal-building booms in Britain, France, and the Low Countries in the late eighteenth century. Some canals, like the duke of Bridgewater's canal in England, connected coal mines to towns or navigable rivers. Others linked navigable rivers and created national transportation networks.

Canals were marvels of construction, with deep cuts, tunnels, and even aqueducts that carried barges over rivers. They also were a sort of school where engineers learned skills they were able to apply to the next great transportation system: the railroads. They laid track across rolling country by cutting deeply into hillsides and erecting daringly long bridges of stone and iron across valleys. Lesser lines snaked their way to small towns hidden in remote valleys. Soon, clanking trains pulled by puffing, smoke-belching locomotives were invading long-isolated districts.

Thus, in the century after industrialization began, the landscape of industrializing countries was transformed more rapidly than ever before. But the ecological changes, like the technological and economic changes that caused them, were only beginning.

Working Conditions

Industrialization offered new opportunities to the enterprising. Carpenters, metalworkers, and machinists were in great demand. Since industrial machines were fairly simple, some workers became engineers or went into business for themselves. The boldest in England moved to the European Continent, the Americas, or India, taking their skills with them to establish new industries.

The successful, however, were a minority. Most industrial jobs were unskilled, repetitive, and boring. Factory work did not vary with the seasons or the time of day but began and ended by the clock. Workdays were long, there were few breaks, and foremen watched constantly. Workers who performed one simple task over and over had little sense of achievement or connection to the final product. Industrial accidents were common and could ruin a family. Unlike even the poorest preindustrial farmer or artisan, factory workers had no control over their tools, jobs, or working hours.

Industrial work, by definition, was physically removed from the home. This had a major impact on women and on family life. Women workers were concentrated in textile mills, partly because of ancient traditions, partly because textile work required less strength than metalworking, construction, or hauling. On average, women earned one-third to one-half as much as men. Young unmarried women worked to support themselves or to save for marriage. Married women took factory jobs when their husbands were unable to support the family. Mothers of infants faced a hard choice: whether to leave their babies with wet-nurses at great expense and danger or to bring them to the factory and keep them quiet with opiates. Rather than working together as family units, husbands and wives increasingly worked in different places.

Even where factory work was available, it was never the main occupation of working women in the early years of industrialization. Most young women who sought paid employment became domestic servants in spite of the low pay, drudgery, and risk of sexual abuse by male employers. Women with small children tried hard to find work they could do at home, such as laundry, sewing, embroidery, millinery, or taking in lodgers.

Even with both parents working, poor families found it hard to make ends meet. As in preindustrial societies, parents thought children should contribute to their upkeep as soon as they were able to. The first generation of workers brought their children with them to the factories and mines as early as age five or six; they had little choice, since there were no public schools or day-care centers. Employers encouraged the practice and even hired orphans. They preferred children because they were cheaper and more docile than adults and were better able to tie broken threads or crawl under machines to sweep the dust.

In Arkwright's cotton mills, two-thirds of the workers were children. In another mill, 17 percent were under ten years of age and 53 percent were between ten and seventeen; they worked 14 to 16 hours a day and were beaten if they made a mistake or fell asleep. Mine operators used children to pull coal carts along the low passageways from the coal face to the mine shaft. In the mid-nineteenth century, when the British government began restricting child labor, mill owners increasingly recruited Irish immigrants.

Cotton Mill in Early-Nineteenth-Century New England These machines, called self-acting mules, could spin hundreds of threads at once. Most of the workers tending the mules were women and children. (The Granger Collection, New York)

American industry began on a somewhat different note than the British. In the early nineteenth century, Americans still remembered their revolutionary ideals. When Francis Cabot Lowell built a cotton mill in Massachusetts, he deliberately hired the unmarried daughters of New England farmers, promising them decent wages and housing in dormitories under careful moral supervision. Other manufacturers eager to combine profits with morality followed his example. But soon the profit motive won out and manufacturers imposed longer hours, harsher working conditions, and lower wages. The young women protested: "As our fathers resisted with blood the lordly avarice of the British ministry, so we, their daughters, never will wear the yoke which has been prepared for us." When they went on strike, the factory owners replaced them with Irish immigrant women willing to accept lower pay and worse conditions.

While the cotton boom enriched planters, merchants, and manufacturers, African-Americans paid for it with their freedom. In the 1790s, 700,000 slaves of African descent lived in the United States, but their numbers were diminishing and the founders of the American republic did not consider slavery a serious problem. The rising demand for cotton and the abolition of the African slave trade in 1808 caused an increase in the price of slaves. As the "Cotton Kingdom" expanded, the number of slaves rose through natural increase and the reluctance of slaveowners to free their slaves. By 1850 the United States had 3,200,000 slaves, 60 percent of whom grew cotton. Similarly, Europe's and North America's surging demand for tea and coffee prolonged slavery in the sugar plantations of the West Indies and caused it to spread to the coffee-growing regions of southern Brazil.

Slavery was not, as white American southerners maintained, a "peculiar institution"—a consequence of biological differences, biblical injunctions, or African traditions. Slavery was part and parcel of the Industrial Revolution, just as much as child labor in Britain, the clothes that people wore, and the beverages they drank.

Changes in Society

Industrialization accentuated the polarization of society and disparities of income. In his novel *Sybil; or, The Two Nations*, the British politician Benjamin Disraeli° (1804–1881) spoke of "Two nations between whom there is no intercourse and no sympathy, who are as ignorant of each other's habits, thoughts, and feelings as if they were dwellers in different zones, or inhabitants of different planets . . . the rich and the poor."

Disraeli (diz-RAY-lee)

In Britain, the worst-off were those who clung to an obsolete skill or craft. The cotton-spinning boom of the 1790s briefly brought prosperity to weavers. Their high wages and low productivity, however, induced inventors to develop power looms. As a result, by 1811 the wages of handloom weavers had fallen by a third; by 1832, by two-thirds. Even by working more hours, they could not escape destitution.

The wages and standard of living of factory workers did not decline steadily like those of handloom weavers; they fluctuated wildly. During the war years 1792 to 1815, the price of food, on which the poor spent most of their income, rose faster than wages. The result was widespread hardship. Then, in the 1820s, real wages and public health began to improve. Industrial production grew at over 3 percent a year, pulling the rest of the economy along. Prices fell and wages rose. Even the poor could afford comfortable, washable cotton clothes and underwear.

Improvement, however, was not steady. One reason was the effect of **business cycles**—recurrent swings from economic hard times to recovery and growth, then back to hard times and a repetition of the sequence. When demand fell, businesses contracted or closed, and workers found themselves unemployed without any savings or insurance. Hard times returned in the "hungry forties." In 1847–1848 the potato crop failed in Ireland. One-quarter of the Irish population died in the resulting famine, and another quarter emigrated to England and America. On the European continent, the negative effects of economic downturns were tempered by the existence of small family farms to which urban workers could return when they were laid off.

Overall, the benefits of industrialization—cheaper food, clothing, and utensils—did not improve workers' standard of living until the 1850s. The real beneficiaries of the Industrial Revolution were the middle class. In Britain, landowning gentry and merchants had long shared wealth and influence. In the late eighteenth century, a new group arose: entrepreneurs whose money came from manufacturing. Most, like Arkwright and Wedgwood, were the sons of middling shopkeepers, craftsmen, or farmers. Their enterprises were usually self-financed, for little capital was needed to start a cotton-spinning or machine-building business. Many tried and some succeeded, largely by plowing their profits back into the business. A generation later, in the nineteenth century, some newly rich industrialists bought their way into high society.

Before the Industrial Revolution, wives of merchants had often participated in the family business; occasionally, widows managed sizable businesses on their own.

With industrialization came a "cult of domesticity" to justify removing middle-class women from contact with the business world. Instead, they became responsible for the home, the servants, the education of children, and the family's social life.

Middle-class people who attributed their success, often correctly, to their own efforts and virtues believed in individual responsibility: if some people could succeed through hard work, thrift, and temperance, then those who did not succeed had no one but themselves to blame for their failure. Many workers, however, newly arrived from rural districts, earned too little to save for the long stretches of unemployment they periodically experienced, and the squalor and misery of life in factory towns led to a noticeable increase in drunkenness on paydays. While the life of the poor remained brutal, the well-to-do—with no hypocrisy—espoused sobriety, thrift, industriousness, and responsibility. This moral position was a middle-class expression of sincere concern coupled with feelings of helplessness in the face of terrible social problems.

IDEOLOGICAL AND POLITICAL RESPONSES TO INDUSTRIALIZATION

Changes as profound as the Industrial Revolution could not occur without political ferment and ideological conflict. So many other momentous events took place during those years—the American Revolution (1776–1783), the French Revolution (1789–1799), the Napoleonic Wars (1804–1815), the reactions and revolts that periodically swept over Europe after 1815—that we cannot neatly separate out the consequences of industrialization from the rest. But it is clear that the Industrial Revolution strengthened the ideas of laissez faire° and socialism and sparked workers' protests.

Laissez Faire and Its Critics

The most celebrated exponent of **laissez faire** ("let them do") was Adam Smith (1723–1790), a Scottish economist. In *The Wealth of Nations* (1776) Smith argued that if individuals

---

laissez faire (lay-say fair)

were allowed to seek their personal gain, the effect, as though guided by an "invisible hand," would be to increase the general welfare. Except to protect private property, the government should refrain from interfering in business; it should even allow duty-free trade with foreign countries.

Although it was true that governments at the time were incompetent at regulating their national economies, it was becoming obvious that industrialization was not improving the general welfare but was for some causing great misery. Two other thinkers, Thomas Malthus (1766–1834) and David Ricardo (1772–1832), attempted to explain the poverty they saw without changing the basic premises of laissez faire. The cause of the workers' plight, Malthus and Ricardo said, was the population boom, which outstripped the food supply and led to falling wages. The workers' poverty, they claimed, was as much a result of "natural law" as the wealth of successful businessmen, and the only way the working class could avoid mass famine was to delay marriage and practice self-restraint and sexual abstinence.

Laissez-faire provided an ideological justification for a special kind of capitalism: banks, stock markets, and chartered companies allowed investors to obtain profits with reasonable risks but with much less government control and interference than in the past. In particular, removing guild and other restrictions allowed businesses to employ women and children and keep wages low.

Business people in Britain eagerly adopted laissez-faire ideas that justified their activities and kept the government at bay. But not everyone accepted the grim conclusions of the "dismal science," as economics was then known. Jeremy Bentham (1748–1832) believed that it was possible to maximize "the greatest happiness of the greatest number," if only a Parliament of enlightened reformers would study the social problems of the day and pass appropriate legislation; his philosophy became known as utilitarianism.

The German economist Friedrich List (1789–1846) rejected laissez faire and free trade as a British trick "to make the rest of the world, like the Hindus, its serfs in all industrial and commercial relations." To protect their "infant" industries from British competition, he argued, countries like Germany had to erect high tariff barriers. On the European continent, List's ideas were as influential as those of Smith and Ricardo and led to the formation of the Zollverein°, a customs union of most of the German states in 1834.

Positivists and Utopian Socialists

Bentham optimistically advocated gradual improvements. In contrast, some French social thinkers, moved by sincere concern for the poor, offered a radically new vision of a just civilization. Espousing a philosophy called **positivism,** the count of Saint-Simon (1760–1825) argued that the scientific method could solve social as well as technical problems. He recommended that the poor, guided by scientists and artists, form workers' communities under the protection of benevolent business leaders. These ideas found no following among workers, but they attracted the enthusiastic support of bankers and entrepreneurs, inspired by visions of railroads, canals, and other symbols of progress.

Meanwhile, the **utopian° socialism** of Charles Fourier (1768–1837), who loathed capitalists, imagined an ideal society in which groups of sixteen hundred workers would live in dormitories and work together on the land and in workshops where music, wine, and pastries would soften the hardships of labor. For this idea, critics called him "utopian"—a dreamer, after the Greek word *utopia* meaning "nowhere."

The person who came closest to creating a utopian community was the Englishman Robert Owen (1771–1858), a successful cotton manufacturer who believed that industry could provide prosperity for all. Conscience-stricken by the appalling plight of the workers, Owen took over the management of New Lanark, a mill town south of Glasgow. He improved the housing and added schools, a church, and other amenities. He also testified before Parliament against child labor and for government inspection of working conditions, thereby angering his fellow industrialists.

Protests and Reforms

Workers benefited little from the ideas of these middle-class philosophers. Instead, they resisted the harsh working conditions in their own ways. They changed jobs frequently. They often were absent, especially on Mondays. And when they were not closely watched, the quality of their work was likely to be poor.

Periodically, workers rioted or went on strike. Protests coincided with periods of high food prices and with downturns in the business cycle that left many unemployed. In some places, craftsmen broke into factories and destroyed the machines that threatened their livelihoods. Such acts of resistance did nothing, however, to change the nature of industrial work. Not until

---

Zollverein (TSOLL-feh-rine)

utopian (you-TOE-pee-uhn)

workers learned to act together could they hope to have much influence.

Gradually they formed benevolent societies and organizations to demand universal male suffrage and shorter workdays. In 1834 Robert Owen organized the Grand National Consolidated Trade Union to lobby for an eight-hour workday; it gained half a million members but failed a few months later in the face of government prosecution of trade-union activities. The Chartist movement had more success, gathering petitions by the thousands to present to Parliament. Although Chartism collapsed in 1848, it left a legacy of labor organizing.

Eventually, mass movements persuaded political leaders to look into the abuses of industrial life, despite the prevailing laissez-faire philosophy. In the 1820s and 1830s, the British Parliament began investigating conditions in the factories and mines. The Factory Act of 1833 prohibited the employment of children under age nine in textile mills. It also limited the working hours of children between the ages of nine and thirteen to eight hours a day and the daily working hours of fourteen- to eighteen-year-olds to twelve. The Mines Act of 1842 prohibited the employment of all women and of boys under age ten underground. Several decades passed before the government appointed enough inspectors to enforce the new laws.

Most important was the struggle over the Corn Laws—tariffs on imported grain. Their repeal in 1846, in the name of "free trade," was designed to lower the cost of food for workers and thereby allow employers to pay lower wages. A victory for laissez-faire, the repeal also represented a victory for the rising class of manufacturers, merchants, and investors over the conservative landowners who had long dominated politics.

The British learned to seek reform through accommodation. On the European continent, in contrast, the revolutions of 1848 revealed widespread discontent with repressive governments but failed to soften the hardships of industrialization.

INDUSTRIALIZATION AND THE NONINDUSTRIAL WORLD

The spread of the Industrial Revolution to western Europe and North America in the early nineteenth century delayed industrialization elsewhere. In most places, trade with the industrial countries meant exporting raw materials, not locally made handicraft products. In the few countries whose governments were tempted to imitate the West, cheap Western imports, backed by the power of Great Britain, thwarted the spread of industry for a century or more.

We will consider three places where industrialization did *not* occur in this period: Russia, whose society and institutions delayed industrialization by a century, and Egypt and India, where industrialization was stifled at the outset. In these three cases, we can discern the outlines of the Western domination that has characterized the history of the world since the late nineteenth century.

Russia

Russia had been in close contact with western Europe since the seventeenth century. Its aristocrats spoke French, its army was modeled on the armies of western Europe, and it participated in European wars and diplomacy. Yet Russia differed from western Europe in one important aspect: it had almost no middle class. Thus industrialization there arose not from the initiative of local entrepreneurs but by government decree and through the work of foreign engineers.

Tsar Nicholas I (r. 1825–1855) built the first railroad in Russia from St. Petersburg, the capital, to his summer palace in 1837. A few years later, he insisted that the trunk line from St. Petersburg to Moscow run in a perfectly straight line. American engineers built locomotive workshops in Russia, and British engineers set up textile mills. These projects, though well publicized, were oddities in a society where most people were serfs tied to the estates of powerful noble landowners and towns were few and far apart.

Until the late nineteenth century, the Russian government's interest in industry was limited and hesitant. An industrial revolution, to be successful, required large numbers of educated and independent-minded artisans and entrepreneurs. Suspicious of Western ideas, especially anything smacking of liberalism, socialism, or revolution, the Russian government feared the spread of literacy and of modern education beyond the minimum needed to train the officer corps and the bureaucracy. Rather than run the risk of allowing a middle class and a working class to arise that might challenge its control, the regime of Nicholas I kept the peasants in serfdom and preferred to import most industrial goods and pay for them with exports of grain and timber.

Russia aspired to Western-style economic development. But fear of political change caused the country to fall further behind western Europe, economically and technologically, than it had been a half-century before. When France and Britain went to war against Russia in 1854, they faced a Russian army equipped with obsolete weapons and bogged down for lack of transportation.

Steam Tractor in India Power machinery was introduced slowly into India because of the abundance of skilled low-cost labor. In this scene, a steam tractor fords a shallow stream, to the delight of onlookers. The towerlike construction on the right is probably a pier for a railroad bridge. (Billie Love Historical Collection)

Egypt

Like Russia, Egypt began to industrialize in the early nineteenth century. The driving force was its ruler, Muhammad Ali (1769–1849), a man who was to play a major role not only in the history of Egypt but in the Middle East and East Africa as well (see Chapter 26). He wanted to build up the Egyptian economy and military in order to become less dependent on the Ottoman sultan, his nominal overlord. To do so, he imported advisers and technicians from Europe and built cotton mills, foundries, shipyards, weapons factories, and other industrial enterprises. To pay for all this, he made the peasants grow wheat and cotton, which the government bought at a low price and exported at a profit. He also imposed high tariffs on imported goods in order to force the pace of industrialization.

Muhammad Ali's efforts, however, fell afoul of the British, who did not want a powerful country threatening to interrupt the flow of travelers and mail cross Egypt, the shortest route between Europe and India. When Egypt went to war against the Ottoman Empire in 1839, Britain intervened and forced Muhammad Ali to eliminate all import duties in the name of free trade. Unprotected, Egypt's fledgling industries could not compete with the flood of cheap British products. Thereafter, Egypt exported raw cotton and imported manufactured goods and became, in effect, an economic dependency of Britain.

India

Until the late eighteenth century, India had been the world's largest producer and exporter of cotton textiles, handmade by skilled spinners and weavers. The British East India Company took over large parts of India just as the Industrial Revolution was beginning in Britain. Thus cheap British factory-made textiles began flooding into India duty-free, putting first spinners and then handloom weavers out of work. Unlike Britain, India had no factories to which displaced handicraft workers could turn for work. Most of them became landless peasants, eking out a precarious living.

Like other tropical regions, India became an exporter of raw materials and an importer of British industrial goods. To hasten the process, British entrepreneurs and colonial officials introduced railroads into the subcontinent. The construction of India's railroad network began in the mid-1850s, along with coal mining to fuel the locomotives and the installation of telegraph lines to connect the major cities.

Some Indian entrepreneurs saw opportunities in the atmosphere of change that the British created. In 1854 the Bombay merchant Cowasjee Nanabhoy Davar imported an engineer, four skilled workers, and several textile machines from Britain and started India's first textile mill. This was the beginning of India's cotton industry. But, despite many gifted entrepreneurs, India's industrialization proceeded at a snail's pace, for the government was in British hands and the British did nothing to encourage Indian industry.

CONCLUSION

In the period from 1760 to 1851, the new technologies of the Industrial Revolution greatly increased humans' power over nature. Goods could be manufactured in vast quantities at low cost. People and messages could travel at unprecedented speeds. In addition to utilizing the energy produced by muscle power, wind, and water, humans gained access to the energy stored in coal. Faster than ever before, humans turned woodland into farmland, dug canals and laid tracks, bridged rivers and cut through mountains, and covered the countryside with towns and cities.

This newfound power over nature, far from benefiting everyone, increased the disparities between individuals and societies. Industrialization brought forth entrepreneurs—whether in the mills of England or on plantations in the American south—with enormous power over their employees or slaves, a power that they found easy and profitable to abuse. Some people acquired great wealth while others lived in poverty and squalor. Middle-class women were restricted to the care of their homes and children. Many working-class women had to leave home to earn wages in factories or as domestic servants. These changes in work and family life provoked intense debates among intellectuals. Some defended the disparities in the name of laissez faire; others criticized the injustices that industrialization brought. Society was slow to bring these abuses under control.

By the 1850s, the Industrial Revolution had spread from Britain to western Europe and the United States, and its impact was being felt around the world. To make a product that was sold on every continent, the British cotton industry used African slaves, American land, British machines, and Irish workers. Iron ships and steam engines shifted the historic balance between Europe and China. After the 1850s—as we shall see in Chapter 29—no part of the world remained untouched by the power of industry.

■ Key Terms

Industrial Revolution	Crystal Palace
agricultural revolution	steam engine
(eighteenth century)	James Watt
mass production	electric telegraph
Josiah Wedgwood	business cycle
division of labor	laissez faire
mechanization	positivism
Richard Arkwright	utopian socialism

■ Suggested Readings

General works on the history of technology give pride of place to industrialization. For an optimistic overview see Joel Mokyr, *The Lever of Riches: Technological Creativity and Economic Progress* (1990). Other important recent works include James McClellan III and Harold Dorn, *Science and Technology in World History* (1999); David Landes, *The Wealth and Poverty of Nations* (1998); and Ian Inkster, *Technology and Industrialization: Historical Case Studies and International Perspectives* (1998).

There is a rich literature on the British industrial revolution, beginning with T. S. Ashton's classic *The Industrial Revolution, 1760–1830*, published in 1948 and often reprinted.

The impact of industrialization on workers is the theme of E. P. Thompson's classic work *The Making of the English Working Class* (1963), but see also E. R. Pike, *"Hard Times": Human Documents of the Industrial Revolution* (1966). The role of women is most ably revealed in Lynn Y. Weiner, *From Working Girl to Working Mother: The Female Labor Force in the United States, 1820–1980* (1985), and in Louise Tilly and Joan Scott, *Women, Work, and Family* (1978).

European industrialization is the subject of J. Goodman and K. Honeyman, *Gainful Pursuits: The Making of Industrial Europe: 1600–1914* (1988); John Harris, *Industrial Espionage and Technology Transfer: Britain and France in the Eighteenth Century* (1998); and David Landes, *The Unbound Prometheus: Technological Change and Industrial Development in Western Europe from 1750 to the Present* (1972). On the beginnings of American industrialization see David Jeremy, *Artisans, Entrepreneurs and Machines: Essays on the Early Anglo-American Textile Industry, 1770–1840* (1998).

On the environmental impact of industrialization see Richard Wilkinson, *Poverty and Progress: An Ecological Perspective on Economic Development* (1973), and Richard Tucker and John Richards, *Global Deforestation in the Nineteenth-Century World Economy* (1983).

The first book to treat industrialization as a global phenomenon is Peter Stearns, *The Industrial Revolution in World History* (1993); see also Louise Tilly's important article "Connections" in *American Historical Review* (February 1994).

■ Note

1. *Nautical Magazine* 12 (1843): 346.

25

NATION BUILDING AND ECONOMIC TRANSFORMATION IN THE AMERICAS,

1800–1890

Independence in Latin America, 1800–1830 • The Problem of Order, 1825–1890 • The Challenge of Economic and Social Change

ENVIRONMENT AND TECHNOLOGY: The McCormick Reaper

SOCIETY AND CULTURE: Villages in New England and Mexico

The Train Station in Orizaba, Mexico, 1877 In the last decades of the nineteenth century, Mexico's political leaders actively promoted economic development. The railroad became the symbol of this ideal.

n 1862, seeing Mexico divided by violent factional conflicts and the United States convulsed by the Civil War, Napoleon III seized the opportunity to project French power into the Americas by sending a large military force to Mexico. Mexican conservatives who resented their government's efforts to introduce democratic reforms and limit the power of the Catholic Church supported the invasion. After driving the liberal president, Benito Juárez°, from Mexico City, Napoleon III and a group of Mexican conservatives in 1864 convinced Archduke Maximilian of Habsburg, brother of Emperor Franz Joseph of Austria, to accept the throne of Mexico.

Although Maximilian embraced Mexican patriotic symbols and accepted some of Juárez's reforms, he failed to win popular support. Armed resistance by Mexican liberals and diplomatic pressure by the United States after the conclusion of the Civil War led to a French pullout. Then, on the morning of June 19, 1867, a Mexican firing squad executed Maximilian. His young wife Charlotte, daughter of King Leopold of Belgium, was in Europe trying to convince the emperor of France or the pope to intervene to save her husband when news of his death swept her into madness. For Mexicans, the defeat and execution of Maximilian signaled an end to intervention and the triumph of republicanism.

The independence of Britain's thirteen North American colonies set in motion a radical transformation of the New World. Spurred by the revolutionary examples of the United States and France (see Chapter 23) and buttressed by Enlightenment ideology, which exalted political freedom, most of the Spanish and Portuguese colonies in the New World gained independence in the early decades of the nineteenth century. As the French intervention in Mexico illustrates, however, European powers were ready to challenge the sovereignty of many of the new American nations.

Through the nineteenth century, the new nations in the Western Hemisphere wrestled with the difficult questions that independence raised. If colonies could

Benito Juárez (beh-NEE-toh WAH-rez)

reject submission to imperial powers, could not regions with distinct cultures, social structures, and economies refuse to accept the political authority of the newly formed nation-states? How could nations born in revolution accept the political strictures of written constitutions—even those they wrote themselves? How could the ideals of liberty and freedom expressed in those constitutions be reconciled with the denial of rights to Amerindians, slaves, recent immigrants, and women?

While trying to resolve these political questions, the new nations also attempted to promote economic growth. But just as the legacy of class and racial division thwarted the realization of political ideals, colonial economic development, with its emphasis on agricultural and mining exports, inhibited efforts to promote diversification and industrialization.

As you read this chapter, ask yourself the following questions:

- What were the causes of the revolutions for independence in Latin America?
- What major political challenges did Western Hemisphere nations face in the nineteenth century?
- How did abolitionism, the movement for women's rights, and immigration change the nations of the Western Hemisphere?
- How did industrialization and new agricultural technologies affect the environment?

INDEPENDENCE IN LATIN AMERICA, 1800–1830

As the eighteenth century drew to a close, Spain and Portugal held vast colonial possessions in the Western Hemisphere, although their power had declined relative to that of their British and French rivals. Both Iberian empires had reformed colonial administration and strengthened their military forces in the eighteenth century. Despite these efforts, the same economic and political forces that had undermined British rule in the colonies that became the United States were present in Spanish America and Brazil.

Roots of Revolution, to 1810

Wealthy colonial residents of Latin America were frustrated by the political and economic power of colonial officials and angered by high taxes and imperial monopolies. By 1800, the examples of the American and French Revolutions had stirred enthusiasm for self-government (see Chapter 23). The great works of the Enlightenment as well as revolutionary documents like the Declaration of Independence and the Declaration of the Rights of Man circulated widely in Latin America. But it was Napoleon's decision to invade Portugal (1807) and Spain (1808), not revolutionary ideas, that ignited Latin America's struggle for independence.

In 1808 the royal family of Portugal fled to Brazil. King John VI maintained his court there for over a decade. In Spain, in contrast, Napoleon forced King Ferdinand VII to abdicate and placed his own brother, Joseph Bonaparte, on the throne. Spanish patriots fighting against the French created a new political body, the Junta° Central, to administer the areas they controlled. Most Spaniards viewed the Junta as a temporary patriotic institution created to govern Spain while the king remained a French prisoner. The Junta, however, claimed the right to exercise the king's powers over Spain's colonies, and this claim provoked a crisis.

Large numbers of colonists in Spanish America, perhaps a majority, favored obedience to the Junta Central. A vocal minority, which included many wealthy and powerful individuals, objected. The dissenters argued that they were subjects of the king, not dependents of the Spanish nation. They wanted to create local juntas and govern their own affairs until Ferdinand regained the throne. Spanish loyalists in the colonies resisted this tentative assertion of local autonomy and thus provoked armed uprisings. In late 1808 and 1809, popular movements overthrew Spanish colonial officials in Venezuela, Mexico, and Bolivia and created local juntas. In each case, Spanish officials quickly reasserted control and punished the leaders. Their harsh repression, however, further polarized public opinion in the colonies and gave rise to a greater sense of a separate American nationality. By 1810 Spanish colonial authorities were facing a new round of revolutions more clearly focused on the achievement of independence.

Junta (HUN-tah)

Simón Bolívar   Simón Bolívar was the greatest of Latin America's independence-era leaders. There are many portraits of Bolívar, each suggesting distinct elements of his political legacy. This portrait shows him in uniform and cape mounted on a white horse. His gaze is focused on the horizon, suggesting his unique ability to foresee the future's challenges.   (Organization of American States)

Spanish South America, 1810–1825

In Caracas (the capital city of modern Venezuela), a revolutionary Junta led by creoles (colonial-born whites) declared independence in 1811. Although this group espoused popular sovereignty and representative democracy, its leaders were large landowners who defended slavery and opposed full citizenship for the black and mixed-race majority. Their aim was to expand their own privileges by eliminating Spaniards from the upper levels of Venezuela's government and from the church. The junta's narrow agenda spurred loyalists in the colonial administration and church hierarchy to rally thousands of free blacks and

CHRONOLOGY

	United States and Canada	Mexico and Central America	South America
	1789 U.S. Constitution ratified		
1800	**1803** Louisiana Purchase		**1808** Portuguese royal family arrives in Brazil
	1812–1815 War of 1812	**1810–21** Mexican movement for independence	**1808–1809** Revolutions for independence begin in Spanish South America
1825	**1837** Texas gains independence from Mexico		**1822** Brazil gains independence
	1845 Texas admitted as a state	**1846–1848** War between Mexico and the United States	
		1847–1870 Caste War	
1850	**1848** Women's Rights Convention in Seneca Falls, New York		
	1861–1865 Civil War	**1862–1867** French invade Mexico	
	1867 Creation of Dominion of Canada		**1865–1870** Argentina, Uruguay, and Brazil wage war against Paraguay
			1870s Governments of Argentina and Chile begin final campaigns against indigenous peoples
1875	**1876** Sioux and allies defeat United States Army in Battle of Little Bighorn		**1879–1881** Chile wages war against Peru and Bolivia
			1888 Abolition of slavery in Brazil

slaves to defend the Spanish Empire. Faced with this determined resistance, the revolutionary movement placed overwhelming political authority in the hands of its military leader **Simón Bolívar°** (1783–1830), who later became the preeminent leader of the independence movement in Spanish South America.

The son of wealthy Venezuelan planters, Bolívar had studied both the classics and the works of the Enlightenment. He used the force of his personality to mobilize political support and to hold the loyalty of his troops. Defeated on many occasions, Bolívar successfully adapted his objectives and policies to attract new allies and build coalitions. Although initially opposed to the abolition of slavery, for example, he agreed to support emancipation in order to draw slaves and freemen to his cause and to gain supplies from Haiti. Bolívar was also capable of

using harsh methods to ensure victory. Attempting to force resident Spaniards to join the rebellion in 1813, he proclaimed: "Any Spaniard who does not . . . work against tyranny in behalf of this just cause will be considered an enemy and punished; as a traitor to the nation, he will inevitably be shot by a firing squad."[1]

Between 1813 and 1817 military advantage shifted back and forth between the patriots and loyalists. Bolívar's ultimate success was aided by his decision to enlist demobilized English veterans of the Napoleonic Wars and by a military revolt in Spain in 1820. The English veterans, hardened by combat, helped improve the battlefield performance of Bolívar's army. The revolt in Spain forced Ferdinand VII—he was restored to the throne in 1814 after the defeat of Napoleon—to accept a constitution that limited the powers of both the monarch and the church. Colonial loyalists who for a decade had fought to maintain the authority of monarch and church viewed those reforms as unacceptably liberal.

Simón Bolívar (see-MOAN bow-LEE-varh)

With the king's supporters divided, momentum swung irreversibly to the patriots. After liberating present-day Venezuela, Colombia, and Ecuador, Bolívar's army occupied the area that is now Peru and Bolivia (named for Bolívar). Finally defeating the last Spanish armies in 1824, Bolívar and his closest supporters attempted to draw the former Spanish colonies into a formal confederation. The first step was to forge Venezuela, Colombia, and Ecuador into a single nation: Gran Colombia (see Map 25.1). With Bolívar's encouragement, Peru and Bolivia also experimented with unification. Despite his prestige, however, all of these initiatives had failed by 1830.

Buenos Aires (the capital city of modern Argentina) was the second important center of revolutionary activity in Spanish South America. In Buenos Aires, news of Ferdinand VII's abdication led to the creation of a junta, organized by militia commanders, merchants, and ranchers, which overthrew the viceroy in 1810. To deflect the opposition of loyalists and Spanish colonial officials, the junta claimed loyalty to the imprisoned king. After Ferdinand regained the Spanish throne, however, junta leaders dropped this pretense. In 1816 they declared independence as the United Provinces of the Río de la Plata.

Patriot leaders in Buenos Aires at first sought to retain control over the territory of the Viceroyalty of Río de la Plata, which had been created in 1776 and included modern Argentina, Uruguay, Paraguay, and Bolivia. But Spanish loyalists in Uruguay and Bolivia and a separatist movement in Paraguay defeated these ambitions. Even within the territory of Argentina, the government in Buenos Aires was unable to control regional rivalries and political differences. As a result, the region rapidly descended into political chaos.

A weak succession of juntas, collective presidencies, and dictators soon lost control over much of the interior of Argentina. However, in 1817 the government in Buenos Aires did manage to support a mixed force of Chileans and Argentines led by José de San Martín° (1778–1850), who crossed the Andes Mountains to attack Spanish military forces in Chile and Peru. During this campaign, San Martín's most effective troops were former slaves, who had gained their freedom by enlisting in the army, and gauchos, the cowboys of the Argentine

pampas (prairies). After gaining victory in Chile, San Martín pushed on to Peru in 1820 but failed to gain a clear victory there. The violent and destructive uprising of Tupac Amaru II in 1780 had traumatized the Andean region and colonists fearful that support for independence might unleash another Amerindian uprising. Unable to make progress, San Martín surrendered command of patriot forces in Peru to Simón Bolívar, who overcame final Spanish resistance in 1824.

Mexico, 1810–1823

In 1810, Mexico was Spain's richest and most populous colony. Its silver mines were the richest in the world, and the colony's capital, Mexico City, was larger than any city in Spain. Mexico also had the largest population of Spanish immigrants among the colonies. Spaniards dominated the government, church, and economy of Mexico. When news of Napoleon's invasion of Spain reached the colony, conservative Spaniards in Mexico City overthrew the local viceroy because he was too sympathetic to the Creoles. This action by Spanish loyalists underlined the new reality: with the king of Spain in a French prison, colonial authority now rested on brute force.

The first stage of the revolution against Spain occurred in central Mexico. In this region wealthy ranchers and farmers had aggressively forced many Amerindian communities from their traditional agricultural lands. A series of crop failures and epidemics further afflicted the region's rural poor. At the same time, miners and the urban poor faced higher food prices and rising unemployment. With the power of colonial authorities weakened by events in Spain, anger and fear spread through towns and villages in central Mexico.

On September 16, 1810, **Miguel Hidalgo y Costilla°**, parish priest of the small town of Dolores, rang the church bells, attracting thousands. In a fiery speech he urged the crowd to rise up against the oppression of Spanish officials. Tens of thousands of the rural and urban poor joined his movement. They lacked military discipline and adequate weapons but knew who their oppressors were, spontaneously attacking the ranches and mines that had been exploiting them. Many Spaniards and colonial-born whites were murdered or assaulted. At first, wealthy Mexicans were sympathetic to Hidalgo's objectives, but they eventually supported Spanish authorities when they recognized the threat that the angry masses following Hidalgo posed to them. The military

Map 25.1 Latin America by 1830   By 1830, patriot forces had overturned the Spanish and Portuguese Empires of the Western Hemisphere. Regional conflicts, local wars, and foreign interventions challenged the survival of many of these new nations following independence.

José de San Martín (hoe-SAY deh san mar-TEEN)
Miguel Hidalgo y Costilla (mee-GEHL ee-DAHL-go ee cos-TEA-ah)

tide quickly turned against Hidalgo, and he was captured, tried, and executed in 1811.

The revolution continued under the leadership of another priest, **José María Morelos°,** a former student of Hidalgo. A more adept military and political leader than his mentor, Morelos created a formidable fighting force and, in 1813, convened a congress that declared independence and drafted a constitution. Despite these achievements, loyalist forces also proved too strong for Morelos. He was defeated and executed in 1815.

Although small numbers of insurgents continued to wage war against Spanish forces, colonial rule seemed secure in 1820. However, news of the military revolt in Spain unsettled the conservative groups and church officials who had defended Spanish rule against Hidalgo and Morelos. In 1821 Colonel Agustín de Iturbide° and other loyalist commanders forged an alliance with remaining insurgents and declared Mexico's independence. The conservative origins of Mexico's transition to independence were highlighted by the decision to create a monarchial form of government and crown Iturbide as emperor. In early 1823, however, the army overthrew Iturbide and Mexico became a republic.

Brazil, to 1831

The arrival of the Portuguese royal family in Brazil in 1808 helped to maintain the loyalty of the colonial elite and to stimulate the local economy. After the defeat of Napoleon in Europe, the Portuguese government called for King John VI to return to Portugal. He at first resisted this pressure. Then in 1820 the military uprising in Spain provoked a sympathetic liberal revolt in Portugal, and the Portuguese military garrison in Rio de Janeiro forced the king to permit the creation of juntas. John recognized that he needed to take dramatic action to protect his throne. In 1821, he returned to Portugal. Hoping to protect his claims to Brazil, he left his son Pedro in Brazil as regent.

By 1820, the Spanish colonies along Brazil's borders had experienced ten years of revolution and civil war, and some, like Argentina and Paraguay, had gained independence. Unable to ignore these struggles, some Brazilians began to reevaluate Brazil's relationship with Portugal. Many Brazilians resented their homeland's economic subordination to Portugal. The arrogance of Portuguese soldiers and bureaucrats led others to talk openly of independence. Rumors circulated that Portuguese troops were being sent to discipline Brazil and force the regent Pedro to join his father in Lisbon.

Unwilling to return to Portugal and committed to maintaining his family's hold on Brazil, Pedro aligned himself with the rising tide of independence sentiment. In 1822, he declared Brazilian independence. Pedro's decision launched Brazil into a unique political trajectory. Unlike its neighbors, which became constitutional republics, Brazil gained independence as a constitutional monarchy with Pedro I, heir to the throne of Portugal, as emperor.

Pedro I was committed both to monarchy and to many liberal principles. He directed the writing of the constitution of 1824, which provided for an elected assembly and granted numerous protections for political opposition. But he made powerful enemies by attempting to protect the Portuguese who remained in Brazil from arbitrary arrest and seizure of their property. More dangerously still, he opposed slavery in a nation dominated by the slave-owning class. In 1823 Pedro I anonymously published an article that characterized slavery as a "cancer eating away at Brazil." Despite opposition, he then concluded a treaty with Great Britain to end Brazilian participation in the slave trade in 1830. The political elite of Brazil's slave-owning regions opposed the treaty and for nearly two decades worked tirelessly to prevent enforcement. Pedro also continued his father's costly commitment of military forces to control neighboring Uruguay. As military losses and costs rose, the Brazilian public grew impatient. A small but vocal minority that opposed the monarchy and sought the creation of a democracy used these issues to rally public opinion against the emperor.

Confronted by street demonstrations and violence between Brazilians and Portuguese, Pedro I abdicated the throne in 1831 in favor of his five-year-old son Pedro II. After a nine-year regency, Pedro II assumed full powers as emperor of Brazil. He reigned until he was overthrown by republicans in 1889.

THE PROBLEM OF ORDER, 1825–1890

All the newly independent nations of the Western Hemisphere had difficulties establishing stable political institutions. The idea of popular sovereignty found broad support across the hemisphere. As a result, written constitutions and elected assemblies were put in place, often before the actual achievement of independence. Even in the hemisphere's two monarchies, Mexico and Brazil, the emperors sought to legitimize their

---

José María Morelos (hoe-SAY mah-REE-ah moh-RAY-los)
Agustín de Iturbide (ah-goos-TEEN deh ee-tur-BEE-deh)

rule by accepting constitutional limits on their authority and by the creation of representative assemblies. Nevertheless, widespread support for constitutional order and for representative government failed to prevent bitter factional conflict, regionalism, and the appearance of charismatic political leaders and military uprisings.

Constitutional Experiments

In reaction to the arbitrary and tyrannical authority of colonial rulers, revolutionary leaders in both the United States and Latin America espoused constitutionalism. They believed that the careful description of political powers in written constitutions offered the best protection for individual rights and liberties. In practice, however, many new constitutions proved unworkable. In the United States, George Washington, James Madison, and other leaders became dissatisfied with the nation's first constitution, the Articles of Confederation. They led the effort to write a new constitution, which was put into effect in 1789. In Latin America, few constitutions survived the rough-and-tumble of national politics. Between 1811 and 1833 Venezuela and Chile alone ratified and then rejected a combined total of nine constitutions.

Important differences in colonial political experience influenced later political developments in the Americas. The ratification of a new constitution in the United States was the culmination of a long historical process that had begun with the development of English constitutional law and continued under colonial charters. Many more residents of the British North American colonies had had the experience of voting and holding political office than was true in the colonial societies of Portuguese or Spanish America. The British colonies provided opportunities for holding elective offices in town governments and colonial legislatures, and, by the time of independence, citizens had grown accustomed to elections, political parties, and factions. In contrast, constitutional government and elections were only briefly experienced in Spanish America between 1812 and 1814—while Ferdinand VII was a prisoner of Napoleon—and this short period was disrupted by the early stages of the revolutions for independence. Brazil had almost no experience with popular politics before independence. Despite these differences in experience and constitutional forms, every new republic in the Americas initially limited the right to vote to free men of property.

Democratic passions and the desire for effective self-rule led to significant political reform in the Americas, even in some of the region's remaining colonies. British Canada was divided into separate colonies and territories each with a separate and distinct government. Political life in each colony was dominated by a provincial governor and appointed advisory councils drawn from the local elite. Elected assemblies existed within each province, but they exercised limited power. Agitation to end oligarchic rule and make government responsive to the will of the assemblies led to armed rebellion in 1837. In the 1840s Britain responded by establishing responsible government in each of the Canadian provinces, allowing limited self-rule. By the 1860s regional political leaders interested in promoting economic development realized that railroads and other internal improvements required a government with a "national" character. Moreover, civil war in the U.S. and raids from U.S. territory into Canada by Irish nationalists focused attention on the need to protect the border. Negotiations led to the **Confederation of 1867,** which included the provinces of Ontario, Quebec, New Brunswick, and Nova Scotia. The Confederation that created the new Dominion of Canada with a central government in Ottawa (see Map 25.2) was hailed by one observer as the "birthday of a new nationality." [2]

The path to effective constitutional government was rockier to the south. Because neither Spain nor Portugal had permitted anything like the elected legislatures and municipal governments of colonial North America, the drafters of Latin American constitutions were less constrained by practical political experience. As a result, many of the new Latin American nations experimented with untested political institutions. For example, Simón Bolívar, who wrote the first constitutions of five South American republics, included in Bolivia's constitution a fourth branch of government that had "jurisdiction over the youth, the hearts of men, public spirit, good customs, and republican ethics."

Most Latin American nations found it difficult to define the political role of the Catholic Church after independence. In the colonial period the Catholic Church was a religious monopoly that controlled all levels of education, and dominated intellectual life. Many early constitutions aimed to reduce this power by making education secular and by permitting the practice of other religions. The church reacted by organizing its allies and financing conservative political movements. In Mexico, Colombia, Chile, and Argentina conflicts between liberals who sought the separation of church and state and supporters of the church's traditional powers dominated political life until late in the nineteenth century.

Limiting the power of the military proved to be another significant stumbling block to the creation of constitutional governments in Latin America. The wars for independence elevated the prestige of military leaders. When the wars were over, Bolívar and other military commanders seldom proved willing to subordinate themselves to civilian authorities. At the same time, frustrated

Map 25.2   Dominion of Canada, 1873   Although independence was not yet achieved and settlement remained concentrated along the U.S. border, Canada had established effective political and economic control over its western territories by 1873.

by the often-chaotic workings of constitutional democracy, few citizens were willing to support civilian politicians in any contest with the military. As a result, many Latin American militaries successfully resisted civilian control. Brazil, ruled by Emperor Pedro I, was the principal exception to this pattern.

Personalist Leaders

Successful patriot leaders in both the United States and Latin America gained mass followings during the wars for independence. They recruited and mobilized popular support by using patriotic symbols and by carefully associating their actions with national objectives. After independence, many patriot military leaders were able to use their personal followings to gain national political leadership. George Washington's ability to dominate the political scene in the early republican United States anticipated the later political ascendancy of revolutionary heroes such as Iturbide in Mexico and Bolívar in Gran Colombia. In each case, military reputation provided the foundation for personal political power. These **personalist leaders** relied on their ability to mobilize and direct the masses of these new nations rather than on the authority of constitutions and laws. Their model was Napoleon, who rose from the French army to become emperor, not John Madison, the primary author of the U.S. Constitution. In Latin America, a personalist leader who gained and held political power without constitutional sanction was called a *caudillo°.*

Latin America's slow development of stable political institutions made personalist politics more influential than was the case in the United States (see Society and Culture: Villages in New England and Mexico). Nevertheless, charismatic politicians in the United States such as Andrew Jackson did sometimes challenge constitutional limits to their authority, as did the caudillos of Latin

caudillo (kouh-DEE-yoh)

Villages in New England and Mexico

Born in Scotland, Fanny Calderón de la Barca lived briefly in Boston. She married a Spanish diplomat who later became ambassador to Mexico. She was a very critical observer of Mexican customs and culture. In this brief selection from Life in Mexico, *published in 1843, she compares village life in Mexico and New England. We can see clearly Calderón de la Barca's obvious affection for her native land and prejudice against Mexico. Historians often deal with biased or prejudiced sources and develop strategies to overcome these weaknesses in order to illuminate the past. This source challenges us to overcome the author's prejudice in order to undertake a comparative analysis of why Mexico and the United States developed so differently in response to the opportunities and challenges of the nineteenth century.*

If anyone wishes to try the effect of strong contrast, let him come direct from the United States to this country; but it is in the villages especially that the contrast is most striking. Travelling in New England, for example, we arrive at a small village. We see four new churches, proclaiming four different sects; religion suited to all customers. These wooden churches or meeting houses are all new, all painted white. . . . Houses, churches, stores, and taverns, all are of a piece. They are suited to the present emergency, whatever that may be, though they will never make fine ruins. Everything proclaims prosperity, equality, consistency; the past forgotten, the present all and all, and the future taking care of itself. . . . No beggars.

Transport yourself in imagination [to] Mexico. The Indian huts, with their half-naked inhabitants, and little gardens full of flowers; the huts themselves built either of clay or the [stones of a ruined building]. . . . [T]he church, gray and ancient, but strong as if designed for eternity; with its saints and virgins, and martyrs and relics, its gold and silver and precious stones, whose value could buy up all the spare lots in the New England village; the [beggar] with scarce a rag to cover him, kneeling on the marble pavement. . . . Here, everything reminds us of the past; of the conquering Spaniards, who seemed to build for eternity; impressing each work with their own solid, grave, and religious character; of the triumphs of Catholicism. . . . It is the present that seems like a dream, a pale reflection of the past. All is decaying and growing fainter, and men seem trusting to some unknown future which they may never see. One government has been abandoned, and there is none in its place. One revolution follows another, yet the remedy is not found. Let them beware lest half a century later, they be awakened from their delusion.

How does Fanny Calderón de la Barca attempt to connect the visual differences between New England and Mexican villages to differences in culture? What does she say about how these two societies regarded their pasts and futures? What threat does the author seem to see in Mexico's future? Find one example of bias in her comparison.

Source: Fanny Calderón de la Barca, *Life in Mexico* (1843), reprinted in an abridged form in Lewis Hanke, ed., *Latin America: A Historical Reader* (Boston: Little, Brown, 1974), 440–441.

America. Unlike Latin America, however, the United States never experienced an armed rebellion that overturned the results of an election.

Throughout the Western Hemisphere, charismatic military men played key roles in attracting mass support for independence movements that were commonly dominated by colonial elites. Although this popular support was often decisive in the struggle for independence, the first constitutions of nearly all the American republics excluded large numbers of poor citizens from full political participation. But nearly everywhere in the Americas marginalized groups found populist leaders to articulate their concerns and challenge these limits on their political participation. Using informal means, these leaders sought to influence the selection of officeholders and to place their concerns in the public arena. Despite their success in overturning the deference-based politics of the colonial past, this populist political style at times threatened constitutional order and led to dictatorship.

Andrew Jackson of the United States and **José Antonio Páez°** of Venezuela were political leaders whose powerful personal followings allowed them to challenge constitutional limits to their authority. During the independence

---

José Antonio Páez (hoe-SAY an-TOE-nee-oh PAH-eez)

wars in Venezuela and Colombia, Páez (1790–1873) organized and led Bolívar's most successful cavalry force. Like most of his followers, Páez was uneducated and poor, but his physical strength, courage, and guile made him a natural guerrilla leader and helped him build a powerful political base in Venezuela. Páez described his authority in the following manner: "[the soldiers] resolved to confer on me the supreme command and blindly to obey my will, confidant . . . that I was the only one who could save them."[3] Able to count on the personal loyalty of his followers, Páez was seldom willing to accept the constitutional authority of a distant president.

After defeating the Spanish armies, Bolívar pursued his dream of forging a permanent union of former Spanish colonies modeled on the federal system of the United States. But he underestimated the strength of nationalist sentiment unleashed during the independence wars. Páez and other Venezuelan leaders resisted the surrender of their hard-won power to Bolívar's Gran Colombia government in distant Bogotá (the capital city of modern Colombia). When Bolívar's authority was challenged by political opponents in 1829, Páez declared Venezuela's independence. Merciless to his enemies and indulgent with his followers, Páez ruled the country as president or dictator for the next eighteen years. Despite implementing an economic program favorable to the elite, Páez remained popular with the masses by skillfully manipulating popular political symbols. Even as his personal wealth grew through land acquisitions and commerce, Páez took care to present himself as a common man.

Andrew Jackson (1767–1845) was the first president of the United States born in humble circumstances. A self-made man who eventually acquired substantial property and owned over a hundred slaves, Jackson was extremely popular among frontier residents, urban workers, and small farmers. Although he was notorious for his untidy personal life as well as for dueling, his courage, individualism, and willingness to challenge authority helped him lead a successful political career as judge, general, congressman, senator, and president.

During his military career, Jackson proved to be impatient with civilian authorities. Widely known because of his victories over the Creek and Seminole peoples, he was elevated to the pinnacle of American politics by his celebrated defeat of the British at the Battle of New Orleans in 1815 and by his seizure of Florida from the Spanish in 1818. In 1824 he received a plurality of the popular votes cast for the presidency, but he failed to win a majority of the electoral votes and was denied the presidency when the House of Representatives chose John Quincy Adams.

Jackson's followers viewed his landslide election victory in 1828 and reelection in 1832 as the triumph of democracy over the entrenched aristocracy. In office Jackson challenged constitutional limits on his authority, substantially increasing presidential power at the expense of Congress and the Supreme Court. Like Páez, Jackson was able to dominate national politics by blending a populist political style that celebrated the virtues and cultural enthusiasms of common people with support for policies that promoted the economic interests of some of the nation's most powerful propertied groups.

Personalist leaders were common in both Latin America and the United States, but Latin America's weaker constitutional tradition, more limited protection of property rights, lower literacy levels, and less-developed communications systems provided fewer checks on the ambitions of popular politicians. The Constitution of the United States was never suspended, and no national election result in the United States was ever successfully overturned by violence. Latin America's personalist leaders, however, often ignored constitutional restraints on their authority, and election results seldom determined access to presidential power. As a result, by 1900, every Latin American nation had experienced periods of dictatorship.

The Threat of Regionalism

After independence, new national governments were generally weaker than the colonial governments they replaced. In debates over tariffs, tax and monetary policies, and, in many nations, slavery and the slave trade, regional elites often were willing to lead secessionist movements or to provoke civil war rather than accept laws that threatened their interests. Some of the hemisphere's newly independent nations did not survive these struggles; others lost territories to aggressive neighbors.

In Spanish America, all of the postindependence efforts to forge large multistate federations failed. Central America and Mexico maintained their colonial-era administrative association following independence in 1821. After the overthrow of Iturbide's imperial rule in Mexico in 1823, however, regional politicians split with Mexico and created the independent Republic of Central America. Regional rivalries and civil wars during the 1820s and 1830s forced the breakup of that entity as well and led to the creation of five separate nations. Bolívar attempted to maintain the colonial unity of Venezuela, Colombia, and Ecuador by creating the nation of Gran Colombia with its capital in Bogotá. But even before his death in 1830, not only Venezuela but also Ecuador had become independent states.

During colonial times, Argentina, Uruguay, Paraguay, and Bolivia had been united in a single viceroyalty with its capital in Buenos Aires. With the defeat of Spain, political leaders in Paraguay, Uruguay, and Bolivia declared their independence from Buenos Aires. Argentina, the area that remained after this breakup, was itself nearly overwhelmed by these powerful centrifugal forces. After independence, Argentina's liberals took power in Buenos Aires. They sought a strong central government to promote secular education, free trade, and immigration from Europe. Conservatives dominated the interior provinces. They supported the Catholic Church's traditional control of education as well as the protection of local textile and winemaking industries from European imports. When, in 1819, political leaders in Buenos Aires imposed a national constitution that ignored these concerns, the conservatives of the interior rose in rebellion.

After a decade of civil war and rebellions, a powerful local caudillo, Juan Manuel de Rosas°, came to power. For more than two decades he dominated Argentina, running the nation as if it were his private domain. The economy expanded under Rosas, but his use of intimidation, mob violence, and assassination created many enemies. In 1852 an alliance of foreign and domestic enemies overthrew him, but a new cycle of provincial rivalry and civil war prevented the creation of a strong central government until 1861.

Regionalism threatened the United States as well. The defense of state and regional interests played an important role in the framing of the U.S. Constitution. Many important constitutional provisions represented compromises forged among competing state and regional leaders. The creation of a Senate with equal representation from each state, for example, was an attempt to calm small states, which feared they might be dominated by larger states. The formula for representation in the House of Representatives was also an effort to compromise the divisions between slave and free states. Yet, despite these constitutional compromises, the nation was still threatened by regional rivalries.

Slavery increasingly divided the nation into two separate and competitive societies. A rising tide of immigration to the northern states in the 1830s and 1840s began to move the center of political power in the House of Representatives away from the south. Many southern leaders sought to protect slavery by expanding it to new territories. They supported the Louisiana Purchase in 1803 (see Map 25.3). This agreement with France transferred to the United States a vast territory extending from the Gulf of Mexico to Canada. Southern leaders also supported statehood for Texas and war with Mexico (discussed later in the chapter).

The territorial acquisitions proved a mixed blessing to the defenders of slavery because they forced a national debate about slavery itself. Should slavery be allowed to expand into new territories? Could slavery be protected if new territories eligible for statehood were overwhelmingly free?

In 1860 Abraham Lincoln (1809–1865), who was committed to checking the spread of slavery, was elected president of the United States. In response, the planter elite in the southern states chose the dangerous course of secession from the federal Union. The seceding states formed a new government, the Confederate States of America, known as the Confederacy. Lincoln was able to preserve the Union, but his victory was purchased at an enormous cost. The U.S. Civil War (1861–1865), waged by southern Confederate forces and northern Union (U.S.) forces, was the most destructive conflict in the history of the Western Hemisphere. More than 600,000 lives were lost before the Confederacy surrendered in 1865. The Union victory led to the abolition of slavery. It also transferred national political power to a northern elite committed to industrial expansion and federal support for the construction of railroads and other internal improvements.

The Confederate States of America was better prepared politically and economically for independence than were the successful secessionist movements that broke up Gran Colombia and other Spanish American federations. Nevertheless, the Confederacy failed, in part because of poor timing. The new nations of the Western Hemisphere were most vulnerable during the early years of their existence; indeed, all the successful secessions occurred within the first decades following independence. In the case of the United States, southern secession was defeated by an experienced national government legitimated and strengthened by more than seventy-five years of stability and reinforced by economic and population growth.

Foreign Interventions and Regional Wars

With the exception of the U.S. Civil War, in the nineteenth century the scale of military conflict was far smaller in the Western Hemisphere than in Europe. Nevertheless, wars often determined national borders, access to natural resources, and control of markets in the hemisphere. Even after independence, some Western Hemisphere nations had to defend themselves against Europe's great powers. Contested national borders and regional rivalries also led to wars between Western Hemisphere nations. By the end of the nineteenth century, the United States, Brazil, Argentina, and Chile

---

Juan Manuel de Rosas (huan man-WELL deh ROH-sas)

Map 25.3 Territorial Growth of the United States, 1783–1853 The rapid western expansion of the United States resulted from aggressive diplomacy and warfare against Mexico and Amerindian peoples. Railroad development helped integrate the trans-Mississippi west and promote economic expansion.

Benito Juárez's Triumph over the French   Benito Juárez overcame humble origins to lead the overthrow of Emperor Maximilian and the defeat of French imperialism. He remains a powerful symbol of secularism and republican virtue in Mexico. In this 1948 mural by José Clemente Orozco, Juárez's face dominates a scene of struggle that pits Mexican patriots against the allied forces of the Catholic Church, Mexican conservatives, and foreign invaders.   (Museo Nacional de Historia/CENIDIAP-INBA)

had successfully waged wars against their neighbors and established themselves as regional powers.

Within thirty years of independence, the United States fought a second war with England—the War of 1812 (1812–1815). The weakness of the new republic was symbolized by the burning of the White House and Capitol by British troops in 1814. This humiliation was soon overcome, however, and by the end of the nineteenth century the United States was the hemisphere's greatest military power. Its war against Spain in 1898–1899 created an American empire that reached from the Philippines in the Pacific Ocean to Puerto Rico in the Caribbean Sea.

Europe also challenged the sovereignty of Latin American nations. During the first decades after independence, Argentina faced British and French naval blockades, and British naval forces systematically violated Brazil's territorial waters to stop the importation of slaves. Mexico faced graver threats to its sovereignty, defeating a weak Spanish invasion in 1829 and then a French assault on the city of Veracruz in 1838.

The French used Mexico's inability to repay a loan as an excuse for an invasion in 1862. Mexico had been weakened by a destructive war between conservatives and liberals (1858–1862), and the conservatives allied themselves with the French invaders. The French army quickly forced the president of Mexico, **Benito Juárez,** to flee Mexico City. The French then installed the Austrian Habsburg Maximilian as emperor of Mexico. Juárez, the orphaned child of Amerindian parents, organized an effective military resistance and after years of warfare drove the French army out of Mexico in 1867. After capturing Maximilian, Juárez ordered his execution.

Wars between Western Hemisphere nations commonly produced more enduring results. The United States greatly expanded its land area through military conflicts. In the 1820s Mexico had encouraged Americans to immigrate to Texas, which at that time was part of Mexico. By the early 1830s Americans outnumbered Mexican nationals in Texas by four to one and were aggressively challenging Mexican laws such as the prohibition of slavery. In 1835 political turmoil in Mexico led to a rebellion in Texas by an alliance of Mexican liberals and American settlers. Mexico was defeated in a brief war, and in 1837 Texas became an independent nation. In

1845 the United States made Texas a state, provoking war with Mexico a year later. Mexican forces fought well, but U.S. forces captured Mexico City, and the United States imposed a punitive peace treaty in 1848. Compounding the loss of Texas in 1837, the treaty of 1848 forced Mexico to cede vast territories to the United States, including present-day Texas, New Mexico, Arizona, and California. In return Mexico received $15 million. When gold was discovered in California in 1848, the magnitude of Mexico's loss became clear.

In two wars with neighbors, Chile established itself as the leading military and economic power on the west coast of South America. Between 1836 and 1839, Chile defeated the Confederation of Peru and Bolivia. In 1879 Chilean and British investors in nitrate mines located in the Atacama Desert, a disputed border region, provoked a new war with Peru and Bolivia. The Chilean army and navy won a crushing victory in 1881, forcing Bolivia to cede its only outlet to the sea and Peru to yield the mining districts.

Argentina and Brazil fought over control of Uruguay in the 1820s, but a military stalemate eventually forced them to recognize Uruguayan independence. In 1865 Argentina and Uruguay joined Brazil to wage war against Paraguay. After five years of warfare, the Paraguayan dictator Francisco Solano López° and more than 20 percent of the population of Paraguay were dead. Paraguay suffered military occupation, lost territory to the victors, and was forced to open its markets to foreign trade.

Native Peoples and the Nation-State

Both diplomacy and military action shaped relations between the Western Hemisphere's new nation-states and the indigenous peoples living within them. During late colonial times, to avoid armed conflict and to limit the costs of frontier defense, Spanish, Portuguese, and British imperial governments attempted to limit the expansion of settlements into territories already occupied by Amerindians. With independence, the colonial powers' role as mediator for and protector of native peoples ended.

Still-independent Amerindian peoples posed a significant military challenge to many Western Hemisphere republics. Weakened by civil wars and constitutional crises, many of the new nations were less able to maintain frontier peace than the colonial governments had been. After independence, Amerindian peoples in Argentina, the United States, Chile, and Mexico succeeded in pushing back some frontier settlements. But despite these early victories, native military resistance was finally overcome by the end of the 1880s in both North and South America.

After the American Revolution, the rapid expansion of agricultural settlements threatened native peoples in North America. Between 1790 and 1810 tens of thousands of settlers entered territories guaranteed to Amerindians in treaties with the United States. In Ohio alone more than 200,000 white settlers were present by 1810. Indigenous leaders responded by seeking the support of British officials in Canada and by forging broad indigenous alliances. American forces decisively defeated one such Amerindian alliance in 1794 at the Battle of Fallen Timbers in Ohio. After 1800 two Shawnee leaders, the brothers **Tecumseh**° and Prophet (Tenskwatawa), created a larger and better-organized alliance among southern and western Amerindian peoples and gained some support from Great Britain. In 1811 American military forces attacked and destroyed the ritual center of the alliance, Prophet Town. The final blow came during the War of 1812 when Tecumseh, fighting alongside his British allies, was killed in battle.

In the 1820s white settlers forced native peoples living in Ohio, southern Indiana and Illinois, southwestern Michigan, most of Missouri, central Alabama, and southern Mississippi to cede their land. The 1828 presidential election of Andrew Jackson, a veteran of wars against native peoples, brought matters to a head. In 1830 Congress passed the Indian Removal Act, forcing the resettlement of the Cherokee, Creek, Choctaw, and other eastern peoples to land west of the Mississippi River. The removal was carried out in the 1830s, and nearly half of the forced migrants died on this journey, known as the Trail of Tears.

Amerindians living on the Great Plains offered formidable resistance to the expansion of while settlement. By the time substantial numbers of white buffalo hunters, cattlemen, and settlers reached the American west indigenous peoples were skilled users of horses and firearms. These technologies had transformed the cultures of the Sioux, Comanche, Pawnee, Kiowa, and other Plains peoples. The improved efficiency of the buffalo hunt reduced their dependence on agriculture. As a result, women, whose primary responsibility had been raising crops, lost prestige and social power to male hunters. Living arrangements also changed as the single-family tepees of migratory buffalo hunters replaced the multigenerational lodges of the traditional farming economy.

During the U.S. Civil War, native peoples experienced a disruption of their trade with Eastern merchants and the suspension of treaty indemnities. After the war,

---

Francisco Solano López (fran-CEES-co so-LAN-oh LOH-pez)

Tecumseh (teh-CUM-sah)

Navajo Leaders Gathered in Washington to Negotiate As settlers, ranchers, and miners pushed west in the nineteenth century, leaders of Amerindian peoples were forced to negotiate territorial concessions with representatives of the U.S. government. In order to impress Amerindian peoples with the wealth and power of the United States, many of their leaders were invited to Washington, D.C. This photo shows Navajo leaders and their Anglo translators in Washington, D.C., in 1874. (#5851 Frank McNill Collection, State Records Center & Archives, Sante Fe, NM)

ever more settlers pushed onto the plains. Buffalo herds were hunted to near extinction for their hides, and land was lost to farmers and ranchers. During nearly four decades of armed conflict with the United States Army, Amerindian peoples were forced to give up their land and their traditional ways. The Comanche, who had dominated the southern plains during the period of Spanish and Mexican rule, were forced by the U.S. government to cede most of their land in Texas in 1865. The Sioux and their allies resisted. In 1876 they overwhelmed General George Armstrong Custer and the Seventh Cavalry in the Battle of Little Bighorn (in the southern part of the present-day state of Montana). But finally the Sioux also were forced to accept reservation life. Military campaigns in the 1870s and 1880s then broke the resistance of the Apache.

The indigenous peoples of Argentina and Chile experienced a similar trajectory of adaptation, resistance, and defeat. Herds of wild cattle provided indigenous peoples with a limitless food supply, and horses and metal weapons increased their military capacities. Thus, for a while, the native peoples of Argentina and Chile effectively checked the southern expansion of agriculture and ranching. Amerindian raiders operated within 100 miles (160 kilometers) of Buenos Aires into the 1860s. Unable to defeat these resourceful enemies, the governments of Argentina and Chile relied on an elaborate system of gift giving and prisoner exchanges to maintain peace on the frontier. By the 1860s, however, population increase, political stability, and military modernization allowed Argentina and Chile to take the offensive.

In the 1870s the government of Argentina used overwhelming military force to crush native resistance. Thousands of Amerindians were killed, and survivors were driven onto marginal land. In Chile the story was the same. When civil war and an economic depression weakened the Chilean government at the end of the 1850s, the Mapuches° (called "Araucanians" by the Spanish) attempted to push back frontier settlements. Despite early successes, the Mapuches were defeated in the 1870s by modern weaponry. In Chile, as in Argentina and the United States, military campaigns against native peoples were justified by demonizing the Amerindians. Newspaper editorials and the speeches of politicians portrayed Amerindians as brutal and cruel, and as obstacles to progress. In April 1859, a Chilean newspaper commented:

> The necessity, not only to punish the Araucanian race, but also to make it impotent to harm us, is well recognized . . . as the only way to rid the country of a million evils. It is well understood that they are odious and prejudicial guests in Chile . . . conciliatory measures have accomplished nothing with this stupid race—the infamy and disgrace of the Chilean nation.[4]

Political divisions and civil wars within the new nations sometimes provided an opportunity for long-pacified native peoples to rebel. In the Yucatán region of Mexico, the owners of henequen (the agave plant that produces fiber used for twine) and sugar plantations had forced

Mapuches (mah-POO-chez)

many Maya° communities off their traditional agricultural lands, reducing thousands of them to peonage. This same regional elite declared itself independent of the government in Mexico City that was convulsed by civil war in the late 1830s. The Mexican government was unable to reestablish control because it faced the greater threat of invasion by the United States. Seeing their oppressors divided, the Maya rebelled in 1847. This well-organized and popular uprising, known as the **Caste War,** nearly returned the Yucatán to Maya rule. Grievances accumulated over more than three hundred years led to great violence and property destruction. The Maya were not defeated until the war with the United States ended. Even then Maya rebels retreated to unoccupied territories and created an independent state, which they called the "Empire of the Cross." Organized around a mix of traditional beliefs and Christian symbols, this indigenous state resisted Mexican forces to 1870. A few defiant Maya strongholds survived until 1901.

THE CHALLENGE OF ECONOMIC AND SOCIAL CHANGE

During the nineteenth century, the newly independent nations of the Western Hemisphere struggled to realize the Enlightenment ideals of freedom and individual liberty that had helped to ignite the revolutions for independence. The achievement of these objectives was slowed by the persistence of slavery and other oppressive colonial-era institutions. Cultural and racial diversity also presented obstacles to reform. Nevertheless, by century's end reform movements in many of the hemisphere's nations had succeeded in ending the slave trade, abolishing slavery, expanding voting rights, and assimilating immigrants from Asia and Europe.

The consequences of increased industrialization and greater involvement in the evolving world economy challenged the region's political stability and social arrangements. A small number of nations embraced industrialization, but most Western Hemisphere economies became increasingly dependent on the export of agricultural goods and minerals during the nineteenth century. While the industrializing nations of the hemisphere became richer than the nations that remained

Maya (MY-ah)

exporters of raw materials, all the region's economies became more vulnerable and volatile as a result of greater participation in international markets. Like contemporary movements for social reform, efforts to assert national economic control produced powerful new political forces.

The Abolition of Slavery

In both the United States and Latin America, strong anti-slavery sentiments were expressed during the struggles for independence. In nearly all the new nations of the Western Hemisphere, revolutionary leaders asserted universal ideals of freedom and citizenship that contrasted sharply with the reality of slavery. Men and women who wanted to outlaw slavery were called **abolitionists.** Despite the efforts of abolitionists, slavery survived in much of the hemisphere until the 1850s. In regions where the export of plantation products was most important—such as the United States, Brazil, and Cuba—the abolition of slavery was achieved with great difficulty.

In the United States, slavery was weakened by abolition in some northern states and by the termination of the African slave trade in 1808. But this progress was stalled by the profitable expansion of cotton agriculture after the War of 1812. In Spanish America, tens of thousands of slaves gained freedom by joining revolutionary armies during the wars for independence. After independence, most Spanish American republics prohibited the slave trade. Counteracting that trend was the growing international demand for sugar and coffee, products traditionally produced on plantations by slaves. As prices rose for plantation products in the first half of the nineteenth century, Brazil and Cuba (the island remained a Spanish colony until 1899) increased their imports of slaves.

During the long struggle to end slavery in the United States, American abolitionists argued that slavery offended both morality and the universal rights asserted in the Declaration of Independence. Abolitionist Theodore Weld articulated the religious objection to slavery in 1834:

> No condition of birth, no shade of color, no mere misfortune of circumstance, can annul the birth-right charter, which God has bequeathed to every being upon whom he has stamped his own image, by making him a free *moral agent* [emphasis in original], and that he who robs his fellow man of this tramples upon right, subverts justice, outrages humanity . . . and sacrilegiously assumes the prerogative of God.[5]

Two groups denied full rights of citizenship under the Constitution, women and free African-Americans, played important roles in the abolition of slavery. Women served on the executive committee of the American Anti-Slavery Society and produced some of the most effective propaganda against slavery. Eventually, thousands of women joined the abolitionist cause, where they provided leadership and were effective speakers and propagandists. When social conservatives attacked this highly visible public role, many women abolitionists responded by becoming public advocates of female suffrage as well.

Frederick Douglass, a former slave, became one of the most effective abolitionist speakers and writers. Other more radical black leaders pushed the abolitionist movement to accept the inevitability of violence. They saw civil war or slave insurrection as necessary for the ending of slavery. One argued passionately that slaves should "RISE AT ONCE, en masse, and THROW OFF THEIR FETTERS" (capitalization in original).

In the 1850s the growing electoral strength of the newly formed Republican Party forced a confrontation between slave and free states. After the election of Abraham Lincoln in 1860, the first of the thirteen southern states that formed the Condeferacy seceded from the Union. During the Civil War, pressure for emancipation rose as tens of thousands of black freemen and escaped slaves joined the Union army. Hundreds of thousands of other slaves fled their masters' plantations and farms for the protection of advancing northern armies. In 1863, in the midst of the Civil War and two years after the abolition of serfdom in Russia (see Chapter 27), President Lincoln began the abolition of slavery by issuing the Emancipation Proclamation, which ended slavery in rebel states not occupied by the Union army. Final abolition was accomplished after the war, in 1865, by the Thirteenth Amendment to the Constitution.

In Brazil slavery survived more than two decades after it was abolished in the United States. Progress toward abolition was not only slower in Brazil but also depended on foreign pressure. In 1830 Brazil signed a treaty with the British ending the slave trade. Despite this agreement, Brazil illegally imported over a half-million more African slaves before the British navy finally forced compliance in the 1850s. In the 1850s and 1860s the Brazilian emperor, Pedro II, and many liberals worked to abolish slavery, but their desire to find a form of gradual emancipation acceptable to slave owners slowed progress.

During the war with Paraguay (1865–1870), large numbers of slaves joined the Brazilian army in exchange for freedom. Their loyalty and heroism undermined the military's support for slavery. Educated Brazilians in-

A Former Brazilian Slave Returns from Military Service   The heroic participation of black freemen and slaves in the Paraguayan War (1885–1870) led many Brazilians to advocate the abolition of slavery. The original caption for this drawing reads: "On his return from the war in Paraguay: Full of glory, covered with laurels, after having spilled his blood in defense of the fatherland and to free a people from slavery, the volunteer sees his own mother bound and whipped! Awful reality!"   (Courtesy, Fundacao Biblioteca Nacional, Brazil)

creasingly viewed slavery as an obstacle to economic development and an impediment to democratic reform. In the 1870s, as abolitionist sentiment grew, reformers forced the passage of laws providing for the gradual emancipation of slaves. When political support for slavery weakened in the 1880s, growing numbers of slaves forced the issue by fleeing from bondage. By the 1880s, however, army leaders were resisting demands that they capture and return runaway slaves. Legislation abolishing slavery finally was passed by the Brazilian parliament and accepted by the emperor in 1888.

The plantations of the Caribbean region received almost 40 percent of all African slaves shipped to the New World. As a result, throughout the region tiny white minorities lived surrounded by slave and free colored majorities. At the end of the eighteenth century, the slave rebellion in Saint Domingue (see Chapter 23) spread terror across the Caribbean. Because of fear that any effort to overthrow colonial rule might unleash new slave rebellions, there was little enthusiasm among free settlers in Caribbean colonies for independence. Nor did local support for abolition appear among white settlers or free colored populations. Thus abolition in most Caribbean colonies commonly resulted from political decisions made in Europe by colonial powers.

Nevertheless, like slaves in Brazil, the United States, and Spanish America, slaves in the Caribbean helped propel the movement toward abolition by rebelling, running away, and resisting in more subtle ways. Although initially unsuccessful, the rebellions that threatened other French Caribbean colonies after the Haitian Revolution (1789–1804)) weakened France's support for slavery. Jamaica and other British colonies also experienced rebellions and saw the spread of communities of runaways. In Spanish Cuba as well, slave resistance forced increases in expenditures for police forces in the nineteenth century.

After 1800, the profitability of sugar plantations in the British West Indian colonies declined, and a coalition of labor groups, Protestant dissenters, and free traders in Britain pushed for the abolition of slavery. Britain, the major participant in the eighteenth-century expansion of slavery in the Americas, ended its participation in the slave trade in 1807. It then negotiated a series of treaties with Spain, Brazil, and other importers of slaves to eliminate the slave trade to the Americas. Once these treaties were in place, British naval forces acted to force compliance.

Slavery in British colonies was abolished in 1834. However, the law compelled "freed" slaves to remain with former masters as "apprentices." Abuses by planters and resistance to apprenticeship by former slaves led to complete abolition in 1838. A decade later slavery in the French Caribbean was abolished after upheavals in France led to the overthrow of the government of Louis Philippe (see Chapter 23).

Slavery lasted longest in Cuba and Puerto Rico, Spain's remaining colonies. Britain's use of diplomatic pressure and naval force to limit the arrival of African slaves weakened slavery after 1820. More important, however, was the growth of support for abolition in these colonies. Both Cuba and Puerto Rico had larger white and free colored populations than did the Caribbean colonies of Britain and France. As a result, there was less fear in Cuba and Puerto Rico that abolition would lead to the political ascendancy of former slaves (as had occurred in Haiti). In Puerto Rico, where slaves numbered approximately thirty thousand, local reformers sought and gained the abolition of slavery in 1873. In the midst of a decade-long war to defeat forces seeking the independence of Cuba, the Spanish government moved

gradually toward abolition. Initially, slave children born after September 18, 1868, were freed but obligated to work for their former masters for eighteen years. In 1880 all other slaves were freed on the condition that they serve their masters for eight additional years. Finally, in 1886, these conditions were eliminated, slavery was abolished, and Cuban patriots forged the multiracial alliance that was to initiate a war for Cuban independence in 1895 (See Chapter 29).

Immigration

During the colonial period, free Europeans were a minority among immigrants to the Western Hemisphere. Between 1500 and 1760, African slaves entering the Western Hemisphere outnumbered European immigrants by nearly two to one. Another 4 million or so African slaves were imported before the effective end of the slave trade at the end of the 1850s. As the African slave trade came to an end, the arrival of millions of immigrants from Europe and Asia in the nineteenth century contributed to the further transformation of the Western Hemisphere. This new wave of immigration fostered rapid economic growth and the occupation of frontier regions in the United States, Canada, Argentina, Chile, and Brazil. It also promoted urbanization. By century's end, nearly all of the hemisphere's fastest-growing cities (Buenos Aires, Chicago, New York, and São Paulo, for example) had large immigrant populations.

During the nineteenth century, Europe provided the majority of immigrants to the Western Hemisphere. For much of the century, these people came primarily from western Europe, but after 1870 most came from southern and eastern Europe. The scale of immigration increased dramatically in the second half of the century. The United States received approximately 600,000 European immigrants in the 1830s, 1.5 million in the 1840s, and then 2.5 million per decade until 1880. In the 1890s an astonishing total of 5.2 million immigrants arrived. European immigration to Latin America also increased dramatically after 1880. Combined immigration to Argentina and Brazil rose from just under 130,000 in the 1860s to 1.7 million in the 1890s. By 1910, 30 percent of the Argentine population was foreign-born, more than twice the proportion in the U.S. population. Argentina was an extremely attractive destination for European immigrants, receiving more than twice as many immigrants as Canada between 1870 and 1930. Even so, immigration to Canada increased tenfold during this period.

Asian immigration to the Western Hemisphere increased after 1850. Between 1849 and 1875, approximately 100,000 Chinese immigrants arrived in Peru and another 120,000 entered Cuba. Canada attracted about 50,000 Chinese in the second half of the century. The United States, however, was the primary North American destination for Chinese immigrants, receiving 300,000 between 1854 and 1882. India also contributed to the social transformation of the Western Hemisphere, sending more than a half-million immigrants to the Caribbean region. British Guiana alone received 238,000 immigrants from the Asian subcontinent.

Despite the obvious economic benefits that accompanied this inflow of people, hostility to immigration mounted in many nations. Nativist political movements argued that large numbers of foreigners could not be successfully integrated into national political cultures. By the end of the century, fear and prejudice led many governments in the Western Hemisphere to limit immigration or to distinguish between "desirable" and "undesirable" immigrants, commonly favoring Europeans over Asians.

Asians faced more obstacles to immigration than did Europeans and were more often victims of violence and extreme forms of discrimination in the New World. In the 1870s and 1880s anti-Chinese riots erupted in many western cities in the United States. Congress responded to this wave of racism by passing the Chinese Exclusion Act in 1882, which eliminated most Chinese immigration. In 1886 fears that Canada was being threatened by "inferior races" led to the imposition of a head tax that made immigration to Canada more difficult for Chinese families. During this same period, strong anti-Chinese prejudice surfaced in Peru, Mexico, and Cuba. Japanese immigrants in Brazil and East Indians in the English-speaking Caribbean faced similar prejudice.

Immigrants from Europe also faced prejudice and discrimination. In the United States, Italians were commonly portrayed as criminals or anarchists. In Argentina, social scientists attempted to prove that Italian immigrants were more violent and less honest than the native-born population. Immigrants from Spain were widely stereotyped in Argentina as miserly and dishonest. Eastern European Jews seeking to escape pogroms and discrimination at home found themselves barred from many educational institutions and professional careers in both the United States and Latin America. Negative stereotypes were invented for German, Swedish, Polish, and Middle Eastern immigrants as well. The perceived grievances used to justify these common prejudices were remarkably similar from Canada to Argentina. Immigrants, it was argued, threatened the well-being of native-born workers by accepting low wages, and they threatened national culture by resisting assimilation.

Many intellectuals and political leaders wondered if the evolving mix of culturally diverse populations could sustain a common citizenship. As a result, efforts were directed toward compelling immigrants to assimilate.

Arrest of Labor Activist in Buenos Aires
The labor movement in Buenos Aires grew in numbers and became more radical with the arrival of tens of thousands of Italian and Spanish immigrants. Fearful of socialist and anarchist unions, the government of Argentina used an expanded police force to break strikes by arresting labor leaders. (Archivo General de la Nacion, Buenos Aires)

Schools became cultural battlegrounds where language, cultural values, and patriotic feelings were transmitted to the children of immigrants. Across the hemisphere, school curricula were revised to promote national culture. Ignoring Canada's large French-speaking population, an English-speaking Canadian reformer commented on recent immigration: "If Canada is to become in a real sense a nation, if our people are to become one people, we must have one language."[6] Fear and prejudice led to the singing of patriotic songs, the veneration of national flags and other symbols, and the writing of national histories that emphasized patriotism and civic virtue. Nearly everywhere in the Americas schools worked to create homogeneous national cultures.

American Cultures Despite discrimination, immigrants continued to stream into the Western Hemisphere, introducing new languages, living arrangements, technologies, and work customs. Immigrants altered the politics of many of the hemisphere's nations as they sought to influence government policies. Where immigrants arrived in the greatest numbers, they put enormous pressure on housing, schools, and social welfare services. To compensate for their isolation from home, language, and culture, immigrants often created ethnically based mutual aid societies, sports and leisure clubs, and neighborhoods. Ethnic organizations and districts provided valuable social and economic support for recent arrivals while sometimes worsening the fears of the native-born that immigration posed a threat to national culture.

Immigrants were changed by their experiences in their adopted nations and by programs that forced them to accept new cultural values through education or, in some cases, service in the military. The modification of the language, customs, values, and behaviors of a group as a result of contact with people from another culture is called **acculturation.** Immigrants and their children, in turn, made their mark on the cultures of their adopted nations. They learned the language spoken in their adopted countries as fast as possible in order to improve their earning capacity. At the same time, words and phrases from their languages entered the language of the host nations. Languages as diverse as Yiddish and Italian strongly influenced American English, Argentine Spanish, and Brazilian Portuguese. Dietary practices introduced from Europe and Asia altered the cuisine of nearly every American nation. In turn, immigrants commonly added native foods to their diets, especially the hemisphere's abundant and relatively cheap meats.

American popular music changed as well. For example, the Argentine tango, based on African-Argentine rhythms, was transformed by new instrumentation and orchestral arrangements brought by Italian immigrants. Mexican ballads blended with English folk music in the U.S. southwest, and Italian operas played to packed houses in Buenos Aires. Sports, games of chance, and fashion also experienced this process of borrowing and exchange.

Union movements and electoral politics in the hemisphere also felt the influence of new arrivals who aggressively sought to influence government and improve working conditions. The labor movements of Mexico, Argentina, and the United States, in particular, were influenced by the anarchist and socialist beliefs of European immigrants. Mutual benevolent societies and less formal ethnic associations pooled resources to help immigrants open businesses, aid the immigration of their relatives, or bury their family members. They also established links with political movements, sometimes exchanging votes for favors.

Women's Rights and the Struggle for Social Justice The abolition of slavery in the Western Hemisphere did not end racial discrimination or provide full political rights for every citizen. Not only blacks but also women, new immigrants, and native peoples in nearly every Western Hemisphere nation suffered the effects of political and economic discrimination. During the second half of the nineteenth century, reformers struggled to remove these limits on citizenship while also addressing the welfare needs of workers and the poor.

In 1848 a group of women angered by their exclusion from an international antislavery meeting issued a call for a meeting to discuss women's rights. The **Women's Rights Convention** at Seneca Falls, New York, issued a statement that said in part, "We hold these truths to be self-evident: that all men and women are equal." While moderates focused on the issues of greater economic independence and full legal rights, increasing numbers of women demanded the right to vote. Others lobbied to provide better conditions for women working outside the home, especially in textile factories. Sarah Grimké responded to criticism of women's activism:

> This has been the language of man since he laid aside the whip as a means to keep woman in subjection. He spares her body, but the war he has waged against her mind, her heart, and her soul, has been no less destructive to her as a moral being. How monstrous is the doctrine that woman is to be dependent on man![7]

Progress toward equality between men and women was equally slow in Canada and Latin America. Canada's first women doctors received their training in the United States because no woman was able to receive a medical degree in Canada until 1895. Full enfranchisement occurred in Canada in the twentieth century, but Canadian women did gain the right to vote in some provincial and municipal elections before 1900. Like women in the United States, Canadian women provided leadership in temperance, child welfare, and labor reform movements. Argentina and Uruguay were among the first Latin American nations to provide public education for women. Both nations introduced coeducation in the 1870s. Chilean women gained access to some careers in medicine and law in the 1870s. In Argentina, the first woman doctor graduated from medical school in 1899. In Brazil, where many women were active in the abolitionist movement, four women graduated in medicine by 1882. Throughout the hemisphere, more rapid progress was achieved in lower status careers that threatened male economic power less directly, and by the end of the century, women dominated elementary school teaching throughout the Western Hemisphere.

From Canada to Argentina and Chile, the majority of working-class women had no direct involvement in these reform movements, but in their daily lives they succeeded in transforming gender relations. By the end of the nineteenth century, large numbers of poor women worked outside the home on farms, in markets, and, increasingly, in factories. Many bore full responsibility for providing for their children. Whether men thought women should remain in the home or not, by the end of the century women were unambiguously present in the economy (see also Chapter 28).

Throughout the hemisphere there was little progress toward eliminating racial discrimination. Blacks were denied the vote throughout the southern United States. They also were subjected to the indignity of segregation—consigned to separate schools, hotels, restaurants, seats in public transportation, and even water fountains. Racial discrimination against men and women of African descent was also common in Latin America, though seldom spelled out in legal codes. Unlike the southern states of the United States, Latin American nations did not insist on formal racial segregation or permit lynching. Nor did they enforce a strict color line. Many men and women of mixed background were able to enter the skilled working class or middle class. Latin Americans tended to view racial identity across a continuum of physical characteristics rather than in the narrow terms of black and white that defined race relations in the United States.

The Children's Aid Society of Toronto   Throughout the Western Hemisphere, women led the effort to develop social welfare institutions. Their leadership was most clearly evident in providing protection for poor and abandoned children. This photo shows a social worker and children sitting on the front step of the Children's Aid Society of Toronto in 1895.   (City of Toronto Archives, #SC1-3)

The successful movements to abolish slavery in Latin America did not lead to an end to racial discrimination. But some of the participants in the abolition struggles later organized to promote racial integration in their societies. They demanded access to education, the right to vote, and greater economic opportunity, pointing out the economic and political costs paid by poor countries that denied full rights to all citizens. Their success depended on political organization and the forging of alliances with sympathetic white politicians. Black intellectuals also struggled to overturn racist stereotypes. In Brazil, Argentina, and Cuba, as in the United States, political and literary magazines celebrating black cultural achievement became powerful weapons in the struggle against racial discrimination. Despite these efforts, men and women of African descent continued to suffer discrimination everywhere in the Americas at century's end.

Development and Underdevelopment

Although the Atlantic economy experienced three periods of economic contraction during the nineteenth century, nearly all the nations of the Western Hemisphere were richer in 1900 than in 1800. The Industrial Revolution, worldwide population growth, and an increasingly integrated world market stimulated economic expansion (see Environment and Technology: The McCormick Reaper). Wheat, corn, wool, meats, and nonprecious minerals joined the region's earlier exports of silver, sugar, dyes, coffee, and cotton. During the nineteenth century, the United States was the only Western Hemisphere nation to industrialize, but nearly every government promoted new economic activities. Throughout the hemisphere investments were made in roads, railroads, canals, and telegraphs to better serve distant markets. In addition, tariff and monetary policies helped to foster economic diversification and growth. Yet only three Western Hemisphere nations—the United States, Canada, and Argentina—achieved individual income levels similar to those in western Europe by 1900.

New demands for copper, zinc, lead, coal, and tin unleashed by the Industrial Revolution led to mining booms in the western United States and in Mexico and Chile. Unlike the small-scale and often short-term gold- and silver-mining operations of the colonial era, the mining companies of the late nineteenth century were heavily capitalized international corporations that could bully governments and buy political favors. During this period, European or North American corporations owned most new mining enterprises in Latin America. Petroleum development, which occurred at the end of the century, followed this pattern as well.

New technology accelerated economic integration, but the high cost of this technology often increased dependence on foreign capital. Many of the hemisphere's governments promoted railroads by granting tax benefits, free land, and monopoly rights to both domestic and foreign investors. By 1890 vast areas of the Great Plains in the United States and Canada, the Argentine pampas, and the northern part of Mexico were producing grain and livestock for foreign markets opened by the development of railroads. Steamships also lowered the cost of transportation to distant markets, and the telegraph stimulated expansion by speeding the spread of information about the demand for and availability of products.

The acquisition of bundles of new technologies at the same time often multiplied the cumulative effects of individual technologies. In Argentina, for example, the railroad, telegraph, barbed wire, and refrigeration all appeared within a single generation in the 1870s and 1880s. Although Argentina had had abundant livestock herds since the colonial period, the great distance separating Argentina from Europe's markets prevented Argentine cattle raisers from efficiently exporting either fresh meat or live animals. Technology changed this situation. The combination of railroads and the telegraph lowered freight costs and improved information about markets. Steamships shortened trans-Atlantic crossings. Refrigerated ships made it possible to sell meat from Argentina's pampas in the markets of Europe. As land values rose and livestock breeding improved, new investments were protected by barbed wire, the first inexpensive fencing available on the nearly treeless plains.

Despite these shared experiences, growing interdependence and increased competition produced deep structural differences among Western Hemisphere economies by 1900. Two distinct economic tracks became clearly visible. One led to industrialization and prosperity, what is now called **development.** The other continued colonial dependence on the export of raw materials and low-wage industries, now commonly called **underdevelopment.** By the end of the nineteenth century, material prosperity was greater and economic development was more diversified in English-speaking North America than in the nations of Latin America. With a temperate climate, vast fertile prairies, and an influx of European immigrants, Argentina was the only Latin American nation to imitate the prosperity of the United States and Canada in the nineteenth century.

These important differences in regional economic development were due in part to cyclical swings in international markets. When the United States gained independence in 1783, the world capitalist economy was in the first years of a four-decade period of rapid growth. With a large merchant fleet, a diversified economy that included some manufacturing, and adequate banking and insurance services, the United States benefited from the expansion of the world economy. Rapid population growth due in large measure to immigration, high levels of individual wealth, widespread landownership, and relatively high literacy rates also fostered rapid economic development in the United States.

Canada's struggle for greater political autonomy, which culminated in the Confederation of 1867, coincided with a second period of global economic expansion. Canada also benefited from its special trading relationship with Britain, the world's preeminent industrial nation, and from a rising tide of immigrants after 1850.

The McCormick Reaper

The McCormick reaper was one of the great industrial success stories of the nineteenth century. McCormick reapers and other agricultural implements dominated agriculture and gained export markets throughout the Western Hemisphere and Europe. By leading the mechanization of agriculture, the McCormick Havesting Machine Company reduced labor costs and promoted the development of large-scale commercial farming in the midwestern United States and Canada. Aided by mechanization, wheat production grew by 70 percent in the 1850s alone.

Cyrus McCormick and his family began building reapers in their blacksmith shop in Rockbridge County, Virginia, in 1840. In the early years, slaves owned by the family helped handcraft the reapers from raw materials found locally. Although McCormick faced competition from other manufacturers, the business grew quickly, in part because McCormick was a great promoter who effectively used advertising to develop his business. As demand rose, he increased production by adding new skilled workers and by licensing other manufacturers to produce the company's reapers.

These licensing agreements caused problems of quality control that led McCormick to move all the company's production to a custom-built factory in Chicago in 1848. Production in the new factory quickly reached 1,500 units per year, far outstripping the 200 units per year produced in the Virginia operation. Nearly all this increase came from adding skilled workers and from the closer supervision of subcontractors who supplied blades and other parts. By 1876, 14,000 reapers were produced.

At the end of the 1870s, Cyrus broke with his brother, Leander, and brought in a factory manager who had worked at Colt firearms and the Wilson Sewing Machine Company. Under this new leadership, the company introduced a new industrial process that emphasized standardization and the use of special-purpose machine tools for fabrication. Production reached 48,000 units in 1885 and then soared to 100,000 in 1889. These changes in technology and production methods, however, changed the work force from skilled to unskilled labor and contributed to increased numbers of strikes and work stoppages.

Source: This discussion follows the analysis in David A. Hounshell, *From the American System to Mass Production, 1800–1932: The Development of Manufacturing Technology in the United States* (Baltimore: Johns Hopkins University Press, 1984), 153–189.

The McCormick Reaper In the nineteenth century, the machine age arrived in the countryside. The McCormick reaper increased productivity and also promoted the concentration of land in grain producing regions of the United States. (Navistar International Harvester Archives)

The Introduction of New Technologies Changes the Mining Industry Powerful hydraulic technologies were introduced in western mining sites in the United States. This early photo shows how high power water jets could transform the natural environment. (Colorado Historical Society)

Nevertheless, some regions within each of these prosperous North American nations—Canada's Maritime Provinces and the southern part of the United States, for example—demonstrated the same patterns of underdevelopment found in Latin America.

Latin American nations gained independence in the 1820s, when the global economy was contracting due to the end of the Napoleonic Wars and market saturation provoked by the early stages of European industrialization. During the colonial period the region's economic resources had been concentrated on the production of agricultural and mining exports. After independence those raw-material exports faced increased competition. Although these sectors experienced periods of great prosperity in the nineteenth century, their markets experienced sharp moves not only up but down. The history of these specialized Latin American economies, subject to periodic problems of oversupply and low prices, was one of boom and bust. The efforts of Latin American

governments to gain competitive market advantages by defeating union activity, holding down wages, and opening markets to foreign manufactures further complicated the movement toward industrialization.

Weak governments, political instability, and, in some cases, civil war also slowed Latin American economic development. A comparative examination of Western Hemisphere economic history makes clear that stable and reliable public administration is a necessary part of the development process. Because Latin America was dependent on capital and technology obtained from abroad, Great Britain and, by the end of the century, the United States often were able to impose unfavorable trade conditions or even intervene militarily to protect investments. The combined impact of these domestic and international impediments to development became clear when Mexico, Chile, and Argentina failed to achieve high levels of domestic investment in manufacturing late in the nineteenth century, despite a rapid accumulation of wealth induced by a rising tide of income derived from traditional exports.

Altered Environments

Population growth, economic expansion, new technologies, and the introduction of plants and animals to new regions dramatically altered the Western Hemisphere's environment. Many of Cuba's forests were cut in the early nineteenth century to expand sugar production. The expansion of livestock raising put heavy pressure on fragile environments in Argentina, Uruguay, southern Brazil, and the southwestern United States. Other forms of commercial agriculture also threatened the environment. Farmers in South Carolina and Georgia gained a short-term increase in cotton production by abandoning crop rotation after 1870, but this practice quickly led to soil exhaustion and erosion. The use of plows on the North American prairies and the Argentine pampa eliminated many native grasses and increased the threat of soil erosion. Coffee planters in Brazil exhausted soil fertility with a destructive cycle of overplanting followed by expansion onto forest reserves cleared by cutting and burning.

Rapid urbanization also put heavy pressure on the environment. New York, Chicago, Rio de Janeiro, Buenos Aires, and Mexico City were among the world's fastest-growing cities in the nineteenth century. Governments strained to keep up with the need for sewers, clean water, and garbage disposal. A rising demand for building materials led to the rapid spread of the timber industry in many countries. Under the Timber and Stone Act of

1878, more than 3.5 million acres (1.4 million hectares) of public land in the United States had been claimed at low cost by 1900. Similar transfers of land from public to private ownership occurred in Argentina and Brazil.

As the mining frontier advanced into Nevada, Montana, and California after 1860, erosion and pollution resulted. Similar results occurred in other mining areas. The expansion of nitrate mining and, later, open-pit copper mining in Chile scarred and polluted the environment. The state of Minas Gerais in Brazil experienced a series of mining booms that began with gold in the late seventeenth century and continued with iron ore in the nineteenth. By the end of the century, its red soil was ripped open, its forests were depleted, and the resulting erosion was uncontrolled. Similar devastation afflicted parts of Bolivia and Mexico.

Efforts to meet increasing domestic demand for food and housing and to satisfy foreign demands for exports led to environmental degradation but also contributed significantly to the growth of the world economy and to regional prosperity. By the end of the nineteenth century, small-scale conservation efforts were under way in many nations, and the first national parks and nature reserves had been created. But when confronted by a choice between economic growth and environmental protection, all of the hemisphere's nations embraced growth.

CONCLUSION

The nineteenth century witnessed enormous changes in the Western Hemisphere. With the exception of Canada and many Caribbean islands, colonial controls were removed by century's end. The powerful new political ideas of the Enlightenment and an increased sense of national identity contributed to the desire for independence and self-rule. The success of the American and Haitian revolutions began the assault on the colonial order, transforming the hemisphere's politics. Napoleon's invasion of Portugal and Spain then helped initiate the movement toward independence in Latin America.

Once colonial rule was overturned, the creation of stable and effective governments proved difficult. Powerful personalist leaders resisted the constraints imposed by constitutions. National governments often confronted divisive regional political movements. From Argentina in the south to the United States in the north regional political rivalries provoked civil wars that challenged the very survival of the new nations. Foreign military interven-

tions and wars with native peoples also consumed resources and determined national boundaries. The effort to fulfill the promise of universal citizenship led to struggles to end slavery, extend civil and political rights to women and minorities, and to absorb new immigrants. These objectives were only partially achieved.

Industrialization had a transforming effect on the hemisphere as well. Wealth, political power, and population were increasingly concentrated in urban areas. Bankers and manufacturers, not farmers and plantation owners, directed national destinies. The United States, the most industrialized nation in the Americas, played an aggressive economic role in the region's affairs and used its growing military power as well. Industrialization altered the natural environment in dramatic ways. Modern factories consumed huge amounts of raw materials and energy. Copper mines in Chile and Mexico, Cuban sugar plantations, Brazilian coffee plantations, and Canadian lumber companies all left their mark on the natural environment, and all had ties to markets in the United States. The concentration of people in cities in the United States and Latin America put pressure on water supplies, sewage treatment, and food supplies.

By 1900, however, the hemisphere's national governments were much stronger than they had been at independence. Latin America lagged behind the United States and Canada in institutionalizing democratic political reforms, but Latin American nations in 1900 were stronger and more open than they had been in 1850. By 1900, all of the hemisphere's nations also were better able to meet the threats of foreign intervention and regionalism. Among the benefits resulting from the increased strength of national governments were the abolition of slavery and the extension of political rights to formerly excluded citizens.

Serious challenges remained. Amerindian peoples were forced to resettle on reservations, were excluded from national political life, and, in some countries, remained burdened with special tribute and tax obligations. Women began to enter occupations previously reserved to men but still lacked full citizenship rights. The baneful legacy of slavery and colonial racial stratification remained a barrier to many men and women. The benefits of economic growth were not equitably distributed among the nations of the Western Hemisphere or within individual nations. In 1900 nearly every American nation was wealthier, better educated, more democratic, and more populous than at independence. But they also were generally more vulnerable to distant economic forces, more profoundly split between haves and have-nots, and more clearly divided into a rich North and a poorer South.

■ Key Terms

Simón Bolívar	Tecumseh
Miguel Hidalgo y Costilla	Caste War
José María Morelos	abolitionists
Confederation of 1867	acculturation
personalist leaders	Women's Rights Convention
Andrew Jackson	development
José Antonio Páez	underdevelopment
Benito Juárez	

■ Suggested Reading

For the independence era in Latin America see John Lynch, *The Spanish American Revolutions, 1808–1826*, 2d ed. (1986); Jay Kinsbruner, *Independence in Spanish America* (1994); and A. J. R. Russell-Wood, ed., *From Colony to Nation: Essays on the Independence of Brazil* (1976).

The postindependence political and economic struggles in Latin America can be traced in David Bushnell and Neil Macaulay, *The Emergence of Latin America in the Nineteenth Century* (1988). Tulio Halperin-Donghi, *The Contemporary History of Latin America* (1993), and E. Bradford Burns, *The Poverty of Progress: Latin America in the Nineteenth Century* (1980), argue in different ways that Latin America's economic and social problems originated in unfavorable trade relationships with more-developed nations. See also an excellent collection of essays, Leslie Bethell, ed., *The Cambridge History of Latin America*, vol. 3, *From Independence to c. 1870* (1985).

There is an enormous literature on politics and nation building in the United States and Canada. Among the many worthy studies of the United States are William J. Cooper, *The South and the Politics of Slavery, 1828–1856* (1978); Kenneth M. Stampp, *America in 1857* (1991); and Lawrence Frederick Kohl, *The Politics of Individualism: Parties and the American Character in the Jacksonian Era* (1989). For Canada see J. M. S. Careless, *The Union of the Canadas: The Growth of Canadian Institutions, 1841–1857* (1967); Ged Martin, ed., *The Causes of Canadian Confederation* (1990); and Arthur I. Silver, *The French-Canadian Idea of Confederation, 1864–1900* (1982).

The social and cultural issues raised in this chapter are also the subject of a vast literature. For an excellent history of the immigration era see Walter Nugent, *Crossing: The Great Transatlantic Migrations, 1870–1914* (1992). See also Gunther Barth, *Bitter Strength: A History of Chinese in the United States, 1850–1870* (1964), and Nicolás Sánchez-Albornoz, *The Population of Latin America: A History* (1974).

On the issue of slavery see David Brion Davis, *Slavery and Human Progress* (1984); George M. Frederickson, *The Black Image in the White Mind: The Debate on Afro-American Character and Destiny, 1817–1914* (1971); and Benjamin Quarles, *Black Abolitionists* (1969). For the women's rights movement see Ellen C. Du Bois, *Feminism and Suffrage: The Emergence of an Indepen-*

dent Woman's Movement in the Nineteenth Century (1984), and Lori D. Ginzberg, *Women and the Work of Benevolence: Morality, Politics, and Class in the Nineteenth-Century United States* (1990). Among numerous excellent studies of Indian policies see Robert M. Utley, *The Indian Frontier of the American West, 1846–1890* (1984). On those topics for Canada see J. R. Miller, *Skyscrapers Hide the Heavens: A History of Indian White Relations in Canada* (1989); Olive Patricia Dickason, *Canada's First Nations* (1993); and Alison Prentice, *Canadian Women: A History* (1988).

For abolition in Latin America and the Caribbean see Rebecca Scott, *Slave Emancipation in Cuba: The Transition to Free Labor, 1860–1899* (1985); Robert Conrad, *The Destruction of Brazilian Slavery, 1850–1888* (1973); and William A. Green, *British Slave Emancipation: The Sugar Colonies and the Great Experiment, 1830–1865*. An introduction to the place of women in Latin American society is found in Francesca Miller, *Latin American Women and the Search for Social Justice* (1991), and Jane Jaquette, ed., *The Women's Movement in Latin America* (1989). See also David Barry Gaspar and Darlene Clark Hine, eds., *More Than Chattel: Black Women and Slavery in the Americas* (1996).

An introduction to environmental consequence of North American development is provided by William Cronon, *Nature's Metropolis: Chicago and the Great West* (1991); Joseph M. Petulla, *American Environmental History* (1973); and Donald Worster, *Rivers of Empire: Water, Aridity, and the Growth of the American West* (1985). For Brazil see Warren Dean, *With Broadax and Firebrand: The Destruction of the Brazilian Atlantic Forest* (1995); and for Argentina, Uruguay, and Chile, Alfred Crosby, *Ecological Imperialism: The Biological Expansion of Europe, 900–1900* (1986).

■ Notes

1. Quoted in Lyman L. Johnson, "Spanish American Independence and Its Consequences," in *Problems in Modern Latin American History: A Reader,* ed. John Charles Chasteen and Joseph S. Tulchin (Wilmington, DE: Scholarly Resources, 1994), 21.
2. Quoted in Margaret Conrad, Alvin Finkel, and Cornelius Jaenen, *History of the Canadian Peoples*, vol. 1 (Toronto: Copp Clark Pittman Ltd., 1993), 606–607.
3. José Antonio Páez, *Autobiografía del General José Antonio Páez*, vol. 1 (Nueva York: Hallety Breen, 1869), 83.
4. Quoted in Brian Loveman, *Chile: The Legacy of Hispanic Capitalism* (New York: Oxford University Press, 1979), 170.
5. Quoted in Bernard Bailyn, David Brion Davis, David Herbert Donald, John L. Thomas, Robert H. Wiebe, and Gordon S. Wood, *The Great Republic: A History of the American People* (Lexington, MA: D. C. Heath, 1981), 398.
6. J. S. Woodsworth in 1909, quoted in R. Douglas Francis, Richard Jones, and Donald B. Smith, *Destinies: Canadian History Since Confederation*, 2d ed. (Toronto: Holt, Rinehart and Winston, 1992), 141.
7. Sarah Grimké, "Reply to the Massachusetts Clergy," in Nancy Woloch, ed., *Early American Women: A Documentary History, 1600–1900* (Belmont, CA: Wadsworth, 1992), 343.

26

AFRICA, INDIA, AND THE NEW BRITISH EMPIRE,

1750–1870

Changes and Exchanges in Africa • India Under Company Rule •
Britain's Eastern Empire
ENVIRONMENT AND TECHNOLOGY: Whaling
SOCIETY AND CULTURE: Ceremonials of Imperial Domination

Indian Railroad Station, 1866 British India built the largest network of railroads in Asia. People of every social class traveled by train.

n 1782 Tipu Sultan inherited the throne of the state of Mysore°, which his father had made the most powerful state in South India. The ambitious and talented new ruler also inherited a healthy distrust of the British East India Company's territorial ambitions. Before the company could invade Mysore, Tipu Sultan launched his own attack in 1785. He then sent an embassy to France in 1788 seeking an alliance against Britain. Neither of these ventures was immediately successful.

Not until a decade later did the French agree to a loose alliance with Tipu Sultan as part of their plan to challenge Britain's colonial and commercial supremacy in the Indian Ocean. General Napoleon Bonaparte invaded Egypt in 1798 to threaten British trade routes to India and hoped to use the alliance with Tipu Sultan to drive the British out of India. The French invasion of Egypt went well enough at first, but a British naval blockade and the ravages of disease crippled the French force. When the French withdrew, another military adventurer, Muhammad Ali, commander of the Ottoman army in Egypt, took advantage of the situation to revitalize Egypt and expand its rule.

Meanwhile, Tipu's struggle with the East India Company was going badly. A military defeat in 1792 forced him to surrender most of his coastal lands. Despite the loose alliance with France, he was unable to stop further British advances. Tipu lost his life in 1799 while defending his capital against a British assault. Mysore was divided between the British and their Indian allies.

As these events illustrate, talented local leaders and European powers were both vying to expand their influence in South Asia and Africa between 1750 and 1870. Midway through that period, it was by no means clear who would gain the upper hand. Britain and France were as likely to fight each other as they were to fight any Asian or African state. In 1800, the two nations were engaged in their third major war for over-

seas supremacy since 1750. By 1870, however, Britain had gained a decisive advantage over France.

The new British empire in the East included the subcontinent of India, settler colonies in Australia and New Zealand, and a growing network of trading outposts. By 1870 Britain had completed the campaign to replace the overseas slave trade from Africa with "legitimate" trade and had spearheaded new Asian and South Pacific labor migrations into a rejuvenated string of tropical colonies.

As you read this chapter, ask yourself the following questions:

- Why were the British able to gain decisive advantages in distant lands?
- Why were Asians and Africans so divided, some choosing to cooperate with the Europeans while others resisted their advances?
- How important an advantage were Britain's weapons, ships, and economic motives?
- How much of the outcome was the result of advance planning, and how much was due to particular individuals or to chance?
- By 1870, how much had the British and the different peoples of Africa and Asia gained or lost?

Changes and Exchanges in Africa

During the century before 1870, Africa underwent dynamic political changes and a great expansion of foreign trade. Indigenous African leaders as well as Middle Eastern and European imperialists built powerful new states or expanded old ones. As the continent's external slave trades to the Americas and to Islamic lands died slowly under British pressure, trade in goods such as palm oil, ivory, timber, and gold grew sharply. In return Africans imported large quantities of machine-made textiles and firearms. These complex changes are best understood by looking at African regions separately.

Mysore (my-SORE)

CHRONOLOGY

	Empire	Africa	India
1750	1763 End of Seven Years War 1769–1778 Captain James Cook explores New Zealand and eastern Australia 1795 End of Dutch East India Company		1756 Black Hole of Calcutta 1765 East India Company (EIC) rule of Bengal begins
1800		1795 Britain takes Cape Colony 1798 Napoleon invades Egypt	1798 Britain annexes Ceylon 1799 EIC defeats Mysore
	1808 Britain outlaws slave trade	1805 Muhammad Ali seizes Egypt 1808 Britain takes over Sierra Leone 1809 Sokoto Caliphate founded 1818 Shaka founds Zulu kingdom 1821 Foundation of Republic of Liberia; Egypt takes control of Sudan	1818 EIC creates Bombay Presidency 1826 EIC annexes Assam and northern Burma 1828 Brahmo Samaj founded
	1834 Britain abolishes slavery	1831–1847 Algerians resist French takeover 1836–1839 Afrikaners' Great Trek 1840 Omani sultan moves capital to Zanzibar	1834 Indentured labor migrations begin
1850	1867 End of Atlantic slave trade 1877 Queen Victoria becomes Empress of India	1869 Jaja founds Opobo 1889 Menelik unites modern Ethiopia	1857–1858 Sepoy Rebellion leads to end of EIC rule and Mughal rule 1885 First Indian National Congress

New States in Southern and Inland West Africa

Internal forces produced clusters of new states in two parts of sub-Saharan Africa between 1750 and 1870. In southern Africa changes in warfare gave rise to a powerful Zulu kingdom and other new states. In inland West Africa Islamic reformers created the gigantic Sokoto° Caliphate and companion states (see Map 26.1).

In the fertile coastlands of southeastern Africa (in modern South Africa), the Nguni° peoples for many centuries had pursued a life based on cattle and agriculture. Small independent chiefdoms suited their political needs until a serious drought hit the region at the beginning of the nineteenth century. Out of the conflict for grazing and farming lands an upstart military genius named Shaka (r. 1818–1828) in 1818 created the **Zulu** kingdom. Strict military drill and close-combat warfare featuring oxhide shields and lethal stabbing spears made the Zulu the most powerful and most feared fighters in southern Africa.

Shaka expanded his kingdom by raiding his African neighbors, seizing their cattle, and capturing their women and children. Breakaway military bands spread this system of warfare and state building inland to the high plateau country, across the Limpopo River (in modern Zimbabwe°), and as far north as Lake Victoria. As the power and population of these new kingdoms increased, so too did the number of displaced and demoralized refugees around them.

To protect themselves from the Zulu, some neighboring Africans created their own states. The Swazi kingdom consolidated north of the Zulu, and the kingdom of Lesotho° grew by attracting refugees to strongholds in

---

Sokoto (SOH-kuh-toh) **Nguni** (ng-GOO-nee) **Zimbabwe** (zim-BAH-bway) **Lesotho** (luh-SOO-too)

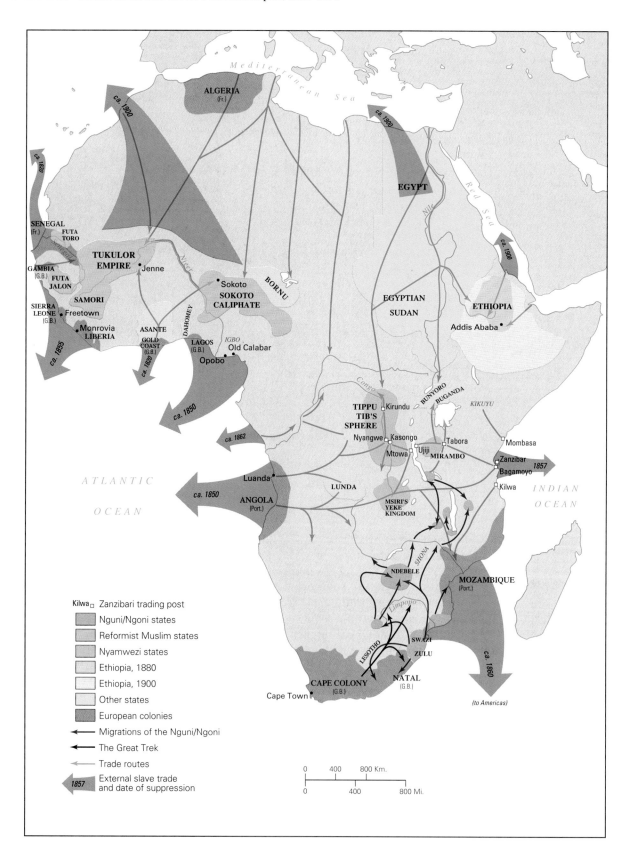

Kilwa☐ Zanzibari trading post

Nguni/Ngoni states

Reformist Muslim states

Nyamwezi states

Ethiopia, 1880

Ethiopia, 1900

Other states

European colonies

← Migrations of the Nguni/Ngoni

← The Great Trek

← Trade routes

1857 External slave trade and date of suppression

Map 26.1   Africa in the Nineteenth Century   Expanding internal and overseas trade drew much of Africa into global networks, but foreign colonies in 1870 were largely confined to Algeria and southern Africa. Growing trade, Islamic reform movements, and other internal forces created important new states throughout the continent.

Zulu in Battle Dress, 1838   Elaborate costumes helped impress opponents with the Zulu's strength. Shown here are long-handled spears and thick leather shields. The stabbing spear is not shown. (Killie Campbell Africana Library. Photo: Jane Taylor/Sonia Halliday)

southern Africa's highest mountains. Both Lesotho and Swaziland survive as independent states to this day.

Although Shaka ruled for little more than a decade, he succeeded in creating a new national identity as well as a new kingdom. He grouped all the young people in his domains by age into regiments. Regiment members lived together and immersed themselves in learning Zulu lore and customs, including fighting methods for the males. A British trader named Henry Francis Fynn expressed his "astonishment at the order and discipline" he found everywhere in the Zulu kingdom. He witnessed public festivals of loyalty to Shaka at which regiments of young men and women numbering in the tens of thousands danced around the king for hours. Parades showed off the king's enormous herds of cattle, a Zulu measure of wealth.

Meanwhile, Islamic reform movements were creating another cluster of powerful states in the savannas of West Africa. Islam had been a force in the politics and cities of this region for centuries, but it had made only slow progress among most rural people. As a consequence, most Muslim rulers had found it prudent to tolerate the older religious practices of their rural subjects. In the 1770s, local Muslim scholars began preaching the need for a vigorous reform of Islamic practices. They condemned the accommodations Muslim rulers had made with older traditions and called for a forcible conquest of rural "pagans." The reformers followed a classic Muslim pattern: a *jihad* (holy war) added new lands, where governments enforced Islamic laws and promoted the religion's spread among conquered people.

The largest of the new Muslim reform movements occurred in the Hausa° states (in what is now northern Nigeria) under the leadership of Usuman dan Fodio° (1745–1817), a Muslim cleric of the Fulani° people. He charged that the Hausa kings, despite their official profession of Islam, were "undoubtedly unbelievers . . . because they practice polytheistic rituals and turn people away from the path of God." Distressed by the lapses of a former pupil, the king of Gobir, Usuman issued a call in

1804 for a jihad to overthrow him. Muslims unhappy with their social or religious position spread the movement to other Hausa states. The successful armies united the conquered Hausa states and neighboring areas under a caliph (sultan) who ruled from the city of Sokoto. The **Sokoto Caliphate** (1809–1906) was the largest state in West Africa since the fall of Songhai in the sixteenth century.

As in earlier centuries, these new Muslim states became centers of Islamic learning and reform. Schools for training boys in Quranic subjects spread rapidly, and the great library at Sokoto attracted many scholars. Although officials permitted non-Muslims within the empire to follow their religions in exchange for paying a special tax, they suppressed public performances of dances and ceremonies associated with traditional religions. During the jihads, many who resisted the expansion of Muslim rule were killed, enslaved, or forced to convert.

Hausa (HOW-suh)
Usuman dan Fodio (OO-soo-mahn dahn FOH-dee-oh)
Fulani (foo-LAH-nee)

Sokoto's leaders sold some captives into the Atlantic slave trade and many more into the trans-Saharan slave trade, which carried ten thousand slaves a year, mostly women and children, across the desert to North Africa and the Middle East. Slavery also increased greatly within the Sokoto Caliphate and other new Muslim states. It is estimated that by 1865 there were more slaves in the Sokoto Caliphate than in any remaining slaveholding state in the Americas.[1] Most of the enslaved persons raised food, making possible the seclusion of free women in their homes in accordance with reformed Muslim practice.

Modernization and Expansion in Egypt and Ethiopia

While new states were arising elsewhere, the ancient African states of Egypt and Ethiopia in northeastern Africa were undergoing a period of growth and **modernization.** Napoleon's invading army had withdrawn from Egypt by 1801, but the shock of this display of European strength and Egyptian weakness was long lasting. The successor to Napoleon's rule was **Muhammad Ali** (1769–1849), who eliminated his rivals and ruled Egypt from 1805 to 1848. He began the political, social, and economic reforms that created modern Egypt.

Muhammad Ali's central aim was to give Egypt sufficient military strength to prevent another European conquest, but he was pragmatic enough to make use of European experts and techniques to achieve that goal. His reforms transformed Egyptian landholding, increased agricultural production, and created a modern administration and army. To train candidates for the army and administration, Muhammad Ali set up a European-style state school system and opened a military college at Aswan°. To pay for these ventures and for the European experts and equipment that he imported, he required Egyptian peasants to cultivate cotton and other crops for export.

In the 1830s Muhammad Ali headed the strongest state in the Islamic world and the first to employ Western methods and technology for modernization. The process was far from a blind imitation of the West. Rather, the technical expertise of the West was combined with Islamic religious and cultural traditions. For example, the Egyptian printing industry, begun to provide Arabic translations of technical manuals, turned out critical editions of Islamic classics and promoted a revival of Arabic writing and literature later in the century.

By the end of Muhammad Ali's reign in 1848, the modernization of Egypt was well under way. The popula-

tion had nearly doubled, trade with Europe had expanded by almost 600 percent, and a new class of educated Egyptians had begun to replace the old ruling aristocracy. Egyptians were replacing many of the foreign experts, and the fledgling program of industrialization was providing the country with its own textiles, paper, weapons, and military uniforms. The demands on peasant families for labor and military service, however, were acutely disruptive.

Ali's grandson Ismail° (r. 1863–1879) placed even more emphasis on westernizing Egypt. "My country is no longer in Africa," Ismail declared, "it is in Europe."[2] His efforts increased the number of European advisers in Egypt—and Egypt's debts to French and British banks. In the first decade of his reign, revenues increased thirty-fold and exports doubled (largely because of a huge increase in cotton exports during the American Civil War). By 1870 there was a network of new irrigation canals, 800 miles (1,300 kilometers) of railroads, a modern postal service, and the dazzling new capital city of Cairo. When the market for Egyptian cotton collapsed after the American Civil War, however, Egypt's debts to British and French investors led to the country's partial occupation.

From the middle of the century, state building and reform also were under way in the ancient kingdom of Ethiopia, whose rulers had been Christian for fifteen hundred years. Weakened by internal divisions and the pressures of its Muslim neighbors, Ethiopia was a shadow of what it had been in the sixteenth century, but under Emperor Téwodros° II (r. 1833–1868) and his successor Yohannes° IV (r. 1872–1889) most highland regions were brought back under imperial rule. The only large part of ancient Ethiopia that remained outside Emperor Yohannes's rule was the Shoa kingdom, ruled by King Menelik° from 1865. When Menelik succeeded Yohannes as emperor in 1889, the merger of their separate realms created the modern boundaries of Ethiopia.

Beginning in the 1840s, Ethiopian rulers purchased modern weapons from European sources and created strong armies loyal to the ruler. Emperor Téwodros also encouraged the manufacture of weapons locally. With the aid of Protestant missionaries his craftsmen even constructed a giant cannon capable of firing a half-ton shell. However, his efforts to coerce more technical aid by holding some British officials captive backfired when the British invaded instead. As the British forces advanced, Téwodros committed suicide to avoid being taken prisoner. Satisfied that their honor was avenged, the British withdrew. Later Ethiopian emperors kept up the program of reform and modernization.

Aswan (AS-wahn)

Ismail (is-MAH-eel)   Téwodros (tay-WOH-druhs)
Yohannes (yoh-HAHN-nehs)   Menelik (MEN-uh-lik)

Téwodros's Mighty Cannon Like other modernizers in the nineteenth century, Emperor Téwodros of Ethiopia sought to reform his military forces. In 1861 he forced resident European missionaries and craftsmen to build guns and cannon, including this 7-ton behemoth nicknamed "Sebastapol" after the Black Sea port that had been the center of the Crimean War. It took five hundred men to haul the cannon across Ethiopia's hilly terrain. (From Hormuzd Rassam, *Narrative of the British Mission to Theodore, King of Abyssinia, II*, London 1869, John Murray)

European Invaders and Explorers

More lasting than Britain's punitive invasion of Ethiopia was France's conquest of Algeria, a move that anticipated the general European "Scramble for Africa" after 1870. Equally pregnant with future meaning was the Europeans' exploration of the inland parts of Africa in the middle decades of the century.

Long an exporter of grain and olive oil to France, the North African state of Algeria had even supplied Napoleon with grain for his 1798 invasion of Egypt. The failure of French governments to repay this debt led to many disputes between Algeria and France and eventually to a serving of diplomatic relations in 1827, after the ruler of Algeria, annoyed with the French ambassador, allegedly struck him with a fly whisk. Three years later an unpopular French government, hoping to stir French nationalism with an easy overseas victory, attacked Algeria on the pretext of avenging this insult.

The invasion of 1830 proved a costly mistake. The French government was soon overthrown, but the war in Algeria dragged on for eighteen years. The attack by an alien Christian power united the Algerians behind 'Abd al-Qadir°, a gifted and resourceful Muslim holy man. To achieve victory, the French built up an army of over 100,000 that broke Algerian resistance by destroying farm animals and crops and massacring villagers by the tens of thousands. After 'Abd al-Qadir was captured and exiled in 1847, the resistance movement fragmented, but the French occupiers faced resistance in the mountains for another thirty years. Poor European settlers, who rushed in to take possession of Algeria's rich coastlands, numbered 130,000 by 1871.

Meanwhile, a more peaceful European intrusion was penetrating Africa's geographical secrets. Small expeditions of adventurous explorers, using their own funds or financed by private geographical societies, were seeking to uncover the mysteries of inner Africa that had eluded Europeans for four centuries. Besides discovering more about the course of Africa's mighty rivers, these explorers wished to assess the continent's mineral wealth or convert the African millions to Christianity.

'Abd al-Qadir (AHB-dahl-KAH-deer)

Many of the explorers were concerned with tracing the course of Africa's great rivers. Explorers learned in 1795 that the Niger River in West Africa flowed from west to east (not the other way as had often been supposed) and in 1830 that the great morass of small streams entering the Gulf of Guinea was in fact the Niger Delta.

The north-flowing Nile, whose annual floods made Egypt bloom, similarly attracted explorers bent on finding the headwaters of the world's longest river. In 1770 Lake Tana in Ethiopia was established as a major source, and in 1861–1862 Lake Victoria (named for the British sovereign) was found to be the other main source.

In contrast to the heavily financed expeditions with hundreds of African porters that searched the Nile, the Scottish missionary David Livingstone (1813–1873) organized modest treks through southern and Central Africa. The missionary doctor's primary goal was to scout out locations for Christian missions, but he was also highly influential in tracing the course of the Zambezi River, between 1853 and 1856. He named its greatest waterfall for the British monarch Queen Victoria. Livingstone also traced the course of the upper Congo River, where in 1871 he was met by the Welsh-American journalist Henry Morton Stanley (1841–1904) on a publicity-motivated search for the "lost" missionary doctor. On an expedition from 1874 to 1877, Stanley descended the Congo River to its mouth.

One of the most remarkable features of the explorers' experiences in Africa was their ability to move unmolested from place to place. The strangers were seldom harmed without provocation. Stanley preferred large expeditions that fought their way across the continent, but Livingstone's modest expeditions, which posed no threat to anyone, regularly received warm hospitality.

Abolition and Legitimate Trade in Coastal West Africa

No sooner was the mouth of the Niger River discovered than eager entrepreneurs began to send expeditions up the river to scout out its potential for trade. Along much of coastal West Africa, commercial relations with Europeans remained dominant between 1750 and 1870. The value of trade between Africa and the other Atlantic continents more than doubled between the 1730s and the 1780s, then doubled again by 1870.[3] Before about 1825 the slave trade accounted for most of that increase, but thereafter African exports of vegetable oils, gold, ivory, and other goods drove overseas trade to new heights.

Europeans played a critical role in these changes in Africa's overseas trade. The Atlantic trade had arisen to serve the needs of the first European empires, and its transformation was linked to the ideas and industrial needs of Britain's new economy and empire.

One step in the Atlantic slave trade's extinction was the successful slave revolt in Saint Domingue in the 1790s (see Chapter 23). It ended slavery in the largest plantation colony in the West Indies, and elsewhere in the Americas it inspired slave revolts that were brutally repressed. As news of the slave revolts and their repression spread, humanitarians and religious reformers called for an end to the slave trade. Since it was widely believed that African-born slaves were more likely to rebel than were persons born into slavery, support for abolition of the slave trade was found even among Americans wanting to preserve slavery. In 1808 both Great Britain and the United States made carrying and importing slaves from Africa illegal for their citizens. Most other Western countries followed suit by 1850, but few enforced abolition with the vigor of the British.

Once the world's greatest slave traders, the British became the most aggressive abolitionists. Britain sent a naval patrol to enforce the ban along the African coast and negotiated treaties allowing the patrol to search other nations' vessels suspected of carrying slaves. During the half-century after 1815, Britain spent some $60 million (£12 million) in its efforts to end the slave trade, a sum equal to the profits British slave traders had made in the fifty years before 1808.

Although British patrols captured 1,635 slave ships and liberated over 160,000 enslaved Africans, the trade proved difficult to stop, for Cuba and Brazil continued to import huge numbers of slaves. Such demand drove prices up and persuaded some African rulers and merchants to continue to sell slaves and to help foreign slavers evade the British patrols. After British patrols quashed the slave trade along the Gold Coast, the powerful king of Asante° even tried to persuade a British official in 1820 that reopening the trade would be to their mutual profit. Because the slave trade moved to other parts of Africa, the trans-Atlantic slave trade did not end until 1867.

The demand for slaves in the Americas claimed the lives and endangered the safety of untold numbers of Africans, but the trade also satisfied other Africans' desires for the cloth, metals, and other goods that European traders brought in return. To continue their access to those imports, Africans expanded their **"legitimate" trade** (exports other than slaves). They revived old trades or developed new exports as the Atlantic slave trade was shut down. On the Gold Coast, for example, annual exports of gold climbed to nearly 25,000 ounces (750 kilograms) in the 1840s and 1850s, compared to 10,000 ounces (300 kilograms) in the 1790s.

Asante (uh-SHAHN-tee)

The most successful of the new exports from West Africa was palm oil, a vegetable oil used by British manufacturers for soap, candles, and lubricants. Though still a major source of slaves until the mid-1830s, the trading states of the Niger Delta simultaneously emerged as the permier exporters of palm oil. In inland forests men climbed tall oil palms and cut down large palm-nut clusters, which women pounded to extract the thick oil. Coastal African traders bought the palm oil at inland markets and delivered it to European ships at the coast.

The dramatic increase in palm-oil exports—from a few hundred tons at the beginning of the century to tens of thousands of tons by midcentury—did not require any new technology, but it did alter the social structure of the coastal trading communities. Coastal traders grew rich and used their wealth to buy large numbers of male slaves to paddle the giant dugout canoes that transported palm oil from inland markets along the narrow delta creeks to the trading ports. Niger Delta slavery could be as harsh and brutal as slavery on New World plantations, but it offered some male and female slaves a chance to gain wealth and power. Some female slaves who married big traders exercised great authority over junior members of trading households. Male slaves who supervised canoe fleets were well compensated, and a few even became wealthy enough to take over the leadership of the coastal "canoe houses" (companies). The most famous, known as "Jaja" (ca. 1021–1091), rose from being a canoe slave to the head of a major canoe house. To escape discrimination by free-born Africans, in 1869 he founded the new port of Opobo, which he ruled as king. In the 1870s Jaja of Opobo was the greatest palm-oil trader in the Niger Delta.

Another effect of the suppression of the slave trade was the spread of Western cultural influences in West Africa. To serve as a base for their anti-slave-trade naval squadron, in 1808 the British had taken over the small colony of Sierra Leone°. Over the next several years, 130,000 men, women, and children taken from "captured" vessels were liberated in Sierra Leone. Christian missionaries helped settle these impoverished and dispirited **recaptives** in and around Freetown, the capital. In time the mission churches and schools made many willing converts among such men and women.

Sierra Leone's schools also produced a number of distinguished graduates. For example, Samuel Adjai Crowther (1808–1891), freed as a youth from a slave ship in 1821 by the British squadron, became the first Anglican bishop in West Africa in 1864, administering a pioneering diocese along the lower Niger River. James

Sierra Leone (see-ER-uh lee-OWN)

King Jaja of Opobo   This talented man rose from slavery in the Niger Delta port of Bonny to head one of the town's major palm-oil trading firms, the Anna Pepple House, in 1863. Six years later, Jaja founded and ruled his own trading port of Opobo. (Reproduced from *West Africa: An Introduction to Its History*, by Michael Crowder, by courtesy of the publishers, Addison Wesley Longman)

Africanus Horton (1835–1882), the son of a slave liberated in Sierra Leone, became a doctor and the author of many studies of West Africa.

Other Western cultural influences came from people of African birth or descent returning to their ancestral homeland in this era. In 1821, to the south of Sierra Leone, free black Americans began a settlement that grew into the Republic of Liberia, a place of liberty at a time when slavery was illegal and flourishing in the

United States. After their emancipation in 1865 other African-Americans moved to Liberia. Emma White, a literate black woman from Kentucky, moved from Liberia to Opobo in 1875, where King Jaja employed her to write his commercial correspondence and run a school for his children. Edward Wilmot Blyden (1832–1912), born in the Danish West Indies and proud of his West African parentage, emigrated to Liberia in 1851 and became a professor of Greek and Latin (and later Arabic) at the fledgling Liberia College. Free blacks from Brazil and Cuba chartered ships to return to their West African homelands, bringing with them Roman Catholicism, architectural motifs, and clothing fashions from the New World. Although the number of Africans exposed to Western culture in 1870 was still small, this influence grew rapidly.

Slaves and Secondary Empires in Eastern Africa

When British patrols hampered the slave trade in West Africa, slavers moved southward and then around the tip of southern Africa to eastern Africa. There the Atlantic slave trade joined an existing trade in slaves to the Islamic world that also was expanding. Two-thirds of the 1.2 million slaves exported from eastern Africa in the nineteenth century went to markets in North Africa and the Middle East; the other third went to plantations in the Americas and to European-controlled Indian Ocean islands.

Slavery also became more prominent within eastern Africa itself. Between 1800 and 1873, Arab and Swahili owners of clove plantations along the coast purchased some 700,000 slaves from inland eastern Africa to do the labor-intensive work of harvesting this spice. The plantations were on Zanzibar Island and in neighboring territories belonging to the Sultanate of Oman, an Arabian kingdom on the Persian Gulf that had been expanding its control over the East African coast since 1698. The sultan had even moved his court to Zanzibar in 1840 to take better advantage of the burgeoning trade in cloves. Zanzibar also was an important center of slaves and ivory. Most of the ivory was shipped to India, where much of it was carved into decorative objects for European markets.

Ivory caravans came to the coast from hundreds of miles inland under the direction of African and Arab merchants. Some of these merchants brought large personal empires under their control by using capital they had borrowed from Indian bankers and modern firearms they had bought from Europeans and Americans. Some trading empires were created by inland Nyamwezi° traders, who worked closely with the indigenous Swahili° and Arabs in Zanzibar to develop the long-distance caravan routes.

The largest of these personal empires, along the upper Congo River, was created by Tippu Tip (ca. 1830–1905), a trader from Zanzibar, who was Swahili and Nyamwezi on his father's side and Omani Arab on his mother's. Livingstone, Stanley, and other explorers who received Tippu Tip's gracious hospitality in the remote center of the continent praised their host's intelligence and refinement. On an 1876 visit, for example, Stanley recorded in his journal that Tippu Tip was "a remarkable man," a "picture of energy and strength" with "a fine intelligent face: almost courtier-like in his manner."

Tippu Tip also composed a detailed memoir of his adventures in the heart of Africa, written in the Swahili language of the coast. In it he mocked innocent African villagers for believing that his gunshots were thunder. As the memoir and other sources make clear, these modern rifles not only felled countless elephants for their ivory tusks but also inflicted widespread devastation and misery on the people of this isolated area.

One can blame Tippu Tip and other Zanzibari traders for the pillage and havoc in the once-peaceful center of Africa, along with their master, the sultan of Oman. However, the circle of responsibility was still broader. Europeans supplied the weapons used by the invaders and were major consumers of ivory and cloves. For this reason histories have referred to the states carved out of eastern Africa by the sultans of Oman, Tippu Tip, and others as "secondary empires," in contrast to the empire that Britain was establishing directly. At the same time, Britain was working to bring the Indian Ocean slave trade to an end in eastern Africa. British officials pressured the sultan of Oman into halting the Indian Ocean slave trade from Zanzibar in 1857 and ending the import of slaves into Zanzibar in 1873.

Egypt's expansion southward during the nineteenth century can also be considered a secondary empire. Muhammad Ali had pioneered the conquest of the upper Nile, in 1821 establishing at Khartoum° a major base that became the capital of the Egyptian Sudan. A major reason for his invasion of Sudan was to secure slaves for his army so that more Egyptian peasants could be left free to grow cotton for export. From the 1840s unscrupulous traders of many origins, leading forces armed with European weapons, pushed south to the modern frontiers of Uganda and Zaire in search of cattle, ivory, and slaves. They set one African community against another and reaped profit from the devastation they sowed.

Nyamwezi (nn-nyahm-WAY-zee)   **Swahili** (swah-HEE-lee)
Khartoum (khar-TOOM)

British Mem–Sahib, ca. 1782   This charming painting by a Bengali artist shows Lady Impey, wife of the British East India Company's chief justice of Bengal, surrounded by her Indian servants in a room that mixes Indian and European decor. The Hindi word *sahib* was an honorific title; *mem-sahib* was the Anglo-Indian feminine term reserved for European women.   (The Art Archive Ltd.)

INDIA UNDER BRITISH RULE

The people of South Asia felt the impact of European commercial, cultural, and colonial expansion more immediately and profoundly than did the people of Africa. While Europeans were laying claim to only small parts of Africa between 1750 and 1870, nearly all of India (with three times the population of all of Africa) came under Britain's direct or indirect rule. During the 250 years after the founding of East India Company in 1600, British interests commandeered the colonies and trade of the Dutch, fought off French and Indian challenges, and picked up the pieces of the decaying Mughal° Empire. By 1763 the French were stymied, in 1795 the Dutch East India Company was dissolved, and in 1858 the last Mughal emperor was dethroned, leaving the vast subcontinent in British hands.

Company Men   As Mughal power weakened in the eighteenth century, Europeans were not the first outsiders to make a move. In 1739, Iranian armies defeated the Mughal forces, sacked Delhi, and returned home with vast amounts of booty. Indian states also took advantage of Mughal weakness to assert their independence. By midcentury, the Maratha° Confederation, a coalition of states in central India, controlled more land than the Mughals did (see Map 26.2). Also ruling their own powerful states were the **nawabs°** (a term used for Muslim princes who were deputies of the Mughal emperor, though in name only): the nawab of Bengal in the northeast; the nawab of Arcot in the southeast, Haidar Ali (1722–1782)—the father of Tipu Sultan and ruler of the southwestern state of Mysore; and many others.

British, Dutch, and French companies were also eager to expand their profitable trade into India in the eighteenth century. Such far-flung European trading

---

Mughal (MOO-guhl

Maratha (muh-RAH-tuh)   **nawab** (NAH-wab)

Map 26.2 India, 1707–1805 As Mughal power weakened during the eighteenth century, other Indian states and the British East India Company expanded their territories.

companies were speculative and risky ventures in 1750. Their success depended on hard-drinking and ambitious young "Company Men," who used hard bargaining, and hard fighting when necessary, to persuade Indian rulers to allow them to establish trading posts at strategic points along the coast. To protect their fortified warehouses from attack by other Europeans or by native states, the companies hired and trained Indian troops

known as **sepoys°.** In divided India these private armies came to hold the balance of power.

In 1691 the East India Company (EIC) had convinced the nawab of the large state of Bengal in northeast India to let the company establish a fortified outpost at the fishing port of Calcutta. A new nawab, pressing claims

sepoy (SEE-poy)

for additional tribute from the prospering port, overran the fort in 1756 and imprisoned a group of EIC men in a cell so small that many died of suffocation. To avenge their deaths in this "Black Hole of Calcutta," a large EIC force from Madras, led by the young Robert Clive, overthrew the nawab. The weak Mughal emperor was persuaded to acknowledge the East India Company's right to rule Bengal in 1765. Fed by the tax revenues of Bengal as well as by profits from trade, the EIC was on its way. Calcutta grew into a city of 250,000 by 1788.

In southern India, Clive had used EIC forces from Madras to secure victory for the British Indian candidate for nawab of Arcot during the Seven Years War (1756–1763), thereby gaining an advantage over French traders who had supported the loser. The defeat of Tipu Sultan of Mysore at the end of the century (described at the start of the chapter) secured south India for the company and prevented a French resurgence.

Along with Calcutta and Madras, the third major center of British power in India was Bombay, on the western coast. There, after a long series of contests with the Maratha Confederation rulers, the East India Company gained a decisive advantage in 1818, annexing large territories to form the core of what was called the "Bombay Presidency." Some states were taken over completely, as Bengal had been, but very many others remained in the hands of local princes who accepted the political control of the company.

The Raj and the Rebellion, 1818–1857

In 1818 the East India Company controlled an Empire with more people than in all of western Europe and fifty times the population of the colonies the British had lost in North America. One thrust of **British raj** (reign) was to remake India on a British model through administrative and social reform, economic development, and the introduction of new technology. But at the same time the company men—like the Mughals before them—had to temper their interference with Indian social and religious customs lest they provoke rebellion or lose the support of their Indian princely allies. For this reason and because of the complexity of the task of ruling such a vast empire, there were many inconsistencies in Britain's policies toward India.

The main policy was to create a powerful and efficient system of government. British rule before 1850 relied heavily on military power—170 sepoy regiments and 16 European regiments. Another policy very much in the interests of India's new rulers was to disarm approximately 2 million warriors who had served India's many states and turn them to civilian tasks, mostly cultivation. A third policy was to give freer rein to Christian missionaries eager to convert and uplift India's masses. Few converts were made, but the missionaries kept up steady pressure for social reforms.

Another key British policy was to substitute ownership of private property for India's complex and overlapping patterns of landholding. In Bengal this reform worked to the advantage of large landowners, but in Mysore the peasantry gained. Private ownership made it easier for the state to collect the taxes that were needed to pay for the costs of administration, the army, and economic reform.

Such policies of "westernization, Anglicization, and modernization," as they have been called, were only one side of British rule. The other side was the bolstering of "traditions"—both real and newly invented. In the name of tradition the Indian princes who ruled nearly half of British India were frequently endowed by their British overlords with greater power and splendor and longer tenure than their predecessors had ever had. Hindu and Muslim holy men were able to expand their "traditional" power over property and people far beyond what had ever been the case in earlier times. Princes, holy men, and other Indians frequently used claims of tradition to resist British rule as well as to turn it to their advantage. The British rulers themselves invented many "traditions"—including elaborate parades and displays—half borrowed from European royal pomp, half freely improvised from Mughal ceremonies (see Society and Culture: Ceremonials of Imperial Domination).

The British and Indian elites danced sometimes in close partnership, sometimes in apparent opposition. But the ordinary people of India suffered. Women of every status, members of subordinate Hindu castes, the "untouchables" and "tribals" outside the caste system, and the poor generally found less benefit in the British reforms and much new oppression in the taxes and "traditions" that exalted their superiors' status.

The transformation of British India's economy was also doubled-edged. On the one hand, British raj created many new jobs as a result of the growth of internal and external trade and the expansion of agricultural production, such as in opium in Bengal—largely for export to China (see Chapter 27)—coffee in Ceylon (an island off the tip of India), and tea in Assam (a state in northeastern India). On the other hand, competition from cheap cotton goods produced in Britain's industrial mills drove many Indians out of the handicraft textile industry. In the eighteenth century India had been the world's greatest exporter of cotton textiles; in the nineteenth century India increasingly shipped raw cotton fiber to Britain.

Ceremonials of Imperial Domination

These excerpts from a letter written to Queen Victoria by the viceroy of India, Lord Lytton, describe the elaborate ceremonies the colony staged in 1876 in anticipation of her being named "Empress of India" and the effects they had on the Indian princes who governed many parts of India. Although British India's power still rested on the threat of military force, its leaders grew increasingly skilled at using symbolic displays of authority and material rewards to win the support of Indian allies.

The day before yesterday (December 23), I arrived, with Lady Lytton and all my staff at Delhi. . . . I was received at the [railroad] station by all the native chiefs and princes, and, . . . after shaking hands . . . , I immediately mounted my elephant, accompanied by Lady Lytton, our two little girls following us on another elephant. The procession through Delhi to the camp . . . lasted upwards of three hours. . . . The streets were lined for many miles with troops; those of the native princes being brigaded with those of your Majesty. The crowd along the way, behind the troops, was dense, and apparently enthusiastic; the windows, walls, and housetops being thronged with natives, who salaamed, and Europeans, who cheered as we passed along. . . .

My reception by the native princes at the station was most cordial. The Maharaja of Jeypore (who has lighted the Viceroy's camp with gas of his own manufacture) informed Sir John Strachey that India had never seen such a gathering as this, in which not only all the great native princes (many of whom have never met before), but also chiefs and envoys from Khelat, Burmah, Siam, and the remotest parts of the East, are assembled to do homage to your Majesty. . . .

On Tuesday (December 26) from 10 A.M. till past 7 P.M., I was, without a moment's intermission, occupied in receiving visits from native chiefs, and bestowing on those entitled to them the banners, medals, and other honours given by your Majesty. The durbar, which lasted all day and long after dark, was most successful. . . . Your Majesty's portrait, which was placed over the Viceregal throne in the great durbar tent, was thought by all to be an excellent likeness of your Majesty. The native chiefs examined it with special interest.

On Wednesday, the 27th, I received visits from native chiefs, as before, from 10 A.M. til 1 P.M., and from 1:30 P.M. to 7:30 P.M., was passed in returning visits. I forgot to mention that on Tuesday and Wednesday evenings I gave great State dinners to the Governors of Bombay and Madras. Every subsequent evening of my stay at Delhi was similarly occupied by state banquets and receptions [for officials, foreign dignitaries, and] many distinguished natives. After dinner on Thursday, I held a levee [reception], which lasted till one o'clock at night, and is said to have been attended by 2,500 persons—the largest, I believe, ever held by any Viceroy or Governor-General in India.

. . . your Majesty will, perhaps, allow me to mention, in connection with [the ruler of Kashmir], one little circumstance which appears to me very illustrative of the effect which the assemblage has had on him and others. In the first interviews which took place months ago between myself and Kashmir, . . . I noticed that, though perfectly courteous, he was extremely mistrustful of the British Government and myself. . . . On the day following the Imperial assemblage, I had another private interview with Kashmir for the settlement of some further details. His whole manner and language on this last occasion were strikingly different. [He said:] "I am now convinced that you mean nothing that is not for the good of me and mine. Our interests are identical with those of the empire. Give me your orders and they shall be obeyed."

What is significant about the fact that Lord Lytton and his family arrived in Delhi by train and then chose to move through the city on elephants? What impression did the viceroy intend to create in the minds of the Indian dignitaries by assembling so many of them together and bestowing banners, medals, and honors on them? What might account for the Indian ruler of Kashmir's remarkable change of attitude toward the viceroy and the empire? How differently might a member of the Indian middle class or an unemployed weaver have reacted?

Source: Lady Betty Balfour, *The History of Lord Lytton's Indian Administration, 1876 to 1880* (London: Longmans, Green, and Co., 1899), 116–121, 132.

Even the beneficial economic changes introduced under Britain rule were disruptive, and there were no safety nets for the needy. Thus local rebellions by displaced ruling elites, disgruntled religious traditionalists, and the economically dispossessed were almost constant during the first half of the nineteenth century. Officials' greatest concern was over the continuing loyalty of Indian sepoys in the East India Company's army. Their numbers had increased to 200,000 in 1857, along with 38,000 British officers. Armed with the latest rifles and disciplined in fighting methods, the sepoys had a potential for successful rebellion that other groups lacked.

In fact, discontent was growing among Indian soldiers. In the early decades of EIC rule, most sepoys came from Bengal, one of the first states the company had annexed. The Bengali sepoys resented the active recruitment of other ethnic groups into the army after 1848, such as Sikhs° from Punjab and Gurkhas from Nepal. Many high-caste Hindus objected to a new law in 1856 requiring new recruits to be available for service overseas in the growing Indian Ocean empire, for their religion prohibited ocean travel. The replacement of the standard military musket by the far more accurate Enfield rifle in 1857 also caused problems. Soldiers were ordered to use their teeth to tear open the ammunition cartridges, which were greased with animal fat. Hindus were offended by this order if the fat came from cattle, which they considered sacred. Muslims were offended if the fat came from pigs, which they considered unclean.

Although the cartridge-opening procedure was quickly changed, the initial discontent grew into rebellion by Hindu sepoys in May 1857. British troubles mushroomed when Muslim sepoys, peasants, and discontented elites joined in. The rebels asserted old traditions to challenge British authority: sepoy officers in Delhi proclaimed their loyalty to the Mughal emperor; others rallied behind the Maratha leader Nana Sahib. The rebellion was put down by March 1858, but it shook this piecemeal empire to its core.

Historians have attached different names and meanings to the events of 1857 and 1858. Concentrating on the technical fact that the uprising was an unlawful action by soldiers, nineteenth-century British historians labeled it the **"Sepoy Rebellion"** or the "Mutiny," and these names are still commonly used. Seeing in these events the beginnings of the later movement for independence, some modern Indian historians have termed it the "Revolution of 1857." In reality, it was much more than a simple mutiny, because it involved more than soldiers, but it was not yet a nationalist revolution, for the rebels' sense of a common Indian national identity was weak.

Sikh (seek)

Political Reform and Industrial Impact, 1858–1900

Whatever it is called, the rebellion of 1857–1858 was a turning point in the history of modern India. Some say it marks the beginning of modern India. In its wake Indians gained a new centralized government, entered a period of rapid economic growth, and began to develop a new national consciousness.

The changes in government were immediate. In 1858 Britain eliminated the last traces of Mughal and Company rule. In their place, a new secretary of state for India in London oversaw Indian policy, and a new government-general in Delhi acted as the British monarch's viceroy on the spot. A proclamation by Queen Victoria in November 1858 guaranteed all Indians equal protection of the law and the freedom to practice their religions and social customs; it also assured Indian princes that so long as they were loyal to the queen British India would respect their control of territories and "their rights, dignity and honour."[4]

British rule continued to emphasize both tradition and reform after 1857. At the top, the British viceroys lived in enormous palaces amid hundreds of servants and gaudy displays of luxury meant to convince Indians that the British viceroys were legitimate successors to the Mughal emperors. They treated the quasi-independent Indian princes with elaborate ceremonial courtesy and maintained them in splendor. When Queen Victoria was proclaimed "Empress of India" in 1877 and periodically thereafter, the viceroys put on great pageants known as **durbars.** The most elaborate of all was the durbar at Delhi in 1902 to celebrate the coronation of King Edward VII, at which Viceroy Lord Curzon honored himself with a 101-gun salute and a parade of 34,000 troops in front of 50 princes and 173,000 lesser visitors.

Behind the pomp and glitter, a powerful and efficient bureaucracy controlled the Indian masses. Members of the elite **Indian Civil Service** (ICS), mostly graduates of Oxford and Cambridge Universities, held the senior administrative and judicial posts. Numbering only a thousand at the end of the nineteenth century, these men visited the villages in their districts, heard lawsuits and complaints, and passed judgments. Beneath them were a far greater number of Indian officials and employees. Recruitment into the ICS was by open examinations. In theory any British subject could take these exams. But they were given in England, so in practice the system worked to exclude Indians. In 1870 only one Indian was a member of the ICS. Subsequent reforms by Viceroy Lord Lytton led to fifty-seven Indian appointments by 1887, but there the process stalled.

The key reason blocking qualified Indians' entry into the upper administration of their country was the racist contempt most British officials felt for the people they ruled. When he became commander-in-chief of the Indian army in 1892, Lord Kitchener declared:

> It is this consciousness of the inherent superiority of the European which had won for us India. However well educated and clever a native may be, and however brave he may have proved himself, I believe that no rank we can bestow on him would cause him to be considered an equal of the British officer.

A second transformation of India after 1857 resulted from involvement with industrial Britain. The government invested millions of pounds sterling in harbors, cities, irrigation canals, and other public works. British interests felled forests to make way for tea plantations, persuaded Indian farmers to grow cotton and jute for export, and created great irrigation systems to alleviate the famines that periodically decimated whole provinces. As a result, India's trade expanded rapidly.

Most of the exports were agricultural commodities for processing elsewhere: cotton fiber, opium, tea, silk, and sugar. In return India imported manufactured goods from Britain, including the flood of machine-made cotton textiles that severely undercut Indian hand-loom weavers. The effects on individual Indians varied enormously. Some women found new jobs, though at very low pay, on plantations or in the growing cities, where prostitution flourished. Others struggled to hold families together or ran away from abusive husbands. Everywhere in India poverty remained the norm.

The Indian government also promoted the introduction of new technologies into India not long after their appearance in Britain. Earlier in the century there were steamboats on the rivers and a massive program of canal building for irrigation. Beginning in the 1840s, a railroad boom (paid for out of government revenues) gave India its first national transportation network, followed shortly by telegraph lines. Indeed, in 1870 India had the greatest rail network in Asia and the fifth largest in the world. Originally designed to serve British commerce, the railroads were owned by British companies, constructed with British rails and equipment, and paid dividends to British investors. Ninety-nine percent of the railroad employees were Indians, but Europeans occupied all the top positions—"like a thin film of oil on top of a glass of water, resting upon but hardly mixing with [those] below," as one official report put it.

Although some Indians opposed the railroads at first because the trains mixed people of different castes, faiths, and sexes, the Indian people took to rail travel with great enthusiasm. Indians rode trains on business, on pilgrimage, and in search of work. In 1870 over 18 million passengers traveled along the network's 4,775 miles (7,685 kilometers) of track, and more than a half-million messages were sent up and down the 14,000 miles (22,500 kilometers) of telegraph wire. By 1900 India's trains were carrying 188 million passengers a year.

But the freer movement of Indian pilgrims and the flood of poor Indians into the cities also promoted the spread of cholera°, a disease transmitted through water contaminated by human feces. Cholera deaths rose rapidly during the nineteenth century, and eventually the disease spread to Europe. In many Indian minds *kala mari* ("the black death") was a divine punishment for failing to prevent the British takeover. This chastisement also fell heavily on British residents, who died in large numbers. In 1867 officials demonstrated the close connection between cholera and pilgrims who bathed in and drank from sacred pools and rivers. The installation of a new sewerage system (1865) and a filtered water supply (1869) in Calcutta dramatically reduced cholera deaths there. Similar measures in Bombay and Madras also led to great reductions, but most Indians lived in small villages where famine and lack of sanitation kept cholera deaths high. In 1900 an extraordinary four out of every thousand residents of British India died of cholera. Sanitary improvements lowered the rate later in the twentieth century.

Rising Indian Nationalism, 1828–1900

Ironically, both the successes and the failures of British India stimulated the development of Indian nationalism. Stung by the inability of the rebellion of 1857 to overthrow British rule, some thoughtful Indians began to argue that the only way for Indians to regain control of their destiny was to reduce their country's social and ethnic divisions and promote Pan-Indian nationalism.

Individuals such as Rammohun Roy (1772–1833) had promoted development along these lines a generation earlier. A Western-educated Bengali from a Brahmin family, Roy was a successful administrator for the British East India Company and a thoughtful student of comparative religion. His Brahmo Samaj° (Divine Society), founded in 1828, attracted Indians who sought to reconcile the values they found in the West with the ancient religious traditions of India. They supported efforts to reform some Hindu customs, including the restrictions on widows and the practice of child marriage. They

cholera (KAHL-uhr-uh)   Bramo Samaj (BRAH-moh suh-MAHJ)

advocated reforming the caste system, encouraged a monotheistic form of Hinduism, and urged a return to the founding principles found in the Upanishads, ancient sacred writings of Hinduism.

Roy and his supporters had backed earlier British efforts to reform or ban some practices they found repugnant. Widow burning (*sati*°) was outlawed in 1829 and slavery in 1843. Reformers sought to correct other abuses of women: prohibitions against widows remarrying were revoked in 1856, and female infanticide was made a crime in 1870.

Although Brahmo Samaj remained an influential movement after the rebellion of 1857, many Indian intellectuals turned to Western secular values and nationalism as the way to reclaim India for its people. In this process the spread of Western education played an important role. Roy had studied both Indian and Western subjects, mastering ten languages in the process, and helped found the Hindu College in Calcutta in 1816. Other Western-curriculum schools quickly followed, including Bethune College in Calcutta, the first secular school for Indian women, in 1849. European and American missionaries played a prominent role in the spread of Western education. In 1870 there were 790,000 Indians in over 24,000 elementary and secondary schools, and India's three universities (established in 1857) awarded 345 degrees. Graduates of these schools articulated a new Pan-Indian nationalism that transcended regional and religious differences.

Many of the new nationalists came from the Indian middle class, which had prospered from the increase of trade and manufacturing. Such educated and ambitious people were angered by the obstacles that British rules and prejudices put in the way of their advancement. Hoping to increase their influence and improve their employment opportunities in the Indian government, they convened the first **Indian National Congress** in 1885. The members sought a larger role for Indians in the Civil Service. They also called for reductions in military expenditures, which consumed 40 percent of the government's budget, so that more could be spent on alleviating the poverty of the Indian masses. The Indian National Congress promoted unity among the country's many religions and social groups, but most early members were upper-caste Western-educated Hindus and Parsis (members of a Zoroastrian religious sect descended from Persians). The Congress effectively voiced the opinions of elite Indians, but until it attracted the support of the masses, it could not hope to challenge British rule.

BRITAIN'S EASTERN EMPIRE

In 1750 Britain's empire was centered on slave-based plantation and settler colonies in the Americas. A century later its main focus was on commercial networks and colonies in the East. In 1750 the French and Dutch were also serious contenders for global dominion. A century later they had been eclipsed by the British colossus straddling the world. Several distinct changes facilitated this expansion and transformation of Britain's overseas empire: a string of military victories pushed aside other rivals for overseas trade and colonies; new policies favored free trade over mercantilism; and changes in shipbuilding techniques increased the speed and volume of maritime commerce. Linked to these changes were new European settlements in southern Africa, Australia, and New Zealand and the growth of a new long-distance trade in indentured labor.

Colonial Rivalries and Trading Networks

As the story of Tipu Sultan told at the beginning of this chapter illustrates, France was still a serious rival to Britain for dominion in the Indian Ocean at the end of the eighteenth century. However, France's defeats in the wars of French Revolution (see Chapter 23) ended Napoleon's dream of restoring French dominance overseas. The wars also dismantled much of the Netherlands' Indian Ocean empire. When French armies occupied the Netherlands, the Dutch ruler, who had fled to Britain in January 1795, authorized the British to take over Dutch possessions overseas, to keep them out of French hands. During 1795 and 1796 British forces quickly occupied the Cape Colony at the tip of southern Africa, the strategic Dutch port of Malacca on the strait between the Indian Ocean and the South China Sea, and the island of Ceylon (see Map 26.3).

Then the British occupied Dutch Guiana° and Trinidad in the southern Caribbean. In 1811 they even seized the island of Java, the center of the Netherlands' East Indian empire. British forces had also attacked French possessions, gaining control of the islands of Mauritius° and Réunion in the southwestern Indian Ocean. At the end of the Napoleonic Wars in 1814, Britain returned Java to the Dutch and Réunion to the French but kept the Cape Colony, British Guiana (once

---

sati (suh-TEE)

Guiana (ghee-AH-nuh)   **Mauritius** (moh-RIH-uhs)

Map 26.3   European Possessions in the Indian Ocean and South Pacific, 1870   After 1750, French and British competition for new territories generally expanded the European presence established earlier by the Portuguese, Spanish, and Dutch. By 1870 the British controlled much of India, were settling Australia and New Zealand, and possessed important trading enclaves throughout the region.

part of Dutch Guiana), Trinidad, Ceylon, Malacca, and Mauritius.

The Cape Colony was valuable because of Cape Town's strategic importance as a supply station for ships making the long voyages between Britain and India. With the port city came some twenty thousand descendants of earlier Dutch and French settlers who occupied far-flung farms and ranches in its hinterland. Despite their European origins, these people thought of themselves as permanent residents of Africa and were beginning to refer to themselves as "Afrikaners°" ("Africans" in their dialect of Dutch). British governors prohibited any expansion of the white settler frontier because such expansion invariably led to wars with indigenous Africans. This decision, along with the imposition of laws protecting African rights within Cape Colony (including the emancipation of slaves in 1834), alienated many Afrikaners.

Between 1836 and 1839, parties of Afrikaners embarked on a "Great Trek," leaving British-ruled Cape Colony for the fertile high *veld* (plateau) to the north that two decades of Zulu wars had depopulated. The Great Trek led to the foundation of three new settler colonies in southern Africa by 1850: the Afrikaners' Orange Free State and Transvaal on the high veld and the British colony of Natal on the Indian Ocean coast. Although firearms enabled the settlers to win some important battles against the Zulu and other Africans, they were still a tiny minority surrounded by the populous and powerful independent African kingdoms that had grown up at the beginning of the century. A few thousand British settlers came to Natal and the Cape Colony by midcentury, but these colonies' strategic importance to Britain was only as stopovers for shipping between Britain and British India.

Meanwhile, another strategic British outpost was being established in Southeast Asia. One prong of the advance was led by Thomas Stamford Raffles, who had governed Java during the period of British occupation from 1811 to 1814. After Java's return to the Dutch, Raffles helped the British East India Company establish a new free port at Singapore in 1824, on the site of a small Malay fishing village with a superb harbor. By attracting British merchants and Chinese businessmen and laborers, Singapore soon became the center of trade and shipping between the Indian Ocean and China. Along with Malacca and other possessions on the strait, Singapore formed the "Straits Settlements," which British India administered until 1867.

Further British expansion in Malaya (now Malaysia) did not occur until after 1874, but in neighboring Burma

Great Trek Aided by African Servants   The ox-drawn wagons of the Afrikaners struggled over the Drakensberg Mountains to the high plains in an effort to escape British control.   (Hulton Getty/ Liaison)

it came more quickly. Burma had emerged as a powerful kingdom by 1750, with plans for expansion. In 1785 Burma tried to annex neighboring territories of Siam (now Thailand) to the east, but a coalition of Thai leaders thwarted Burmese advances by 1802. Burma next attacked Assam to the west, but this action led to war with British India, which was concerned for the security of its own frontier with Assam. After a two-year war, India annexed Assam in 1826 and occupied two coastal provinces of northern Burma. As rice and timber trade from these provinces grew important, the occupation became permanent, and in 1852 British India annexed the port of Rangoon and the rest of coastal Burma.

Imperial Policies and Shipping

Through such piecemeal acquisitions, by 1870 Britain had added several dozen colonies to the twenty-six colonies it had in 1792, after the loss of the thirteen in North America (see Chapter 23). Nevertheless, historians usually portray Britain in this period as a reluctant empire builder, its leaders unwilling to acquire new outposts

Afrikaner (af-rih-KAHN-uhr)

that could prove difficult and expensive to administer. This apparent contradiction is resolved when one recognizes that the underlying goal of most British imperial expansion during these decades was trade rather than territory. Most of the new colonies were meant to serve as ports in the growing network of shipping that encircled the globe or as centers of production and distribution for those networks.

This new commercial expansion was closely tied to the needs of Britain's growing industrial economy and reflected a new philosophy of overseas trade. Rather than rebuilding the closed, mercantilist network of trade with its colonies, Britain sought to trade freely with all parts of the world. Free trade was also a wise policy in light of the independence of so many former colonies in the Americas (see Chapter 25).

Whether colonized or not, more and more African, Asian, and Pacific lands were being drawn into the commercial networks created by British expansion and industrialization. As was pointed out earlier, uncolonized parts of West Asia became major exporters to Britain of vegetable oils for industrial and domestic use and forest products for dyes and construction, while areas of eastern Africa free of European control exported ivory that ended up as piano keys and decorations for the elegant homes of the industrial middle class. From the far corners of the world came coffee, cocoa, and tea for the tables of the new industrial classes in Britain and other parts of Europe (along with sugar to sweeten these beverages), and indigo dyes and cotton fibers for their expanding textile factories.

In return, the factories of the industrialized nations supplied manufactured goods at very attractive prices. By the mid-nineteenth century a major part of their textile production was destined for overseas markets. Sales of cotton cloth to Africa increased 950 percent from the 1820s to the 1860s. British trade to India grew 350 percent between 1841 and 1870 while India's exports increased 400 percent. Trade with other regions also expanded rapidly. In most cases such trade benefited both sides, but there is no question that the industrial nations were the dominant partners.

A second impetus to global commercial expansion was the technological revolution in the construction of oceangoing ships under way in the nineteenth century. The middle decades of the century were the golden age of the sailing ship. Using iron to fasten timbers together permitted shipbuilders to construct much larger vessels. Merchant ships in the eighteenth century rarely exceeded 300 tons, but after 1850 swift American-built **clipper ships** of 2,000 tons were commonplace in the British merchant fleet. Huge canvas sails hung from tall masts made the streamlined clippers faster than earlier vessels. Ships from the East Indies or India had taken six months to reach Europe in the seventeenth century; after 1850 the new ships could complete the voyage in half that time.

This increase in size and speed lowered shipping costs and further stimulated maritime trade. The growth in size and numbers of ships increased by the tonnage of British merchant shipping by 400 percent between 1778 and 1860. To extend the life of such ships in tropical lands, clippers intended for Eastern service generally were built of teak and other tropical hardwoods from new British colonies in South and Southeast Asia. Although tropical forests began to be cleared for rice and sugar plantations as well as for timbers, the effects on the environment and people of Southeast Asia came primarily after 1870.

Colonization of Australia and New Zealand

The development of new ships and shipping contributed to a third form of British rule in the once-remote South Pacific. In contrast to the rule over an indigenous population in India or the commercial empire overseen from Singapore and Cape Town, in the new British colonies of Australia and New Zealand British settlers displaced indigenous populations, just as they had done in North America.

Portuguese mariners had sighted the continent of Australia in the early seventeenth century, but its remoteness made the land of little interest to Europeans. However, after the English adventurer Captain James Cook made the first systematic European exploration of New Zealand and the fertile eastern coast of Australia between 1769 and 1778, expanding shipping networks brought in growing numbers of visitors and settlers.

At the time of Cook's visits Australia was the home of about 650,000 hunting and gathering people, whose Melanesian° ancestors had settled there some 40,000 years earlier. The two islands of New Zealand, lying 1,000 miles (1,600 kilometers) southeast of Australia, were inhabited by about 250,000 Maori°, who practiced hunting, fishing, and simple forms of agriculture, which their Polynesian ancestors had introduced around 1200 C.E. Because of their long isolation from the rest of humanity, the populations of Australia and New Zealand were as vulnerable as the Amerindians had been to unfamiliar

Melanesian (mel-uh-NEE-zhuhn)
Maori (MOW-ree [*ow* as in *cow*])

diseases introduced by new overseas contacts. By the late nineteenth century only 93,000 aboriginal Australians and 42,000 Maori survived. By then they were outnumbered and dominated by British settler populations.

The first permanent British settlers in Australia were 736 convicts, of whom 188 were women, sent into exile from British prisons in 1788. For the next few decades Australian penal colonies grew slowly and had only slight contact with the indigenous population, whom the British called "Aborigines." However, the discovery of gold in 1851 brought a flood of free European settlers (and some Chinese) and hastened the end of the penal colonies. After 1850 tens of thousands of British settlers received government-subsidized passages "down under" on the improved sailing ships of that era, although the voyage still took more than three months. By 1860 the settler population had reached 1 million, and it doubled over the next fifteen years.

British settlers were drawn more slowly to New Zealand. Some of the first were temporary residents along the coast who slaughtered seals and exported seal pelts to Western countries to be made into men's felt hats. A single ship in 1806 took away sixty thousand sealskins. By the early 1820s overhunting had nearly exterminated the seal population. Sperm whales were also hunted extensively near New Zealand for their oil, used for lubrication, soap, and lamps; ambergris°, an ingredient in perfume; and bone, used in women's corsets (see Environment and Technology: Whaling). Military action that overcame Maori resistance, a brief gold rush, and the availability of faster ships and subsidized passages attracted more British immigrants after 1860. The colony especially courted women immigrants to offset the preponderance of single men. By the early 1880s, fertile agricultural lands of this farthest frontier of the British Empire had a settler population of 500,000.

The model that in 1867 had formed the giant Dominion of Canada out of the very diverse and thinly settled colonies of British North America was applied to the newer colonies in Australia and New Zealand. In 1901 Australia emerged from the federation of six separate colonies. New Zealand became a separate colony in 1840 and a self-governing dominion in 1907.

Britain's policies toward its settler colonies in Canada and the South Pacific were shaped by a desire to avoid the conflicts that had led to the American Revolution in the eighteenth century. By gradually turning over governing power to the colonies' inhabitants, Britain accomplished three things. It satisfied the settlers' desire

ambergris (AM-ber-grees)

British Proclamation to the Australian Aborigines, ca. 1830
Affixed to trees in rural areas, this poster was intended to convey to the indigenous population the message that the European settlers wanted to be their friends and the settler government would punish murders of either race with equal severity. The poster failed to produce mutual trust.   (Tasmanian Museum & Art Gallery)

for greater control over their own territories, it muted demands for independence, and it made the colonial governments responsible for most of their own expenses. Indigenous peoples were outvoted by the settlers or even excluded from voting. An 1897 Australian law segregated the remaining Aborigines onto reservations, where they lacked the rights of Australian citizenship. The requirement that voters had to be able to read and write English kept Maori from voting in early New Zealand elections, but four seats in the lower house of the legislature were reserved for Maori from 1867.

Whaling

The rapid expansion of whaling aptly illustrates the growing power of technology over nature in this period. Many contemporaries, like many people today, were sickened by the killing of the planet's largest living mammals. American novelist Herman Melville captured the conflicting sentiments in his epic whaling story, *Moby Dick* (1851). One of his characters enthusiastically explains why the grisly and dangerous business existed:

> But, though the world scorns us as whale hunters, yet does it unwittingly pay us the profoundest homage; yea, an all abounding adoration! for almost all the tapers, lamps, and candles that burn around the globe, burn, as before so many shrines, to our glory!

Melville's character overstates the degree to which whale oil dominated illumination and does not mention its many other industrial uses. Neither does he describe the commercial importance of whalebone (baleen). For a time its use in corsets allowed fashionable women to achieve the hourglass shape that fashion dictated. Whalebone's use for umbrella stays, carriage springs, fishing rods, suitcase frames, combs, brushes, and many other items made it the plastic of its day.

New manufacturing technologies went hand in hand with new hunting technologies. The revolution in ship design enabled whalers from Europe and North America to extend the hunt into the southern oceans off New Zealand. By the nineteenth century whaling ships were armed with guns that shot a steel harpoon armed with vicious barbs deep into the whale. In the 1840s explosive charges on harpoon heads ensured the whale's immediate death. Yet, as this engraving of an expedition off New Zealand shows, flinging small harpoons from rowboats in the open sea continued to be part of the dangerous work.

Another century of extensive hunting devastated many whale species before international agreements finally limited the killing of these giant sea creatures.

South Pacific Whaling   One boat was swamped, but the hunters killed the huge whale.   (The Granger Collection, New York)

Asian Laborers in British Guiana
The manager of the sugar estate reposes on the near end of the gallery of his house with the proprietor's attorney. At the other end of the gallery European overseers review the plantation's record books. In the yard, cups of lifeblood are being drained from bound Chinese and Indian laborers. This allegorical drawing by a Chinese laborer represents the exploitation of Asian laborers by Europeans. (Boston Athenaeum)

In other ways the new settler colonies were more progressive. Australia developed very powerful trade unions, which improved the welfare of skilled and semi-skilled urban white male workers, promoted democratic values, and exercised considerable political clout. In New Zealand, where sheep raising was the main occupation, populist and progressive sentiments promoted the availability of land for the common person. Australia and New Zealand were also among the first states in the world to grant women the right to vote, beginning in 1894.

New Labor Migrations

Europeans were not the only people to transplant themselves overseas in the mid-nineteenth century. Between 1834 and 1870 large numbers of Indians, Chinese, and Africans responded to labor recruiters, especially to work overseas on sugar plantations. In the half-century after 1870 tens of thousands of Asians and Pacific Islanders made similar voyages. The scale of such population movements and fact that many of these migrants traveled halfway around the world show the capacities of the new sailing ships. The power and interdependence of the British Empire are revealed in the fact that British India was the greatest source of such laborers and other British colonies were their principal destinations.

After Britain's emancipation of slaves in 1834, the freed Africans were no longer willing to work the long hours they had been forced to work as slaves. When given full freedom of movement in 1839, many men and women left the plantations. British colonies had to find other laborers if they were to compete successfully with sugar plantations in Cuba, Brazil, and the French Caribbean that were still using slave labor.

India's impoverished people seemed one obvious alternative. After planters on Mauritius successfully introduced Indian laborers, the Indian labor trade was extended to the British Caribbean in 1838. Free Africans were another possibility. In 1841, the British government allowed Caribbean planters to recruit Africans whom British patrols had rescued from slave ships and brought to liberation depots in Sierra Leone and elsewhere. By 1870, over a half-million Indians had left their homes for Mauritius or the British Caribbean along with nearly 40,000 Africans and over 18,000 Chinese for the British Caribbean colonies. After the French abolished slavery in 1848, their colonies also recruited 19,000 laborers from Africa and nearly 80,000 from India. Also ending slavery in 1848, Dutch Guiana recruited 57,000 new Asian workers for its plantations.

Although African slave labor was not abolished in Cuba until 1886, the rising cost of slaves led the burgeoning sugar plantations to recruit 138,000 new laborers from China between 1847 and 1873. Such labor recruitment also became the mainstay of new sugar plantations in places that had never known slave labor: after 1850 American planters in Hawaii recruited labor from China and Japan; British planters in Natal recruited from India; and those in Queensland (in northeastern Australia) relied on laborers from neighboring South Pacific islands.

Larger, faster ships made transporting laborers halfway around the world affordable, though voyages from Asia to the Caribbean still took an average of three months. Despite close regulation and supervision of shipboard conditions, the crowded accommodations on the long voyages encouraged the spread of cholera and other contagious diseases that took many migrants' lives.

All of these laborers served under **contracts of indenture,** which bound them to work for a specified period (usually from five to seven years) in return for free passage to their overseas destination. They were also paid a small salary and were provided with housing, clothing, and medical care. Indian indentured laborers also received the right to a free passage home if they worked a second five-year contract. British Caribbean colonies required that forty women be recruited for every hundred men as a way to promote family life. So many Indians chose to stay on in Mauritius, Trinidad, British Guiana, and Fiji that they constituted a third or more of the total population of these colonies by the early twentieth century.

Although many early recruits from China and the Pacific Islands were kidnapped or otherwise coerced into leaving their homes, in most cases the new indentured migrants had much in common with contemporary emigrants from Europe (described in Chapter 24). Both groups chose to leave their homelands in hopes of improving their economic and social conditions. Both earned modest salaries. Many saved to bring money back with them when they returned home, or they used their earnings to buy land or to start a business in their new countries, where large numbers chose to remain. One major difference was that people recruited as indentured laborers were generally so much poorer than emigrants from Europe that they had to accept lower-paying jobs in less desirable areas because they could not pay their own way. However, it is also true that many European immigrants into distant places like Australia and New Zealand had their passages subsidized but did not have to sign a contract of indenture. This shows that racial and cultural preferences, not just economics, shaped the flow of labor into European colonies.

A person's decision to accept an indentured labor contract could also be shaped by political circumstances. In India, disruption brought by British colonial policies and the suppression of the 1857 rebellion contributed significantly to people's desire to emigrate. Poverty, famine, and warfare had not been strangers in precolonial India. Nor were these causes of emigration absent in China and Japan (see Chapter 27).

Not simply the creation of Western imperialism, the indentured labor trade both allured and repelled the Asians and Africans. The commercial and industrial expansion of the West created an unequal relationship but not an entirely one-sided one. Most men and women who signed indentured contracts were trying to improve their lives by emigrating, and many succeeded in manipulating the system to their own advantage. Whether for good or ill, more and more of the world's peoples saw their lives being influenced by the existence of Western colonies, Western ships, and Western markets.

CONCLUSION

What is the global significance of these complex political and economic changes in southern Asia, Africa, and the South Pacific? One perspective stresses the continuing exploitation of the weak by the strong, of African, Asian, and Pacific peoples by aggressive Europeans. In this view, the emergence of Britain as a dominant power in the Indian Ocean basin and South Pacific continues the European expansion that the Portuguese and the Spanish pioneered and the Dutch continued. Likewise, Britain's control over the densely populated lands of South and Southeast Asia and over the less populated lands of Australia and New Zealand can be seen as a continuation of the conquest and colonization of the Americas.

From another perspective what was most important about this period was not the political and military strength of the Europeans but their growing dominance of the world's commerce, especially through long-distance ocean shipping. In this view, like other Europeans, the British were drawn to Africa and southern Asia by a desire to obtain new materials.

Britain's commercial expansion in the nineteenth century, however, was increasingly the product of

Easterners' demand for industrial manufactures. The growing exchanges could be mutually beneficial. African and Asian consumers found industrially produced goods far cheaper and sometimes better than the handicrafts they replaced or supplemented. Industrialization created new markets for African and Asian goods, as in the case of the vegetable-oil trade in West Africa or cotton in Egypt and India. There also was a negative impact, in the case of the weavers of India and the damage to species of seals and whales.

The emphasis on Europeans' military and commercial strength did not mean that African, Asian, and Pacific peoples were reduced to appendages of Europe. The balance of power was shifting in the Europeans' favor between 1750 and 1870, but local cultures were still vibrant and local initiatives often dominant. Islamic reform movements and the rise of the Zulu nation had greater significance for their respective regions of Africa than did Western forces. Despite some ominous concessions to European power, Southeast Asians were still largely in control of their own destinies. Even in India, most people's lives and beliefs showed more continuity with the past than the change due to British rule.

Finally, it must not be imagined that Asians and Africans were powerless in dealing with European expansion. The Indian princes who extracted concessions from the British in return for their cooperation and the Indians who rebelled against the raj both forced the system to accommodate their needs. Moreover, some Asians and Africans were beginning to use European education, technology, and methods to transform their own societies. Leaders in Egypt, India, and other lands, like those in Russia, the Ottoman Empire, China, and Japan—the subject of Chapter 27—were learning to challenge the power of the West on its own terms. In 1870 no one could say how long and how difficult that learning process would be, but Africans and Asians would continue to shape their own futures.

■ Key Terms

Zulu	British raj
Sokoto Caliphate	Sepoy Rebellion
modernization	durbar
Muhammad Ali	Indian Civil Service
"legitimate" trade	Indian National Congress
recaptives	clipper ship
nawab	contract of indenture
sepoy	

■ Suggested Reading

Volumes 2 and 3 of *The Oxford History of the British Empire*, ed. William Roger Louis, (1998, 1999), are the most up-to-date global surveys of this period. Less Anglocentric in their interpretations are Immanuel Wallerstein's *The Modern World-System III: The Second Era of Great Expansion of the Capitalist World-Economy, 1730–1840s* (1989) and William Wodruff's *Impact of Western Man: A Study of Europe's Role in the World Economy, 1750–1960* (1982). Atlantic relations are well handled by David Eltis, *Economic Growth and the Ending of the Transatlantic Slave Trade* (1987). For the Indian Ocean basin see Sugata Bose, ed., *South Asia and World Capitalism* (1990).

Roland Oliver and Anthony Atmore provide a brief introduction to Africa in *Africa Since 1800*, 4th ed. (1994). More advanced works are J. F. Ade Ajayi, ed., *UNESCO General History of Africa*, vol. 6, *Africa in the Nineteenth Century until the 1880s* (1989), and John E. Flint, ed., *The Cambridge History of Africa*, vol. 5, *From c. 1790 to c. 1870* (1976). Although specialized literature has refined some of their interpretations, the following are excellent introductions to their subjects: J. D. Omer-Cooper, *The Zulu Aftermath* (1966); Murray Last, *The Sokoto Caliphate* (1967); A. G. Hopkins, *An Economic History of West Africa* (1973); Robert W. July, *The Origins of Modern African Thought* (1967); and Robert I. Rotberg, ed., *Africa and Its Explorers: Motives, Methods, and Impact* (1970). For eastern and northeastern Africa see Norman R. Bennett, *Arab Versus European: War and Diplomacy in Nineteenth Century East Central Africa* (1985); P. J. Vatikiotis, *The History of Modern Egypt: From Muhammad Ali to Mubarak*, 4th ed. (1991); and, for the negative social impact of Egyptian modernization, Judith Tucker, "Decline of the Family Economy in Mid-Nineteenth-Century Egypt," *Arab Studies Quarterly 1* (1979): 245–271.

Very readable introductions to India in this period are Sugata Bose and Ayeshia Jalal, *Modern South India* (1998); Burton Stein, *A History of India* (1998); and Stanley Wolpert, *A New History of India*, 6th ed. (1999). More advanced treatments in the "New Cambridge History of India" series are P. J. Marshall, *Bengal: The British Bridgehead: Eastern India, 1740–1828* (1988); C. A. Bayly, *Indian Society and the Making of the British Empire* (1988); Sugata Bose, *Peasant Labour and Colonial Capital: Rural Bengal Since 1700* (1993); and Kenneth W. Jones, *Socio-Religious Reform Movements in British India* (1989). Environmental and technological perspectives on India are offered in the appropriate parts of Daniel Headrick, *The Tentacles of Progress: Technology Transfer in the Age of Imperialism, 1850–1940* (1988); Mashav Gadgil and Ramachandra Guha, *This Fissured Land: An Ecological History of India* (1992); and David Arnold, *Colonizing the Body: State Medicine and Epidemic Disease in Nineteenth-Century India* (1993).

A good introduction to the complexities of Southeast Asian history is D. R. SarDesai, *Southeast Asia: Past and Present*, 2d ed. (1989). More detail can be found in the appropriate chapters of Nicholas Tarling, ed., *The Cambridge History of South East Asia*, 2 vols. (1992). The second and third volumes of *The Oxford History of Australia*, ed. Geoffrey Bolton (1992, 1988), deal with the period covered by this chapter. A very readable multicultural and gendered perspective is provided by *Images of Australia,* ed. Gillian Whitlock and David Carter (1992). *The Oxford Illustrated History of New Zealand,* ed. Keith Sinclair (1990), provides a wide-ranging introduction to that nation.

For summaries of recent scholarship on the indentured labor trade see David Northrup, *Indentured Labor in the Age of Imperialism, 1834–1922* (1995), and Robin Cohen, ed., *The Cambridge Survey of World Migration,* part 3, "Asian Indentured and Colonial Migration" (1995).

An outstanding analysis of British whaling is Gordon Jackson's *The British Whaling Trade* (1978). Edouard A. Stackpole's *Whales & Destiny: The Rivalry Between America, France, and Britain for Control of the Southern Whale Fishery, 1785–1825* (1972) is more anecdotal.

■ Notes

1. Paul E. Lovejoy and Jan S. Hogendorn, *Slow Death for Slavery: The Course of Abolition in Northern Nigeria, 1897–1936* (New York: Cambridge University Press, 1993).
2. Quoted in P. J. Vatikiotis, *The History of Modern Egypt: From Muhammad Ali to Mubarak,* 4th ed. (Baltimore: Johns Hopkins University Press, 1991), 74.
3. David Eltis, "Precolonial Western Africa and the Atlantic Economy," in *Slavery and the Rise of the Atlantic Economy,* ed. Barbara Solow (New York: Cambridge University Press, 1991), table 1.
4. Quoted by Bernard S. Cohn, "Representing Authority in Victorian India," in *The Invention of Tradition,* ed. Eric Hobsbawm and Terence Ranger (Cambridge, England: Cambridge University Press, 1983), 165.

27

THE OTTOMAN EMPIRE AND EAST ASIA,

1800–1870

The Ottoman Empire and the European Model • The Qing Empire and Foreign Coercion • Japan from Shogunate to Empire
ENVIRONMENT AND TECHNOLOGY: The Web of War
SOCIETY AND CULTURE: Fighting the Opium Trade

Netting Whales During the Tokugawa, the Japanese began using nets to catch large numbers of whales, and many provinces became dependent on the new industry.

When the emperor of the Qing° (the last empire to rule China) died in 1799, the imperial court received a shock. For decades officials had known that the emperor was indulging his handsome young favorite, Heshen°, allowing him extraordinary privileges and power. Senior bureaucrats hated Heshen, suspecting him of overseeing a widespread network of corruption. They believed he had been scheming to prolong the inconclusive wars against the native Miao° peoples of southwest China in the late 1700s. Glowing reports of successes against the rebels had poured into the capital, and enormous sums of government money had flowed to the battlefields. But there was no adequate accounting for the funds, and the war persisted.

After the emperor's death, Heshen's enemies ordered his arrest. When they searched his mansion, they discovered a magnificent hoard of silk, furs, porcelain, furniture, and gold and silver. His personal cash alone exceeded what remained in the imperial treasury. The new emperor ordered Heshen to commit suicide with a rope of gold silk. The government seized Heshen's fortune, but the financial damage could not be undone. The expenses of the government were so great that it was permanently bankrupt. The declining agricultural base could not replenish the state coffers, and pressures for internal police and military action rose after 1800. Repeated investigations of the bureaucracy revealed growing corruption. Thus, in the 1800s, the Qing Empire faced increasing challenges from Europe and the United States with an empty treasury, a stagnant economy, and a troubled society.

The Qing Empire's problems were not unique. They were common to all of the land-based empires of Eurasia. During the early 1800s, rapid population growth and slow agricultural growth affected much of Eurasia. Earlier military expansion had overstretched the resources of the imperial treasuries. As these traditional regimes were experiencing economic and social crises in the 1800s, the militarily advanced sea-based powers of western Europe were pressing them for economic concessions. The result was general indebtedness—either through direct loans or failure to pay indemnities after losing military conflicts—to France, Britain, and other Western powers.

This chapter concentrates on the experiences of the Ottoman and Qing Empires. To understand the significance of the similarities between them, it is necessary to examine a dramatic contrasting case: Japan. Like the Ottoman and Qing Empires, Japan in the 1800s was in the late decades of a long-lived political system—the Tokugawa Shogunate. Also like the imperial Ottomans and Qing, the Tokugawa government saw revenues steeply declining, the agricultural base stagnating, and the central government engulfed in corruption. And finally, Japan like other East Asian countries experienced the shock of military and economic confrontation with a foreign power in the mid-1800s. But the decentralized system of rule under the Tokugawa made it impossible for Japan to attempt the top-down reforms tried by the Ottomans and Qing. Instead, Japan's first direct contact with a foreign sea power led to the destruction, not reform, of the traditional state. It was replaced by a centralized and relatively efficient order whose leaders were determined to avoid becoming victims of European expansion and to participate in the evolving colonial order in Asia.

As you read this chapter, ask yourself the following questions:

- Why did the Ottoman and Qing Empires find themselves at a disadvantage during their encounters with Europeans in the 1800s?
- What were the best options for the land-based empires facing military challenges from Europe?
- Why was Japan's experience so different from that of China?

Qing (ching)   **Heshen** (huh-shun)   **Miao** (mee-ow)

CHRONOLOGY

	Ottoman Empire	Qing Empire	Japan
			Since 1600 Decentralized rule of Tokugawa Shogunate
1800	**1789–1807** Rule of Selim III	**1794–1804** White Lotus Rebellion	
	1826 Janissary corps dissolved **1829** Greek independence **1839** Abdul Mejid begins Tanzimat reforms	**1839–1842** Opium War	
1850	**1853–1856** Crimean War	**1850–1864** Taiping Rebellion	**1853** First visit by Commodore Matthew Perry **1854** Perry returns **1858** Treaty of Kanagawa
		1856–1860 Arrow War **1860** Sack of Beijing **1862–1875** Reign of Tongzhi	**1867** Civil war **1868** Meiji Restoration
	1876 First constitution by an Islamic government		

THE OTTOMAN EMPIRE AND THE EUROPEAN MODEL

Though the Ottoman Empire experienced the problems and challenges sketched above, its position close to Europe gave it relatively early exposure to European ambitions and capabilities. The Ottoman rulers were earlier than the rulers of other Eurasian empires to experiment with financial and military modernization. Not until the mid-1800s, however, did the Ottoman government overcome entrenched opposition to change and put into place a series of reforms designed to remove the influence of religious elites from many areas of the state and economy. The reforms could not move rapidly enough to preserve the empire's independence from western Europe, but they created momentum for centralization, helped promote nationalism in the late nineteenth century, and created a practical base for the creation of a Turkish republic in the twentieth century.

Early Struggles for Reform, 1793–1807

At the end of the eighteenth century Sultan Selim° III (r. 1789–1807) introduced reforms to strengthen the military, bring provincial governors under the control of the central government, and standardize taxation and land tenure. The rise in government expenditures to implement the reforms was supposed to be offset by taxes on selected items, primarily tobacco and coffee.

These reforms failed for political reasons, more than economic. The most violent and persistent opposition came from the **Janissaries°,** the traditional corps of Ottoman military slaves. The Janissaries were originally Christian boys required to convert to Islam and serve for life in the Ottoman army. Over the years, the Janissaries became a significant political force, and their conservative attitudes dissuaded many Ottoman rulers and officials from pursuing reform.

At times the disapproval of the Janissaries produced military uprisings. An early example occurred in the

---

Selim (seh-LEEM)   **Janissaries** (JAN-nih-say-rees)

Change with Tradition Change in the Ottoman armies was gradual, beginning with the introduction of European guns and artillery. To use the new weapons efficiently and safely, the Janissaries were required to modify their dress and their beards. Beards were trimmed, and elaborate headgear was reserved for ritual occasions. Traditional military units attempted to retain distinctive dress whenever possible, and one compromise was the brimless cap, the fez (shown here), adapted from the high hats that some Janissaries had traditionally worn. (Courtesy, Turkish Ministry of Culture and Tourism. Photo: Necmettin Kulahci)

The Janissaries were not the only opponents of reform. In some parts of the empire, including Anatolia, revolts by the Janissaries were encouraged by noblemen who had been supporters of earlier imperial reforms but now feared that further reform would result in new taxes. Also opposed to reform were the congregations of Muslim councilors, the *ulama*, who distrusted the secularization of law and taxation that Selim proposed. In the face of widespread rejection of his reforms, Selim suspended his program in 1806. Nevertheless, a massive military uprising occurred at Istanbul, and the sultan was deposed and imprisoned. Reform forces rallied and recaptured the capital, but not before Selim had been executed.

Army and Society in the Early Tanzimat, 1826–1853

In 1826 Selim's cousin Sultan Mahmud° II (r.1808–1839) revived the reform movement. The fate of Selim III had taught the Ottoman court that reform needed to be more systematic and imposed more forcefully. Mahmud II was able to use the loss of Greece, formerly an Ottoman colony, as a sign of the weakness of the empire and the pressing need for reform.

Greek independence in 1829 was a complex event that had dramatic international significance. Earlier Ottoman rulers had pointed to the shattering of Byzantine rule over Greece and Anatolia as a triumph of Islamic civilization and proof of God's favor. Europeans and Russians, however, saw the capture of the former Byzantine capital, Constantinople—now the Ottoman capital, Istanbul—as justification for a new holy war to be waged

Balkans, in the Ottoman territory of **Serbia,** where Janissaries acted as provincial governors. Their control in Serbia was intensely resented by the local residents, particularly Orthodox Christians who claimed that the Janissaries abused them. In response to the charges, Selim threatened to reassign the Janissaries to the Ottoman capital at Istanbul. Suspecting that the sultan's threat signaled the beginning of the end of their political power, the Janissaries in 1805 revolted against Selim, and massacred Christians in Serbia. Selim was unable to reestablish central Ottoman rule over Serbia. Instead, the Ottoman court had to rely on the ruler of Bosnia, another Balkan province, who joined his troops with the peasants of Serbia to suppress the Janissary uprising. The threat of Russian intervention prevented the Ottomans from disarming the victorious Serbians, so Serbia became effectively independent.

Mahmud (MACH-mood)

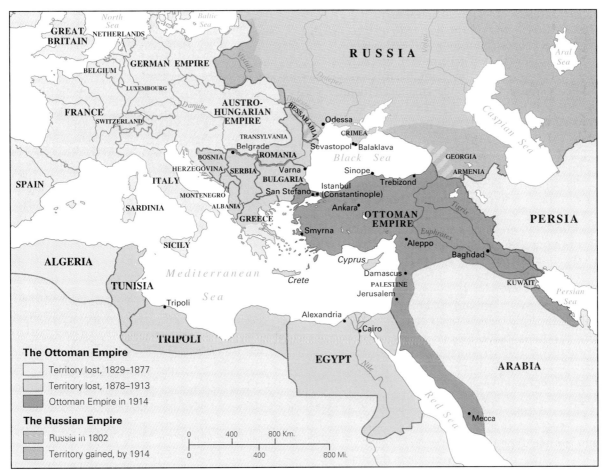

Map 27.1   Disintegration of the Ottoman Empire, 1829–1914   At its height the Ottoman Empire controlled most of the perimeter of the Mediterranean Sea. But in the 1800s Ottoman territory shrank as many countries gained their independence—frequently with the aid of France or Russia. The Black Sea, which left the Turkish coast vulnerable to assault by the Russian navy, was a weak spot that intensely contested in the Crimean dispute.

by Christian countries against the Ottoman Empire. By the early nineteenth century, interest in the classical age of Greece and Rome had intensified Europeans' desire to encourage and if possible aid the Greeks' struggle for independence from Ottoman rule. Europeans considered the war for Greek independence a campaign to recapture the classical roots of their civilization from Muslim despots, and many—including the "mad, bad and dangerous to know" English poet Lord Byron, who lost his life in the war—went to Greece to fight as volunteers. The Ottomans depended on Ibrahim Pasha° of Egypt (son of Muhammad Ali°) to preserve their rule in Greece, but the combined squadrons of the British, French, and Russian

Ibrahim Pasha (EEB-RAH-heem PAH-shah)
Muhammad Ali (moo-HAM-mad AH-lee)

fleets handily defeated him. Not only did Ottoman control of Greece end, but the Ottoman's tenuous rule in Egypt was further damaged (see Map 27.1).

Europeans trumpeted the victory of the Greeks as a triumph of European civilization over the Ottoman Empire, and Mahmud II agreed that the loss of Greece indicated a profound weakness—he considered it backwardness—in Ottoman military and financial organization. Like his predecessors, Mahmud believed that the Janissaries should be destroyed, and with popular outrage over the loss of Greece strong, he made his move in 1826. First he announced the creation of a new army corps, which would be open to the Janissaries. Then, when the Janissaries rose in revolt, he ordered loyal troops to attack the Janissary barracks and obliterate the force.

Mahmud also reduced the political power of the religious elite. To accomplish this reform, he had to restructure the bureaucracy, because education and law were to be under the authority of the civil government. Property laws too were amended, to make the charitable trusts by which religious communities and families managed their wealth subject to civil review and regulation. Even the public judgments of the ulama were to be bureaucratically regulated.

In attempting to secularize the state, Mahmud relied heavily on establishing a uniform code of civil law. Many of his ideas received their widest expression in the **Tanzimat°** ("restructuring"), a series of reforms announced by his sixteen-year-old son and successor, Abdul Mejid°, in 1839. One proclamation guaranteeing basic political rights has been compared to England's Magna Carta (1215). It called for public trials and equal protection under the law for all, whether Muslim, Christian, or Jew. It also guaranteed some rights of privacy, equalized the eligibility of men for conscription into the army, and provided for a new, formalized method of tax collecting that legally ended tax farming in the Ottoman Empire. No Islamic country had ever produced anything so nearly approaching a constitution, and the Ottoman Empire enjoyed a renewed reputation as a progressive influence in the Middle East.

The successors to Mahmud II and Abdul Mejid were less zealous in their legal ideologies and later created a mixed court system that permitted *qadi°* (religious judges) to decide certain matters. Nevertheless, the distinction between religious and secular law continued to be observed. In the mid-1800s, the commercial code was remodeled along the lines of the French system, and the rulers affirmed that trade and finance were outside the jurisdiction of religious law.

Military cadets were sent to France and the German states for training, and military uniforms were modeled on those of France. In the 1830s an Ottoman imperial school of military sciences was established at Istanbul. Instructors imported from western Europe taught chemistry, engineering, mathematics, and physics in addition to military history. Reforms in military education became the model for more general educational reforms. In 1838 the first medical school was established, for army doctors and surgeons. Later, a national system of preparatory schools was created. The subjects that were taught and many of the teachers were foreign, so the issue of whether Turkish would be a language of instruction in the new schools was a serious one. Because it was easier to import and use foreign textbooks than to write

---

Tanzimat (TAHNZ-ee-MAT) **Abdul Mejid** (ab-dul MAY-jeed)
qadi (KAW-dee)

European Exposure Increasing exposure to French and British influence stimulated the programs of the Ottoman rulers to modernize their armies. By the time of the Crimean War, the Janissaries had been replaced by a professional military, trained in special schools, adept in the use of modern artillery, and dressed in the fashion of the European infantry and cavalry. (Hulton Getty Liaison)

new ones in Turkish, French became the preferred language in all advanced professional and scientific training. The translation of fundamental works into Turkish was still not completed by the end of the 1800s.

The importance of educational institutions in the early reforms accelerated the growth in wealth and influence of the urban elites. At Istanbul, the capital, a cosmopolitan milieu embracing European language and culture, as well as military professionalism and an interest in progressive political reform, thrived. Newspapers—most of them in French—were founded at Istanbul, and travel to Europe—particularly to England and France—by wealthy Turks became more common. Interest in importing European military, industrial, and communications technology remained strong through the 1800s.

The Ottoman rulers quickly learned that limited improvements in military technology had unforeseen cultural and social effects. The introduction of modern weapons and drill required a change in traditional military dress. Beards were deemed unhygienic and, in artillery units, a fire hazard. They were restricted, along with the wearing of loose trousers and turbans. Military headgear also became controversial. European military caps, which had leather bills on the front to protect against the glare of the sun, were not acceptable because they interfered with Muslim soldiers' touching their foreheads to the ground during daily prayers. The compromise was the brimless cap now called the *fez*, which was adopted by the military and then by Ottoman civil officials in the early years of Mahmud II's reign.

Military castes had been important in traditional Ottoman society, and the changes in military dress—so soon after the suppression of the Janissaries—were recognized as an indication of the change in the social meaning of military service. A conscript army was created, and with it came educational reforms that attempted to promote secular, international, urban cultural attitudes. Among self-consciously progressive men, European dress became the fashion in the Ottoman cities of the later 1800s. Traditional dress became a symbol of the religious, the rural, and the parochial.

Secularization of the legal code had profound implications for the non-Muslim subjects of the Ottomans. Non-Muslims frequently had been required to pay extra taxes and had been excluded from certain professions, including the military, unless they converted to Islam. In addition, the role of Islamic judges in the legal process had limited non-Muslim's access to the law courts. Secularization of the law, however, gave all male subjects access to the courts. It also resulted in equalization of taxation.

The public rights and political participation granted during the Tanzimat were explicitly restricted to men. Private life, including everything connected to marriage and divorce, was left within the sphere of religious law, and at no time was there a question of political participation or reformed education for women. Indeed, the reforms actually decreased the influence of women. The political changes ran parallel to economic changes that also narrowed women's opportunities.

The influx of silver from the Americas that began in the 1600s increased the monetarization of some sectors of the Ottoman economy, particularly in the cities. Workers were increasingly paid in cash rather than goods, and businesses associated with banking, finance, and law developed. Competition drove women from the work force. Early industrial labor and the professions were not open to women, and traditional "woman's work" such as weaving was increasingly mechanized and done by men.

Nevertheless, well into the 1800s some women retained considerable power in the management and disposal of their own property. After marriage a woman was often pressured to convert her landholdings to cash in order to transfer her personal wealth to her husband's family, with whom she and her husband would reside. Until the 1820s, many women retained their say in the distribution of property through the creation of charitable trusts for their sons. Because these trusts were set up in the religious courts, they could be designed to conform to the wishes of family members, and they gave women of wealthy families an opportunity to exercise significant indirect control over property. Then, in the 1820s and 1830s, the secularizing reforms of Mahmud II transferred jurisdiction over the charitable trusts from religious courts to the state and ended women's control over their own and their families' property. In addition, reforms in the military, higher education, the professions, and commerce all bypassed women. By the late 1800s, the seclusion of women had become a highly valued symbol of Turkish nativism and Muslim traditionalism.

The Crimean War, 1853–1856

Since the reign of Peter the Great (r. 1689–1725) the Russian Empire had been attempting to expand southward at the Ottomans' expense. By 1815 Russia had pried the Georgian region of the Caucasus away from the Ottomans, and the threat of Russian intervention in Serbia had prevented the Ottomans from crushing Serbian independence. Russia seemed poised to exploit Ottoman weakness and seize key territories in the Balkans, Central Asia, and possibly the Middle East.

Between 1853 and 1856 the **Crimean° War** raged on the Black Sea and its northern shore. This extremely destructive conflict was nominally a war between the Russian and Ottoman Empires about whether Russia could claim to protect Christians in the Ottoman domains. But also involved in the dispute were Austria, Britain, France, and the Italian kingdom of Sardinia-Piedmont, all of whom sided—actively or passively—with the Ottoman Empire. These European nations feared Russia's power and influence, which they suspected would increase because of the Ottomans' weakness. The war was fought at sea as well as on land. During the prolonged sea conflict, Britain and France trapped the Russian fleet in the Black Sea. The lack of railways hampered Russian attempts to supply both its land and its sea forces. Tsar Alexander II (r. 1855–1881) abandoned the key fortress of Sevastopol in 1855 and sued for peace.

A formal alliance among Britain, France, and the Ottoman Empire blocked Russian expansion into eastern Europe and the Middle East. The terms of peace also

Crimean (cry-ME-uhn)

The Web of War

The lethal military technologies of the mid-nineteenth century used on battlefields in the United States, Russia, India, and China were rapidly transmitted from one conflict to the next. This dissemination was due not only to the rapid development of communications but also to the existence of a new international network of soldiers who moved from one trouble spot to another, bringing with them expertise in the use of new techniques.

General Charles Gordon (1833–1885), for instance, was commissioned in the British army in 1852, then served in the Crimean War after Britain entered on the side of the Ottomans. In 1860 he was dispatched to China. He served British forces during the Arrow War and took part in the sack of Beijing. Afterward, he stayed in China and was seconded to the Qing imperial government until the suppression of the Taipings in 1864, earning himself the nickname "Chinese" Gordon. Gordon later served the Ottoman rulers of Egypt as governor of territory along the Nile. He was killed in Egypt in 1885 while attempting to lead his Egyptian troops in defense of the city of Khartoum against an uprising by the local religious leader, the Mahdi.

Journalism played an important part in the developing web of telegraph communications that speeded orders to and from the battlefields. Readers in London could learn details of the drama occurring in the Crimea or in China within a week—or in some cases days—after they occurred. Print and, later, photographic journalism created new "stars" from these war experiences. Charles Gordon was one. Florence Nightingale was another.

In the great wars of the 1800s, the vast majority of deaths resulted from infec-tion or excessive bleeding, not from the wounds themselves. Florence Nightingale (1820–1910), while still a young woman, became interested in hospital management and nursing. She went to Prussia and France to study advanced techniques and before the outbreak of the Crimean War was credited with bringing about marked improvement in British health care. When the public reacted to news reports of the suffering in the Crimea, the British government sent Nightingale to the region. Within a year of her arrival the death rate in the military hospitals there dropped from 45 percent to under 5 percent. Her techniques for preventing septicemia and dysentery and for promoting healing therapies were quickly adopted by those working for and with her. On her return to London, Nightingale established institutes for nursing that soon were recognized around the world as leaders. She herself was lionized by the British public and received the Order of Merit in 1907, three years before her death.

The importance of Nightingale's innovations in public hygiene is underscored by the life of her contemporary, Mary Seacole (1805–1881). A Jamaican woman who volunteered to nurse British troops in the Crimean War, Seacole was excluded repeatedly from nursing service by British authorities. She eventually went to Crimea and used her own funds to run a hospital there, bankrupting herself in the process. The drama of the Crimean War moved the British public to support Seacole after her sacrifices were publicized. She was awarded medals by the British, French, and Turkish governments and today is recognized with her contemporary Florence Nightingale as an innovative field nurse and a champion of public hygiene in peacetime.

With Florence Nightingale in Crimea Readers could see as well as read about war dramas with vivid illustrations and telegraphed copy. (The Granger Collection, New York)

We Have Got the Maxim Gun   These two representatives of the Qing Empire visited northern England after the Taiping Rebellion to examine and, if possible, purchase new weapons. They posed for a photograph after watching the famous Maxim gun shoot a tree in half.   (Peter Newark's Military Pictures)

gave Britain and France a means of checking each other's colonial ambitions in the Middle East: neither, according to the agreement that ended the war, was entitled to take Ottoman territory for its exclusive use.

The Crimean War brought significant changes to all the combatants. The tsar and his government, already beset by demands for the reform of serfdom, education, and the military, were further discredited. They plunged into reforms that slightly improved Russia's economy but profoundly destabilized its political system. In Britain and France the conflict was accompanied by massive propaganda campaigns. For the first time newspapers were an important force mobilizing public support for a war. Press accounts of British participation in the war were often so glamorized that ever since the false impression has lingered that Ottoman and Egyptian troops played a negligible role in the conflict. At the time, however, British and French military commanders noted the massive losses among Turkish troops in particular. The French press, dominant in Istanbul, promoted a sense of unity between Turkish and French society that continued to influence many aspects of Turkish urban culture.

The larger significance of the Crimean War was that it marked the transition from traditional to modern warfare (see Environment and Technology: The Web of War). The high casualty count of the war resulted in part from the clash of mechanized and unmechanized means of killing. All the combatant nations in the Crimean War once prided themselves on their effective use of highly trained cavalry to smash through the front lines of infantry. Cavalry coexisted with firearms until the early 1800s, primarily because early rifles were awkward to load, vulnerable to explosion, and not very accurate. Swift and expert cavalry could storm infantry lines during the intervals between volleys and even penetrate artillery barrages. Then in the 1830s and 1840s, **percussion caps** were widely adopted in Europe. In Crimean War battles, many cavalry units were destroyed by the rapid and relatively accurate fire of **breech-loading rifles.** That was the fate of the British "Light Brigade," which was sent to relieve an Ottoman unit surrounded by Russian troops. Cavalry were not the only victims of the new speed of the guns. Many traditional infantry units came to grief attempting to use ranks of marching, brightly coated soldiers to overwhelm lines of rapidly firing riflemen.

In the great conflicts that followed the Crimean War—the Indian Uprising, the Taiping° Rebellion in China, and the American Civil War—percussion-cap technology in combination with new designs of repeating guns led to

Taiping (tie-PING)

the creation of machine guns. Originally called Agar guns, then Gatling guns, machine guns resulted in a new scale of battlefield fatalities, mounting into many hundreds of thousands over only a few years. New manufacturing techniques allowed unprecedented precision in the fitting of caps and bullets within the firing chambers, creating propulsive force never before encountered so widely. Railways permitted the rapid transfer of heavy weaponry toward the front, as well as the transport of the wounded to hospitals, and also aided in the conveyance of iron and coal to manufacturing centers.

The transformation of decisive weaponry meant a change in the general ways of war. Cavalry did not immediately disappear, but the emphasis on speed and the use of light, accurate firearms by riders created more and more deadly conditions for mounted soldiers. Heavily armed infantry units pinned each other down in trenches for weeks, waiting for the enemy to be wiped out by disease or despair. Long-range artillery took on greater strategic significance and was combined with mines, early hand grenades, and mustard gas. Soldiers were reorganized, taught to scatter and shoot from trenches or from behind natural barriers, and dressed in inconspicuous colors. In such circumstances, the military began to lose its traditional connection with the aristocracy, with horses, and with ceremonial uniforms. Conscript armies took on new importance, and warfare became a political issue. Though the transformation of traditional warfare was not completed in the cycle of regional conflicts that began with the Crimean War, the process began that led toward the patterns of warfare that were to become familiar in the twentieth century.

European Patronage and Economic Decline, to 1878

After the Crimean War, declining state revenues and increasing integration with European commercial networks created hazardous economic conditions in the Ottoman Empire. Mahmud II's successors continued to secularize Ottoman financial and commercial institutions, modeling them closely on European counterparts. The Ottoman imperial bank was founded in 1840, and a few years later currency reform pegged the value of Ottoman gold coins to the British pound. Sweeping changes in the 1850s expedited the creation of banks, insurance companies, and legal firms throughout the empire. These and other reforms facilitating trade contributed to a strong demographic shift in the Ottoman Empire between about 1850 and 1880, as many people from the countryside headed for the cities Within this period many of the major cities of the empire—Istanbul, Ankara, Damascus, Cairo—doubled in size. A strong urban professional class emerged, as well as a considerable class of wage laborers. This shift was magnified by an influx into the northern Ottoman territories of refugees from Poland and Hungary, where rivalry between the European powers and the Russian Empire caused political tension and sporadic warfare.

The Ottoman reforms stimulated commerce and urbanization, but no reform could repair the chronic insolvency of the imperial government. Ottoman finances were damaged by declining revenues from agricultural yields and by widespread corruption. Some of the corruption received spectacular exposure in the early 1840s. From the conclusion of the Crimean War in 1856 on, the Ottoman government became heavily dependent on foreign loans. In return for loans, Ottoman tariffs were lowered to favor European imports, and European banks opened for business in Ottoman cities. The Ottoman currency was changed to allow more systematic conversion to European currencies. Europeans were allowed to live in Istanbul and other commercial centers in their own enclaves, subject to their own laws and exempt from Ottoman jurisdiction. This status was known as **extraterritoriality.**

As the cities prospered, they became attractive to laborers, and still more people moved from the countryside. But opportunities for wage workers reached a plateau in the bloated cities. Foreign trade brought in large numbers of imports, but—apart from the Turkish opium that American traders took to China to compete against the Indian opium of the British—few exports were sent abroad. Together with the growing national debt, these factors in the mid-1800s aggravated inflationary trends that left urban populations in a precarious position.

In the 1860s and 1870s, reform groups demanded a constitution, the possibility of a law permitting all men to vote was discussed, the prospect of the Muslims' loss of all political privilege arose. The Muslim majority was disturbed by the apparent signal that the Ottoman Empire was no longer a Muslim society. Muslims also were suspicious of the motives of Christians, many of whom were not of Turkish descent. Many Ottoman Muslims remembered attempts by Russia and France to interfere in Ottoman affairs in order to benefit Christians. Hostilities against Christians in Ottoman territories in Europe, Armenia, and the Middle East could be rationalized on the grounds of Turkish patriotism.

The decline of Ottoman power and prosperity had a strong impact on a group of urban and well-educated young men who aspired to wealth and influence. They believed that the Ottoman rulers would be forced to—or would be willing to—allow the continued domination of the empire's political, economic, and cultural life by Europeans. Inspired by the European nationalist movements of 1848 (see Chapter 23), they began to band together in the 1860s as the "Young Turks." The granting of a constitution in 1876 was regarded abroad as a great achievement because it was the first constitution to be adopted by an Islamic government. The apparent triumph of liberal reform was short lived. A *coup d'état* resulted in the enthroning of a new ruler who was hostile to democratization. A threat of war over the Balkans arose, and the imperial government used the crisis to disable the new Parliament and suspend the Constitution in 1877. But it did not quash the movement by Turks for greater independence from foreign interference. To the Young Turks, freedom from European domination required the destruction of the Ottoman Empire from within. They proposed to replace it with a Turkish national state, their "Fatherland." Though nationalism continued to be fostered by the leaders of the Young Turks—who exploited the new institutions of newspapers and private schools to spread their message—the Ottoman Empire continued its weakened existence under the sponsorship of Western powers until 1922.

THE QING EMPIRE AND FOREIGN COERCION

In 1800 the Qing Empire faced many of the crises the Ottomans had encountered, but no early reform movement of the kind initiated by Selim III emerged in China. The reasons are not difficult to understand. The Qing Empire, created by the Manchus, had distinguished itself in the 1600s for its adept maneuverings against Russia, both strategic and diplomatic. The Qing rulers had earned the admiration of the Jesuits, who transmitted to Europe a very appealing image of the emperors in China as enlightened philosopher-kings. But the failure in 1793 of the British attempt to establish diplomatic and trade relations with the Qing—the Macartney mission—turned European opinion against China, and in the very early 1800s few Europeans apart from traders based in Canton had much contact with or interest in China. For their part, the Qing rulers and bureaucrats were embroiled in some serious crises and had neither the time nor the inclination to explore new contacts with far-off Europeans. Complaints from European merchants at Canton, who

chafed against the restrictions of the "Canton system" by which the Qing limited and controlled foreign trade, were brushed off.

The empire's troubles were primarily domestic and seemed depressingly familiar to Chinese historians and officials: rebellions by displaced indigenous peoples and the poor, and protests against the injustice of the local magistrates. These troubles, it was thought, could be dealt with in the usual way, by suppressing rebels and dismissing incompetent or untrustworthy officials. Unlike the Ottoman rulers of the same period, the Qing rulers of 1800 had no compelling reason to think that cataclysmic challenges were headed their way.

Economic and Social Disorder

Early Qing successes gave rise to much of the domestic and political chaos of the later period. The Qing conquest in the 1600s brought stability to central China, previously subjected to decades of rebellion and agricultural shortages. The Qing emperors encouraged the recovery of farmland, the opening of previously uncultivated areas, and the restoration and expansion of the road and canal systems. The result was a great expansion of the agricultural base together with a doubling of the population between about 1650 and about 1800. Enormous numbers of farmers, merchants, and day laborers migrated across the Qing Empire in search of less crowded conditions, and a permanent floating population of the unemployed and homeless emerged. By 1800, population strain on the land had caused serious environmental damage in some parts of central and western China. Deforestation, erosion, and soil exhaustion left swollen populations stranded on rapidly deteriorating land.

Many groups had serious grievances against the government. Minority peoples in central and southwestern China resented having been driven off their lands during the boom of the 1700s. Mongols resisted the appropriation of their grazing lands and the displacement of their traditional elites. Village vigilante organizations had grown used to policing and practically governing regions that the Qing government had become too weak to manage. And growing numbers of people mistrusted the government, suspecting that all officials were corrupt. Discontent was aggravated by the growing presence of foreign merchants and missionaries in Canton and in the Portuguese colony of Macao.

In some parts of China the Qing were hated because they themselves were a foreign conquest regime and were suspected of having sympathies with the Europeans. Indeed as the nineteenth century opened, the

White Lotus Rebellion (1794–1804)—partly inspired by a mystical ideology that predicted the restoration of the Chinese Ming dynasty and the coming of the Buddha—was raging across central China and could not be suppressed until 1804.

The White Lotus was the first large rebellion in a series of internal conflicts that continued through the 1800s. Ignited by deepening social instabilities, these movements were sometimes intensified by local ethnic conflicts and by unapproved religions. The magnitude of the conflicts was increased by the improving ability of some village militias to defend themselves (and attack others). Some of these techniques were effectively utilized by southern coastal populations attempting to fend off British invasion.

The Opium War, 1839–1842

Unlike the Ottomans, the Qing believed that the Europeans were remote and only casually interested in trade. They knew little of the enormous fortunes being made in the early 1800s by European and American merchants smuggling opium into China. They did not know that silver gained in this illegal trade was helping to finance the industrial transformation of England and the United States. But Qing officials slowly learned that Britain was not really so far away. It had colonies in India, where opium was grown. And it had a major naval base at Singapore, through which it could transport opium to East Asia.

For more than a century, British officials had been frustrated by the enormous trade deficit caused by the British demand for tea and the Qing refusal to facilitate the importation to China of any British product. In the early 1700s, a few European merchants and their Chinese partners were importing small quantities of opium, and in 1729 the first Qing law making it illegal to import opium was promulgated. By 1800, however, smuggling had increased the quantity of annual imports of opium to as many as four thousand chests. British merchants had discovered an extremely profitable trade, and a large Chinese commerce had arisen around the distribution of the drugs that foreigners brought to shore. British importers were competing with Americans, and in the early 1820s a price war raised demand so sharply that by the 1830s as many as thirty thousand chests were being imported. Addiction spread to people at all levels of Qing society, including a large number of very high-ranking officials. For a time the Qing emperor and his officials debated whether to legalize and tax opium or to more strictly enforce the existing ban on the drug. They decided to root out the use and the importation of opium,

and in 1839 they sent Lin Zexu° to Canton to deal with the matter (see Society and Culture: Fighting the Opium Trade).

Britain considered the Qing ban on the importation of opium an intolerable restraint of trade, a direct threat to Britain's economic health, and indirectly a cause for war. British naval and marine forces arrived at the south China coast in late 1839. The significance of naval power, which the Ottomans had understood but not learned to master in the Mediterranean and Black Seas, dawned on the Qing slowly. Indeed, the difference between a naval invasion and piracy was not clear to Qing strategists until the Opium War was nearly ended.

The **Opium War** (1839–1842) broke out when negotiations between the Qing and British representatives became stalemated. The war exposed the fact that the traditional, hereditary soldiers of the Qing Empire—the **Bannermen**—were, like the Janissaries of the Ottoman Empire, hopelessly obsolete. As in the Crimean War, the British attempted to keep most confrontations on the sea, where they had a distinct technological advantage. British ships landed marines who pillaged coastal cities and then returned to their ships and sailed to new destinations (see Map 27.2). The Qing had no imperial navy, and until they were able to engage the British in prolonged fighting on land, they were unable to defend themselves against British attacks. Even in the land engagements, Qing resources proved woefully inadequate. The British could quickly transport their forces by sea along the coast. Qing troops, in contrast, moved primarily on foot. Moving Qing reinforcements from central to eastern China took more than three months, and when the defense forces arrived, they were exhausted and basically without weapons.

Against the British invaders, the Bannermen used the few muskets the Qing had imported during the 1700s. The weapons were matchlocks, which required the soldiers to ignite the load of gunpowder in them by hand. Firing the weapons was dangerous, and the canisters of gunpowder that each musketeer carried on his belt was likely to explode if a fire broke out nearby—a frequent occurrence in encounters with the British artillery. A majority of the Bannermen, however, had no guns and fought with swords, knives, spears, and clubs. Soldiers under British command—many of them were Indians—carried percussion-cap rifles, which were far quicker, safer, and more accurate than the matchlocks. In addition, the long-range artillery of the British could be moved from place to place and proved deadly in the cities and villages of eastern China.

Lin Zexu (lin zuh-SHOO)

Fighting the Opium Trade

In early 1839, Lin Zexu resigned his post as a provincial governor in order to act as a special imperial commissioner at Canton. The Qing court suspected that local officials were partial to the interests of the Canton merchants, and that enforcement of an anti-opium policy would be impossible without an agent as determined and honest as Lin Zexu. Shortly after his imperial appointment, Lin wrote to Queen Victoria, hoping to persuade her to prevent British merchants from continuing the opium trade.

We find that your country is [very far] from China. Yet there are barbarian ships that strive to come here for trade for the purpose of making a great profit. . . . That is to say, the great profit made by barbarians is all taken from the rightful share of China. By what right do they in return use the poisonous drug to injure the Chinese people? Even though the barbarians may not necessarily intend to do us harm, yet in coveting profit to an extreme, they have no regard for injuring others. Let us ask, where is your conscience? I have heard that the smoking of opium is very strictly forbidden by your country; that is because the harm caused by opium is clearly understood. Since it is not permitted to do harm to your own country, then even less should you let it be passed on to the harm of other countries—how much less to China! Of all that China exports to foreign countries, there is not a single thing which is not beneficial to people: they are of benefit when eaten, or of benefit when used, or of benefit when resold: all are beneficial. Is there a single article from China that has done harm to other countries?

When open warfare broke out between the Qing and British Empires, the governments of both countries blamed Lin for the conflict. The Qing court banished him to remote Xinjiang province. In a letter to a friend he reflected on the consequences of Qing technology gap with Britain.

When I was in office in [Canton] I had made plans regarding the problems of ships and cannon and a water force. Afraid that there was not enough time to build ships, I at first rented them. Afraid that there was not enough time to cast cannon and that it would not be done according to the regulations, I at first bought foreign ones. The most painful thing was that when the [harbor] was broken into, a large number of good cannon fell into the hands of the rebellious barbarians. I recall that after I had been punished two years ago, I still took the risk of calling the Emperor's attention to two things: ships and guns.

Though Lin's analysis of the predicament that the empire found itself in because of its neglect of technology was penetrating, it came too late. By the time Lin arrived at this conclusion, the Qing Empire was under such pressure from European powers and the United States that systematic, centralized reforms were very difficult to accomplish.

How do the attitudes expressed in these two passages from Lin's writings contrast with each other? How do they compare with the attitudes of Ottoman elites in the 1830s and 1840s?

Source: Adapted from Ssu-Yu Teng, Ssu-Tu-Teng, and John King Fairbank, *China's Response to the West: A Documentary Survey, 1839–1923* (Cambridge, MA: Harvard University Press, 1979), 24–29. Reprinted by permission of the publisher. Copyright © 1979 by the President and Fellows of Harvard College.

Qing commanders thought that British gunboats would ride so low in the water that they would not be able to sail up Chinese rivers, and that evacuating the coasts would protect the country from the British threat. But the British deployed new gunboats able to proceed in shallow water and moved without difficulty up the Yangzi River.

When the invaders approached Nanjing, the revered former Ming capital, the Qing decided to negotiate an end to the war. In 1842 the terms of the **Treaty of Nanking** (the British name for Nanjing) were concluded. The old Canton system was broken. The number of **treaty ports**—cities opened to foreign residents—was increased from one (Canton) to five (Canton, Xiamen,

Map 27.2 Conflicts in the Qing Empire, 1839–1870 In both the Opium War of 1839–1842 and the Arrow War of 1856–1860, the sea coasts saw most of the action. Since the Qing had no imperial navy, the well-armed British ships encountered little resistance as they shelled the southern coasts. In inland conflicts, such as the Taiping Rebellion, the opposing armies were massive and slow moving. Battles on land were often prolonged attempts by one side to starve out the other side before making a major assault.

Fuzhou, Ningbo, and Shanghai°), and the island of Hong Kong became a permanent British colony. British residents in China were granted the rights of extraterritoriality. The Qing government had to agree to a low tariff of 5 percent on imports and to pay an indemnity of 21 million ounces of silver to Britain as a penalty for having started the war. A supplementary treaty the following year guaranteed **most-favored nation status** to Britain: any privileges that China granted to another country would be automatically extended to Britain as well. This provision effectively prevented the colonization of China, because giving land to one country would have necessitated giving it to all.

With each round of treaties came a new round of privileges for foreigners. In 1860 a new treaty legalized the right of foreigners to import opium. Later, French treaties established the rights of foreign missionaries to travel extensively in the Chinese countryside and preach their religion. The number of treaty ports grew, too; by 1900 they numbered more than ninety.

The treaty system in China resulted in the colonization of small pockets of Qing territory, where foreign

---

Shanghai (shahng-hie)

merchants enjoyed the rights of extraterritoriality (the same system existed in the Ottoman Empire and elsewhere in Asia). As in the case of the Ottoman Empire, the greatest territorial losses for the Qing resulted from the actual or nominal independence of outlying regions it had dominated. In the early 1800s, Britain and Russia were both active in attempts to erase the last traces of Qing sovereignty in Central Asia. In the late 1800s France forced the court of Vietnam to end its vassalage to the Qing, while Britain encouraged Tibetan independence.

In Canton, Shanghai, and other coastal cities, Europeans and Americans maintained offices and factories in which all but a few of the local Chinese were assigned to menial labor. The foreigners built comfortable housing in zones where Chinese were not permitted to live, and they entertained themselves in exclusive restaurants and bars. Around the foreign establishments, gambling and prostitution offered employment to some of the local urban population.

Often, the work of Christian missionaries both in the cities and in the countryside was regarded as benevolent, as when the congregations sponsored hospitals, shelters, and soup kitchens or gave stipends to Chinese who attended church. But just as often the missionaries themselves were regarded as another evil. They seemed to subvert Confucian beliefs, whether by condemning ancestor worship, pressuring poor families to put their children into orphanages, or fulminating against footbinding. The growing numbers of foreigners, and their growing privileges, quickly became a target of resentment for a deeply dissatisfied, daily more impoverished, and increasingly militarized society.

The Taiping Rebellion, 1850–1864

The most startling demonstration of the inflammatory mixture of social unhappiness and foreign intrusion was the great civil war usually called the **Taiping Rebellion.** In Guangxi, where the Taiping movement originated, entrenched social problems had been generating disorders for half a century. Agriculture in the region was unstable, and many people made their living from arduous and despised trades such as disposing of human waste, making charcoal, and mining. Ethnic divisions complicated economic distress. A minority group, the Hakkas, were frequently to be found in the lowliest trades, and tensions between them and the majority were rising. It is possible that the local economy had been affected by the sharp rises and falls in the trade of opium, which after 1842 flooded the coastal and riverine portions of China, then collapsed as domestically grown opium began to dominate the market. Also, the area was

close enough to Canton to feel the cultural and economic impact of the growing number of Europeans and Americans.

All these factors were significant in the experience of Hong Xiuquan°, the founder of the Taiping movement. Hong came from a humble Hakka background. After years of study, he competed in the provincial Confucian examinations, hoping for a post in government. He failed the examinations repeatedly, and it appears that in his late thirties he suffered a nervous breakdown. Afterward he spent some time in Canton, where he met both Chinese and American Protestant missionaries, who inspired him with their teachings. Hong had his own interpretation of the Christian message. He saw himself as the younger brother of Jesus, commissioned by God to found a new kingdom on earth and drive the Manchu conquerors, the Qing, out of China. The result would be universal peace. Hong called his new religious movement the "Heavenly Kingdom of Great Peace."

Hong quickly attracted a community of believers, primarily Hakkas like himself. They believed in the prophecy of dreams and claimed they could walk on air. Hong and his rivals for leadership in the movement went in and out of ecstatic trances. They denounced the Manchus as creatures of Satan. News of the heresy reached the government, and Qing troops were sent to arrest the Taiping leaders. But the Taipings soundly repelled the imperial troops. Local loyalty to the Taipings spread quickly, their numbers multiplied, and they began to enlarge their domain.

It appears that at first the Taipings relied on Hakka sympathy and the charismatic appeal of their religious doctrine to attract followers. But as their numbers and power grew, they altered their methods of preaching and governing. They stopped enlisting Hakkas with anti-Chinese appeals and began to enlist Chinese with anti-Manchu rhetoric. They forced the populations of captured villages to join their movement, and once people were absorbed, the Taipings strictly monitored their activities. They segregated men and women and organized them into work and military teams. Women were forbidden to bind their feet (the Hakkas had never practiced footbinding), and they participated fully in farming and laboring. Brigades of women soldiers took to the field against Qing forces.

As the movement grew, it began to move toward eastern and northern China (see Map 27.2). Panic preceded the Taipings. Villagers feared being forced into Taiping units, and Confucian elites recoiled in horror from the bizarre ideology of foreign gods, totalitarian rule, and walking, working, warring women. But the

Hong Xiuquan (hoong shee-OH-chew-an)

Nanjing Encircled   For a decade the Taipings held the city of Nanjing as their capital. For years Qing and international troops attempted to break the Taiping hold. By the summer of 1864, Qing forces had built tunnels leading to the foundations of Nanjing's city walls and had planted explosives. The detonation of the explosives signaled the final Qing assault on the rebel capital. As shown here, the common people of the city, along with their starving livestock, were caught in the cross-fire. Many of the Taiping leaders escaped the debacle at Nanjing, but nearly all were hunted down and executed.   (Roger-Viollet)

huge numbers the Taipings were able to muster overwhelmed attempts at local defense. The tremendous growth in the number of Taiping followers required the movement to establish a permanent base. When the rebel army conquered Nanjing in 1853, the Taiping leaders decided to settle there and make it the capital of the new "Heavenly Kingdom of Great Peace."

At the time the Taipings were brought to a halt by the growth of their population and their organization, Qing forces attempting to defend north China against them were becoming more successful. Increasing Qing military success was due mainly to the flexibility of the imperial military commanders in the face of an unprecedented challenge. In addition, the military commanders received strong backing from a group of civilian provincial governors who had studied the techniques developed by local militia forces for self-defense. In essence, certain of the provincial governors, especially Zeng Guofan°, combined their knowledge of civilian self-defense and local terrain with more efficient organization and the use of modern weaponry. The result was the formation of new military units, in which many of the Bannermen voluntarily served under civilian governors. The Qing court agreed to special taxes to fund the new armies and acknowledged the new combined leadership of the civilian and professional force.

Zeng Guofan (zung gwoh-FAN)

When the Taipings settled into Nanjing, the new Qing armies surrounded the city, hoping to starve out the rebels. The Taipings, however, had provisioned and fortified themselves well. They also had the services of several brilliant young military commanders, who mobilized enormous campaigns in nearby parts of eastern China, scavenging supplies and attempting to break the encirclement of Nanjing. For more than a decade the Taiping leadership remained ensconced at Nanjing, and the "Heavenly Kingdom" endured.

In 1856, Britain and France, freed from their preoccupation with the Crimean War, turned their attention to China. European and American missionaries had visited Nanjing, curious to see what their fellow Christians were up to. The reports they sent home were discouraging. Hong Xiuquan and the other leaders appeared to lead lives of indulgence and abandon, and more than one missionary accused them of homosexual practices. Now having no fear of being accused of quashing an appealing Christian movement, the British and French considered the situation. Though the Taipings were not going to topple the Qing, the outbreak of a rebellion by the Nian in northern China in the 1850s was ominous. A series of simultaneous large insurrections might indeed destroy the empire. Perhaps more important, Britain and France were now considering making war on the Qing again themselves. The Qing had not observed the provisions of the treaties signed after the Opium War, and European patience was exhausted.

In 1856 the British and French launched a series of swift, brutal coastal attacks—a second opium war, called the Arrow War (1856–1860)—which culminated in a British and French invasion of Beijing and the sacking of the Summer Palace in 1860. A new round of treaties punished the Qing for not enacting all the provisions of the Treaty of Nanking. Having secured their principal objective, the British and French forces now joined the Qing in the campaign against the Taipings. Attempts to coordinate the international forces were sometimes riotous and sometimes tragic, but the injection of European weaponry and money aided in the quelling of both the Taiping and the Nian Rebellions during the 1860s.

The Taiping Rebellion ranks as the world's bloodiest civil war and the greatest armed conflict before the twentieth century. Estimates of deaths range from 20 million to 30 million. The loss of life was due primarily to starvation and disease, for most engagements consisted of surrounding the enemy holed up in fortified cities and waiting until they died, surrendered, or were so weakened that they could be easily defeated. Many sieges continued for months, and people within some cities found that after starving for a year under the occupation of the rebels they had to starve for another year under the occupation of the imperial forces. Reports of people eating grass, leather, hemp, and human flesh were widespread. The dead were rarely buried properly, and epidemic disease was common.

The area of early Taiping fighting was close to the regions of southwest China where bubonic plague had been lingering for centuries. When the rebellion was suppressed, many Taiping followers sought safety in the highlands of Laos and Vietnam, which soon showed infestation by plague. Within a few years the disease reached Hong Kong. From there it spread to Singapore, San Francisco, Calcutta, and London. In the late 1800s there was intense apprehension over the possibility of a worldwide outbreak, and Chinese immigrants were regarded as likely carriers. This fear became a contributing factor in the passage of discriminatory immigration bans on Chinese in the United States in 1882.

The Taiping Rebellion devastated the agricultural centers of China. Many of the most intensely cultivated regions of central and eastern China were depopulated and laid barren. Decades later, some were still uninhabited, and provincial population figures show that major portions of the country did not recover until the twentieth century. Cities, too, were hard hit. Shanghai, a treaty port of modest size before the rebellion, saw its population multiplied many times by the arrival of refugees from the war-blasted neighboring provinces. The city then endured months of siege by the Taipings. Major cultural centers in eastern China lost masterpieces of art and architecture, imperial libraries were burned or their collections exposed to the weather, and the printing blocks used to make books were destroyed. While the empire faced the mountainous challenge of dealing with the material and cultural destruction from the war, it also was burdened by a major ecological disaster in the north: the Yellow River changed course in 1855, destroying the south part of impoverished Shandong province with flood and leaving the former riverbed in northern Shandong to decades of drought.

Decentralization at the End of the Qing Empire

The Qing government emerged from the 1850s with no hope of achieving solvency. The treasury had been bankrupted by the corruption of the 1700s, the attempts in the very early 1800s to restore waterworks and roads, and declining yields from land taxes. By 1850, before the Taiping Rebellion had begun, the Qing government already was spending ten times more than it took in. The burden of indemnities demanded by Europeans after the Opium and Arrow Wars foreclosed any hope that the Qing would get out of debt. Vast stretches of formerly productive rice land were devastated, the population was dispersed, immediate relief for refugees was demanded, and the imperial, volunteer, foreign, and mercenary troops that had suppressed the Taipings were demanding their unpaid wages.

With the Qing government so deeply in their debt, Britain and France became active participants in the period of recovery in China that followed the rebellion. This period is sometimes called the "Tongzhi Restoration," since it occurred during the reign of Tongzhi (r. 1862–1875). To ensure that the Qing government began repaying its debt to Britain, Robert Hart was installed as inspector-general of a newly created Imperial Maritime Customs Service. The revenues he collected were split between Britain and the Qing. Britons and Americans put themselves in the employ of the Qing government as advisers and ambassadors, attempting to smooth communications between the Qing, Europe, and the United States while the imperial government started up the diplomatic machinery demanded by Europe in its latest treaties.

The real work of the recovery, however, was managed by the provincial governors who had come to the forefront in the struggle against the Taipings. To prosecute the war, they had won the right to levy their own taxes, raise their own troops, and run their own bureaucracies. These special powers were not entirely canceled when the war ended. Chief among these governors was Zeng Guofan, who oversaw programs to restore agriculture, communications, education, and publishing, as well as efforts to reform the military and industrialize armaments manufacture.

Like many provincial governors, Zeng preferred to look to the United States rather than to Britain for models and aid. He hired American advisers to run his weapons factories, shipyards, and military academies. He sponsored a daring program in which promising Chinese boys were sent to Hartford, Connecticut, to learn English, science, mathematics, engineering, and history. They returned to China to assume some of the positions previously held by foreign advisers. Though Zeng was never an advocate of participation in public life by women, he was a firm adherent of the Confucian elite view that educated mothers were a necessity, perhaps now more than ever. He not only encouraged but partly oversaw the advanced classical education of his own daughters. Zeng's death in 1872 deprived the empire of a major force for reform.

The period of recovery marked a fundamental structural change in the Qing Empire. Although the emperors after 1850 were ineffective rulers, a coalition of aristocrats supported the reform and recovery programs. If they had been unwilling to legitimate the new powers of provincial governors such as Zeng Guofan, the empire

Cixi's Allies In the 1860s and 1870s, Cixi was a supporter of reform. In later years she was widely regarded as corrupt and self-centered and as an obstacle to reform. Her greatest allies were the court eunuchs. Introduced to palace life in early China as managers of the imperial harems, eunuchs became powerful political parties at court. The first Qing emperors refused to allow the eunuchs any political influence, but by Cixi's time the eunuchs once again were a political factor. (Freer Gallery, Smithsonian Institution)

might have evaporated within a generation. A crucial member of this alliance was Cixi°, after the 1880s known as the "Empress Dowager." Later observers, both Chinese and foreign, reviled her as a monster of corruption and arrogance. But in the 1860s and 1870s Cixi was a supporter of the provincial governors, some of whom became so powerful that they were managing Qing foreign policy as well as domestic affairs.

No longer a conquest regime dominated by a Manchu military caste and its Chinese civilian appointees, the empire came under the control of a group of reformist aristocrats and military men, independently powerful civilian governors, and a small number of foreign advisers. The Qing lacked strong, central, unified leadership, and could not recover their powers of taxation, legislation, and military command once they had been granted to the provincial governors. From the 1860s forward, the Qing Empire disintegrated into a set of large power zones in which provincial governors handed over leadership to their protégés in a pattern that the Qing court eventually could only ritually legitimate.

JAPAN FROM SHOGUNATE TO EMPIRE

The Qing Empire in the 1600s and 1700s had worked systematically to establish centralized control over China and its neighboring regions. In Japan, a completely different political organization was in place. For a thousand years Japan had had a ruler who in English is called an "emperor," but this ruler had no political power. Instead, since the twelfth century Japan had been governed by shogunates—decentralized secular government under a military leader (*shogun*) who was loyal to the emperor. This was an effective solution to the civil wars that on occasion afflicted Japan. Local lords were permitted to control their lands and populations with very little interference from the shogunate, and enough of the lords remained loyal to the shogun to prevent very frequent changes of regime.

In times of threat from outside, this system showed many weaknesses. It did not permit the coordination of resources and communications on a national scale that would be necessary to resist a major invasion from abroad. Shoguns and their advisers understood the basic weakness of the system and attempted to minimize ex-

posure to and possible threat from foreign powers. In the early 1600s they prohibited foreigners from entering Japan and Japanese from going abroad.

The penalties for breaking these laws was death, but many Japanese ignored them anyway. The most flagrant violations were by powerful local lords in southern Japan, who ran large and very successful pirate operations or black-market trade in stolen or faked passes granting entry into the carefully regulated Qing trading ports. In their entrepreneurial activities these local lords benefited from the decentralization of the shogunal political system. But when a genuine foreign threat was suggested—as when, in 1792, Russian and British ships were spotted off the Japanese coast in separate incidents—the local lords realized that their relative independence would be no help if there was a foreign invasion.

For a time, the Tokugawa Shogunate responded to the threat of foreign invasion by attempting to strengthen its finances and its military forces, much as the more centralized Ottoman and Qing Empires had done. But unlike those empires, the Tokugawa government was limited in the measures it could decree to improve national preparedness, and it was not able to carry out a single policy to resist European and American encroachment. Instead, some of the regional lords of Japan, who did not believe the Tokugawa Shogunate had the ability or the will to protect the islands, developed their own reformed armies, arsenals, and shipyards. In 1853 the arrival of a small U.S. fleet with demands for an opening of Japan to trade with the United States started a process that ended with the destruction of the Tokugawa Shogunate by leaders of the more powerful provinces.

Collapse of the Shogunate

By the 1800s, several of the regional provinces had emerged as much wealthier and more ambitious than others. This was particularly true of Satsuma° and Choshu°, two large domains in southern Japan (see Map 27.3). Because the ancestors of their ruling houses had not been supporters of the Tokugawa lineage, they were punished by being given sparsely settled lands far from the shogunal court. Over time, this location proved to offer a distinct advantage. These regions could rapidly expand their agricultural base when more central regions had reached their limits, and Satsuma and Choshu enjoyed high rates of growth in revenue and population during the early 1800s. The remoteness and the economic vigor of these provinces also fostered a strong sense of local self-reliance.

Map 27.3 Tokugawa Japan, to 1867 The Tokugawa Shogunate was the last of the decentralized governments of Japan that put primary power into the hands of a military leader and protector of the emperor. Under the Tokugawa regime, provincial leaders at the western extreme of Honshu Island—regarded as an undesirable site in the early Tokugawa period—experienced higher rates of economic growth and managerial innovation than did provincial leaders in the central provinces.

The economic and political weakness of the shogunate prompted some leaders in the Tokugawa government to attempt a restrengthening, primarily by placing new burdens on the hereditary provincial governors. Some provincial academies for aspiring soldiers, scholars, and bureaucrats became centers for the development and dissemination of a new ideology of loyalty to the shoguns, who depended on the politically weak emperors of Japan for their legitimacy. But the arrival of the American Commodore Matthew C. Perry and his fleet of what the Japanese called "black ships" in 1853 shattered the shogunate's attempts to restore its influence across the provinces. While the Japanese, like other East Asians, had been focused on intruders from their west such as the Dutch, British, French, and Russians, the Americans'

search for a route to bring pelts from northwest America across the Pacific had led them to surprise Japan with an approach from the east. Perry demanded that Japan open its ports to U.S. ships for refueling and for trade when he returned in 1854.

Perry's terms sparked a crisis in the shogunate. Consultation among the provincial governors and the shogunal officials was extensive. In the end, the shogunal advisers advocated capitulation to Perry. They pointed to China's humiliating defeats in the Opium and Arrow Wars and expressed doubt that the treaty powers in China would be discouraged from seeking other ports in East Asia. Leaders of the provincial governors opposed this view. They pointed out that the United States was not a formidable power like Britain and predicted that a

Arrivals from the East   In 1853 Commodore Matthew Perry's ships surprised the Tokugawa Shogunate by appearing not in Kyushu or southern Honshu, where European ships previously had been spotted, but at Uraga on the coast of eastern Honshu. The Japanese soon learned that Perry had come not from the south but across the Pacific from the east. The novelty of the threat unsettled the provincial leaders, who were largely responsible for their own defense. In this print done after the Meiji Restoration, the traditionally dressed local samurai go out to confront the mysterious "black ships."   (Courtesy of the Trustees of the British Museum)

refusal by Japan would result only in the Americans seeking an easier refueling location elsewhere.

In 1854, Perry's fleet returned, and representatives of the Tokugawa shogun indicated their willingness to sign the Treaty of Kanagawa°—modeled on the unequal treaties between China and the Western powers. Before provincial leaders considered the discussion closed, shogunal representatives signed the treaty in 1858. Angry and disappointed, some provincial governors began to encourage an underground movement calling for the destruction of the Tokugawa regime and the banning of foreigners from Japan.

___

Kanagawa (KAH-nah-GAH-wah)

Tensions between the shogunate and some provincial leaders, particularly in Choshu and Satsuma, increased in the early 1860s. British and French shelling of the southwestern coasts in 1864 further enraged provincial samurai who rejected the Treaty of Kanagawa and resented the Shogunate's inability to protect the country. Young, ambitious, educated men who faced mediocre prospects under the rigid Tokugawa class system emerged as provincial leaders. Among them, the Choshu leaders Yamagata Aritomo and Ito Hitobumi were outstanding. They realized in 1867 that they should stop warring with their rival province, Satsuma, and instead join forces to lead a rebellion against the shogunate. The civil war was intense but brief. In 1868, a new government was founded, and the young emperor Mutsuhito (r. 1868–1912) was declared "restored."

The Meiji Restoration

To destroy the old state was one thing; to create a new state with the resources and will to deal with economic and military problems was quite another. Though Japan is smaller than the landmass of either the Qing or the Ottoman Empire, its many islands are far-flung and its natural resources extremely limited. Thus the size of Japan was not necessarily a major explanation for the apparent ease with which it was reformed. Perhaps more important was the fact that, unlike the Qing and Ottoman Empires, Japan was of no great strategic importance to Europe or the United States.

American merchants expected that Japan, like China, would be a rich market for their goods, and American naval planners wanted a reprovisioning station in Japan to facilitate the movement of U.S. ships along the China coast. But neither of these considerations would have propelled the United States to initiate war with Japan in the 1850s. Also, the European powers showed only a casual interest in Japan. Thus there was no foreign effort to economically or strategically sustain the Tokugawa Shogunate, and when it was destroyed, the small group who controlled the new government—often called the Meiji° oligarchs—were unimpeded in their plans for a centralized, industrialized national state.

The ideology of the new state, known by Mutsuhito's reign name, *Meiji*, ("enlightened rule"), was one source of its power. By "restoring" the emperor, the new leaders claimed to have ended centuries of imperial seclusion and disempowerment by the shoguns. The mysticism of the emperors, nationalism, and anxiety over the foreign threat were all combined to create a decade of focused effort on the transformation of Japan from a decentralized, traditional military government to a centralized, civil, industrializing state. The nationalistic ideology of the Meiji Restoration coexisted with intense interest in European practices in government, education, industry, dress, and even popular culture.

The achievements of the **Meiji Restoration** were remarkable. The oligarchs were extraordinarily talented and far-sighted men. They overcame regional resistance to political and social reform, and gradually but systematically they effected the dissolution of the traditional provincial governorships and of the samurai class. Though the Tokugawa government had been poor, there was

Meiji (MAY-gee)

wealth in some of the provinces. The literacy rate may have been as high as 35 percent—certainly the highest in Asia at the time—and the oligarchs shrewdly exploited it in their introduction of new educational systems, a conscript army, and new communications. The government was able to establish heavy industry through the use of judicious deficit financing without extensive foreign debt, thanks to decades of experimentation with industrial development and financing in the provinces in the earlier 1800s. With a conscript army and a revamped educational system the oligarchs attempted to create a new citizenry that was literate and competent but also loyal and obedient.

CONCLUSION

The response of Japan to the challenge of the industrializing nations was a striking contrast to the responses of the Ottoman and Qing Empires. An important point of comparison is the relationship between financial resources and reform from the elite levels downward. In the Ottoman and Qing (as well as the Russian) Empires, the imperial courts attempted to mandate reforms in the military. To meet the cost, these revenue-starved empires debased their currencies, thereby stimulating inflation. To continue the reforms, they became dependent on foreign loans, which ultimately led to control of their finances, commercial strategies, and in some cases revenue-producing organs by European powers. Japan, in contrast, experienced comparatively few top-down major reforms under the Tokugawa shoguns. Instead, the decentralized provinces provided their own means of experimenting with local military improvement, new educational programs, and deficit financing before the Meiji Restoration of 1868. Afterward, they could compare their experiences and apply what they had learned.

Japan's exposure to the military and economic pressure of the sea powers was much more limited than that of the Ottoman and Qing Empires. One reason for this difference was that Japan was not an empire in the same sense. It did not control extensive trade networks and urban centers to which Britain and France wished to gain privileged access. Nor was its position, on the far eastern of the Eurasian continent, regarded as strategically significant in the West. The treaty that the United States forced on Japan was practically Japan's only experience with unequal treaties. In contrast, the Treaty of Nanking of 1842 ushered in the period of unequal treaties that resulted in the installation of a vast system of foreign privilege in China. European and American pressure on the Qing Empire became so intense that the Chinese could neither learn to finance the industries necessary for a strong military nor find a period of peace in which to develop the educational institutions that would have produced a new generation of leaders.

The Meiji oligarchs hoped that Japan's relatively remote location and relatively insignificant political status would permit it breathing space to make the revolutionary changes they envisaged. The Qing and the Ottoman rulers could only hope that mutual distrust by the European powers would limit the ambitions of any individual European state. This strategy—in China known as "using the barbarians against the barbarians"—continually embroiled the Qing Empire in short, localized wars or threatened wars with aspiring signatories in the unequal treaty system.

In the Qing territories and in the Ottoman Empire, Europeans and Americans did not need to establish colonies in order to enjoy privileged status. Neither Ottoman nor Qing lands were in need of "development" by colonial forces. Pockets of wealth—primarily in the cities—could be exploited, and this maneuvering was best done through strategic alliances or diplomacy, not by the expensive and risky methods of colonization. It is not a coincidence that both of the empires whose territorial integrity the European powers—and, in the case of China, the United States—swore to defend were ultimately derided as the "sick men" of Eurasia, unable to defend themselves against their defenders, and kept in a state of low-grade survival to provide markets, raw materials, and strategic advantages to smaller, more dynamic nations.

The Crimean War and Taiping Rebellion were watershed events in the loss of centralization and autonomy for, respectively, the Ottoman and Qing Empires. In each conflict the Eurasian empire in question emerged as nominally victorious. But both land-based empires were overextended. They suffered from declining revenues and social dislocation. Ironically, within these empires were enclaves of merchants and artisans who were enriched by the trade with Europe and America, but the imperial governments never found a way to tax these new incomes.

Much domestic wealth flowed from the Ottoman and Qing Empires to foreign countries in payment for legal as well as illegal commodities, and state resources for arms and education could not be found. Increasing pressure from Britain and France deepened the financial woes and political tensions of both empires and heightened the elite's awareness of the necessity for military reform. During the Crimean War and the Taiping Rebellion, the financial obligations of each empire and the strategic advantages of its existence led to the formation of alliances with Britain and France. And in the aftermath of the conflicts, each empire experienced serious problems with decentralization, loss of control over its borders, permanent indebtedness and inflation, a progressive loss of international and domestic credibility, and new dependence on foreign protection.

The differences between the Ottoman and Qing also are illuminating. The Ottomans made an attempt to modernize their military and make their government more efficient before the end of the 1700s. Their proximity to Europe gave them direct experience with the Napoleonic era and the rising nationalism of the 1800s. The intense struggle between France and Russia, in particular, gave the Ottomans a strategic position that made it distinctly to the advantage of France to side with the Ottomans in their territorial struggles. For their part, the Ottomans were comparatively swift in their adaptation of aspects of French culture, military practices, and commercial institutions. This adaptability sustained Ottoman political credibility in Europe through the critical period of the war for Greek independence, and later it allowed design and implementation of the reform program under Mahmud II. On the strength of that recentralization, the secular programs that defined a civil sphere and a Turkish identity gave strength to the very nationalist movement that eventually helped destroy the empire.

Unlike the Ottomans, the Qing were not able to achieve even a modest degree of recentralization. Suppression of the Taiping Rebellion required the dissolution of the traditional military structures, the regionalization of command and support, and finally the use of foreign troops. The alliance formed by Britain and France at this time was to become more active in the very late 1800s, as the European powers and the United States attempted repeatedly to prevent the colonization of Qing territory by Japan.

■ Key Terms

Janissaries	Opium War
Serbia	Bannermen
Tanzimat	Treaty of Nanking
Crimean War	treaty ports
percussion cap	most-favored-nation status
breech-loading rifle	Taiping Rebellion
extraterritoriality	Meiji Restoration

■ Suggested Reading

For the Ottoman Empire there is a large and interesting literature, much of it based on original documents, some in translation, relating to Ottoman administration throughout Europe and the Middle East. For widely available general histories see Stanford Shaw, *History of the Ottoman Empire and Modern Turkey* (1976–1977), and J.P.D.B. Kinross, *The Ottoman Centuries: The Rise and Fall of the Turkish Empire* (1977).

On the economy and society of the nineteenth-century Ottoman Empire see Huri Islamoglu-Inan, ed., *The Ottoman Empire and the World-Economy* (1987); Resat Kasaba, *The Ottoman Empire and the World Economy: The Nineteenth Century* (1988); Sevket Pamuk, *The Ottoman Empire and European Capitalism, 1820–1913: Trade, Investment, and Production* (1987); Kemal H. Karpat, *Ottoman Population, 1830–1914: Demographic and Social Characteristics* (1985); and Carter V. Findley, *Bureaucratic Reform in the Ottoman Empire: The Sublime Porte, 1789–1922* (1980). On the reform program and the emergence of national concepts see also Selim Deringil, *The Well-Protected Domains: Ideology and the Legitimation of Power in the Ottoman Empire, 1876–1909* (1998).

On the Qing Empire of the nineteenth century see Pamela Kyle Crossley, *Orphan Warriors: Three Manchu Generations and the End of the Qing World* (1990), and for a more detailed political history see Mary C. Wright, *The Last Stand of Chinese Conservatism: The T'ung-chih Restoration, 1862–1874* (1971). There is a very large literature on both the Opium War and the Taiping Rebellion, including reprinted editions of contemporary observers. For general histories of the Opium War see Peter Ward Fay, *The Opium War, 1840–1842: Barbarians in the Celestial Empire in the Early Part of the Nineteenth Century and the War by Which They Forced Her Gates Ajar* (1975); Christopher Hibbert, *The Dragon Wakes: China and the West, 1793–1911* (1970); and the classic study by Chang Hsin-pao, *Commissioner Lin and the Opium War* (1964). For a recent, more monographic study on Qing political thought in the period of the Opium War see James M. Polachek, *The Inner Opium War* (1992). On the Taiping Rebellion, enduring sources are S. Y. Têng, *The Taiping Rebellion and the Western Powers: A Comprehensive Survey* (1971), and C. A. Curwen, *Taiping Rebel: the Deposition of Li Hsiuch'eng* (1976); see also Caleb Carr, *The Devil Soldier: the Story of Frederick Townsend Ward* (1992). The most recent study is Jonathan D. Spence, *God's Chinese Son: The Taiping Heavenly Kingdom of Hong Xiuquan* (1996).

The classic work on the period leading to the Meiji Restoration in Japan is Albert M. Craig, *Choshu in the Meiji Restoration* (1961). See also Conrad Totman, *The Collapse of the Tokugawa Bakufu, 1862–1868* (1980), Bob Tadashi Wakabayashi, *Anti-Foreignism and Western Learning in Early-Modern Japan: The New Theses of 1825* (1986); Peter Booth Wiley with Korogi Ichiro, *Yankees in the Land of the Gods: Commodore Perry and the Opening of Japan* (1990); and George M. Wilson, *Patriots and Redeemers in Japan : Motives in the Meiji Restoration* (1992).

GLOSSARY

The glossary for *The Earth and Its Peoples,* 2/e is for the complete text, Chapters 1 through 35.

Abbas the Great (1571–1629) Shah of Iran (r. 1587–1629). The most illustrious ruler of the **Safavid Empire,** he moved the imperial capital to Isfahan in 1598, where he erected many palaces, mosques, and public buildings. (*p. 533*)

Abbasid Caliphate Descendants of the Prophet Muhammad's uncle, al-Abbas, the Abbasids overthrew the **Umayyad Caliphate** and ruled an Islamic empire from their capital in Baghdad (founded 762) from 750 to 1258. (*p. 234*)

abolitionists Men and women who agitated for a complete end to slavery. British abolitionists pressed for the abolition of the transatlantic slave trade in 1808 and slavery in 1834. In the United States the activities of abolitionists were one factor leading to the Civil War (1861–1865). (*p. 636*)

absolutism The theory popular in France and other early modern European monarchies that royal power should be free of constitutional checks. (*p. 452*)

Acheh Sultanate Muslim kingdom in northern Sumatra. Main center of Islamic expansion in Southeast Asia in the early seventeenth century, it declined after the Dutch seized **Malacca** from Portugal in 1641. (*p. 541*)

acculturation The adoption of the language, customs, values, and behaviors of host nations by immigrants. (*p. 640*)

acllas Women selected by Inca authorities to serve in religious centers as weavers and ritual participants. (*p. 318*)

Aden Port city in the modern south Arabian country of Yemen. It has been a major trading center in the Indian Ocean since ancient times. (*p. 385*)

African National Congress An organization dedicated to obtaining equal voting and civil rights for black inhabitants of South Africa. Founded in 1912 as the South African Native National Congress, it changed its name in 1923. Though it was banned and its leaders were jailed for many years, it eventually helped bring majority rule to South Africa. (*p. 809*)

Afrikaners South Africans descended from Dutch and French settlers of the seventeenth century. Their Great Trek founded new settler colonies in the nineteenth century. Though a minority among South Africans, they held political power after 1910, imposing a system of racial segregation called apartheid after 1949. (*pp. 665, 735*)

Agricultural Revolution(s) (ancient) The change from food gathering to food production that occurred between ca. 8000 and 2000 B.C.E. Also known as the Neolithic Revolution. (*p. 17*)

Agricultural Revolution (eighteenth century) The transformation of farming that resulted in the eighteenth century from the spread of new crops, improvements in cultivation techniques and livestock breeding, and the consolidation of small holdings into large farms from which tenants and sharecroppers were forcibly expelled. (*p. 600*)

Aguinaldo, Emilio (1869–1964) Leader of the Filipino independence movement against Spain (1895–1898). He proclaimed the independence of the Philippines in 1899, but his movement was crushed and he was captured by the United States Army in 1901. (*p. 743*)

Akbar I (1542–1605) Most illustrious sultan of the Mughal Empire in India (r. 1556–1605). He expanded the empire and pursued a policy of conciliation with Hindus. (*p. 536*)

Akhenaten Egyptian pharaoh (r. 1353–1335 B.C.E.). He built a new capital at Amarna, fostered a new style of naturalistic art, and created a religious revolution by imposing worship of the sun-disk. The Amarna letters, largely from his reign, preserve official correspondence with subjects and neighbors. (*p. 66*)

Alexander (356–323 B.C.E.) King of Macedonia in northern Greece. Between 334 and 323 B.C.E. he conquered the Persian Empire, reached the Indus Valley, founded many Greek-style cities, and spread Greek culture across the Middle East. Later known as Alexander the Great. (*p. 136*)

Alexandria City on the Mediterranean coast of Egypt founded by Alexander. It became the capital of the Hellenistic kingdom of the **Ptolemies.** It contained the famous Library and the Museum—a center for leading scientific and literary figures. Its merchants engaged in trade with areas bordering the Mediterranean and the Indian Ocean. (*p. 138*)

Allende, Salvador (1908–1973) Socialist politician elected president of Chile in 1970 and overthrown by the military in 1973. He died during the military attack. (*p. 856*)

All-India Muslim League Political organization founded in India in 1906 to defend the interests of India's Muslim minority. Led by Muhammad Ali Jinnah, it attempted to negotiate with the **Indian National Congress.** In 1940, the League began demanding a separate state for Muslims, to be called Pakistan. (See also **Jinnah, Muhammad Ali.**) (*p. 813*)

amulet Small charm meant to protect the bearer from evil. Found frequently in archaeological excavations in Mesopotamia and Egypt, amulets reflect the religious practices of the common people. (*p. 37*)

Anasazi Important culture of what is now the southwest of the United States (1000–1300 C.E.). Centered on Chaco Canyon in New Mexico and Mesa Verde in Colorado, the Anasazi culture built multistory residences and worshipped in subterranean buildings called kivas. (*p. 308*)

aqueduct A conduit, either elevated or under ground, using gravity to carry water from a source to a location—usually a city—that needed it. The Romans built many aqueducts in a period of substantial urbanization. (*p. 156*)

Arawak Amerindian peoples who inhabited the Greater Antilles of the Caribbean at the time of Columbus. (*p. 423*)

Arkwright, Richard (1732–1792) English inventor and entrepreneur who became the wealthiest and most successful textile manufacturer of the early **Industrial Revolution.** He invented the water frame, a machine that, with minimal human supervision, could spin many strong cotton threads at once. (*p. 604*)

Armenia One of the earliest Christian kingdoms, situated in eastern Anatolia and the western Caucasus and occupied by speakers of the Armenian language. (*p. 221*)

Asante African kingdom on the **Gold Coast** that expanded rapidly after 1680. Asante participated in the Atlantic economy, trading gold, slaves, and ivory. It resisted British imperial ambitions for a quarter century before being absorbed into Britain's Gold Coast colony in 1902. (*p. 736*)

Ashikaga Shogunate (1336–1573) The second of Japan's military governments headed by a shogun (a military ruler). Sometimes called the Muromachi Shogunate. (*p. 365*)

Ashoka Third ruler of the **Mauryan Empire** in India (r. 270–232 B.C.E.). He converted to Buddhism and broadcast his precepts on inscribed stones and pillars, the earliest surviving Indian writing. (*p. 184*)

Ashur Chief deity of the Assyrians, he stood behind the king and brought victory in war. Also the name of an important Assyrian religious and political center. (*p. 94*)

Asian Tigers Collective name for South Korea, Taiwan, Hong Kong, and Singapore—nations that became economic powers in the 1970s and 1980s. (*p. 861*)

Atahualpa (1502?–1533) Last ruling Inca emperor of Peru. He was executed by the Spanish. (*p. 438*)

Atlantic system The network of trading links after 1500 that moved goods, wealth, people, and cultures around the Atlantic Ocean basin. (*p. 497*)

Augustus (63 B.C.E.–14 C.E.) Honorific name of Octavian, founder of the **Roman Principate,** the military dictatorship that replaced the failing rule of the **Roman Senate.** After defeating all rivals, between 31 B.C.E. and 14 C.E. he laid the groundwork for several centuries of stability and prosperity in the Roman Empire. (*p. 151*)

Auschwitz Nazi extermination camp in Poland, the largest center of mass murder during the **Holocaust.** Close to a million Jews, Gypsies, Communists, and others were killed there. (*p. 800*)

australopithecines The several extinct species of humanlike primates that existed during the Pleistocene era (genus *Australopithecus*). (*p. 9*)

autocracy The theory justifying strong, centralized rule, such as by the **tsar** in Russia or **Haile Selassie** in Ethiopia. The autocrat did not rely on the aristocracy or the clergy for his or her legitimacy. (*p. 553*)

ayllu Andean lineage group or kin-based community. (*p. 312*)

Aztecs Also known as Mexica, the Aztecs created a powerful empire in central Mexico (1325–1521 C.E.). They forced defeated peoples to provide goods and labor as a tax. (*p. 305*)

Babylon The largest and most important city in Mesopotamia. It achieved particular eminence as the capital of the Amorite king **Hammurabi** in the eighteenth century B.C.E. and the

Neo-Babylonian king Nebuchadnezzar in the sixth century B.C.E. (*p. 29*)

balance of power The policy in international relations by which, beginning in the eighteenth century, the major European states acted together to prevent any one of them from becoming too powerful. (*p. 455*)

Balfour Declaration Statement issued by Britain's Foreign Secretary Arthur Balfour in 1917 favoring the establishment of a Jewish national homeland in Palestine. (*p. 761*)

Bannermen Hereditary military servants of the **Qing Empire,** in large part descendants of peoples of various origins who had fought for the founders of the empire. (*p. 684*)

Bantu Collective name of a large group of sub-Saharan African languages and of the peoples speaking these languages. (*p. 219*)

Batavia Fort established ca.1619 as headquarters of Dutch East India Company operations in Indonesia; today the city of Jakarta. (*p. 543*)

Battle of Midway U.S. naval victory over the Japanese fleet in June 1942, in which the Japanese lost four of their best aircraft carriers. It marked a turning point in World War II. (*p. 795*)

Battle of Omdurman British victory over the Mahdi in the Sudan in 1898. General Kitchener led a mixed force of British and Egyptian troops armed with rapid-firing rifles and machine guns. (*p. 730*)

Beijing China's northern capital, first used as an imperial capital in 906 and now the capital of the People's Republic of China. (*p. 351*)

Bengal Region of northeastern India. It was the first part of India to be conquered by the British in the eighteenth century and remained the political and economic center of British India throughout the nineteenth century. The 1905 split of the province into predominantly Hindu West Bengal and predominantly Muslim East Bengal (now Bangladesh) sparked anti-British riots. (*p. 812*)

Berlin Conference (1884–1885) Conference that German chancellor Otto von Bismarck called to set rules for the partition of Africa. It led to the creation of the Congo Free State under King **Leopold II** of Belgium. (See also **Bismarck, Otto von.**) (*p. 732*)

Bhagavad-Gita The most important work of Indian sacred literature, a dialogue between the great warrior Arjuna and the god Krishna on duty and the fate of the spirit. (*p. 185*)

bipedalism The ability to walk upright on two legs, characteristic of hominids. (*p. 9*)

Bismarck, Otto von (1815–1898) Chancellor (prime minister) of Prussia from 1862 until 1871, when he became chancellor of Germany. A conservative nationalist, he led Prussia to victory against Austria (1866) and France (1870) and was responsible for the creation of the German Empire in 1871. (*p. 714*)

Black Death An outbreak of **bubonic plague** that spread across Asia, North Africa, and Europe in the mid-fourteenth century, carrying off vast numbers of persons. (*p. 397*)

Bolívar, Simón (1783–1830) The most important military leader in the struggle for independence in South America. Born in Venezuela, he led military forces there and in Colombia, Ecuador, Peru, and Bolivia. (*p. 623*)

Bolsheviks Radical Marxist political party founded by Vladimir Lenin in 1903. Under Lenin's leadership, the Bolsheviks seized power in November 1917 during the Russian Revolution. (See also **Lenin, Vladimir.**) (*p. 761*)

Bonaparte, Napoleon. See **Napoleon I.**

Borobudur A massive stone monument on the Indonesian island of Java, erected by the Sailendra kings around 800 C.E. The winding ascent through ten levels, decorated with rich relief carving, is a Buddhist allegory for the progressive stages of enlightenment. (*p. 193*)

bourgeoisie In early modern Europe, the class of well-off town dwellers whose wealth came from manufacturing, finance, commerce, and allied professions. (*p. 459*)

Brant, Joseph (1742–1807) Mohawk leader who supported the British during the American Revolution. (*p. 581*)

breech-loading rifle Gun into which the projectiles had to be individually inserted. Later guns had magazines, a compartment holding multiple projectiles that could be fed rapidly into the firing chamber. (*p. 681*)

British raj The rule over much of South Asia between 1765 and 1947 by the East India Company and then by a British government. (*p. 659*)

bubonic plague A bacterial disease of fleas that can be transmitted by flea bites to rodents and humans; humans in late stages of the illness can spread the bacteria by coughing. Because of its very high mortality rate and the difficulty of preventing its spread, major outbreaks have created crises in many parts of the world in many countries. (See also **Black Death.**) (*pp. 280, 332*)

Buddha (563–483 B.C.E.) An Indian prince named Siddhartha Gautama, who renounced his wealth and social position. After becoming "enlightened" (the meaning of *Buddha*) he enunciated the principles of Buddhism. This doctrine evolved and spread throughout India and to Southeast, East, and Central Asia. (See also **Mahayana Buddhism; Theravada Buddhism.**) (*p. 180*)

business cycles Recurrent swings from economic hard times to recovery and growth, then back to hard times and a repetition of the sequence. (*p. 615*)

Byzantine Empire Historians' name for the eastern portion of the Roman Empire from the fourth century onward, taken from "Byzantion," an early name for Constantinople, the Byzantine capital city. The empire fell to the Ottomans in 1453. (See also **Ottoman Empire.**) (*p. 250*)

caliphate Office established in succession to the Prophet Muhammad, to rule the Islamic empire; also the name of that empire. (See also **Abbasid Caliphate; Sokoto Caliphate; Umayyad Caliphate.**) (*p. 232*)

capitalism The economic system of large financial institutions—banks, stock exchanges, investment companies—that first developed in early modern Europe. *Commercial capitalism,* the trading system of the early modern economy, is often distinguished from *industrial capitalism,* the system based on machine production. (*p. 506*)

caravel A small, highly maneuverable three-masted ship used by the Portuguese and Spanish in the exploration of the Atlantic. (*p. 427*)

Cárdenas, Lázaro (1895–1970) President of Mexico (1934–1940). He brought major changes to Mexican life by distributing millions of acres of land to the peasants, bringing representatives of workers and farmers into the inner circles of politics, and nationalizing the oil industry. (*p. 820*)

Carthage City located in present-day Tunisia, founded by **Phoenicians** ca. 800 B.C.E. It became a major commercial center and naval power in the western Mediterranean until defeated by Rome in the third century B.C.E. (*p. 107*)

Caste War A rebellion of the Maya people against the government of Mexico in 1847. It nearly returned the Yucatán to Maya rule. Some Maya rebels retreated to unoccupied territories where they held out until 1901. (*p. 636*)

Catholic Reformation Religious reform movement within the Latin Christian Church, begun in response to the **Protestant Reformation.** It clarified Catholic theology and reformed clerical training and discipline. (*p. 447*)

Celts Peoples sharing a common language and culture that originated in Central Europe in the first half of the first millennium B.C.E.. After 500 B.C.E. they spread as far as Anatolia in the east, Spain and the British Isles in the west, and later were overtaken by Roman conquest and Germanic invasions. Their descendants survive on the western fringe of Europe (Brittany, Wales, Scotland, Ireland). (*p. 90*)

Champa A state formerly located in what is now southern Vietnam. It was hostile to Annam and was annexed by Annam and destroyed as an independent entity in 1500. (*p. 366*)

Champa rice Quick-maturing rice that can allow two harvests in one growing season. Originally introduced into Champa from India, it was later sent to China as a tribute gift by the Champa state. (See also **tributary system.**) (*p. 295*)

Chang'an City in the Wei Valley in eastern China. It became the capital of the Zhou kingdom and the Qin and early Han Empires. Its main features were imitated in the cities and towns that sprang up throughout the Han Empire. (*p. 164*)

Charlemagne (742–814) King of the Franks (r. 768–814); emperor (r. 800–814). Through a series of military conquests he established the Carolingian Empire, which encompassed all of Gaul and parts of Germany and Italy. Though illiterate himself, he sponsored a brief intellectual revival. (*p. 250*)

chartered companies Groups of private investors who paid an annual fee to France and England in exchange for a monopoly over trade to the West Indies colonies. (*p. 498*)

Chavín The first major urban civilization in South America (900–250 B.C.E.). Its capital, Chavín de Huántar, was located high in the Andes Mountains of Peru. Chavín became politically and economically dominant in a densely populated region that included two distinct ecological zones, the Peruvian coastal plain and the Andean foothills. (*p. 89*)

Chiang Kai-shek (Jiang Jieshi; 1887–1975) General and leader of Nationalist China after 1925. Although he succeeded **Sun Yat-sen** as head of the **Guomindang,** he became a military dictator whose major goal was to crush the communist movement led by **Mao Zedong.** (*p. 788*)

chiefdom Form of political organization with rule by a hereditary leader who held power over a collection of villages and towns. Less powerful than kingdoms and empires, chiefdoms were based on gift giving and commercial links. (*p. 311*)

Chimú Powerful Peruvian civilization based on conquest. Located in the region earlier dominated by **Moche.** Conquered by **Inca** in 1465. (*p. 314*)

chinampas Raised fields constructed along lake shores in Mesoamerica to increase agricultural yields. (*p. 301*)

city-state A small independent state consisting of an urban center and the surrounding agricultural territory. A characteristic political form in early Mesopotamia, Archaic and Classical Greece, Phoenicia, and early Italy. (See also **polis.**) (*p. 32*)

civilization An ambiguous term often used to denote more complex societies but sometimes used by anthropologists to describe any group of people sharing a set of cultural traits. (*p. 28*)

Cixi, Empress Dowager (1835–1908) Empress of China and mother of Emperor Guangxi. She put her son under house arrest, supported antiforeign movements, and resisted reforms of the Chinese government and armed forces. (*p. 721*)

clipper ship Large, fast, streamlined sailing vessel, often American built, of the mid-to-late nineteenth century rigged with vast canvas sails hung from tall masts. (*p. 666*)

Cold War (1945–1991) The ideological struggle between communism (Soviet Union) and capitalism (United States) for world influence. The Soviet Union and the United States came to the brink of actual war during the **Cuban missile crisis** but never attacked one another. The Cold War came to an end when the Soviet Union dissolved in 1991. (See also **North Atlantic Treaty Organization; Warsaw Pact.**) (*p. 831*)

colonialism Policy by which a nation administers a foreign territory and develops its resources for the benefit of the colonial power. (*p. 731*)

Columbian Exchange The exchange of plants, animals, diseases, and technologies between the Americas and the rest of the world following Columbus's voyages. (*p. 472*)

Columbus, Christopher (1451–1506) Genoese mariner who in the service of Spain led expeditions across the Atlantic, reestablishing contact between the peoples of the Americas and the Old World and opening the way to Spanish conquest and colonization. (*p. 430*)

Confederation of 1867 Negotiated union of the formerly separate colonial governments of Ontario, Quebec, New Brunswick, and Nova Scotia. This new Dominion of Canada with a central government in Ottawa is seen as the beginning of the Canadian nation. (*p. 627*)

Confucius Western name for the Chinese philosopher Kongzi (551–479 B.C.E.). His doctrine of duty and public service had a great influence on subsequent Chinese thought and served as a code of conduct for government officials. (*p. 62*)

Congress of Vienna (1814–1815) Meeting of representatives of European monarchs called to reestablish the old order after the defeat of **Napoleon I.** (*p. 594*)

conquistadors Early-sixteenth-century Spanish adventurers who conquered Mexico, Central America, and Peru. (See **Cortés, Hernán; Pizarro, Francisco.**) (*p. 436*)

Constantine (285–337 C.E.) Roman emperor (r. 312–337). After reuniting the Roman Empire, he moved the capital to Con-

stantinople and made Christianity a favored religion. (*p. 159*)

Constitutional Convention Meeting in 1787 of the elected representatives of the thirteen original states to write the Constitution of the United States. (*p. 583*)

constitutionalism The theory developed in early modern England and spread elsewhere that royal power should be subject to legal and legislative checks. (*p. 452*)

contract of indenture A voluntary agreement binding a person to work for a specified period of years in return for free passage to an overseas destination. Before 1800 most **indentured servants** were Europeans; after 1800 most indentured laborers were Asians. (*p. 670*)

Cortés, Hernán (1485–1547) Spanish explorer and conquistador who led the conquest of Aztec Mexico in 1519–1521 for Spain. (*p. 437*)

Cossacks Peoples of the Russian Empire who lived outside the farming villages, often as herders, mercenaries, or outlaws. Cossacks led the conquest of Siberia in the sixteenth and seventeenth centuries. (*p. 552*)

cottage industries Weaving, sewing, carving, and other small-scale industries that can be done in the home. The laborers, frequently women, are usually independent. (*p. 353*)

cotton The plant that produces fibers from which cotton textiles are woven. Native to India, cotton spread throughout Asia and then to the New World. It has been a major cash crop in various places, including early Islamic Iran, Yi Korea, and nineteenth-century Egypt and the United States. A related species was exploited for fiber in pre-Columbia America. (*p. 363*)

Council of the Indies The institution responsible for supervising Spain's colonies in the Americas from 1524 to the early eighteenth century, when it lost all but judicial responsibilities. (*p. 476*)

***coureurs des bois* (runners of the woods)** French fur traders, many of mixed Amerindian heritage, who lived among and often married with Amerindian peoples of North America. (*p. 489*)

creoles In colonial Spanish America, term used to describe someone of European descent born in the New World. Elsewhere in the Americas, the term is used to describe all non-native peoples. (*p. 482*)

Crimean War (1853–1856) Conflict between the Russian and Ottoman Empires fought primarily in the Crimean Peninsula. To prevent Russian expansion, Britain and France sent troops to support the Ottomans. (*p. 679*)

Crusades (1096–1291) Armed pilgrimages to the Holy Land by Christians determined to recover Jerusalem from Muslim rule. The Crusades brought an end to western Europe's centuries of intellectual and cultural isolation. (*p. 270*)

Crystal Palace Building erected in Hyde Park, London, for the Great Exhibition of 1851. Made of iron and glass, like a gigantic greenhouse, it was a symbol of the industrial age. (*p. 606*)

Cuban missile crisis (1962) Brink-of-war confrontation between the United States and the Soviet Union over the latter's placement of nuclear-armed missiles in Cuba. (*p. 839*)

cultural imperialism Domination of one culture over another by a deliberate policy or by economic or technological superiority. (*p. 894*)

Cultural Revolution (China) (1966–1969) Campaign in China ordered by **Mao Zedong** to purge the Communist Party of his opponents and instill revolutionary values in the younger generation.(*p. 848*)

culture Socially transmitted patterns of action and expression. *Material culture* refers to physical objects, such as dwellings, clothing, tools, and crafts. Culture also includes arts, beliefs, knowledge, and technology. (*p. 11*)

cuneiform A system of writing in which wedge-shaped symbols represented words or syllables. It originated in Mesopotamia and was used initially for Sumerian and Akkadian but later was adapted to represent other languages of western Asia. Because so many symbols had to be learned, literacy was confined to a relatively small group of administrators and **scribes**. (*p. 39*)

Cyrus (600–530 B.C.E.) Founder of the Achaemenid Persian Empire. Between 550 and 530 B.C.E. he conquered Media, Lydia, and Babylon. Revered in the traditions of both Iran and the subject peoples, he employed Persians and Medes in his administration and respected the institutions and beliefs of subject peoples. (*p. 117*)

czar See **tsar.**

Dalai Lama Originally, a title meaning "universal priest" that the Mongol khans invented and bestowed on a Tibetan lama (priest) in the late 1500s to legitimate their power in Tibet. Subsequently, the title of the religious and political leader of Tibet. (*p. 556*)

Daoism Chinese school of thought, originating in the Warring States Period with Laozi (604–531 B.C.E.). Daoism offered an alternative to the Confucian emphasis on hierarchy and duty. Daoists believe that the world is always changing and is devoid of absolute morality or meaning. They accept the world as they find it, avoid futile struggles, and deviate as little as possible from the *Dao,* or "path" of nature. (See also **Confucius.**) (*p. 63*)

Darius I (ca. 558–486 B.C.E.) Third ruler of the Persian Empire (r. 521–486 B.C.E.). He crushed the widespread initial resistance to his rule and gave all major government posts to Persians rather than to Medes. He established a system of provinces and tribute, began construction of Persepolis, and expanded Persian control in the east (Pakistan) and west (northern Greece). (*p. 118*)

Darwin, Charles (1809–1882) English naturalist. He studied the plants and animals of South America and the Pacific islands, and in his book *On the Origin of Species by Means of Natural Selection* (1859) set forth his theory of **evolution.** (*p. 715*)

Declaration of the Rights of Man (1789) Statement of fundamental political rights adopted by the French **National Assembly** at the beginning of the French Revolution. (*p. 586*)

deforestation The removal of trees faster than forests can replace themselves. (*p. 462*)

Delhi Sultanate (1206–1526) Centralized Indian empire of varying extent, created by Muslim invaders. (*p. 374*)

democracy A system of government in which all "citizens" (however defined) have equal political and legal rights, privileges, and protections, as in the Greek city-state of Athens in the fifth and fourth centuries B.C.E. (*p. 127*)

demographic transition A change in the rates of population growth. Before the transition, both birth and death rates are high, resulting in a slowly growing population; then the death rate drops but the birth rate remains high, causing a population explosion; finally the birth rate drops and the population growth slows down. This transition took place in Europe in the late nineteenth and early twentieth centuries, in North America and East Asia in the mid-twentieth, and, most recently, in Latin America and South Asia. (*p. 867*)

Deng Xiaoping (1904–1997) Communist Party leader who forced Chinese economic reforms after the death of **Mao Zedong.** (*p. 862*)

development In the nineteenth and twentieth centuries, the economic process that led to industrialization, urbanization, the rise of a large and prosperous middle class, and heavy investment in education. (*p. 642*)

devshirme "Selection" in Turkish. The system by which boys from Christian communities were taken by the Ottoman state to serve as **Janissaries.** (*p. 526*)

dhow Ship of small to moderate size used in the western Indian Ocean, traditionally with a triangular sail and a sewn timber hull. (*p. 382*)

Diagne, Blaise (1872–1934) Senegalese political leader. He was the first African elected to the French National Assembly. During World War I, in exchange for promises to give French citizenship to Senegalese, he helped recruit Africans to serve in the French army. After the war, he led a movement to abolish forced labor in Africa. (*p. 809*)

Dias, Bartolomeu (1450?–1500) Portuguese explorer who in 1488 led the first expedition to sail around the southern tip of Africa from the Atlantic and sight the Indian Ocean. (*p. 428*)

diaspora A Greek word meaning "dispersal," used to describe the communities of a given ethnic group living outside their homeland. Jews, for example, spread from Israel to western Asia and Mediterranean lands in antiquity and today can be found throughout the world. (*p. 103*)

Dirty War War waged by the Argentine military (1976–1982) against leftist groups. Characterized by the use of illegal imprisonment, torture, and executions by the military. (*p. 857*)

divination Techniques for ascertaining the future or the will of the gods by interpreting natural phenomena such as, in early China, the cracks on oracle bones or, in ancient Greece, the flight of birds through sectors of the sky. (*p. 59*)

division of labor A manufacturing technique that breaks down a craft into many simple and repetitive tasks that can be performed by unskilled workers. Pioneered in the pottery works of Josiah Wedgwood and in other eighteenth-century factories, it greatly increased the productivity of labor and lowered the cost of manufactured goods. (See also **Wedgwood, Josiah.**) (*p. 603*)

driver A privileged male slave whose job was to ensure that a slave gang did its work on a plantation. (*p. 503*)

Druids The class of religious experts who conducted rituals and preserved sacred lore among some ancient Celtic peoples. They provided education, mediated disputes between kinship groups, and were suppressed by the Romans as a potential focus of opposition to Roman rule. (See also **Celts.**) (*p. 92*)

durbar An elaborate display of political power and wealth in British India in the nineteenth century, ostensibly in imitation of the pageantry of the **Mughal Empire.** (*p. 661*)

Dutch West India Company (1621–1794) Trading company chartered by the Dutch government to conduct its merchants' trade in the Americas and Africa. (*p. 498*)

economic sanctions Boycotts, embargoes, and other economic measures that one country uses to pressure another country into changing its policies. (*p. 889*)

Edison, Thomas (1847–1931) American inventor best known for inventing the electric light bulb, acoustic recording on wax cylinders, and motion pictures. (*p. 703*)

Einstein, Albert (1879–1955) German physicist who developed the theory of relativity, which states that time, space, and mass are relative to each other and not fixed. (*p. 774*)

El Alamein Town in Egypt, site of the victory by Britain's Field Marshal Bernard Montgomery over German forces led by General Erwin Rommel (the "Desert Fox") in 1942–1943. (*p. 793*)

electricity A form of energy used in telegraphy from the 1840s on and for lighting, industrial motors, and railroads beginning in the 1880s. (*p. 702*)

electric telegraph A device for rapid, long-distance transmission of information over an electric wire. It was introduced in England and North America in the 1830s and 1840s and replaced telegraph systems that utilized visual signals such as semaphores. (See also **submarine telegraph cables.**) (*p. 609*)

encomienda A grant of authority over a population of Amerindians in the Spanish colonies. It provided the grant holder with a supply of cheap labor and periodic payments of goods by the Amerindians. It obliged the grant holder to Christianize the Amerindians. (*p. 479*)

Enlightenment A philosophical movement in eighteenth-century Europe that fostered the belief that one could reform society by discovering rational laws that governed social behavior and were just as scientific as the laws of physics. (*pp. 468, 574*)

equites In ancient Italy, prosperous landowners second in wealth and status to the senatorial aristocracy. The Roman emperors allied with this group to counterbalance the influence of the old aristocracy and used the *equites* to staff the imperial civil service. (*p. 152*)

Estates General France's traditional national assembly with representatives of the three estates, or classes, in French society: the clergy, nobility, and commoners. The calling of the Estates General in 1789 led to the French Revolution. (*p. 585*)

Ethiopia East African highland nation lying east of the Nile River. (See also **Menelik II; Selassie, Haile.**) (*p. 221*)

ethnic cleansing Effort to eradicate a people and its culture by means of mass killing and the destruction of historical buildings and cultural materials. Ethnic cleansing was used by both sides in the conflicts that accompanied the disintegration of Yugoslavia in the 1990s. (*p. 883*)

European Community (EC) An organization promoting economic unity in Europe formed in 1967 by consolidation of earlier, more limited, agreements. Replaced by the European Union (EU) in 1993. (*p. 834*)

evolution The biological theory that, over time, changes occurring in plants and animals, mainly as a result of **natural selection** and genetic mutation, result in new species. (*p. 6*)

extraterritoriality The right of foreign residents in a country to live under the laws of their native country and disregard the laws of the host country. In the nineteenth and early twentieth centuries, European and American nationals living in certain areas of Chinese and Ottoman cities were granted this right. (*p. 682*)

Faisal I (1885–1933) Arab prince, leader of the Arab Revolt in World War I. The British made him king of Iraq in 1921, and he reigned under British protection until 1933. (*p. 760*)

Fascist Party Italian political party created by Benito Mussolini during World War I. It emphasized aggressive nationalism and was Mussolini's instrument for the creation of a dictatorship in Italy from 1922 to 1943. (See also **Mussolini, Benito.**) (*p. 786*)

fief In medieval Europe, land granted in return for a sworn oath to provide specified military service. (*p. 256*)

First Temple A monumental sanctuary built in Jerusalem by King Solomon in the tenth century B.C.E. to be the religious center for the Israelite god Yahweh. The Temple priesthood conducted sacrifices, received a tithe or percentage of agricultural revenues, and became economically and politically powerful. The First Temple was destroyed by the Babylonians in 587 B.C.E., rebuilt on a modest scale in the late sixth century B.C.E., and replaced by King Herod's Second Temple in the late first century B.C.E. (destroyed by the Romans in 70 C.E.) (*p. 102*)

Five-Year Plans Plans that Joseph Stalin introduced to industrialize the Soviet Union rapidly, beginning in 1928. They set goals for the output of steel, electricity, machinery, and most other products and were enforced by the police powers of the state. They succeeded in making the Soviet Union a major industrial power before World War II. (See also **Stalin, Joseph.**) (*p. 781*)

foragers People who support themselves by hunting wild animals and gathering wild edible plants and insects. (*p. 13*)

Forbidden City The walled section of Beijing where emperors lived between 1121 and 1924. A portion is now a residence for leaders of the People's Republic of China. (*p. 355*)

Franklin, Benjamin (1706–1790) American intellectual, inventor, and politician He helped to negotiate French support for the American Revolution. (*p. 577*)

free-trade imperialism Economic dominance of a weaker country by a more powerful one, while maintaining the legal independence of the weaker state. In the late nineteenth century, free-trade imperialism characterized the relations between the Latin American republics, on the one hand, and Great Britain and the United States, on the other. (*p. 744*)

fresco A technique of painting on walls covered with moist plaster. It was used to decorate Minoan and Mycenaean palaces and Roman villas, and became an important medium during the Italian Renaissance. (*p. 73*)

Funan An early complex society in Southeast Asia between the first and sixth centuries C.E. It was centered in the rich rice-growing region of southern Vietnam, and it controlled the passage of trade across the Malaysian isthmus. (*p. 191*)

Gama, Vasco da (1460?–1524) Portuguese explorer. In 1497–1498 he led the first naval expedition from Europe to sail to India, opening an important commercial sea route. (*p. 428*)

Gandhi, Mohandas K. (Mahatma) (1869–1948) Leader of the Indian independence movement and advocate of nonviolent resistance. After being educated as a lawyer in England, he returned to India and became leader of the **Indian National Congress** in 1920. He appealed to the poor, led nonviolent demonstrations against British colonial rule, and was jailed many times. Soon after independence he was assassinated for attempting to stop Hindu-Muslim rioting. (*p. 813*)

Genghis Khan (ca. 1167–1227) The title of Temüjin when he ruled the Mongols (1206–1227). It means the "oceanic" or "universal" leader. Genghis Khan was the founder of the Mongol Empire. (*p. 325*)

gens de couleur Free men and women of color in Haiti. They sought greater political rights and later supported the Haitian Revolution. (See also **L'Ouverture, François Dominique Toussaint.**) (*p. 593*)

gentry In China, the class of prosperous families, next in wealth below the rural aristocrats, from which the emperors drew their administrative personnel. Respected for their education and expertise, these officials became a privileged group and made the government more efficient and responsive than in the past. The term *gentry* also denotes the class of landholding families in England below the aristocracy. (*p. 166*)

Ghana First known kingdom in sub-Saharan West Africa between the sixth and thirteenth centuries C.E. Also the modern West African country once known as the Gold Coast. (*p. 215*)

Gold Coast (Africa) Region of the Atlantic coast of West Africa occupied by modern Ghana; named for its gold exports to Europe from the 1470s onward. (*p. 428*)

Golden Horde Mongol khanate founded by Genghis Khan's grandson Batu. It was based in southern Russia and quickly adopted both the Turkic language and Islam. Also known as the Kipchak Horde. (*p. 333*)

Gorbachev, Mikhail (b. 1931) Head of the Soviet Union from 1985 to 1991. His liberalization effort improved relations with the West, but he lost power after his reforms led to the collapse of Communist governments in eastern Europe. (*p. 863*)

Gothic cathedrals Large churches originating in twelfth-century France; built in an architectural style featuring pointed arches, tall vaults and spires, flying buttresses, and large stained-glass windows. (*p. 405*)

Grand Canal The 1,100-mile (1,700-kilometer) waterway linking the Yellow and the Yangzi Rivers. It was begun in the **Han** period and completed during the Sui Empire. (*p. 277*)

Great Circuit The network of Atlantic Ocean trade routes between Europe, Africa, and the Americas that underlay the **Atlantic system.** (*p. 508*)

Great Ice Age Geological era that occurred between ca. 2 million and 11,000 years ago. As a result of climate shifts, large numbers of new species evolved during this period, also called the Pleistocene epoch. (See also **Holocene.**) (*p. 9*)

"great tradition" Historians' term for a literate, well-institutionalized complex of religious and social beliefs and practices adhered to by diverse societies over a broad geographical area. (See also **"small tradition."**) (*p. 217*)

Great Western Schism A division in the Latin (Western) Christian Church between 1378 and 1417, when rival claimants to the papacy existed in Rome and Avignon. (*p. 411*)

Great Zimbabwe City, now in ruins (in the modern African country of Zimbabwe), whose many stone structures were built between about 1250 and 1450, when it was a trading center and the capital of a large state. (*p. 385*)

guild In medieval Europe, an association of men (rarely women), such as merchants, artisans, or professors, who worked in a particular trade and banded together to promote their economic and political interests. Guilds were also important in other societies, such as the Ottoman and Safavid empires. (*p. 403*)

Gujarat Region of western India famous for trade and manufacturing; the inhabitants are called Gujarati. (*p. 380*)

gunpowder A mixture of saltpeter, sulfur, and charcoal, in various proportions. The formula, brought to China in the 400s or 500s, was first used to make fumigators to keep away insect pests and evil spirits. In later centuries it was used to make explosives and grenades and to propel cannonballs, shot, and bullets. (*p. 289*)

Guomindang Nationalist political party founded on democratic principles by **Sun Yat-sen** in 1912. After 1925, the party was headed by **Chiang Kai-shek,** who turned it into an increasingly authoritarian movement. (*p. 769*)

Gupta Empire (320–550 C.E.) A powerful Indian state based, like its Mauryan predecessor, on a capital at Pataliputra in the Ganges Valley. It controlled most of the Indian subcontinent through a combination of military force and its prestige as a center of sophisticated culture. (See also **theater-state.**) (*p. 186*)

Habsburg A powerful European family that provided many Holy Roman Emperors, founded the Austrian (later Austro-Hungarian) Empire, and ruled sixteenth- and seventeenth-century Spain. (*p. 449*)

hadith A tradition relating the words or deeds of the Prophet Muhammad; next to the **Quran,** the most important basis for Islamic law. (*p. 241*)

Hammurabi Amorite ruler of **Babylon** (r. 1792–1750 B.C.E.). He conquered many city-states in southern and northern Mesopotamia and is best known for a code of laws, inscribed on a black stone pillar, illustrating the principles to be used in legal cases. (*p. 34*)

Han A term used to designate (1) the ethnic Chinese people who originated in the Yellow River Valley and spread throughout regions of China suitable for agriculture and (2) the dynasty of emperors who ruled from 206 B.C.E. to 220 C.E. (*p. 164*)

Hanseatic League An economic and defensive alliance of the free towns in northern Germany, founded about 1241 and most powerful in the fourteenth century. (*p. 401*)

Harappa Site of one of the great cities of the Indus Valley civilization of the third millennium B.C.E. It was located on the northwest frontier of the zone of cultivation (in modern Pakistan), and may have been a center for the acquisition of raw materials, such as metals and precious stones, from Afghanistan and Iran. (*p. 48*)

Hatshepsut Queen of Egypt (r. 1473–1458 B.C.E.). She dispatched a naval expedition down the Red Sea to Punt (possibly Somalia), the faraway source of myrrh. There is evidence of opposition to a woman as ruler, and after her death her name and image were frequently defaced. (*p. 66*)

Hebrew Bible A collection of sacred books containing diverse materials concerning the origins, experiences, beliefs, and practices of the Israelites. Most of the extant text was compiled by members of the priestly class in the fifth century B.C.E. and reflects the concerns and views of this group. (*p. 99*)

Hellenistic Age Historians' term for the era, usually dated 323–30 B.C.E., in which Greek culture spread across western Asia and northeastern Africa after the conquests of **Alexander the Great**. The period ended with the fall of the last major Hellenistic kingdom to Rome, but Greek cultural influence persisted until the spread of Islam in the seventh century C.E. (*p. 137*)

Helsinki Accords (1975) Political and human rights agreement signed in Helsinki, Finland, by the Soviet Union and western European countries. (*p. 839*)

Henry the Navigator (1394–1460) Portuguese prince who promoted the study of navigation and directed voyages of exploration down the western coast of Africa. (*p. 425*)

Herodotus (ca. 485–425 B.C.E.) Heir to the technique of *historia*—"investigation"—developed by Greeks in the late Archaic period. He came from a Greek community in Anatolia and traveled extensively, collecting information in western Asia and the Mediterranean lands. He traced the antecedents of and chronicled the **Persian Wars** between the Greek city-states and the Persian Empire, thus originating the Western tradition of historical writing. (*p. 128*)

Herzl, Theodore (1860–1904) Austrian journalist and founder of the Zionist movement urging the creation of a Jewish national homeland in Palestine. (*p. 760*)

Hidalgo y Costilla, Miguel (1753–1811) Mexican priest who led the first stage of the Mexican independence war in 1810. He was captured and executed in 1811. (*p. 625*)

Hidden Imam Last in a series of twelve descendants of Muhammad's son-in-law Ali, whom **Shi'ites** consider divinely appointed leaders of the Muslim community. In occlusion since ca. 873, he is expected to return as a messiah at the end of time. (*p. 532*)

hieroglyphics A system of writing in which pictorial symbols represented sounds, syllables, or concepts. It was used for official and monumental inscriptions in ancient Egypt. Because of the long period of study required to master this system, literacy in hieroglyphics was confined to a relatively small group of **scribes** and administrators. Cursive symbolforms were developed for rapid composition on other media, such as **papyrus**. (*p. 44*)

high culture Canons of artistic and literary masterworks recognized by dominant economic classes. (*p. 897*)

Hinduism A general term for a wide variety of beliefs and ritual practices that have developed in the Indian subcontinent since antiquity. Hinduism has roots in ancient Vedic, Buddhist, and south Indian religious concepts and practices. It spread along the trade routes to Southeast Asia. (*p. 181*)

Hiroshima City in Japan, the first to be destroyed by an atomic bomb, on August 6, 1945. The bombing hastened the end of World War II. (*p. 797*)

history The study of past events and changes in the development, transmission, and transformation of cultural practices. (*p. 11*)

Hitler, Adolf (1889–1945) Born in Austria, Hitler became a radical German nationalist during World War I. He led the National Socialist German Workers' Party—the **Nazi Party**—in the 1920s and became dictator of Germany in 1933. He led Europe into World War II. (*p. 786*)

Hittites A people from central Anatolia who established an empire in Anatolia and Syria in the Late Bronze Age. With wealth from the trade in metals and military power based on chariot forces, the Hittites vied with New Kingdom Egypt for control of Syria-Palestine before falling to unidentified attackers ca. 1200 B.C.E. (See also **Ramesses II.**) (*p. 64*)

Holocaust Nazis' program during World War II to kill people they considered undesirable. Some 6 million Jews perished during the Holocaust, along with millions of Poles, Gypsies, Communists, Socialists, and others. (*p. 800*)

Holocene The geological era since the end of the **Great Ice Age** about 11,000 years ago. (*p. 21*)

Holy Roman Empire Loose federation of mostly German states and principalities, headed by an emperor elected by the princes. It lasted from 962 to 1806. (*pp. 260, 449*)

hominid The biological family that includes humans and humanlike primates. (*p. 9*)

Homo erectus An extinct human species. It evolved in Africa about 2 million years ago. (*p. 10*)

Homo habilis The first human species (now extinct). It evolved in Africa about 2.5 million years ago. (*p. 9*)

Homo sapiens The current human species. It evolved in Africa about 200,000 years ago. It includes archaic forms such as Neanderthals (now extinct) and all modern humans. (*p. 10*)

hoplite A heavily armored Greek infantryman of the Archaic and Classical periods who fought in the close-packed phalanx formation. Hoplite armies—militias composed of middle- and upper-class citizens supplying their own equipment—were for centuries superior to all other military forces. (*p. 126*)

horse collar Harnessing method that increased the efficiency of horses by shifting the point of traction from the animal's neck to the shoulders; its adoption favors the spread of horse-drawn plows and vehicles. (*p. 269*)

House of Burgesses Elected assembly in colonial Virginia, created in 1618. (*p. 486*)

humanists (Renaissance) European scholars, writers, and teachers associated with the study of the humanities (grammar, rhetoric, poetry, history, languages, and moral philosophy), influential in the fifteenth century and later. (*p. 408*)

Hundred Years War (1337–1453) Series of campaigns over control of the throne of France, involving English and French royal families and French noble families. (*p. 413*)

Husain, Saddam (b. 1937) President of Iraq since 1979. Waged war on Iran in 1980–1988. In 1990 he ordered an invasion of Kuwait but was defeated by United States and its allies in the Gulf War (1991). (*p. 860*)

Ibn Battuta (1304–1369) Moroccan Muslim scholar, the most widely traveled individual of his time. He wrote a detailed account of his visits to Islamic lands from China to Spain and the western Sudan. (*p. 373*)

Ibn Khaldun (1332–1406) Arab historian. He developed an influential theory on the rise and fall of states. Born in Tunis, he spent his later years in Cairo as a teacher and judge. In 1400 he was sent to Damascus to negotiate the surrender of the city, where he met and exchanged views with **Timur.** (*p. 336*)

Il-khan A "secondary" or "peripheral" khan based in Persia. The Il-khans' khanate was founded by Hülegü, a grandson of **Genghis Khan,** was based at Tabriz in modern Azerbaijan. It controlled much of Iran and Iraq. (*p. 333*)

import-substitution industrialization An economic system aimed at building a country's industry by restricting foreign trade. It was especially popular in Latin American countries such as Mexico, Argentina, and Brazil in the mid-twentieth century. It proved successful for a time but could not keep up with technological advances in Europe and North America. (*p. 823*)

Inca Largest and most powerful Andean empire. Controlled the Pacific coast of South America from Ecuador to Chile from its capital of Cuzco. (*p. 316*)

indentured servant A migrant to British colonies in the Americas who paid for passage by agreeing to work for a set term ranging from four to seven years. (*p. 486*)

Indian Civil Service The elite professional class of officials who administered the government of British India. Originally composed exclusively of well-educated British men, it gradually added qualified Indians. (*p. 661*)

Indian National Congress A movement and political party founded in 1885 to demand greater Indian participation in government. Its membership was middle class, and its demands were modest until World War I. Led after 1920 by Mohandas K. Gandhi, it appealed increasingly to the poor, and it organized mass protests demanding self-government and independence. (See also **Gandhi, Mohandas K.**) (*pp. 663, 812*)

Indian Ocean maritime system In premodern times, a network of seaports, trade routes, and maritime culture linking countries on the rim of the Indian Ocean from Africa to Indonesia. (*p. 207*)

indulgence The forgiveness of the punishment due for past sins, granted by the Catholic Church authorities as a reward for a pious act. Martin Luther's protest against the sale of indulgences is often seen as touching off the **Protestant Reformation.** (*p. 446*)

Industrial Revolution The transformation of the economy, the environment, and living conditions, occurring first in England in the eighteenth century, that resulted from the use of steam engines, the mechanization of manufacturing in factories, and innovations in transportation and communication. (*p. 599*)

investiture controversy Dispute between the popes and the Holy Roman Emperors over who held ultimate authority over bishops in imperial lands. (*p. 261*)

Iron Age Historians' term for the period during which iron was the primary metal for tools and weapons. The advent of iron technology began at different times in different parts of the world. (*p. 85*)

iron curtain Winston Churchill's term for the Cold War division between the Soviet-dominated East and the U.S.-dominated West. (*p. 831*)

Iroquois Confederacy An alliance of five northeastern Amerindian peoples (after 1722 six) that made decisions on military and diplomatic issues through a council of representatives. Allied first with the Dutch and later with the English, the Confederacy dominated the area from western New England to the Great Lakes. (*p. 488*)

Islam Religion expounded by the Prophet Muhammad (570–632 C.E.) on the basis of his reception of divine revelations, which were collected after his death into the **Quran.** In the tradition of Judaism and Christianity, and sharing much of their lore, Islam calls on all people to recognize one creator god—Allah—who rewards or punishes believers after death according to how they led their lives. (See also **hadith.**) (*p. 231*)

Israel In antiquity, the land between the eastern shore of the Mediterranean and the Jordan River, occupied by the Israelites from the early second millennium B.C.E. The modern state of Israel was founded in 1948. (*p. 98*)

Jackson, Andrew (1767–1845) First president of the United States born in humble circumstances. He was popular among frontier residents, urban workers, and small farmers. He had a successful political career as judge, general, congressman, senator, and president. After being denied the presidency in 1824 in a controversial election, he won in 1828 and was reelected in 1832. (*p. 629*)

Jacobins Radical republicans during the French Revolution. They were led by Maximilien Robespierre from 1793 to 1794. (See also **Robespierre, Maximilien.**) (*p. 588*)

Janissaries Infantry, originally of slave origin, armed with firearms and constituting the elite of the Ottoman army from the fifteenth century until the corps was abolished in 1826. See also **devshirme.** (*p. 526, 675*)

Jesuits Members of the Society of Jesus, a Roman Catholic order founded by Ignatius Loyola in 1534. They played an important part in the **Catholic Reformation** and helped create conduits of trade and knowledge between Asia and Europe. (*p. 548*)

Jesus (ca. 5 B.C.E.–34 C.E.) A Jew from Galilee in northern Israel who sought to reform Jewish beliefs and practices. He was executed as a revolutionary by the Romans. Hailed as the Messiah and son of God by his followers, he became the central figure in Christianity, a belief system that developed in the centuries after his death. (*p. 155*)

Jinnah, Muhammad Ali (1876–1948) Indian Muslim politician who founded the state of Pakistan. A lawyer by training, he joined the **All-India Muslim League** in 1913. As leader of the League from the 1920s on, he negotiated with the British and the **Indian National Congress** for Muslim participation in Indian politics. From 1940 on, he led the movement for the independence of India's Muslims in a separate state of Pakistan, founded in 1947. (*p. 816*)

joint-stock company A business, often backed by a government charter, that sold shares to individuals to raise money for its trading enterprises and to spread the risks (and profits) among many investors. (*p. 460*)

Juárez, Benito (1806–1872) President of Mexico (1858–1872). Born in poverty in Mexico, he was educated as a lawyer and rose to become chief justice of the Mexican supreme court and then president. He led Mexico's resistance to a French invasion in 1863 and the installation of Maximilian as emperor. (*p. 633*)

junk A very large flatbottom sailing ship produced in the **Tang** and **Song Empires,** specially designed for long-distance commercial travel. (*p. 288*)

Kamakura Shogunate The first of Japan's decentralized military governments. (1185–1333). (*p. 294*)

kamikaze The "divine wind," which the Japanese credited with blowing Mongol invaders away from their shores in 1281. (*p. 365*)

Kangxi (1654–1722) Qing emperor (r. 1662–1722). He oversaw the greatest expansion of the **Qing Empire.**

karma In Indian tradition, the residue of deeds performed in past and present lives that adheres to a "spirit" and determines what form it will assume in its next life cycle. The doctrines of karma and reincarnation were used by the elite in ancient India to encourage people to accept their social position and do their duty. (*p. 177*)

keiretsu Alliances of corporations and banks that dominate the Japanese economy. (*p. 861*)

khipu System of knotted colored cords used by preliterate Andean peoples to transmit information. (*p. 312*)

Khomeini, Ayatollah Ruhollah (1900?–1989) Shi'ite philosopher and cleric who led the overthrow of the shah of Iran in 1979 and created an Islamic republic. (*p. 859*)

Khubilai Khan (1215–1294) Last of the Mongol Great Khans (r. 1260–1294) and founder of the **Yuan Empire.** (*p. 351*)

Kievan Russia State established at Kiev in Ukraine ca. 879 by Scandinavian adventurers asserting authority over a mostly Slavic farming population. (*p. 267*)

Korean War (1950–1953) Conflict that began with North Korea's invasion of South Korea and came to involve the United Nations (primarily the United States) allying with South Korea and the People's Republic of China allying with North Korea. (*p. 836*)

Koryo Korean kingdom founded in 918 and destroyed by a Mongol invasion in 1259. (*p. 292*)

Kush An Egyptian name for Nubia, the region alongside the Nile River south of Egypt, where an indigenous kingdom with its own distinctive institutions and cultural traditions arose beginning in the early second millennium B.C.E. It was deeply influenced by Egyptian culture and at times under the control of Egypt, which coveted its rich deposits of gold and luxury products from sub-Saharan Africa carried up the Nile corridor. (*p. 70*)

labor union An organization of workers in a particular industry or trade, created to defend the interests of members through strikes or negotiations with employers. (*p. 709*)

laissez faire The idea that government should refrain from interfering in economic affairs. The classic exposition of laissez-faire principles is Adam Smith's *Wealth of Nations* (1776). (*p. 615*)

lama In Tibetan Buddhism, a teacher. (*p. 351*)

Las Casas, Bartolomé de (1474–1566) First bishop of Chiapas, in southern Mexico. He devoted most of his life to protecting Amerindian peoples from exploitation. His major achievement was the New Laws of 1542, which limited the ability of Spanish settlers to compel Amerindians to labor for them. (See also **encomienda.**) (*p. 476*)

Latin West Historians' name for the territories of Europe that adhered to the Latin rite of Christianity and used the Latin language for intellectual exchange in the period ca. 1000–1500. (*p. 394*)

League of Nations International organization founded in 1919 to promote world peace and cooperation but greatly weakened by the refusal of the United States to join. It proved ineffectual in stopping aggression by Italy, Japan, and Germany in the 1930s, and it was superseded by the **United Nations** in 1945. (*p. 763*)

Legalism In China, a political philosophy that emphasized the unruliness of human nature and justified state coercion and control. The **Qin** ruling class invoked it to validate the authoritarian nature of their regime and its profligate expenditure of subjects' lives and labor. It was superseded in the **Han** era by a more benevolent Confucian doctrine of governmental moderation. (*p. 62*)

"legitimate" trade Exports from Africa in the nineteenth century that did not include the newly outlawed slave trade. (*p. 654*)

Lenin, Vladimir (1870–1924) Leader of the Bolshevik (later Communist) Party. He lived in exile in Switzerland until 1917, then returned to Russia to lead the Bolsheviks to victory during the Russian Revolution and the civil war that followed. (*p. 761*)

Leopold II (1835–1909) King of Belgium (r. 1865–1909). He was active in encouraging the exploration of Central Africa and became the ruler of the Congo Free State (to 1908). (*p. 732*)

Li Shimin (599–649) One of the founders of the **Tang Empire** and its second emperor (r. 626–649). He led the expansion of the empire into Central Asia. (*p. 277*)

liberalism A political ideology that emphasizes the civil rights of citizens, representative government, and the protection of private property. This ideology, derived from the **Enlightenment,** was especially popular among the property-owning middle classes of Europe and North America. (*p. 713*)

Library of Ashurbanipal A large collection of writings drawn from the ancient literary, religious, and scientific traditions of Mesopotamia. It was assembled by the sixth century B.C.E. Assyrian ruler Ashurbanipal. The many tablets unearthed by archaeologists constitute one of the most important sources of present-day knowledge of the long literary tradition of Mesopotamia. (*p. 98*)

Linear B A set of syllabic symbols, derived from the writing system of **Minoan** Crete, used in the Mycenaean palaces of the Late Bronze Age to write an early form of Greek. It was used primarily for palace records, and the surviving Linear B tablets provide substantial information about the economic organization of Mycenaean society and tantalizing clues about political, social, and religious institutions. (*p. 75*)

Little Ice Age A century-long period of cool climate that began in the 1590s. Its ill effects on agriculture in northern Europe were notable. (*p. 462*)

llama A hoofed animal indigenous to the Andes Mountains in South America. It was the only domesticated beast of burden in the Americas before the arrival of Europeans. It provided meat and wool. The use of llamas to transport goods made possible specialized production and trade among people living in different ecological zones and fostered the integration of these zones by **Chavín** and later Andean states. (*p. 90*)

loess A fine, light silt deposited by wind and water. It constitutes the fertile soil of the Yellow River Valley in northern China. Because loess soil is not compacted, it can be worked with a simple digging stick, but it leaves the region vulnerable to devastating earthquakes. (*p. 58*)

Long March (1934–1935) The 6,000-mile (9,600-kilometer) flight of Chinese Communists from southeastern to northwestern China. The Communists, led by **Mao Zedong,** were pursued by the Chinese army under orders from **Chiang Kai-shek.** The four thousand survivors of the march formed the nucleus of a revived Communist movement that defeated the **Guomindang** after World War II. (*p. 789*)

L'Ouverture, François Dominique Toussaint (1743–1803) Leader of the Haitian Revolution. He freed the slaves and gained effective independence for Haiti despite military interventions by the British and French. (*p. 593*)

ma'at Egyptian term for the concept of divinely created and maintained order in the universe. Reflecting the ancient Egyptians' belief in an essentially beneficent world, the divine ruler was the earthly guarantor of this order. (See also **pyramid.**) (*p. 42*)

Macartney mission (1792–1793) The unsuccessful attempt by the British Empire to establish diplomatic relations with the **Qing Empire.** (*p. 560*)

Magellan, Ferdinand (1480?–1521) Portuguese navigator who led the Spanish expedition of 1519–1522 that was the first to sail around the world. (*p. 431*)

Mahabharata A vast epic chronicling the events leading up to a cataclysmic battle between related kinship groups in early India. It includes the Bhagavad-Gita, the most important work of Indian sacred literature. (*p. 185*)

Mahayana Buddhism "Great Vehicle" branch of Buddhism followed in China, Japan, and Central Asia. The focus is on reverence for **Buddha** and for bodhisattvas, enlightened persons who have postponed nirvana to help others attain enlightenment. (*p. 181*)

Malacca Port city in the modern Southeast Asian country of Malaysia, founded about 1400 as a trading center on the Strait of Malacca. Also spelled Melaka. (*p. 387*)

Malay peoples A designation for peoples originating in south China and Southeast Asia who settled the Malay Peninsula, Indonesia, and the Philippines, then spread eastward across the islands of the Pacific Ocean and west to Madagascar. (*p. 190*)

Mali Empire created by indigenous Muslims in western Sudan of West Africa from the thirteenth to fifteenth century. It was famous for its role in the trans-Saharan gold trade. (See also **Timbuktu.**) (*p. 375*)

Malthus, Thomas (1766–1834) Eighteenth-century English intellectual who warned that population growth threatened future generations because, in his view, population growth would always outstrip increases in agricultural production. (*p. 867*)

Mamluks Under the Islamic system of military slavery, Turkic military slaves who formed an important part of the armed forces of the **Abbasid Caliphate** of the ninth and tenth centuries. Mamluks eventually founded their own state, ruling Egypt and Syria (1250–1517). (*pp. 236, 344*)

Manchuria Region of Northeast Asia bounded by the Yalu River on the south and the Amur River on the east and north. (*p. 354*)

Manchus Federation of Northeast Asian peoples who founded the **Qing Empire.** (*p. 556*)

Mandate of Heaven Chinese religious and political ideology developed by the **Zhou,** according to which it was the prerogative of Heaven, the chief deity, to grant power to the ruler of China and to take away that power if the ruler failed to conduct himself justly and in the best interests of his subjects. (*p. 61*)

mandate system Allocation of former German colonies and Ottoman possessions to the victorious powers after World War I, to be administered under League of Nations supervision. (*p. 770*)

manor In medieval Europe, a large, self-sufficient landholding consisting of the lord's residence (manor house), outbuildings, peasant village, and surrounding land. (*p. 254*)

mansabs In India, grants of land given in return for service by rulers of the **Mughal Empire.** (*p. 536*)

Mansa Kankan Musa Ruler of Mali (r. 1312–1337). His pilgrimage through Egypt to **Mecca** in 1324–1325 established the empire's reputation for wealth in the Mediterranean world. (*p. 376*)

manumission A grant of legal freedom to an individual slave. (*p. 505*)

Mao Zedong (1893–1976) Leader of the Chinese Communist Party (1927–1976). He led the Communists on the **Long March** (1934–1935) and rebuilt the Communist Party and Red Army during the Japanese occupation of China (1937–1945). After World War II, he led the Communists to victory over the **Guomindang.** He ordered the **Cultural Revolution** in 1966. (*p. 789*)

maroon A slave who ran away from his or her master. Often a member of a community of runaway slaves in the West Indies and South America. (*p. 505*)

Marshall Plan U. S. program to support the reconstruction of western Europe after World War II. By 1961 more than $20 billion in economic aid had been dispersed. (*p. 834*)

Marx, Karl (1818–1883) German journalist and philosopher, founder of the Marxist branch of **socialism.** He is known for two books: *The Communist Manifesto* (1848) and *Das Kapital* (Vols. I–III, 1867–1894). (*p. 709*)

mass deportation The forcible removal and relocation of large numbers of people or entire populations. The mass deportations practiced by the Assyrian and Persian Empires were meant as a terrifying warning of the consequences of rebellion. They also brought skilled and unskilled labor to the imperial center. (*p. 95*)

mass production The manufacture of many identical products by the division of labor into many small repetitive tasks. This method was introduced into the manufacture of pottery by Josiah Wedgwood and into the spinning of cotton thread by Richard Arkwright. (See also **Arkwright, Richard; Industrial Revolution; Wedgwood, Josiah.**) (*p. 602*)

Mauryan Empire The first state to unify most of the Indian subcontinent. It was founded by Chandragupta Maurya in 324 B.C.E. and survived until 184 B.C.E. From its capital at Pataliputra in the Ganges Valley it grew wealthy from taxes on agriculture, iron mining, and control of trade routes. (See also **Ashoka.**) (*p. 184*)

Maya Mesoamerican civilization concentrated in Mexico's Yucatán Peninsula and in Guatemala and Honduras but never unified into a single empire. Major contributions were in mathematics, astronomy, and development of the calendar. (*p. 302*)

Mecca City in western Arabia; birthplace of the Prophet **Muhammad,** and ritual center of the Islamic religion. (*p. 230*)

mechanization The application of machinery to manufacturing and other activities. Among the first processes to be mechanized were the spinning of cotton thread and the weaving of cloth in late-eighteenth- and early-nineteenth-century England. (*p. 603*)

medieval Literally "middle age," a term that historians of Europe use for the period ca. 500 to ca. 1500, signifying its intermediate point between Greco-Roman antiquity and the Renaissance. (*p. 250*)

Medina City in western Arabia to which the Prophet Muhammad and his followers emigrated in 622 to escape persecution in Mecca. (*p. 231*)

megaliths Structures and complexes of very large stones constructed for ceremonial and religious purposes in **Neolithic** times. (*p. 23*)

Meiji Restoration The political program that followed the destruction of the **Tokugawa Shogunate** in 1868, in which a collection of young leaders set Japan on the path of centralization, industrialization, and imperialism. (See also **Yamagata Aritomo.**) (*p. 694*)

Memphis The capital of Old Kingdom Egypt, near the head of the Nile Delta. Early rulers were interred in the nearby **pyramids.** (*p. 43*)

Menelik II (1844–1911). Emperor of Ethiopia (r. 1889–1911). He enlarged Ethiopia to its present dimensions and defeated an Italian invasion at Adowa (1896). (*p. 737*)

mercantilism European government policies of the sixteenth, seventeenth, and eighteenth centuries designed to promote overseas trade between a country and its colonies and accumulate precious metals by requiring colonies to trade only with their motherland country. The British system was defined by the Navigation Acts, the French system by laws known as the *Exclusif.* (*p. 506*)

Meroë Capital of a flourishing kingdom in southern Nubia from the fourth century B.C.E. to the fourth century C.E. In this period Nubian culture shows more independence from Egypt and the influence of sub-Saharan Africa. (*p. 71*)

mestizo The term used by Spanish authorities to describe someone of mixed Amerindian and European descent. (*p. 484*)

Middle Passage The part of the **Great Circuit** involving the transportation of enslaved Africans across the Atlantic to the Americas. (*p. 508*)

Ming Empire (1368–1644) Empire based in China that Zhu Yuanzhang established after the overthrow of the **Yuan Empire.** The Ming emperor **Yongle** sponsored the building of the **Forbidden City** and the voyages of **Zheng He.** The later years of the Ming saw a slowdown in technological development and economic decline. (*pp. 355, 554*)

Minoan Prosperous civilization on the Aegean island of Crete in the second millennium B.C.E. The Minoans engaged in far-flung commerce around the Mediterranean and exerted powerful cultural influences on the early Greeks. (*p. 73*)

mit'a Andean labor system based on shared obligations to help kinsmen and work on behalf of the ruler and religious organizations. (*p. 312*)

Moche Civilization of north coast of Peru (200–700 C.E.). An important Andean civilization that built extensive irrigation networks as well as impressive urban centers dominated by brick temples. (*p. 313*)

Moctezuma II (1466?–1520) Last Aztec emperor, overthrown by the Spanish conquistador Hernán Cortés. (*p. 437*)

modernization The process of reforming political, military, economic, social, and cultural traditions in imitation of the early success of Western societies, often with regard for accommodating local traditions in non-Western societies. (*p. 652*)

Mohenjo-Daro Largest of the cities of the Indus Valley civilization. It was centrally located in the extensive floodplain of the Indus River in contemporary Pakistan. Little is known about the political institutions of Indus Valley communities, but the large-scale of construction at Mohenjo-Daro, the orderly grid of streets, and the standardization of building materials are evidence of central planning. (*p. 48*)

moksha The Hindu concept of the spirit's "liberation" from the endless cycle of rebirths. There are various avenues—such as physical discipline, meditation, and acts of devotion to the gods—by which the spirit can distance itself from desire for the things of this world and be merged with the divine force that animates the universe. (*p. 179*)

monasticism Living in a religious community apart from secular society and adhering to a rule stipulating chastity, obedience, and poverty. It was a prominent element of medieval Christianity and Buddhism. Monasteries were the primary centers of learning and literacy in medieval Europe. (*p. 261*)

Mongols A people of this name is mentioned as early as the records of the **Tang Empire,** living as nomads in northern

Eurasia. After 1206 they established an enormous empire under **Genghis Khan,** linking western and eastern Eurasia. (*p. 325*)

monotheism Belief in the existence of a single divine entity. Some scholars cite the devotion of the Egyptian pharaoh **Akhenaten** to the Aten (sun-disk) and his suppression of traditional goals as the earliest instance. The Israelite worship of Yahweh developed into an exclusive belief in one god, and this concept passed into Christianity and Islam. (*p. 102*)

monsoon Seasonal winds in the Indian Ocean caused by the differences in temperature between the rapidly heating and cooling landmasses of Africa and Asia and the slowly changing ocean waters. These strong and predictable winds have long been ridden across the open sea by sailors, and the large amounts of rainfall that they deposit on parts of India, Southeast Asia, and China allow for the cultivation of several crops a year. (*pp. 174, 371*)

Morelos, José María (1765–1814) Mexican priest and former student of Miguel Hidalgo y Costilla, he led the forces fighting for Mexican independence until he was captured and executed in 1814. (See also **Hidalgo y Costilla, Miguel.**) (*p. 626*)

most-favored-nation status A clause in a commercial treaty that awards to any later signatories all the privileges previously granted to the original signatories. (*p. 686*)

movable type Type in which each individual character is cast on a separate piece of metal. It replaced woodblock printing, allowing for the arrangement of individual letters and other characters on a page, rather than requiring the carving of entire pages at a time. It may have been invented in Korea in the thirteenth century. (See also **printing press.**) (*p. 293*)

Mughal Empire Muslim state (1526–1857) exercising dominion over most of India in the sixteenth and seventeenth centuries. (*p. 536*)

Muhammad (570–632 C.E.) Arab prophet; founder of religion of Islam. (*p. 230*)

Muhammad Ali (1769–1849) Leader of Egyptian modernization in the early nineteenth century. He ruled Egypt as an Ottoman governor, but had imperial ambitions. His descendants ruled Egypt until overthrown in 1952. (*p. 652*)

mulatto The term used in Spanish and Portuguese colonies to describe someone of mixed African and European descent. (*p. 484*)

mummy A body preserved by chemical processes or special natural circumstances, often in the belief that the deceased will need it again in the afterlife. In ancient Egypt the bodies of people who could afford mummification underwent a complex process of removing organs, filling body cavities, dehydrating the corpse with natron, and then wrapping the body with linen bandages and enclosing it in a wooden sarcophagus. (*p. 46*)

Muscovy Russian principality that emerged gradually during the era of Mongol domination. The Muscovite dynasty ruled without interruption from 1276 to 1598. (*p. 551*)

Muslim An adherent of the Islamic religion; a person who "submits" (in Arabic, *Islam* means "submission") to the will of God. (*p. 231*)

Mussolini, Benito (1883–1945) Fascist dictator of Italy (1922–1943). He led Italy to conquer Ethiopia (1935), joined Germany in the Axis pact (1936), and allied Italy with Germany in World War II. He was overthrown in 1943 when the Allies invaded Italy. (*p. 786*)

Mycenae Site of a fortified palace complex in southern Greece that controlled a Late Bronze Age kingdom. In Homer's epic poems Mycenae was the base of King Agamemnon, who commanded the Greeks besieging Troy. Contemporary archaeologists call the complex Greek society of the second millennium B.C.E. "Mycenaean." (*p. 74*)

Napoleon I (1769–1832). Overthrew French Directory in 1799 and became emperor of the French in 1804. Failed to defeat Great Britain and abdicated in 1814. Returned to power briefly in 1815 but was defeated and died in exile. (*p. 591*)

Nasir al-Din Tusi (1201–1274) Persian mathematician and cosmologist whose academy near Tabriz provided the model for the movement of the planets that helped to inspire the Copernican model of the solar system. (*p. 337*)

National Assembly French Revolutionary assembly (1789–1791). Called first as the Estates General, the three estates came together and demanded radical change. It passed the **Declaration of the Rights of Man** in 1789. (*p. 585*)

nationalism A political ideology that stresses people's membership in a nation—a community defined by a common culture and history as well as by territory. In the late eighteenth and early nineteenth centuries, nationalism was a force for unity in western Europe. In the late nineteenth century it hastened the disintegration of the Austro-Hungarian and Ottoman Empires. In the twentieth century it provided the ideological foundation for scores of independent countries emerging from **colonialism.** (*p. 713*)

natural selection The biological process by which variations that enhance a population's ability to survive in a particular environment become dominant in a species over very long periods and lead to the **evolution** of a new species. (*p. 6*)

nawab A Muslim prince allied to British India; technically, a semi-autonomous deputy of the Mughal emperor. (*p. 657*)

Nazi Party German political party joined by Adolf Hitler, emphasizing nationalism, racism, and war. When Hitler became chancellor of Germany in 1933, the Nazi Party became the only legal party and an instrument of Hitler's absolute rule. Its formal name was National Socialist German Workers' Party. (See also **Hitler, Adolf.**) (*p. 786*)

Nehru, Jawaharlal (1889–1964) Indian statesman. He succeeded Mohandas K. Gandhi as leader of the **Indian National Congress.** He negotiated the end of British colonial rule in India and became India's first prime minister (1947–1964). (*p. 815*)

Neo-Assyrian Empire An empire extending from western Iran to Syria-Palestine, conquered by the Assyrians of northern Mesopotamia between the tenth and seventh centuries B.C.E. They used force and terror and exploited the wealth and labor of their subjects. They also preserved and continued the cultural and scientific developments of Mesopotamian civilization. (*p. 93*)

Neo-Babylonian kingdom Under the Chaldaeans (nomadic kinship groups that settled in southern Mesopotamia in the early first millennium B.C.E.), **Babylon** again became a major political and cultural center in the seventh and sixth centuries B.C.E. After participating in the destruction of Assyrian power, the monarchs Nabopolassar and Nebuchadnezzar took over the southern portion of the Assyrian domains. By destroying the **First Temple** in Jerusalem and deporting part of the population, they initiated the **diaspora** of the Jews. (*p. 110*)

Neolithic The period of the Stone Age associated with the ancient **Agricultural Revolution(s).** It follows the **Paleolithic** period. (*p. 11*)

Nevskii, Alexander (1220–1263) Prince of Novgorod (r. 1236–1263). He submitted to the invading Mongols in 1240 and received recognition as the leader of the Russian princes under the Golden Horde. (*p. 339*)

New Economic Policy Policy proclaimed by Vladimir Lenin in 1924 to encourage the revival of the Soviet economy by allowing small private enterprises. Joseph Stalin ended the N.E.P. in 1928 and replaced it with a series of **Five-Year Plans.** (See also **Lenin, Vladimir.**) (*p. 766*)

New France French colony in North America, with a capital in Quebec, founded 1608. New France fell to the British in 1763. (*p. 489*)

New Imperialism Historians' term for the late-nineteenth- and early-twentieth-century wave of conquests by European powers, the United States, and Japan, which were followed by the development and exploitation of the newly conquered territories for the benefit of the colonial powers. (*p. 726*)

Newly Industrialized Economies (NIEs) Rapidly growing, new industrial nations of the late twentieth century, including the **Asian Tigers.** (*p. 861*)

new monarchies Historians' term for the monarchies in France, England, and Spain from 1450 to 1600. The centralization of royal power was increasing within more or less fixed territorial limits. (*p. 414*)

nomadism A way of life, forced by a scarcity of resources, in which groups of people continually migrate to find pastures and water. (*p. 326*)

nonaligned nations Developing countries that announced their neutrality in the **Cold War.** (*p. 846*)

nongovernmental organizations (NGOs) Nonprofit international organizations devoted to investigating human rights abuses and providing humanitarian relief. Two NGOs won the Nobel Peace Prize in the 1990s: International Campaign to Ban Landmines (1997) and Doctors Without Borders (1999). (*p. 892*)

North Atlantic Treaty Organization (NATO) Organization formed in 1949 as a military alliance of western European and North American states against the Soviet Union and its east European allies. (See also **Warsaw Pact.**) (*p. 832*)

nuclear nonproliferation Goal of international efforts to prevent countries other than the five declared nuclear powers (United States, Russia, Britain, France, and China) from obtaining nuclear weapons. The first Nuclear Non-Proliferation Treaty was signed in 1968. (*p. 890*)

Olmec The first Mesoamerican civilization. Between ca. 1200 and 400 B.C.E., the Olmec people of central Mexico created a vibrant civilization that included intensive agriculture, wide-ranging trade, ceremonial centers, and monumental construction. The Olmec had great cultural influence on later Mesoamerican societies, passing on artistic styles, religious imagery, sophisticated astronomical observation for the construction of calendars, and a ritual ball game. (*p. 86*)

Oman Arab state based in Musqat, the main port in the southwest region of the Arabian peninsula. Oman succeeded Portugal as a power in the western Indian Ocean in the eighteenth century. (*p. 542*)

Opium War (1839–1842) War between Britain and the **Qing Empire** that was, in the British view, occasioned by the Qing government's refusal to permit the importation of opium into its territories. The victorious British imposed the one-sided **Treaty of Nanking** on China. (*p. 684*)

Organization of Petroleum Exporting Countries (OPEC) Organization formed in 1960 by oil-producing states to promote their collective interest in generating revenue from oil. (*p. 849*)

Ottoman Empire Islamic state founded by Osman in northwestern Anatolia ca. 1300. After the fall of the **Byzantine Empire,** the Ottoman Empire was based at Istanbul (formerly Constantinople) from 1453 to 1922. It encompassed lands in the Middle East, North Africa, the Caucasus, and eastern Europe. (*p. 522*)

Páez, José Antonio (1790–1873) Venezulean soldier who led Simón Bolívar's cavalry force. He became a successful general in the war and built a powerful political base. He was unwilling to accept the constitutional authority of Bolívar's government in distant Bogotá and declared Venezuela's independence from Gran Colombia in 1829. (*p. 629*)

Paleolithic The period of the Stone Age associated with the **evolution** of humans. It predates the **Neolithic** period. (*p. 11*)

Panama Canal Ship canal cut across the isthmus of Panama by United States Army engineers; it opened in 1915. It greatly shortened the sea voyage between the east and west coasts of North America. The United States turned the canal over to Panama on January 1, 2000. (*p. 746*)

papacy The central administration of the Roman Catholic Church, of which the pope is the head. (*pp. 258, 445*)

papyrus A reed that grows along the banks of the Nile River in Egypt. From it was produced a coarse, paperlike writing medium used by the Egyptians and many other peoples in the ancient Mediterranean and Middle East. (*p. 44*)

Parthians Iranian ruling dynasty between ca. 250 B.C.E. and 226 C.E. (*p. 204*)

patron/client relationship In ancient Rome, a fundamental social relationship in which the patron—a wealthy and powerful individual—provided legal and economic protection and assistance to clients, men of lesser status and means, and in return the clients supported the political careers and economic interests of their patron. (*p. 149*)

Paul (ca. 5–65 C.E.) A Jew from the Greek city of Tarsus in Anatolia, he initially persecuted the followers of Jesus but, after receiving a revelation on the road to Syrian Damascus, became a Christian. Taking advantage of his Hellenized background and Roman citizenship, he traveled throughout Syria-Palestine, Anatolia, and Greece, preaching the new religion and establishing churches. Finding his greatest success among pagans ("gentiles"), he began the process by which Christianity separated from Judaism. (*p. 156*)

pax romana Literally, "Roman peace," it connoted the stability and prosperity that Roman rule brought to the lands of the Roman Empire in the first two centuries C.E. The movement of people and trade goods along Roman roads and safe seas allowed for the spread of cultural practices, technologies, and religious ideas. (*p. 154*)

Pearl Harbor Naval base in Hawaii attacked by Japanese aircraft on December 7, 1941. The sinking of much of the U.S. Pacific Fleet brought the United States into World War II. (*p. 793*)

Peloponnesian War A protracted (431–404 B.C.E.) and costly conflict between the Athenian and Spartan alliance systems that convulsed most of the Greek world. The war was largely a consequence of Athenian imperialism. Possession of a naval empire allowed Athens to fight a war of attrition. Ultimately, Sparta prevailed because of Athenian errors and Persian financial support. (*p. 135*)

percussion caps Gunpowder filled capsules that, when struck by the hammer of a gun, ignite the explosive charge in a gun. Their use meant that guns no longer needed to be ignited by hand. (*p. 681*)

perestroika Policy of "openness" that was the centerpiece of Mikhail Gorbachev's efforts to liberalize communism in the Soviet Union. (See also **Gorbachev, Mikhail.**) (*p. 863*)

Pericles (ca. 495–429 B.C.E.) Aristocratic leader who guided the Athenian state through the transformation to full participatory democracy for all male citizens, supervised construction of the Acropolis, and pursued a policy of imperial expansion that led to the **Peloponnesian War.** He formulated a strategy of attrition but died from the plague early in the war. (*p. 130*)

Perón, Eva Duarte (1919–1952) Wife of **Juan Perón** and champion of the poor in Argentina. She was a gifted speaker and popular political leader who campaigned to improve the life of the urban poor by founding schools and hospitals and providing other social benefits. (*p. 824*)

Perón, Juan (1895–1974) President of Argentina (1946–1955, 1973–1974). As a military officer, he championed the rights of labor. Aided by his wife **Eva Duarte Perón,** he was elected president in 1946. He built up Argentinean industry, became very popular among the urban poor, but harmed the economy. (*p. 823*)

Persepolis A complex of palaces, reception halls, and treasury buildings erected by the Persian kings **Darius I** and Xerxes in the Persian homeland. It is believed that the New Year's festival was celebrated here, as well as the coronations, weddings, and funerals of the Persian kings, who were buried in cliff-tombs nearby. (*p. 119*)

Persian Wars Conflicts between Greek city-states and the Persian Empire, ranging from the Ionian Revolt (499–494 B.C.E.) through Darius's punitive expedition that failed at Marathon (490 B.C.E.) and the defeat of Xerxes' massive invasion of Greece by the Spartan-led Hellenic League (480–479 B.C.E.). This first major setback for Persian arms launched the Greeks into their period of greatest cultural productivity. **Herodotus** chronicled these events in the first "history" in the Western tradition. (*p. 131*)

personalist leaders Political leaders who rely on charisma and their ability to mobilize and direct the masses of citizens outside the authority of constitutions and laws. Nineteenth-century examples include José Antonio Páez of Venezuela and Andrew Jackson of the United States. Twentieth-century examples include Getulio Vargas of Brazil and Juan Perón of Argentina. (See also **Jackson, Andrew; Paez, José Antonio; Perón, Juan; Vargas, Getulio.**) (*p. 628*)

Peter the Great (1672–1725) Russian tsar (r. 1689–1725). He enthusiastically introduced Western languages and technologies to the Russian elite, moving the capital from Moscow to the new city of St. Petersburg. (*p. 552*)

pharaoh The central figure in the ancient Egyptian state. Believed to be an earthly manifestation of the gods, he used his absolute power to maintain the safety and prosperity of Egypt. (*p. 42*)

Phoenicians Semitic-speaking Canaanites living on the coast of modern Lebanon and Syria in the first millennium B.C.E. From major cities such as Tyre and Sidon, Phoenician merchants and sailors explored the Mediterranean, engaged in widespread commerce, and founded **Carthage** and other colonies in the western Mediterranean. (*p. 103*)

pilgrimage Journey to a sacred shrine by Christians seeking to show their piety, fulfill vows, or gain absolution for sins. Other religions also have pilgrimage traditions, such as the Muslim pilgrimage to **Mecca** and the pilgrimages made by early Chinese Buddhists to India in search of sacred Buddhist writings. (*p. 270*)

Pilgrims Group of English Protestant dissenters who established Plymouth Colony in Massachusetts in 1620 to seek religious freedom after having lived briefly in the Netherlands. (*p. 487*)

Pizarro, Francisco (1475?–1541) Spanish explorer who led the conquest of the **Inca** Empire of Peru in 1531–1533. (*p. 438*)

Planck, Max (1858–1947) German physicist who developed quantum theory and was awarded the Nobel Prize for physics in 1918. (*p. 774*)

plantocracy In the West Indian colonies, the rich men who owned most of the slaves and most of the land, especially in the eighteenth century. (*p. 502*)

polis The Greek term for a **city-state,** an urban center and the agricultural territory under its control. It was the characteristic form of political organization in southern and central Greece in the Archaic and Classical periods. Of the hundreds of city-states in the Mediterranean and Black Sea regions settled by Greeks, some were oligarchic, others democratic, depending on the powers delegated to the Council and the Assembly. (*p. 125*)

popular culture Entertainment spread by mass communications and enjoying wide appeal. (*p. 897*)

positivism A philosophy developed by the French count of Saint-Simon. Positivists believed that social and economic problems could be solved by the application of the scientific method, leading to continuous progress. Their ideas became popular in France and Latin America in the nineteenth century. (*p. 616*)

postmodernism Post-World War II intellectual movement and cultural attitude focusing on cultural pluralism and release from the confines and ideology of Western high culture. (*p. 900*)

Potosí Located in Bolivia, one of the richest silver mining centers and most populous cities in colonial Spanish America. (*p. 479*)

printing press A mechanical device for transferring text or graphics from a woodblock or type to paper using ink. Presses using movable type first appeared in Europe in about 1450. See also **movable type.** (*p. 409*)

Protestant Reformation Religious reform movement within the Latin Christian Church beginning in 1519. It resulted in the "protesters" forming several new Christian denominations, including the Lutheran and Reformed Churches and the Church of England. (*p. 446*)

proxy wars During the **Cold War,** local or regional wars in which the superpowers armed, trained, and financed the combatants. (*p. 855*)

Ptolemies The Macedonian dynasty, descended from one of Alexander the Great's officers, that ruled Egypt for three centuries (323–30 B.C.E.). From their magnificent capital at Alexandria on the Mediterranean coast, the Ptolemies largely took over the system created by Egyptian pharaohs to extract the wealth of the land, rewarding Greeks and Hellenized non-Greeks serving in the military and administration. (*p. 138*)

Puritans English Protestant dissenters who believed that God predestined souls to heaven or hell before birth. They founded Massachusetts Bay Colony in 1629. (*p. 487*)

pyramid A large, triangular stone monument, used in Egypt and Nubia as a burial place for the king. The largest pyramids, erected during the Old Kingdom near Memphis with stone tools and compulsory labor, reflect the Egyptian belief that the proper and spectacular burial of the divine ruler would guarantee the continued prosperity of the land. (See also **ma'at.**) (*p. 42*)

Qin A people and state in the Wei Valley of eastern China that conquered rival states and created the first Chinese empire (221–206 B.C.E.). The Qin ruler, **Shi Huangdi,** standardized many features of Chinese society and ruthlessly marshalled subjects for military and construction projects, engendering hostility that led to the fall of his dynasty shortly after his death. The Qin framework was largely taken over by the succeeding **Han** Empire. (*p. 163*)

Qing Empire Empire established in China by Manchus who overthrew the **Ming Empire** in 1644. At various times the Qing also controlled Manchuria, Mongolia, Turkestan, and Tibet. The last Qing emperor was overthrown in 1911. (*p. 556*)

Quran Book composed of divine revelations made to the Prophet Muhammad between ca. 610 and his death in 632; the sacred text of the religion of **Islam.** (*p. 232*)

railroads Networks of iron (later steel) rails on which steam (later electric or diesel) locomotives pulled long trains at high speeds. The first railroads were built in England in the 1830s. Their success caused a railroad-building boom throughout the world that lasted well into the twentieth century. (*p. 704*)

Rajputs Members of a mainly Hindu warrior caste from northwest India. The Mughal emperors drew most of their Hindu officials from this caste, and **Akbar I** married a Rajput princess. (*p. 537*)

Ramesses II A long-lived ruler of New Kingdom Egypt (r. 1290–1224 B.C.E.). He reached an accommodation with the **Hittites** of Anatolia after a standoff in battle at Kadesh in Syria. He built on a grand scale throughout Egypt. (*p. 68*)

Rashid al-Din (d.1318) Adviser to the **Il-khan** ruler Ghazan, who converted to Islam on Rashid's advice. (*p. 334*)

recaptives Africans rescued by Britain's Royal Navy from the illegal slave trade of the nineteenth century and restored to free status. (*p. 655*)

reconquest of Iberia Beginning in the eleventh century, military campaigns by various Iberian Christian states to recapture territory taken by Muslims. In 1492 the last Muslim ruler was defeated, and Spain and Portugal emerged as united kingdoms. (*p. 414*)

Renaissance (European) A period of intense artistic and intellectual activity, said to be a "rebirth" of Greco-Roman culture. Usually divided into an Italian Renaissance, from roughly the mid-fourteenth to mid-fifteenth century, and a Northern (trans-Alpine) Renaissance, from roughly the early fifteenth to early seventeenth century. (*pp. 407, 445*)

Revolutions of 1848 Democratic and nationalist revolutions that swept across Europe. The monarchy in France was overthrown. In Germany, Austria, Italy, and Hungary the revolutions failed. (*p. 595*)

Rhodes, Cecil (1853–1902) British entrepreneur and politician involved in the expansion of the British Empire from South Africa into Central Africa. The colonies of Southern Rhodesia (now Zimbabwe) and Northern Rhodesia (now Zambia) were named after him. (*p. 736*)

Robespierre, Maximilien (1758–1794) Young provincial lawyer who led the most radical phases of the French Revolution. His execution ended the Reign of Terror. See **Jacobins.** (*p. 589*)

Roman Principate A term used to characterize Roman government in the first three centuries C.E., based on the ambiguous title *princeps* ("first citizen") adopted by Augustus to conceal his military dictatorship. (*p. 151*)

Roman Republic The period from 507 to 31 B.C.E., during which Rome was largely governed by the aristocratic **Roman Senate.** (*p. 148*)

Roman Senate A council whose members were the heads of wealthy, landowning families. Originally an advisory body to the early kings, in the era of the **Roman Republic** the Senate effectively governed the Roman state and the growing empire. Under Senate leadership, Rome conquered an empire of unprecedented extent in the lands surrounding the Mediterranean Sea. In the first century B.C.E. quarrels among powerful and ambitious senators and failure to address social and economic problems led to civil wars and the emergence of the rule of the emperors. (*p. 148*)

Romanization The process by which the Latin language and Roman culture became dominant in the western provinces of the Roman Empire. The Roman government did not actively seek to Romanize the subject peoples, but indigenous peoples in the provinces often chose to Romanize because of the political and economic advantages that it brought, as well as the allure of Roman success. (*p. 155*)

Romanov, Mikhail (1596–1645) Russian tsar (r. 1613–1645) A member of the Russian aristocracy, he became tsar after the old line of Muscovite rulers was deposed. (*p. 551*)

Royal African Company A trading company chartered by the English government in 1672 to conduct its merchants' trade on the Atlantic coast of Africa. (*p. 507*)

sacrifice A gift given to a deity, often with the aim of creating a relationship, gaining favor, and obligating the god to provide some benefit to the sacrificer, sometimes in order to sustain the deity and thereby guarantee the continuing vitality of the natural world. The object devoted to the deity could be as simple as a cup of wine poured on the ground, a live animal slain on the altar, or, in the most extreme case, the ritual killing of a human being. (*p. 127*)

Safavid Empire Iranian kingdom (1502–1722) established by Ismail Safavi, who declared Iran a Shi'ite state. (*p. 531*)

Sahel Savanna Belt south of the Sahara; literally "coastland" in Arabic. (*p. 215*)

samurai Literally "those who serve," the hereditary military elite of the **Tokugawa Shogunate.** (*p. 563*)

Sandinistas Members of a leftist coalition that overthrew the Nicaraguan dictatorship of Anastasia Somoza in 1979 and attempted to install a socialist economy. The United States financed armed opposition by the Contras. The Sandinistas lost national elections in 1990. (*p. 857*)

Sasanid Empire Iranian empire, established ca. 226, with a capital in Ctesiphon, Mesopotamia. The Sasanid emperors established **Zoroastrianism** as the state religion. Islamic Arab armies overthrew the empire ca. 640. (*p. 225*)

satrap The governor of a province in the Achaemenid Persian Empire, often a relative of the king. He was responsible for protection of the province and for forwarding tribute to the central administration. Satraps in outlying provinces enjoyed considerable autonomy. (*p. 118*)

savanna Tropical or subtropical grassland, either treeless or with occasional clumps of trees. Most extensive in **sub-Saharan Africa** but also present in South America. (*p. 217*)

schism A formal split within a religious community. See **Great Western Schism.** (*p. 260*)

scholasticism A philosophical and theological system, associated with Thomas Aquinas, devised to reconcile Aristotelian philosophy and Roman Catholic theology in the thirteenth century. (*p. 408*)

Scientific Revolution The intellectual movement in Europe, initially associated with planetary motion and other aspects of physics, that by the seventeenth century had laid the groundwork for modern science. (*p. 466*)

"scramble" for Africa Sudden wave of conquests in Africa by European powers in the 1880s and 1890s. Britain obtained most of eastern Africa, France most of northwestern Africa. Other countries (Germany, Belgium, Portugal, Italy, and Spain) acquired lesser amounts. (*p. 731*)

scribe In the governments of many ancient societies, a professional position reserved for men who had undergone the lengthy training required to be able to read and write using **cuneiforms, hieroglyphics,** or other early, cumbersome writing systems. (*p. 35*)

seasoning An often difficult period of adjustment to new climates, disease environments, and work routines, such as that experienced by slaves newly arrived in the Americas. (*p. 504*)

Selassie, Haile (1892–1975) Emperor of Ethiopia (r. 1930–1974) and symbol of African independence. He fought the Italian invasion of his country in 1935 and regained his throne during World War II, when British forces expelled the Italians. He ruled **Ethiopia** as a traditional **autocracy** until he was overthrown in 1974. (*p. 809*)

Semitic Family of related languages long spoken across parts of western Asia and northern Africa. In antiquity these languages included Hebrew, Aramaic, and Phoenician. The most widespread modern member of the Semitic family is Arabic. (*p. 32*)

"separate spheres" Nineteenth-century idea in Western societies that men and women, especially of the middle class, should have clearly differentiated roles in society: women as wives, mothers, and homemakers; men as breadwinners and participants in business and politics. (*p. 711*)

sepoy A soldier in South Asia, especially in the service of the British. (*p. 658*)

Sepoy Rebellion The revolt of Indian soldiers in 1857 against certain practices that violated religious customs; also known as the Sepoy Mutiny. (*p. 661*)

Serbia The Ottoman province in the Balkans that rose up against **Janissary** control in the early 1800s. After World War II the central province of Yugoslavia. Serb leaders struggled to maintain dominance as the Yugoslav federation dissolved in the 1990s. (*p. 676*)

serf In medieval Europe, an agricultural laborer legally bound to a lord's property and obligated to perform set services for the lord. In Russia some serfs worked as artisans and in factories; serfdom was not abolished there until 1861. (*pp. 254, 553*)

shaft graves A term used for the burial sites of elite members of Mycenaean Greek society in the mid-second millennium B.C.E. At the bottom of deep shafts lined with stone slabs, the bodies were laid out along with gold and bronze jewelry, implements, weapons, and masks. (*p. 75*)

shamanism The practice of identifying special individuals (shamans) who will interact with spirits for the benefit of the community. Characteristic of the Korean kingdoms of the early medieval period and of early societies of Central Asia. (*p. 292*)

Shang The dominant people in the earliest Chinese dynasty for which we have written records (ca. 1750–1027 B.C.E.). Ancestor worship, divination by means of oracle bones, and the use of bronze vessels for ritual purposes were major elements of Shang culture. (*p. 59*)

Shi Huangdi Founder of the short-lived **Qin** dynasty and creator of the Chinese Empire (r. 221–210 B.C.E.). He is remembered for his ruthless conquests of rival states, standardization of practices, and forcible organization of labor for military and engineering tasks. His tomb, with its army of life-size terracotta soldiers, has been partially excavated. (*p. 163*)

Shi'ites Muslims belonging to the branch of Islam believing that God vests leadership of the community in a descendant of Muhammad's son-in-law Ali. Shi'ism is the state religion of Iran. (See also **Sunnis.**) (*pp. 225, 531*)

Siberia The extreme northeastern sector of Asia, including the Kamchatka Peninsula and the present Russian coast of the Arctic Ocean, the Bering Strait, and the Sea of Okhotsk. (*p. 551*)

Sikhism Indian religion founded by the guru Nanak (1469–1539) in the Punjab region of northwest India. After the Mughal emperor ordered the beheading of the ninth guru in 1675, Sikh warriors mounted armed resistance to Mughal rule. (*p. 538*)

Silk Road Caravan routes connecting China and the Middle East across Central Asia and Iran. (*p. 203*)

"small tradition" Historians' term for a localized, usually non-literate, set of customs and beliefs adhered to by a single society, often in conjunction with a **"great tradition."** (*p. 217*)

socialism A political ideology that originated in Europe in the 1830s. Socialists advocated government protection of workers from exploitation by property owners and government ownership of industries. This ideology led to the founding of socialist or labor parties throughout Europe in the second half of the nineteenth century. (See also **Marx, Karl.**) (*p. 709*)

Socrates Athenian philosopher (ca. 470–399 B.C.E.) who shifted the emphasis of philosophical investigation from questions of natural science to ethics and human behavior. He attracted young disciples from elite families but made enemies by revealing the ignorance and pretensions of others, culminating in his trial and execution by the Athenian state. (*p. 133*)

Sokoto Caliphate A large Muslim state founded in 1809 in what is now northern Nigeria. (*p. 651*)

Solidarity Polish trade union created in 1980 to protest working conditions and political repression. It began the nationalist opposition to communist rule that led in 1989 to the fall of communism in eastern Europe. (*p. 863*)

Song Empire Empire in central and southern China (960–1126) while the Liao people controlled the north. Empire in southern China (1127–1279; the "Southern Song") while the Jin people controlled the north. Distinguished for its advances in technology, medicine, astronomy, and mathematics. (*p. 285*)

Srivijaya A state based on the Indonesian island of Sumatra, between the seventh and eleventh centuries C.E. It amassed wealth and power by a combination of selective adaptation of Indian technologies and concepts, control of the lucrative trade routes between India and China, and skillful showmanship and diplomacy in holding together a disparate realm of inland and coastal territories. (See also **theater-state.**) (*p. 192*)

Stalin, Joseph (1879–1953) Bolshevik revolutionary, head of the Soviet Communist Party after 1924, and dictator of the Soviet Union from 1928 to 1953. He led the Soviet Union with an iron fist, using **Five-Year Plans** to increase industrial production and terror to crush all opposition. (*p. 780*)

Stalingrad City in Russia, site of a Red Army victory over the Germany army in 1942–1943. The Battle of Stalingrad was the turning point in the war between Germany and the Soviet Union. Today Volgograd. (*p. 793*)

Stanley, Henry Morton (1841–1904) British-American explorer of Africa, famous for his expeditions in search of Dr. David Livingstone. Stanley helped King **Leopold II** establish the Congo Free State. (*p. 732*)

steam engine A machine that turns the energy released by burning fuel into motion. Thomas Newcomen built the first crude but workable steam engine in 1712. **James Watt** vastly improved his device in the 1760s and 1770s. Steam power was later applied to moving machinery in factories and to powering ships and locomotives. (*p. 607*)

steel A form of iron that is both durable and flexible. It was first mass-produced in the 1860s and quickly became the most widely used metal in construction, machinery, and railroad equipment. (*p. 701*)

steppes Treeless plains, especially the high, flat expanses of northern Eurasia, which usually have little rain and are covered with coarse grass. They are good lands for nomads and their herds. Living on the steppes promoted the breeding of horses and the development of military skills that were essential to the rise of the Mongol Empire. (*pp. 217, 326*)

stirrup Device for securing a horseman's feet, enabling him to wield weapons more effectively. First evidence of the use of stirrups was among the Kushan people of northern Afghanistan in approximately the first century C.E. (*p. 206*)

stock exchange A place where shares in a company or business enterprise are bought and sold. (*p. 460*)

Stone Age The historical period characterized by the production of tools from stone and other nonmetallic substances. It was followed in some places by the Bronze Age and more generally by the Iron Age. (*p. 11*)

submarine telegraph cables Insulated copper cables laid along the bottom of a sea or ocean for telegraphic communication. The first short cable was laid across the English Channel in 1851; the first successful transatlantic cable was laid in 1866. (See also **electric telegraph.**) (*p. 704*)

sub-Saharan Africa Portion of the African continent lying south of the Sahara. (*p. 216*)

Suez Canal Ship canal dug across the isthmus of Suez in Egypt, designed by Ferdinand de Lesseps. It opened to shipping in 1869 and shortened the sea voyage between Europe and Asia. Its strategic importance led to the British conquest of Egypt in 1882. (*p. 726*)

Suleiman the Magnificent (1494–1566) The most illustrious sultan of the **Ottoman Empire** (r. 1520–1566); also known as Suleiman Kanuni, "The Lawgiver." He significantly expanded the empire in the Balkans and eastern Mediterranean. (*p. 526*)

Sumerians The people who dominated southern Mesopotamia through the end of the third millennium B.C.E. They were responsible for the creation of many fundamental elements of Mesopotamian culture—such as irrigation technology, **cuneiform,** and religious conceptions—taken over by their **Semitic** successors. (*p. 32*)

Sunnis Muslims belonging to branch of Islam believing that the community should select its own leadership. The majority religion in most Islamic countries. (See also **Shi'ites.**) (*p. 225*)

Sun Yat-sen (1867–1925) Chinese nationalist revolutionary, founder and leader of the **Guomindang** until his death. He attempted to create a liberal democratic political movement in China but was thwarted by military leaders. (*p. 768*)

Swahili Bantu language with Arabic loanwords spoken in coastal regions of East Africa. (*p. 542*)

Swahili Coast East African shores of the Indian Ocean between the Horn of Africa and the Zambezi River; from the Arabic *sawahil,* meaning "shores." (*p. 383*)

Taiping Rebellion (1853–1864) The most destructive civil war before the twentieth century. A Christian-inspired rural rebellion threatened to topple the **Qing Empire.** (*p. 687*)

Tamil kingdoms The kingdoms of southern India, inhabited primarily by speakers of Dravidian languages, which developed in partial isolation, and somewhat differently, from the Aryan north. They produced epics, poetry, and performance arts. Elements of Tamil religious beliefs were merged into the Hindu synthesis. (*p. 185*)

Tang Empire Empire unifying China and part of Central Asia, founded 618 and ended 907. The Tang emperors presided over a magnificent court at their capital, Chang'an. (*p. 277*)

Tanzimat "Restructuring" reforms by the nineteenth-century Ottoman rulers, intended to move civil law away from the control of religious elites and make the military and the bureacracy more efficient. (*p. 678*)

tax farming A government's use of private collectors to collect taxes. Individuals or corporations contract with the government to collect a fixed amount for the government and are permitted to keep as profit everything they collect over that amount. (*p. 334*)

technology transfer The communication of specific plans, designs, or educational programs necessary for the use of new technologies from one society or class to another. (*p. 358*)

Tecumseh (1768–1813) Shawnee leader who attempted to organize an Amerindian confederacy to prevent the loss of additional territory to American settlers. He became an ally of the British in War of 1812 and died in battle. (*p. 634*)

Tenochtitlan Capital of the Aztec Empire, located on an island in Lake Texcoco. Its population was about 150,000 on the eve of Spanish conquest. Mexico City was constructed on its ruins. (*p. 305*)

Teotihuacan A powerful **city-state** in central Mexico (100–75 C.E.). Its population was about 150,000 at its peak in 600. (*p. 300*)

Terrorism Political belief that extreme and seemingly random violence will destabilize a government and permit the terrorists to gain political advantage. Though an old technique, terrorism gained prominence in the late twentieth century with the growth of worldwide mass media that, through their news coverage, amplified public fears of terrorist acts. (*p. 890*)

theater-state Historians' term for a state that acquires prestige and power by developing attractive cultural forms and staging elaborate public ceremonies (as well as redistributing valuable resources) to attract and bind subjects to the center. Examples include the **Gupta Empire** in India and **Srivijaya** in Southeast Asia. (*p. 186*)

Thebes Capital city of Egypt and home of the ruling dynasties during the Middle and New Kingdoms. Amon, patron deity of Thebes, became one of the chief gods of Egypt. Monarchs were buried across the river in the Valley of the Kings. (*p. 43*)

Theravada Buddhism "Way of the Elders" branch of Buddhism followed in Sri Lanka and much of Southeast Asia. Therevada remains close to the original principles set forth by the **Buddha;** it downplays the importance of gods and emphasizes austerity and the individual's search for enlightenment. (*p. 181*)

third-century crisis Historians' term for the political, military, and economic turmoil that beset the Roman Empire during much of the third century C.E.: frequent changes of ruler, civil wars, barbarian invasions, decline of urban centers, and near-destruction of long-distance commerce and the monetary economy. After 284 C.E. Diocletian restored order by making fundamental changes. (*p. 157*)

Third World Term applied to a group of developing countries who professed nonalignment during the **Cold War.** (*p. 846*)

three-field system A rotational system for agriculture in which one field grows grain, one grows legumes, and one lies fallow. It gradually replaced two-field system in medieval Europe. (*p. 396*)

Tiananmen Square Site in Beijing where Chinese students and workers gathered to demand greater political openness in 1989. The demonstration was crushed by Chinese military with great loss of life. (*p. 862*)

Timbuktu City on the Niger River in the modern country of Mali. It was founded by the Tuareg as a seasonal camp sometime after 1000. As part of the **Mali** empire, Timbuktu became a major major terminus of the trans-Saharan trade and a center of Islamic learning. (*p. 388*)

Timur (1336–1405) Member of a prominent family of the Mongols' Jagadai Khanate, Timur through conquest gained control over much of Central Asia and Iran. He consolidated the status of Sunni Islam as orthodox, and his descendants, the Timurids, maintained his empire for nearly a century and founded the **Mughal Empire** in India. (*p. 336*)

Tiwanaku Name of capital city and empire centered on the region near Lake Titicaca in modern Bolivia (375–1000 C.E.). (*p. 315*)

Tokugawa Shogunate (1600–1868) The last of the three shogunates of Japan. (*p. 563*)

Toltecs Powerful postclassic empire in central Mexico (900–1168 C.E.). It influenced much of Mesoamerica. Aztecs claimed ties to this earlier civilization. (*p. 305*)

tophet A cemetery containing burials of young children, possibly sacrificed to the gods in times of crisis, found at **Carthage** and other **Phoenician** settlements in the western Mediterranean. (*p. 108*)

trans-Saharan caravan routes Trading network linking North Africa with **sub-Saharan Africa** across the Sahara. (*p. 210*)

Treaty of Nanking (1842) The treaty that concluded the **Opium War.** It awarded Britain a large indemnity from the **Qing Empire,** denied the Qing government tariff control over some of its own borders, opened additional ports of residence to Britons, and ceded the island of Hong Kong to Britain. (*p. 685*)

Treaty of Versailles (1919) The treaty imposed on Germany by France, Great Britain, the United States, and other Allied Powers after World War I. It demanded that Germany dismantle its military and give up some lands to Poland. It was resented by many Germans. (*p. 763*)

treaty ports Cities opened to foreign residents as a result of the forced treaties between the **Qing Empire** and foreign signatories. In the treaty ports, foreigners enjoyed **extraterritoriality.** (*p. 685*)

tributary system A system in which, from the time of the **Han** Empire, countries in East and Southeast Asia not under the direct control of empires based in China nevertheless enrolled as tributary states, acknowledging the superiority of the emperors in China in exchange for trading rights or strategic alliances. (*p. 279*)

tribute system A system in which defeated peoples were forced to pay a tax in the form of goods and labor. This forced transfer of food, cloth, and other goods subsidized the development of large cities. An important component of the Aztec and Inca economies. (*p. 307*)

trireme Greek and Phoenician warship of the fifth and fourth centuries B.C.E. It was sleek and light, powered by 170 oars arranged in three vertical tiers. Manned by skilled sailors, it was capable of short bursts of speed and complex maneuvers. (*p. 132*)

tropical rain forest High-precipitation forest zones of the Americas, Africa, and Asia lying between the Tropic of Cancer and the Tropic of Capricorn. (*p. 217*)

tropics Equatorial region between the Tropic of Cancer and the Tropic of Capricorn. It is characterized by generally warm or hot temperatures year-round, though much variation exists due to altitude and other factors. Temperate zones north and south of the tropics generally have a winter season. (*p. 370*)

Troy Site in northwest Anatolia, overlooking the Hellespont strait, where archaeologists have excavated a series of Bronze Age cities. One of these may have been destroyed by Greeks ca. 1200 B.C.E., as reported in Homer's epic poems. (*p. 76*)

Truman Doctrine Foreign policy initiated by U.S. president Harry Truman in 1947. It offered military aid to help Turkey and Greece resist Soviet military pressure and subversion. (*p. 836*)

tsar (czar) From Latin *caesar*, this Russian title for a monarch was first used in reference to a Russian ruler by Ivan III (r. 1462–1505). (*pp. 340, 551*)

Tulip Period (1718–1730) Last years of the reign of Ottoman sultan Ahmed III, during which European styles and attitudes became briefly popular in Istanbul. (*p. 530*)

Tupac Amaru II Member of Inca aristocracy who led a rebellion against Spanish authorities in Peru in 1780–1781. He was captured and executed with his wife and other members of his family. (*p. 493*)

tyrant The term the Greeks used to describe someone who seized and held power in violation of the normal procedures and traditions of the community. Tyrants appeared in many Greek **city-states** in the seventh and sixth centuries B.C.E., often taking advantage of the disaffection of the emerging middle class and, by weakening the old elite, unwittingly contributing to the evolution of **democracy.** (*p. 127*)

Uigurs A group of Turkic-speakers who controlled their own centralized empire from 744 to 840 in Mongolia and Central Asia. (*p. 284*)

ulama Muslim religious scholars. From the ninth century onward, the primary interpreters of Islamic law and the social core of Muslim urban societies. (*p. 238*)

Umayyad Caliphate First hereditary dynasty of Muslim caliphs (661 to 750). From their capital at Damascus, the Umayyads ruled an empire that extended from Spain to India. Overthrown by the **Abbasid Caliphate.** (*p. 232*)

umma The community of all Muslims. A major innovation against the background of seventh-century Arabia, where traditionally kinship rather than faith had determined membership in a community. (*p. 231*)

underdevelopment The condition experienced by economies that depend on colonial forms of production such as the export of raw materials and plantation crops with low wages and low investment in education. (*p. 642*)

United Nations International organization founded in 1945 to promote world peace and cooperation. It replaced the **League of Nations.** (*p. 833*)

Universal Declaration of Human Rights A 1946 United Nations covenant binding signatory nations to the observance of specified rights. (*p. 892*)

universities Degree-granting institutions of higher learning. Those that appeared in Latin West from about 1200 onward became the model of all modern universities. (*p. 407*)

Urdu A Persian-influenced literary form of Hindi written in Arabic characters and used as a literary language since the 1300s. (*p. 388*)

utopian socialism A philosophy introduced by the Frenchman Charles Fourier in the early nineteenth century. Utopian socialists hoped to create humane alternatives to industrial capitalism by building self-sustaining communities whose inhabitants would work cooperatively. (See also **socialism.**) (*p. 616*)

Vargas, Getulio (1883–1954) Dictator of Brazil from 1930 to 1945 and from 1951 to 1954. Defeated in the presidential election of 1930, he overthrew the government and created Estado Novo ("New State"), a dictatorship that emphasized industrialization and helped the urban poor but did little to alleviate the problems of the peasants. (*p. 823*)

variolation The technique of enhancing immunity by exposing patients to dried mucous taken from those already infected. (*p. 559*)

varna/jati Two categories of social identity of great importance in Indian history. *Varna* are the four major social divisions: the *Brahmin* priest class, the *Kshatriya* warrior/administrator class, the *Vaishya* merchant/farmer class, and the *Shudra* laborer class. Within the system of *varna* are many *jati*, regional groups of people who have a common occupational sphere, and who marry, eat, and generally interact with other members of their group. (*p. 177*)

vassal In medieval Europe, a sworn supporter of a king or lord committed to rendering specified military service to that king or lord. (*p. 256*)

Vedas Early Indian sacred "knowledge"—the literal meaning of the term—long preserved and communicated orally by

Brahmin priests and eventually written down. These religious texts, including the thousand poetic hymns to various deities contained in the Rig Veda, are our main source of information about the Vedic period (ca. 1500–500 B.C.E.). (*p. 175*)

Victorian Age The reign of Queen Victoria of Great Britain (r. 1837–1901). The term is also used to describe late-nineteenth-century society, with its rigid moral standards and sharply differentiated roles for men and women and for middle-class and working-class people. (See also **"separate spheres."**) (*p. 711*)

Vietnam War (1954–1975) Conflict pitting North Vietnam and South Vietnamese communist guerrillas against the South Vietnamese government, aided after 1961 by the United States. (*p. 838*)

Villa, Francisco "Pancho" (1878–1923) A popular leader during the Mexican Revolution. An outlaw in his youth, when the revolution started, he formed a cavalry army in the north of Mexico and fought for the rights of the landless in collaboration with **Emiliano Zapata.** He was assassinated in 1923. (See also **Zapata, Emiliano.**) (*p. 819*)

Wari Andean civilization culturally linked to **Tiwanaku**, perhaps beginning as colony of Tiwanaku. (*p. 314*)

Warsaw Pact The 1955 treaty binding the Soviet Union and countries of eastern Europe in an alliance against the **North Atlantic Treaty Organization.** (*p. 836*)

Washington, George (1732–1799) Military commander of the American Revolution. He was the first elected president of the United States (1789–1799). (*p. 581*)

water wheel A mechanism that harnesses the energy in flowing water to grind grain or to power machinery. It was used in many parts of the world but was especially common in Europe from 1200 to 1900. (*p. 398*)

Watt, James (1736–1819) Scot who invented the condenser and other improvements that made the **steam engine** a practical source of power for industry and transportation. The watt, an electrical measurement, is named after him. (*p. 607*)

Wedgwood, Josiah (1730–1795) English industrialist whose pottery works were the first to produce fine-quality pottery by industrial methods. (*p. 603*)

Western Front A line of trenches and fortifications in World War I that stretched without a break from Switzerland to the North Sea. Scene of most of the fighting between Germany, on the one hand, and France and Britain, on the other. (*p. 757*)

Wilson, Woodrow (1856–1924) President of the United States (1913–1921) and the leading figure at the Paris Peace Conference of 1919. He was unable to persuade the U.S. Congress to ratify the **Treaty of Versailles** or join the **League of Nations.** (*p. 762*)

witch-hunt The pursuit of people suspected of witchcraft, especially in northern Europe in the late sixteenth and seventeenth centuries. (*p. 464*)

Women's Rights Convention An 1848 gathering of women angered by their exclusion from an international antislavery meeting. They met at Seneca Falls, New York to discuss women's rights. (*p. 640*)

World Bank A specialized agency of the United Nations that makes loans to countries for economic development, trade promotion, and debt consolidation. Its formal name is the International Bank for Reconstruction and Development. (*p. 834*)

World Trade Organization (WTO) An international body established in 1995 to foster and bring order to international trade. (*p. 889*)

Xiongnu A confederation of nomadic peoples living beyond the northwest frontier of ancient China. Chinese rulers tried a variety of defenses and stratagems to ward off these "barbarians," as they called them, and finally succeeded in dispersing the Xiongnu in the first century C.E. (*p. 168*)

Yamagata Aritomo (1838–1922) One of the leaders of the **Meiji Restoration.** (*p. 722*)

Yi kingdom (1392–1910) The Yi dynasty ruled Korea from the fall of the **Koryo** kingdom to the colonization of Korea by Japan. (*p. 362*)

yin/yang In Chinese belief, complementary factors that help to maintain the equilibrium of the world. Yin is associated with masculine, light, and active qualities; yang with feminine, dark, and passive qualities. (*p. 63*)

Yongle Reign period of Zhu Di (1360–1424), the third emperor of the **Ming Empire** (r. 1403–1424). He sponsored the building of the **Forbidden City,** a huge encyclopedia project, the expeditions of **Zheng He,** and the reopening of China's borders to trade and travel. (*p. 355*)

Yuan Empire (1271–1368) Empire created in China and Siberia by **Khubilai Khan.** (*p. 349*)

Yuan Shikai (1859–1916) Chinese general and first president of the Chinese Republic (1912–1916). He stood in the way of the democratic movement led by **Sun Yat-sen.** (*p. 768*)

Zapata, Emiliano (1879–1919) Revolutionary and leader of peasants in the Mexican Revolution. He mobilized landless peasants in south-central Mexico in an attempt to seize and divide the lands of the wealthy landowners. Though successful for a time, he was ultimately defeated and assassinated. (*p. 819*)

Zen The Japanese word for a branch of **Mahayana Buddhism** based on highly disciplined meditation. It is known in Sanskrit as *dhyana*, in Chinese as *chan*, and in Korean as *son*. (*p. 289*)

Zheng He (1371–1433) An imperial eunuch and Muslim, entrusted by the Ming emperor **Yongle** with a series of state voyages that took his gigantic ships through the Indian Ocean, from Southeast Asia to Africa. (*pp. 355, 122*)

Zhou The people and dynasty that took over the dominant position in north China from the **Shang** and created the concept of the **Mandate of Heaven** to justify their rule. The Zhou era, particularly the vigorous early period (1027–771 B.C.E.), was remembered in Chinese tradition as a time of prosperity and benevolent rule. In the later Zhou period (771–221 B.C.E.), centralized control broke down, and warfare among many small states became frequent. (*p. 61*)

ziggurat A massive pyramidal stepped tower made of mud-bricks. It is associated with religious complexes in ancient Mesopotamian cities, but its function is unknown. (*p. 37*)

Zoroastrianism A religion originating in ancient Iran with the prophet Zoroaster. It centered on a single benevolent deity—Ahuramazda—who engaged in a twelve-thousand-year struggle with demonic forces before prevailing and restoring a pristine world. Emphasizing truth-telling, purity, and reverence for nature, the religion demanded that humans choose sides in the struggle between good and evil. Those whose good conduct indicated their support for Ahuramazda would be rewarded in the afterlife. Others would be punished. The religion of the Achaemenid and Sasanid Persians, Zoroastrianism may have spread within their realms and influenced Judaism, Christianity, and other faiths. (*p. 120*)

Zulu A people of modern South Africa whom King Shaka united beginning in 1818. (*p. 649*)

INDEX